D1535239

Chesterton
and the Jews

Chesterton and the Jews

Friend, Critic, Defender

∾

Ann Farmer

 Angelico Press

For information, address:
4709 Briar Knoll Dr.
Kettering, OH 45429
angelicopress.com
www.angelicopress.com

ISBN 978-1-62138-130-3 (pbk: alk. paper)
ISBN 978-1-62138-131-0 (cloth: alk. paper)

Cover Design: Michael Schrauzer

CONTENTS

Acknowledgments

My grateful thanks for their invaluable assistance and support in the writing of *Chesterton and the Jews* go to Stratford Caldecott, R.I.P., Dale Ahlquist, Father Ian Boyd, Denis Conlon, Sheridan Gilley, Gloria Garafulich-Grabois, and John Riess.

Dedication

Dedicated to Stratford Caldecott (1953–2014), who provided invaluable encouragement and assistance for *Chesterton and the Jews*, R.I.P.

1

Introduction
Chesterton: Pro- or Anti-Semite?

GILBERT KEITH CHESTERTON, best known for his clerical detective Father Brown, was enormously popular in the first half of the twentieth century. He was loved for the quirky English humor of his poetry ("For there is good news yet to hear and fine things to be seen, / Before we go to Paradise by way of Kensal Green."[1] "I think I will not hang myself today."[2]) and for his defense of the humble—including donkeys: "Fools! For I also had my hour; / One far fierce hour and sweet: / There was a shout about my ears, / And palms before my feet."[3] His more serious verse proved inspirational as England faced the fires of the Blitz and the threat of Nazi invasion:

> The fires of the Great Army
> That was made of iron men,
> Whose lights of sacrilege and scorn
> Ran around England red as morn,
> Fires over Glastonbury Thorn—
> Fires out on Ely Fen.[4]

Intellectually brilliant and widely read, he could nonetheless put into words his readers' feelings: "The Christian ideal has not been tried and found wanting. It has been found difficult; and left untried."[5] He also challenged them with the paradoxical "[i]f a thing is worth doing, it is worth doing badly."[6] His influence touched J. R. R. Tolkien, C. S. Lewis, Marshall McLuhan, Hannah Arendt,

---

1. G. K. Chesterton, "The Rolling English Road," *The Works of G. K. Chesterton* (Ware, Herts.: Wordsworth Poetry Library, 1995), 150.
2. G. K. Chesterton, "Ballade of Suicide," (ibid., 144).
3. G. K. Chesterton, "The Donkey," (ibid., 248).
4. G. K. Chesterton, "Ballad of the White Horse," (ibid., 164).
5. G. K. Chesterton, "The Unfinished Temple," *What's Wrong with the World* (USA: Quiet Vision Publishing, 1910/2003), 16.
6. G. K. Chesterton, "Folly and Female Education," (ibid., 108).

Orson Welles, Graham Greene, Philip Yancey, Mahatma Gandhi, Alfred Hitchcock, Dorothy L. Sayers, and Michael Collins and his biography of Charles Dickens inspired a revival. Although not a theologian his book on St. Thomas Aquinas was praised by a prominent Thomist scholar.[7] A century after he burst onto the public stage with his paradoxical insights and literary pyrotechnics he is enjoying a worldwide revival as the "secret people who have not spoken yet"[8] rediscover Chestertonian wit and wisdom, and see his "family and property" system, Distributism, as a sane alternative to capitalism and communism.

He has been regarded as an innocent abroad, a jolly optimist, praised as a philosopher and even a theologian. He can amuse and offend—sometimes at the same time—but is never dull. But his enduring appeal poses problems linked to his equally enduring reputation regarding anti-Semitism, especially in difficult economic times, which, historically, have always posed particular dangers for Jews.[9] In view of this, there is a moral imperative to ask whether Chesterton was anti-Semitic or a candidate for sainthood;[10] a prophet[11] or a pariah.

Evidence has been adduced with equal sincerity for both views, but concerns about anti-Semitism are closely linked to that unique expression of Jew-hatred,[12] the Holocaust[13] (or *Shoah*) which destroyed six million Jews as well as millions of others. Its goal was the attempted extermination of every Jewish man, woman, and child.[14] Fears of its "repetition," embodied in the expression

---

7. Étienne Gilson praised Chesterton's work on St. Thomas Aquinas (Joseph Pearce, *Wisdom and Innocence: A Life of G. K. Chesterton* [London: Hodder & Stoughton, 1997], 432–433). C. S. Lewis was inspired by *The Everlasting Man* and Dorothy L. Sayers by *Orthodoxy*. Popular editions of Charles Dickens's works still cite Chesterton's 1903 biography. Gandhi was inspired by Chesterton's piece on Indian nationalism in the *Illustrated London News* of September 18, 1909; see: J. R. McCleary, *The Historical Imagination of G. K. Chesterton: locality, patriotism, and nationalism* (London: Routledge, 2009).

8. G. K. Chesterton, "The Secret People," *The Works of G. K. Chesterton*, op. cit., 133; see Chapters Two and Seven.

9. See: Abraham H. Foxman, *Jews and Money: The Story of a Stereotype* (New York: Palgrave Macmillan, 2010).

10. William Oddie, ed., introduction to *The Holiness of G. K. Chesterton* (Leominster, Herefordshire: Gracewing, 2010), 2.

11. For example, Aidan Mackey's *G. K. Chesterton: A Prophet for the 21st Century* (Kempston, Bedford: A. Mackey, 2008).

12. See: Steven T. Katz, *The Holocaust in Historical Context, Vol. I: The Holocaust and Mass Destruction before the Modern Age* (Oxford: Oxford University Press, 1994).

13. David Lodge, *The Novelist at the Crossroads and other essays on Fiction and Criticism* (London: Ark Paperbacks, 1986), 146.

14. Other victims included the physically and mentally disabled, Christians, political opponents, sexual minorities and petty criminals; see: Michael Berenbaum, ed., *A Mosaic of Victims: Non-Jews Persecuted and Murdered by the Nazis* (London: I. B. Tauris & Co. Ltd., 1990); for the role of the Nazis' infamous Wannsee Conference in the plan to exterminate all Jews see: William D. Rubinstein, *Genocide: A History* (Harlow, Essex: Pearson Longman, 2004), 164.

"never again," have led to "constant vigilance" against anti-Semitism.[15] And if concerns about anti-Semitism have been influenced by the Holocaust, so have opinions of Chesterton's "anti-Semitism," as will be seen. Nonetheless he gained this reputation, especially among Jews, during his lifetime. Even in his own era he was seen as a backward-looking little Englander. Could this supposedly out-dated philosopher still have something to say to the world? Of the historian who says that historical figures may deserve credit allowing for the ideas of their time, Chesterton himself observed: "There will never be really good history until the historian says, 'I think they were worthy of praise, allowing for the ideas of my time.'"

Only by setting Chesterton in the appropriate historical, sociological, and political contexts is it possible to determine whether he is worthy of praise. In examining the problem from every angle, *Chesterton and the Jews* will help the post-Holocaust reader understand his views on the "Jewish question" and their root causes; in so doing it will paint a more rounded portrait than has hitherto appeared. And that is something that Chesterton, himself a well-rounded fig-ure, would have appreciated.

Aims and Approaches, Methodology and Materials, Terminology and Themes

In studying Chesterton's major ideological influences we will trace the develop-ment of his thinking about Jews and Jewish issues as it was shaped by his per-sonality, his relationships with Jews and Gentiles, and his responses to rapidly unfolding events. In examining these interlocking aspects of his life and thought we come as close as possible to the real truth of Chesterton and the Jews. The aim is not to whitewash Chesterton—in fact, in the pursuit of truth the smallest hint of anti-Semitism is examined—but to ask whether he deserves to be seen as an anti-Semite; whether he is still relevant in the twenty-first cen-tury; and finally, with the knowledge gained, to recognize and avoid anti-Semitism in our own time.

Chesterton's prolific output of fiction, non-fiction, and poetry will be studied not only in relation to Jewish issues but for any clues that may help to explain his stance on them. Secondary works will be examined in order to compare con-temporary perceptions of Chesterton and others with those of later commenta-tors; Jewish periodicals will be studied to see how he has been perceived by the Jewish community; and correspondence in the British Library's Chesterton Collection will offer a glimpse of the private Chesterton, his family and friends.

---

15. Isabel Wollaston, *A War Against Memory? The Future of Holocaust Remembrance* (London: SPCK, 1996), 80.

Regarding methodology, Chesterton's writings on Jews and on Jewish issues have been set in their original contexts. His remarks, restored to their original settings, often reveal a meaning which in some cases is the exact opposite of later interpretations. Often they have been quoted by commentators in support of a pre-existing view—negative or positive, as evidence for prosecution or defense. By considering both sets of evidence a more nuanced conclusion has been reached, offering a more objective picture of Chesterton's attitudes and motivations. Any alterations in his stance, what may have influenced them, and whether they were part of a pattern, will be noted. Although an admirer of Chesterton, I began the work, which built on my research in Jewish-Christian relations,[16] with no definite view on whether he was pro- or anti-Semitic. My sympathetic view of Jewish issues pre-dated this work by many years,[17] but my interest in Chesterton's approach to the "Jewish question" flowed from my interest in his opposition to eugenics and questions regarding the apparent dissonance in his positions. In this connection, *Chesterton and the Jews* subjects various historical approaches to the "Jewish question"—especially conspiracy theories—to rigorous scrutiny, highlighting the apparently logical steps that paradoxically may lead, as Chesterton himself knew, to illogicality, persecution, and cultural or religious paranoia. In order to assess Chesterton's enduring worth as a philosopher his positions on Jewish and other relevant, crucial issues will be compared and contrasted to those of some of his contemporaries whose views on these issues tend to be less known.

The early chapters will address interpretive problems arising from Holocaust influence, removing simple misunderstandings and misconstructions of Chesterton and by removing the layers of varnish distorting the picture of Chesterton's relationship with "the Jews," the way is cleared for later chapters to study more fundamental problems.

Regarding terminology, post-Holocaust attempts to define anti-Semitism[18] have been fraught with subjectivity. Louis Jacobs states that not "everyone who dislikes Jews [should] be dubbed an anti-Semite. Simple prejudice, unfortunate though it is, hardly constitutes a philosophy of Jew-hatred."[19] In view of this,

16. Ann E. Farmer, *Has the Holocaust Influenced Views of G. K. Chesterton's 'Anti-Semitism'* (Master's degree dissertation, unpublished) (Cambridge: The Centre for Jewish-Christian Relations, Anglia Polytechnic University, 2004).

17. My mother's first job, aged 14, was with an East End of London Jewish tailoring firm; my father's, at age 16, with a Jewish bakery. Both clearly remembered the Fascist marches of the 1930s and the signs in Jewish shops urging a boycott of German goods. Both supported the State of Israel. My reading on the Holocaust and interest in the Jewish roots of Christianity also influenced my sympathy for Jewish issues.

18. Gisela C. Lebzelter, *Political Anti-Semitism in England* 1918–1939 (London: Macmillan Press Ltd., 1978), 1–2.

19. Louis Jacobs, *The Jewish Religion: A Companion* (Oxford: Oxford University Press, 1995), 29.

"anti-Semitism" and its variants have been used to denote persecution or unjust discrimination against Jews (rather than Semitic peoples),[20] and are rendered in quotes when opinion on individuals is inconclusive. Used without such qualification, anti-Semitism and its variants will be used regarding individuals whose words, actions, and personal relationships unequivocally demonstrate that their primary driving force was hatred for all Jews. Post-Holocaust, "race" and its derivatives have been seen as referring to the discriminatory and exterminatory racial theories embraced by Hitler and other Nazis; unless this was indeed the case regarding individuals under discussion, therefore, such terminology will also be rendered in parentheses. The term "Jewish problem" was used by Jews and Gentiles to refer to the cycle of anti-Jewish violence and expulsions that tended to follow the apparently successful settlement of Jewish communities in the "Diaspora" (the Jewish "dispersal" throughout the nations), and the problem of how to break this cycle; a more neutral version of this term was "Jewish question," also used by Jews and Gentiles, and used in this work for the same reason.[21]

The following chapters will study various themes illuminating Chesterton's attitude to, and relationship with, the Jewish people. Chapter Two will examine his fondness for that curious animal, the underdog, and its unique place in British politics. Chapter Three will study Chesterton's fiction in the context of inter-War Golden Age detective fiction—an allegorical gold mine, where clues to his attitudes to Jews and anti-Semitism are abundant. In Chapter Four we investigate Chesterton's friendships with fellow anti-capitalists George Bernard Shaw and H.G. Wells, comparing and contrasting their treatment of Jewish characters and themes in their fiction. In Chapter Five we see how the political philosophies of the three friends fared in the age of dictators, and ask whether these literary giants of the early twentieth century deserve to be seen as prophets in the twenty-first. Chapter Six examines Chesterton's response to the "Jewish question" in the context of his relationship with his brother Cecil and the influence of their close friend and colleague Hilaire Belloc. Chapter Seven explores Chesterton's Zionism, comparing and contrasting his views with those of Jewish and Gentile Zionists, as well as anti-Zionists, to determine whether it betokened pro- or anti-Semitism. In Chapter Eight we ask whether Chesterton's family, and his non-Jewish and Jewish non-political friends, shaped his views on "the Jews"; and whether his developing religious beliefs might have influenced him toward "anti-Semitism."

In conclusion, Chapter Nine looks at the influence of the multicultural approach that emerged from concerns about the Holocaust, and which has

---

20. *Collins Dictionary of the English Language* (London: Collins, 1987).
21. For Jewish usage of such terms, see Chapters Six and Seven.

come to dominate Western society, but also asks whether multicultural considerations are leading us down the same tragic pathway. The "new anti-Semitism" is subjected to the same critical examination as the approach of the *Chesterbelloc* circle, comprising Chesterton, his brother Cecil, and their friend Hilaire Belloc,[22] to "financial" Jews, comparing and contrasting reactions of present-day commentators on the "Israel question" with Chesterton's responses to the "Jewish question." It will ask whether the real test of a philosopher—whether he or she is of enduring value—is not perfection as tested by hindsight, but the readiness to change direction in response to events that signal the falsity of his or her position. Such a readiness is a true test of humility, and a further indication of whether his or her driving force is hatred or love.

Regarding the Holocaust, Yuri Slezkine warns: "In a world without God, evil and victimhood are the only absolutes. . . ."[23] The final chapter asks what will happen to the Jewish people in a world without God, with a subjective view of evil and a fickle choice of victims; and whether studying Chesterton's approach to the "Jewish question" in the context of his own time can hold important lessons on anti-Semitism for our own age, and for an increasingly uncertain future.

The present chapter continues with a short biography of G. K. Chesterton, followed by a brief historical overview of anti-Semitism. It concludes with a study of the influence of the Holocaust on views of Chesterton.

Gilbert Keith Chesterton (1874–1936)

The son of a London estate agent, both Gilbert and his only brother, Cecil were day pupils at St Paul's public school. Here Gilbert founded the Junior Debating Club, from which sprang many life-long friendships with Jews and non-Jews. During a spell at the Slade School of Art he suffered from severe depression, and left without graduating.[24] After a short period in publishing, his career was spent chiefly as a journalist, addressing every topic imaginable, from running after one's hat[25] to the neglect of cheese in European literature.[26]

---

22. "Chesterbelloc" was Shaw's name for the ungainly pantomime animal that he saw as expressing the attempted union of Chesterton's and Belloc's philosophies, which he saw as conflicting (M. Ward, *Return to Chesterton* [London: Sheed & Ward, 1952], 59); the term came to be associated with Chesterton's and Belloc's collaborative literary efforts (M. Ward, *Gilbert Keith Chesterton* [New York: Sheed & Ward, 1943], 549).

23. Yuri Slezkine, *The Jewish Century* (Princeton: Princeton University Press, 2004), 370.

24. In October 1893 Chesterton entered the Slade School, then part of University College, and attended lectures in other faculties; he spent one year studying art and two studying English, French, and history (I. Ker, *G. K. Chesterton: A Biography* [Oxford: Oxford University Press, 2011], lvii–lxvii).

25. G. K. Chesterton, "On Running After One's Hat," *All Things Considered* (USA: Feather Tail Press, 1908/2009), 14.

26. G. K. Chesterton, "Cheese," *Alarms and Discursions* (London: Methuen & Co. Ltd., 1939), 57–61.

His first volume of poetry, *Greybeards at Play* (1900), was followed by articles for newspapers and journals, popular philosophical works, biographies, introductions to books, poetry, plays and detective fiction. He illustrated his own works and those of his friend and colleague Hilaire Belloc. Chesterton suffered a near-fatal brain illness at the beginning of the Great War[27] and, when Cecil volunteered for active service, took over the editor's chair at his political journal, *The New Witness*, until 1923. After it ceased he established *G.K.'s Weekly*, which he edited from 1925 until his death. He lectured as far afield as America, gave radio talks, and took part in debates. After a youthful flirtation with socialism he returned to liberalism, although as a severe critic. Notoriously absentminded, on one occasion he is said to have telegraphed his wife with the message: "Am in Market Harborough. Where ought I to be?"[28]

Anti-Semitism and the Influence of the Holocaust on Views of Chesterton

Anti-Semitism, more recently defined as "prejudice, discrimination, and hatred of Jews as a national, ethnic, religious, or racial group"[29] was a feature of pagan times, but continued under the Christian Roman Empire; and under Islamic dominance Jews were treated as second-class citizens. In Medieval Europe it took the form of religious denunciation, expulsion, and massacre. Many Jews converted to Christianity, but suspicions that the conversions were not genuine led to the Inquisition and even more severe penalties. Anti-Jewish conspiracy theories included such ideas as Jews being accused of using Christian blood, especially children's, to bake matzos (the "blood libel"); poisoning wells; and causing epidemics and crop failures.[30] Protestant attitudes were generally more favorable, but Martin Luther's initial fervor for the Jewish people turned sour, and anti-Semitism spread to the New World in the seventeenth century.[31] European Jews were emancipated as religious influence declined in the eighteenth

---

27. Chesterton collapsed at home and "sank into a coma"; in order to promote his recovery doctors advised that he be prevented from using his brain (M. Ward, *Gilbert Keith Chesterton* [New York: Sheed & Ward, 1943], 384–387).

28. Maisie Ward, *Gilbert Keith Chesterton* (New York: Sheed & Ward, 1943), 257.

29. Jewish Virtual Library, accessed May 17, 2012, http://www.jewishvirtuallibrary.org/jsource/antisem.html at.

30. See: Leon Poliakov, *The History of Anti-Semitism: From the Time of Christianity to the Court Jews*, Vol. I, trans. R. Howard (Philadelphia, PA: University of Pennsylvania Press, 2003); also: P. Goldstein, *A Convenient Hatred: The History of Antisemitism*, accessed at http://www.facinghistory.org).

31. See: Edwin G. Burrows, Mike Wallace, *Gotham: A History of New York City to 1898* (New York: Oxford University Press, 1999), 60; see Chapter Eight.

and nineteenth centuries, but with the rise of science, new theories of Jewish inferiority emerged, based on "race."[32] The late nineteenth century saw Tsarist pogroms in Russia and a resurgence of anti-Jewish feeling in some Muslim lands.[33] The Dreyfus affair polarized French opinion in the late nineteenth/early twentieth century. The British largely sympathized with the Jewish Captain Dreyfus, wrongly accused of spying, but anti-Semitic violence erupted during riots in Wales in 1911.[34] After the Russian Revolution, in which some Jews figured prominently,[35] conspiracy theories emerged regarding Jewish bids for world domination, most notoriously *The Protocols of the Elders of Zion*, purportedly revealing an age-old Jewish plot to take over the world.[36] The Russian Jewish position improved under the Soviets, but Zionism was suppressed and after the Second World War anti-Semitism returned in the guise of tackling "rootless cosmopolitans," as the Soviet Union turned against the fledgling State of Israel.[37]

In 1930s Europe, Fascists exploited fears of Jewish conspiracy in the quest for political power.[38] With the rise of Hitler under the Nazi Third Reich from 1933–1945, anti-Jewish persecution plumbed depths of hatred and depravity previously unseen in history.[39] The Holocaust ["sacrifice by fire"] or *Shoah* ["calamity"] was arguably the most monstrous work of Man, a combination of bestiality and bureaucracy described by Hannah Arendt as the "banality of evil."[40] Hitler's "apocalyptic" anti-Semitism had religious overtones, with a

32. See: Houston Stewart Chamberlain, *The Foundations of the Nineteenth Century*, Vol. I (London: John Lane the Bodley Head); Vol. II (London/New York: John Lane, 1911), originally published as *Grundlagen des neunzehnten Jahr hunderts Kristische Urteile* (1899). Chamberlain was ambiguous about Darwinism, but acknowledged Darwin's influence regarding "the struggle for existence and selection through breeding" (Richard Weikart, *From Darwin to Hitler: Evolutionary Ethics, Eugenics, and Racism in Germany* [New York/Basingstoke, Hants.: Palgrave Macmillan, 2004], 124–125); Chamberlain's work influenced the Nazi Party, which he joined (Dennis Sewell, *The Political Gene: How Darwin's Ideas Changed Politics* [London: Picador, 2010], 133).

33. See: Benny Morris, *Righteous Victims: A History of the Zionist-Arab Conflict 1881–1999* (New York/Toronto: Vintage Books, 2001).

34. 1753 saw the "Jew Bill" riots (Geoffrey Alderman, "The Anti-Jewish Riots of August 1911 in South Wales," *Current research on antisemitism: studies on modern antisemitism* 1870–1933–39, 1, Germany—Great Britain—France (3), (1993): 365–375; 365; see Chapters Six and Seven.

35. See: Y. Slezkine, *The Jewish Century*, op. cit.

36. See: Norman Cohn, *Warrant for Genocide: The myth of the Jewish world-conspiracy and the Protocols of the Elders of Zion* (London: Eyre & Spottiswoode, 1967); see Chapter Seven.

37. See: Robert S. Wistrich, ed., *The Left Against Zion: Communism, Israel and the Middle East* (London: Vallentine, Mitchell, 1979); see Chapter Seven.

38. Martin Pugh, *Hurrah for the Blackshirts! Fascists and Fascism in Britain Between the Wars* (London: Jonathan Cape, 2005), 218.

39. See: Martin Gilbert, *The Holocaust: The Jewish Tragedy* (London: Fontana Press, 1986).

40. Hannah Arendt, *Eichmann in Jerusalem: A report on the Banality of Evil* (London: Faber & Faber, 1963).

"millennial and messianic" urgency that ushered in his Thousand Year Reich.[41] But the Nazi amalgam of religious, cultural, and political anti-Semitism was based on the "science" of race, and, as often in times of economic hardship, the enduring search for a scapegoat ended with the persecution of that most enduring of religious, cultural, and racial communities, "the Jews."[42] Antagonism to Jews has always existed, but it has been exploited by Gentile authorities orchestrating systematic persecutions. Jews were often involved in usury— lending money at interest—and, as will be seen, rulers could win easy popularity and wipe out their debts by expelling Jewish communities. In 1290 King Edward I issued an Edict expelling all Jews from England, although they were readmitted by Cromwell in 1656. In Spain and Portugal there were persecutions and expulsions in the fourteenth and fifteenth centuries. Much later the Russian Tsars organized pogroms, while in France the innocent Dreyfus was used as a scapegoat by the military authorities.

Nonetheless, throughout history Jew and non-Jew have lived side-by-side and have co-operated with each other and been a positive influence on each other; and there have been pro-Semites as well as anti-Semites.[43] During the Holocaust, many Jews lost their lives because of non-Jews, but many owed their lives to non-Jews.[44] The frank discussion of the "Jewish question" pre-Holocaust owed much to society's Enlightenment influences: Jews were seen as equal to other men and judged not on what they were but on their actions. It was regarded as a mark of civilization that Jew and Gentile could engage in debate on equal terms.

Despite this, the Holocaust continues to cast its long, sinister shadow in the twenty-first century, eclipsing positive relationships and distorting views of those who lived and wrote long before it occurred. Chesterton did not live to see the Second World War or the Holocaust, but his unavoidable absence from that period of history has not prevented critics from seeing him against its background, even though for some time after the Second World War he was

---

41. Charles B. Strozier, K. A. Boyd, "The Apocalyptic," in Strozier et al, *The Fundamental Mindset: Psychological Perspectives on Religion, Violence, and History* (New York: Oxford University Press, 2010), 29–37.

42. See: A. H. Foxman, *Jews and Money: The Story of a Stereotype*, op. cit.

43. See: W.D. Rubinstein, H.L. Rubinstein, *Philosemitism* (London: Macmillan Press, 1999); as Bernard Lazare noted, while urging anti-Jewish legislation, throughout history the Popes condemned violence against Jews (see: B. Lazare, *Anti-Semitism: its History and Causes*, 1894), accessed July 8, 2012, http://archive.org/details/Anti-semitismItsHistoryAndCausesByBernardLazare. One of my treasured possessions is a photograph taken in the garden of my mother's home in East London in 1934, depicting her family with a little girl, Sybil Pallenbaum, who lived downstairs in the same house, the daughter of a Jewish dentist and his wife.

44. See: Martin Gilbert, *The Righteous: the unsung heroes of the Holocaust* (London: Black Swan, 2003).

seen as a "political prophet" regarding Hitler and Nazism[45]—a view that persisted until the 1960s.[46] By the late twentieth century, however, his reputation as an anti-Semite seemed assured. This about-turn in perceptions was linked to the rise in interest in the Holocaust, which itself changed Western attitudes toward anti-Semitism so drastically that focusing on the Jewish origins of individuals, or attributing specific characteristics to Jews, became unacceptable. Inevitably, commentators on Chesterton have been affected by this unprecedented evil, which represented a watershed in history.[47] As David Lodge notes: "The death of some six million European Jews under Hitler's Nazi regime was arguably the most traumatic episode in modern European history. . . ."[48] Margaret Canovan remarks that Chesterton "lived and wrote before World War II" and that to such radicals "the economic and political power of the Jews all over the Western world seemed as secure and unchallengeable as does that of America now"; that "the idea of a Final Solution seemed as incredible then as the destruction of America now. . . ."[49] Nonetheless, Chesterton did offend some Jews during his lifetime, and although there is equally compelling evidence of his unequivocal anti-Nazi stance, some criticism has come from admirers such as Canovan.[50]

If emotive debates on Chesterton's "guilt" or "innocence" resemble a posthumous trial it is due to the crime against humanity that was the Holocaust, which increased awareness of anti-Semitism and its unacceptability, but also influenced perceptions of earlier attitudes to Jews.[51] Chesterton's biographer Maisie Ward noted a "strange crank peculiar to the *ChesterBelloc*—their out-

---

45. "[I]n the universal reaction from the war-spirit to Pacifism the truths he was urging received scant attention, his really amazing prophecies fell on deaf ears. . . . Only one thing, said the *New Witness*, would make for a stable peace: remove Prussia from her position at the head of Germany: make her regaining of it impossible. Make a strong Poland, and a strong Italy, as well as a strong France" (M. Ward, *Gilbert Keith Chesterton*, op. cit., 425–426); I. Brown, "A Multiple Man" (1944), in Denis Joseph Conlon, ed., *G.K. Chesterton: The Critical Judgments Part I: 1900–1937* (Antwerp: Antwerp Studies in English Literature, 1976), 58. Frank Sheed compiled Chesterton's prophetic articles in *The End of the Armistice* (1940) for this reason (Ian Ker, *G.K. Chesterton: A Biography* [Oxford: Oxford University Press, 2011], 693).

46. Malcolm Muggeridge, "GKC" (1963), D.J. Conlon, ed., *G.K. Chesterton: A Half Century of Views* (Oxford: Oxford University Press, 1987), 226; R. Hamilton, "Rationalist in Fairyland" (1967), in ibid., 237.

47. Tony Kushner, *The persistence of prejudice: Antisemitism in British Society during the Second World War* (Manchester: Manchester University Press, 1989), 57.

48. D. Lodge, *The Novelist at the Crossroads and other essays on Fiction and Criticism*, op. cit., 146.

49. Margaret Canovan, *G.K. Chesterton: Radical Populist* (New York: Harcourt Brace Jovanovich, 1977), 140.

50. For example M. Canovan, *G.K. Chesterton: Radical Populist* (ibid., 136).

51. Dan Stone, *Responses to Nazism in Britain, 1933–1939: Before the War and the Holocaust* (Basingstoke, Hants: Palgrave Macmillan, 2003), 3.

look towards Jews."[52] But in pre-Holocaust England this "crank" was not so "strange." There was no persecution, but in polite circles anti-Semitism took "the form of pinpricks of mere contempt."[53] Harold Nicolson, discussing Foreign Office recruitment with his friends Virginia Woolf and her Jewish husband Leonard, recorded: "The awkward question of the Jews arises. I admit that is the snag. Jews are more interested in international life than are Englishmen, and if we opened the service it might be flooded by clever Jews"; but, he added that "[i]t was a little difficult to argue this point frankly with Leonard there."[54] George Orwell believed that anti-Semitism was "pretty widespread"[55] although he himself was not immune to such views,[56] and official fears of rousing anti-Semitism influenced British inter-War immigration policy.[57] But if Jews were seen as foreign, so was violent anti-Semitism. Harold Nicolson later reported his disgust at the treatment of Viennese Jews;[58] as the British Union of Fascists increased their violence, their popularity among "respectable" people declined.[59] In some senses post-Holocaust England has reconstructed its past[60] by "forgetting" its "anti-Semitism,"[61] therefore discussion of the "Jewish question" by pre-Holocaust writers can easily shock,[62] as can the light tone of the Jewish refugee debate of the 1930s.[63] The Holocaust prompted research into anti-Semitism,[64] but the very unacceptability of anti-Semitism in Western soci-

52. M. Ward, *Gilbert Keith Chesterton*, op. cit., 414–415.

53. B. Jacobs, "An Enquiry into Anti-Semitism," Interview, the *Jewish Chronicle*, October 23, 1925, 20; G. C. Lebzelter, *Political Anti-Semitism in England* 1918–1939, op. cit., 34.

54. Diary entry, July 11, 1930, Harold Nicolson, *Harold Nicolson: Diaries and Letters* 1930–39, N. Nicolson, ed. (London: Collins, 1967), 53.

55. George Orwell, *As I Please: The Collected Essays, Journal and Letters of George Orwell, Vol. III, 1943–5* (London: Secker and Warburg, 1968), 338.

56. He believed there was "no real Jewish 'problem' in England. The Jews are not numerous or powerful enough" (G. Orwell, *As I Please: The Collected Essays, Journal and Letters of George Orwell, Vol. III, 1943–5*, op. cit., 332–333).

57. Tony Kushner, *The persistence of prejudice*, op. cit., 34.

58. "There is a devilish sort of humour in their cruelty. . . . They made the Jewish gentlemen take off all their clothes and walk on all fours on the grass. They made the old Jewish ladies get up into the trees by ladders and sit there. They then told them to chirp like birds" (Letter, H. Nicolson to Vita Sackville-West, June 17, 1938, H. Nicolson, *Harold Nicolson: Diaries and Letters* 1930–39, op. cit., 347–348).

59. M. Pugh, *Hurrah for the Blackshirts! Fascists and Fascism in Britain Between the Wars*, op. cit., 167–169.

60. Maurice Halbwachs, *On Collective Memory* (Chicago: The University of Chicago Press, 1992), 182.

61. Peter Novick, *The Holocaust and Collective Memory* (London: Bloomsbury, 2001), 170.

62. W. D. Rubinstein, *A History of the Jews in the English-Speaking World: Great Britain* (London: Macmillan Press Ltd., 1996), 293.

63. Ibid., 320.

64. G. C. Lebzelter, *Political Anti-Semitism in England* 1918–1939, op. cit., 1.

eties—its marginalization rather than eradication—has hampered post-Holo-caust understanding of pre-Holocaust society as younger generations of commentators struggle to distinguish between anti-Semitic writings, humor-ous material, and serious philosophical discussion, sometimes conflating all these with Hitler's approach.

Like many of his contemporaries Chesterton equated anti-Semitism not with discussing the "Jewish question" but with violence against Jews, associated with the Tsarist pogroms and the Swansea riots. He insisted that he represented a middle way, "more reasonable than those of the people that wreck their shops; and much more reasonable than those of the people who justify them on all occasions."[65]

The post-Holocaust change in attitudes to anti-Semitism is illustrated by the fact that in 1947 Evelyn Waugh saw Chesterton's *The Man Who Was Thursday* as overturning Jewish conspiracy theories. He mentioned the Holocaust without linking it to Chesterton's "anti-Semitism,"[66] but fifty years later, British Parlia-mentarian Gerald Kaufman compared Chesterton's approach to that of Hitler in an article redolent with Holocaust influence, *Chesterton's final solution*.[67] Furthermore, it has been claimed that Chesterton's admirers have ignored his "anti-Semitism,"[68] but while not all post-Holocaust commentators on Chester-ton have discussed the issue,[69] later biographies have not avoided it. None, however, have studied it in depth,[70] and if Chesterton's admirers have mini-mized his "anti-Semitism" critics have minimized his "pro-Semitism." Interest

65. G. K. Chesterton, "Taffy," *Illustrated London News*, September 16, 1911, in *The Uses of Diversity* (London: Methuen & Co. Ltd., 1920/1927), 158; see Chapter Eight.

66. Evelyn Waugh, E., "The Man Who Was Thursday," in D. J. Conlon, ed., *G. K. Chesterton: A Half Century of Views*, op. cit., 73–74.

67. Gerald Kaufman, "Chesterton's final solution," *Times Educational Supplement*, January 2, 1998.

68. Jay P. Corrin, *G. K. Chesterton and Hilaire Belloc: The Battle Against Modernity* (Athens: Ohio University Press, 1981), 63; D. Lodge, *The Novelist at the Crossroads and other essays on Fiction and Criticism*, op. cit., 155.

69. Out of 56 short commentaries from 1946 to 1985, 35 (by 30 authors) mention neither anti-Semitism nor the Holocaust (Denis J. Conlon, ed., *G. K. Chesterton: A Half Century of Views*, op. cit.).

70. D. J. Conlon, ed., *G. K. Chesterton: A Half Century of Views*, op. cit., included critical pieces, as did John Sullivan, ed., *G. K. Chesterton: A Centenary Appraisal* (London: Paul Elek, 1974), notably I. Boyd (ibid., 40–57). The English Chesterton Society invited Kaufman, a critic of Chesterton's "anti-Semitism" to address them on the subject (*Jewish Chronicle*, November 14, 1997) and he subsequently accepted an invitation to become Vice-president (D. J. Conlon, Secretary, The Chesterton Society, personal communication, September 21, 2004). Those discussing the issue at length include Canovan (*G. K. Chesterton: Radical Populist*, op. cit.), Pearce (*Wisdom and Innocence: A Life of G. K. Chesterton*, op. cit.) and Michael Coren (*Gilbert: The Man Who Was G. K. Chesterton* [Vancouver: Regent College Publishing, 1990]).

in the problem has been increasingly linked to the Holocaust, and has waxed rather than waned with the passage of time. Holocaust interest has stimulated a growing historiography,[71] which, paradoxically, has encouraged anachronistic assumptions that those living at the time must have known about it; in fact, post-Holocaust judgment has also fallen on Jews of that era for failing those who perished.[72] But only with the liberation of Hitler's death camps did its full horror begin to dawn upon the public consciousness.[73] Even after the War, the raising of the Iron Curtain, the emergence of the Cold War, and the plight of thousands of displaced persons in Europe, distracted full attention from the public's ability to absorb the unthinkable, especially as the physical and emotional trauma of Holocaust survivors, and post-War dislocations, meant that not all their experiences were recorded straight away. The term "Holocaust" only emerged in 1961 in connection with the Nazi Adolf Eichmann's trial in Jerusalem.[74] As the Holocaust recedes into history the task of gathering first-hand testimony from the dwindling number of survivors becomes more urgent.[75] But the increased stock of knowledge holds uncomfortable lessons: one important factor in the world's unwillingness to confront the Holocaust was that even in 1961 "[m]any people in many parts of the world still believe[d] that by 1933 Germany was 'dominated by the Jews,'" since this "'fact,' supported with well-selected statistics," was "pumped into each visitor to the Reich and disseminated from every Nazi agency abroad."[76]

As interest in the Holocaust has grown it has influenced criticism of remarks Chesterton wrote long before the rise of Nazism. For example, Lodge, acknowledging the unfairness of reading Chesterton in the light of a posthumous event nonetheless says that he and Belloc were "playing with fire; fire that (though the possibility never crossed their minds and would have shocked and horrified them had it done so) eventually burned in the ovens of Auschwitz. . . ." On Chesterton's "whimsica[l]" suggestion that English Jews should wear Arab dress Lodge admits: "[O]ne cannot help thinking forward to the yellow stars stitched to the sleeves of Hitler's victims. . . ."[77] Lawrence Clipper, with "horrible antici-

---

71. Dan Stone, *Constructing the Holocaust: A Study in Historiography* (London: Vallentine Mitchell, 2003), xiii.

72. W.D. Rubinstein, *The Myth of Rescue: Why the democracies could not have saved more Jews from the Nazis* (London: Routledge, 1997), 4–8; 12–13.

73. See Chapter Five.

74. P. Novick, *The Holocaust and Collective Memory*, op. cit., 133.

75. For example, the Steven Spielberg Film and Video Archive, housed by the United States Holocaust Memorial Museum, aimed during the 1990s to record oral testimony from 50,000 Holocaust survivors.

76. James Parkes, *Antisemitism* (London: Vallentine, Mitchell, 1963), 88.

77. D. Lodge, *The Novelist at the Crossroads and other essays on Fiction and Criticism*, op. cit., 155–156.

pation," saw in Chesterton's Zionist proposals a "final solution" with "steps toward identification (yellow stars of David)" and "segregation in some sort of self-governing enclave." He detected the "odor of Auschwitz and Belsen" that "mock" and "impeach" Chesterton's entire worldview.[78] Chesterton's Open Letter to Rufus Isaacs (written in 1918, to be studied in Chapter Six), has been seen as "distasteful . . . especially in the light of the holocaust which was to follow."[79] That interest in Chesterton's "anti-Semitism" has grown in inverse proportion to the distance in time from the Holocaust is demonstrated by the fact that Garry Wills' *Chesterton* (1961) contained one brief mention of anti-Semitism,[80] but in its re-issue forty years later Wills admitted he had been insufficiently "strict" on Chesterton's "faults," including "his anti-Semitism."[81] In *Papal Sin: Structures of Deceit* (2000) he devotes 59 pages to the Holocaust, anti-Semitism, and related issues.[82]

David Lodge notes that after the Holocaust, society "gradually [came] to realize" that the "guilt and responsibility" could not be "confined to the Nazis alone," citing Norman Cohn's *Warrant for Genocide* (1967) and James Parkes' *Antisemitism* (1963) as portraying "Hitler's 'final solution'" as "the ghastly climax to two thousand years of Christian prejudice." However, Lodge believed that Christianity experienced a change of heart, "prompted" by Gordon C. Zahn's *German Catholics and Hitler's Wars* (1964), and "goaded" by "polemics" like Rolf Hochhuth's play *The Representative* (1963).[83] Growing acceptance of the idea of associated guilt for the Holocaust, expressed in such titles as *While Six Million Died*, *Blind Eye to Murder*, and *Murder in Our Midst* has raised public consciousness regarding pre-Holocaust commentators on the "Jewish question."[84]

Chesterton's Zionism was once assumed to be proof against charges of anti-

---

78. Lawrence Clipper, *G.K. Chesterton* (New York: Indiana University at South Bend, Twayne Publishers Inc., 1974), 57; despite these "flaws (if they are flaws)" Clipper concludes that Chesterton's romances "do not deserve the oblivion in which they languish at present" (ibid., 143).

79. M. Coren, *Gilbert: The Man Who Was G.K. Chesterton*, op. cit., 203.

80. Garry Wills, *Chesterton* (New York: Image Books, 1961/2001), 141.

81. Ibid., xvii.

82. Garry Wills, *Papal Sin: Structures of Deceit* (London: Darton, Longman & Todd, 2000), 13–69; there was no mention of Chesterton.

83. D. Lodge, *The Novelist at the Crossroads and other essays on Fiction and Criticism*, op. cit., 146; the references are to J. Parkes, *Antisemitism*, op. cit.; Gordon C. Zahn, *German Catholics and Hitler's Wars: A Study in Social Control* (London/New York: Sheed & Ward, 1964); R. Hochhuth's play is also translated as *The Deputy* (1963); see Chapter Nine.

84. Arthur D. Morse, *While Six Million Died* (London: Secker & Warburg, 1968); Tom Bower, *Blind Eye to Murder: Britain, America and the Purging of Nazi Germany—A Pledge Betrayed* (London: Andre Deutsch, 1981); Omer Bartov, *Murder in Our Midst: The Holocaust, Industrial Killing, and Representation* (New York: Oxford University Press, 1996).

Semitism[85] but, as Chapter Seven shows, post-Holocaust critics have been similarly "strict" on pre-Holocaust non-Jewish Zionists. For example, Gerald Kaufman quotes from an unnamed source Chesterton's "vile" language about Jews (shown in italics) which, when restored to its original context (*The New Jerusalem* [1920]) is capable of bearing a different interpretation:

> Rightly or wrongly, certain people in Palestine fear the coming of the Jews as they fear the coming of the locusts; they regard them as [*parasites that feed on a community by a thousand methods of financial intrigue and economic exploitation*]. I could understand the Jews indignantly denying this, or eagerly disproving it, or best of all, explaining what is true in it while exposing what is untrue. What is strange, I might almost say weird, about the attitude of some quite intelligent and sincere Zionists, is that they talk, write and apparently think as if there were no such thing in the world.[86]

Kaufman regarded Chesterton as a proto-Nazi, equating his Zionism with Hitler's anti-Semitism, and citing his reference to "a strange swarthy little creature with a hooked nose" as evidence of Chesterton's view of "the archetypal Jew."[87] In fact the description referred to Chesterton's first meeting with his

---

85. K. Whitehorn, "The Return of G. K. Chesterton" (1974), in Conlon, D. J., ed., *G. K. Chesterton: A Half Century of Views*, op. cit., 305–309.

86. G. K. Chesterton, *The New Jerusalem* (1920), quoted in G. Kaufman, "Chesterton's Final Solution," op. cit.

87. G. Kaufman, "Chesterton's final solution," *Times Educational Supplement*, January 2, 1998. Citing Chesterton's interest in George MacDonald's tales of fairies and goblins, Simon Mayers sees in this reminiscence evidence that he "maintained this caricature of the Jew as a warped and grotesque creature throughout his life," noting that William Oddie cites the incident as "evidence of Chesterton's philosemitism" while omitting the unflattering description (W. Oddie, *Chesterton and the Romance of Orthodoxy: The Making of GKC, 1874–1908* [Oxford: Oxford University Press, 2008], 126–127); S. Mayers, *Chesterton's Jews: Stereotypes and Caricatures in the Literature and Journalism of G. K. Chesterton* (CreateSpace Independent Publishing Platform, 2013), 56–64. However, Mayers fails to note the life-long mutual friendship that sprang out of the incident, quoting from Chesterton's *The New Jerusalem* (1920) his description of rabbis having hair "like the horns of a devil," and that "one need not be an Anti-Semite to say that the face is often made to match," suggesting that they were "ugly, or even horrible" (S. Mayers, ibid, 63–64). However, Chesterton adds: "But though they may be ugly, or even horrible, they are not vulgar like the Jews of Brighton"; that the former "trail behind them too many primeval traditions and laborious loyalties, along with their grand though often greasy robes of bronze or purple velvet," as such resembling far more closely the paintings of Rembrandt than John Singer Sargent; for Rembrandt, "the Rabbi was, in a special and double sense, a distinguished figure," while Sargent's portrayals of his "sitters as solid citizens of England or America" made his pictures "direct provocations to a pogrom. But the light that Rembrandt loved falls not irreverently on the strange hairy haloes that can still be seen on the shaven heads of the Jews of Jerusalem." Furthermore, Chesterton rejects violence against them, concluding: "And I should be sorry for any pogrom that brought down any of their grey wisps or whiskers in sorrow to the grave" (G. K. Chesterton, *The New Jerusalem* [1920], *G. K. Chesterton Collected Works Vol. XX* [San Francisco: Ignatius Press, 2001], 262–263).

lifelong Jewish friend Lawrence Solomon, when in school he "extricat[ed] a strange swarthy little creature with a hooked nose from being bullied or rather being teased."[88] Kaufman interpreted Chesterton's lines "Thou has a right to rule thyself: to be / The thing thou wilt: to grin, to fawn, to creep" as meaning that when "a Jew acknowledged himself to be a Jew and went off to Palestine to rule himself as Chesterton so generously advocated, even there [the Jew] was still horrible." In fact, the poem, *To a Certain Nation*, was written in defense of Captain Dreyfus, and the "certain nation" was France.[89]

Nonetheless, Ian Ker notes that the anti-Jewish pogroms of the late nineteenth and early twentieth century "should have made Chesterton more cautious in what he said,"[90] and although he died before the Holocaust, it would be more useful to ask whether Chesterton helped to cause it by fostering anti-Semitism. Despite this, inevitably, post-Holocaust commentators have found it difficult to divest themselves of Holocaust influence. Canovan found it "impossible to read" Chesterton's remarks about Jews wearing Arab dress "without being chilled by the recollection of the Nazis' Nuremberg Laws; but of course [he] was quite innocent of any such connection, and had no idea of making such separate dress a mark of shame and an incitement to mob violence."[91] Chesterton himself saw the suggestion as "a joke,"[92] a "pleasing if flippant fancy" that British Jews should be allowed to occupy any public office—even that of Archbishop of Canterbury—provided that they dressed as Arabs, an idea "often offered symbolically as a solution to the Jewish problem."[93] The idea did represent something more than a joke,[94] but it also exemplified Chesterton's enduring fascination with the symbolism of dress—he wore a cloak and carried a sword-stick,[95] and his prized possession was an alarmingly large knife.[96] He found noses of any description, as well as the very fact of walking on two legs, hilarious. The "ugliest thing that Europe ever produced," he claimed, was "its modern dress";[97] in contrast, the long robes of Eastern males,

88. G.K. Chesterton, *Autobiography* (Sevenoaks, Kent: Fisher Press, 1937/1992), 72.

89. G. Kaufman, "Chesterton's final solution," op. cit.; the lines quoted are from "To a Certain Nation" (G.K. Chesterton, *The Works of G.K. Chesterton*, op. cit., 274).

90. I. Ker, *G.K. Chesterton: A Biography*, op. cit., 422.

91. M. Canovan, *G.K. Chesterton: Radical Populist*, op. cit., 137.

92. G.K. Chesterton, *Eyewitness*, July 24, 1913.

93. G.K. Chesterton, *The New Jerusalem* (1920), in Vol. XX of *G.K. Chesterton Collected Works* (San Francisco: Ignatius Press, 2001), 397.

94. See Chapter Seven.

95. M. Ward, *Gilbert Keith Chesterton*, op. cit., 158.

96. M. Ward, *Return to Chesterton* (London: Sheed & Ward, 1952), 130.

97. G.K. Chesterton, *Sidelights on New London and Newer York and Other Essays* (London: Sheed & Ward, 1932), 165.

reminiscent of medieval costume, enhanced their dignity.[98] He believed that the "skirt mean[t] female dignity, not female submission," "proved" by the fact that "when men wish to be safely impressive, as judges, priests or kings, they do wear skirts, the long, trailing robes of female dignity."[99]

Nonetheless, the Nazis' yellow stars took their inspiration from medieval dress distinctions for different social categories, including religious minorities in Islamic and Christian countries.[100] It is against this pre-Holocaust background, rather than that of the Holocaust, that Chesterton should be seen. In fact, his Jewish contemporaries did see him against the backdrop of historical anti-Semitism, as they made clear in several critical pieces in the *Jewish Chronicle* and *Jewish World*[101] sparked by *Chesterbelloc* allegations of Jewish lack of patriotism in the Great War.[102] Belatedly reviewing *Manalive* (1912) the *Chronicle* drew attention to passages seen as impugning Jewish patriotism,[103] and up until 1921 Chesterton's "disparaging remarks about Jews" provoked 35 editorials, news reports, and letters.[104] Neither the *Jewish Chronicle* nor the *Jewish World* reviewed *The New Jerusalem*, and when in 1933 the *Chronicle* interviewed him about his denunciations of Nazi anti-Semitism the editor classed Chesterton with "the most confirmed anti-Semites" and with "bosoms hitherto . . . irrevocably hardened against the Hebrew."[105] But in headlining Chesterton's attacks on Hitler the editor highlighted the fact that many Jews were desperate

---

98. G.K. Chesterton, *The New Jerusalem*, op. cit., 214–215.

99. G.K. Chesterton, "The Coldness of Chloe," *What's Wrong with the World*, op. cit., 60. Chesterton blames Western assumptions for misunderstandings about the function of the hat in Hebrew ritual: "It may be true, and personally I think it is true, that the Hebrew covering of the head signifies a certain stress on the fear of God, which is the beginning of wisdom, while the Christian uncovering of the head suggests rather the love of God that is the end of wisdom. But this has nothing to do with the taste and dignity of the ceremony; and to do justice to these we must treat the Jew as an oriental; we must even dress him as an oriental" because "[t]o throw those loose draperies over the head is decidedly a dignified and even poetic gesture" (G.K. Chesterton, *The New Jerusalem*, op. cit., 396); see Chapter Seven.

100. The Nazis introduced yellow stars for Jews in Poland in 1939, and throughout the Reich in 1941 for all Jews over six years old; the Fourth Lateran Council (1215) introduced distinctive clothing for Jews and Muslims and forbade sexual contact with Christians; in England Jews had to wear the "Tablets of the Law" although enforcement gradually declined; sumptuary laws mandating distinctive clothing for different social categories were also aimed at preventing commoners dressing like aristocrats and to restrict extremes of fashion and luxury; prostitutes were required to wear distinctive clothing and Muslims to wear a crescent-shaped patch or Eastern dress; distinctive dress for Christians and Jews was a feature in Muslim territories from the sixth or seventh centuries.

101. D. Rapp, "The Jewish Response to G.K. Chesterton's Antisemitism, 1911–1933," *Patterns of Prejudice* 24 (2–4), (1990): 76.

102. Ibid., 78–79.

103. *Jewish Chronicle*, November 5, 1915, 29, in ibid., 79–80; see Chapter Six.

104. Ibid., 75–86.

105. Interview with G.K. Chesterton, *Jewish Chronicle*, September 22, 1933, 14; see Chapter Five.

for recognition of their own view on the Nazi threat. At such a time, and with such a history, Jews were understandably alert to injustice against Jews—but an anti-Semite who shared their concerns was clearly worth a headline.

Primo Levi described the concentration camp inmates' fear that, even if they escaped, nobody would believe their story.[106] With Holocaust denial gaining ground, the very idea of the Holocaust is beginning to come under pressure,[107] and soon, Holocaust remembrance may become a thing of the past:

> When all the survivors are dead, people will forget about the Shoah. In 35 years, they will not believe that it ever happened.[108]

According to Michael McGarry, the Holocaust is "not only a part of Jewish history, but more importantly a part of Christian history," and "in the post-Auschwitz age, Christian history must include as a significant chapter the experience of the holocaust."[109] But in trying to avoid a repetition of the greatest crime in history, we risk being trapped in the same cycle of mistakes and misunderstanding. In response to Jewish criticism Chesterton denied anti-Semitism; but his complex stance did not find favor among anti-Semites either. Paradoxically, the complexity of his attitude to Jews—as well as "the Jews"—can make a positive contribution to contemporary Jewish/non-Jewish relations by deepening our understanding of pre-Holocaust inter-communal exchanges, with their good intentions, but with their mistakes and missed opportunities.

One such misunderstanding is that post-Holocaust interpretations have placed Chesterton on the political Right, when his populist approach was more redolent of socialism. His preoccupation with the plight of the underdog—perennial concern of the political Left—will be studied in the next chapter.

---

106. Primo Levi, "The Drowned and the Saved," in John K. Roth, Michael Berenbaum, eds., *Holocaust: Religious and Philosophical Implications* (St Paul, Minnesota: Paragon House, 1989), 107.

107. See Chapter Nine.

108. Son of a Holocaust survivor, film producer Branko Lustig, who won an Oscar for *Schindler's List*, commenting on the fact that 2011 was "the first year for nearly 50 years that not a single Oscar or Golden Globe entry has focused on the horrors of the Shoah" ("Is this the end of the road for films on the Holocaust?" *Jewish Chronicle*, February 18, 2011); see Chapter Nine.

109. Michael McGarry, "The Holocaust as an orientating Event for Christianity," in H. P. Fry, ed., *Christian-Jewish Dialogue: A Reader* (Exeter: University of Exeter Press, 1996), 67.

2

Chesterton and the Underdog

THE BRITISH UNDERDOG, though less familiar than the British bull-dog, has played a constant yet ever-changing role in British politics, and this phenomenon is essential to understanding Chesterton's relationship with "the Jews." The politically radical Chesterton wanted to "put a chain and collar of Responsibility, not on the Underdog, but on the Top-dog."[1] He certainly refused to obey the maxim "never discuss politics and religion," for politics, like Judaism and its offspring Christianity, should be concerned with the just cause, with the weakest in society.[2] But when politics became a secular religion there was a danger of deifying the just cause instead of the uncaused Cause—worshipping creation instead of the Creator. Replacing the theocentric with the anthropocentric led to the philosophical approach of Tolstoy, who "erase[d] theology altogether" and formed a "purely ethical theory that love should be the instrument of reform"; but following a "purely ethical theory" could easily lead to unethical practices, and Tolstoy ended, Chesterton said, by "maintaining that we have no right to strike a man if he is torturing a child before our eyes."[3]

Since "[e]very man carries about with him his own theory of the world," with each "living in a separate Cosmos,"[4] there were as many causes as there were men, and the radical often used the plight of their underdog to attack

---

1. G.K. Chesterton, *Autobiography* (Sevenoaks, Kent: Fisher Press, 1936/1992), 184.

2. For example, "Thou shalt not wrest the judgment of thy poor in his cause" (Ex. 23:6); "Thou shalt not pervert the judgment of the stranger, nor of the fatherless; nor take a widow's raiment to pledge" (Deut. 25:17); "Cursed be he that perverteth the judgment of the stranger, fatherless, and widow" (Deut. 27:19); "Blessed are they that keep judgment, and he that doeth righteousness at all times" (Psalm 106:3); "But let judgment run down as waters, and righteousness as a mighty stream" (Amos 5:24); the New Testament continues this emphasis on justice for the weak (Acts 6:1) (*The Holy Bible* King James Version [London: Collins, 1953]).

3. G.K. Chesterton, *Leo Tolstoy* (1903) in Vol. XVIII of *G.K. Chesterton Collected Works* (San Francisco: Ignatius Press, 1991), 38.

4. G.K. Chesterton, *Thomas Carlyle* (1902) in Vol. XVIII of *G.K. Chesterton Collected Works* (San Francisco: Ignatius Press, 1991), 29–30.

political opponents. For example, George Bernard Shaw and Chesterton, whose love of the underdog was part of their liberal make-up,[5] took anti-Semitism so seriously that they often used the issue to attack each other. In fact, many radicals identified so closely with their underdog that they became one by proxy, although lack of constancy was a continuous danger. To the poor, however, Chesterton remained unequivocally loyal, noting that as slavery went out, the workhouses came in.[6]

It is possible to adopt more than one underdog, and as a young man Chesterton espoused the cause of suffering Jewry. In 1906 he used Jewish suffering to highlight Irish suffering, and said that he had "no doubt that the Russians have grossly oppressed the Jews. In the same way I have ... no doubt that the English have grossly oppressed the Irish."[7] In 1913 he claimed that his interest in Jews was real, unlike those "who publish little pamphlets about the persecution of Jews in Russia." They were "not interested in Jews at all" but only in "certain imaginary good old men with patriarchal beards and ragged gabardines who are made to wander about in the snow because they never did anyone any harm," while omitting "[a]ll the interesting part of the Jewish problem, good as well as bad."[8] Much later he claimed that although the English were never "in a mood to enjoy the massacre of Catholics and Celts" they nonetheless "tolerated the massacre of Catholic and Celts."[9] As to the Jews—the minority suffering the most enduring prejudice—Canovan remarks: "The jokes about pork and noses, which we read as bullying taunts against the weak, were often meant by their writers as brave gestures defying the mighty."[10] Anthony Julius notes that anti-Semitism presented itself "*both* as a pseudo-ethical obligation *and* as a sanctioned exception to the rules of ethical behaviour." With its "moral appeal" it also sought "the suspension of the categorical imperative in respect of Jews" and, thus, "[h]atred represents itself as an exercise in virtue, spite masquerades

5. I. Boyd, *The Novels of G.K. Chesterton: A Study in Art and Propaganda* (London: Paul Elek, 1975), 154. The Catholic Emancipation Act was passed in 1829. Full equality for Jews and Catholics was not achieved until 1890, although heirs to the throne may not be Catholic and any member of the royal family who marries a Catholic automatically forfeits his or her claim to the throne.

6. G.K. Chesterton, *A Short History of England* (London: Chatto & Windus, 1917), 582.

7. G.K. Chesterton, *Illustrated London News*, April 21, 1906, in *Gilbert Magazine* 12 (2 & 3), (November/December 2008): 58, accessed May 19, 2011, http://www.209.236.72.127/wordpress/wp-content/uploads/2010/12/gilbert_12.2_5.pdf.

8. G.K. Chesterton, *Illustrated London News*, July 19, 1913, in *Gilbert Magazine* 12 (2 & 3), (November/December 2008): 8, accessed May 19, 2011, http://www.209.236.72.127/wordpress/wp-content/uploads/2010/12/gilbert_12.2_5.pdf.

9. G.K. Chesterton, *Illustrated London News*, September 20, 1930, in *Gilbert Magazine* 12 (2 & 3), (November/December 2008): 9, accessed May 19, 2011, http://209.236.72.127/wordpress/wp-content/uploads/2010/12/gilbert_12.2_5.pdf.

10. M. Canovan, *G.K. Chesterton: Radical Populist* (New York: Harcourt Brace Jovanovich, 1977), 140.

as righteous indignation. The Jew is injured in the interests of justice" and in defending "the interests of the poor, the disadvantaged, the downtrodden," and Julius concludes that Chesterton's "compassion for the poor and speaking openly about the Jews' harmful influence" were "of a piece."[11]

Chesterton, Cobbett, and the Underdog

Canovan notes that Chesterton's "intellectual ancestor" from the French revolutionary period was not Edmund Burke but William Cobbett.[12] His biography of Cobbett (1925) offers insights into his approach to the problem of competing radical causes. Cobbett, an English patriot who travelled from Tory to Radical without settling anywhere, also sympathized with the poor and the agricultural classes, as well as the American and French Republics. As an orthodox Anglican, the plight of Catholics as the underdogs of the Reformation provided the old soldier with ammunition for his attack on the Established Church. He also excoriated "money men"—Jews and Quakers: "[T]hat sect, the Quakers . . . arose in England: they were engendered by the Jewish system of usury. Till *excises* and *loanmongering* began, these vermin were never heard of in England."[13] Chesterton says Cobbett saw "the sprawling omnipotence of financiers over patriots";[14] that his inner consciousness (to which "nobody ever went . . . least of all himself") was full of questions such as "[w]hy ought not a Radical to dislike peasants being oppressed by Jews?"[15] Cobbett's "bitter generalizations"[16] were, Chesterton said, part of the "traditions of the past and the instincts of the people," intimately and inextricably bound up with countryside "common sense" about Yorkshiremen, Kentishmen, or gypsies: "Most people are still allowed to express these general impressions until they come to the case of the Jews. There (for some reason I have never understood), the whole natural tendency has been to stop; and anybody who says anything whatever about Jews as Jews is supposed to wish to burn them at the stake."[17]

A sympathetic biographer, Chesterton's analysis of Cobbett's inner consciousness is revealing: a champion of underdogs should have understood that Yorkshiremen and Kentishmen are on a more equal footing than were gypsies and Jews, the eternal outsiders, with the majority population. Although wealthy "outsiders" were better placed in a civilized society, in uncivilized times

11. Anthony Julius, *Trials of the Diaspora: A History of Anti-Semitism in England* (Oxford: Oxford University Press, 2010), 14.

12. M. Canovan, *G.K.C.: Radical Populist*, op. cit., 34.

13. William Cobbett, *Rural Rides* (London: Penguin Books, 1830/2001), 442.

14. G.K. Chesterton, *William Cobbett* (London: Hodder and Stoughton Ltd., 1925), 15.

15. Ibid., 138–139.

16. Ibid., 219.

17. Ibid., 193.

wealth was an added incentive to plunder. Cobbett's love for his countrymen was such that he tended to load the universal vices of greed, treachery, and miserliness onto the shoulders of Scotsmen and Jews as a warning to his countrymen, while praising the French and Americans as good examples of the radical tendency. Chesterton was also a patriot, although he preferred to laugh at foreigners rather than fight them. In Cobbett's inner consciousness he seems to have discovered a view of foreigners remarkably similar to his own, involving a similar clash of underdogs.

The Jew and the Papist: Underdogs?

Bernard Shaw was a close friend of Chesterton's but his antagonism to his religion[18] was apparent in the militant pacifist's firing of "anti-Semitism" hyperbole: "We cannot massacre the Jews without carting them all to Russia, which is hardly feasible"—a hypothesis raised neither by Chesterton's biography on Cobbett, to which Shaw referred, nor anywhere else by Chesterton.[19] Chesterton in turn ridiculed Shaw's notion that "to breed a man like a cart-horse was the true way to attain that higher civilisation, of intellectual magnanimity and sympathetic insight, which may be found in cart-horses."[20] Two of Chesterton's chief preoccupations were contending against eugenics and anti-Catholicism; the latter, "no doubt too cynically," was said to be "the default religion of the English," re-emerging in the nineteenth century in response to Irish mass immigration and "crypto-Romanism" fears regarding the Oxford movement.[21] The Irish were caricatured as backward and troublesome, the implication being that Catholicism was to blame. The Victorian age spawned a "huge volume of 'No Popery' literature,"[22] and the works of Charlotte Brontë, Harriet Beecher Stowe, Charles Kingsley, and Henry James, as well as many lesser known writers, were noted for their strident anti-Catholicism.[23] The anti-clerical persecu-

18. William Furlong, *Shaw and Chesterton: The Metaphysical Jesters* (University Park/London: Pennsylvania State University Press, 1970), 178.

19. "We must put up with the Jews, just as we must put up with the Irish" (G. B. Shaw, Review, *The New Statesman*, May 13, 1916, 133–136, in D. J. Conlon, ed., *G. K. Chesterton: The Critical Judgments Part I: 1900–1937* (Antwerp: Antwerp Studies in English Literature, 1976), 346. Julius West was sympathetic to Chesterton (*G. K. Chesterton: A Critical Study* [London: Martin Secker, 1915], 182), although he noted and objected to his "anti-Semitism" (ibid., 160).

20. G. K. Chesterton, introduction to *Eugenics and Other Evils* (London: Cassell & Company, 1922).

21. Aidan Nichols, *G. K. Chesterton, Theologian* (Darton: Longman & Todd Ltd., 2009), 188.

22. E. R. Norman, *Anti-Catholicism in Victorian England* (London: Geo. Allen & Unwin Ltd., 1968), 13.

23. See: Susan Griffin, *Anti-Catholicism in Nineteenth Century Fiction* (Cambridge: Cambridge University Press, 2004); also: A. Farmer, "A Strange Romance: Catholicism in the Life and Works of Charlotte Brontë," *Catholic Life*, January 2003; February 2003.

tion associated with the French Revolution had softened British attitudes toward some Catholics, if not toward Catholicism,[24] just as the Nazi anti-Jewish persecution would act as a watershed for vocal British anti-Semitism.[25] But at the beginning of the twentieth century, anti-Catholicism re-emerged, seemingly ingrained in the national consciousness.[26] Its reemergence was closely linked to Irish immigration and fuelled by the claim of the eugenics movement that Catholics would "out-breed" everyone else. Even before he became a Catholic Chesterton's underdog of choice was Ireland. In the wake of the Easter Rising of 1916, seen as an act of treachery against England during the Great War, his *Irish Impressions* (1919) was a bold attempt to present Ireland as a victim. Jews were already seen as victims by English liberals, and it was even, Chesterton claimed, "regarded as a rabid and insane form of religious persecution to suggest that a Jew very probably comes of a Jewish family"; at the same time, English rulers, confronted with an influx of poor Irish Catholics, saw eugenics "as a reasonable opportunity for . . . infanticide."[27] Chesterton meant birth control, the eugenics weapon which was, however, forbidden to the Irish by their religion. In this context, therefore, Irish and Italian immigrants—but also poor Jews from Russia[28]—were seen as threats to the English race, already regarded as dwelling on an overcrowded island.[29]

After his brief flirtation with socialism Chesterton returned to the Liberals, but as a severe critic of their Boer War policy. Those in his circle saw themselves as representing authentic Liberal values and maintained that the Boer War exemplified what was wrong with England in its Imperialistic bullying of a small people—denying their patriotic aspirations in the name of patriotism. Chesterton, himself a patriot, famously remarked that saying "my country right or wrong" was like saying "my mother, drunk or sober."[30]

24. After the anti-Catholic Gordon Riots set London aflame in 1778, many French priests and nuns sought refuge from the Revolution (Ernest E. Reynolds, *The Roman Catholic Church in England and Wales: A Short History* [Wheathampstead, Herts.: Anthony Clarke Books, 1973], 321).

25. W. D. Rubinstein, *A History of the Jews in the English-Speaking World: Great Britain* (London: Macmillan Press Ltd., 1996), 112; see Chapter One.

26. G. K. Chesterton, "A Century of Emancipation," *The Well and the Shallows* (London: Sheed & Ward, 1935), 178–195; see also: G. K. Chesterton, *The Catholic Church and Conversion* (San Francisco: Ignatius Press, 1926/2006).

27. G. K. Chesterton, *Irish Impressions* (1919) in Vol. XX of *G. K. Chesterton Collected Works* (San Francisco: Ignatius Press, 2001), 109.

28. See: W. D. Rubinstein, *A History of the Jews in the English-Speaking World: Great Britain* (London: Macmillan Press Ltd., 1996).

29. Alice Jenkins, abortion campaign pioneer, eugenicist and Neo-Malthusian, made such claims, warning of the dangers of "Rome" "reconquering" England (A. Jenkins, *Law for the Rich* [London: Charles Skilton Ltd., 1964], 43–45).

30. G. K. Chesterton, "A Defence of Patriotism," *The Defendant* (1902), accessed July 3, 2008, http://www.chesterton.org./gkc/murderer/defence_d_stories.htm.

Chesterton, along with his brother Cecil and Hilaire Belloc, criticized the Liberals over what he saw as their increasing illiberality—imposing reforms on the people rather than restoring the lost freedom of self-government. He continued to sympathize with conservative middle-class values[31] while deploring big business and the power of millionaires. His political writings, to which his "anti-Semitism" was mainly confined, were aimed at the middle and working classes, but his populist approach was characterized by the fact that, unlike socialist intellectuals who dismissed the anti-Semitism of the poor (Shaw dismissed the poor themselves),[32] Chesterton took their views seriously: "The popular legend is never quite wrong."[33] He looked up at the people that everyone else looked down on, praising the humor that enabled them to forget the poverty that "we (the moderately rich) ought never to forget."[34] Despite this, during the 1930s, unlike the socialist-turned-populist Sir Oswald Mosley, he did not exploit anti-Semitism nor did it predominate in his writing, which aimed to persuade the "small man" that there was an alternative to socialism and the vested interests that wiped out small players. He disapproved of Jewish capitalists but approved of Jewish anti-capitalists;[35] his diatribes against millionaires and capitalism appealed to socialists, although he also committed the unforgivable sin of attacking socialism.[36]

The Liberals' social reforms were partly aimed at repulsing the challenge posed by the Labour Party, but the 1923 General Election spelled the end of the Liberal Party as a major force competing for the working-class vote.[37] Because

31. Julia Stapleton, *Christianity, Patriotism, and Nationhood: The England of G.K. Chesterton* (Lanham MD/Plymouth: Lexington Books, 2009), 192.

32. See Chapter Four.

33. G.K. Chesterton, *St. Thomas Aquinas* (1933); *Thomas of Aquinas; St. Francis of Assisi* (San Francisco: Ignatius Press, 2002), 65.

34. G.K. Chesterton, "Cockneys and their Jokes," *All Things Considered* (USA: Feather Tail Press, 1908/2009), 8–9.

35. See Chapter Five.

36. "The Capitalist is an ingenious person, and has many polished characteristics; but I think the most singular thing about him is his staggering lack of shame" (G.K. Chesterton, "The New Raid," *Utopia of Usurers* [Norfolk VA: IHS Press, 1917/2002], 50); however, he begins "The Mask of Socialism": "The chief aim of all honest Socialists just now is to prevent the coming of Socialism" (ibid., 44); see Chapter Six.

37. Many working people voted Liberal or for a Liberal-sponsored Labour candidate before the Labour Party could muster candidates for every parliamentary seat. There was no overall victory in the December 1923 Election; in January 1924 Ramsay MacDonald formed a minority Labour Government which lasted until November 1924. See: Paul Adelman, *The Decline of the Liberal Party 1910–1931* (London: Longman, 1995). In 1918 all adult males were allowed the vote, also married women aged 30 and over; in 1928, all adult men and women were allowed the vote. Conservatives saw older women's votes as a counterweight to the newly enfranchised working men who were more inclined to vote Labour; see: M. Phillips, *The Ascent of Woman: A History of the Suffragette Movement and the Ideas Behind It* (London: Abacus, 2003), 230; 308.

of this—although many on the Left were "convinced that they were the natural vehicle of popular political aspirations, if only people would realise it!"[38]— many working men already voted Tory. The widening of the franchise was expected to benefit parties of the Left, but instead the Conservative Party became "one of the most successful parties known to modern Western democracy."[39] Chesterton believed that the "Common Labourer of England" was not a socialist and bore "no more resemblance" to a Labour Member of Parliament than to "a City Alderman or a Die-Hard Duke."[40] Working men purchased Tory newspapers, which became increasingly anti-Semitic after the Russian Revolution as Russia withdrew from the Great War and murdered its royal family.[41] Jewish patriotism was questioned by the *Times*, and the *Morning Post* warned that "those who know him know that the Russian Jew will remain what he has ever been since hostilities began, an enemy alien at heart."[42] Notwithstanding Disraeli, who made no secret of his Jewish roots,[43] and the fact that Arthur Balfour pledged a Jewish homeland in Palestine, the Conservative Party was not free of anti-Semitism.[44]

Neither was the Left, an amalgam of intellectuals strongly influenced by materialistic atheism and internationalism (including the Fabian movement of Shaw, Sidney and Beatrice Webb, and Bertrand Russell), and a working-class trade union movement.[45] In the late nineteenth century a surge of primarily Jewish immigrants from Eastern Europe was seen as competing for housing and employment, and the trade unions opposed what they saw as imported cheap labor. Some Labour supporters joined with Liberals—including Chesterton's circle—in opposing the Boer War, believing it was caused by a largely Jewish capitalist conspiracy.[46]

---

38. Stuart Ball and Ian Holliday, *Mass Conservatism: The Conservatives and the Public since the 1880s* (London: Frank Cass, 2002), xi.

39. Ibid., 1.

40. G. K. Chesterton, *Miscellany of Men* (Norfolk VA: IHS Press, 1912/2004), 139.

41. Tsarina Alexandra was a granddaughter of Queen Victoria.

42. March 9, 1918, 3, in Harry Defries, *Conservative Party Attitudes to Jews 1900–1950* (London: Frank Cass, 2001), 39; see Chapter Seven.

43. Thom Braun, *Disraeli the Novelist* (London: Geo. Allen & Unwin, 1981), 118–119.

44. See: H. Defries, *Conservative Party Attitudes to Jews 1900–1950*, op. cit. From 1920 to 1948, under a League of Nations Mandate, the British ruled the geo-political region of Palestine, now referred to as Mandatory Palestine.

45. E. P. Thompson, *The Making of the English Working Class* (London: Penguin Books, 1984), 34; see: H. A. Clegg, A. Fox, *A History of British Trade Unions since 1889 Vol. I, 1889–1910* (Oxford: Clarendon, 1964); H. A. Clegg, *A History of British Trade Unions since 1889 Vol. II, 1911–1933* (Oxford: Clarendon, 1985).

46. H. Defries, *Conservative Party Attitudes to Jews 1900–1950*, op. cit., 16.

Chesterton and the "Jewish Conspiracy"

But belief in Jewish capitalist conspiracies paled beside widespread fears of Jewish communist conspiracies. The latter were a growing feature of the right wing press, which was more comfortable with the idea of capitalist Jews; this led Chesterton to joke that Karl Marx, communism's founding father, was "by real or racial extraction . . . a Jew"—but so was Disraeli, "Queen Victoria's favourite Prime Minister."[47] The atheist Marx's anathematization of Judaism as a religion of hucksters was less well known,[48] but when the Russian Revolution rocked the Western world, socialism and communism became notorious as Jewish phenomena.[49] Although Jews were also capitalists, conspiracy theorists explained that both tendencies were secretly in league to achieve world domination. Rejecting such theories, Chesterton wrote:

> [I]t is true that [Jews] fattened on the worst forms of Capitalism; and it is inevitable that, on losing these advantages of Capitalism, they naturally took refuge in its other form, which is Communism. For both Capitalism and Communism rest on the same idea: a centralisation of wealth which destroys private property.[50]

Unfortunately, his self-consciously rational approach suggests that on losing financial power Jews turned to political means of getting their hands on other people's property. Many people saw Jewish engagement in a variety of (sometimes contradictory) fields[51]—normal among Gentiles—as suspicious. This prepared the way for the resurrection of *The Protocols of the Elders of Zion*, a Tsarist forgery, whose exposure by the *Times* in 1921 did not prevent the millionaire industrialist Henry Ford from funding the publication of half a million copies.[52]

---

47. G.K. Chesterton, *The Well and the Shallows*, op. cit., 126.

48. K. Marx, *On the Jewish Question* (1844 [Paris]); Marx argued that the Jewish religion did not need to disappear because it was already part of bourgeois society.

49. Baptized a Christian, Vladimir Ilyich Lenin had some Jewish ancestry; very few of the Revolution's leaders were "proletarians" (Albert S. Lindemann, *Esau's Tears: Modern Anti-Semitism and the Rise of the Jews* [Cambridge: Cambridge University Press, 1997], 432). Jews were disproportionately drawn to revolutionary movements in response to oppression, with Leon Trotsky and other prominent revolutionaries of Jewish ancestry if not allegiance, thus exacerbating "hostility among broad strata of the population toward both Communism and the Jewish people. Rather than breaking down hostility between nationalities, the conspicuous presence of Jews in the party served to augment traditional anti-Jewish resentment" (Jonathan Frankel, ed., *Dark Times, Dire Decisions: Jews and Communism* [New York: Oxford University Press, Inc., 2004], 4–5); see: David Cesarani, *The Jews and the Left: The Left and the Jews* (London: Labour Friends of Israel, 2004); also Chapter Seven.

50. G.K. Chesterton, "The Judaism of Hitler," *G.K.'s Weekly*, July 20, 1933, in *End of the Armistice* (London: Sheed & Ward, 1940), 95.

51. See: Y. Slezkine, *The Jewish Century* (Princeton, NJ: Princeton University Press, 2004).

52. See: N. Cohn, *Warrant for Genocide: The myth of the Jewish world-conspiracy and the Protocols of the Elders of Zionism* (London: Eyre & Spottiswoode, 1967); see Chapter Seven.

In the "underdog wars," criticizing a minority is only permissible if, despite appearances, it is really the "top-dog." The cognitive dissonance involved in this reversal of reality is addressed by arguing that it wields a secret power, thus making it a legitimate target—in reality a scapegoat. The *Chesterbelloc* argued with self-conscious rationalism that although some Jews were millionaires, most Jews were powerless, and in 1908 Chesterton satirized secret conspiracy theories in *The Man Who Was Thursday*. The story highlights the irony of dismissing the threat of anarchists who openly discuss murder over breakfast[53] while remaining obsessed by secret conspiracies—especially when capitalism openly conspired to monopolize trade and put rivals out of business.[54] Likewise and in the same year, Chesterton noted in *Orthodoxy* that madmen saw conspiracies everywhere.[55] *Utopia of Usurers* (1917), a collection of articles written 1913–14 for the left-wing *Daily Herald*, is almost free of "anti-Semitism" (despite its title and the fact that the *Herald*'s editor refused to censor contributions—Chesterton was even allowed to attack socialism) and within which he dismissed the Marconi case, involving Jewish and non-Jewish politicians as "a conspiracy of a very few millionaires."[56]

Chesterton's literary circle despised money-making,[57] and with Shaw and Wells they saw capitalism as an informal conspiracy against the public, aided and abetted by politicians and the newspapers. He saw communism as a reaction to capitalism: both were materialistic systems that sought to fulfill the spiritual needs of Man. Now, however, Russian communism seemed to be evolving into state capitalism, suggesting that there might be a kind of atavistic capitalism emerging in Jewish Bolsheviks. When Chesterton appeared to teeter on the brink of believing in world Jewish conspiracy, uncharacteristically, it was under the influence of an American millionaire who took such theories seriously. In *What I Saw in America* Chesterton maintained of Ford: "If a man of that sort

53. G. K. Chesterton, *The Man Who Was Thursday* (Harmondsworth, Middx.: Penguin, 1908/1967), 53–54.

54. G. K. Chesterton, *The Outline of Sanity* (London: Methuen & Co. Ltd., 1926), 101–102.

55. G. K. Chesterton, *Orthodoxy* (1908) in Vol. I of *G. K. Chesterton Collected Works* (San Francisco: Ignatius Press, 1986), 221–222.

56. G. K. Chesterton, "The Tyranny of Bad Journalism," *Utopia of Usurers*, op. cit., 107–110. Jewish references are fleeting and peripheral: he criticizes "[l]iterary men" for "being employed to praise a big business man personally, as men used to praise a king," for example, T. P. O'Connor on "some people called Salmon and Glückstein" and "Sir Joseph Lyons—the man who runs those teashop places. . . . I like best the passage where he said that Lyons's charming social accomplishments included a talent for 'imitating a Jew' . . . accompanied with a large and somewhat leering portrait of that shopkeeper, which makes the parlour-trick in question particularly astonishing" ("Letters and the New Laureates," [ibid., 21–22]); George Lansbury's left-wing *Daily Herald* published contributions from syndicalists, suffragists and pacifists, as well as Chesterton and Belloc: see Chapter Six.

57. I. Boyd, *The Novels of G. K. Chesterton: A Study in Art and Propaganda*, op. cit., 149.

has discovered that there is a Jewish problem, it is because there is a Jewish problem. It is certainly not because there is an Anti-Jewish prejudice." If there was, the cosmopolitan, pacifist, and non-religious Ford "would have been about the very last sort of man to have it." Chesterton insisted: "[E]ven if I did have a dislike of Jews, it would be illogical to call dislike a prejudice. Prejudice is a very lucid Latin word meaning the bias which a man has before he considers a case."[58]

What I Saw in America, published in 1926, originally appeared in article form in *The New Witness* when Cecil's death still exerted a strong influence, but even then Chesterton would not support the allegation that "the Jews" were engaged in a conscious conspiracy.[59] But Chesterton had previously ridiculed the fears of Bolshevism that prompted anti-Jewish riots during the Great War, namely, that a poor Jewish tailor who "called himself by a German name merely because he lived for a short time in a German town" was "instantly mobbed in Whitechapel for his share in the invasion of Belgium."[60] Chesterton believed that Jews were foreign—not that it excused anti-Jewish violence—but there was more to fear from capitalism, an insidious power, than from open, honest revolution, and he continued to support the Jewish Bolshevik against the Jewish capitalist, observing that the English "used to lecture the Russians for oppressing the Jews, before we heard the word Bolshevist and began to lecture them for being oppressed by the Jews."[61] After the Revolution such "pro-Semites" had changed their tune about "the persecuted Jews in Russia": "I fear there are a great many middle-class Englishmen already who wish that Trotsky had been persecuted a little more."[62] This was typical of the "underdog wars," for Chesterton used this example of English hypocrisy to attack views of the Irish as disorganized "idealists and dreamers" incapable of self-governance, regardless of

---

58. G. K. Chesterton, *What I Saw in America* (London: Hodder & Stoughton Ltd., 1922), 140–141.

59. The first article appeared on February 18, 1921 (I. Ker, *G. K. Chesterton: A Biography* [Oxford: Oxford University Press, 2011], 454). Simon Mayers notes that Chesterton makes similar points in articles written around the same time, in response to H. G. Wells' assertions that Bolshevism was not a "Jewish" movement, asserting that it was "not necessary to have every man a Jew to make a thing a Jewish movement; it is at least clear that there are quite enough Jews to prevent it from being a Russian movement" (G. K. Chesterton, "The Beard of the Bolshevist," *The New Witness*, January 14, 1921, 22); S. Mayers, *Chesterton's Jews: Stereotypes and Caricatures in the Literature and Journalism of G. K. Chesterton* (CreateSpace Independent Publishing Platform, 2013), 36; however, he added that "the very simple explanation" of worldwide Marxism was "that very half-conscious conspiracy which [Wells] hesitates or refuses to credit," which "simply" arose from the fact that "Marx was a Jew and the Jews are in every nation, to advertise him as an international prophet" (G. K. Chesterton, "The Beard of the Bolshevist," *The New Witness*, January 14, 1921, 23).

60. G. K. Chesterton, *The New Jerusalem* (1920) in Vol. XX of *G. K. Chesterton Collected Works* (San Francisco: Ignatius Press, 2001), 398.

61. G. K. Chesterton, *What I Saw in America*, op. cit., 142.

62. Ibid., 48–49.

flourishing Irish communities in America.[63] But his high hopes of the Russian Revolution appeared dashed by an apparent conspiracy between Jews of Left and Right, posited in the same work:

> The cosmopolitan Jews who are the Communists in the East will not find it so very hard to make a bargain with the cosmopolitan Jews who are the Capitalists in the West. The Western Jews would be willing to admit a nominal Socialism. The Eastern Jews have already admitted that their Socialism is nominal. It was the Bolshevist leader himself who said, "Russia is again a Capitalist country." But whoever makes the bargain, and whatever is its precise character, the substance of it will be servile.[64]

Chesterton feared that in the absence of a homeland to absorb their formidable energies and talents, Jews would direct their loyalties to each other; now, he believed this tendency would lead to "bargains" among Jews with apparently conflicting interests.[65] Chesterton insisted, however, that he criticized individuals as individuals, and the last sentence, apparently vague but characteristically precise as to meaning, excludes the idea of a true Jewish conspiracy, which would be a conspiracy of all Jews against all Gentiles. This does not exclude the possibility of anti-Semitism, and later, when Chesterton defended Jews from the Nazis he nevertheless claimed that "many" German Jews "toiled at that obscure conspiracy against Christendom, which some of them can never abandon," marked "sometimes ... not by obscurity but obscenity."[66] This remark will be explored further in Chapter Five, but once again the qualifying adjective "many" excludes an unqualified acceptance of "Jewish conspiracy," and also racial interpretations.

His own journal, *G.K.'s Weekly* (1925–1936), offered greater freedom to expound anti-Semitism but even though it was trying to attract the class of underdogs most exposed to the anti-Semitism of Fleet Street it never acquired the reputation of Cecil's *New Witness*. Instead, Chesterton used his paper to promote Distributism as the only rational alternative to capitalism and communism. Both were "equally impersonal and inhuman" according to *The Outline of Sanity* (1926), a Distributist work containing few Jewish references.[67]

---

63. G. K. Chesterton, *What I Saw in America*, op. cit., 48–51.

64. "It will be servile in the only rational and reliable sense; that is, an arrangement by which a mass of men are ensured shelter and livelihood, in return for being subjected to a law which obliges them to continue to labour" (ibid., 247); Hilaire Belloc envisaged a State in which workers were forced to toil in exchange for material security from the state (*The Servile State* [London: Constable & Co. Ltd., 1912/1950], 6); see Chapters Three and Seven.

65. See Chapters Six and Seven.

66. G. K. Chesterton, "The Judaism of Hitler," *G.K.'s Weekly*, July 20, 1933, in *End of the Armistice*, op. cit., 95.

67. G. K. Chesterton, *The Outline of Sanity*, op. cit., 19.

In 1929, in *The Thing*, there is no reference to a "Jewish conspiracy," while the Ku Klux Klan and Freemasons are cited as open conspirators. Chesterton also satirized allegations that he was pursuing a secret Catholic conspiracy against Jews: "It would be an exaggeration to say that it is my daily habit to leap upon aged Jews in Fleet Street and tear out their teeth; so, given my admitted monomania on the subject, it only remains to suppose that my private house is fitted up like a torture chamber for this mode of mediaeval dentistry. Catholic crimes are not plotted in public, so it stands to reason that they must be plotted in private."[68]

Despite teetering on the brink of the "Jewish conspiracy" theory after Cecil's death, Chesterton viewed historical injustices not as the product of conspiracies, but of wrong actions caused by the recurrence of wrong, though attractive, ideas. These "heresies," the first and worst of which was pride, he saw reappearing in the guise of "Prussianism" or "race."[69] His twin beliefs in Enlightenment reason and revealed religion conflicted with irrational prejudice, but he was more sympathetic to "folk" prejudice than scientific prejudice. His personal faith bound him in loyalty to the Jews, who brought God's moral order to men,[70] providing the foundation on which the Church erected her doctrines "in order that man might enjoy general human liberties."[71] Ultimately, it was Faith and Reason, inextricably linked, which would underpin his defence of the Jews against recurring prejudice, this time in scientific form: "race."

Chesterton continued to defend Jewish revolutionary tendencies and see big business as an open conspiracy,[72] but in 1936 he dismissed secret Jewish conspiracy theories: "Capitalism and Communism are so very nearly the same thing, in ethical essence, that it would not be strange if they did take leaders from the same ethnological elements."[73] In contrast, after Poland's defeat, convinced anti-Semites believed that "the omnipotent Jews in the plutocratic countries would call off the war against Germany."[74]

GKC, Religion and Race

There was no conflict between Chesterton's Enlightenment view of the equality of man and his Christianity. In fact, these influences alerted him to the new aris-

---

68. G. K. Chesterton, "Who are the conspirators?," *The Thing* (London: Sheed & Ward, 1929), 40–141.

69. See: Chesterton, G. K., *Heretics* (1905) in Vol. I of *G. K. Chesterton Collected Works* (San Francisco: Ignatius Press, 1986); see Chapter Five.

70. G. K. Chesterton, *Orthodoxy*, op. cit., 271.

71. Ibid., 305.

72. G. K. Chesterton, *The Outline of Sanity*, op. cit., 97–100.

73. G. K. Chesterton, *Autobiography*, op. cit., 73.

74. Max Weinreich, *Hitler's Professors: The Part of Scholarship in Germany's Crimes Against the Jewish People* (New Haven and London: Yale University Press, 1946/1999), 88.

tocracy constructed by nineteenth century Darwinist race theorists who saw humanity as a pyramid of racial groups with specific characteristics, with the "Aryan" top-dog at the pinnacle of human development and the poor and non-white underdogs at the bottom, jostling for precedence with the other animals.[75]

Alongside religious terminology Chesterton used "racial" terms throughout his career.[76] Like many in that era he employed them in a general sense regarding groups of people or the human race.[77] While such usage did not necessarily signify a common viewpoint with Nazism,[78] initially at least Chesterton was concerned about the effect of racial theory on the English rather than the Jews. Moreover, although he attacked the rich, including rich Jews, and defended the poor, including poor Jews, as will be seen, the latter defenses were less straightforward than may appear.[79] Crucially, attacking rich Jews gave a negative impression about all Jews, verging on the racial.

Nonetheless, Chesterton adhered to the view that no man was intrinsically better or worse because of his race, which he could not choose. Both underdog and topdog were responsible for their actions, for Chesterton's approach was based on equality under God: "The brotherhood of men is a fact: which in the long run wears down all other facts."[80] Regarding people's allegedly "racial" tendencies, the "most important thing" to ask of a "rascal" was "what he has done with himself"; secondly, to ask "what other people have done to him." He goes on to explain: "[I]f anyone asks, 'What has made the Jew secretive or tenacious or restless or inspiring, or whatever we may think him to be?' The first answer is that the Jew has made the Jew secretive or tenacious or whatever he may be. The next most important fact is what the Gentiles have done to the Jews." Such a position was not an ethnological one about "Semitic skulls," but not a totally environmental one either; it was about what people did—not what

75. M. Burleigh, W. Wippermann, *The Racial State: Germany* 1933–1945 (Cambridge: Cambridge University Press, 2003), 23.

76. Cheyette gives a very early example when Chesterton "racially define[d] anti-Semitism" as a "phenomenon that 'flourish[es] tauntingly the image of a martyred Jew upon an Aryan gibbet'" ("Jews Old and New," *The Speaker*, March 2, 1901, in *The Chesterton Review* IX (1), (February 1983): 601–602, quoted in Bryan Cheyette, *Constructions of "the Jew" in English literature and society: Racial representations, 1875–1945* [Cambridge: Cambridge University Press, 1995], 191); he still employed both racial and religious terminology at the end of his career, referring to "Aryans" and "Anglo-Saxons" (G.K. Chesterton, *Autobiography*, op. cit., 73), but also "Jew or Gentile" (ibid., 319); see Chapter Seven.

77. See: Ivan Hannaford, *Race: The History of an Idea in the West* (Baltimore/London: Johns Hopkins University Press, 1996).

78. D. Stone, *Responses to Nazism in Britain, 1933–1939: Before the War and the Holocaust* (Basingstoke, Hants: Palgrave Macmillan, 2003), 38–39.

79. See Chapter Six.

80. G.K. Chesterton, *New Witness*, June 18, 1914, in *Gilbert Magazine* 12 (2 & 3), (November/December 2008): 12, accessed May 19, 2011, http://www.209.236.72.127/wordpress/wp-content/uploads/2010/12/gilbert_12.2_5.pdf.

their remote ancestors were. It was "nothing to do" with blaming "the Jew or the enemies of the Jew," but simply acknowledging that the Jew was "mainly the result of what he does and what other people do; not merely the result of the physical type of the remote tribe from which he sprang." Once again taking Ireland for an analogy, Chesterton observed: "Ireland made Ireland; with some unintentional assistance from England."[81]

Race theory abolished free will, intrinsic to both democracy and religion. Christianity, specifically the Catholic Church, enshrined the "popular instinct" —a "deep and democratic and dramatic instinct"—not for man to do as he pleased, but to use his freedom to do the right thing. This was the "idea of free will operating under conditions of design," in which "there is an aim and it is the business of a man to aim at it." Free will, the "primary power of choice" that gave "a supernatural power of creation," was the "essential form of freedom" for "a free man."[82] Free will was also the basis of a progressive democracy, since reform required action, and action required a choice between right and wrong, as well as choosing the person who would best represent the people's decision. Throughout his career religious belief influenced Chesterton's politics,[83] including his approach to racial theories. In *The Well and the Shallows* (1935) the belief that a person's "blood" determined their characteristics and actions, and therefore their fate, is equated with the Calvinist doctrine of predestination,[84] a perspective recalling that of historian Lord Acton.[85] According to Ian Crowther, "fundamental to Chesterton's philosophy" was the belief that "each individual has an immortal soul and destiny."[86] For Chesterton, even economics was affected by original sin;[87] democracy was dependent on Christianity[88] and reason on organized religion.[89] Crucially, progress was

---

81. G.K. Chesterton, *New Witness*, September 23, 1921, in *Gilbert Magazine* 12 (2 & 3), (November/December 2008): 10, accessed May 19, 2011, http://www.209.236.72.127/wordpress/wp-content/uploads/2010/12/gilbert_12.2_5.pdf.

82. G.K. Chesterton, *The Everlasting Man* (San Francisco: Ignatius Press, 1925/1993), 241–242. For example, William McDougall, deeply influenced by Darwinism and the "most celebrated British psychologist" of the early twentieth century, promoted "instinct psychology" (M. Thomson, *Psychological Subjects: Identity, Culture, and Health in Twentieth-Century Britain* [Oxford: Oxford University Press, 2006], 55); but his theory lost out to "a more determined behaviourism" (ibid., 60–61). His "left-wing" theory emphasized the ability of Man to learn and thus improve, but gave way to the harsher, right-wing, eugenicist view that lesser-evolved humans could never learn.

83. G.K. Chesterton, *Autobiography*, op. cit., 355.

84. G.K. Chesterton, *The Well and the Shallows*, op. cit., 275.

85. Roland Hill, *Lord Acton* (New Haven/London: Yale University Press, 2000), 412.

86. Ian. Crowther, *Thinkers of Our Time: G.K. Chesterton* (London: The Claridge Press, 1991), 87.

87. G.K. Chesterton, *The Outline of Sanity*, op. cit., 41.

88. G.K. Chesterton, "About Changing Human Nature," *As I Was Saying* (London: Methuen & Co. Ltd., 1935), 34.

89. G.K. Chesterton, *Orthodoxy*, op. cit., 237.

indivisible from free will,[90] which was explored in his fiction; neither did he exclude Jews from the "essential form of freedom...."[91] Unlike racists he believed that no one was incapable of change, for better or worse, due to their "blood," and saw racial loyalties as more dangerous than national loyalties. *Heretics* (1905) rejects Darwinist ideas of evolution and race, warning of the potential for Imperialistic exploitation:

> When a wealthy nation like the English discovers the perfectly patent fact that it is making a ludicrous mess of the government of a poor nation like the Irish, it pauses for a moment in consternation, and then begins to talk about Celts and Teutons.[92]

By 1935 he saw threats to patriotism in attempts to link Englishmen with Americans as Anglo-Saxons, or with Germans as Nordics and Teutons. These "racial" movements aimed at uniting peoples across national boundaries were mere "pedantic fads" based on spurious scientific grounds and adorned with "preposterous prehistoric theories."[93]

But the racial preoccupations of the late nineteenth/early twentieth century were not exclusive to Gentiles.[94] Benjamin Disraeli's racial philosophy,[95] a secular version of Genesis 24 and 29, Ezekiel 9:1 and Tobit 4:4, was promulgated in his novels.[96] A "scientific" interpretation of the Chosen People idea, it saw the Jewish people as a distinct racial group with superior qualities, explaining their emergence from persecution in terms of Darwinian notions of struggle and survival.[97] It also emphasized the importance of preserving the "purity" of Jewish

90. G.K. Chesterton, *The Blatchford Controversies* (1904) in Vol. I of *G.K. Chesterton Collected Works* (San Francisco: Ignatius Press, 1986), 394–395; originally published as *The Religious Doubts of Democracy* (1904).

91. G.K. Chesterton, *The Man Who Knew Too Much* (Thirsk, N. Yorks.: House of Stratus, 1922/2001), 331; see Chapter Three.

92. G.K. Chesterton, *Heretics* (1905), op. cit., 132.

93. G.K. Chesterton, *Explaining the English* (1935) in Vol. XX of *G.K. Chesterton Collected Works* (San Francisco: Ignatius Press, 2001), 629.

94. I. Hannaford, *Race: The History of an Idea in the West*, op. cit., 272–276.

95. Stanley Weintraub, *Disraeli: A Biography* (London: Hamish Hamilton Ltd., 1993), 246.

96. T. Braun, *Disraeli the Novelist*, op. cit., 118–119; see B. Disraeli, *Alroy* (London: Longmans, Green & Co., 1833/1881), 59–60; *Coningsby, or the New Generation* (London: John Lehmann Ltd., 1844/1948), 203–204; 310; *Tancred or The New Crusade* (London: Longmans, Green & Co., 1847/1881), 148–149; 188–196; 251; 265; *Endymion* (Montreal: Dawson Bros., 1880), 250–252; and *Lothair* (London: John Lane, The Bodley Head Ltd., 1870/1927), xvi.

97. Disraeli was keenly interested in Robert Chambers's *Vestiges of the Natural History of Creation* (1844) on evolution (S. Weintraub, *Disraeli: A Biography*, op. cit., 260–261), one of many theories circulating before Darwin's *On the Origin of Species by Means of Natural Selection* (1859) (Stephen J. Gould, *Dinosaur in a Haystack: Reflections in Natural History* [London: Jonathan Cape, 1996], 430); Darwin himself claimed the direct influence of T.R. Malthus and his theory of population (*Autobiography*, 1876).

blood by remaining separate. Disraeli, though a Christian convert,[98] and Jews like the Zionist Ze'ev Jabotinsky,[99] in response to Gentile perceptions of Jewish inferiority, embraced the theory defensively[100] although it remained controversial among Jews.[101] In contrast, Oscar Levy, a Jewish admirer of Friedrich Nietzsche, uniquely envisioned an aristocracy of race, and blamed society's ills on the Jewish religion (via Christianity), horrifying many Jews but garnering praise from anti-Semites.[102]

Chesterton, no fan of Nietzsche, did call Levy the "only intelligent Nietzschite,"[103] and his belief in Jewish "difference" might indicate racial anti-Semitism[104] on par with Eugene Düring, the German socialist philosopher who had advocated Jewish "separateness" to avoid "Judaization" of "Aryan" "blood."[105] But Liberal thinkers J.A. Hobson and Goldwin Smith also believed in Jewish "difference,"[106] as did Conservative Arthur Balfour, whose Declaration formed the foundation of the Jewish homeland in Palestine.[107] So did many if not most Jews. Moreover, with Jewish emancipation helping to weaken social bonds,[108]

98. A baptized Christian, Disraeli celebrated his Jewish origins, describing Christianity as completed Judaism (S. Weintraub, *Disraeli: A Biography*, op. cit., 267), and the Church as "the only Jewish Institution remaining" (Helen M. Swartz, Marvin Swartz, eds., *Disraeli's Reminiscences* [London: Hamish Hamilton Ltd., 1975], 103), whose purpose was "the promulgation and maintenance in Europe of certain Asian principles, which, altogether located in their birth, are of divine origin, and of universal and eternal application" (B. Disraeli, *Tancred or The New Crusade*, op. cit., viii).

99. David J. Goldberg, *To the Promised Land: A History of Zionist Thought* (London: Penguin, 1996), 180–181. Ze'ev (Vladimir) Jabotinsky (1880–1940), author, orator and Zionist, during Passover 1920 led the Haganah Jewish defense organization against the Arab riots in Jerusalem; sentenced to 15 years hard labor by the British Mandatory Government, he received an amnesty and was released from prison after a public outcry (Jewish Virtual Library, accessed October 16, 2014, https://www.jewishvirtuallibrary.org/jsource/biography/jabotinsky.html).

100. H. Arendt, *The Origins of Totalitarianism* (San Diego: Harcourt Inc., 1994), 73.

101. "[British] Chief Rabbi Dr. Jonathan Sacks has rejected a claim by an influential Jewish philanthropist and communal leader that prevailing attitudes to intermarriage are 'racist'" (*Jewish Chronicle*, October 10, 2004, 17). The London School of Economics cancelled a lecture by "controversial" German banker Thilo Sarrazin "following threats from anti-fascist demonstrators" after he claimed in *Germany Does Away With Itself* (2010) that "'[a]ll Jews share a particular gene'" (ibid., February 18, 2011, 4).

102. D. Stone, *Breeding Superman: Nietzsche, Race and Eugenics in Edwardian and Interwar Britain* (Liverpool: Liverpool University Press, 2002), 22.

103. G.K. Chesterton, *Orthodoxy* (1908), op. cit., 327.

104. H. Arendt, *The Origins of Totalitarianism*, op. cit., 28.

105. E. Düring, *The Jewish Question, as a Question of Race, Morals and Culture* (1881), in D.J. Goldberg, J.D. Rayner, *The Jewish People: Their History and Their Religion* (London: Penguin, 1987), 159.

106. W.D. Rubinstein, *A History of the Jews in the English-Speaking World: Great Britain*, 109.

107. Balfour thought Jews "however patriotic, able, and industrious . . . still by their own action, remained a people apart" (H. Defries, *Conservative Party Attitudes to Jews 1900–1950*, op. cit., 5).

108. Shmuel Almog, *Zionism and History: The Rise of the New Jewish Consciousness* (New York: St. Martin's Press, 1987), 9.

many Jews also emphasized a diversity of thought and opinion, not solely based on religion, before the Holocaust drew a sharp and tragic distinction between Jews and Gentiles.[109] From a Christian viewpoint Chesterton acknowledged the "unusual and unique ... position of the Jews"[110] as a "family ... generally divided among the nations."[111] He insisted: "All men know in their hearts that Jews are Jews, and there is nothing like them in the world. Israel, like the Lord her God, is one"; there was "no other tribe to share with her either the admiration or the power or the persecution that attend her on her wandering way."[112] Chesterton, while sharing some of the Conservative Disraeli's early political ideas,[113] was not alone in seeing him as ambitious.[114] Disraeli played a leading role in British Imperialism diametrically opposed to Chesterton's Liberal Little Englander stance.[115] Chesterton described him as a "genius ... not a gentleman,"[116] his view of Disraeli's "pride" undoubtedly influenced by his own objections to secular philosophies of "chosenness."[117]

Chesterton's distrust of race theories was linked to the fact that "the learned" were "more liable" to the "extraordinary delusion" of this "sham science" than the "ignorant": if he trusted "a peasant or any such plain man more than most intellectual aristocrats," it was because the former knew "quite well" that a Jew was a Jew, "whether or no he was ever a Semite," and that "an Irishman was an Irishman, whether or no he was ever a Celt."[118] Chesterton wrote about Jews in religious terms, and in *Orthodoxy* (1908) acknowledged Christianity's origins in Judaism in the face of progressive secularism;[119] he re-emphasized the point in

109. Morris N. Kertzer, *What is a Jew?* (New York: Touchstone, 1996), 114–115.

110. G.K. Chesterton, *The Everlasting Man*, op. cit., 85.

111. G.K. Chesterton, *The New Jerusalem* (1920), op. cit., 404.

112. G.K. Chesterton, *New Witness*, September 23, 1921, in *Gilbert Magazine* 12 (2 & 3), (November/December 2008), 10, accessed May 19, 2011, http://www.209.236.72.127/wordpress/wp-content/uploads/2010/12/gilbert_12.2_5.pdf.

113. G.K. Chesterton, *G.K. Chesterton Collected Works Vol. VIII*, D. Barr, ed. (San Francisco: Ignatius Press, 1999), 38–39.

114. Disraeli's ambition was widely acknowledged (H. Arendt, *The Origins of Totalitarianism*, op. cit., 68; C.C. Eldridge, *Disraeli and the Rise of a New Imperialism* [Cardiff: University of Wales Press, 1996], 3); indeed, Disraeli's early novels celebrated ambition (T. Braun, *Disraeli the Novelist*, op. cit., 56–57).

115. W.D. Rubinstein, *A History of the Jews in the English-Speaking World: Great Britain*, op. cit., 108; C.C. Eldridge, *Disraeli and the Rise of a New Imperialism*, op. cit., 72.

116. G.K. Chesterton, *Heretics* (1905), op. cit., 150.

117. G.K. Chesterton, *Orthodoxy* (1908), op. cit., 358.

118. G.K. Chesterton, *New Witness*, September 23, 1921, in *Gilbert Magazine* 12 (2 & 3), (November/December 2008): 10, accessed May 19, 2011, http://www.209.236.72.127/wordpress/wp-content/uploads/2010/12/gilbert_12.2_5.pdf.

119. G.K. Chesterton *Orthodoxy* (1908), op. cit., 383.

response to Nazi attempts to "de-Judaize" Christianity.[120] The same influence prompted him to concede specifically to the Jewish people the "concept of the chosen people,"[121] something he had criticized in *The New Jerusalem* (1920) as a potential source of racial pride.[122]

Chesterton's reverence for religious Jews and criticism of secular Jews suggests a "dual image" of "the Jew," which could excite "horror, fear, hatred" but also "wonder, awe, and love,"[123] the product of Christian views of a "deicide nation" that nevertheless "could also potentially 'redeem mankind.'"[124] Chesterton was undoubtedly awed by the Jewish religion and believed that the idea of the Chosen People had "a certain tragic grandeur" for the Jews, "as of men separated and sealed and waiting for a unique destiny." But among Gentiles this idea was dangerous—indeed, until it was "utterly destroyed" among Christians, they would "never restore Christendom."[125] Chesterton, who associated almost exclusively with secular or assimilated Jews, nonetheless increasingly warned against the dangers of Jewish assimilation for both Jew and Gentile. Coupled with his enduring reverence toward Judaism and the Old Testament, his approach suggests the dual image theory, under which Jews were seen as acceptable provided they conformed to Gentile expectations. Even so, in comparison to modern intellectual movements, Chesterton regarded all religions as superior:

> [M]y sympathies, when I go beyond the things I myself believe, are with all the poor Jews who do believe in Judaism and all the Mahometans who do believe in Mahometanism, not to mention so obscure a crowd as the Christians who do believe in Christianity. I feel I have more morally and even intellectually in common with these people, and even the religions of these people, than with the supercilious negations that make up the most part of what is called enlightenment.[126]

---

120. G.K. Chesterton, "The Religion of Fossils," *The Well and the Shallows*, op. cit., 27–29; see also: J.S. Conway, *The Nazi Persecution of the Churches 1933–1945* (Vancouver: Regent College Publishing, 2001), 168–201. Some Enlightenment thinkers saw Christianity as inferior on account of Jesus' Jewishness (Charlotte Allen, *The Human Christ: The Search for the Historical Jesus* [Oxford: Lion Publishing, 1998], 116–119); the Nazis abhorred Christianity's Jewish roots: see: *The Persecution of the Catholic Church in the Third Reich: Facts and Documents* (London: Burns Oates, 1940).

121. G.K. Chesterton, "The Judaism of Hitler," *G.K.'s Weekly*, July 20, 1933, in *The End of the Armistice*, op. cit., 97.

122. G.K. Chesterton, *The New Jerusalem* (1920), op. cit., 213–214; see Chapters Five and Seven.

123. Harold Fisch, *The Dual Image: A Study of the figure of the Jew in English Literature* (London: Lincolns-Prager Ltd., 1959), 89, in B. Cheyette, *Constructions of "the Jew" in English Literature and Society: Racial Representations 1875–1945*, op. cit., 264.

124. H. Fisch, *The Dual Image: A Study of the figure of "the Jew" in English Literature*, in B. Cheyette, *Constructions of "the Jew" in English Literature and Society: Racial Representations 1875–1945*, op. cit., 270.

125. G.K. Chesterton, "The Judaism of Hitler," *The End of the Armistice*, op. cit., 97.

126. G.K. Chesterton, *The New Jerusalem* (1920), op. cit., 296.

One of Chesterton's chief preoccupations was the need for religious ortho-doxy and the need to defend it; this explains his approach to secular Jews, who could not choose their race but could choose their religion—could choose to be chosen by God—but chose not to be. His opposition to Jewish secularity and assimilation can be seen at its most insouciant in an interview with the *Jewish Chronicle* (to be explored in Chapter Seven):

> [I] am no anti-Semite. I respect and have the deepest regard for Jews, for their wonderful history, for their wonderful faith, and for the remarkably fine qualities, mental and moral, which the Jew evinces in his natural state. Of course, I can't stand the Jew who, having struck oil, oils himself all over; he is only a little more repugnant in my eyes than the non-Jew who does like wise, because he is a Jew with infinitely finer potentialities. The sort of Jew that I am against is the one who is unfaithful to his race, who, saying he is proud about being a Jew, strives his utmost to assimilate.[127]

Doubtless influenced by his mode of expression, Chesterton's claim to respect and admire the Jewish faith has been questioned, and a study by Bryan Cheyette sees Chesterton's article *Jews Old and New* (1901) associating "Jews in general with an untranscendent worldliness."[128] A much less uncomplimentary compliment than that expressed in the *Jewish Chronicle* interview, the remark's full context was that Jewish "worldliness" was based on "the survival of the blinding simplification of existence" caused by the impact of the "enormous philosophic truth" of "the unity of creation."[129]

Clearly Chesterton might have been protecting his Christian faith by empha-sizing its roots in Judaism, a possibility further examined in Chapter Eight. Cheyette argues that Chesterton's religious influences played a defensive, nega-tive role; that he "venerated" "the narrow-minded Jew" only because the reli-gious Jew "maintained a distinct 'boundary line' between his Jewishness and Christendom," not attempting to "lose" himself in his "'adopted' European nation."[130] Moreover, he interprets Chesterton's defense of Lord Swaythling,

127. "G.K.C.: Interview for the Jewish Chronicle with Mr. G.K. Chesterton," *Jewish Chronicle*, April 28, 1911, 18; see: Sr. M. Loyola, "Chesterton and the Mystery of Israel," *The Chesterton Review* 13 (2), (1987): 155–156.

128. B. Cheyette, *Constructions of "the Jew" in English Literature and Society: Racial Representa-tions 1875–1945*, op. cit., 189.

129. G.K. Chesterton, "Jews Old and New," *The Speaker*, March 2, 1901, 7; Chesterton praises Nordau for his theory of the degeneration of culture even though it was based on a Darwinian model of human development (Max Nordau, *Degeneration* [Lincoln, NE/London: University of Nebraska Press, 1895/1993], xv–xvi).

130. B. Cheyette, *Constructions of "the Jew" in English Literature and Society: Racial Representa-tions 1875–1945*, op. cit., 182.

criticized for bequeathing money to his children on condition they remained Jews, as evidence of his early (but "short-lived") "uncompromising racial division of 'the Jew'" into "'international' financiers and 'orthodox' emblems of religious virtue," quoting Chesterton:

> The wealthy Semite sits in the inmost chamber of the State; he controls it by a million filaments of politics and finance. But the only pebble you throw at the poor old man, you throw at his most honourable moment, when the schemes are over and his riches vain, and with a gesture, momentarily sublime, he bears witness to the God of his fathers. This does not strike me as respecting a religion—or even tolerating it.[131]

Notwithstanding Chesterton's use of "Semite," undoubtedly a more culturally acceptable euphemism, his view of Swaythling as redeemed in his "momentarily sublime" gesture of bearing "witness to the God of his fathers" shows religious rather than "racial" influence; portraying Swaythling as representative of all Jews, however, came close to "racism," and one religious Jew objected:

> Lash these Jewish evil-doers, as devoid of Judaism as they are of conscience, as mercilessly as you please; but do it in such wise as to make it clear that they are an insignificant fraction of their race.[132]

Nonetheless, Chesterton's belief in Swaythling's capacity to change was based on a fundamental Christian belief[133] incompatible with racial theories of the inherently "good" or "bad" qualities of different races.[134] Cheyette maintains that Chesterton "still believed in the potential for Jews to change for the better" but that "any improvement of 'the Jew' was to take place outside the borders of England."[135] But Chesterton clearly believed that Swaythling, although based in England, could—indeed had—changed.

In an attempt to avoid the dangers of Holocaust influence, Cheyette adopts a post-modern, non-judgmental approach to a number of nineteenth and twentieth century English writers. Avoiding pejorative terms such as "anti-Semitism," he instead studies them in the light of the influence of poet and critic Matthew Arnold and his views of culture, especially those regarding race and

131. G. K. Chesterton, Letter to the *Nation*, March 18, 1911, in Sr. M. Loyola, "Chesterton and the Mystery of Israel," op. cit., 146–147, in B. Cheyette, *Constructions of "the Jew" in English Literature and Society: Racial Representations 1875–1945*, op. cit., 185.

132. Rev. Morris Joseph, letter, *Jewish Chronicle*, June 23, 1911, 14.

133. Alister E. McGrath, *Christian Theology* (Oxford: Blackwell Publications Ltd., 1999), 427.

134. J. Maritain, *Antisemitism* (London: Geoffrey Bles: The Centenary Press, 1939), 13.

135. B. Cheyette, *Constructions of "the Jew" in English Literature and Society: Racial Representations 1875–1945*, op. cit., 184.

transformation.[136] However, emphasizing his subjects' "racial" influences in this Arnoldian framework[137] is equally problematical, since racial terms, despite their neutral origins, have acquired similar connotations through association with the Holocaust. Post-Holocaust, racial theories have been associated with Imperialistic Europe's extermination of "lesser races,"[138] with prejudice and discrimination, but even more with Nazi adaptations of Darwinian notions to redefine the German "race"[139] and Hitler's obsession with a pure Aryan body biologically menaced by Jewish impurity[140]—an obsession leading to the Holocaust.[141]

Nonetheless, in view of Chesterton's emphasis on change, Cheyette's chosen context is apt. Arnold, like Chesterton, idealized yet criticized Jews, and his attitudes were also influenced by religion[142] (as Cheyette notes), although his initial enthusiasm for transforming Jews foundered over a growing personal dislike.[143] In contrast, although equally suggestive of prejudice, Chesterton liked all the Jews he met but disliked the "financial Jews" he seldom met. Initially he sympathized with the Jewish underdog Alfred Dreyfus, but as Chapter Six shows, he retreated somewhat from that stance. However, Chesterton criticized Arnold's

136. B. Cheyette, *Constructions of "the Jew" in English Literature and Society: Racial Representations 1875–1945*, op. cit., xii–xiii. Arnold's benign view of Jews (I. Hannaford, *Race: The History of an Idea in the West*, op. cit., 281–282) is noted by Cheyette but also his later change of attitude (*Constructions of "the Jew" in English literature and society: Racial representations, 1875–1945*, op. cit., 19). In 1869 Arnold stated: "Science has now made visible . . . the great and pregnant elements of difference which lie in race, and . . . how . . . they make the genius and history of an Indo-European people vary from those of a Semitic people. . . . But nothing more strongly marks the essential unity of man than the affinities we can perceive . . . between members of one family of peoples and members of another . . . than that likeness in the strength and promise of the moral fibre, which, notwithstanding immense elements of difference, knits in some special sort the genius and history of us English . . . to the genius and history of the Hebrew people" (Matthew Arnold, *Culture and Anarchy: An Essay in Political and Social Criticism* [McLean, VA: IndyPublish.com], 64).

137. B. Cheyette, *Constructions of the Jew in English Literature and Society: Racial Representations 1875–1945*, op. cit., 21.

138. Sven Lindqvist, *Exterminate all the Brutes* (London: Granta Books, 1997), 122–130.

139. I. Hannaford, *Race: The History of an Idea in the West*, op. cit., 365; Michael Burleigh, Wolfgang Wippermann, *The Racial State: Germany 1933–1945*, op. cit., 28–30.

140. Adolf Hitler, *Mein Kampf* (London: Pimlico, 1925–6/2001), 272; Ian Kershaw, *Hitler: Hubris 1889–1936* (London: Penguin, 1998), xxviii; S. T. Katz, *The Holocaust in Historical Context Vol. I: The Holocaust and Mass Destruction before the Modern Age* (Oxford: Oxford University Press, 1994), 59.

141. P. Bell, "Hitler's War? The Origins of the Second World War in Europe," in Paul Hayes, ed., *Themes in Modern European History 1890–1945* (London: Routledge, 1992), 231; Henry Friedlander, *The Origins of Nazi Genocide: from Euthanasia to the Final Solution* (Chapel Hill/London: University of North Carolina Press, 1995), xii.

142. M. Arnold, *Culture and Anarchy: An Essay in Political and Social Criticism*, op. cit., xxii.

143. B. Cheyette, *Constructions of the Jew in English Literature and Society: Racial Representations 1875–1945*, op. cit., 18–19.

"racial" philosophy in 1933, having earlier praised him:[144] he saw modern race theory as a substitute for religion,[145] and in 1929 remarked that "anybody who likes" could belong to a traditional religion, "whereas it is not very clear what is to be done with the people who do not happen to belong to the race."[146]

Much earlier Chesterton had taken Henry Ford's prejudice seriously, but in his Distributist work *The Outline of Sanity* he reverts to his customary view of millionaires, influenced by his views on "race." In "The Free Man and the Ford Car" he comments on riding "in a Ford car, like that in which I remember riding over Palestine, and in which (I suppose) Mr. Ford would enjoy riding over Palestinians."[147] In referring to "Palestinians" Chesterton was using the term customarily applied to Jews living in British-ruled Palestine before the advent of the State of Israel. He also ridiculed those who, like Ford, held Darwinistic beliefs— "men who talk about superior and inferior races; I never heard a man say: 'Anthropology shows that I belong to an inferior race.'" Ford was "a good man, so far as it is consistent with being a good millionaire,"[148] but there are no good millionaires in *The Outline of Sanity* and in Chesterton's fiction the millionaire "is always a fool or a criminal,"[149] and likely to be murdered. In *Sidelights* (1932) there are no disquisitions on "Jewish power," and while Chesterton "hate[d] Americanization" he did "not hate America." America's "great virtue" was that it did "really remain democratic," but this was despite "progress and practical success" and "in spite of Ford and Fords."[150]

Chesterton: Eugenics, Race, and Religion

Chesterton's waning admiration for Henry Ford was also influenced not only by Ford's attitude to Palestinian Jews, but by his espousal of eugenics,

144. Arnold "made himself specially and supremely the apostle of cosmopolitan culture" and was "affected by the universal fashion of ethnology and worried by the racial generalizations" (G.K. Chesterton, introduction to Richard Ferrar Patterson, *Six Centuries of English Literature: Meredith to Rupert Brooke* [1933], reproduced in G.K. Chesterton, "From Meredith to Rupert Brooke," *The Common Man* [London: Sheed & Ward, 1950], 81–82); earlier he had maintained that "[o]ne of the immense benefits conferred on us by Matthew Arnold lay in the fact that he recalled to us the vital fact that we are Europeans"; he "was not deluded by any separatist follies about the superiority of a Teutonic race. If he admired the Germans it was for being European" (G.K. Chesterton, introduction to Matthew Arnold, *Essays Literary and Critical* [London, 1906], reproduced in G.K. Chesterton, *G.K.C. as M.C.*, J.P. de Fonseka, ed. [London: Methuen & Co. Ltd., 1929], 26); see: John Coates, *Chesterton and the Edwardian Cultural Crisis* (Hull: Hull University Press, 1984), 28.

145. G.K. Chesterton, *Heretics* (1905), op. cit., 133.

146. G.K. Chesterton, "The Call to the Barbarians," *The Thing*, op. cit., 114.

147. G.K. Chesterton, "The Free Man and the Ford Car," *The Outline of Sanity*, op. cit., 173.

148. G.K. Chesterton, "The Free Man and the Ford Car" (ibid., 176–177).

149. I. Boyd, *The Novels of G.K. Chesterton: A Study in Art and Propaganda*, op. cit., 149.

150. G.K. Chesterton, *Sidelights on New London and Newer York and Other Essays* (London: Sheed & Ward, 1932), 164–165.

prompted by the renewed threat of that philosophy to Chesterton's favored underdog, the poor. As he notes in *Eugenics and Other Evils* (1922), he had believed that eugenics had been killed off by the Great War, along with other aspects of "Prussianism." An absence of Jewish references suggests that at this stage Chesterton did not link "race" and eugenics or see either as a threat to Jews. Later eugenics became intrinsically linked to Nazi anti-Semitism,[151] but in 1905, in contrast to racists, for whom "blood mixing" was a matter of deep and enduring interest, Chesterton wrote:

> How much of the blood of the Angles and Saxons (whoever they were) there remains in our mixed British, Roman, German, Dane, Norman, and Picard stock is a matter only interesting to wild antiquaries.[152]

As to the United States, that "melting pot" of European nations:[153]

> [H]ow much of the diluted blood can possibly remain in that roaring whirlpool of America into which a cataract of Swedes, Jews, Germans, Irishmen, and Italians is perpetually pouring, is a matter only interesting to lunatics.[154]

Listing Jews as a nationality reflected Chesterton's Zionist beliefs and emphasized Jewish "difference" which he claimed they retained in America—as did the Irish,[155] as well as emphasizing the difference between "national" and "racial" characteristics. One of very few prominent English opponents of eugenics,[156] Chesterton's recognition of its dangers helped him recognise similar dangers in Nazism ahead of other commentators. In *Eugenics and Other Evils*, a chapter entitled "The Anarchy from Above" discusses the dangers of unlimited state power.[157] His definition of anarchy was the inability of governments to "leave off governing,"[158] particularly relevant to the totalitarian nature of Nazism, noted by Hannah Arendt.[159] English eugenicists had already achieved the segregation of the "unfit" via the Mental Deficiency Act of 1913, which allowed "feeble-minded" and "mentally defective" children and adults to be placed in institutions, including women "in receipt of poor relief at the time

---

151. M. Burleigh, *Death and Deliverance: "Euthanasia" in Germany* 1900–1945 (Cambridge: Cambridge University Press, 1994), 231–237; H. Friedlander, "Euthanasia and the Final Solution," in D. Cesarani, ed., *The Final Solution: Origins and Implementation* (London: Routledge, 1996), 51–61.

152. G.K. Chesterton, *Heretics* (1905), op. cit., 133.

153. G.K. Chesterton, *What I Saw in America*, op. cit., 15.

154. G.K. Chesterton, *Heretics* (1905), op. cit., 133.

155. G.K. Chesterton, *What I Saw in America*, op. cit., 35.

156. I. Hannaford, *Race: The History of an Idea in the West*, op. cit., 370; see Chapter Six.

157. G.K. Chesterton, *Eugenics and Other Evils*, op. cit., 30.

158. Ibid., 83.

159. H. Arendt, *The Origins of Totalitarianism*, op. cit., 392.

of giving birth to an illegitimate child or when pregnant with such a child."[160] A 1927 Amendment, also the work of the Eugenics Society, went further, ensuring that "moral defectives" could be placed in an institution without committing an offence, on account of their "strongly vicious and criminal propensities."[161] In contrast to convicted criminals they could be confined indefinitely. *Eugenics and Other Evils* warned of the dangers of unlimited State power to label men as "mad," and this attack on civil liberties would have ramifications for opponents of both Stalinism and Nazism.[162] In 1917 Chesterton noted:

> The man's punishment refers to the past, which is supposed to have been investigated. But his restraint refers to the future, which his doctors, keepers, and wardens have yet to investigate. . . . [A] man can be punished for a crime because he is born a citizen; while he can be constrained because he is born a slave.[163]

But segregation was merely the first step; English and German eugenicists realized that sterilization was cheaper than institutionalization, and that killing was cheaper than both.[164] The Nazis passed the Nuremberg laws of 1933, prohibiting marriages between "Aryans" and "non-Aryans," and legalizing eugenic sterilization and abortion—although not euthanasia, which would be carried out secretly—but the English sterilization and euthanasia campaigns carried on regardless.[165] In 1934 Chesterton attacked the "German Dictator" for his racial and eugenic theories, most especially his "compulsory action to keep the breed in an artificial state of bestial excellence; of nosing out every secret of sex or origin, so that nobody may survive who is not Nordic; of setting a hundred quack

---

160. Four categories were listed: "Idiots," "Imbeciles," "feeble-minded persons," and "moral defectives" (Mental Deficiency Act 1913 [London: His Majesty's Stationery Office], 136–137).

161. Mental Deficiency Act 1927 (London: His Majesty's Stationery Office), Sec. 2, 414.

162. G. K. Chesterton, *Eugenics and Other Evils*, op. cit., 22–30.

163. G. K. Chesterton, *Utopia of Usurers*, op. cit., 102–103.

164. Wing-Commander A. W. H. James in his 1932 Parliamentary Bill to legalize sterilization calculated that it cost £1,440,000 to administer the Mental Deficiency Acts in 1929, and £2,421,000 to administer Lunacy laws (Eugenics Society Records [SA/EUG/C190]); however, English eugenicists admitted privately that disabled people were being sterilized without legislation (A. Farmer, *By Their Fruits: Eugenics, Population Control, and the Abortion Campaign* [Washington, D.C.: Catholic University of America, 2008], 126). Berthold Kihn argued that expenditure on "ballast existences" was unnecessary; that "30,000 institutionalised idiots" cost 45 million Reichmarks to keep every year: "[K]illing these people would remove the burden on the tax payer and release considerable reserves of labour tied up in their care" (Lecture, "The eradication of the less valuable from society," *Allgemeine Zeitschrift für Psychiatrie* [1932], in M. Burleigh, *Death and Deliverance: "Euthanasia" in Germany* 1900–1945, op. cit., 38). Between 1933 and 1945 17,000 German deaf people were sterilized; after War began they were murdered ("The Deaf Holocaust: Deaf People and Nazi Germany," *See Hear*, BBC2 TV, February 7, 2005).

165. A. Farmer, *By Their Fruits: Eugenics, Population Control, and the Abortion Campaign*, op. cit., 111–122.

doctors to preserve an imaginary race in its imaginary purity."[166] Later he remarked on "the most modern governments" that "organise sterilisation today [and] may organise infanticide tomorrow," and warned of the "concentration camp."[167]

Cheyette describes claims of Chesterton's anti-Nazism as "extravagant," and as not contradicting his "racial" view of Jews,[168] but in fact Chesterton rejected race theory early in his career, and it was Nazi anti-Semitism that prompted him to emphasize his rejection of racial theories about Jews. He noted that while the Church "excommunicates" the "State . . . exterminates,"[169] and that "[t]he Nordic man of the Nazi type in Germany is a very slow thinker" but "swift to shed innocent blood."[170] Moreover, while believing that in other nations it was still a source of racial pride that brought disaster, as seen, he conceded the concept of the chosen people specifically to "the Jews."

Nonetheless, Cheyette maintains that Chesterton "condemned Nazism in general terms as an example of the worst kind of Prussianism" and that his condemnations were a reprise of his Great War writings.[171] This is correct, but during the Great War Chesterton, who described Frederick the Great's Prussia as a "commonwealth that . . . can of its nature eat other commonwealths,"[172] had seen "Prussianism" acting out of "racial supremacy."[173] In a 1934 pamphlet *Germany's National Religion,* he attacked Nazism as a "racial religion"[174] and the natural outcome of "Prussianism."[175] While acknowledging that "a 'Prussian' Nazism genuinely appalled Chesterton" Cheyette insists: "[S]o did the all-powerful 'Semite.'"[176] Chesterton would continue to see "Jewish finance" as a problem—although in more qualified terms—even while attacking Nazi anti-Semitism. George Bernard Shaw and H.G. Wells also remained critical on the

---

166. G.K. Chesterton, "On the Instability of the State," *Avowals and Denials* (London: Methuen & Co. Ltd., 1934), 134–135.

167. G.K. Chesterton, *The Well and the Shallows*, op. cit., 241–242.

168. Cheyette suggests that Coren (*Gilbert: The Man Who Was G.K. Chesterton* [1989], 210–212) was "misled" by Ward (*Gilbert Keith Chesterton* [1944], 265): B. Cheyette, *Constructions of "the Jew" in English Literature and Society: Racial Representations 1875–1945*, op. cit., 202, note 58).

169. G.K. Chesterton, *The Well and the Shallows*, op. cit., 246–247.

170. Ibid., 249–250.

171. B. Cheyette, *Constructions of "the Jew" in English Literature and Society: Racial Representations 1875–1945*, op. cit., 200–201.

172. G.K. Chesterton, *A Short History of England*, op. cit., 194.

173. G.K. Chesterton, *The Barbarism of Berlin* (London: Cassell & Company Ltd., 1914), 59.

174. G.K. Chesterton, introduction to *Germany's National Religion*, Lord Tyrell, ed. (London: Friends of Europe, 1934), 1–2, published as "The Tribal Triumph" in G.K. Chesterton, *The End of the Armistice*, op. cit., 65–69; see Chapter Five.

175. G.K. Chesterton, "The Judaism of Hitler," *G.K.'s Weekly*, July 20, 1933 (ibid., 97).

176. B. Cheyette, *Constructions of "the Jew" in English Literature and Society: Racial Representations 1875–1945*, op. cit., 201.

"Jewish question" while condemning Nazi anti-Semitism,[177] and the claim that Chesterton saw Nazis and Jews as "equally pernicious forces"[178] is not substantiated by his writings. His anti-Nazi attacks were scattered broadside, many in articles of general interest, without being "balanced" by anti-Jewish criticism.[179] Moreover, Chesterton specifically addressed the racial persecution of German Jews:

> As for persecution, it has become a grim joke in the case of the Jews; nor is it less persecution if we call it the persecution of a race and not the persecution of a religion.[180]
>
> Herr Hitler and his group have done many things of which I cannot approve.... They beat and bully poor Jews in concentration camps. They talk about preserving the purity of their blood. They commit every crime.[181]

In *Eugenics and Other Evils* Chesterton's chief target was "positive" eugenics: he ridiculed the desire of Shaw and other progressives to breed a better man as they might breed a carthorse. He also saw eugenics as part of class warfare. If strikes were the weapons of the workers, wielded more in helplessness than as a prelude to revolution, eugenics was a plot by the wealthy to head off revolution by controlling the poor with contraception and sterilization. Chesterton's choice of the poor as underdog was in part a reaction to progressive intellectuals like Shaw. As anti-capitalists they were on the same side, but they treated the poor with impatience and disdain, and while attacking anyone they deemed anti-Semitic they reserved the right to their own prejudices.

Chesterton's own gradual reappraisal of priorities began in the 1920s during his Palestine visit: "I have lived to see people who accused me of Anti-Semitism become far more Anti-Semitic than I am or ever was. I have heard people talking with real injustice about the Jews, who once seemed to think it an injustice to talk about them at all."[182] So shocked was he by Arab animosity that it moved him to defend the Jews, although "[t]o talk of the Jews always as the oppressed and never as the oppressors" was "simply absurd."[183] Furthermore,

---

177. See Chapter Five.

178. B. Cheyette, *Constructions of "the Jew" in English Literature and Society: Racial Representations 1875–1945*, op. cit., 201.

179. For example, "About Impenitence" (G.K. Chesterton, *As I Was Saying*, op. Cit., 23); "About Puritanism" (ibid., 48); "About Voltaire" (ibid., 61); "About Blondes" (ibid., 83–84); "About Meredith" (ibid., 99–100); "About Shirts" (ibid., 114); "About Impermanence" (ibid., 126); "About Relativity" (ibid., 144); "About Historians" (ibid., 155); "About Bad Comparisons" (ibid., 158–159); "About Education" (ibid., 179); and "About Sacrifice" (ibid., 222).

180. G.K. Chesterton, "About Changing Human Nature" (ibid., 150).

181. G.K. Chesterton, "On War Books," *The End of the Armistice*, op. cit., 192.

182. G.K. Chesterton, *The New Jerusalem* (1920), op. cit., 392–393.

183. Ibid., 191.

although eugenics was an important factor in his changing view of Jews as top-dogs,[184] after the Great War his New Witness League colleagues emphasized eugenics as a Jewish plot. In reality, both Jews and Gentiles supported eugenics, and Jews and Gentiles opposed it. The dividing line was not "race" but religious belief. As Chapter Seven shows, Chesterton's Jewish friendships also influenced his opposition to eugenics.

A further factor in this opposition was his sympathy for the family, especially the poor family, which became one of the first victims of the Nazis' drive for political and biological domination, as the Hereditary Courts ordered the sterilization of the poor and disabled, against family opposition.[185] If the Nazi eugenics program touched on Chesterton's love for the family, it also recalled his admiration for Jewish family life. It must have seemed as though the clock had been turned back to his schooldays when he had defended a Jewish pupil from a crowd of bullies—now the Nazi bully was persecuting harmless Jews. Other champions of the underdog were hampered in their response to the Age of Dictators by their espousal of eugenics, but eugenics led Chesterton to oppose Nazi anti-Semitism, and these and other influences on his anti-Nazism will be explored in later chapters.

Another overlapping preoccupation of "race" and eugenics theorists was the effect on mankind of the non-white races. Hitler railed against the stationing of black African troops in the Rhineland because of its supposed effects on the German "race";[186] but, as seen, the sympathies of Liberal dissidents were for the Boers: "[n]ot at any stage did Chesterton consider the original native races of South Africa," those with "dark skins" who "had certainly been oppressed by the Boers," the "under-underdogs."[187] In fact, it was British anti-slavery laws that sparked the Boers' Great Trek out of British territory.[188] Chesterton's trajectory of opinion on non-white races mirrored that of his response to the "Jewish question," and was similarly influenced by his religion. If converts to Catholi-

---

184. See Chapter Five.

185. Dr. Laetitia Fairfield noted the increasingly coercive application of the Nazi sterilization laws: at first, disabled Catholics and their relations "put up some gallant fights" but by 1934 the police would call early in the morning: "[T]hey drag [the disabled person] to the operating theatre and lay him on the operating table. If the parents refuse to surrender their children, the police can make a forcible entry and take away the child. The same may be done in a charitable institution" (L. Fairfield, *Catholics and the German Law of Sterilisation*, 1938).

186. Hitler blamed this "contamination" on the French and the "ice-cold calculation of the Jew thus to begin bastardising the European continent at its core and to deprive the white race of the foundations for a sovereign existence through infection with lower humanity" (*Mein Kampf*, op. cit., 569).

187. M. Ward, *Return to Chesterton* (London: Sheed & Ward, 1952), 54.

188. David Olusoga, Casper W. Erichsen, *The Kaiser's Holocaust: Germany's Forgotten Genocide* (London: Faber & Faber, 2011), 23.

cism like Chesterton were attracted because of their perceptions of solid dogma,[189] the same authority placed them on the same spiritual level as those whom they considered culturally inferior. The practice of equality may not have equated with its theory, but the theory contrasted dramatically with eugenics theories of biological inequality, and for Chesterton the theory had to be right.

According to Quentin Lauer, Chesterton's attitude to non-white races was characterized by a "complete lack of sympathy with blacks, whom he consistently refers to as 'niggers' (always scornfully), or sometimes as 'wooly savages,'" seeing them, along with "Asiatics" as "quite clearly . . . inferior to whites." This attitude was "far more amazing than his alleged anti-Semitism," which was "aimed at the wealthy and the powerful." Chesterton's sympathies, Lauer maintains, lay not with "the cause of the native Africans" during the Boer War, and it was not enough to say that "he thought as did any Englishman in his day; one looks for something better in Chesterton!"[190] Lauer also notes that Chesterton was strongly influenced by the views of ordinary people,[191] and he certainly scorned the "superior" wisdom of intellectuals, especially the political Mrs. Jellybys, who favored faraway causes over the needs of the domestic poor. Once again it was a clash of underdogs, with Chesterton espousing the language (although not always, as will be seen) as well as the "cause" of the man in the street, who happened to be poor and white.

But, as we will see, while Shaw approved of Mussolini controlling "savage" Abyssinian tribes,[192] Chesterton thought the Nazis more barbarous. He admired Charles Dickens for defending the right to life of "savages," eschewing the modern "brutalitarian" extremes of wronging people "because they are nasty" or excusing them like the humanitarians who could not "be just to them without pretending that they are nice."[193] True justice meant being just even to people you did not like. And it was the universality of the Catholic Church that attracted him: "Becoming a Catholic broadens the mind." It was only when the convert entered the Church that he found it was "much larger inside than it is outside,"[194] and he discovered that he "could not cease to be a Catholic, except by becoming something more narrow than a Catholic. A man must narrow his mind in order to lose the universal philosophy. . . ."[195] Chesterton was a liberal

---

189. See Chapter Eight.

190. Quentin Lauer, *G. K. Chesterton: Philosopher without Portfolio* (New York: Fordham University Press, 1988/1991), 143.

191. Ibid., 10.

192. See Chapter Five.

193. G. K. Chesterton, *"American Notes, and Pictures from Italy"* (London, 1908), in *Appreciations and Criticisms of the Works of Charles Dickens* (London: J. M. Dent & Sons, Ltd., 1911), 48.

194. G. K. Chesterton, *The Catholic Church and Conversion*, op. cit., 80–81.

195. G. K. Chesterton, *The Well and the Shallows*, op. cit., 71.

who actually became the underdog he defended. In *The Catholic Church and Conversion* (1926) he still saw the Church as the underdog,[196] but found it was not quite the same on the inside looking out as on the outside looking in.

Like many Victorians, Chesterton struggled to include non-whites in his view of the equality of man, but with his adherence to Enlightenment universalism and universal religion, and with the plight of the underdog as a goad to his sense of injustice, he defended the religion of dervishes against "progressive" Imperialists who ranked thought above religion, and would allow capitalists to "mow down men like grass in the Soudan, to steal their land and desecrate their tombs" because they were not considered "thinking human beings."[197] He also realized that the pernicious "scientific" creed of race affected blacks, warning that "science might easily corrupt" culture "as in the American South" it was used "to legitimate racism."[198] Evolutionary theories had had a disastrous, retrograde effect on human solidarity:[199] the imposition of a new biological, Nietzschean aristocracy.[200] Chesterton believed that "man is the image of God" and "[i]n the presence of this mysterious monopoly," men's differences were "like dust."[201] Too much emphasis on difference worked "against the unity of the human race," which was to him a theological truth.[202] He doubted whether, had slavery survived until "the age of Rhodes and Roosevelt and evolutionary imperialism," there would ever have been emancipation.[203] He also opposed the prophets and priests of the reproductive movement, which strove to control the numbers of non-whites.[204] In New York in 1906 a Congolese pygmy, Ota Benga, was exhibited at the Bronx Zoo in the same cage as an orangutan for people to draw their own Darwinist conclusions.[205] In *What I Saw in America* Chesterton maintained:

> An ape cannot be a priest, but a negro can be a priest. The dogmatic type of Christianity, especially the Catholic type ... riveted itself irrevocably to the manhood of all men. Where its faith was fixed by creeds and councils it could not save itself even by surrender. It could not gradually dilute democracy, as

196. G. K. Chesterton, *The Catholic Church and Conversion*, op. cit., 73–74.

197. G. K. Chesterton, Letter, "The Jew in Modern Life," *The Nation*, April 8, 1911, 58–59, in J. Stapleton, *Christianity, Patriotism, and Nationhood: The England of G. K. Chesterton*, op. cit., 142.

198. G. K. Chesterton, *Illustrated London News*, July 5, 1924, 6 (ibid., 195).

199. G. K. Chesterton, *What I Saw in America*, op. cit., 300.

200. Q. Lauer, *G. K. Chesterton: Philosopher without Portfolio*, op. cit., 115.

201. G. K. Chesterton, "The Secret Society of Mankind," *Fancies Versus Fads* (London: Methuen & Co. Ltd., 1923), 122–123.

202. A. Nichols, *G. K. Chesterton, Theologian*, op. cit., 173.

203. G. K. Chesterton, *What I Saw in America*, op. cit., 301.

204. See: A. Farmer, *By Their Fruits: Eugenics, Population Control, and the Abortion Campaign*, op. cit.

205. D. Sewell, *The Political Gene: How Darwin's Ideas Changed Politics* (London: Picador, 2010), 1.

could a merely sceptical or secular democrat. There stood, in fact or in possibility, the solid and smiling figure of a black bishop.[206]

Chesterton defended the English pastime of laughing at the strange and foreign, not because it was inferior but because it was strange and foreign, insisting that it was "far better to laugh at a negro for having a black face than to sneer at him for having a sloping skull."[207] As usual, there was a deeper reason: "Nobody laughs at what is entirely foreign; nobody laughs at a palm tree. But it is funny to see the familiar image of God disguised behind the black beard of a Frenchman or the black face of a Negro."[208] In America, where he believed "[t]he new dreams of the 18th century" had already vanished, "the ancient dogmas of the Catholic Church remained." Catholics might also forget brotherhood, but "[t]he church would always continue to ordain negroes and canonize beggars and labourers."[209]

He believed it "absurd" to make, for example, white and black pugilists "representative of races and causes that they do not represent."[210] In *What I Saw in America* he had not, he said, "attempted" to "deal adequately with the question of the negro" for the "somewhat sensational" reason that he did "not have anything particularly valuable to say or suggest." He did not "profess to understand this singularly dark and intricate matter" and could see "no use in men who have no solution filling up the gap with sentimentalism." Nonetheless, "[t]he chief thing that struck me about the coloured people I saw was their charming and astonishing cheerfulness."[211] As always, personal contact was important to Chesterton, and he found that black Americans exhibited the same good humor shown by all poor people under oppression. Some saw this as proof of their inferiority, but Chesterton saw it as the mark of equality.

If the charge of anti-Semitism was serious enough to be used as a weapon against opponents in the "underdog wars," "racist" remarks attracted less controversy. Chesterton recalled one *New Witness* debate that began with his brother Cecil doubting H. G. Wells' understanding of "the difficulties" of Booker T. Washington, "famous negro publicist in America . . . and by inference those of the White South in which he worked." This was followed by "a letter dated from Bexley, which warned everybody of the real dangers of racial admixture and intermarriage," signed "White Man." This "produced a fiery letter from Mr. Wells, humorously headed 'The White Man of Bexley,'" saying that

206. G. K. Chesterton, *What I Saw in America*, op. cit., 302–303.

207. G. K. Chesterton, *What I Saw in America*, op. cit., 3.

208. G. K. Chesterton, "Cockneys and their Jokes," *All Things Considered*, op. cit., 9.

209. Quoted in M. Ward, *Gilbert Keith Chesterton*, op. cit., 572.

210. G. K. Chesterton, "The Silver Goblets," *The Uses of Diversity* (London: Methuen & Co. Ltd, 1920/1927), 103–104.

211. G. K. Chesterton, *What I Saw in America*, op. cit., 158–159.

"he did not know what life was like 'among the pure whites of Bexley'" but that "elsewhere meeting people did not always mean marrying them." Next came someone Chesterton presumed was "a real negro" who "intervened in the debate about his nature and destiny," signing himself "Black Man"; following this, a letter signed "Brown Man" from "I should guess . . . some Brahmin or Parsee student at some college" asked "what view was taken of intermarriage with the races of Asia." The correspondence closed with a letter from someone complaining about the "considerable pain" intermarriage had caused "to many innocent persons, who, by no fault of their own, but by the iron laws of nature," had inherited "a complexion uncommon among their fellow-creatures and attractive only to the elite." The letter, which begged readers regardless of "race or colour" to "work hand in hand for the broadening of the brotherhood of humanity," was signed "Mauve Man with Green Spots."[212]

More seriously, in *The Resurrection of Rome* (1930) Chesterton describes a visit to the Vatican where he saw Pope Pius XI and found himself influenced by the "proximity of the Judaic elements and origins of Christianity."[213] He reflected, in response to a suggestion that "[w]e may yet have a black Pope":

> In a spirit of disgraceful compromise, I suggested meekly that (if not quite ready for that) I should be delighted to see a black Cardinal. I was conscious of some shadowy pleasure in the image; and I recalled the imperial bust of black marble with the red robe, and wondered if there is something pro- phetic or significant in our fancies. Then I remembered the great King who came to Bethlehem, heavy with purple and crimson and with a face like night; and I was ashamed.[214]

From Underdog to Scapegoat—and Back

Chesterton started out with liberal sympathies for the Jewish people but his sympathies waned as he discovered the Irish and he began to speak out for the English poor—the "secret people" who, he hoped, would yet speak out.[215] He began by defending "the Jews," but went through a period when he believed that Jewish financial power was damaging the interests of the poor; it was extreme foreign anti-Semitism and British indifference to it that shocked him into once again defending Jews. Much later, Anthony Julius categorized "disin-

---

212. Gilbert thought he could "trace [Ada's] hand, as well as the editor's, in one of the most admi- rably absurd correspondences I have ever seen in the columns of journalism" (G.K. Chesterton, *Autobiography*, op. cit., 195–196); see Chapter Four regarding Wells and "race."

213. G.K. Chesterton, *The Resurrection of Rome* (London: Hodder & Stoughton Ltd., 1930), 65.

214. Ibid., 320; the early Church saw three popes from North Africa: St. Victor I, St. Miltiades and St. Gelasius I, from the North African region later conquered by Islam.

215. G.K. Chesterton, "The Secret People" (1907) *The Works of G.K. Chesterton* (Ware, Herts.: Wordsworth Poetry Library, 1995), 133; see Chapters Seven and Eight.

terested" anti-Semitism as coming from "the voluntary enemy": political campaigners, often left wing, sometimes depending on one-sided information, who support the Palestinian cause against Israel. This kind of campaigner "acts without regard to his own interests, rather than in their defence" and is "an interferer," although "often with good reasons."[216]

Such a categorization could apply to Chesterton who, like many political campaigners, suffered from the underdog complex in which the radical from a privileged background studies a cause so intensely that he becomes "a professor of the fact," identifying so strongly with the victim of injustice that he almost becomes that victim. But when a new underdog is discovered, who is judged to be more oppressed and thus more worthy of help, the old underdog can swiftly be replaced. The rules of engagement in the "underdog wars" decree that only powerful institutions and majorities may be attacked, but prejudice can easily magnify the size of an underdog in order to provide a legitimate target for criticism. Thus, depending on how dispensable he is, the underdog may become a scapegoat. However, while some radicals pushed the Jewish people away when they came under existential attack, blaming them for their own plight, Chesterton blamed the Nazis.[217]

In the task of unravelling Chesterton's approach to the "Jewish question," an understanding of the "underdog complex," a major component of his worldview, is essential. Nonetheless, his chief preoccupations continued to be the old heresies re-emerging as new fashions—racial theory and eugenics, and the old sins of greed and pride, presumption and despair, manifesting themselves in capitalism, "Prussianism," utopianism, and pessimism. His defense against all these was the democratic nation state under God, which also happened to be his answer to the "Jewish question." In the next chapter we study the trajectory of his relationship with "the Jews" as he addressed such concerns in his fiction.

216. A. Julius, *Trials of the Diaspora: A History of Anti-Semitism in England*, op. cit., 9–10; see Chapter Seven.
217. See Chapters Four and Five.

3

Chesterton and the Golden Age of Anti-Semitism

G.K. CHESTERTON'S FICTION has been called as a witness for the prosecution regarding allegations of anti-Semitism, but all too frequently his declared motivations have been overlooked in preparing the case against him: "My first impulse to write, and almost my first impulse to think, was a revolt of disgust with the Decadents and the aesthetic pessimism of the 'nineties.'"[1] Chesterton's stories certainly reflect this long argument; but it could be argued that he saw "the Jew" as responsible for the decadence and pessimism. But once they are set in the context of their genre, and with his nonfiction as an interpretive tool, his stories throw further light on his views of the "Jewish question," revealing developments in his thought that have been neglected under the influence of the Holocaust.

Chesterton's Times

The Golden Age[2] of detective fiction came between the First and Second World Wars, a time of political and social turbulence. The Russian Revolution during the Great War dealt a shock to the British mind, leading to "a Red Scare."[3] British Imperialism, global capitalism, and air transport had brought the world and its problems ever closer, but greater proximity did not, as H.G. Wells posited, make for greater harmony.[4] Golden Age fiction reflected the British distrust of foreigners, and this included Jews.[5] According to Malcom J. Turnbull,

---

1. G.K. Chesterton, "Milton and Merry England," *A Gleaming Cohort* (London: Methuen & Co. Ltd., 1926), 183.
2. Malcolm J. Turnbull, *Victims or Villains: Jewish Images in Classic English Detective Fiction* (Bowling Green, OH: Bowling Green State University Popular Press, 1998), 1.
3. Pier Brendon, *The Dark Valley: A Panorama of the 1930s* (NY: Alfred A. Knopf, 2000), 13–14.
4. See Chapter Four.
5. Gisela C. Lebzelter, *Political Anti-Semitism in England 1918–1939* (London: Macmillan Press Ltd., 1978), 1–2.

negative Jewish references in crime fiction reached a peak in the 1920s and 1930s.[6] But unflattering stereotypes could sometimes disguise a more sympathetic approach that only became apparent on closer acquaintance:

> He had a jutting nose, a full-lipped mouth and a look about him that said he was not a man to play tricks with, yet a hint he could be pleasant enough if folks were pleasant with him. . . . "And yes," thought Miss Pettigrew; "somewhere in his ancestry there has been a *Jew*. . . ."[7]

By the 1870s the most famous "eternal foreigner" in British literature, Charles Dickens's villainous Fagin (more of whom later) had transmogrified into Anthony Trollope's wealthy and powerful "Melmotte," who "had once been imprisoned for fraud at Hamburg, and had come out of gaol a pauper; friendless, with all his wretched antecedents against him. Now he was a member of the British House of Parliament . . . a commercial giant whose name was a familiar word on all the exchanges of the two hemispheres."[8] Nearly forty years later, Jewish involvement in the Marconi scandal,[9] which Chesterton's brother Cecil helped expose, appeared to reinforce the idea of Jewish financial power, but when Jews became involved in the Russian Revolution,[10] it stirred fears of a secret alliance between capitalist and communist Jews rather than being regarded as a reflection of non-Jewish political diversity.[11] The Left warned of powerful capitalist Jews; the Right was equally certain of "Jewish power," although they approved of it being used in the interests of capitalism. But if capitalist Jews were so powerful, and yet had allowed the Russian Revolution to happen, it seemed they were no longer to be trusted.

Against a background of economic depression, British middle-class readers of crime fiction were caught between envy of rich Jews and fear of poor ones.[12] In Graham Greene's *Brighton Rock* (1938) the "capitalist Jew" has "a neat round belly" and eyes that "gleamed like raisins,"[13] but since the Russian Revolution the fictional Jewish Bolshevik spy had joined an ever-lengthening queue of Jewish criminals, money-lenders, pawnbrokers, and (as some rose from poverty-

6. M. J. Turnbull, *Victims or Villains: Jewish Images in Classic English Detective Fiction*, op. cit., 7.

7. W. Watson, *Miss Pettigrew Lives for a Day* (London: Persephone Books, 1938/2004), 6; despite this Miss Pettigrew proves not unsympathetic to the Jewish character thus described.

8. Anthony Trollope, *The Way We Live Now* (Oxford: Oxford University Press, 1875/1991), 298.

9. M. J. Turnbull, *Victims or Villains: Jewish Images in Classic English Detective Fiction*, op. cit., 8; see Chapter Six.

10. See Chapters Two and Seven.

11. M. J. Turnbull, *Victims or Villains: Jewish Images in Classic English Detective Fiction*, op. cit., 9.

12. Ibid., 25.

13. G. Greene, *Brighton Rock: An Entertainment* (Harmondsworth, Middx.: Penguin Books Ltd., 1938/1968), 63.

stricken immigrant roots) flashy middle-class parvenus.[14] Racists believed that certain crimes were typically Jewish,[15] and despite Hitler's racial crimes it took some time for Golden Age stereotypes to fade.[16]

Catholics had also taken the part of foreigners in English literature. Charlotte Brontë had mocked Methodists for their religious enthusiasm,[17] but took Catholics seriously enough to portray them as villains:

> These Romanists are strange beings. Such a one among them—whom you know no more than the last Inca of Peru or the first Emperor of China—knows you and all your concerns, and has his reasons for saying to you so and so, when you simply thought the communication sprang impromptu from the instant's impulse, his plan in bringing it about that you shall come on such a day, to such a place, under such and such circumstances, when the whole arrangement seems to your crude apprehension the ordinance of chance or the sequel of exigency.[18]

Brontë's evil Madame Walravens in *Villette* is a hideous dwarf[19] and, while Jewish villains have gone out of fashion, the bitter and twisted disabled villain remains fashionable to this day, despite the fact that thousands of disabled people were murdered both before and during the Holocaust.[20] More recently, Dan Brown's *The Da Vinci Code* featured a sinister, murderous albino monk.[21] Agatha Christie saw Catholics as exotic, if less threatening,[22] but Golden Age fiction was thronged with Jews and foreigners of all descriptions, some of which persisted until the 1950s and 1960s, perhaps explaining why Chesterton's characters were rarely singled out for comment.[23] Nonetheless, there was some Jew-

14. M. J. Turnbull, *Victims or Villains: Jewish Images in Classic English Detective Fiction*, op. cit., 7.

15. J. Maritain, *Antisemitism* (London, Geoffrey Bles: The Centenary Press, 1939), 6.

16. M. J. Turnbull, *Victims or Villains: Jewish Images in Classic English Detective Fiction*, 10–11.

17. "Terrible, most distracting to the ear, was the strained shout in which the last stanza [of the hymn] was given. . . . The roof did *not* fly off, which speaks volumes in praise of its solid slating" (C. Brontë, *Shirley* (London: Collins, 1849/1968), 127).

18. C. Brontë, *Villette* (London: Collins, 1853/1970), 382.

19. "She might be three feet high, but she had no shape. Her skinny hands rested upon each other, and pressed the gold knob of a wand-like ivory staff. Her face was large, set not upon her shoulders but before her breast; she seemed to have no neck. I should have said there were a hundred years in her features, and more perhaps in her eyes—her malign, unfriendly eyes, with thick gray brows above and livid lids all round" (ibid., 378).

20. See Chapters Two and Five.

21. The monk was supposed to belong to a religious organization within the Catholic Church, Opus Dei, which has no monks and no record of murder either (as far as known).

22. "The old woman drew herself up. 'I am a good Catholic, Monsieur'" (Agatha Christie, "The Last Séance," (1936) *Agatha Christie: the collected short stories* [London: HarperCollins, 2002], 432).

23. Those who did not comment on them included Maurice Baring, *The Puppet Show of Memory* (London: William Heinemann, 1922); Gerald Cumberland, *Written in Friendship* (London: Grant Richards, 1923); Carl Arns, *Gilbert Keith Chesterton: Umniss seiner KünsHerpersönlichkeit und Proben-seiner schaffens* (Dortmund: Würzburg), 1925. Baring was a friend of Chesterton's (see Chapter Eight),

ish criticism of Chesterton,[24] although, perhaps befitting its subject, not all of it was expressed seriously.[25] One non-Jewish admirer, Reginald Arkell, wrote:

> For Gilbert oft discloses,
> As only Gilbert can,
> His curious hate for noses
> Worn by the sons of Moses,
> He'd like them, one supposes,
> Built on a different plan
> But what nobody knows, is
> How first the feud began.[26]

Elsewhere Arkell somewhat inaccurately furnishes his caricature of the Jewish sculptor, Jacob Epstein, with a hooked nose[27] and the light-hearted tone of most criticism suggests that in the scale of Golden Age anti-Semitism Chesterton's fictional Jew was not regarded as seriously offensive.[28]

Regarding *The Man Who Was Thursday* and *The Duel of Doctor Hirsch*, William Rubinstein remarks that Chesterton was "a particularly difficult figure to come to terms with" because of his "deep love of paradox—a sense that things were not as they seemed—nor yet, on the other hand, were *not* not as they seemed," an atmosphere that was "all-pervasive." His stories were "peppered

---

but although others did notice they made no further comment (R. Lynd, "Mr. Chesterton's Holy War," *The Daily News*, February 25, 1910, in D. J. Conlon, ed., *G. K. Chesterton: The Critical Judgments Part I: 1900–1937* [Antwerp: Antwerp Studies in English Literature, 1976], 219–221; J. Douglas, review of *The Ball and the Cross*, *The Star*, February 26, 1910, in ibid., 221–224); one noticed with apparent approval ("Mimnermus," "A Licensed Jester," *Freethinker*, October 16, 1910, in ibid., 240–242), although another generally sympathetic critic complained (Julius West, *G. K. Chesterton: A Critical Study* [London: Martin Secker, 1915], 182; 160); see: A. Farmer, "Has the Holocaust Influenced Views of G. K. Chesterton's 'Anti-Semitism?'" (unpublished) (Anglia Polytechnic University, 2005). "Exotic" foreigners continued to feature in popular literature, including children's stories like those of Enid Blyton, and the books of Dennis Wheatley, well into the 1950s and 1960s; Huncoat Primary School near Accrington, Lancashire, removed copies of Blyton's books with references to gypsies, gollywogs and a dog with a racially-charged named in order to "gain a Race Equality Mark from the local authority prior to opening a new library" (MailOnline, December 7, 2013, accessed at http://www.dailymail.co.uk/news/article-2519806/Enid-Blyton-Famous-Five-childrens-classics-axed-school-win-race-equality-award.html at September 25, 2014). See also: Phil Baker, *The devil is a gentleman: the life and times of Dennis Wheatley* (Sawtry, Cambridgeshire: Dedalus, 2009).

24. D. Rapp, "The Jewish Response to G. K. Chesterton's Antisemitism, 1911–1933," *Patterns of Prejudice*, 24, (2–4), (1990): 76; see Chapters One and Six.

25. For example the Anglo-Australian Jewish scientist Joseph Jacobs (J. Jacobs, *Jewish Contributions to Civilization: An Estimate* [Philadelphia: The Jewish Publication Society of America, 1919], 40, in Stone, D., *Responses to Nazism in Britain, 1933–1939: Before the War and the Holocaust* [Basingstoke, Hants.: Palgravemacmillan, 2003], 220).

26. Reginald Arkell, *Meet these People* (London: Herbert Jenkins Ltd., 1928), 139.

27. Ibid., 66.

28. See Chapter One.

with the mindless stereotypical characters of the period, and the journals with which he was associated like *New Witness* and *G. K.'s Weekly* of course attacked Jewish 'plutocrats.'" But it was "not easy to categorise his attitude toward the Jews with precision." Rubinstein concludes that Chesterton's attitude was a "curious mixture of Christian (i.e., Catholic) patriot and English patriot; the Jews were undesirable and alien because they were neither." Nevertheless, this attitude "distinguished him from most post-1880 anti-Semitism, which was, increasingly, purely 'racial' in nature," and while few readers would be "happy" with the theme of *The Duel of Dr. Hirsch* their "dissatisfaction" would be "equally felt by Chesterton's most bigoted and anti-Semitic readers."[29] In fact, Rubinstein sees Chesterton as part of a general intellectual trend away from anti-Semitism, which encompassed all political shades in Britain after 1933.[30]

The Genre

Post-Holocaust, difficulties in interpreting earlier English literature—of distinguishing between political comment, humor, and gratuitous insult—have been compounded by the nature of Golden Age crime fiction. Crowded as it was with stereotypes, Jewish readers may not have felt too singled out by seeing the Jewish financier, moneylender, pawnbroker and parvenu sneering, jeering and leering across the pages. Even so, the portrayal of Jews as foreign villains reflected a view of them as innately aggressive and inferior;[31] sometimes, as in Marjorie Allingham's unmasking of an underworld mastermind, criminally overweight: "An immense Jew standing with his back to the doorway suddenly raised his voice above the din. 'Put 'em up quick, both of you. Sit on 'em, boys.'"[32] Agatha Christie's *The Secret of Chimneys* discloses rumors of oil discoveries in "Herzoslovakia": "I've a feeling in my bones . . . that people are getting ready to be interested in that unimportant little country.... Hebraic people. Yellow-faced financiers in city offices."[33] Jews were so closely associated with finance[34] that characters desperate for cash were described simply as "going to the Jews." In Dorothy L. Sayers's *Gaudy Night* Lord Peter Wimsey's nephew, "struck by a melancholy association of ideas," says that as an uncle

29. W.D. Rubinstein, *A History of the Jews in the English-speaking World: Great Britain* (London: Macmillan Press Ltd., 1996), 114–116.

30. Ibid., 297; W.D. Rubinstein, H.L. Rubinstein, *Philosemitism* (London: Macmillan Press, 1999), 123.

31. G.C. Lebzelter, *Political Anti-Semitism in England 1918–1939*, op. cit., 96.

32. Margery Allingham, *Mystery Mile* (Suffolk: St. Edmundsbury Press Ltd., 1930/1989), 171.

33. A. Christie, *The Secret of Chimneys* (London: Pan Books Ltd., 1925/1961), 16.

34. A.H. Foxman, *Jews and Money: The Story of a Stereotype* (New York: Palgrave Macmillan, 2010), 52.

Lord Peter is "a dashed sight more accommodating than the Jewish kind."[35] John Buchan's *The Thirty-Nine Steps* (1915) informs the reader: "[I]f you're on the biggest kind of job and are bound to get to the real boss, ten to one you are brought up against a little white-faced Jew in a bath-chair with an eye like a rattlesnake."[36] Chesterton's friend E.C. Bentley writes in *Trent's Last Case* (1913): "In Paris a well-known banker walked quietly out of the Bourse and fell dead upon the broad steps among the raving crowd of Jews, a phial crushed in his hand."[37]

Neither were Jewish women and children immune from literary barbs.[38] In Graham Greene's *Brighton Rock* "[a] little Jewess sniffed at [Pinkie] bitchily and then talked him over with another little Jewess on a settee."[39] The closest Chesterton's fiction came to such ungallant references was *The Fool of the Family* (1922) which mentions "a flashy South American Jewess with a fortune."[40] Golden Age crime fiction featured "[t]emperamental, exotic, and dubious continentals of all descriptions," with Jews filling this role most frequently,[41] such that a Jewish commentator rather forlornly pointed out that the number of Jews involved in crime was disproportionately low.[42]

From the 1880s Jews were associated with the more mundane clothing and boot trades, with furniture-making, food, and entertainment. As to finance, "contrary to what one might expect, the more the best-known Jewish banking house, the Rothschilds, decreased in international importance, the more the Jew in literature is described as a cosmopolitan financier with money-interests spread all over the world." Despite this, Jews continued to be identified with "the wicked rich" because of their historical "role as money-lenders,"[43] and Golden Age fiction implied that Jews were determined to get their hands on other people's property by any means, legal or illegal: there was a foreigner

35. D.L. Sayers, "Gaudy Night," *Dorothy L. Sayers, Three Complete Lord Peter Wimsey Novels* (New York: Wings Books, 1936/1992), 410.

36. John Buchan, *The Thirty-Nine Steps* (London: Penguin Books, 1915/1994), 8.

37. E.C. Bentley, *Trent's Last Case* (New York: Harper & Row, Publishers, 1913/1978), 6.

38. C.L. Klein, "The changing image of the Jew in modern English literature," *Patterns of Prejudice*, 5(2) (1971): 30.

39. G. Greene, *Brighton Rock*, op. cit., 63.

40. G.K. Chesterton, *The Man Who Knew Too Much* (Thirsk, N. Yorks.: House of Stratus, 1922/2001), 135.

41. M.J. Turnbull, *Victims or Villains: Jewish Images in Classic English Detective Fiction*, op. cit., 3–4.

42. "A most careful investigation has proved conclusively that the allegations against the Jew . . . are utterly baseless. . . . This fact has, to some extent, been obscured by an obnoxious practice of a section of the Press of giving the religion of the offender if he is a Jew, but omitting it if he is not" (Sidney Salomon, *The Jews of Britain* [London: Jarrolds Publishers, 1938], 104.)

43. C.L. Klein, "The changing image of the Jew in modern English literature," op. cit., 27–28.

behind every plot, a red under every bed, and a Jew behind every lamp post. In real life, the scarcity of Jews partly explained their ubiquitous presence in literature since (like Catholics) their very exoticism came from being rare: the reader, not to mention the writer, was less able to distinguish fantasy from the reality of their own experience. As to crime, for middle class Britons, inter-War London was a much safer place than Chicago or even Paris,[44] making fictional murder appear exotic, even cosy, rather than an unwelcome reminder of ghastly reality.

In *Snobbery with Violence*, Colin Watson comments on the "racialist flavour" of Golden Age fiction.[45] In *Bloody Murder*, Julian Symons sees crime writers' attitudes to foreigners ranging from the "casual anti-Semitism" of Lord Peter Wimsey[46] to the "markedly xenophobic" "Bulldog Drummond" stories of Herman McNeile.[47] But while Golden Age fiction feasted on foreignness it ignored political turmoil and the conditions of the poor, and he says that "almost all" British Golden Age authors and "most" Americans "were unquestionably right-wing. This is not to say that they were openly anti-Semitic or anti-Radical, but that they were overwhelmingly conservative in feeling." To create a Jewish detective or a working-class version "aggressively conscious of his origins" would have seemed "quite incongruous" to them. In Symons's view, "We are very far in these books from the radicalism of Chesterton, and a long way even from . . . Bentley's denunciation of [the banker] Sigsbee Manderson" in *Trent's Last Case*.[48] Even socialists G.D.H. and Margaret Cole "never treated seriously the social realities with which in life they were so much concerned."[49] In Golden Age crime fiction, it would appear that Chesterton's stories stood out not so much for their "anti-Semitism" as for their political awareness.

The Co-Accused

Nonetheless, Turnbull has severely criticized Chesterton while dismissing Christie's and Sayers's "anti-Semitic" allusions as "generally . . . fleeting and peripheral," a product of their time and class. Sayers' "personal, and passionate, fealty to mainstream Christian Orthodoxy . . . incorporated a degree of theological anti-Semitism" and none of Christie's Jewish characters "ever turns out to be the culprit."[50] Of Margery Allingham, another Golden Age detective fic-

---

44. J. Symons, *Bloody Murder* (London: Pan Books, 1972/1992), 129.

45. Colin Watson, *Snobbery with Violence: English Crime Stories and their Audience* (London: Methuen, 1971/1987), 123–136.

46. Julian Symons, *Bloody Murder*, op. cit., 124.

47. Ibid., 273.

48. Ibid., 118–119.

49. Ibid., 128–129.

50. M.J. Turnbull, *Victims or Villains: Jewish Images in Classic English Detective Fiction*, op. cit., 86–87.

tion writer, he remarks: "True, an immense Jew stage-manages a punch-up and is summarily dealt with," but the character "appears only fleetingly," one of "a cosmopolitan gang of toughs," thus "he is only one player in a virtual League of Nations of odd ethnics."[51] While noting other, positive Golden Age Jewish portraits,[52] Turnbull overlooks Chesterton's "Mr. Lever" in *The Queer Feet*, relying instead on a "racial" interpretation of the story.[53] He also notes the use of anti-Semitic prejudice to mislead the reader in Herbert Adams's *The Sloane Square Mystery*,[54] but not E.C. Bentley's[55] and John Buchan's;[56] or Chesterton's in *The Loyal Traitor*.[57] Turnbull does however cite Canovan's defense of Chesterton against anachronistic criticism.[58]

The tone of any piece of writing is crucial to its interpretation, and some Golden Age fiction is decidedly tongue-in-cheek. It might be argued, however, that this trivialized anti-Jewish prejudice, and Turnbull quotes Chesterton to show that he "remained convinced of the essential otherness of the Jew,"[59] although the same could be argued of many of the Golden Age authors and, as seen in Chapter Two, of many Jews. Turnbull also notes that political reality eventually intruded upon Golden Age writers who as a consequence changed their approach to Jewish characterization, recording Buchan's Zionist sympathies and Greene's condemnations of fascism.[60] Despite this, he overlooks Chesterton's much earlier work *The Return of Don Quixote* (1927) in which "Murrel" describes the idea of the English being ruled by a "strong man" as "too horrible."[61] Turnbull also neglects Chesterton's political awareness expressed in *The Moderate Murderer* (1930): "Believe me, the reactionary Extremists are quite as likely to go to extremes [as revolutionary Extremists]. The history of faction fights will show acts of violence by Patricians as well as

51. Ibid., 72.

52. Ibid., 74.

53. Ibid., 35–36; this story will be examined in more depth later in this chapter.

54. Ibid., 58–59.

55. Ibid., 36.

56. Ibid., 38.

57. Ibid., 55–56.

58. Ibid., 47; see Chapter One.

59. G.K. Chesterton, *Autobiography* (London, 1936), 75–77, in M.J. Turnbull, *Victims or Villains: Jewish Images in Classic English Detective Fiction*, op. cit., 47–48; Chesterton adds that the perceived "foreignness" of Jews "did not prevent friendship and affection, especially in my own case; but then it never has prevented it in the case of ordinary foreigners" (*Autobiography* [Sevenoaks, Kent: Fisher Press, 1936/1992], 74); see Chapters Seven and Eight.

60. M.J. Turnbull, *Victims or Villains: Jewish Images in Classic English Detective Fiction*, op. cit., 100–102.

61. G.K. Chesterton, *The Return of Don Quixote* (1927, 261), in M. Canovan, *G.K. Chesterton: Radical Populist* (New York and London: Harcourt Brace Jovanovich), 145.

Plebians, by . . . Orangemen as well as Fenians, by Fascists as well as Bolshevists, by the Ku-Klux-Klan as well as the Black Hand."[62] Buchan and Greene lived to see the War, which appeared to trigger a change in attitude.[63] Chesterton died before the War, but there is additional, albeit subtle evidence of change long before it became impossible to avoid the evidence from Nazi Germany, although Jewish stereotypes were remarkably resistant to such realities,[64] notably those of writer Sydney Horler.[65]

Personal preference may partly explain conflicting reactions to Golden Age authors. Despite noting their "generalised defects," including "most glaringly, an extensive and untenable racism," Turnbull retained "a nostalgic fondness" for Christie.[66] Symons "still enjoy[ed] enormously the best work of the Golden Age detective story writers,"[67] and he saw Chesterton as one of those still capable of being re-read[68]—with Father Brown one of the "two most successful Supermen detectives of the period."[69] He mentions *The Queer Feet* and *The Purple Wig*, seen by Turnbull as anti-Semitic, without reference to such concerns. Symons considered that Chesterton's detective stories "sometimes topple into absurdity because the premises of the tale are too fantastic," nonetheless "[o]ften the points he is making are beautifully put"; he further states that *The Queer Feet* was "among the finest short crime stories ever written."[70] Whereas Turnbull's and Symons's fondness for the Golden Age influenced their more nuanced responses to offensive attitudes, Colin Watson, in deriding the prejudice of Golden Age authors, conveyed his own dislike for the genre.[71]

---

62. G. K. Chesterton, "The Moderate Murderer," *Four Faultless Felons* (New York: Dover Publications Inc., 1930/1989), 54. "[D]uring the twenties and thirties Chesterton consistently refused to look upon the Left as a political danger. His position on this question does not change in his final novel. Socialism and Communism are dismissed as false but not dangerous philosophies, except to the extent that they are distractions from the real danger of the Servile State which they unconsciously help to introduce" (I. Boyd, *The Novels of G. K. Chesterton: a study in art and propaganda* [London: Paul Elek, 1975], 184).

63. M. J. Turnbull, *Victims or Villains: Jewish Images in Classic English Detective Fiction*, op. cit., 104.

64. Ibid., 127–139.

65. Ibid., 120–121.

66. Ibid., 2.

67. J. Symons, *Bloody Murder*, op. cit., 26.

68. Ibid., 87; the other was Stanley Ellin.

69. Ibid., 91; the other was Professor S. F. X. Van Dusen.

70. Ibid., 94–95.

71. Colin Watson, *Snobbery with Violence: English Crime Stories and their Audience*, op. cit., 123; 105; 174–175; despite his criticism of Golden Age crime writers' lack of realism, Watson's "Flaxborough" series, set in a quiet and respectable rural English backwater, describes the kind of gruesome events more closely associated with a modern urban setting.

The Wider Chesterton: Race and Anti-Semitism in Chesterton's Fiction

In response to "anti-Semitism" claims made against *Four Faultless Felons* (1930) Chesterton responded: "I do take my real opinions seriously, though not the stories that sometimes embody them."[72] Turnbull, however, while studying the wider literary output of T.S. Eliot, Ezra Pound, D.H. Lawrence, and Wyndham Lewis for clues regarding anti-Semitism,[73] neglects Chesterton's "real opinions" in his non-fiction, and also his wider fiction. In selectively quoting Chesterton regarding anti-Semitism he draws heavily on Cheyette's study of "race" in fiction.[74] Nonetheless, despite Holocaust influences, the latter's "racial" approach can help interpret Chesterton's fiction, when his non-fiction is also taken into account.

Cheyette notes that in *The Curse of the Golden Cross* (1926) Father Brown "makes a point of denying" that Jews were persecuted in the Middle Ages: "[I]f you want to satirize medievalism, you could make a good case by saying that some poor Christian might be burned alive for making a mistake about the Homoousion, while a rich Jew might walk down the street openly sneering at Christ and the Mother of God." Cheyette adds that Chesterton's "earlier distinctions between 'rich and poor' or 'orthodox and broad' Jews" had been "elided in the all-embracing context of 'Semitic trouble,'"[75] a view echoed by Turnbull.[76]

But the reference in *The Curse of the Golden Cross* to a rich Jew makes the distinction between Jews that Chesterton is supposed to have discarded: according to the legend of the Golden Cross, as recounted by a vicar, the cross fell into the hands of "a Jew money-lender" along with the tools and possessions of the local goldsmith who had fallen on hard times after a "series of inexplicable accidents"; the money-lender, "cynically tolerated" by the lord of the manor, was "ruthlessly burnt" by order of the local Lord's newly-religious son, determined to uphold Christianity—all under the curse of the cross.[77] Father Brown knows

---

72. In response to an anonymous review in the *News Chronicle* (G.K. Chesterton, *Illustrated London News*, September 20, 1930, in *Gilbert Magazine*, 12 [2 & 3], [November/December 2008]): 9, accessed May 19, 2011, http://www.209.236.72.127/wordpress/wp-content/uploads/2010/12/gilbert_12.2_5.pdf.

73. M.J. Turnbull, *Victims or Villains: Jewish Images in Classic English Detective Fiction*, op. cit., 70.

74. Ibid., 7, 33, 36, 45, 48.

75. G.K. Chesterton, "The Curse of the Golden Cross" (1926, 118) in B. Cheyette, *Constructions of "the Jew" in English literature and society: Racial representations, 1875–1945* (Cambridge: Cambridge University Press, 1995), 200 (referred to as "The Ghost of the Golden Cross"); the Council of Nicaea (AD 325) used "Homoousion" to express the divinity of Christ.

76. M.J. Turnbull, *Victims or Villains: Jewish Images in Classic English Detective Fiction*, op. cit., 45.

77. Chesterton, G.K., *The Curse of the Golden Cross* (1926) *The Complete Father Brown* (London: Penguin, 1981), 396–397.

that the "vicar" is no historical expert (in fact he is the villain) since it was "illegal for a money-lender to distrain on a man's shop and tools," and it was unlikely that a man's Guild would not save him, "especially if he were ruined by a Jew." The story is not unsympathetic to the fate of Jews, for the "vicar" admits that rich Jews were only tolerated because of their wealth and ruthlessly discarded when no longer useful. Father Brown is not attacking Jews but defending the Medieval Church in pointing out that a Christian would be more likely to be burnt for heresy than a Jew. Furthermore, even while defending the medieval Guild system he admits: "Those people had vices and tragedies of their own; they sometimes tortured and burned people." Moreover, he makes the political point that the "idea of a man . . . crawling away to die because nobody cared whether he lived—that is not a mediaeval idea. That's a product of our economic science and progress." However, when challenged: "[S]urely you won't deny that Jews were persecuted in the Middle Ages?" Father Brown responds: "It would be nearer the truth . . . to say they were the only people who weren't persecuted in the Middle Ages."[78] Although Chesterton was not supporting the persecution of Jews, they were ill-treated and murdered in medieval times, and even if they converted to Christianity, which many did out of fear, they could be burnt for heresy. While pointing out that poor Jews were more likely to be persecuted than rich Jews, who could, it claims, openly sneer at Christian beliefs, the story nevertheless gives the impression that anti-Jewish persecution was not so bad, and if it did occur it was the fault of Jews.[79]

Regarding Edward I's expulsion of the Jews, Chesterton's *Short History of England* (1917) attempts to reconcile what he saw as two opposed views of history, that of the Jews and the poor people of England: "The problem is so much misunderstood and mixed with notions of a stupid spite against a gifted and historic race as such, that we must pause for a paragraph upon it." Medieval Jews, he said, "were as powerful as they were unpopular. They were the capitalists of the age, the men with wealth banked ready for use. It is very tenable that in this way they were useful; it is certain that in this way they were used. It is also quite fair to say that in this way they were ill-used." This had nothing to do with King John pulling out Jews' teeth—in fact, "a story against King John"— but "the real unfairness of the Jews' position was deeper and more distressing to a sensitive and highly civilised people." They "might reasonably say that Chris-

78. Ibid., 402–403. The villain poses as the Reverend Walters after murdering him.

79. Having been confined to money-lending (and heavily taxed for it) Jews often found themselves at the mercy of the mobs, easily stirred to persecution when a prominent non-Jew was unable or unwilling to repay a debt, as Chesterton's bogus vicar recounts; on the most notorious occasion, in 1190—following anti-Jewish riots in Norwich, Dunstable and Stamford—the Jews of York, led by their Rabbi, "committed suicide rather than fall prey to the mob" (D. J. Goldberg, J. D. Rayner, *The Jewish People: Their History and Their Religion* [London: Penguin, 1987], 103).

tian kings and nobles, and even Christian popes and bishops, used for Christian purposes (such as the Crusades and the cathedrals) the money that could only be accumulated in such mountains by a usury they inconsistently denounced as unchristian, and in times of economic hardship, "gave up the Jew to the fury of the poor, whom that useful usury had ruined. That was the real case for the Jew; and no doubt he really felt himself oppressed," but "[u]nfortunately it was the case for the Christians that they, with at least equal reason, felt him as the oppressor; and that *mutual* charge of tyranny is the Semitic trouble in all times." Chesterton concludes: "It is certain that in popular sentiment, this Anti-Semitism was not excused as uncharitableness, but simply regarded as charity."[80] Chesterton, as ever on the side of the poor, provides a "reasonable" explanation for their apparently unreasoning prejudice, and tries to redefine the oppressor—the mob—as the underdog; but it is doubtful whether the persecuted Jews regarded their "fury" as "charity."

In a sense, however, Chesterton did discard Jewish distinctions, for he drew attention to the sufferings not only of poor Jews but also of wealthy Jews. Throughout his career he claimed that the activities of a few wealthy Jews were responsible for the sufferings of poor Jews as well as poor non-Jews, continuing to distinguish between perceived actions and intrinsic characteristics. It could be argued that actions spring from characteristics, but his avoidance of a monolithic view of Jews undermines perceptions of him as "racist."

Chesterton's disapproval of "financial" and "political" Jews can be seen in another story in 1926 in which a French monarchist insists: "Our only claim is to be a wall across Christendom against the Jew pedlars and pawnbrokers, against the Goldsteins and the—" to which an English Duke responds: "Nobody but dirty Radicals can say a word against Goldstein." The Frenchman, whose eyes "shone" with "that steel which is the mind of France," asserts: "You have ruled England for four hundred years. By your own account you have not made the countryside endurable to men ... you are hand in glove with those very money-grubbers and adventurers whom gentlemen have no other business but to keep at bay. I do not know what your people will do; but my people would kill you."[81] But in the same collection Chesterton treats the Jewish people reverently: "[T]he Jew is a genuine peculiar case. The Wandering Jew is not a wandering cad. He is a highly civilized man in a highly difficult position; the world being divided, and his own nation being divided, about whether he can do anything else except wander."[82] This might be seen as unwillingness to

80. G. K. Chesterton, *A Short History of England* (1917) *The Collected Works of G. K. Chesterton Vol. XX* (San Francisco: Ignatius Press, 2001), 497–498.

81. G. K. Chesterton, "Dukes," *A Gleaming Cohort*, op. cit., 127–128.

82. G. K. Chesterton, "The Aristocratic 'Arry'" (ibid., 113–114).

attack the roots of his own religion, an issue explored in Chapter Eight, but in his *Short History* Chesterton says "the Roman soldiers killed Christ,"[83] and even refers to "this Semite God."[84] In his non-fiction his view of "good and bad Jews" was closely linked to religious practice.[85] In *The Curse of the Golden Cross*, although he portrayed both Jews and anti-Semites as oppressed, wealth is a key factor, and the theme of the poor religious Jew as morally superior to the wealthy secular Jew is pursued in *The Ball and the Cross*[86] and *The Paradoxes of Mr. Pond*.[87]

Dickens shows a similar "dual approach" in *Oliver Twist* when the evil Fagin faces the hangman's noose: "Venerable men of his own persuasion had come to pray beside him, but he had driven them away with curses. They renewed their charitable efforts, and he beat them off."[88] Even so, in *The Flying Inn* (1914) Chesterton treats sympathetically the dubious origins of Dr. Moses Meadows, describing his atheism and milk-watering scam humorously.[89] Dr. Simeon Wolfe, the implicitly Jewish atheist in *The Poet and the Lunatics* (1929) turns out to be guilty, although acting under someone else's authority. Moreover, in a significant twist, both Wolfe (albeit with his face "wrinkled with a Semitic sneer")[90] and Starkey, the equally guilty non-Jewish doctor,[91] are shown as capable of redemption.[92] Chesterton is sympathetic to nearly all his Jewish characters, even the worst, attributing their wrongdoing to circumstances they cannot help. Naturally, he selected negative storylines for them but, considered as a whole, his fiction shows that far from discarding all differences between Jewish characters, which would suggest a racist approach, he continued to distinguish between rich and poor Jews, and furthermore was sympathetic even to atheist Jews.

83. G. K. Chesterton, *A Short History of England* (1917), op. cit., 431.

84. Ibid., 466.

85. G. K. Chesterton, Letter to *The Nation*, April 28, 1911, in Sr. M. Loyola, "Chesterton and the Mystery of Israel," *The Chesterton Review* 13, (2), (1987): 150.

86. G. K. Chesterton, *The Ball and the Cross* (London: House of Stratus, 1909/2001), 31.

87. G. K. Chesterton, *The Paradoxes of Mr. Pond* (New York: Dover Publications Inc., 1937/1990), 119 (to be studied).

88. C. Dickens, *Oliver Twist* (Ware, Herts.: Wordsworth Classics, 1837–38/1996), 346.

89. The scientist Dr Moses Meadows "had certainly come in the first instance from a little town in Germany" (G.K. Chesterton, *The Flying Inn* [Harmondsworth, Middx.: Penguin, 1914/1958], 210); when challenged about his famous "health cure" he shakes his fists aloft "in a way unknown to all the English around him"; Meadows, "like even the most genuine sceptics such as Bradlaugh, was as legal as he was sceptical" (ibid., 213).

90. G. K. Chesterton, *The Poet and the Lunatics: Episodes in the Life of Gabriel Gale* (London: Cassell & Company Ltd., 1929), 259.

91. Ibid., 261.

92. Ibid., 263; somehow Gale reads Wolfe's mind and finds it, as a result of atheism, a "chaos of exceptions" (ibid., 259).

Unlike Disraeli, Chesterton did not explicate racial theories in his fiction, but in *Manalive* (1912), Cheyette sees evidence for such views in the character Moses Gould, in whom, he claims, Chesterton abolished his earlier distinctions between "wealthy Jewish cosmopolitans and poor 'orthodox' Jews." As his friends listen reverently to a letter that defends the hero, "Innocent Smith," in mystical terms, Gould smiles "a certain smile. It was the smile of the Cynic Triumphant, which has been the tocsin for many a cruel riot in Russian villages or medieval towns."[93] Chesterton differentiates Gould from the non-Jewish characters when he interjects cynically: "Oh, 'oly, 'oly, 'oly!"; at this, "English reverence, Irish mysticism, American idealism, looked up" at Gould, and Chesterton adds: "[W]henever there is conflict, crises come in which any soul, personal or racial, unconsciously turns on the world the most hateful of its hundred faces."[94] This suggests that Gould is immune to spirituality, although he might possess a "racial soul." This "immunity" must be a Jewish trait, since it caused historical anti-Jewish persecution. Despite this, Chesterton describes such riots as "cruel" and, as will be seen, there is a deeper level of meaning to this passage.[95] Elsewhere, Gould laughs at the non-Jewish characters "with the shameless rationality of another race," and Cheyette sees Chesterton's differentiation as showing that Gould is unable to attain the "spiritual transfiguration that he so desperately needs."[96] But some of this differentiation is positive. Gould may possess a "shameless rationality" but the "subconscious transcendentalism" of his non-Jewish friends leads them to demonstrate it by picnicking on the roof of the boarding house: "suicidal athletics" in which he refuses to join.[97]

This humorous approach,[98] while not excluding the possibility of anti-Semitism, lessens the impact of references that appear threatening when seen in isolation, and the novel's characteristically allegorical nature[99] offers a particularly useful interpretive tool. Chesterton claimed the book, like all his writing, was a response to "the Decadents and the Pessimists" that had contributed to

93. G.K. Chesterton, *Manalive* (1912, 215–216), in B. Cheyette, *Constructions of "the Jew" in English literature and society: Racial representations, 1875–1945*, op. cit., 186.

94. G.K. Chesterton, *Manalive* (London: House of Stratus, 2001), 138.

95. "What is usually missed by those who quote this passage as evidence of Chesterton's anti-Semitism, is that, cynic or sceptic as he may be, Moses Gould is right in his reactions, and English reverence, Irish mysticism and American idealism are wrong in their reactions to "Raymond Percy." Of course, being right has never spared anyone in a riot" (D.J. Conlon, "New and Original Views," 2012 [unpublished]).

96. G.K. Chesterton, *Manalive* (1912, 43), in B. Cheyette, *Constructions of "the Jew" in English literature and society: Racial representations, 1875–1945*, op. cit., 186.

97. G.K. Chesterton, *Manalive*, op. cit., 24.

98. Lynette Hunter, *G.K. Chesterton: Explorations in Allegory* (London: The Macmillan Press Ltd., 1979), 109.

99. Maurice Evans, *G.K. Chesterton* (London: Cambridge University Press, 1939), 78.

his period of youthful depression, and "ruled the culture of the age."[100] Lynette Hunter regards the novel as portraying a "pure artist express[ing] his meaning through living."[101] Innocent Smith acts out his belief that familiarity breeds contempt by repeatedly eloping with his wife and stealing his own possessions. The clergyman Raymond Percy remarks in his defense: "His creed of wonder was Christian by this absolute test; that he felt it continually slipping from himself as much as from others."[102] As will be seen, Moses Gould was one of these "others" at risk of losing this "wonder." While his "negro vitality and vulgarity" suggests racial connotations,[103] the story's plethora of racial and national[104] types makes a consistent Jew/non-Jew differentiation problematical: Chesterton mentions the "intellectual cruelty of . . . the Celt,"[105] and that "the Jew [Gould] and the American [Pym]" are of "sensitive and excitable stocks";[106] furthermore, the Irish, "when gathered together into gangs and conspiracies" seemed to "lose altogether that lovable good-nature and readiness to accept anything one tells them."[107]

Gould, however, is also described as "the gayest of godless little dogs," and a "performing monkey," prompting Cheyette to see "semitic depths" underlying his "godless bestiality."[108] A description of Gould as a "thoroughly wholesome animal"[109] suggests, post-Holocaust, a Hitlerian view of less-than-human "non-Aryans."[110] But in *Manalive*, Gentile character Innocent Smith also suffers anthropological comparison, likened to "a monkey swung by his tail,"[111] a "huge, half-human figure" which, when it ran, "rather suggested a baboon,"[112] his "great apish figure"[113] "leaping like a gorilla."[114] Gould may look "like a dog" with "two dark eyes on each side of his protuberant nose" that "glistened

100. G. K. Chesterton, *Autobiography*, op. cit., 92.

101. L. Hunter, *G. K. Chesterton: Explorations in Allegory*, op. cit., 96.

102. G. K. Chesterton, *Manalive*, op. cit., 134.

103. G. K. Chesterton, *Manalive* (1912, 19), in B. Cheyette, *Constructions of "the Jew" in English literature and society: Racial representations, 1875–1945*, op. cit., 186.

104. I. Boyd, *The Novels of G. K. Chesterton: A Study in Art and Propaganda*, op. cit., 59.

105. G. K. Chesterton, *Manalive*, op. cit., 39.

106. Ibid., 109.

107. Ibid., 116.

108. G. K. Chesterton, *Manalive* (1912, 32; 19), in B. Cheyette, *Constructions of "the Jew" in English literature and society: Racial representations, 1875–1945*, op. cit., 186.

109. G. K. Chesterton, *Manalive*, op. cit., 138.

110. M. Biddiss, "Mind at the end of its tether: political ideology and cultural confusion, 1914–1945," in P. Hayes, ed., *Themes in Modern European History 1890–1945* (London: Routledge, 1992), 281; A. Hitler, *Mein Kampf* (London: Pimlico, 1925–26/2001), 263.

111. G. K. Chesterton, *Manalive*, op. cit., 14.

112. Ibid., 77.

113. Ibid., 184.

114. Ibid., 124.

gloomily like black buttons,"[115] but Innocent Smith has "a prominent pointing nose, a little like a dog's."[116]

Gould has "a short dark figure with a walk apparently founded on the imperfect repression of a negro breakdown,"[117] and Chesterton's remark about a "racial soul" could refer to the idea of animals or races having souls,[118] but such teasing references to evolutionary and racial theories are more redolent of Chesterton's skepticism about modern fads[119] rather than an acceptance of them. Nothing is as it seems in *Manalive*: the hero is accused of burglary, desertion, polygamy, and attempted murder but it is all a matter of perception. Chesterton humorously dismissed evolutionary theories in *The Everlasting Man* (1925)[120] and in *Manalive* the evolutionary "red herrings" are summarily dismissed by Smith's friend "Michael Moon": "All we know of the Missing Link is that he is missing—and he won't be missed either."[121] Furthermore, Gould's declaration that he has "got a conscience"[122] defines him as human in Chesterton's book, since he believed that "God has given all men a conscience";[123] in fact, Gould is the only Chesterton character to merit this description.

Nonetheless, Turnbull echoes Cheyette in diagnosing "racial" preoccupations in Chesterton's "Mr. Lever," the Jewish hotelier in *The Queer Feet*.[124] Lever[125] and Gould[126] are quite different, but both are treated sympathetically and share the positive attribute of being kindly. Lever is "not untouched by spirituality,"[127] but despite noting such positive qualities Cheyette sees a racial connection between the two in their "Jewish" inability to transcend materialism. Lever makes a fortune by making his hotel difficult to get into, loans

---

115. Ibid., 18.

116. Ibid., 11.

117. Ibid., 69.

118. The idea of a "racial" soul was connected to the fascination with "fair Aryans" who, it was claimed, originated in India but ended up in Germany (Alfred Rosenberg, *The Myth of the Twentieth Century* 1925–1930, accessed March 28, 2004, http://www.ety.com/HRP/booksonline/mythos/mythostoc.htm); such ideas featured in the Nazi quest for a source of spiritual power (see: N. Goodrick-Clarke, *The Occult Roots of Nazism: Secret Aryan Cults and their Influence on Nazi Ideology* [London: I. B. Tauris & Co. Ltd., 1992]).

119. B. Bergonzi, "Chesterton and/or Belloc" (1959), in D.J. Conlon, ed., *G.K. Chesterton: A Half Century of Views* (Oxford: Oxford University Press, 1987), 183.

120. G.K. Chesterton, *The Everlasting Man* (San Francisco: Ignatius Press, 1925/1993), 26; 40–42.

121. G.K. Chesterton, *Manalive*, op. cit., 175.

122. Ibid., 160.

123. Ibid., 237.

124. M.J. Turnbull, *Victims or Villains: Jewish Images in Classic English Detective Fiction*, op. cit., 35–36.

125. G.K. Chesterton, "The Queer Feet" (1911) *The Complete Father Brown*, op. cit., 40.

126. G.K. Chesterton, *Manalive*, op. cit., 138.

127. G.K. Chesterton, "The Queer Feet" (1911) *The Complete Father Brown*, op. cit., 49.

money to dukes, and is "torn in two" by his anxieties over cleanliness and the need to show hospitality toward the muddy Father Brown; according to Cheyette: "[T]he madness of Lever's 'good manners' abolishes the most profound of spiritual relations with a 'higher' world," substituting "a series of false material 'limitations.'" He further notes that "'the Jew' signifies the confusion which arises when false or wordly (*sic*) distinctions blur the timeless boundary between God and man."[128] When valuable cutlery is stolen, Cheyette sees Lever reverting to his "racial type" by speaking with a "deepening accent" and turning a "sickly yellow."[129] Chesterton did portray Jews signaling their origins by reverting to foreign accents in a crisis,[130] but frequently described both Jewish and non-Jewish characters with yellow faces,[131] and Lever's reaction to the loss of cutlery could be seen as typical of hoteliers rather than one specific race.

Hunter has seen *The Queer Feet* as illustrating Father Brown's prosaic methods of detection rather than supernatural powers,[132] while Symons has interpreted it as a vehicle for social criticism because the snobbish witnesses fail to notice the fundamental equality of thief, gentleman, and waiter.[133] Chesterton gently satirizes Lever's approach to hotel management but also the solemn but meaningless ritual of gullible Gentiles anxious to be admitted to his exclusive hotel.[134] In fact, *The Queer Feet* typifies Chesterton's approach to his creations: far from stereotypes, both Jews and Gentiles exhibit positive and negative characteristics but each one is unique. Chesterton said a detective story writer "despises" his work when he makes "the common error" of constructing his characters as "stock figures," for "even in order that the novelist should kill people, it is first necessary that he should make them live."[135]

---

128. G.K. Chesterton, "The Queer Feet" (1911, 58–59) in B. Cheyette, *Constructions of "the Jew" in English literature and society: Racial representations, 1875–1945*, op. cit., 187.

129. G.K. Chesterton, "The Queer Feet" (1911, 73–74) in ibid., 188.

130. G.K. Chesterton, "The Moderate Murderer," *The Four Faultless Felons*, op. cit., 33; G.K. Chesterton, *Tales of the Long Bow* (London: House of Stratus, 1925/2001), 141.

131. For example, the Jewish Dr. Wolfe (G.K. Chesterton, *The Poet and the Lunatics: Episodes in the Life of Gabriel Gale*, op. cit., 260); the Jewish "Lorraine" ("The Five of Swords," *The Man Who Knew Too Much*, op. cit., 308); "Morse," a financier of obscure origins ("The Moderate Murderer," *The Four Faultless Felons*, op. cit., 23). However, so does a butler and a Cornishman ("The Trees of Pride," *The Man Who Knew Too Much*, op. cit., 223; 193); an Arab ("The Bottomless Well," [ibid., 68]); an Italian ("The Hole in the Wall," [ibid., 91]); an aristocrat ("The Vengeance of the Statue," [ibid., 164]); a French sea captain ("The Garden of Smoke," [ibid., 258]); an Admiral ("The Vampire of the Village," *The Complete Father Brown*, op. cit., 712).

132. L. Hunter, *G.K. Chesterton: Explorations in Allegory*, op. cit., 141.

133. J. Symons, *Bloody Murder*, op. cit., 94.

134. G.K. Chesterton, "The Queer Feet" (1911) *The Complete Father Brown*, op. cit., 40.

135. G.K. Chesterton, "Errors about Detective Stories," *Illustrated London News*, August 28, 1920, in *The Chesterton Review*, XXXVII (1 & 2), (Spring/Summer 2011): 17.

A Bewildering Variety of Characters

Traditional literary analysis, utilizing context and comparison[136] demonstrates that Chesterton's diverse Jewish creations are not indicative of "racial" anti-Semitism. However, Cheyette's study of authors, which includes Chesterton, Belloc and Buchan, Shaw and Wells, found their "indeterminate, fluid reading of 'the Jews'"[137] to be a sign of "racial" views. Some of Chesterton's creations do have stereotypical characteristics such as lisps,[138] but they also display more universal features: Gould is "as good a fellow in his way as ever lived; far kinder to his family than more refined men of pleasure, simple and steadfast in his admirations, a thoroughly wholesome animal, and a thoroughly genuine character."[139] Lever sends for the nearest "Popish priest" for a sick waiter.[140] The banker Isidor Simon "had never taken any title though many had been offered to him."[141] The downtrodden Mr. Leveson is driven to drink by his teetotalling Gentile employer Lord Ivywood.[142] Only one, Dr. Amiel, who tries to save a monk's life, is portrayed without debatably negative features;[143] only one is portrayed as totally bad: the implicitly Jewish Dr. Hirsch who, with echoes of the Dreyfus case (as Cheyette notes) is likened to Judas "laughing horribly and surrounded by capering flames of hell."[144]

Somewhat earlier, *The Ball and the Cross* described the Dreyfus affair as "a wrong thing,"[145] but despite the hellish description Hirsch is shown as redeemable: Father Brown finds excuses for his apparent treachery, saying "gently" and with ironic humor: "You mustn't be too hard on [Darwinists].... It's not entirely their fault; but they have no instincts.... They've been taught that it's all a matter of degree."[146] If, as Ker says, "[t]he voice of Father Brown is often

136. M.H. Gelber, "What is Literary Antisemitism?" *Jewish Social Studies* 47, XLVI (1), (1985): 17.

137. B. Cheyette, *Constructions of "the Jew" in English literature and society: Racial representations, 1875–1945*, op. cit., 8.

138. For example, "Low" in *Tales of the Long Bow*, op. cit., 142, and "Schiller" in *The Paradoxes of Mr. Pond*, op. cit., 119; see: Edgar Rosenberg, *From Shylock to Svengali: Jewish Stereotypes in English Fiction* (London: Peter Owen, 1961), 18.

139. G.K. Chesterton, *Manalive*, op. cit., 137–138.

140. G.K. Chesterton, "The Queer Feet" (1911) *The Complete Father Brown*, op. cit., 41.

141. G.K. Chesterton, "The Loyal Traitor," *Four Faultless Felons*, op. cit., 160.

142. G.K. Chesterton, *The Flying Inn*, op. cit., 138.

143. G.K. Chesterton, "The Tower of Treason," *The Man Who Knew Too Much*, op. cit., 338.

144. B. Cheyette, *Constructions of "the Jew" in English literature and society: Racial representations, 1875–1945*, op. cit., 192; Hirsch's name suggests his origins; he was "born in France" rather than French; "in short, was more like a German than a Frenchman" (G.K. Chesterton, "The Duel of Dr Hirsch" [1914] *The Complete Father Brown*, op. cit., 196).

145. G.K. Chesterton, *The Ball and the Cross*, op. cit., 46–47.

146. G.K. Chesterton, "The Duel of Dr Hirsch" (1914) *The Complete Father Brown*, op. cit., 203; "Darwin brought man from his former special position in the cosmos down to the animal level. Man was now to struggle with a blind and purposeless nature without having the advantage of a special

audibly the voice of Chesterton"[147] it is not a hateful one. When at last it is clear that Hirsch cannot be innocent Father Brown says that he is not guilty of treason: "No; only of ambition—like Caesar." Written in 1914,[148] this could be interpreted as meaning that Jews were incapable of treason because they were incapable of true loyalty. The point is not elaborated, and in *The Loyal Traitor*, written much later, Simon the banker is shown as a true patriot by refusing patriotic honors.

Despite his view that Golden Age writers provided some balance with "more positive characterizations and references,"[149] Turnbull echoes Watson in seeing Chesterton as "psychotic"[150] about Jews, his fiction regarded as proof that he was "paranoid" on the subject.[151] Chesterton's lack of solidly negative Jewish characters fails to substantiate this conclusion. He dismissed the idea that Dickens introduced Riah, "the kind old Jew" in *Our Mutual Friend* because "some Jewish correspondent" complained that "the bad Jew in 'Oliver Twist' conveyed the suggestion that all Jews were bad." This principle, he said, was "so light-headedly absurd" that it was "hard to imagine any literary man submitting to it for an instant." But Dickens did submit to it: "It pleased him to be mistaken for a public arbiter: it pleased him to be asked (in a double sense) to judge Israel."[152] Later, Chesterton remarked that "[i]n a moral sense" there was "no doubt" that Dickens had "introduced the Jew [Aaron] with a philanthropic idea of doing justice to Judaism," which "he was told he had affronted by the great gargoyle of Fagin." If that was his motive, Chesterton added, "morally" it was a "most worthy one," but it was "unfortunate for the Hebrew cause that the bad Jew should be so very much more convincing than the good one." "Old Aaron," he said, was "not an exaggeration of Jewish virtues; he is simply not Jewish, because he is not human." The character did not suggest "the nobler sort of Jew" like "Spinoza or Mr. Zangwill," but was "simply a public apology, and like

creation or free will. Bertrand Russell wrote that Darwin had made everything a 'matter of degree' and so with his triumph 'all splendid things vanished'" (H. Grisewood, ed., *Ideas and Beliefs of the Victorians* [London, 1949, 23], in J.P. Corrin, *G.K. Chesterton and Hilaire Belloc: The Battle Against Modernity* [Athens/London: Ohio University Press, 1981], 6).

147. I. Ker, *G.K. Chesterton: A Biography* (Oxford: Oxford University Press, 2011), 286.

148. G.K. Chesterton, "The Duel of Dr Hirsch" (1914) *The Complete Father Brown*, op. cit., 204.

149. M.J. Turnbull, *Victims or Villains: Jewish Images in Classic English Detective Fiction*, op. cit., 10.

150. Ibid., 46; C. Watson, *Snobbery with Violence: English Crime Stories and their Audience*, op. cit., 131.

151. M.J. Turnbull, *Victims or Villains: Jewish Images in Classic English Detective Fiction*, op. cit., 148.

152. G.K. Chesterton, *Charles Dickens* (London: Methuen & Co. Ltd., 1906/1913), 217; Cheyette claims Chesterton "had already accused Dickens of attempting in a 'double sense' to 'judge Israel'" by introducing Riah (B. Cheyette, *Constructions of "the Jew" in English literature and society: Racial representations, 1875–1945*, op. cit., 181).

most public apologies, he is very stiff and not very convincing." Anyone who knew "a low Jew by sight or hearing" would know that the story was "literally full of Jews" because "[l]ike all Dickens's best characters they are vivid; we know them. And we know them to be Hebrew." Messrs. Veneering, Lammle, and Fledgeby were the "particular types that people hate in Jewry, the types that are the shame of all good Jews." Such characters "absolutely run riot in this book, which is supposed to contain an apology to them."[153] Chesterton thought that "at first sight" Dickens's apology appeared to be "one hideous sneer. It looks as if he put in one good Jew whom nobody could believe in, and then balanced him with ten bad Jews whom nobody could fail to recognise." This notion was, however, "not admissible." Dickens was a "good Liberal" who "would have been horrified at the notion of making so venomous a vendetta against one race or creed," but he was also "so wonderfully sensitive" to impending social changes that he instinctively portrayed these "bad Jews" as assimilated.[154] In fact the "good liberal" Dickens portrays "the good old man" Riah[155] speaking out against anti-Semitism, but also has him pondering the fact that as a money-lender he has given all Jews a bad name.[156]

While in real life he praised Israel Zangwill (who was not religious, although neither he nor Spinoza were plutocrats),[157] in his fiction Chesterton did not "balance" good and bad Jews but depicted the whole spectrum of morality, with the good, bad, and indifferent Leveson, Gluck, and Meadows in *The Flying Inn* and the nice and nasty Simon and Loeb in *The Loyal Traitor*. But he did seem to "balance" the bad Jew with the bad non-Jew, painting negative portraits of Gentile as well as Jewish doctors, scientists, and millionaires.[158] *The Five of Swords*, which as Cheyette notes portrays "cosmopolitan moneylenders" and in which "lurks the undeniable fact of the 'Jew,'"[159] is included in the same

---

153. G. K. Chesterton, *Appreciations and Criticisms of the Works of Charles Dickens* (London: J. M. Dent & Sons, Ltd., 1911), x–xi.

154. Ibid., xi–xiii.

155. C. Dickens, *Our Mutual Friend* (Ware, Herts.: Wordsworth Classics, 1864–65/2002), 409.

156. C. Dickens, *Our Mutual Friend* (Ware, Herts.: Wordsworth Classics, 1864–65/2002), 686. "Mortimer Lightwood" discusses Riah with "Eugene Wrayburn": "I have had an interview today, Eugene, with a Jew, who seems determined to press us hard. Quite a Shylock, and quite a Patriarch" (C. Dickens, *Our Mutual Friend* [Ware, Herts.: Wordsworth Classics, 1864–65/2002], 506).

157. G. K. Chesterton, *Appreciations and Criticisms of the Works of Charles Dickens*, op. cit., x–xi.

158. Non-Jewish doctors are negatively portrayed in *Manalive*, op. cit., 65, and *The Poet and the Lunatics: Episodes in the Life of Gabriel Gale*, op. cit., 261; the latter also contains a bad non-Jewish scientist (ibid., 36–67); a Canadian millionaire is an "undesirable alien" in "The Face in the Target" (*The Man Who Knew Too Much*, op. cit., 8); a Baptist millionaire oppresses the poor in "The Ecstatic Thief" (*Four Faultless Felons*, op. cit., 111); three American millionaires are murdered in "The Arrow of Heaven" (1926) (*The Complete Father Brown*, op. cit., 349–350).

159. B. Cheyette, *Constructions of "the Jew" in English literature and society: Racial representations, 1875–1945*, op. cit., 198.

collection as the very sympathetic Dr. Amiel in *The Tower of Treason*.[160] Nonetheless, Cheyette sees in the very diversity of Chesterton's and other writers' Jewish creations a "bewildering variety of contradictory and over-determined representations of 'the Jew.'" Nuances in the characters' construction and handling are seen by Cheyette as indications not of the rejection of Jewish stereotypes but as evidence of the hidden polarities in texts: Jews "were constructed *at one and the same time* both as embodying the aspirations of an enlightened State and as undermining the essential characteristics of a particularist nation," with the portrayal of Jewish characters as good and evil as "embod[ying] simultaneously both 'culture' *and* 'anarchy.'"[161]

This may well apply to Chesterton, whose view of the "Jewish question" was intrinsic to his patriotism[162] and, as Chapter Four shows, like H.G. Wells he used "Jewish materialism" to illustrate what he saw as the deleterious effects of capitalism on England. In distinguishing between anti-Semitic intentions and "literary conventions,"[163] however, it is clear that indeterminate characters create the indeterminacy demanded by detective fiction.[164] There would be no genre if writers did not engage in what John Cawelti calls "the kind of basic reversal in assumption so important to a truly effective scheme of mystification."[165] Chesterton attempted to get away from stale stereotypes, but even if the results are unrealistic,[166] a literary criticism that distinguishes between "metaphor and statement, creation and criticism,"[167] and which defines authors' attitudes to Jews with reference to their non-fiction[168], would be eminently suited to Chesterton, who used his characters to express his social and political views[169] through humor, nonsense, and allegory.[170]

---

160. G.K. Chesterton, "The Tower of Treason," *The Man Who Knew Too Much*, op. cit.; originally published in *Hearst's International*, February 1919 (D.J. Conlon, personal communication).

161. B. Cheyette, *Constructions of "the Jew" in English literature and society: Racial representations, 1875–1945*, op. cit., 268–269.

162. See Chapter Seven.

163. M.H. Gelber, "Pedagogical Guidelines for Literary Antisemitism," *Patterns of Prejudice*, 20 (1), (1986): 39.

164. W.D. Rubinstein, *A History of the Jews in the English-Speaking World: Great Britain*, op. cit., 293; J. Cawelti, "The Study of Literary Formulas," in Robin W. Winks, ed., *Detective Fiction: A Collection of Critical Essays* (Englewood Cliffs, NJ: Prentice-Hall, Inc., 1980), 127.

165. Ibid., 189.

166. E. Rosenberg, *From Shylock to Svengali: Jewish Stereotypes in English Fiction*, op. cit., 18.

167. Ibid., 17.

168. Ibid., 301.

169. I. Boyd, *The Novels of G.K. Chesterton: A Study in Art and Propaganda*, op. cit., 5–9.

170. L. Hunter, *G.K. Chesterton: Explorations in Allegory*, op. cit., 116; Ker argues that in general, apart from *The Man Who Was Thursday*, Chesterton's non-fiction was funnier (I. Ker, "Humour and Holiness in Chesterton," in W. Oddie, ed., introduction to *The Holiness of G.K. Chesterton* [Leominster, Herefordshire: Gracewing, 2010], 53).

Only when Chesterton's non-fiction is studied alongside his fiction does his Jewish "dual image" emerge: the former maintained a reverent attitude toward Judaism and Old Testament Jews while criticizing "financial Jews," but his fiction contained no religious Jews; *The Ball and the Cross*,[171] *The Flying Inn*,[172] *The Poet and the Lunatics*,[173] and *The Paradoxes of Mr. Pond* all link the secularization of Jews to their bad behavior.[174] Despite this, Chesterton's secular Jews, whether good or bad, are mostly treated sympathetically, and he takes the trouble to explain the origins of their behavior. Even so, Chesterton portrayed far fewer Jewish than Gentile villains, especially in his Father Brown stories.[175] His belief in free will, explored in his fiction, was antagonistic to racial theory; in fact, it was crucial to Father Brown's method of solving crime,[176] and, as seen, Chesterton did not exclude Jews from this concept.

"Racial" interpretations of Chesterton's fiction make an important contribution to the debate on literary anti-Semitism by highlighting the tendency for texts to reflect the experience of the dominant culture; but there is relevant concrete, coherent evidence that offers a more plausible interpretation of his attitude to Jews. The diagnosis in Chesterton of an "indeterminate, fluid reading of 'the Jew'"[177] might seem appropriate in view of such binary opposites as Gould and Simon, although the very diversity of his creations does not convey a monolithic view of Jews.

Hitler's avowedly racist approach to Jews has led to post-Holocaust assumptions of a Jewish "monolith," but Jews were divided by religion and background, and on issues like assimilation and Zionism; they also shared political and philosophical views with Gentiles. Both Jews and Gentiles commented on Chesterton's "anti-Semitism"; but, whereas a truly "racial" anti-Semite crime writer (or a lazy one) might paint a sinister, monochromatic, Jewish stereotype, Chesterton's was a diverse collection of characters—evidence not of racial theories about Jews but a rebuttal of them. Doubtless they appeared refreshingly

---

171. G.K. Chesterton, *The Ball and the Cross*, op. cit., 31.

172. G.K. Chesterton, *The Flying Inn*, op. cit., 213.

173. G.K. Chesterton, *The Poet and the Lunatics: Episodes in the Life of Gabriel Gale*, op. cit., 259.

174. G.K. Chesterton, *The Paradoxes of Mr. Pond*, op. cit., 119.

175. Out of 52 Father Brown stories (including *The Donnington Affair* (1914) in *Thirteen Detectives* [New York: Dodd, Mead and Company, 1987]) 11 have Jewish elements; out of 13 Jewish characters three are guilty. In *The Wisdom of Father Brown* (1914) two out of 12 stories contain three Jewish characters between them, two of whom turn out to be guilty; in contrast in *The Scandal of Father Brown* (1935) one out of nine stories contains a Jewish character—the murder victim (*The Complete Father Brown*, op. cit.).

176. G.K. Chesterton, "The Secret of Father Brown" (1927) *The Complete Father Brown*, op. cit., 464–465; see: L. Hunter, *G.K. Chesterton: Explorations in Allegory*, op. cit., 138.

177. B. Cheyette, *Constructions of "the Jew" in English literature and society: Racial representations, 1875–1945*, op. cit., 8.

different to the "cardboard" figures of Jewish "villainy," heirs of that archetypal Victorian Jewish stereotype, Fagin.[178]

Exploding Stereotypes

Although the foreign villain is part of an English literary tradition stretching back to Chaucer,[179] some Golden Age authors—arguably the best—came to see the villainous Jew in the same light as the villainous butler. In 1928 Father Ronald Knox drew up rules for the Detection Club, of which Chesterton was the first president, sternly warning: "No Chinaman must figure in the story."[180] Allingham's "immense Jew" began to shrink and fade into the background as the anti-Semitism of Nazi Germany took center stage. Agatha Christie met her "first Nazi" in Iraq, her first "hint of what was to come later from Germany," and she recalls that in the early 1930s, "for ordinary people . . . there was a complete lack of foreknowledge."[181] This prompted her to moderate her fiction,[182] and although, as in *The Body in the Library* (1942) these changes can appear unconvincing, their very clumsiness suggests a genuine desire to avoid giving offence:

> "Why the hell should I [clear out] because you told me to? I was enjoying myself."
> "Yes—with that filthy brute Rosenberg. You know what *he's* like."
> "You were jealous, that's all."
> "Don't flatter yourself. I hate to see a girl I like who can't hold her drink and lets a disgusting Central European paw her about."[183]

Even earlier, Chesterton's *The Song of the Flying Fish* (1927) is chock-full of foreigners, and when "Mrs. Robinson" says "darkly" that "[f]oreign is as foreign does,"[184] Chesterton constructs a double-bluff in which the foreigner actually did do it. His most outrageous example of this practice, a prologue to a Detection Club collaborative effort *The Floating Admiral* (1931) has been taken seri-

---

178. W. D. Rubinstein, *A History of the Jews in the English-Speaking World: Great Britain*, op. cit., 292–293.

179. G. Orwell, *As I Please: The Collected Essays, Journal and Letters of George Orwell Vol. III*, 1943–5 (London: Secker & Warburg, 1968), 338; however Orwell also praises Chesterton (ibid., 6, 65, 175, 284).

180. Commandment V (R. A. Knox, "A Detective Story Decalogue," introduction to *The Best Detective Stories of 1928* [London: Faber & Faber, 1929], in R. W. Winks, ed., *Detective Fiction: A Collection of Critical Essays* [Englewood Cliffs, N.J.: Prentice-Hall, Inc., 1980], 200–202.)

181. A. Christie, *Agatha Christie: An Autobiography* (London: HarperCollins, 1977/1993), 482.

182. W. D. Rubinstein, *The Myth of Rescue* (London: Routledge, 1997), 58–59.

183. A. Christie, *The Body in the Library* (London: HarperCollins, 1942/2000), 32.

184. G. K. Chesterton, "The Song of the Flying Fish" (1927) *The Complete Father Brown*, op. cit., 497–498.

ously by Turnbull: "And then a swarthy little Jew, who was born in Budapest but had lived in Whitechapel, struck up in piping tones a song he had heard there: 'Every nice girl loves a sailor.' And in his song there was a sneer that was some day to be seen on the face of Trotsky, and to change the world."[185] As Dorothy L. Sayers reveals in her Introduction to *The Floating Admiral*, Chesterton's "picturesque Prologue . . . was written last,"[186] and since there are no Jews in the book it is clear that the character is a particularly juicy red herring, playing on the "red menace" fears that Turnbull notes,[187] an early example of Postmodern irony. Chesterton's view was that "the great detective story deals with small things; while the small or silly detective story generally deals with great things," such as "diabolical diplomatists darting about between Vienna and Paris and Petrograd; with vast cosmopolitan conspiracies ramifying through all the cellars of Europe."[188]

In a further dig at right-wing obsessions Chesterton described the Detection Club as "a very small and quiet conspiracy" whose deadly secret initiation ceremony he publicized in an article "thereby setting a good example to the Mafia, the Ku Klux Klan, the Illuminati . . . and all the other secret societies which now conduct the greater part of public life, in the age of Publicity and Public Opinion." He says that the "subtler joke underlying" *The Floating Admiral* was that each chapter, "contributed by an amateur detective," was "a satire on the personal peculiarities of the last amateur detective."[189] Agatha Christie used common prejudices to mislead her readers,[190] as did Buchan in *The Thirty-Nine Steps*. German spies posing as dull Englishmen, not "Jew-anarchists," are behind everything.[191] As to *Trent's Last Case*, seen as endorsing myths of Jewish domination,[192] we never find out why Bentley's crowd of Jews is raving, but the scene misleadingly suggests that international businessman Sigsbee Mander-

185. M. J. Turnbull, *Victims or Villains: Jewish Images in Classic English Detective Fiction*, op. cit., 46.

186. A. Christie, et al., *The Floating Admiral* (New York: Charter Books, 1931/1984), 3.

187. "Chesterton . . . targeted Jews and the 'red menace' briefly in his Prologue to the Detection Club's collaborative novel *The Floating Admiral*" (M. J. Turnbull, *Victims or Villains: Jewish Images in Classic English Detective Fiction*, op. cit., 46).

188. G. K. Chesterton, "The Domesticity of Detectives," *The Uses of Diversity* (London: Methuen & Co. Ltd, 1920/1927), 27.

189. G. K. Chesterton, *Strand Magazine*, May 1933, in M. Ward, *Gilbert Keith Chesterton* (New York: Sheed & Ward, 1943), 550–552.

190. W. D. Rubinstein, *The Myth of Rescue*, op. cit., 58. In "Swan Song" (1934) Mr Cowan (who "had a way of slurring his 's's' which was not quite a lisp, but came perilously near to it," and whose "father's name had probably been Cohen") is not the culprit (A. Christie, *Agatha Christie the collected short stories*, op. cit., 445).

191. J. Buchan, *The Thirty-Nine Steps*, op. cit., 102.

192. M. J. Turnbull, *Victims or Villains: Jewish Images in Classic English Detective Fiction*, op. cit., 36.

son, nicknamed "Colossus" for his heavy-handed treatment of the poor, has been murdered because of his financial dealings.[193] The scene was an isolated "red herring" exploiting anti-Semitic beliefs. Bentley himself called the book "an exposure of detective stories."[194] Chesterton also introduced foreign, and Jewish, characters as suspects that turn out to be innocent: in *The Actor and the Alibi*, the "dark, curly-haired youth of somewhat Semitic profile bearing the name of Aubrey Vernon" ("the curly-headed youth with the nose") is superfluous to the plot.[195]

Nonetheless, unlike the "fleeting and peripheral" allusions of Christie and Sayers,[196] Chesterton's Jewish characters played more important roles. His Jewish characterization was sometimes explicit and sometimes implicit,[197] but general trends are discernible: his unpublished *Basil Howe* (1893–1894) is infused with Old Testament references and a Jewish friend is given a starring role.[198] During his early, "pro-Semitic" period, there is a dearth of Jewish references;[199] while his "middle period," dating from about 1914, was characterized by negativity on the "Jewish question" and reached its nadir in the early 1920s. In his later fiction, Ian Boyd traces his changing attitudes to Imperialism, the monarchy and Germany, and a "new tolerance" towards Jews.[200] But even during the "middle period" the negativity is not absolute: *The Five of Swords* (1922) has

193. E.C. Bentley, *Trent's Last Case*, op. cit., 5.

194. E.C. Bentley, *Those Days* (London: Constable & Co. Ltd., 1940), 254; see Chapter Eight.

195. G.K. Chesterton, "The Actor and the Alibi" (1927) *The Complete Father Brown*, op. cit., 513–514.

196. M.J. Turnbull, *Victims or Villains: Jewish Images in Classic English Detective Fiction*, op. cit., 87.

197. "Gluck" and "Meadows" are gradually revealed as Jewish (G.K. Chesterton, *The Flying Inn*, op. cit., 24; 219); the "swarthy" secretary "Leveson" (suggesting "Levy's son") is efficient (ibid., 68; 108), as is "Low," the Jewish manager in *Tales of the Long Bow*, op. cit., 47.

198. See Chapter Eight.

199. L.A. Hetzler, "Chesterton's Political Views, 1892–1914," *The Chesterton Review*, VII (2), (1981): 131; see: W. Oddie, *Chesterton and the Romance of Orthodoxy: The Making of GKC 1874–1908* (Oxford: Oxford University Press, 2008). There are no Jewish characters in *The Napoleon of Notting Hill* (1904) or *The Club of Queer Trades* (1905); in *The Man Who Was Thursday* (1908) "Wednesday" "might be a Jew; he might be something deeper yet in the dark heart of the East" but more likely a red herring (*The Man Who Was Thursday* [Harmondsworth, Middx.: Penguin, 1967], 59) typical of Chesterton's Kafkaesque setting (C.S. Lewis, "On Stephens on Chesterton" [1946], in D.J. Conlon, ed., *G.K. Chesterton: A Half Century of Views*, op. cit., 69); parts of *The Man Who Was Thursday* "went back to [Chesterton's] schooldays" (I. Ker, *G.K. Chesterton: A Biography*, op. cit., 125).

200. Boyd notes that "for the first time [Jews] are represented in something like a favourable light" (Ian Boyd, *The Novels of G.K. Chesterton: A Study in Art and Propaganda*, op. cit., 197). *The Return of Don Quixote* (1926, although according to its dedication planned before the Great War) has no Jewish characters; *The Poet and the Lunatics* (1927) contains one main Jewish character, although the unsympathetic Dr. Wolfe acts for a non-Jewish villain (*The Poet and the Lunatics: Episodes in the Life of Gabriel Gale*, op. cit., 259).

been seen by Cheyette as supporting his theory of consistent racial anti-Semitism,[201] while *The Bottomless Well*, a chapter in the novel *The Man Who Knew Too Much* (1922) contains a diatribe against "Jewish money power."[202] And yet, in the same collection, *The Tower of Treason* (written around 1919), while containing a similar critique, also includes Chesterton's most favorable Jewish character and an ironic rejection of "Jewish conspiracy."[203] *Tales of the Long Bow* (1925) is chiefly concerned with the restoration of rural England.[204] It depicts "Rosenbaum Low" as engineering the law for personal gain and lending money to the Prime Minister,[205] but the theme is that all are redeemable and this included Jews.[206] Atheism is the chief target of *The Poet and the Lunatics* (1929) which contains positive references to the Jewish religion, has Aubrey Vernon as a "red herring," and a wicked Gentile doctor alongside the wicked Dr. Simeon Wolfe, who is represented as manipulated rather than manipulator.[207]

But *The Loyal Traitor* in *Four Faultless Felons* (1930) has been viewed as anti-Semitic[208] and Cheyette sees it as exemplifying the continuity of Chesterton's "racial" attitude, because in it he reiterates "the 'formidable normality' of 'the Jews'" by saying it was "'absolutely characteristic' for a 'little Jew to have a little champagne, but very expensive, and to have black coffee, the proper digestive, after it.'"[209] The remark is made by Grimm, the aptly named Pavonian police chief who, hunting a revolutionary, looks for clues in the remains of a meal found in the house of Jewish millionaire pawnbroker Lobb—real name Loeb,[210] who is long deceased.[211] The incident is another example of Chesterton using anti-Jewish prejudice to mislead and, moreover, the story contains a passage that militates against a "racial" interpretation: Simon, the Jewish banker (Lobb's antithesis, being cultured, sensitive and disinterested)[212]

201. B. Cheyette, *Constructions of "the Jew" in English literature and society: Racial representations, 1875–1945*, op. cit., 197–198.

202. G. K. Chesterton, *The Man Who Knew Too Much*, op. cit., 79; I. Boyd, *The Novels of G.K. Chesterton: A Study in Art and Propaganda*, op. cit., 83; 92.

203. D. Barr, introduction to *G. K. Chesterton Collected Works Vol. VIII* (San Francisco: Ignatius Press, 1999), 41.

204. I. Boyd, *The Novels of G. K. Chesterton: A Study in Art and Propaganda*, op. cit., 99.

205. G. K. Chesterton, *Tales of the Long Bow*, op. cit., 152.

206. Ibid., 72.

207. In a story with no references to Jews, a bird is an "undesirable alien" and a "Yellow Peril" (G. K. Chesterton, "The Yellow Bird," *The Poet and the Lunatics: Episodes in the Life of Gabriel Gale*, op. cit., 45).

208. M. Gardner, introduction to G. K. Chesterton, *Four Faultless Felons*, op. cit., xiii.

209. G. K. Chesterton, *The Loyal Traitor* (1930, 260), in B. Cheyette, *Constructions of "the Jew" in English literature and society: Racial representations, 1875–1945*, op. cit., 189.

210. G. K. Chesterton, "The Loyal Traitor," *Four Faultless Felons*, op. cit., 169–170.

211. Ibid., 197–198.

212. Ibid., 160.

"explains" concepts of Jewish miserliness and greed:[213]

> [N]o Jew was ever a miser. . . . Avarice is not a Jewish vice; it's a peasant's vice, a vice of people who want to protect themselves with personal possessions in perpetuity. Greed is the Jewish vice: greed for luxury; greed for vulgarity; greed for gambling; greed for throwing away other people's money and their own on a harem or a theatre or a grand hotel or some harlotry—or possibly on a grand revolution. But not hoarding it. That is the madness of sane men; of men who have a soil.[214]

Chesterton is attributing an alleged Jewish vice to the lack of a homeland, something with a political remedy, rather than to their blood, as did racial anti-Semites.[215] His use of a sympathetic Jewish character—a banker, moreover—as a mouthpiece suggests a desire to avoid anti-Semitism, but one contemporary reviewer said the passage proved he was "a professed Anti-Semite." Chesterton responded: "[M]y Jew was defending Jews from the much more common but completely mistaken charge of being stingy and mean"; he was surprised at the reviewer's claim that "no Jew could ever talk like that" because he had "heard several Jews talk exactly like that." The critic, he said, was "apparently unaware of one of the very real virtues of the Jew—his capacity for detachment and objective criticism. Jews sometimes pursue (unwisely, I think) an external policy of silence and suppression in the Press and the political world," which they defended privately "on the ground of real peril from real persecution." It was "perfectly sound psychology to make a man repel a charge against his race as untrue by admitting that another and almost contrary charge is true"; nearly "all patriots" did, who combined "patriotism with any kind of balance of liberality of mind." But the critic had "misse[d] the whole point by omitting the preceding sentence."[216]

Chesterton's characterization of a Jewish banker as a patriot at a time of growing anti-Semitism constitutes a milestone in the development of his thought. As Boyd notes, for the first time in one of his stories, he credits "both a

213. Regarding miserliness as a Jewish vice in English fiction, (see E. Rosenberg, *From Shylock to Svengali: Jewish Stereotypes in English Fiction*, op. cit., 4–5), the philosopher Eugene Düring claimed the Jewish people were the "worst branch of the Semitic race": greedy, exploitative and bent on world domination (E. Düring, *The Jewish Question, as a Question of Race, Morals and Culture* [1881], in D. J. Goldberg, J. D. Rayner, *The Jewish People: Their History and Their Religion*, op. cit., 159).

214. G. K. Chesterton, "The Loyal Traitor," *Four Faultless Felons*, op. cit., 161–162; "[t]he avarice of [French] peasants means the independence of [French] peasants" ("French and English," *A Gleaming Cohort*, op. cit., 42).

215. I. Hannaford, *Race: The History of an Idea in the West* (Baltimore/London: Johns Hopkins University Press, 1996), 356; 320.

216. Regarding a review in the *News Chronicle* (Chesterton, G. K., *Illustrated London News*, September 20, 1930, in *Gilbert Magazine*, 12 (2 & 3), (November/December 2008): 9, accessed May 19, 2011, http://209.236.72.127/wordpress/wp-content/uploads/2010/12/gilbert_12.2_5.pdf).

Jewish financier and a discredited politician" with patriotism—Chesterton's "basic national virtue."[217] Earlier, in *The Man Who Knew Too Much*, Horne Fisher remarks: "Patriotism is not the first virtue. Patriotism rots into Prussianism when you pretend it is the first virtue. But patriotism is sometimes the last virtue. A man will swindle or seduce who will not sell his country. But who knows?" Horne Fisher's uncle turns out to be the traitor,[218] and an Irish traitor features in *The Flying Inn* (1914).[219] In Chesterton's theory of nationality, patriotism was closely connected to the land, and was not easily transferable. The appearance of doing so was questionable, and when Jews were forced to move from country to country because of persecution, although they might feel patriotic, they could feel true patriotism only for other Jews—a good thing in itself but detrimental to England. With their mystical history tying them to a special place, however, their patriotism could be safely "absorbed" by a Jewish homeland in Palestine.[220] This is why Simon's inclusion among the "four chief rulers of Pavonia" in a state committee to discuss the threat of revolution[221] represents, Boyd notes, a subtly expressed but important development in his thinking.[222] In *Four Faultless Felons* Simon the banker is not the "loyal traitor" but the "loyal Jew";[223] despite this, Turnbull blames Chesterton's "deep-seated neuroses" for his "sneer" about champagne and coffee.[224]

In *A Tall Story* (1936) Chesterton once again "explodes" Jewish conspiracy theories but, true to his belief that writers should create believable characters—that victims should be defended not because they were "nice" but because they were victims—this time with a less idealistic creation.[225] Once again Turnbull overlooks this evidence, following the lead of Cheyette, for whom the story provides yet more evidence of Chesterton's "racial" continuity because in the story he was "able to blame the victim for the rise of Nazism." Cheyette cites the non-Jewish "Gahagan" as saying it was "'a damned shame' that 'hundreds and thousands of poor little fiddlers and actors and chess-players . . . should be kicked out of' Nazi Germany," but that he "quickly goes on to qualify his sympathy" by "averring that 'I fancy they must be kicking themselves, for having been so faithful to Germany and even, everywhere else, pretty generally pro-

217. I. Boyd, *The Novels of G. K. Chesterton: A Study in Art and Propaganda*, op. cit., 174.

218. G. K. Chesterton, *The Man Who Knew Too Much*, op. cit., 164.

219. G. K. Chesterton, *The Flying Inn*, op. cit., 28.

220. See Chapters Five, Seven, and Eight.

221. G. K. Chesterton, "The Loyal Traitor," *Four Faultless Felons*, op. cit., 186.

222. I. Boyd, *The Novels of G. K. Chesterton: A Study in Art and Propaganda*, op. cit., 174.

223. Ibid., 169.

224. M. J. Turnbull, *Victims or Villains: Jewish Images in Classic English Detective Fiction*, op. cit., 70.

225. G. K. Chesterton, "A Tall Story," *The Paradoxes of Mr. Pond*, op. cit., 119–120.

German.'"[226] But in the next sentence Mr. Pond corrects his friend: "Even that can be exaggerated."[227] Here Chesterton employs the literary technique of using contradiction to put his own view of anti-Semitism.[228] Furthermore, in his essay "About Loving Germans," despite "never underrat[ing]" the "real problem" of the "international position of the Jews," Chesterton ridicules German beliefs that the "complete surrender of all the German armies" in the Great War was "brought about by the Jews."[229] This explicates Pond's story, related to Gahagan, about spy mania during the Great War, in which he recalls that he had warned a Jewish shopkeeper about using an "absurd German name":

> I know very well this is no quarrel of yours. I am well aware ... that you never invaded Belgium. I am fully conscious that your national tastes do not lie in that direction. I know that you had nothing to do with burning the Louvain Library or sinking the *Lusitania*. Then why the devil can't you say so?[230]

Pond satirizes the claim that Jews were responsible for the Great War but—in line with Chesterton's Zionism—also treats the shopkeeper's German connection as purely nominal. Such warnings have been seen as threats, but since name changes (sometimes imposed on Jews upon immigration) have been associated with anti-Semitic riots in England,[231] Pond's warning appears genuine—even the British Royal family changed its name because of anti-German feeling during the Great War.[232] Nonetheless, Cheyette sees further evidence in *A Tall Story* for his "continuity of race" theory, quoting from Chesterton's *The New Jerusalem* (1920) to the effect that anti-Jewish riots during the Great War were "partly at least the fault of the Jew himself, and of the whole of that futile and unworthy policy which had led him to call himself Bernstein when his name was Benjamin."[233] The preceding sentences, however, refer to a "poor little Jewish tailor" who "called himself by a German name merely because he lived for a short time in a German town" and who, during the Great War, was

---

226. G.K. Chesterton, "A Tall Story" (1937, 232), in B. Cheyette, *Constructions of "the Jew" in English literature and society: Racial representations, 1875–1945*, op. cit., 200–201.

227. G.K. Chesterton, "A Tall Story," *The Paradoxes of Mr. Pond*, op. cit., 114.

228. D. Walden, "Three Cases of Literary Antisemitism," *Sh'ma*, (7/124), (1976): 26–28, in M.H. Gelber, "What is Literary Antisemitism?," op. cit., 16.

229. G.K. Chesterton, "About Loving Germans," *As I Was Saying* (London: Methuen & Co. Ltd., 1936), 16; Hitler made this claim in *Mein Kampf*: see Chapter Seven.

230. G.K. Chesterton, "A Tall Story," *The Paradoxes of Mr. Pond*, op. cit., 119.

231. Geoffrey Wheatcroft, *The Controversy of Zion: or How Zionism tried to resolve the Jewish Question* (London: Sinclair-Stevenson, 1996), 157–159.

232. King George V, angry with his cousin Kaiser Wilhelm for German bombing raids on London, in 1917 changed the family name from Saxe-Coburg and Gotha to Windsor.

233. G.K. Chesterton, *The New Jerusalem* (1920, 272–273), in B. Cheyette, *Constructions of "the Jew" in English literature and society: Racial representations, 1875–1945*, op. cit., 202.

"instantly mobbed in Whitechapel for his share in the invasion of Belgium."[234] Once again Chesterton is satirizing the idea that Jews were responsible for the War, which sparked the anti-Semitic riots.

Although *A Tall Story* looked back to the Great War it was prompted by much more recent events. It opens with the line: "They had been discussing the new troubles in Germany...."[235] Superficially the story could be seen as Chesterton's vindication of his earlier warnings regarding Jewish name-changes; but while it highlights the folly of the practice, it does not blame Jews for anti-Jewish persecution. Pond's warning, and other references to their plight, appear motivated by concern. Although there is an element of Chesterton vindicating his historical theory of anti-Semitism as the "mutual trouble" of Jews and non-Jews, the story is sympathetic in intent, prompted by Nazi anti-Semitism and written not in triumph but in sorrow. For a confirmed anti-Semite to draw attention to anti-Jewish persecution and to ridicule Jewish conspiracy theories in a specially created fictional vehicle would be a more fantastic "tall story" than *The Tall Story*.

In fact, the story reinforces the view that significant developments were occurring in Chesterton's approach to Jewish issues: Pond's encounter with the Jewish shopkeeper is very similar to a scene in *The Ball and the Cross* (1910) where "Turnbull" (an atheist but unusually for Chesterton, a hero) encounters another Jew with an antiquities shop and an allegedly questionable name.[236] But whereas Turnbull discusses whether the shopkeeper "Gordon" should be "killed like a cockroach" (as Cheyette notes)[237] speaks with "grating contempt," threatens to run Gordon through the body, ties him up and gags him,[238] in *A Tall Story* Pond warns the Jewish shopkeeper regarding his safety "with an earnest gaze."[239] Turnbull remarks sarcastically that he will "leave the religion of humanity" in Gordon's hands,[240] while Pond implores: "Why can't you call

234. G. K. Chesterton, *The New Jerusalem* (1920) *G. K. Chesterton Collected Works Vol. XX* (San Francisco: Ignatius Press, 2001), 398.

235. G. K. Chesterton, *The Paradoxes of Mr. Pond*, op. cit., 113; originally published in *Storyteller*, February 1936.

236. West points out that though Chesterton "jeers" at the shopkeeper Gordon's "Scottish ancestry," he was "probably unaware that there are large numbers of Jews bearing that name in Russia" (J. West, *G. K. Chesterton: A Critical Study*, op. cit., 40); Conlon speculates that Chesterton's error may have been the result of having Jewish friends from Sephardic (Mediterranean) communities rather than Ashkanazim (D. J. Conlon, "New and Original Views" [unpublished], 2012).

237. G. K. Chesterton, *The Ball and the Cross* (1910, 53–54), in B. Cheyette, *Constructions of "the Jew" in English literature and society: Racial representations, 1875–1945*, op. cit., 182.

238. G. K. Chesterton, *The Ball and the Cross*, op. cit., 32.

239. G. K. Chesterton, "A Tall Story," *The Paradoxes of Mr. Pond*, op. cit., 119.

240. G. K. Chesterton, *The Ball and the Cross*, op. cit., 32; Turnbull, an atheist who publicly challenges the Old Testament, is lampooned by Chesterton (ibid., 17–18).

yourself Levy, like your fathers before you—your fathers who go back to the most ancient priesthood of the world?"[241] Cheyette interprets this incident as Chesterton's "consistent...championing of distinctly identifiable Jews, as opposed to indistinct Jewish 'cosmopolitans.'"[242] Malcolm Turnbull follows his lead, but claims the story involves "a German spy named Levy" who "attempts to change his name to Schiller (because 'there'th a lot of prejudith againth my rathe')" and is "admonished" by Pond.[243] The lisping Levy merely puts the name "Schiller" over his shop,[244] but a real German spy named Schiller is at large,[245] prompting Pond to warn the shop-keeper about name-changes, thus provoking Levy's explanation about prejudice.[246]

As Pond recalls: "Mr. Levy was certainly not a German; and it was very improbable that he was a real enthusiast for Germany"; but adds that "it was not altogether impossible to suppose, in the tangle and distraction of all the modern international muddle, that he might be some sort of tool, conscious or unconscious, of a real German conspiracy. So long as that was possible, he must be watched."[247] Pond recalls the story in response to Gahagan's claim that Jews were "pretty generally pro-German,"[248] and in so doing reinforces the point that neither English nor German Jews were "behind" Germany and that German Jews should not be blamed for anti-Jewish persecution. Levy turns out not to be a spy but another of Chesterton's red herrings, playing on anti-Jewish prejudice not only to explode Jewish conspiracy theory, but to make a point about a possible German conspiracy—although the real spy turns out to be an Italian.[249] As will be seen, Chesterton had personal reasons for drawing attention to the Nazi persecution of Jews that made it even less likely that he was gloating over it.[250]

Nonetheless, Cheyette says Chesterton portrayed a "racial inter-connection between poor Jewish communists and rich Jewish capitalists" in *The Ghost of Gideon Wise* (1926) in which "three Jewish millionaires and three Jewish Bolsheviks...are not opposed to each other, as most think, but are in cahoots." Cheyette concludes: "Any subtleties in Chesterton's thinking on these

241. G.K. Chesterton, "A Tall Story," *The Paradoxes of Mr. Pond*, op. cit., 119.

242. B. Cheyette, *Constructions of "the Jew" in English literature and society: Racial representations, 1875–1945*, op. cit., 202.

243. M.J. Turnbull, *Victims or Villains: Jewish Images in Classic English Detective Fiction*, op. cit., 48.

244. G.K. Chesterton, "A Tall Story," *The Paradoxes of Mr. Pond*, op. cit., 119.

245. Ibid., 114.

246. Ibid., 119.

247. Ibid., 120.

248. Ibid., 114.

249. Ibid., 126.

250. See Chapter Eight.

matters had, clearly, long since past."(*sic*)[251] In fact, only one millionaire ("Stein") is Jewish, as well as only one Bolshevist ("Elias"); it is Stein and the Gentile millionaire "Gallup" who are "in cahoots" to force the third millionaire, the Gentile "Gideon Wise," to combine his business with theirs. Meanwhile Wise and the Gentile Bolshevist "Horne" are "in cahoots" to murder both the Jewish millionaire Stein and the Gentile millionaire Gallup.[252] No Jews are "in cahoots," and the story is yet another example of Chesterton using prejudice as a literary device, carefully constructing the similarities between Stein and Elias to suggest they are the same man.[253]

This certainly played on suspicions that Jews could assume any identity they found convenient, and Cheyette maintains that the story had been "anticipated" by *What I Saw in America*[254]—in which Chesterton does speculate on a possible bargain between communist and capitalist Jews, but veers away from a "Jewish conspiracy" conclusion.[255] Turnbull says Chesterton "acknowledged early on" that *The Protocols of the Elders of Zion* were forged, but "the persistent theory of a union between Jewish money and Jewish revolutionaries clearly continued to strike a chord."[256] Jay Corrin also sees *What I Saw in America* and *Four Faultless Felons* as demonstrating Chesterton's view of Jews as "the moving forces behind both communism and capitalism."[257] But Chesterton's chief concerns appear to be not that the communists are Jews in disguise but that the communists are capitalists in disguise, and that an agreement between them would lead to industrial slavery for the poor. Despite this, and despite overlooking similar exploded stereotypes in *The Loyal Traitor, The Poet and the Lunatics*, and *A Tall Story* Cheyette concludes: "The extent of the semitic uncertainty spread by these all-powerful conspiracies can be found in a great many stories by Chesterton."[258]

This interpretation of Chesterton's fiction was influenced by the theory of Robert Casillo, who believed that the poet Ezra Pound assigned "difference and 'confused otherness' to 'the Jews'" and saw "the Jew" as "the carrier of . . .

251. B. Cheyette, *Constructions of "the Jew" in English literature and society: Racial representations, 1875–1945*, op. cit., 200.

252. G.K. Chesterton, "The Ghost of Gideon Wise" (1926) *The Complete Father Brown*, op. cit., 457–458.

253. Ibid., 446.

254. G.K. Chesterton, *What I Saw in America* (1922, 247), in B. Cheyette, *Constructions of "the Jew" in English literature and society: Racial representations, 1875–1945*, op. cit., 200.

255. See Chapters Two and Seven.

256. M.J. Turnbull, *Victims or Villains: Jewish Images in Classic English Detective Fiction*, op. cit., 45.

257. J.P. Corrin, *G.K. Chesterton and Hilaire Belloc: The Battle Against Modernity*, op. cit., 66.

258. B. Cheyette, *Constructions of "the Jew" in English literature and society: Racial representations, 1875–1945*, op. cit., 199–200.

uncertainty and the archetypal transgressor of boundaries."[259] Consequently Cheyette saw the absence of "racial stereotyping" by Chesterton and other authors not as indicating a lack of racial anti-Semitism, but as indicating their belief in the "dangerous indeterminacy of 'the Jews,'" whom they constructed "as a potent threat."[260] Casillo's theory, inspired by Pound's use of metaphors about Jews, including "the swamp, bacilli, plague, castration, parthenogenesis, erosion, the parasite," is influenced by Joseph Hillis Miller's theory "that the 'parasite' is often characterized by a threatening confusion and uncertainty, particularly in the eyes of those belonging to the closed community in which the parasite appears." Hillis Miller applies this theory to texts,[261] following Jacques Derrida's Deconstructionism. Heavily influenced by Freudian psychoanalysis, Deconstructionism sees supposedly objective statements marginalizing or suppressing alternative—often minority—perspectives, and posits that they are thus dependent on them for their existence—"parasitic."[262] Hillis Miller's belief that the "parasite" threatened "confusion and uncertainty" in "closed communities"[263] was applied by Casillo to Pound's texts, from which he believed anti-Semitism was frequently inseparable, and where he saw "the parasite" as "moving freely across (and thus transgressing and obscuring) all margins."[264]

The inherent danger in applying such approaches to literature is the marginalization and suppression of objective truth itself, representing a retreat from Enlightenment "reason." This holds grave implications for philosophical debate, even regarding the Holocaust,[265] especially when texts completely unrelated to anti-Semitism are "deconstructed," supposedly to reveal what an author really thinks about Jews. To introduce the term "parasite" into a study of Chesterton's fiction inevitably associates it with Hitler's denunciations of Jews,[266] although before the Holocaust it had less sinister connotations. For example, Disraeli in *Lothair* refers humorously to a "lively social parasite."[267]

259. Robert Casillo, *Genealogy of Demons: Anti-Semitism, Fascism, and the Myths of Ezra Pound* (1988, 18) in ibid., 11.

260. Ibid., 270.

261. R. Casillo, *Genealogy of Demons: Anti-Semitism, Fascism, and the Myths of Ezra Pound* (Evanston, Illinois: Northwestern University Press, 1988), 17–18.

262. Jonathan Rée, J. O. Urmson, eds., *The Concise Encylopaedia of Western Philosophy*, 3rd Edition (London: Routledge, 2005), 88–89.

263. J. Hillis Miller, "The Critic as Host," in Harold Bloom et al., *Deconstruction and Criticism* (New York: Seabury, 1979), 219.

264. R. Casillo, *Genealogy of Demons: Anti-Semitism, Fascism, and the Myths of Ezra Pound*, op. cit., 18.

265. See Chapter Nine.

266. A. Hitler, *Mein Kampf*, op. cit., 138–139; 144; 276–277; 280; 292; 296; 512.

267. B. Disraeli, *Lothair* (London: John Lane, The Bodley Head Ltd., 1870/1927), 34.

Cheyette gives no examples of Chesterton's use of the metaphor in connection with Jews although, as seen in Chapter One, Kaufman misinterpreted one example, and Colin Holmes claims that in *G. K.'s Weekly*, Belloc and Chesterton "continued to assert their hostility to Jews, repeating their distrust of Jewish separateness, describing Jews as a 'parasitic organism.'"[268] In the article cited, Chesterton comments on the Zionist Israel Zangwill's remark about Jews forming an "imperfect economic organism," stating: "If the Jews could become a self-contained organism, nobody could possibly pretend that they were a parasitic organism."[269] None of these critics mention Chesterton's non-Jewish "parasitic" character (to be discussed).

Despite such factors, Cheyette, applying the Casillo/Hillis Miller theory of Pound, sees in Chesterton's fiction "semitic confusion," "spiritual confusion," "spiritual and national confusion," "semitic uncertainty" and "fateful indeterminacy" generated in him by "the Jew."[270] In fact Pound (whose anti-Semitism was firmly based on racial theories)[271] like many anti-Semites, complained of Jewish "separateness" because he believed it stemmed from their feelings of superiority: "Didn't realize the Pup kept 'em in the ghetto till 1850. Trouble not that they got OUT of the ghetto, but that they carried the ghetto [deletion] everywhere they got into. With all that is worst in it. And no refuge for communities that wd/ like to have a little territory to themselves."(*sic*)[272] Nevertheless, in support of his approach Cheyette cites Chesterton's love of boundaries, linking it to his "deliberately 'nasty' construction of the 'broad-minded Jew,'" quoting from Chesterton's recollection of the toy theater his father made.[273] As an artist Chesterton was familiar with the concepts of "framing" and outlines; he illustrated his own and Belloc's works, and the descriptions in his fiction are vivid. He wrote about familiar things, "framing" them to get people to see them afresh. Like his hero William Cobbett he believed injustice was accepted because it was familiar: the monastic ruins and poor peasants in the paintings commissioned by wealthy landowners were no peaceful backdrop but told the

268. Colin Holmes, *Anti-Semitism in British Society 1876–1939* (London: Edward Arnold, 1979), 212.

269. G.K. Chesterton, "Zangwill and Zionism," *G.K.'s Weekly*, June 6, 1925, 246.

270. B. Cheyette, *Constructions of "the Jew" in English literature and society: Racial representations, 1875–1945*, op. cit., 193; 188; 196; 199.

271. R. Casillo, *Genealogy of Demons: Anti-Semitism, Fascism, and the Myths of Ezra Pound*, op. cit., 4.

272. Ezra Pound, Letter to Olivia Rossetti Agresti, April 4, 1950, D.P. Tryphonopoulous, L. Surette, eds., *I Cease Not to Yowl: Ezra Pound's Letters to Olivia Rossetti Agresti* (Illinois: University of Illinois Press, 1998), 48; the reference is to Pope Pius IX and the Rome ghetto.

273. B. Cheyette, *Constructions of "the Jew" in English literature and society: Racial representations, 1875–1945*, op. cit., 182; the toy theater remark is in G.K. Chesterton, *Autobiography*, op. cit., 28.

story of Reformation plunder and pillage. One of his characters, Audrey Smith, an artist, maintains: "'Literary people let words get between them and things. We [artists] do at least look at the things and not the names of the things.'"[274] Chesterton's love of boundaries did not prevent him from condemning the injustice of enclosing open spaces during the Reformation and the eighteenth century, which involved imposing boundaries on what had been common land.[275]

Nonetheless, it is possible that Chesterton's love of boundaries subconsciously influenced his treatment of Jewish characters and themes, and Chesterton's enduring fascination with the Jewish people will be analyzed in greater detail.[276] Although overall his treatment of Jewish characters was sympathetic, he did tend to portray them as different, reflecting his belief in Jewish foreignness. In *What's Wrong With the World* (1910) Chesterton set out his view of limits in the context of owning property: "Every man should have something that he can shape in his own image, as he is shaped in the image of heaven. But because he is not God, but only a graven image of God, his self-expression must deal with limits; property with limits that are strict and even small." This did not mean, he added, that "the Rothschilds and the Rockefellers were on the side of property." On the contrary, they were "the enemies of property" because they were "enemies of their own limitations." They did not want "their own land; but other people's," and it was "the negation of property that the Duke of Sutherland should have all the farms on one estate; just as it would be the negation of marriage if he had all our wives in one harem."[277] Chesterton viewed as blasphemy the disregard of material limits because it encroached on the prerogative of God, who alone had no limits; he insisted that ever since the forbidden fruit in the Garden of Eden, the idea of limits had formed "the core of ethics."[278]

Chesterton does mention boundaries and limits in his fiction in a variety of contexts, but most are unrelated to Jews: for example, an "elfin turret chamber" and modern art;[279] alcohol and drugs, friendship and romance;[280] "crazy regulations and conditions";[281] but also a forbidden tree in a garden that hid the

274. G.K. Chesterton, *Tales of the Long Bow*, op. cit., 23.

275. See Chapter Eight for a discussion of this theme in his poetry.

276. See Chapter Seven.

277. G.K. Chesterton, *What's Wrong with the World* (USA: Quiet Vision Publishing, 1910/2003), 19.

278. G.K. Chesterton, "Fairy Tales," *All Things Considered* (USA: Feather Tail Press, 1908/2009), 87.

279. G.K. Chesterton, *The Flying Inn*, op. cit., 119; 228.

280. G.K. Chesterton, "The Garden of Smoke," *The Man Who Knew Too Much*, op. cit., 271; 277–278.

281. G.K. Chesterton, *Manalive*, op. cit., 29.

corpse of a murdered money-lender, the implicitly Jewish "Morse."[282] Chesterton distrusted Benjamin Disraeli, who notably widened the cosmopolitan horizons of non-Jewish Imperialists, and he explored the theme of Jewish cosmopolitan tendencies when he portrayed Rosenbaum Low, in *Tales of the Long Bow* (1925) describing the "illimitable veldt,"[283] although Chesterton attributed the expression to Joseph Chamberlain.[284] In *Manalive* the hero echoes *What's Wrong With the World*: "I think God has given us the love of special places, of a hearth and of a native land, for a good reason." Otherwise, he says, men might worship "[e]ternity . . . the largest of the idols—the mightiest of the rivals of God."[285] Chesterton regarded sin, not virtue, as imposing limitations on individuals—"if we build our palace on some unknown wrong it turns very slowly into our prison"[286]—but also believed that limits were necessary to preserve the individual's freedom.[287] But his most explicit use of the idea of the need for limits in his fiction is in *The Poet and the Lunatics* where he emphasizes the need for limits to preserve the individual's sanity.[288] In his *Autobiography* he describes being unable to distinguish the boundary between fantasy and reality:

> At this time I did not very clearly distinguish between dreaming and waking; not only as a mood, but as a metaphysical doubt, I felt as if everything might be a dream. . . . I was not mad, in any medical or physical sense; I was simply carrying the scepticism of my time as far as it would go.[289]

In *The Flying Inn* (1914), however, Cheyette saw "spiritual and national confusion" "generated by 'the Jew,'" a confusion "opposed to a boundary-ridden Englishness" that was "threatened by an increasingly intricate and expansive set of conspiracies."[290] In this work Chesterton links his theory that limits are necessary to human sanity, with his view that a lack of limits is the sole prerogative of God. Hunter has also seen the work as primarily portraying "[t]he opposing forces [of] Moslem against Christian . . . East against West,"[291] and as Chester-

282. G.K. Chesterton, "The Honest Quack," *Four Faultless Felons*, op. cit., 57–103.

283. G.K. Chesterton, *Tales of the Long Bow*, op. cit., 133.

284. G.K. Chesterton, *A Miscellany of Men* (Norfolk VA: IHS Press, 1912/2004), 51.

285. G.K. Chesterton, *Manalive*, op. cit., 157.

286. G.K. Chesterton, "The Macbeths," *The Spice of Life*, Collins, D., ed. (Beaconsfield, Bucks.: Darwen Finlayson Ltd., 1964), 47.

287. I. Crowther, *Thinkers of Our Time: G.K. Chesterton* (London: The Claridge Press, 1991), 80.

288. G.K. Chesterton, *The Poet and the Lunatics: Episodes in the Life of Gabriel Gale*, op. cit., 65–66.

289. G.K. Chesterton, *Autobiography*, op. cit., 89.

290. B. Cheyette, *Constructions of "the Jew" in English literature and society: Racial representations, 1875–1945*, op. cit., 196.

291. L. Hunter, *G.K. Chesterton: Explorations in Allegory*, op. cit., 107.

ton's "eventual novelistic response to Shavianism,"[292] although such serious interpretations are of later provenance.[293] *The Flying Inn* does link Muslims and Jews, mainly regarding diet and noses;[294] but the main threat is the "Islam-icisation" of England as a result of the "madness" of teetotalling, atheist non-Jew Lord Ivywood.[295] Ivywood's obsession with all things Eastern leads him to come under what Misysra Ammon, the "Prophet of the Moon," calls the "'unlimitable influence'" of Islam.[296] Ivywood introduces an alcohol ban under which the implicitly Jewish Leveson, his downtrodden secretary, suffers.[297] The story does, however, involve a threat to England's physical boundaries, culminating in an invasion by Turkish soldiers.[298]

In addition, the Jewish German government minister, Gluck, aids the Muslim threat, effortlessly changing his national allegiance in order to negotiate peace.[299] This could suggest that Chesterton believed in Jewish "indeterminacy," and he did believe that as "foreigners" Jews could not represent their nations of residence, a point he made regarding Herbert Samuel.[300] Nonetheless, as to Gluck's "race," "Captain Dalroy" remarks: "It's not the race he was— if it was one race—it's the Sort he was. A coarse, common, Levantine nark and eavesdropper."[301] Chesterton saw the Jewish people as coming "from the East,"[302] although Gluck, and Meadows—the implicitly Jewish doctor who profits from the alcohol ban with a health drink made from watered milk— are specifically linked to Prussia,[303] but Boyd notes that "Gluck ('the German Minister with the far from German face') . . . enables Chesterton to express his

---

292. A. Nichols, *G.K. Chesterton, Theologian* (Darton, Longman & Todd Ltd., 2009), 38.

293. I. Boyd, *The Novels of G.K. Chesterton: A Study in Art and Propaganda*, op. cit., 65–66; M. Evans, *G.K. Chesterton*, op. cit., 16; 75; one (unnamed) contemporary reviewer wrote: "He seems to have some extremely serious idea at the back of his mind which has a depressing influence on the ostentatious irresponsible fun of his fantastic story" (*Times Literary Supplement*, January 22, 1914, in D.J. Conlon, ed., *G.K. Chesterton: The Critical Judgments Part I: 1900–1937*, op. cit., 324–325).

294. The Muslim "Misysra Ammon" has a "Jewish nose" (G.K. Chesterton, *The Flying Inn*, op. cit., 110; 70); Ammon agrees with Lord Ivywood's view that "[i]n the gradual emergence of mankind from a gross and sanguinary mode of sustenance, the Semite has led the way" (ibid., 115).

295. I. Boyd, *The Novels of G.K. Chesterton: A Study in Art and Propaganda*, op. cit., 65.

296. G.K. Chesterton, *The Flying Inn*, op. cit., 31.

297. Ibid., 221–222.

298. Ibid., 286.

299. Ibid., 108.

300. G.K. Chesterton, *The New Jerusalem* (1920), op. cit., 393–394; Sir Herbert Samuel was Postmaster-General during the Marconi case; see Chapters Six and Seven.

301. G.K. Chesterton, *The Flying Inn*, op. cit., 123.

302. G.K. Chesterton, *The New Jerusalem* (1920), op. cit., 395.

303. G.K. Chesterton, *The Flying Inn*, op. cit., 133; 212.

dual obsession with Prussian militarism and cosmopolitan Jewish finance."[304] Chesterton satirized Gluck in verse, along with race theories and vegetarians:

> Oh I knew a Dr Gluck,
> And his nose it had a hook,
> And his attitudes were anything but Aryan;
> So I gave him all the pork
> That I had, upon a fork
> Because I am myself a Vegetarian.[305]

The suggestion that *The Flying Inn* represents a boundary-less "Eastern" coalition of Jews and Turks is further complicated by Chesterton's claim elsewhere that Islam "owed nothing whatever to Asia."[306] The dangerous coalition in *The Flying Inn* is, in fact, between Muslim "monomania"[307] and atheism. Although an atheist, Ivywood embraces Islam for its "simplicity," thereby unleashing his Nietzschean lack of limitations.[308] In his thirst for unlimited progress he ends in total insanity as a kind of "Nietzschean Superman."[309] Chesterton's Turkish invasion theme, seen as "bizarre,"[310] had historical provenance:[311] in the 1870s British anti-Semitism was stirred by the "Bulgarian Horrors," Turkish massacres of "rebellious Bulgarian Christians in 1875." Gladstone's "moral passions were galvanized" but Disraeli "judged it in the interest of Great Britain to continue to support the Turks against the Russians."[312] Turkey sided with Germany in the Great War, leading to the break-up of the Ottoman Empire. Chesterton portrays Ivywood the atheist as parasitic, not only on the labors of the people, but in his philosophy, since he clings to Islam merely because he has ceased to cling to "out-moded" Christianity. Despite his emphasis on Pound and parasites, Cheyette overlooks such clues to this tendency in Lord Ivywood, despite his name.[313]

---

304. I. Boyd, *The Novels of G.K. Chesterton: A Study in Art and Propaganda*, op. cit., 68; Chesterton saw Prussian pride (indirectly, via Protestantism) influenced by Jews: see Chapter Five.

305. G.K. Chesterton, *The Flying Inn*, op. cit., 123; published as "The Logical Vegetarian," *The Works of G.K. Chesterton* (Ware, Herts.: Wordsworth Poetry Library, 1995), 153.

306. G.K. Chesterton, *The Everlasting Man*, op. cit., 234.

307. G.K. Chesterton, *The New Jerusalem*, op. cit., 218.

308. J. Coates, *Chesterton and the Edwardian Cultural Crisis* (Hull: Hull University, 1984), 112.

309. L. Hunter, *G.K. Chesterton: Explorations in Allegory*, op. cit., 107.

310. J. Coates, *Chesterton and the Edwardian Cultural Crisis*, op. cit., 87–88. The story begins at a Mediterranean Peace Conference (G.K. Chesterton, *The Flying Inn*, op. cit., 16–25).

311. The Ottoman Empire, which played an aggressive role in international affairs during the Great War, was involved in regional conflict during the nineteenth and early twentieth century; the use of Asian troops was based on historical fact: in 1878 Disraeli dispatched Indian troops to Malta through the Suez Canal without Parliamentary consent (C.C. Eldridge, *Disraeli and the Rise of a New Imperialism* [Cardiff: University of Wales Press, 1996], 59).

312. A.S. Lindemann, *Esau's Tears: Modern Anti-Semitism and the Rise of the Jews* (Cambridge: Cambridge University Press, 1997), 249.

313. G.K. Chesterton, *The Flying Inn*, op. cit., 267–268.

Little Englander?

Chesterton did meet Pound at Max Beerbohm's villa in Rapallo in 1929,[314] where they discussed Social Credit, a topic that interested Distributists.[315] Pound then contributed a poem and several articles to *G.K.'s Weekly* in 1934 and 1935 where he attacked the banking system and claimed that Distributism had become state policy in Mussolini's Italy.[316] But it was not Pound's racism that influenced Chesterton's Jewish characters and themes; these were shaped by his own theory of patriotism, although Cheyette cites Grainger to support his claim that "Chesterton's sense of religious 'boundaries'" was "central both to his model of Christian individualism and his national construction of a 'small oppugnant' English *patria*."[317] Chesterton did see England, and other European nations, as Christian entities,[318] but in the instance cited by Cheyette, Grainger notes that Chesterton needed a Christian "dogma" for contending with the "fashionable rationalisms of the age," specifically, Imperialism.[319] This supports Crowther's interpretation of *The Flying Inn*'s dominant theme as the need to combat "rationalisms."[320] Cheyette acknowledges Chesterton's perspective on the importance of limits when he quotes Hunter regarding *The Ball and the Cross* that "Gordon's denial of 'human limitation' is, as Hunter has pointed out, the 'root of madness.'"[321] But Hunter's reference is not to Gordon, the Jewish shopkeeper, but to Turnbull's and McIan's dreams "occur[ring] in an asylum which harbours lunatics who believe themselves perfect."[322]

Chesterton believed that unthinking patriotism was the last resort of the scoundrel, and imperialism the first resort of the unthinking patriot. *The Napoleon of Notting Hill* (1904) illustrates the belief that while nationalism can inspire,[323] when it transgresses its boundaries it becomes Imperialism and

---

314. The Chestertons were returning from Rome (I. Ker, *G.K. Chesterton: A Biography*, op. cit., 608–609); see Chapter Eight.

315. J. Pearce, *Wisdom and Innocence: A Life of G.K. Chesterton* (London: Hodder & Stoughton, 1997), 383.

316. Brocard Sewell, *G.K.'s Weekly: An Appraisal* (Wirral, Cheshire: Aylesford Press, 1990), 40; despite its title, "With *Usura*," Pound's Canto XLV makes no mention of Jews.

317. J.H. Grainger, *Patriotisms* (1986, 104), in B. Cheyette, *Constructions of "the Jew" in English literature and society: Racial representations, 1875–1945*, op. cit., 182.

318. See: J. Stapleton, *Christianity, Patriotism, and Nationhood: The England of G.K. Chesterton* (Lanham MD/Plymouth, England: Lexington Books, 2009).

319. J.H. Grainger, *Patriotisms: Britain 1900–1939* (London: Routledge and Kegan Paul, 1986), 104–105.

320. I. Crowther, *Thinkers of Our Time: G.K. Chesterton*, op. cit., 25.

321. L. Hunter, (1979, p. 62), in B. Cheyette, *Constructions of "the Jew" in English literature and society: Racial representations, 1875–1945*, op. cit., 182.

322. L. Hunter, *G.K. Chesterton: Explorations in Allegory*, op. cit., 62.

323. G.K. Chesterton, *The Napoleon of Notting Hill* (Ware, Herts.: Wordsworth Classics, 1904/1996), 133.

tramples on other countries' rights to self-determination.[324] The belief that "[t]he patriot loves his own country, the Imperialist wants to swallow other countries"[325] underpinned Chesterton's opposition to "cosmopolitanism." The more powerful culture, while declaring the value of uniting all cultures, would swallow up the weaker cultures, as the Nicaraguan patriot explains to the English "moderns."[326] *The Napoleon of Notting Hill* has no Jewish element, and Chesterton's private writings of the 1890s reveal his deep concern for Jewish suffering under the Tsarist pogroms. His views on English nationality were not, therefore, shaped by anti-Semitism. Chesterton's Zionism fitted into his views on patriotism, not the other way round.[327] *Manalive* (1912) contains a plethora of national (sometimes regional)[328] characters, each a mixture of good and bad, and while Moses Gould is distinguished on account of his "shameless rationality," it is portrayed as a positive attribute, thus there is no consistent "good English/bad Jew" dichotomy.

It was an essential feature of Chesterton's patriotism that it supported the aspirations of non-English patriots, which to him included Jewish patriots, although his fiction did reflect a view of Jews as foreign. In *Manalive* it is proposed, for no stated reason, to try Moses Gould for "patriotism" at the "High Court of Beacon"—and yet in *Manalive* there is a reason for everything. The "holy fool" Innocent Smith, who blows in on a gale, overturns the conventional lives of the boarding house dwellers, and also their philosophical assumptions; and in this feverish atmosphere the barrister Michael Moon mocks the view that British justice had "evolved" since Magna Carta, becoming increasingly just, arguing to the contrary that it had become more and more trivial and intrusive. His idea for a "tribunal that was a parody on the pompous anomalies of English law" was conceived at a time when "he had never been more sarcastic, and even inhuman." This tribunal's frivolous aspects appealed to his friends, who sought legal rulings on matters like spilling sauce on the tablecloth or shutting the window. But if Gould's crime is seen as one of false patriotism, a mere imitation, the patriotism he is imitating is theirs, and the fact that they view the seriousness of the charge as comparable to spilling sauce on the tablecloth shows their own patriotism to be a shallow affair. No wonder that his trial never took place because it "was rather above the heads of the company, especially of the criminal."[329]

---

324. Ibid., 115.

325. M. Ward, *Return to Chesterton* (London: Sheed & Ward, 1952), 55.

326. G. K. Chesterton, *The Napoleon of Notting Hill*, op. cit., 15–16; see also: M. Canovan, *G. K. Chesterton: Radical Populist*, op. cit., 106–107.

327. W. Oddie, *Chesterton and the Romance of Orthodoxy: The Making of GKC 1874–1908*, op. cit., 79–81; see Chapter Seven.

328. G. K. Chesterton, *Manalive*, op. cit., 182.

329. Ibid., 32–33.

Nevertheless, the passage about Gould's cynicism being the kind that sparked riots appears to reveal the superficially good-humored Cockney as a materialist, in stark contrast to his Gentile friends. Like the remark about Jews and heresy in *The Curse of the Golden Cross* it seems to be Chesterton's attempt to "explain" the "mutual" oppression of Jews and non-Jews, specifically as it involved the ordinary people with whom he sympathized, rather than the upper classes who cynically discarded Jewish money-lenders when it suited them. To Chesterton, the mob was not "mindless" but the basis of democracy,[330] although he did not apply the same reasoning to the common man's enthusiasm for Imperialism, to which he was antagonistic.[331] In most other cases he saw rights as inalienable from the "mob of free men" rather than dependent on laws handed down from the same courts that had criminalized the mob.

It was not until 1915 that the *Jewish Chronicle* commented on Moses Gould: "[O]nce again we have to deplore the fact that the author should so prostitute his talents by his anti-Semitic bias." The paper claimed that rather than "direct attacks," Chesterton used "innuendo," but that his Jewish character was "always a villain." Worse, it was "skilfully shown" that the villain was not "an individual but a type." Since Jews were "not generally guilty of murder or wife-beating" he portrayed them "as the embodiment of selfishness and pushfulness . . . indifferent to the claims of humanity and idealism." It was "very noticeable" that in the *Daily News* and *Illustrated London News* his "venom" was "restrained." In those periodicals he was "silent" about Jews: "But he rewards himself when he is his own master." The paper continued by saying that Moses Gould's explanation of anti-Jewish riots was "one of the wickedest things" Chesterton had ever written; this "most original excuse for pogrom" was compounded by the proposed "trial" of Gould for patriotism, which, since the outbreak of the Great War, had become a controversial topic: "Even if Mr. Chesterton were ignorant of the part played by the Jews in the Boer War," he must "surely be aware" of the "magnificent" Jewish response to the present war. The *Jewish Chronicle* asked whether he considered the "anxiety" he caused to Jewish soldiers who had "given up everything to fight for England," leaving their families exposed to his "virulence." The Jewish soldier was fighting for Chesterton "in the trenches," while he was "safe and secure in his study . . . sowing the seeds of pogroms."[332]

---

330. Chesterton cites St. Thomas Aquinas's fondness for "phrases like 'a mob of free men' as the essential material of a city; and he is emphatic upon the fact that law, when it ceases to be justice, ceases even to be law" (G. K. Chesterton, *St Thomas Aquinas* [1923] *St Thomas Aquinas; St Francis of Assisi* [San Francisco: Ignatius Press], 172).

331. M. Canovan, *G. K. Chesterton: Radical Populist*, op. cit., 76–77.

332. *Jewish Chronicle*, November 5, 1915, 28–29.

Although *Manalive* was published well before the War, it appeared after the Swansea riots. But Moses Gould was a sympathetic figure and, moreover, the controversial passage contained a deeper layer of meaning: the American criminologist Cyrus Pym is the real cynic, for when the true story of Innocent Smith unfolds Pym is ready with "one of his more pedantic interpellations." In contrast, Moses understands. He "suddenly struck his forefinger on his nose, with an expression of extreme astonishment and intelligence in his brilliant eyes." While Pym relies on "science" to explain Smith—an approach demolished by Michael Moon,[333] Moses possesses one of Chesterton's cardinal virtues, common sense.[334] Initially he believed Smith guilty because even if he didn't "believe most of the things they tell you in church in Sundays," his "conscience" urged him to defend "all those poor girls" Smith had supposedly betrayed.[335] But when Moon says, "If one could keep as happy as a child or a dog, it would be by being as innocent as a child, or as sinless as a dog," he detects "a look of skepticism" on the face of his "old friend Moses. Mr. Gould does not believe that being perfectly good in all respects would make a man merry." Moses drops his own merry façade: "'No,' said Gould, with an unusual and convincing gravity," upon which Moon "quietly" says: "Which of us has ever tried it?"[336] If Gould is cynical about human goodness, he has good reason to be. Thus, after apparently excusing pogroms, Chesterton explains at the story's conclusion what he sees as the real cause—the failure of Gentiles to strive for goodness.

Even while Chesterton portrayed English Jews as foreign, he tended to portray foreign Jews as true citizens of their countries of residence. In *The Secret Garden* (1911) Dr. Simon, the implicitly Jewish friend of Father Brown, is a "typical French scientist,"[337] while Dr. Hirsch (*The Duel of Dr. Hirsch* [1914]) is French enough to be a traitor. Simon, the Jewish banker (*The Loyal Traitor* [1930]) is portrayed as a patriotic Pavonian. In *The Tower of Treason* (1922) it is a suspicious Englishman who describes good Dr. Amiel, a denizen of Eastern Europe, as "a Frenchman, or, rather, a French Jew" who, when bareheaded, seems "only a dark, rather distinguished-looking French man of science," but when he dons his red smoking cap, he "suddenly" resembles "something much lower than a Turk; and I see all Asia sneering and leering at me across the Levant." Later, however, the Englishman admits that "perhaps it's a fancy of the fit I'm in."[338] The red smoking cap is eventually discarded among Chesterton's other red herrings.

333. G. K. Chesterton, *Manalive*, op. cit., 175.
334. Ibid., 70.
335. Ibid., 160–161.
336. Ibid., 178–179.
337. G. K. Chesterton, "The Secret Garden" (1911) *The Complete Father Brown*, op. cit., 37.
338. G. K. Chesterton, "The Tower of Treason," *The Man Who Knew Too Much*, op. cit., 324.

Anti-Semitism: Clue or Red Herring?

In Golden Age fiction, what at first sight appear to be gratuitous anti-Semitic slurs often turn out to be clues or red herrings; the Jewish suspect frequently turns out to be a cardboard cut-out that fades into the background. Chesterton's full range of fiction, with its diversity of Jewish characters, does not suggest he was "racially" anti-Semitic in the sense of seeing all Jews negatively, especially as even his negative portrayals are not completely negative. But Chesterton did use those characters to express his views on the "Jewish question," and his popularity might suggest that his readers shared those views.

Through the lens of the Holocaust, even when seen in context, Jewish references in Golden Age fiction have the power to discomfit, and Turnbull found such "unflattering" remarks "disconcerting" and "derogatory."[339] Rubinstein agrees they are "disconcerting . . . and certainly indicative of a strand of popular fiction," but argues that "more should not be made of this than meets the eye," since "the overwhelming proportion of popular British fiction of this type contained no Jewish characters, while virtually all identifiable groups—ethnic, national, occupational and class-based—are stereotyped in this way. Until the rise of Nazism . . . such negative group stereotyping was a commonplace device of lazy writers, even those of some distinction."[340] Dilys Winn, however, insists: "For all the reasons a reader may be drawn to English mysteries of the Twenties and Thirties—nostalgia, a certain elegance of phrasing and tone, that classic plotting—there is an equally good reason for slamming the books shut and tossing them from one's home: a strain of anti-Semitism that runs deep, constant and pervasive." This, she said, included Chesterton.[341] Turnbull sees such writing as part of a much wider problem. Negative images of Jews "were a reflection of mainstream attitudes to Jews as a group within British society."[342] Golden Age crime fiction was enormously popular.[343] Thriller writer Sydney Horler was one of three noted "propagandists" for a world view of British "intellectual, ethical, physical and racial superiority"[344] who by the early Thirties sold "an estimated two million volumes . . . suggest[ing] that his insular views were shared by a large number of readers."[345]

But Turnbull also acknowledges "strong disagreement" among historians of

339. M.J. Turnbull, *Victims or Villains: Jewish Images in Classic English Detective Fiction*, op. cit., 4–5.

340. W.D. Rubinstein, *A History of the Jews in the English-speaking World: Great Britain*, op. cit., 292–293.

341. Dilys Winn, *Murder Ink* (New York: Workman Publishing, 1984), 133.

342. M.J. Turnbull, *Victims or Villains: Jewish Images in Classic English Detective Fiction*, op. cit., 5.

343. Ibid., 1.

344. Ibid., 2–3.

345. Ibid., 63.

Anglo-Jewry as to the "significance of antisemitism in British society," particularly regarding the inter-War period, with younger historians less forgiving than those of Rubinstein's generation.[346] As seen, even when care is taken to avoid Holocaust influence, a "racial" approach to interpreting fiction inevitably imbues it with that influence, as Winn amply demonstrates: "[T]he number of gratuitous insults dangled upon Jews in these books quite exceeds the reprimands, slights and minor indignities suffered on (sic) anyone else. Something more powerful is operating here than a casual disdain of the outsider; it is a virulent, insidious attempt to verbally annihilate a race."[347] It is clear that Jewish caricatures did not dent the popularity of Golden Age authors. Nonetheless, "even among such clearly prejudiced commentators as McNeile, Horler, Oppenheim or Freeman" Turnbull notes that Jewish characters were "rarely" responsible for murder.[348] In Chesterton's fiction, at least, they were rarely the victims of murder.

In addressing the question of whether these Jewish references were merely clues and red-herrings, or the product of an anti-Semitic mindset that Golden Age authors apparently shared with their readers, it is useful to turn to Dorothy L. Sayers's introduction to *The Floating Admiral*—to which each member of the Detection Club contributed a chapter—which supplies useful insights as she describes the attempts of each writer to outguess the other:

> [I]t is here, perhaps, that the game approximates most closely to real life. We judge one another by our outward actions, but in the motive underlying those actions our judgment may be widely at fault. Preoccupied by our own private interpretation of the matter, we can see only the one possible motive behind the action, so that our solution may be quite plausible, quite coherent, and quite wrong.[349]

If Golden Age writers were merely products of their age, that age, to the post-Holocaust reader, must have been very anti-Semitic, raising the question as to whether authors influenced their readers toward anti-Semitism. And yet it would be difficult, if not impossible to prove that people read such works spe-

---

346. Ibid., 12–13.

347. D. Winn, *Murder Ink*, op. cit., 133. Watson asks whether the rise of British fascism owed a debt to "Bulldog Drummond" but comments: "Popular fiction is not evangelistic; it implants no new ideas. Fascism sprang, in Britain as elsewhere, from frustration caused by economic chaos and political ineptitude" (C. Watson, *Snobbery with Violence: English Crime Stories and their Audience*, op. cit., 71); however, there was "no argument" about the fact that the survival of a great many of those depicted negatively in Alister McAllister's *Deductions of Colonel Gore* (i.e., Jews) were "past praying for" as a result of that war (ibid., 136).

348. M.J. Turnbull, *Victims or Villains: Jewish Images in Classic English Detective Fiction*, op. cit., 75.

349. D.L. Sayers, introduction to A. Christie, *et al*, *The Floating Admiral*, op. cit., 4.

cifically for the anti-Semitism in them. Even though to be a Golden Age for-eigner (which included being Jewish) was sometimes a capital offence,[350] there is no concrete evidence that people read crime fiction as a substitute for, or even as a precursor to, violent action against Jews. Deterministic theories of Marxist or Freudian origin, used to diagnose social or psychological influences on readerships, have been advanced, but they are impossible to prove.[351] In attempting to diagnose suppressed anti-Semitism in people's choice of reading matter, such diviners of the public psyche may have seen in the bottom of the well the reflection of their own preoccupations. In the same way, it has been claimed that the working classes, suffering from false consciousness about their repressed state, reveal in their choice of reading matter a "displaced" desire for revolution, concealed deep in their subconscious.[352] Cawelti comments: "Some scholars see the whole range of formulaic literature as an opiate for the masses, a ruling-class stratagem for keeping the majority of the people content with a daily ration of pleasant distractions,"[353] which suggests that they never read Chesterton.

Judging by the overall infrequency of Jewish references in most works it seems unlikely that anti-Semitism, even as understood pre-Holocaust, was the driving force of most authors. Moreover, Golden Age writers, including Ches-terton, frequently utilized common prejudices to mislead readers,[354] but despite having their prejudices mocked, people continued to buy Golden Age detective books in huge quantities. Notwithstanding common prejudices, this suggests that neither writers nor readers were solely motivated by anti-Semitism.

As Symons points out, "one of the most marked features" of the Anglo-American detective story is that it is "strongly on the side of law and order," and this did reflect public sympathies.[355] In fact, the crime novel of the Golden Age was not so much the descendant of the novel as the child of the pantomime, where nothing is quite what it seems, and good triumphs over evil in the end. When God has been all but banished from our Universe we must find a substi-tute to restore order to the chaos—and who better than an omniscient Miss Marple, Hercule Poirot, or Father Brown?

350. G. Grella, "The Formal Detective Novel," in R.W. Winks, ed., *Detective Fiction: A Collection of Critical Essays*, op. cit., 97.

351. See: J. Cawelti, "The Study of Literary Formulas" (ibid., 133).

352. See: Dennis Dworkin, *Cultural Marxism in Postwar Britain: History, the New Left, and the Origins of Cultural Studies* (Durham/London: Duke University Press, 1997).

353. J. Cawelti, "The Study of Literary Formulas," in R. W. Winks, ed., *Detective Fiction: A Collec-tion of Critical Essays*, op. cit., 133.

354. Jewish characters rarely committed murder (M.J. Turnbull, *Victims or Villains: Jewish Images in Classic English Detective Fiction*, op. cit., 75).

355. Such sympathies were more characteristic of "better educated" readers (J. Symons, *Bloody Murder: from the Detective Story to the Novel: a History*, op. cit., 22–23).

Guilty or Not Guilty?

If attempts to put a well-rounded peg like Chesterton into a racist square hole ultimately fail, the problem with deconstructing the deconstruction of his fiction is that it can give the impression that it presents no problems regarding anti-Semitism. Although, as seen, the Father Brown stories are mostly free of such issues, the longer works—often strung together from series of short stories but connected by an overarching theme—present a more serious problem. And it is possible that a rounded character articulating a carefully constructed philosophy about Jews would be more influential than a patently absurd cardboard stereotype. Most Golden Age writers were not political philosophers (although John Buchan became a Conservative Member of Parliament) and merely used current events as backgrounds for their plots. But Chesterton (like Bernard Shaw and H.G. Wells, to be examined in the next chapter) used his stories to expound his religious, philosophical, and political views, and his non-fiction offers a valuable means of interpreting the problematical *The Man Who Knew Too Much* (1922). This collection features Horne Fisher, a member of the British upper class who knows too much about the sordid political machinations of his own social milieu for his peace of mind, but cannot expose them because of personal loyalties. Chesterton, characteristically, treats such matters soberly, avoiding triumphalism: Boyle, a character outside Fisher's circle, reacts to his "revelations" with "bewilderment that was almost fear, and had even a touch of distaste," remarking that "there seems to be something rather horrid about the things you know." Fisher replies: "There is . . . I am not at all pleased with my small stock of knowledge and reflection."[356] As in *The Flying Inn* the tale ends with revolution and an invasion by "mysterious Eastern armies,"[357] at which point Fisher is at last able to put loyalty to country above personal loyalties.

As noted before, the good Jewish doctor, Amiel, is found in the same collection, and not all stories concern Jewish influence. Some much-needed humor is provided when an "undesirable alien" turns out to be a Canadian millionaire.[358] Nonetheless, one contemporary reviewer remarked: "Brilliant as those essays in the incredible are, there are too many King Charles's heads among them. There is hardly a tale in which the Jew, or the scientist, or the plutocrat, or the antiquarian, or the politician does not offer his head to be hit."[359] Ches-

---

356. G.K. Chesterton, *The Man Who Knew Too Much*, op. cit., 79.

357. I. Boyd, *The Novels of G.K. Chesterton: A Study in Art and Propaganda*, op. cit., 96.

358. G.K. Chesterton, *The Man Who Knew Too Much*, op. cit., 21.

359. Unsigned review, *The Observer*, November 19, 1922, in D. J. Conlon, ed., *G.K. Chesterton: The Critical Judgments Part I: 1900–1937*, op. cit., 402; "Mr Dick" helplessly bemoans the constant intrusion of "King Charles's head" into the Memorial of his own life that he is writing (C. Dickens, *David Copperfield* [Ware, Herts.: Wordsworth Editions Ltd, 1849–50/2000]).

terton's dreary and weary amateur detective is improbably on the scene of several murders, but in a Golden Age story this is excusable, even essential. What is more improbable is that the same culprit should be behind most of the economic and social problems of England, directing foreign policy, bleeding the nation, and lending money "to half the Cabinet."[360] A Jewish "self-made captain of industry" is really a "damned blood-sucking blackmailer,"[361] and "cosmopolitan cads . . . only help themselves."[362] But the "dirty foreigner" should not be cursed, rather "the English . . . because they allowed such vermin to crawl into the high places of their heroes and their kings."[363] The "foreign financiers" are to blame for introducing cheap Chinese labor into the country, reducing the "workmen and peasants to starvation."[364] As seen, the real traitor is Fisher's own uncle, but that could be because he is seen as authentically English.

The negativity continues in *The Five of Swords*, a short story in which the internationally respected firm of Miller, Moss, and Hartmann ("as big as the Bank of England") mostly consists of "cosmopolitan moneylenders" and is the sinister force behind a murder. A record four Jewish characters are found to be guilty.[365] In *The Tower of Treason*, the last story in the collection, the "scientist and humanitarian" Dr. Amiel is ultimately exonerated from suspicion of treason, but earlier, the sympathetic "Father Stephen" articulates a deliberately misleading passage:

> [I]t is perfectly true that the Jews have woven over these nations a net that is not only international, but anti-national; and it is quite true that inhuman as is their usury and inhuman as is often their oppression of the poor, some of them are never so inhuman as when they are idealistic, never so inhuman as when they are humane. . . . I could take your hint about the scarlet smoking-cap, and say it was a signal and the symbol of a secret society; that a hundred Jews in a hundred smoking-caps were plotting everywhere, as many of them really are; I could show a conspiracy ramifying from the red cap of Amiel as it did from the *Bonnet Rouge* of Almereyda. . . .[366]

While satirizing secret Jewish conspiracy theories, the story claims that "the Jews" have openly undermined nationalism while practicing usury and oppressing the poor, although their materialism is more humane than their idealism. There is no formal conspiracy, but Jews are linked in patriotism to

360. G.K. Chesterton, *The Man Who Knew Too Much*, op. cit., 79.
361. Ibid., 125.
362. Ibid., 133.
363. Ibid., 151.
364. Ibid., 159.
365. Ibid., 306–310.
366. G.K. Chesterton, "The Tower of Treason" (ibid., 331–332).

each other, a problem for which Chesterton has a political solution, Zionism. Cheyette says that Chesterton, having once sympathized with Dreyfus's plight, became less certain under the influence of Hilaire Belloc, consonant with his "fictional construction of 'the Jew' as a site for spiritual confusion." This "'fog' of conspiratorial uncertainty" was particularly evident in *The Duel of Dr. Hirsch*. Father Brown, after speculating that Dreyfus "was both innocent *and* guilty," realizes that Hirsch has played a double game, accusing himself in order to attain glory when he is exonerated. Like Dreyfus, he is "worse than 'guilty'" because his acts "knowingly divided France."[367]

The implicitly Jewish atheist Dr. Hirsch has been "playing the Dreyfus card" in order to gain a popular audience for his views by posing as the underdog. Both Dr. Hirsch and his critic, the patriotic "Dubosc," seem sincere, prompting Father Brown to wonder how it is possible—not in the "ordinary police mystery where one man is more or less lying and the other man more or less telling the truth," but in a case like that of Dreyfus—for both parties to be telling the whole truth. He insists: "I don't mean [the French authorities] behaved well [in accusing Dreyfus]; I mean they behaved as if they were sure."[368]

The patriotic Duc de Valognes is deeply disappointed when Hirsch appears not to be guilty after all. He claims the whole affair was "some plot of the Jews and Freemasons . . . meant to work up glory for Hirsch."[369] This leads Father Brown to the truth. The plot is not the work of Jews and Freemasons but of one individual atheist Jew (Hirsch) to "work up glory" for himself. Chesterton makes the point that individual Jews could sometimes be guilty, while once again discarding Jewish conspiracy theories. Brown's friend Flambeau (an ex-burglar but a French patriot) is also deeply disappointed when Hirsch appears to be innocent,[370] and both he and the Duc de Valognes are right. Hirsch is guilty but he orchestrated his own "non-crime," whereas Dreyfus was not guilty of an actual crime, and so was a real victim. The story reverses this reality, portraying a victim, supposedly the underdog, who is actually the victimizer. Nonetheless, the Dreyfus case did divide France, with Dreyfusards and anti-Dreyfusards equally convinced of their own "truth." Father Brown's dilemma of being faced by two equally sincere and equally fervent parties reflects Chesterton's dilemma of being faced by those who believed Dreyfus could not be guilty, and those who believed he could not be innocent, and he gently mocks those

---

367. B. Cheyette, *Constructions of "the Jew" in English literature and society: Racial representations, 1875–1945*, op. cit., 190–193; M. J. Turnbull, *Victims or Villains: Jewish Images in Classic English Detective Fiction*, op. cit., 33–34.

368. G. K. Chesterton, "The Duel of Dr Hirsch" (1914) *The Complete Father Brown*, op. cit., 202–203.

369. Ibid., 204.

370. Ibid., 200.

who continue to believe against all the evidence—like the disappointed patriots who refused to accept Dreyfus's innocence despite the facts.[371]

These included Belloc, his close and trusted friend, whom Chesterton met after the Dreyfus affair. Dreyfus was exonerated in 1906, and Father Brown does not question this outcome, but the story suggests that Jews, as foreigners, could not be expected to be patriotic to their country of residence and could not, therefore, be guilty of betrayal, although they *could* cause division. As Chapter Six finds, Chesterton was influenced by Belloc's doubts in the Dreyfus case.

Belloc also influenced *The Man Who Knew Too Much*, Chesterton's gloomiest fictional foray into the "Jewish question." Although published in 1922 it emphasized "Edwardian financiers and Jewish money-lenders," harking back to Belloc's political novels.[372] Like many of his collections it was drawn from earlier material, but was more explicitly and pessimistically painted. But the intervening years had seen the Marconi affair, the Great War, the Russian Revolution, and the *Protocols of the Elders of Zion*. While rejecting Jewish conspiracy theories, Chesterton continued to see capitalist rather than Bolshevik Jews as the real danger. It was capitalist Jews who had shown questionable probity in the Marconi case, and Chesterton, who admired Jewish revolutionary tendencies, still saw revolution as a laudable reaction to injustice: "It may be we shall rise the last as Frenchmen rose the first, / Our wrath come after Russia's wrath and our wrath be the worst."[373] He would continue to interpret working class history in terms of revolt against injustice, just as Marxists like E.P. Thompson would see revolutionary tendencies in working class movements throughout history.[374] Thus in the 1920s, while continuing to view "Jewish money power" as demonstrating the corruption of the Jewish revolutionary spirit, he went against the flow of popular opinion by rejecting the belief in an ages-old, worldwide Jewish conspiracy and that communism was a greater threat than capitalism.

Although overall most of Chesterton's Jewish characters turn out to be not guilty, 1922 reached a peak, with four guilty Jewish characters in *The Five of Swords*, a story in *The Man Who Knew Too Much*. But a gradual change of emphasis followed until in *The Three Horsemen*, in *The Paradoxes of Mr. Pond* (1937) there are no Jewish characters and Prussianism is portrayed as the threat.

---

371. J. Parkes, *Antisemitism* (London: Vallentine Mitchell & Co. Ltd., 1963), 37.

372. I. Boyd, *The Novels of G. K. Chesterton: A Study in Art and Propaganda*, op. cit., 83–84.

373. Composed around the time of the first Russian Revolution (1905–1907) the poem showed that it was "arousing within him not the reactions of a natural conservative, but rather a hankering for the same thing to happen in England, if possible with a little more violence" (W. Oddie, *Chesterton and the Romance of Orthodoxy: The Making of GKC 1874–1908*, op. cit., 372).

374. See: D. Dworkin, *Cultural Marxism in Postwar Britain: history, the New Left, and the Origins of Cultural Studies*, op. cit.

Nonetheless there was sometimes an undercurrent of blame, as in *The Loyal Traitor*, when John Conrad's revolution scam is provoked by Lobb's bad treatment.[375] As Boyd remarks: "That Lobb should be Jewish fits in perfectly with Chesterton's belief that Jews, and particularly, Jewish financiers, are equally disposed to become capitalists or revolutionaries."[376] But Lobb was not a revolutionary, and in *The Fool of the Family* (1922) Sir Francis Verner turns out to be a German[377] while old Squire Hawker, whom Verner blackmails and ruins, is said to have imprisoned his wife and bigamously married "a flashy South American Jewess with a fortune."[378]

In Chesterton's fiction not all Jewish characters are explicit, but the best are explicitly so, for example, Dr. Amiel in *The Tower of Treason* and Simon the patriotic banker in *The Loyal Traitor*, while the ethnicity of the worst, such as Sir Isaac Hook in *The Fad of the Fisherman*, is merely implied. Moreover, even in stories where the Jewish character is guilty he is seldom treated unsympathetically, as in the murder of young "Waldo Lorraine" by fellow Jewish criminals:

> [Forain] stood a minute or two in silence, looking down at the fallen figure across the table with pity and something almost like admiration. "Strange," he said at last, "that he should die just here, with his head in all that dustbin of curiosities that he was born among and had such a taste for. You saw he was a Jew, of course, but, my God, what a genius! Like your young Disraeli— and he might have succeeded too and filled the world with his fame."[379]

Horne Fisher carries a heavy burden of knowledge, and when a Jewish character is murdered (as a result of his own misdeeds) the tone is more tragic than triumphant, as with the implicitly Jewish moneylender Melchior Morse in *The White Pillars Murder* (1925): the detective Weir remarks: "I believe [Dr. Hyde] tripped up the poor old usurer and stamped on him on the stone steps with those monstrous boots."[380] Although in *The Honest Quack* (1930) the "late lamented" moneylender Isaac Morse is clearly unlamented,[381] there is no sense of what George Grella described as a "murderable" victim "worthy of his

---

375. Loeb "was not a nice old gentleman" ("The Loyal Traitor," *Four Faultless Felons*, op. cit., 197).

376. I. Boyd, *The Novels of G. K. Chesterton: A Study in Art and Propaganda*, op. cit., 171.

377. "[S]omething about the turn of his fair moustache and the lie of his flat hair ... suddenly revealed that his name was Franz Werner" (G. K. Chesterton, "The Fool of the Family," *The Man Who Knew Too Much*, op. cit., 145–146); Turnbull includes Sir Francis Verner in a list of negative Jewish characters in this collection (M. J. Turnbull, *Victims or Villains: Jewish Images in Classic English Detective Fiction*, op. cit., 45).

378. G. K. Chesterton, "The Fool of the Family," *The Man Who Knew Too Much*, op. cit., 135.

379. G. K. Chesterton, "The Five of Swords" (ibid., 304–305).

380. G. K. Chesterton, *Thirteen Detectives*, op. cit., 26.

381. G. K. Chesterton, *Four Faultless Felons*, op. cit., 100.

fate."[382] Notwithstanding his views on "balancing" good and bad Jewish characters, in the overwhelming majority of his own creations criticism is tempered with praise or exculpation, and bad Jews are "balanced" by bad Gentiles. In the Golden Age of Jewish and foreign stereotypes he created a diversity of Jewish characters, some explicit and some implicit, although their occupations were influenced by his Zionism.[383] While Moses Gould's occupation is never stated there are two Bolshevists, four scientists, one lawyer, one wine merchant, five bankers/financiers, one count, one hotelier, two shopkeepers, one businessman, one philanthropist/businessman, one diplomat, four doctors, two millionaires, two moneylenders, one pawnbroker, one secretary, one actor, one servant, one artistic individual, one school friend, and five full-time criminals.

It is easier to gather two or three fictional plotters in one Edwardian drawing room than to describe the complexities of politics and finance, and Chesterton attempted to distil those complexities in his fiction. But even though he softened the edges of his characters, they retain the texture of cardboard from his beloved toy theater, where the boundaries between good and evil were clearly marked. Chesterton continued to view the real world with little "confusion" in his mind about right and wrong—and Right and Left.

The influence of Chesterton's views can be gauged by the fact that the majority of those who enjoyed his fiction did not read *The New Witness* or *G.K.'s Weekly*; that Distributism did not become a mass movement suggests that too much can be made of the power of such stories, especially if we ignore the fact that they are fiction. And yet, if such representations of "the eternal alien"[384] are dismissed as harmless, it may not be long before "bad Jew"—or "bad Israeli"—stereotypes are once again met with approval rather than "discomfort."[385]

A Case to Answer?

Chesterton's revolt against pessimism certainly seemed to suffer a setback with *The Man Who Knew Too Much*, but the book marked the nadir of his gloom on Jewish issues. His writing career was indeed one side of a long argument, stemming from his need to defend the things he held dear, like the small nations treated so shamefully by the English—but also the English themselves, the revolutionary, the poor, Catholicism, and religion in general. His defense of the

382. G. Grella, "The Formal Detective Novel," op. cit., 96.

383. See Chapter Seven.

384. As depicted in George du Maurier's "Trilby" (M.J. Turnbull, *Victims or Villains: Jewish Images in Classic English Detective Fiction*, op. cit., 18–19).

385. The BBC television series *Spooks* has frequently portrayed Israel and Israelis (as well as America and Americans) as dangerous "rogue" forces, discovered to be behind various terrorist outrages, while neglecting more obvious types of terrorist; see Chapter Nine.

detective story is further proof that, as in *The Man Who Was Thursday*, Chesterton saw the good conspiracy as more powerful than the bad:

> The romance of the police force is ... the whole romance of man. It is based on the fact that morality is the most dark and daring of conspiracies. It reminds us that the whole noiseless and unnoticeable police management by which we are ruled and protected is only a successful knight-errantry.[386]

His loyalty to the Catholic Middle Ages was linked to his defense of the poor and the democracy of Everyman, against prejudiced elitists who dismissed the era as a time of ignorance, squalor, and superstition. In contrast, Chesterton saw their way of life as more democratic than that of the poor slum dwellers of industrial Britain. He never dismissed folk tales, arguing that they had a basis in reality,[387] but his defense of the poor and the Middle Ages meant taking their prejudices seriously, hence the ghost of the Jewish moneylender oppressing the poor that hovered over his fiction.

Even though Jewish characters and themes did not predominate in Chesterton's fiction, there is a case to answer. His primary foes continued to be pessimism and decadence, but if he did not blame Jews for pessimism and decadence, he did appear to blame them for the worst aspects of capitalism and political chicanery, aspects of his worldview that will be explored in forthcoming chapters. Nevertheless, most of his fictional Jews were sympathetically drawn. The very complexity of that treatment shows that he thought deeply about such issues; certainly he did not see himself as prejudiced.[388] Only by viewing Chesterton's works narrowly, through the lens of the Holocaust, is it possible to see him as driven primarily by anti-Semitism, or diagnose in him a "racial," all-embracing antipathy to Jews, an approach almost guaranteed to result in a guilty verdict.

Chesterton's "long argument," beginning with the birth of his brother Cecil,[389] continued with his friends George Bernard Shaw and H.G. Wells, whose approach to Jewish issues will be explored in the next chapter, in the context of their fiction.

---

386. G.K. Chesterton, "A Defence of Detective Stories," *The Defendant* (1902), accessed July 3, 2008, http://www.chesterton.org./gkc/murderer/defence_d_stories.htm.
387. See Chapter Eight.
388. G.K. Chesterton, *Autobiography*, op. cit., 71–76.
389. Ibid., 199.

4

The ChesterShaWells and the Jews: a Fictional Friendship?

G EORGE BERNARD SHAW, H.G. Wells, and G.K. Chesterton, the three literary giants of the early twentieth century, like many other writers, included Jewish characters and themes in their fiction. But while Chesterton's approach has been tried and found wanting, the reputations of Shaw and Wells have survived relatively unscathed. This chapter will ask whether such responses are justified. None was trained in philosophy,[1] each promoting his worldview in popular format to a wide audience. Their close friendship gave birth to the ChesterShaWells, a fabulous monster fit to rival the *Chesterbelloc*. In fact the philosophies of Chesterton, Shaw, and Wells conflicted even more than those of the *Chesterbelloc*. All turned away from capitalism, but when it came to positive programs the three heads strained in different directions, putting their friendship in even greater danger of splitting at the seams. Judging from their exchanges on the "Jewish question," it may be supposed that this issue contributed to that tension. By studying their fiction in the light of the philosophies that underpinned it, we may be able to judge whether their friendship with "the Jews" was genuine, or simply a weapon in the "underdog wars" conducted by three radicals determined to defeat the common enemy, capitalism, while combating the personal philosophies of the other two, united in friendly rivalry.

The Fiction of Shaw

George Bernard Shaw was a middle-class Protestant[2] who came to England from Dublin in 1876 and, after several difficult years, achieved success in the 1890s.[3] He is best remembered for the sparkling wit of his plays, didactic vehi-

---

1. See: Q. Lauer, *G.K. Chesterton: Philosopher without Portfolio* (New York: Fordham University Press, 1991).

2. "The Shaws made no secret of being aristocrats" (Michael Holroyd, *Bernard Shaw Vol. I, 1856–1898: The Search for Love* [London: Chatto & Windus, 1988], 5).

3. Ibid., 401.

cles for a philosophy opposed to yesterday's theories of natural selection. Shaw and writers like Samuel Butler "were no longer Darwinians, but neo-Lamarcki-ans." This allowed potential for social reform,[4] although some believed that only revolution would bring the drastic reforms that were needed. However, Darwinism had enveloped British Marxian politics with the comforting belief that revolution was inevitable. The socialist Shaw was not content to wait for revolution to "just happen," but was determined to make it happen. As Ches-terton remarked, the "Larmarckian suggestion" was that "the will counts. . . ."[5] Shaw's Life Force, "creative evolution" with its powerful mystique, was a reli-gion designed to serve his politics, but it lulled some of the more convention-ally religious into believing that he had not rejected Christianity.[6] Dismissing a Parliamentary career, Shaw worked instead through culture: through "an effort of will and a sustained act of faith" he created "the new drama" in "a series of parables" that "could rewrite history and set it on a new course."[7] *Man and Superman* (1903), influenced by Wagner's Ring Cycle, explores eugenics, Cre-ative Evolution,[8] and Zionism. Shaw's Jewish brigand leader "Mendoza," a socialist, will "not be the last to volunteer" when "the Zionists need a leader to reassemble our race on its historic soil of Palestine."[9] The liberal Shaw praises the Mosaic Law for forbidding more than forty lashes as punishment,[10] and it is Shaw's view of Judaism that Mendoza articulates: "Our elaborate sanitary code makes us unduly contemptuous of the Gentile."[11] Thanks to Mendoza, Shaw was regarded as a friend of the Jewish people. His Jewish doctor in *The Doctor's Dilemma* (1906) was seen as refreshingly different from the usual stereotypes, although Shaw's treatment bore all the hallmarks of his even-handedness, seen by some Jews as ambivalence.[12] In the "Revolutionist's Hand-book" accompanying the play Shaw expounds Shavian law: equality is essential

4. André Maurois, *Prophets and Poets*, trans. H. Miles, (Milton Keynes, Bucks.: Lightning Source UK Ltd., 1935/n.d.), 10; Jean-Baptiste Lamarck posited that acquired characteristics in humans could be passed on, thus human beings could be improved by improving their environment.

5. G.K. Chesterton, "The Soul in Every Legend," *The Spice of Life*, D. Collins, ed. (Beaconsfield, Bucks.: Darwen Finlayson Ltd., 1964), 39.

6. Shaw carried on a long correspondence with Dame Laurentia McLachlan of Stanbrook Abbey.

7. Using the "Hegelian triad" of socialist philosopher E. Belfort Bax, "reconciling opposites" brought "harmony" to Shaw's life (M. Holroyd, *Bernard Shaw Vol. II, 1898–1918: The Pursuit of Power* [London: Chatto & Windus, 1989], 72).

8. Ibid., 13.

9. G.B. Shaw, *Man and Superman*, *The Bodley Head Bernard Shaw Collected Plays with Prefaces Vol. II* (London: The Bodley Head, 1971), 618–619.

10. G.B. Shaw, "The Revolutionist's Handbook" (ibid., 769).

11. G.B. Shaw, *Man and Superman*, *The Bodley Head Bernard Shaw Collected Plays with Prefaces Vol. II*, op. cit., 626.

12. "I saw 'The Doctor's Dilemma' . . . and was both embarrassed and excited by the character of Dr. Leo Schutzmacher, the polished physician. Here, for the first and practically only time during the

to good breeding (in the eugenic sense) but incompatible with property. Happy marriages produce the best offspring, but with the emphasis on mating, "not . . . marrying."[13]

Shaw's Superman was not simply a pastiche of Nietzsche's amoral power figure, but a unity of speech and action, reflecting Shaw's own politico-religious stance. Creative evolution demanded that the world must not wait for a superman but must produce super men. Until every man in England was a Cromwell, every Frenchman a Napoleon, every Roman a Caesar, and every German a Luther, the world would be imperfect.[14] Shaw condemned "proletarian democracy," calling instead for a "Democracy of Supermen."[15] He rejected the dynamite of the assassin, for "in spite of all 'movements' and all revolutions," until his nature was changed, Man would "return to his idols and his cupidities."[16] Shaw saw socialism as "the socialization of the selective breeding of Man"— "human evolution." Society must "eliminate the Yahoo" or his vote would "wreck the commonwealth." To this end he suggested a private company specializing in "human live stock" that sounds, post-Holocaust, like the Nazi *Lebensborn* program.[17]

Shaw's "Maxims for Revolutionists" state: "Democracy substitutes election by the incompetent many for appointment by the corrupt few." Attempting to force society to reappraise its conventional views after the manner of Proudhon's "all property is theft,"[18] Shaw constructed a series of philosophical equations redolent of relativism. For example, he claimed "the vilest abortionist is he who attempts to mould a child's character"; imprisonment was "as irrevocable as death"; "[a]ssassination on the scaffold" was "the worst form" because it was "invested with the approval of society." Marriage or similar forms of "promiscuous amoristic monogamy" were "fatal to large States" because they prevented "the deliberate breeding of man as a political animal." His more "Chestertonian" maxims included: "He who gives money he has not earned is generous with other people's labour"; "What is the matter with the poor is poverty"; "The reasonable man adapts himself to the world: the unreasonable one

first decade of the century, was a Jew who spoke and behaved like a rational being on the stage, and had caustic honest remarks to make, both about the Jew and about the Englishman. Shaw, of course, was always in advance of his times" (Charles Landstone, "Stage Jews," *Jewish Chronicle*, July 2, 1971, ii–iv); see Chapter Five.

13. G. B. Shaw, "The Revolutionist's Handbook," *Man and Superman, The Bodley Head Bernard Shaw Collected Plays with Prefaces Vol. II*, op. cit., 743–745.

14. Ibid., 751.

15. Ibid., 755.

16. Ibid., 763.

17. Ibid., 776.

18. "La propriété, c'est le vol!" (Pierre-Joseph Proudhon, *What is Property? Or, an Inquiry into the Principle of Right and of Government* [1840]).

persists in trying to adapt the world to himself. Therefore all progress depends on the unreasonable man."[19]

Shaw's preface to *Major Barbara* (1905)[20] reclaims the Nietzschean idea of the Superman from perceptions of selfish bullying. Nietzsche's "Ubermensch" was to save Mankind in the shape of a Napoleonic Superman, in contrast, Shaw proposed a whole race of Supermen.[21] The unegalitarian Nietzsche maintained that the "tendency must be towards the rendering extinct of the wretched, the deformed, the degenerate," advocating "positive" and "negative" eugenics. Marriage should be for the "fit" alone— "[c]oncubinage is enough for all the rest, with measures to prevent conception. . . . These geese must not marry! . . . Go through the towns and ask yourselves whether these people should reproduce! Let them go to their whores!"[22]

Shaw's approach was more humorous, but his egalitarianism struggled against his love of aristocracy, resulting in some nimble philosophical acrobatics. He believed that it was "quite useless" to believe all men were born free unless they were born good: "Guarantee a man's goodness and his liberty will take care of itself."[23] But like many political radicals who believed in the perfectibility of Man, when confronted with imperfect men, Shaw swiftly moved from libertarianism to authoritarianism. As a socialist he emphasized the material causes of crime; dismissing conventional approaches he claimed "morality and law" were "only conventions, fallible and continually obsolescing."[24] All that was needed to maintain public order was to have laws that commanded "public assent."[25] His character, Salvation Army officer Major Barbara, attempts to

---

19. Shaw's "Maxims for Revolutionists" equated "Poverty, obedience, and celibacy" with the "canonical vices" (G.B. Shaw, *Man and Superman*, *The Bodley Head Bernard Shaw Collected Plays with Prefaces Vol. II*, op. cit., 789); decency was "[i]ndecency's Conspiracy of Silence" (ibid., 792); home was "the girl's prison and the woman's workhouse" (ibid., 794); he claimed: "All men mean well" (ibid., 792) but "[t]hose who minister to poverty and disease are accomplices in the two worst of all the crimes" (ibid., 793); however, he acknowledged: "Decadence can find agents only when it wears the mask of progress" (ibid., 795), and "[t]he artificial sterilization of marriage makes it possible for marriage to fulfil its accidental function whilst neglecting its essential one" (ibid., 785).

20. Influenced by Samuel Butler's *Luck or Cunning* (M. Holroyd, *Bernard Shaw Vol. I, 1856–1898: The Search for Love*, op. cit., 212–213).

21. G.B. Shaw, *Major Barbara*, *The Bodley Head Bernard Shaw Collected Plays with Prefaces Vol. III* (London: The Bodley Head, 1971), 48.

22. Friedrich Nietzsche, *Nachgelassene Fragmente Anfang 1880 bis Sommer 1882* (G. Colli, M. Montinare, eds., *Nietzsches Sämtliche Werke* [Munich, 1980], Vol. 9, 250: 189), in M. Burleigh, W. Wippermann, *The Racial State: Germany 1933–1945* (Cambridge: Cambridge University Press, 2003), 34–35.

23. G.B. Shaw, preface to *Major Barbara*, *The Bodley Head Bernard Shaw Collected Plays with Prefaces Vol. III*, op. cit., 48.

24. Ibid., 58.

25. Ibid., 56.

minister to the sometimes violent and undeserving poor. Shaw believed that charity was merely a sticking plaster on the wounds of society. Any church that really preached the gospel would not be tolerated by the ruling classes.[26]

Barbara's father, Andrew Undershaft, is an armaments manufacturer, but his partner Lazarus, "a gentle romantic Jew who cares for nothing but string quartets and stalls at fashionable theatres" is blamed for his non-Jewish partners' "rapacity in money matters, poor fellow!"[27] Here Shaw attempts to break with Jewish stereotypes but his sensitive arms manufacturer is scarcely more credible than the "exploitative Jew." In *John Bull's Other Island* (1906), Broadbent, an English stereotype among many Irish ones,[28] claims that if his name were Breitstein and he had "a hooked nose and a house in Park Lane" he would "carry a Union Jack handkerchief and a penny trumpet," and tax the people's food "to support the Navy League," while clamoring for "the destruction of the last remnants of national liberty."[29] Against this, Larry voices Chestertonian views of Jews as intellectuals: "[W]e Irishmen were never made to be farmers; and we'll never do any good at it. We're like the Jews: the Almighty gave us brains, and bid us farm them, and leave the clay and the worms alone."[30]

Jews and the Irish also feature in *Back to Methuselah* (1921). In the Ireland of 2170, a tale is told of how the Irish once laid claim to Jerusalem, marching on the city and forcing the Jews to scatter, although, when they found the land barren they returned to Ireland. The younger Irish, seeing the equally stony nature of Irish ground, abandoned it and dispersed, never revealing their true identity. The Jews follow suit, fearing they would be sent back to Palestine, thus both Irish and Jewish identities vanish peacefully from the face of the earth, illustrating Shaw's anti-nationalist philosophy.[31] Such non-violent abolitions of peoples or races were viewed as "exterminations." In *On The Rocks* (1933) Shaw called capital punishment extermination by the state, which should be "put on a scientific basis" if it was to be "carried out humanely and apologetically as

---

26. Ibid., 51.

27. "Undershaft" to "Cusins" (G. B. Shaw, *Major Barbara*, in B. Cheyette, *Constructions of "the Jew" in English literature and society: Racial representations, 1875–1945* [Cambridge: Cambridge University Press, 1995], 111).

28. Superstitious Catholic "Patsy Farrell" is afraid of a talking grasshopper, repeatedly crossing himself: "Oh Holy Mother an all the Saints! Oh murdher! Murdher!" (G. B. Shaw, *John Bull's Other Island*, The Bodley Head Bernard Shaw Collected Plays with Prefaces Vol. II, op. cit., 416); Broadbent's valet "Hodson" is a "Home Ruler" because "Oi want a little attention pide to my aown cantry" (ibid., 435).

29. G. B. Shaw, *John Bull's Other Island* (ibid., 407).

30. Ibid., 430–431.

31. G. B. Shaw, *Back to Methuselah: Tragedy of an Elderly Gentleman*, The Complete Plays of Bernard Shaw (London: Odhams Press Ltd, 1937), 917–918.

well as thoroughly."[32] Extermination had been "advocated [and] actually attempted" in the quest for wealth, against "whole races and classes." The extermination of the peasant and anyone who did not fit the Soviet template was "in active progress in Russia" and the "extirpation of the Jew as such" had "figured for a few mad moments in the program of the Nazi party in Germany."[33] Shaw equated land clearances and evictions with "extermination,"[34] but like Binding and Hoche, who inspired the Nazi euthanasia program,[35] he wanted to eradicate the "old doctrine of the sacredness of human life," which "still terrifies us into wasting the lives of capable people in preserving the lives of monsters" while "murderers, heretics, traitors" could be "legally killed." Having constructed a false moral equivalence between murder and the state punishment of murderers, Shaw demanded "capital punishment" for the physically and mentally disabled,[36] but would not allow murderers a "merciful release."

Another Ulster posited that the Balfour Declaration (1917), laying the foundation of the Jewish state, was a reward for the chemist Chaim Weizmann's contribution to the British War effort. David Nathan notes that in 1938 Shaw "supported the establishment of a Jewish-Arab Committee to Combat British Imperialism," a Marxist venture appealing to both communities to "unite in one socialist party for the sake of the anti-Imperialist struggle"; however, Balfour and Weizmann's exchange raised "the interesting question of whether the propagation of the antisemitic assumption that Jews are, above all, interested in money ('I do not ask for money'—'There must be some misunderstanding. I was informed that you are a Jew') is less harmful—or more—when it comes from a writer who was more or less free from antisemitism."[37]

This was Shaw's joke against anti-Semitism rather than a reflection of it, but Allied strategic interests in the Great War[38] make the play's premise dubious and it was never performed. Given Arab violence against the Jewish settlements,[39]

---

32. G.B. Shaw, preface to *Plays Political: On the Rocks* (Harmondsworth, Middx.: Penguin Books Ltd., 1986), 142.

33. Ibid., 145.

34. Ibid., 148–149.

35. German jurist Karl Binding and psychologist Alfred Hoche published *Die Freigabe der Vernichtung Lebensunwertem Lebens* (*Allowing the Destruction of Life Unworthy of Life*) (Leipzig, 1920) advocating the killing of the chronically sick, disabled and incurably mentally ill.

36. G.B. Shaw, preface to *Plays Political: On the Rocks*, op. cit., 152–154.

37. Written in June 1936 as *Arthur and the Acetone* (David Nathan, *Jewish Chronicle*, October 27, 1989, 28). Cheyette comments that in the play "Shaw went on to further debunk Jewish national aspirations in terms of Irish history" (B. Cheyette, *Constructions of "the Jew" in English literature and society: Racial representations, 1875–1945*, op. cit., 115).

38. See: Howard M. Sachar, *A History of Israel: From the Rise of Zionism to our Time*, New York, Alfred A. Knopf, 2007.

39. See Chapter Seven.

the play's pessimistic conclusion that Britain had created another Ulster was more realistic than the fantasy about the Balfour Declaration. Shaw satirizes the anti-Semitism of a civil servant, but his suggestion that the Jewish national home sprang from a Jewish chemist's demands would have fuelled Jewish conspiracy theory and damaged the Zionist cause.

Geneva (published in 1939 but revised several times until 1946) delivers another Shavian mixed message as a diverse group of characters gather at the League of Nations to articulate their view of current events. One, called simply "The Jew," demands: "Can I deny that there are good reasons for disliking Jews? On the contrary, I dislike most of them myself."[40] This could be Shaw emphasizing that minorities should not be massacred even if they were not "nice," especially as The Jew pleads: "[W]hat is your grievance compared to mine? Have you been robbed? Have you been battered with clubs? gassed? massacred? Have you been commercially and socially ruined? Have you been imprisoned in concentration camps commanded by hooligans? Have you been driven out of your country to starve in exile?" His plea is challenged by a character called "The Newcomer": "[B]ut if the people vote for it there is no violation of democratic principle in it." To his protest that he has been "cast out" of the country in which he was born, The Newcomer responds: "You oughtnt to have been born there. You ought to have been born in Jerusalem."[41] This exchange emphasizes Shaw's belief in the right of democracies to impose their own rules.

The League's secretary hates every nationality, including Jews: "Two nationalities are worse than one."[42] The judge describes The Jew as a "harmless Jewish gentleman"[43] but (like Shaw) dismisses tales of Soviet repression.[44] Shaw ridicules anti-Semitism in the character of the "devout" Catholic widow who would "shoot every Jew in the country."[45] Divorce, she maintains, is "a deadly sin," but adds: "I hate, loathe, and abhor [the Jew]. He would steal my child and cut it in pieces and sprinkle its blood on the threshold. He is a Jew." The Commissar blames their "corruption" on capitalism: "Come to Russia. Jews do not do such things there." The Jew responds: "Lies! lies! Excuses for robbing and murdering us."[46] The widow links Jews to the East: "You have taste, you Jews.

---

40. G.B. Shaw, *Plays Political: Geneva*, op. cit., 345.

41. Shaw's spelling reflected his belief in rational English (ibid., 387).

42. Ibid., 396.

43. Ibid., 400.

44. "It is evident that the lady [Begonia Brown] is wrong as to the facts because the inhabitants of a country conducted as she supposes Russia to be conducted would all be dead in a fortnight" (ibid., 402).

45. When The Jew points out that Jesus was a Jew she protests: "Oh, what a horrible blasphemy!" Reaching for her pistol: "You will be telling me next that King David was a Jew" (ibid., 388–389).

46. Ibid., 391.

You have appetites. You are vital, in your oriental fashion. And you have boundless ambition and indefatigable pertinacity: you never stop asking for what you want until you possess it." Eventually she agrees to dine with him providing he pays and she can keep her pistol handy.[47]

Shaw's dictators are less violent than the widow and sound more reasonable (i.e. Shavian). His Italian "Bombardone" says: "Thank your stars you have never known democracy in England. I have rescued my country from all that by my leadership." Battler, the German, agrees: "British democracy is a lie. I have said it."[48] No character goes unchallenged: "Sir Orpheus Midlander" is challenged by the Judge on the evils of bombing civilians; the Judge by "the Russian Commissar," on capital punishment.[49] The Jew complains of Battler's "attempt to exterminate the flower of the human race" and Battler retorts: "I am sorry. I cannot be everywhere; and all my agents are not angels.... Keep away; and you will be neither beaten nor robbed."[50]

Battler insists: "[M]y support is no dead Jew, but a mighty movement in the history of the world.... I have snapped my fingers in the face of all your Jewish beliefs and Roman traditions." He urges Bombardone to avoid being "a tool of that accursed [Jewish] race."[51] A third dictator, the Catholic "Flanco," abuses them both. Battler calls him "nine tenths a Jew."[52] The Judge then rebukes all the dictators: "There are a thousand good things to be done in your countries. They remain undone for hundreds of years; but the fire and the poison are always up to date." He continues in eugenic vein: "Man is a failure as a political animal. The creative forces which produce him must produce something better."[53] When a new Ice Age is predicted, Sir Orpheus says: "Only the Jews, with the business faculty peculiar to their race, will profit by our despair.... our Jewish friend ... is instructing his stockbroker to sell gilt-edged in any quantity, at any price, knowing that if this story gets about before settling day he will be able to buy it for the price of waste paper and be a millionaire until the ice-cap overtakes him." Meanwhile, Battler breaks down at the thought of losing his pet dog to the impending ice.[54] The Judge concludes: "They blustered: they defied us. But they came."[55] In giving his most anti-Semitic lines to unsympathetic characters Shaw mocked anti-Semitism, but gave a painfully false

---

47. Ibid., 405.
48. Ibid., 416–417.
49. Ibid., 424–425.
50. Ibid., 429–431.
51. Ibid., 439.
52. Ibid., 445–446.
53. Ibid., 450–451.
54. Ibid., 454–456.
55. Ibid., 460–461.

impression of the power balance between Jew and dictator, which he did not correct after the Holocaust became known.

Shaw and "Race"

Shaw was a Fabian, and socialists prided themselves on critiquing anti-Semitism,[56] described by August Bebel as "the socialism of fools."[57] Enlightened radicals emphasized the equality of man. In overthrowing the class hierarchy they expected newly-emancipated Jews to abandon their identity, but many still wanted to be Jews, appearing reluctant to take up the revolutionary socialist mantle. Like Martin Luther, Leftists showed impatience at the Jewish refusal to "convert" from religion and capitalism to secular radicalism.[58]

Cheyette's study of "racial" constructions of "'the Jew'" sees Shaw and Wells as part of a late Victorian "radical anti-capitalist tradition" in which such constructions constituted a "potent symbol of capitalist disorder." Judaism was "irredeemably capitalist" but the "universalized 'Jew'" was central to the "radical transformation of society," associated with the emerging world utopia, therefore all distinctions of race and class, and "all forms of Jewish particularity" would have to vanish.[59] Anti-capitalists praised "Jewish" qualities, but wanted the qualities to remain and Jews to disappear. Shaw's apparently ambivalent Jewish images exemplified these tensions in his political philosophy.

Chesterton's Jewish "dual image," which straddled his fiction and non-fiction, contrasted secular Jews unfavorably with religious Jews, whereas Shaw's Jewish representations, Cheyette notes, were "the embodiment of a Hebraic liberal capitalism" but also "the most revolutionary of 'races.'" Shaw's counterpointed images of worldly Jew and revolutionary Jew emphasized the need for synthesis to produce his world-changing Superman. Nevertheless, between the Wars Shaw and Wells tended to link Jews not with society's "progressive evolution" but with "regressive forces" stalling society's "rational development."[60] Like Luther and Matthew Arnold, initial hopes of transformation of and from "the Jews" were followed by disappointment, just as Chesterton's initial defenses of Jews as underdogs gave way to criticism of them as top-dogs.

56. See Chapter Two.

57. The non-Jewish Bebel was one of the founders of the German Social Democratic Party (A.S. Lindemann, *Esau's Tears: Modern Anti-Semitism and the Rise of the Jews* [Cambridge: Cambridge University Press, 1997], 175).

58. See Chapter Eight.

59. B. Cheyette, *Constructions of "the Jew" in English literature and society: Racial representations, 1875–1945*, op. cit., 94.

60. Cheyette sees Shaw's Jewish characters as "pointedly transient . . . because they were deemed to be outside of the evolutionary Life Force"; nevertheless they "often had a considerable dramatic impact as a necessary counter to the supra-worldly 'superman'" (ibid., 94–95).

Cheyette sees *Major Barbara* as dramatizing the Devil's argument in *Man and Superman* that the Life Force can also be the Death force.[61] *Back to Methuselah* was Shaw's fantasia about the natural death of Jewish identity, and the direct extermination of the "unfit."[62] Cheyette notes a further disturbing development in Shaw's espousal of eugenics as an approach to diversity. In a letter to Beatrice Webb, Shaw "constructs Jews as a potentially 'undesirable' 'strain'" in saying that "we" should "tackle the Jewish question" by "admitting the right of States" to experiment eugenically "by weeding out any strains that they think undesirable," while doing it as "humanely" as such states could afford so as not to "shock civilization" with "such misdemeanors as the expulsion and robbery of Einstein."[63] According to Cheyette, Shaw dismissed the Nazi concentration camps due to the "understandable naïveté" of his "essentially late Victorian assumptions"; stuck in an "Edwardian" "semitic discourse" that positioned Jews and Aryans as "racial 'opposites,'" he continued to cling to his *Man and Superman* theme of synthesis. Cheyette adds that he saw Hitler, Mussolini "and, especially, Stalin" as "Great Men" with the "power as individuals to transform mankind," and that *Geneva*, redrafted several times between 1939 and 1946, with its continued focus on a "progressive synthesis between 'the Jew' and a Hitlerite Superman" was "at best, wildly optimistic."[64] Shaw's "hopes for the rational progress of history," glimpsed through Battler, are apparently contradicted in the play's final version by the dictator's emotion about his pet dog, undermining the idea of Battler as Superman. But as Cheyette notes, elsewhere Shaw suggested that if Hitler "had not acquired a Hebraic Messiah complex" he might "have helped evolve a more rational future," thus Shaw appears to blame the Jewish religion for Hitler appointing himself leader of a German chosen race.[65]

Chesterton and Wells agreed on the irony that Hitler had adopted a Jewish

---

61. Ibid., 109.

62. "Zoo" warns the Elderly Gentleman (Joseph Popham Bolge Bluebin Barlow, OM): "You are a child; an evil child. We kill evil children here. We do it even against our own wills, by instinct"; "abnormal" individuals are weeded out (G.B. Shaw, *Back to Methuselah: Tragedy of an Elderly Gentleman, The Complete Plays of Bernard Shaw*, op. cit., 923–925); the Elderly Gentleman is required to explain words like "landlord," "trespass," and "sneer," but not "stupid," "normal," and "abnormal" (ibid., 913).

63. G.B. Shaw, *Bernard Shaw: Collected Letters 1926–1950*, D.H. Laurence, ed. (London, 1988), 493, in B. Cheyette, *Constructions of "the Jew" in English literature and society: Racial representations, 1875–1945*, op. cit., 115–116.

64. Ibid., 116–118.

65. Shaw refused to agree that Britain was "fighting for democracy," which was "'nothing but Anglo-Semitic plutocracy' in Adolf Hitler's 'unanswerable retort'" (G.B. Shaw, *Everybody's Political What's What?* [1944, 351], in ibid., 119–120); in the final version of *Geneva* and in his 1945 preface Shaw noted Hitler's appropriation of the Chosen People idea (ibid., 120).

prerogative, but Shaw believed that, divested of his anti-Semitism, Hitler could be a Superman. His extreme nationalism was no disqualification: like Napoleon, he could impose improvements on every nation. This conclusion is chilling, since Shaw viewed Nazi eugenics as an improvement on traditional marriage and reproduction, which he regarded as primitive stages of evolution. Even shorn of his anti-Semitism, Hitler would seek to eugenically "improve" Jews. And Shaw evidently thought they needed it: the brave and enlightened Mendoza in *Man and Superman* degenerated into The Jew in *Geneva*, an inferior creature, no match for the far nobler Battler and Bombadone. Shaw's belief in modified evolution, the Life Force, meant he transferred his Superman hopes from "the Jew" to "the Dictator." While he continued to see the potential of a Hitler divested of anti-Semitism, he no longer believed "the Jew" would divest himself of his Jewishness. He rejected anti-Semitism but thought that Germany's eugenics program was Germany's business, and if it happened to include Jews, as a pacifist he would not support armed intervention.

Shaw and Chesterton

On their first meeting "Shaw talked Gilbert down,"[66] but called Chesterton "a man of colossal genius."[67] The Shaws and Chestertons became friends,[68] and although by 1930 Chesterton and Shaw no longer met regularly, their intellectual rapport endured to the end.[69] When the actress Mrs. Patrick Campbell threatened to publish Shaw's love letters he confided in Chesterton.[70] Chesterton's play *Magic* was the outcome of good-humored badgering by Shaw, who tried the same with Belloc.[71] The socialist Shaw even advised Chesterton on business acumen, something he sorely lacked,[72] but his didacticism belied real

---

66. According to Lucien Oldershaw, recalling his first meeting in Paris with Chesterton, "one of the few great conversationalists—perhaps the only one—who would really rather listen than talk" (M. Ward, *Gilbert Keith Chesterton*, op. cit., 154–155).

67. M. Ward, *Return to Chesterton*, op. cit., 4.

68. M. Ward, *Gilbert Keith Chesterton*, op. cit., 239–240.

69. W.B. Furlong, *Shaw and Chesterton: The Metaphysical Jesters* (London: The Pennsylvania State University Press, 1970), 183.

70. M. Holroyd, *Bernard Shaw Vol. III, 1918–1950: The Lure of Fantasy* (London: Penguin, 1993), 117.

71. M. Ward, *Gilbert Keith Chesterton*, op. cit., 368; Shaw urged him to write a play about St. Augustine re-visiting England and even began the scenario for him (G.B. Shaw, Letter, October 30, 1909 [ibid., 234–236]); Shaw asked Chesterton: "Do you think it would be possible to make Belloc write a comedy? If he could only be induced to believe in some sort of God instead of in that wretched little conspiracy against religion which the pious Romans have locked up in the Vatican, one could get some drive into him. . . . If he must have a Pope, there is quite a possible one at Adelphi Terrace" (G.B. Shaw, Letter, October 30, 1909 [ibid., 236]).

72. G.B. Shaw, Letter (undated), M. Ward, *Gilbert Keith Chesterton*, op. cit., 237–239.

kindness. After Chesterton's death Shaw promised to return all his own letters to enhance the value of Frances Chesterton's correspondence. It seemed, Shaw said, "the most ridiculous thing in the world" that he, who was 18 years older than Gilbert, "should be heartlessly surviving him," but if she had "any temporary bothers that I can remove, a line on a postcard (or 3 figures) will be sufficient. The trumpets are sounding for him; and the slightest interruption must be intolerable."[73]

Like Chesterton, Shaw expressed strong views on world affairs, in response to the smug indifference of the English middle classes to the "intolerable" social conditions of the poor. Wells and Belloc, Chesterton and Shaw were reminding the English upper and middle classes ("by a series of earthquakes" if necessary) that they lived "in an unreal world."[74] Many were inclined to ignore such "earthquakes," but Shaw and Chesterton were happy to encourage fears of labor unrest, and that the terrible conditions of the poor would lead to "bloody revolution."[75]

But it was Shaw's belief in the Life Force, an inadequate preparation for the reality of death, which caused trouble at Jane Wells' funeral as he began to "behave badly," firing off jokes to make Wells laugh: "All Shaw's comedy and philosophy were marshalled against these fears" of infirmity and death.[76] Shaw's "optimism" was the result of willing himself not to give in to pain and suffering, but his Life Force necessitated death for some in order to improve life for others. In contrast, Chesterton's answer to the problems of life was not death; his optimism, which inspired him to fight against pain and suffering, was based on his respect for the will of God, the author of life.

Even regarding capitalism the two disagreed. While Chesterton regarded the Marconi affair as pivotal, Shaw called it "The Wireless Indignation"—just "a lot of hot air."[77] Their common distrust of science[78] foundered on eugenics, illustrating another fundamental difference: "Chesterton had a profound and noble respect for the poor: Shaw declared that they were 'useless, dangerous, and ought to be abolished.'"[79] Chesterton and Belloc viewed Shaw's "wholesome

73. G. B. Shaw, Letter to Frances Chesterton, June 15, 1936, G.B. Shaw, *Bernard Shaw: Collected Letters 1926–1950 Vol. IV*, D.H. Laurence, ed. (London: Max Reinhardt, 1988), 433; he also helped the Webbs financially (M. Holroyd, *Bernard Shaw Vol. III, 1918–1950: The Lure of Fantasy*, op. cit., 361–362), and was kind about Maurice Baring's plays even though they did badly (*Maurice Baring: a postscript [with some letters and verse]*, L. Lovat, ed. [London: Hollis & Carter, 1947], 14).

74. M. Ward, *Gilbert Keith Chesterton*, op. cit., 221.

75. M. Ward, *Return to Chesterton*, op. cit., 57.

76. M. Holroyd, *Bernard Shaw Vol. III, 1918–1950: The Lure of Fantasy*, op. cit., 207.

77. M. Holroyd, *Bernard Shaw Vol. II, 1898–1918: The Pursuit of Power*, op. cit., 272.

78. W.B. Furlong, *Shaw and Chesterton: The Metaphysical Jesters*, op. cit., 178.

79. M. Ward, *Gilbert Keith Chesterton*, op. cit., 221–222.

discipline" of socialism as policing the private lives of the poor.[80] Most people thought Shaw a humorist who said controversial things for the sake of controversy but Chesterton understood him.[81] No "paradox-monger," Shaw was "a wild logician, far too simple even to be called a sophist."[82]

Shaw "would not accept the old Scriptural orthodoxy; G.K. refused to accept the new Agnostic orthodoxy." Where Shaw said: "Abolish private property which has produced this ghastly poverty," Chesterton said: "Abolish ghastly poverty by restoring property." Both were sincere, and prepared to fight the matter out "endlessly,"[83] but it was in their differences that the two men most influenced each other: "Until G.K.C. turned up G.B.S. had the world of controversy to himself. But as soon as G.K. stepped into the ring he had to watch his step in a new way . . . G.K. could always get through the old man's guard." But their disagreements were always good-humored and their debates "Do We Agree?" chaired by Belloc under the aegis of *G.K.'s Weekly*, were hugely popular.[84] Shaw advised Chesterton: "In a really hostile debate it is better to be as strict as possible; but as this is going to be a performance in which three Macs who are on the friendliest terms in private will belabour each other recklessly on wooden scalps and pillowed waistcoats and trouser seats, we need not be particular."[85] Some, however, saw the debates as "a sham fight or a display of fireworks, as indeed it always partly was; for each of them would have died rather than really hurt the other."[86] After Shaw reviewed Chesterton's biography on him, one critic even suggested that in the tunnel connecting Adelphi with the Strand the "saturnine Shaw" left off his beard, his clothes, his "Shaw expression of countenance . . . all the Shaw theories" and donned "the immense padding of chest . . . the Chesterton sombrero hat and cloak and pince-nez" and went forth to secretly enjoy "meat, food and strong drink." After delivering

---

80. "A Socialist state might make the lazy man work, the fat man diet or take exercise. It might limit the number of glasses of beer allowed to an individual. . . . Shaw emitted a howl of joy at the thought of a Chesterton forced to perform reducing exercises and perhaps to become a vegetarian" (M. Ward, *Return to Chesterton*, op. cit., 61).

81. M. Ward, *Gilbert Keith Chesterton*, op. cit., 222–223.

82. G.K. Chesterton, *George Bernard Shaw* (London: House of Stratus, 1909/2000), 70; Shaw could "also utter judgments whose terms [were] in collision," but "any contradiction between them" existed only for "a superficial mind that contents itself with some current acceptation of terms, ignoring the richness of meaning human language can yield" (A. Nichols, *G.K. Chesterton, Theologian* [London: Darton, Longman & Todd Ltd., 2009], 93).

83. M. Ward, *Gilbert Keith Chesterton*, op. cit., 224–225.

84. M. Ward, *Return to Chesterton*, op. cit., 224.

85. G.B. Shaw, Letter, October 27, 1911, Ward, M., *Gilbert Keith Chesterton* (New York: Sheed & Ward, 1943), 365–366.

86. M. Ward, *Gilbert Keith Chesterton*, op. cit., 220.

his "Chesterton" manuscripts to the publisher he would change back into the Shaw regalia ready to write "sardonic letters to the *Times*."[87]

Shaw accused Chesterton of "going too far" by becoming a Catholic[88] but, contrary to the claims of Shaw's biographer, Shaw never accused Chesterton of falling "[w]ith viperish violence . . . upon the Jews."[89] Chesterton's conversion did allow Shaw to claim he was under orders from the Pope, but Chesterton never needed orders, for example in attacking eugenics. He had been a fierce anti-eugenicist for many years, and the Church's stance was simply an added attraction.[90]

Chesterton on Shaw

Chesterton was an equally trenchant critic of Shaw, although unlike Shaw he always ladled high praise with the criticism. *Heretics* (1905) portrays Shaw as a humorist who should be taken seriously. Far from doing "anything to startle and amuse" he was "thoroughly consistent," applying the "Shaw test rapidly and rigorously to everything." If he disliked lawlessness, he disliked it as much in the socialist as in the individualist and he disliked "the fever of patriotism . . . in Boers and Irishmen as well as in Englishmen."[91] But Shaw's "The Golden rule is that there is no Golden rule" struck at Chesterton's belief in free will, and he insisted that Shaw's approach, while pretending to free men, was "itself a golden rule, or rather . . . an iron rule, a fetter on the first movement of a man,"

---

87. Review, *The Bystander*, September 1, 1909, in M. Ward, *Gilbert Keith Chesterton*, op. cit., 236–237.

88. M. Ward, *Return to Chesterton*, op. cit., 75.

89. According to Hesketh Pearson, Shaw continued: "Forgetting with characteristic absence of mind that Jesus Christ was distinctly Hebraic, you implied that all the dark and dirty dealings in the world were directly traceable to the malign activities of that race"; that the outburst was prompted by eugenics, because Chesterton, at Belloc's behest, had become a Catholic, and "[b]ecause the Roman Church says that the indiscriminate breeding of babies is the first duty of civilized man—meaning, of course, babies born for the Church of Rome," Gilbert had "turned and rent the Eugenists, whose sole crime is that they prefer healthy babies to diseased ones"; allegedly, Gilbert "even suggested that Sir Francis Galton, a charming old gentleman of unblemished moral character, must have been a prurient blackguard whose loathsome lewdness was fitly camouflaged by the imposition of this obscene science upon the world"; Ker comments: "The story of Shaw offensively attacking Chesterton for converting . . . recounted by Hesketh Pearson in "G.B.S. v. G.K.C.," *Adelphi Magazine* (Sept. 1923), repr. in (*Chesterton on Shaw, G. K. Chesterton Collected Works Vol. XI* [San Francisco: Ignatius Press, 2000], 577–583), and repeated in William B. Furlong, *Shaw and Chesterton: The Metaphysical Jesters* (University Park, PA: Pennsylvania State University Press, 1970), 121–133, is a total fabrication. For the hoax, see Hesketh Pearson, *Thinking it over: The Reminiscences of Hesketh Pearson* (London: Hamish Hamilton, 1938), 221" (I. Ker, *G. K. Chesterton: A Biography* [Oxford: Oxford University Press, 2011], 496).

90. See Chapter Eight.

91. G. K. Chesterton, *Heretics* (1905) *G. K. Chesterton Collected Works Vol. I* (San Francisco: Ignatius Press, 1986), 64–65.

since it restrained him from making rules, "the only thing that men want to do." Shaw actually said: "The golden rule is that there are no golden rules,"[92] but in fact he wanted a completely new set of rules. He "mocked at the faiths in the forgotten past," while discovering "in the unimaginable future" the Superman. Thus Shaw, "on the practical side perhaps the most humane man alive" was "in this sense inhumane"; under his "new master, Nietzsche," he believed that the greater and stronger the man, "the more he would despise other things."[93] Shaw asked "not for a new kind of philosophy, but for a new kind of man," regardless of the fact that "[a]ll the empires and the kingdoms have failed, because of this inherent and continual weakness, that they were founded by strong men . . . upon strong men." In contrast, Christianity was "founded on a weak man" and thus was "indestructible. For no chain is stronger than its weakest link."[94] Chesterton's biography of Shaw (1909) showed startling prescience: Nietzsche had influenced Shaw with "a new superstition, which bids fair to be the chief superstition of the dark ages which are possibly in front of us . . . [that of] the Superman."[95]

In Shaw's Fabian evolutionary view of politics, the Superman was bound to emerge because socialism was so obviously better than capitalism that men would vote for it. But Shaw began to view democracy not as a vehicle for the socialist utopia but an obstacle to it when voters failed to agree with his stance. Despite his egalitarianism, his elitist project aimed to produce a politically enlightened Man, by nature if not by nurture. Chesterton thought that Shaw was not a democrat but "an aristocrat"—a "Calvinist,"[96] saved simply by being "one of the elect." Shaw simply could not comprehend Jack the Giant Killer and Chesterton needed to "summon up the physical presence of Shaw, his frank gestures, kind eyes, and exquisite Irish voice" to cure him of "contempt" for Shaw's doctrine that "the strength of the strong is admirable, but not the valour of the weak."[97] Shaw had lost faith in education; better men could only be bred,[98] although he never ceased teaching the masses what to think. Chesterton believed Shaw's Superman would more likely be a criminal, and if this led cer-

---

92. Ibid., 67; Chesterton also misquotes him in *George Bernard Shaw*, op. cit., 39; the phrase came from Shaw's "Maxims for Revolutionists" in *Man and Superman*.

93. G. K. Chesterton, *Heretics* (1905) *G. K. Chesterton Collected Works Vol. I*, op. cit., 67–68.

94. Ibid., 70.

95. G. K. Chesterton, *George Bernard Shaw*, op. cit., 75; Ward notes Chesterton's neglect of Shaw's debt to Samuel Butler, especially regarding the Life Force (M. Ward, *Gilbert Keith Chesterton*, op. cit., 231).

96. G. K. Chesterton, *George Bernard Shaw*, op. cit., 15.

97. Ibid., 57–58.

98. Ibid., 77; Shaw "discovered that Plato was a more advanced mind than Shakespeare" and "suddenly ceased to believe in educational progress" (A. Nichols, *G. K. Chesterton, Theologian*, op. cit., 45).

tain "weak-minded followers" to see the criminally-minded as superior, Shaw could not restrain their "follies."[99]

In *Heretics* Chesterton claimed he knew "perfectly well what Mr. Bernard Shaw will be saying thirty years hence; he will be saying what he has always said."[100] Thirty years later his revised Shaw biography displayed the same ability to interpret his philosophy and predict how it would respond to the totalitarian challenge, claiming that Shaw had "horrified all the other Socialists by expressing approval of the Fascists." His "last political phase" was "largely a general loathing of anarchy; and a disposition to accept whatever can reduce it to rational order, whether it be Fascism or Bolshevism."[101] Shaw had predicted the demise of patriotism, but the new nationalism was knocking at the door "with police clubs and Prussian sabres."[102] The Golden Rule had indeed led to the Iron Rule. In casting out "contemptuously" the "sense of a conscience working from within" Shaw had "nothing left except compulsion . . . from without." After the Great War "nearly everybody" had turned pacifist, but "just when the World was really moving towards the World State, just when everybody agreed that Bernard Shaw had been right . . . then came the shock that . . . changed all the politics of the West. Steel Helmets and Storm Troops swept a whole vast civilisation like a storm." This "ruthless militarism" did not erupt, as Shaw and others had predicted, among "the negro population of Paris," or in Belgium, Britain, America or "the other Allies" but in Germany, "exactly" as the *Chesterbelloc* had said, and "in spite of the widespread influence of Mr. Bernard Shaw's plays." Shaw was "conspicuously courageous and splendidly sincere," but he was wrong. Chesterton made "no apology" for prioritizing the issue, since it was "the great historical event on which many things will turn."[103]

Shaw's "Paradise," his fantasy of killing off people for "purely sociological considerations," was simply "the Inferno of Aldous Huxley."[104] Christianity was "the one and only philosophy that [had] refused to despair of Man," whereas Shaw's "evolutionism" was "rooted in a despair about Man."[105] The philosopher Shaw was "not trying to get rid of the troubles of men" but was "trying to get rid of men because they are the troubles of the philosopher." All "normal" socialists "professed fraternity with the working-classes," but Shaw "never had

99. G. K. Chesterton, *George Bernard Shaw*, op. cit., 88.
100. G. K. Chesterton, *Heretics* (1905) *G. K. Chesterton Collected Works Vol. I*, op. cit., 65.
101. G. K. Chesterton, *George Bernard Shaw*, op. cit., 262.
102. Ibid., 272.
103. Ibid., 277–281.
104. Ibid., 286.
105. Ibid., 288–289; "unless you have a permanent standard of good, how do you know when [man] has been surpassed?" (ibid., 287).

any feeling about the working-classes except a desire to abolish them, and replace them by sensible people."[106]

Shaw on Chesterton

Shaw's response was equally forthright: he had spent his life answering the charge of being a Puritan, and Chesterton's biography "might just as well have been entitled: *Gilbert Keith Chesterton by Himself.*"[107] Shaw made this claim about all Shaw biographies,[108] and he re-wrote two of them.[109] When Archibald Henderson's authorized version was "spectacularly outshone" by Chesterton's,[110] Shaw claimed he could get "a splash or two in on the right spot."[111] Regarding Chesterton's proposed newspaper, the old controversialist lectured: "Mere controversy is a waste of time," and advised him not to pursue "pseudo-race feuds" against Jews.[112] In fact, their extensive correspondence made little mention of the "Jewish question," while Shaw alleged that Belloc was wasting his talents in the Pope's service and that he had led Gilbert up the same "blind alley."[113] Shaw did recognize, however, that Chesterton and Wells had something he lacked: people loved them.[114]

Shaw and Wells among the Fabians

Though all Victorians by birth if not by temperament, in their prime Shaw (1856–1950), Herbert George Wells (1866–1946), and Arnold Bennett (1867–1931) were seen by young intellectuals like Leonard Woolf as "leaders . . . struggling against a religious and moral code of cant and hypocrisy" that "produced and condoned such social crimes and judicial murders as the condemnation of

---

106. Ibid., 290–291.

107. W. B. Furlong, *Shaw and Chesterton: The Metaphysical Jesters*, op. cit., 127.

108. M. Holroyd, *Bernard Shaw Vol. II, 1898–1918: The Pursuit of Power*, op. cit., 213–214.

109. Pearson's biography (authorized) and Harris's (said to be unauthorized); Pearson suggested brackets around the amended paragraphs but Shaw was adamant, swearing Pearson to secrecy; however, when the book was a success, Shaw himself revealed the secret of its authorship (M. Holroyd, *Bernard Shaw Vol. III, 1918–1950: The Lure of Fantasy*, op. cit., 370–371); Shaw also amended Ward's Chesterton biography (M. Ward, *Gilbert Keith Chesterton*, op. cit., opposite 224).

110. M. Holroyd, *Bernard Shaw Vol. III, 1918–1950: The Lure of Fantasy*, op. cit., 178–179.

111. Shaw also made this claim about St. John Ervine (ibid., 366).

112. "The Irish will not support an English journal because it occasionally waves a green flag far better than they can wave it themselves. And the number of Jews who will buy you just to see what you say about them is not large enough to keep you going" (Shaw, G. B., Letter, February 16, 1923, M. Ward, *Gilbert Keith Chesterton*, op. cit., 488–489); Ker corrects the text from the original letter (BL Add. MS 73198, fo. 89, I. Ker, *G. K. Chesterton: A Biography*, op. cit., 496–497); see Chapter Six.

113. Ibid., 219.

114. Ibid., 214.

Dreyfus."[115] The fiction of Shaw and Wells helped swing middle-class Liberals toward Labour by creating "a middle class with expectations of swift social change"; the same "turn in allegiance by progressive individuals" gave "rise to the new Fabian boom."[116] But as Chesterton warned, being fashionable today means being unfashionable tomorrow, and intellectuals increasingly turned to Eliot, Joyce, Pound, Proust, D.H. Lawrence, and Aldous Huxley.[117] In the beginning, Wells' writings intrigued the Fabian Shaw. His fellow doyens of progressive socialism, Beatrice and Sidney Webb thoroughly approved of Wells' "New Republicans," the benevolent technocratic elite of *Anticipations* who would regenerate the nation. Shaw and the Webbs began a "pincer movement" to get Wells into the Fabians. Beatrice considered him "an interesting though somewhat unattractive personality," but "a good instrument for propagating ideas."[118] The association proved tempestuous. Shaw prevailed, while still admiring his vanquished opponent, but "the worse Wells behaved the more he was indulged," his ego soothed by the Fabian "old guard." "[G]lamorously popular"—particularly among young female Fabians—many pleaded with him not to leave.[119]

The Shaws often visited the Wells family. Shaw remained keen to work with Wells in promoting socialism,[120] but the friendship was an explosive mix of antagonism and admiration, an intellectual power struggle with disagreements especially over science. The young Wells tolerated Shaw's relentless lecturing and admired his plays, but under his admiration "boiled a vast irritation." Shaw thought he and Wells were "both in the same boat" and "must pull together,"[121] but based his amoral artist in *Doctor's Dilemma* partly on Wells.[122] Only a concerted effort by the Webbs and Shaw kept Wells in the Fabians, a resentful prisoner of their persuasiveness. Michael Holroyd sees Wells as "an escapologist" whose need to bail out was central to everything from politics to love affairs. But despite her disapproval, Beatrice Webb thought that "'in the present stage of sociology' Wells was 'useful.'" Wells grudgingly agreed to stay, but while the

115. Ibid., 149.

116. Ibid., 253.

117. Shaw's play *The Apple Cart* prompted accusations that he was turning into his old adversary Hilaire Belloc, but the play was later seen as prophetic (M. Holroyd, *Bernard Shaw Vol. III, 1918–1950: The Lure of Fantasy*, op. cit., 160).

118. H.G. Wells, *Anticipations of the Reaction of Mechanical and Scientific Progress Upon Human Life and Thought* (London: Chapman & Hall Ltd., 1901/1902). M. Holroyd, *Bernard Shaw Vol. II, 1898–1918: The Pursuit of Power*, op. cit., 131–132; *A Modern Utopia* prompted hero-worship among radical Fabians (ibid., 136).

119. Ibid., 146.

120. Ibid., 180.

121. Ibid., 133–134.

122. Ibid., 165.

Fabians wanted to make the world socialist by stealth, Wells wanted to "dismantle [socialism] altogether." He claimed he was "going to turn the Fabian Society inside out . . . and then throw it into the dustbin."[123] The newspapers said Wells' socialism meant all wives being "held in common," and although Shaw defended him on behalf of the Fabians, Wells did want to "repudiate bourgeois marriage."[124] In fact his philosophy drew many young women to the organization, and when his real-life affairs became known it seemed the newspapers were right.[125]

During the Great War, the semi-pacifist Shaw appealed to Chesterton, who responded that although Shaw was a great man "the epoch is growing greater: but you are not"; however, he "neither sent this letter to Shaw nor published it."[126] Chesterton collapsed with a severe brain illness before its completion,[127] but on recovering he instantly picked up the threads of the argument. Still, the letter was never finished or sent.[128] Shaw was simply being consistent in his response to the War. If he had been German, he would have criticized Germany. Wells was as pro-War as Chesterton, to begin with at least, and complained that Shaw's constant barrage of criticism made him "an almost unendurable nuisance."[129] Shaw could forgive, indeed, he never seemed to take offence in the first place, but Wells could not: "Their friendly antagonism extended into a macabre postscript" when each was asked to write an obituary for the other. Shaw's was "an even-handed recollection of a spoilt man of genius, temperamental yet 'without malice,'" but it seemed he was over generous, since Wells alleged that the "mental and moral consequences" of Shaw's "prolonged virginity" had given rise to a "secondary, vindictive personality . . . whose method of self-assertion was 'to inflict pain.'"[130]

Unlike the "platonic displays" of Shaw and Chesterton, the Shaw and Wells debates "turned too deadly."[131] Seeking revenge, Wells picked a public quarrel

123. Ibid., 135–137.
124. Ibid., 256–257.
125. Ibid., 252.
126. Ibid., 355–356.
127. I. Ker, *G. K. Chesterton: A Biography*, op. cit., 354–355.
128. "When I first recovered full consciousness . . . I am told that I asked for *Land and Water*, in which Mr. Belloc had already begun his well-known series of war articles, the last of which I had read, or been able to understand, being the news of the new hope from the Marne. When I woke again to real things, the long battles before Ypres were over and the long trench war had begun. The nurse, knowing that I had long been incapable of really reading anything, gave me a copy of the paper at random, as one gives a doll to a sick child. But I suddenly asserted in a loud and clear voice that this was an old number dealing with the first attempt before Nancy; and that I wanted all the numbers of the paper that had appeared since the Battle of the Marne" (G. K. Chesterton, *Autobiography* [Sevenoaks, Kent: Fisher Press, 1936/1992], 257–258).
129. M. Holroyd, *Bernard Shaw Vol. II, 1898–1918: The Pursuit of Power*, op. cit., 355–356.
130. M. Holroyd, *Bernard Shaw Vol. III, 1918–1950: The Lure of Fantasy*, op. cit., 207–208.

with Shaw over the controversial issue of vivisection, which the latter opposed. Chesterton refused to take sides, and Wells lost.[132] The pacifist Shaw was the better strategist and fighter, and unlike Wells he won without being unkind.[133] That kindness drove him to lecture Wells about his wife's illness, leading to a serious breach.[134] William Furlong notes: "Only on the superficial level of camaraderie" could Wells "ever be said to have an advantage over G.B.S. where G.K.C. was concerned." Between Shaw and Chesterton, the "inner understanding" was "profound. For Shaw knew the private Chesterton as well as the public Chesterton, just as G.K.C. knew the private Shaw as well as the public Shaw."[135]

The Fiction of Wells

Like Shaw, H.G. Wells, the son of a maid and a gardener, was an established author before Chesterton arrived on the scene. The family rose to lower-middle-class status when they took on an unsuccessful china shop. Wells rebelled against his mother's ambition for him to go into the drapery business, failed to graduate from a science course under T.H. Huxley, and tried teaching before achieving worldwide popularity as a writer. His *History of Mr. Polly* (1910) was seen as championing the "little man," but also chronicled the little man's attempts to escape marriage and the lower middle class. Wells' science fiction was seen as a warning against Man's hubristic attempts to harness the power of science and misuse it, with disastrous results. As Mr. Bedford, the businessman-turned-astronaut, cries in *The First Men in the Moon*: "It's this accursed Science. . . . It's the very Devil. The medieval priests and persecutors were right, and the moderns are all wrong. . . . Old passions and new weapons—now it upsets your religion, now it upsets your social ideas, now it whirls you off to desolation and misery!"[136] *The Time Machine* (1895) warns that the quest for a comfortable civilization would lead to the eclipse of the comfortable classes. In *The Island of Doctor Moreau* (1896) a scientist obsessed with turning animals into men via cruel and hideous experiments is killed by his "creations." In *The Invisible Man* (1897) a science student soon discovers the drawbacks to invisibility, and in attempting to become visible again wreaks havoc on the ordinary

131. M. Holroyd, *Bernard Shaw Vol. II, 1898–1918: The Pursuit of Power*, op. cit., 252.

132. M. Coren, *The Invisible Man: The Life and Liberties of H.G. Wells* (London: Bloomsbury, 1994), 178–180.

133. M. Holroyd, *Bernard Shaw Vol. II, 1898–1918: The Pursuit of Power*, op. cit., 144.

134. G.B. Shaw, Letter, August 4, 1927, G. B. Shaw, *Bernard Shaw: Collected Letters 1926–1950 Vol. IV*, op. cit., 57–60; Wells ignored Shaw's lengthy letter on cancer treatments for his sick wife, and Mrs. Shaw wrote entreating Wells not to be angry (C. Shaw, Letter, September 1, 1927 [ibid., 60–61]).

135. W.B. Furlong, *Shaw and Chesterton: The Metaphysical Jesters*, op. cit., 35.

136. H.G. Wells, *The First Men in the Moon* (1901) *The Complete Science Fiction Treasury of H.G. Wells* (New York: Avenel Books, 1934/1978), 447.

people he disdains. In *The Food of the Gods* (1904) careless scientists allow a new super-food to create a race of giants who are more human than the humans who attack them. *The War of the Worlds* appears to show Wells taking the side of extra-terrestrial forces against mankind:

> Yet so vain is man and so blinded by his vanity, that no writer, up to the very end of the nineteenth century, expressed any idea that intelligent life might have developed . . . beyond its earthly level. . . . And before we judge of [the Martians] too harshly we must remember what ruthless and utter destruction our own species has wrought, not only upon animals . . . but upon its own inferior races.[137]

The Moon dwellers in *The First Men in the Moon*, astonished at tales of war and conquest on Earth, "[w]ith knowledge . . . grew and changed; mankind stored their knowledge about them and remained brutes."[138] The hero of *In the Days of the Comet* wishes a comet "or some such thing would indeed strike this world—and wipe us all away, strikes, wars, tumults, loves, jealousies, and all the wretchedness of life!"[139]

Wells gained a reputation for prescience but made some significant errors: he caricatured Winston Churchill as a "potential dictator" in *The Autocracy of Mr. Parham* (1929), although Churchill became "one of the British Union of Fascists' most vociferous opponents," who "understood the nature of fascism better than most of his contemporaries." Mr. Parham, obsessed with destroying Russian communism,[140] provokes war with the United States, upon which Germany's "accumulated resentment of ten years of humiliation and frustration blazed to fury."[141] With Parham's repression of domestic unrest and instigation of world war set against the German dictator's reasonableness, the story is a warning not against fascism but against Churchill. Wells angered the Nazis with his satire on dictators, *The Holy Terror*, although, as will become apparent, that too was more complex than might appear.

Wells' fiction contains no heroic Shavian Jews. His Jewish characters lack

137. H. G. Wells, *The War of the Worlds* (1898), ibid., 266.

138. H. G. Wells, *The First Men in the Moon* (1901), ibid., 525.

139. H. G. Wells, *In the Days of the Comet* (1906), ibid., 705.

140. M. Coren, *The Invisible Man: The Life and Liberties of H. G. Wells*, op. cit., 185–186. In 1934 Wells stated: "The Autocracy of Mr. Parham is all about dictators, and dictators are all about us, but it has never struggled through to a really cheap edition. Work of this sort gets so stupidly reviewed nowadays that it has little chance of being properly read. People are simply warned that there are ideas in my books and advised not to read them. . . . Who wants the invented humours of Mr. Parham in Whitehall, when day by day we can watch Mr. Hitler in Germany?" (Preface to *The Complete Science Fiction Treasury of H. G. Wells*, op. cit., 2).

141. H. G. Wells, *The Autocracy of Mr. Parham: His Remarkable Adventures in This Changing World* (London: William Heinemann Ltd., 1930), 285.

Chesterton's deliberate diversity. In *The Invisible Man* (1897) an "old Polish Jew in a long grey coat and greasy slippers"[142] is described as having "staring eyes and thick-lipped bearded face,"[143] an "ugly little Jew of a landlord," although the description comes from Wells' anti-hero.[144] *In the Days of the Comet* features Gurker, Jewish Chancellor of the Exchequer, is one of many politicians improved by a mysterious green vapor from outer space. With his "deep throaty voice, a big nose, a coarse mouth with a drooping everted lower lip, eyes peering amidst folds and wrinkles" he "made his confession for his race. 'We Jews . . . have gone through . . . this world, creating nothing, consolidating many things, destroying much. Our racial self-conceit has been monstrous'"; using their "ample coarse intellectuality . . . to develop and master and maintain the convention of property, to turn life into a sort of mercantile chess" and spend their "winnings grossly," Jews had "no sense of service to mankind." They made beauty, which was "a godhead," into "a possession."[145] Like Chesterton's banker Simon, Gurker is Wells' mouthpiece for his view of the "Jewish question," but influenced by "race" rather than nationalism.

Tono-Bungay (1909) is Wells' "self-consciou[s] parody" of itself.[146] With echoes of Chesterton's *The Man Who Knew Too Much*, the Jewish "Lichtensteins" take over the country house where the hero George Ponderevo grew up, their influence epitomizing the "Hebraization" of England: "They are a very clever people, the Jews, but not clever enough to suppress their cleverness."[147] But there is no deliberate Jewish conspiracy and George dismisses anti-Catholic literature as "rubbish."[148] "Uncle Edward Ponderevo" hastens to join the plutocrats when he makes a fortune out of his fake cure-all, Tono-Bungay, but his wife describes some "Plutocratic ladies" with "infinite disgust," saying, "It's the old pawnshop in the blood," and then adding: "They run their hands over your clothes—they paw you." A sympathetic character, Mrs. Ponderevo's "verdict" creates a negative feeling.[149] But a "Roumanian Jew" sea captain refuses to transport the dangerous material, "Quap," to England on behalf of Uncle Ponderevo, and lectures George on morality. The latter appeals to the unsociable-looking first mate: "[F]rom that time forth I knew that I could depend on him

---

142. H. G. Wells, *The Invisible Man* (1897) *The Complete Science Fiction Treasury of H. G. Wells*, op. cit., 225.

143. Ibid., 227.

144. Ibid., 234.

145. "One got a queer impression that except perhaps for Gurker or Revel these men had not particularly wanted the power they held" (H. G. Wells, *In the Days of the Comet* [1906], ibid., 818–819).

146. B. Cheyette, *Constructions of "the Jew" in English literature and society: Racial representations, 1875–1945*, op. cit., 130.

147. H. G. Wells, *Tono-Bungay* (London: Penguin, 1909/2005), 16.

148. Ibid., 26.

149. Ibid., 247.

and that he and I were friends."[150] Cheyette says the captain "embodies both the racial exclusivism and moral inclusivism of Wells' semitic discourse,"[151] but the captain's "Hebraizing" influence fails signally with George, and the next sentence conveys authorial irony: "It happens I never did have to depend upon [the first mate], but that does not affect our relationship."[152]

Such wry humor reduces the level of threat in some of Wells' Jewish references. Nonetheless, *Tono-Bungay*, which contains elements of autobiography and expounds Wells' worldview,[153] paints a picture of "a kingdom of Bladesovers, all much shaken and many altogether in decay, parasitically occupied, insidiously replaced by alien, unsympathetic and irresponsible elements." Croydon and "tragic impoverished West Ham" are "wedges of foreign settlement embedded in the heart of this yeasty English expansionism." The novel also describes "a shabbily bright foreign quarter, shops displaying Hebrew placards and weird unfamiliar commodities, and a concourse of bright-eyed, eagle-nosed people talking some incomprehensible gibberish." Wells frequently applied biological terminology in sociological contexts, describing a "tumorous growth-process," which "bursts all the outlines of the affected carcass and protrudes such masses as ignoble comfortable Croydon."[154] He also portrayed Christians as foolish, cowardly, and hypocritical, and in *Tono-Bungay* as a downright nuisance when they attempt to convert Uncle Ponderevo on his deathbed.[155]

The New Machiavelli unites Jewish themes with politics and "feminism," all heavily influenced by eugenics. The modern state, it insisted, must be based "not upon the irresponsible man-ruled family" from which women should be freed, but "upon the matriarchal family, the citizenship and freedom of women

---

150. The sea captain has been seen as based on Wells' friend Joseph Conrad (B. Cheyette, *Constructions of "the Jew" in English literature and society: Racial representations, 1875–1945*, op. cit., 132–133); the character also resembles the Swedish sea captain in Conrad's *Heart of Darkness*: "He was a young man, lean, fair, and morose, with lanky hair and a shuffling gait"; he "tossed his head contemptuously at the shore. 'Been living there?' he asked. I said, 'Yes.' 'Fine lot these government chaps—are they not?' he went on, speaking English with great precision and considerable bitterness" (Joseph Conrad, *Heart of Darkness* [London: Penguin Books, 1902/1973], 21).

151. B. Cheyette, *Constructions of "the Jew" in English literature and society: Racial representations, 1875–1945*, op. cit., 132.

152. H.G. Wells, *Tono-Bungay*, op. cit., 323–324.

153. Wells' mother was housekeeper in a country house like "Bladesover"; Uncle Edward Ponderevo and his wife manage a small shop similar to that of Wells' parents, and inhabit a narrow, dreary, squalid, dirty, clumsy world; the hero becomes a student in London, gets married and has an affair; his wife leaves him and takes a small country farm; he helps her financially; see: David C. Smith, *H.G. Wells: Desperately Mortal: A Biography* (New Haven/London: Yale University Press).

154. H.G. Wells, *Tono-Bungay*, op. cit., 102–103.

155. Ibid., 359–363.

and the public endowment of motherhood."[156] The hero's main achievement is to introduce this "endowment" as a "practical form of Eugenics . . . into English politics."[157] Wellsian "feminism" has the hero's mistress tearfully telling him: "You and I, Master, we've got to be men."[158] The character Lewis (based on Herbert Samuel, one of the "Marconi" politicians)[159] lives near his cousins "the Solomons and the Hartsteins" and is "a brilliant representative of his race, able, industrious and invariably uninspired, with a wife a little in revolt against the racial tradition of feminine servitude and inclined to the suffragette point of view."[160] Wells' own record on feminine servitude was not unblemished, as will be seen.

Marriage reprises *Tono-Bungay*'s theme, but less humorously: Marjorie Trafford's corruption by her Jewish friends illustrates the corruption of English society by "Jewish" materialism. Her pious Anglican home is full of Bible texts, pictures of Jerusalem and the Holy Land, religious souvenirs and "kindred trash." Clearly, Christian veneration for the Bible and Holy Land encouraged uncritical acceptance of modern secular Jews, despite their essential foreignness.[161] Marjorie tries to emulate the wealthy Jewish Carmel sisters who (despite an explicit rejection of racial theories)[162] are described by ex-draper's shop assistant Wells as possessing the "racial trick of acute appraisement."[163] When the Traffords embark on an expedition to a distant frozen wilderness, Marjorie repents of her pointless acquisitiveness. Her husband declares: "You're going to be a non-shopping woman now. You've to come out of Bond Street, you and your kind, like Israel leaving the Egyptian flesh-pots."[164] The counterpointed biblical themes of Israel's tendency to fall into idolatry and Israel purified could be seen as expressing a Jewish "dual image" uncharacteristic of Wells.

Throughout the story Wells links Jews to the Orient. At one point both Jews and non-Jews wear long Persian robes. Sir Rupert Solomonson is transformed into a "turbaned Oriental who might have come out of a picture by Carpac-

---

156. H.G. Wells, *The New Machiavelli* (London: Penguin, 1911/2005), 325–326.

157. Ibid., 356.

158. Ibid., 372; the politician hero says: "I made [my mistress] what she is—as I never made [my wife]"; his wife muses sadly: "We women are trained to be so dependent on a man. I've got no life of my own at all" (ibid., 410).

159. B. Cheyette, *Constructions of "the Jew" in English literature and society: Racial representations, 1875–1945*, op. cit., 136; Michael Foot notes that Wells included many of his acquaintance in *The New Machiavelli*: the Webbs joked about their portraits (op. cit., xvii–xviii).

160. Ibid., 203.

161. H.G. Wells, *Marriage* (London: no publisher, 1912/1933), 20.

162. Ibid., 158.

163. Ibid., 142.

164. Ibid., 305.

cio."[165] Cheyette sees racial connotations in the portrayal of Solomonson who, despite his public school and university background, "lapsed undisguisedly into the Oriental" but, as with Chesterton, the picture is humorous and even complimentary.[166] But Sir Roderick Dover launches into a eugenics tirade, lambasting women for marrying "things" just "for the sake of the homes and the clothes. Nasty little beasts they'll breed without turning a hair. All about us we see girls and women marrying ugly dyspeptic wrecks, sickly young fools, human rats—rats!"[167] When Trafford visits the Lees, a Jewish family, and sees them taking pleasure in their large family, Wells extends the eugenics theme to Jews. Trafford is resentful that his own daughter "had no cloth elephant to ride, no elaborate cubby-house to get into." He was not "above the normal human vanity of esteeming his own race and type the best, and certain vulgar aspects of what nowadays one calls Eugenics crossed his mind."[168] But it is the Traffords who see child-rearing materialistically and go off to the wilderness, leaving their children without a backward glance. Wells' "feminist" hero seeks a mother-figure who will put his whims before the needs of her "other" children. His "happy ending" sees Marjorie begging forgiveness for treating her husband as her servant when it should have been the other way round: "Don't please make me ... one of those little parasitic, parroting wives.... Don't forget a woman isn't a man."[169]

Wells expands such themes in *The Wife of Sir Isaac Harman*. Lady Harman is rescued from her obsessively jealous Jewish husband—wealthy, but old and ugly—and re-partnered with the liberal-minded non-Jewish Mr. Brumley, unsubtly drawing attention to the Jewish roots of the "restrictive" Christian sexual mores Wells repudiated. Victoria Glendinning, like other commentators, emphasizes Wells' "feminism," failing to see it as intrinsic to his male-centered eugenics worldview, claiming that "the stereotype of the close Jewish family, and the uxoriousness of the Jewish marriage" gave Wells "a successful working model for the sexual possessiveness" that his social discussion novels "set out to challenge." Wells makes the neat comparison between Sir Isaac's exploitative and acquisitive business methods and mistreating his wife. Harman's Jewishness was implied by his "name and his entrepreneurial activity" and, based on this and on Jewish characters in his other works, "one critic at least ... accused Wells of anti-Semitism." Glendinning speculates that Wells may have avoided being "explicit about Sir Isaac's Jewishness" to "avoid just such a charge," con-

165. Ibid., 199.

166. H.G. Wells, *The New Machiavelli* (1911, 246), in B. Cheyette, *Constructions of "the Jew" in English literature and society: Racial representations, 1875–1945,* op. cit., 137; see Chapter One.

167. "Dover" may have been based on T.H. Huxley (H.G. Wells, *Marriage,* op. cit., 147).

168. Ibid., 203.

169. Ibid., 297–298.

cluding that "here as elsewhere" Wells was "not so much anti-Jewish as Jew-conscious. Jews seem to have fascinated and impressed him, and Jewish businessmen had an energy and appetite for life that he admired."[170]

As seen, however, elsewhere Wells expressed disgust at Jewish "mercantile" tendencies. Furthermore, Michael Draper comments that the "racist assumptions" that "infect" *Anticipations* are reflected in *When the Sleeper Awakes*,[171] where Wells portrays black people as a threat, although the hero deems it just retribution for past oppression when blacks are used by the ruling powers to quell rebellious whites.[172] This is a Wellsian Dystopia in keeping with his earlier science fiction, but the pitiless creed he expounds in *Anticipations, A Modern Utopia*, and *Mankind in the Making* (discussed in the next chapter) is articulated by the villain Ostrog, who declares democracy dead. The only hope for the poor, stupid, and servile, he says, is the "Over-man" who will subdue or eliminate them as their inferiority deserves; they are doomed by evolution anyway.[173] Draper notes that Wells' time travelers' emancipation from the material world "does not open the way to transcendence but to a painful and irreconcilable tension between the actual and the ideal."[174] Wells saw *The War of the Worlds*, like *The Time Machine*, as "another assault on human self-satisfaction," a "wake-up call" to society,[175] but Chesterton satirized such elitist attitudes to solving poverty in *The Ball and the Cross* (1909) in which the "Unemployables" are destroyed from the air.[176] Wells admitted that in writing *The War of the Worlds* he took vicarious pleasure in killing his neighbors "in painful and eccentric ways ... selecting South Kensington for feats of peculiar atrocity."[177] Wells did not reject science but romanticized it,[178] although his stories tackle the problems he avoided in his non-fiction: "Breaking out of the prison of the mundane, Wells' characters can really only find themselves in a bigger, more imposing prison." Despite this, "some of them, unable to face such a truth, insist on calling it utopia and inviting us to follow them there."[179] Perhaps this

---

170. V. Glendinning, introduction to H.G. Wells, *The Wife of Sir Isaac Harman* (London: Hogarth Press, 1914/1986).

171. Michael Draper, *H.G. Wells* (London: Macmillan Publishers Ltd., 1987), 65.

172. H.G. Wells, *When the Sleeper Wakes* (London: J. M. Dent, 1999), 213–214.

173. Ibid., 162–167.

174. M. Draper, *H.G. Wells* (London: Macmillan Publishers Ltd., 1987), 39; in *The First Men in the Moon* Wells took account of Huxley's criticisms of Plato's Utopia in portraying a super-efficient but inhuman state (Huxley, T.H.H., *Evolution and Ethics* [1893], 22–29 [ibid., 56]).

175. H.G. Wells, preface to *The Complete Science Fiction Treasury of H.G. Wells*, op. cit., 1.

176. G.K. Chesterton, *The Ball and the Cross* (London: House of Stratus, 1909/2001), 192.

177. Norman MacKenzie, Jeanne MacKenzie, *The Time Traveller* (London: Weidenfeld & Nicolson, 1973), 113, quoted in M. Draper, *H.G. Wells*, op. cit., 60.

178. Ibid., 19.

179. Ibid., 117.

was because Wells saw the real world as far more prison-like than his fictional world, in which love at least was free.

Real prisons played little part in Wells' Utopian idea, because, as in *The Shape of Things to Come* (1933), large swathes of the population would be culled, including irredeemable misfits, the disabled and chronically sick, as well as anyone who tolerated bad conditions, or was not sufficiently dynamic and revolution-minded.[180] Wells' fictionalized "futuristic history," wrong on so many counts, was right about the wholesale extermination of disabled persons. The story is based on actual events up until 1933, seen from the future through the character Dr. Philip Raven. He recounts that in 1933 it appeared, from the rise of fascism in Italy and Nazism in Germany, that the "cosmopolitan idea was everywhere in retreat before the obsessions of race, creed and nationalism"; and yet "all the while the germs of the Modern State were growing, everywhere its votaries were learning and assembling force."[181] Raven says the Second World War commenced in 1940 and was started by the Poles, with a gas that could kill or sterilize.[182] Much earlier, "Jewish intelligences" had "redeemed" the "mathematical and psychological ineptitudes" of the "German brain,"[183] but with violent campaigns targeting Jews, communists, and speculators, and the "brisk, silly little" swastika,[184] a pathological hatred grew for the Jewish "whipping-boys of the Western civilization."[185] War was sparked when a Nazi shot a Polish Jew for making faces, when he was merely struggling to adjust an ill-fitting dental plate. The Poles and French had been waiting for some pretext to launch a pre-emptive strike, and Poland leapt to the occasion, but was faced with German "non-resistance"; the French were unsure whether to be disappointed or relieved. The Poles devastated Berlin with gas bombs but, apart from "the youth of the fascisti" and Nazi, public schoolboy and scoutmaster types, Europeans were unenthusiastic for this localized war. Indeed, the "main Polish masses never came into actual contact with the German troops." Italy, closely allied with the "Teutonic powers," did become embroiled, but Britain, Japan, China and the Americas remained neutral.

The Shape of Things to Come notes that there was "no direct continuity" (since the "fascisti were intensely nationalist") but this "self-appointed, self-disciplined elite" constituted a "distinct step" towards the modern world state; at

---

180. H. G. Wells, *The Shape of Things to Come: The Ultimate Revolution* (London: J. M. Dent, 1933/1999), 40.
181. Ibid., 29.
182. Ibid., 161.
183. Ibid., 177.
184. Ibid., 180–181.
185. Ibid., 185.

least they did not oppose it.[186] After the air raids, torture, deaths, rape and plunder of the 1940s, in which Japanese soldiers suffered enormously,[187] the adolescent fascist, communist, and Nazi organizers "became Modern State men" in middle age.[188] According to Dr. Raven, anti-Semitism played little part in "the Polish wars." Perhaps the only thing that Wells got right was that "Germany as a unity did not survive."[189]

The Shape of Things to Come blamed Marx ("son of a Christianized Jewish lawyer") for imbuing socialism with the idea that revolution was inevitable, thus removing the urgency from radical politics. Like Shaw, Wells believed that revolutionaries would have to be bred.[190] Dr. Raven's war did not directly lead to a world state, rather the reverse,[191] but after capitalism had weakened the family the state took over parental rights: "Citizens were begotten in the home but they were no longer MADE in the home." Democracy's "error" was in asking people what they wanted instead of deciding "what they ought to want if society is to be saved. Then you have to tell them what they want and see that they get it."[192] This capitalistic marketing technique delivered "ten thousand active and devoted minds" pursuing the same goal, "not in any single consciousness but in the consciousness of the race." There would be no "class insurrection" but "a revolution of the competent."[193] The idea suggests communist brainwashing, but Russia, he says, had shown that appealing to "the mere insurrectionary impulse of the downtrodden was to invite the specialist demagogue." The state would "abolish toil," which meant abolishing the "toiling class." Raven does record the "toiling classes" showing signs of revolt, but, ironically, it is against the World State's population control and "hideous invasion of the most private moments in life."[194] Wells' narrator also notes resistance from Italian fascists in alliance with "Pope Alban III," marking a new religious conflict, until the Pope is gas-bombed.[195] As Raven comments, all alternative worldviews,

186. Ibid., 190–199; there was antagonism to the World State idea from "local self-appointed bodies" (ibid., 316).

187. Ibid., 202.

188. Ibid., 402.

189. Ibid., 214.

190. Ibid., 40.

191. The Great War was followed by a nationalist upsurge (ibid., 227).

192. Ibid., 248–250.

193. Ibid., 255–257.

194. Ibid., 297–298; there would be "no sense in bringing children into the world" without work for them to do (ibid., 315).

195. Ibid., 324; the Pope and the fascists were knocked unconscious, their fates unrecorded, but although the Pope showed greater courage than the fascists, Wells' knockabout scenario stands in stark contrast to the savage suppression of religion in the Russian and Mexican Revolutions (ibid., 340).

including religion, were "wrong and misleading,"[196] but eventually, human behavior would improve as material want was removed, and against Man's nature there would be more love and less jealousy.[197] *The Shape of Things to Come* promulgated Wells' own worldview, presented as an inevitable development as the young rejected the "rotting banners" of outdated nationalism, thus ushering in his Utopia:[198] "[Y]ear by year the old order and those who have anchylosed to the old order, die and pass away, and the unhampered children of the new time grow up about us."[199] If only the present generation could produce "a few thousand of such men and women . . . with a common faith and a common understanding," the "work" would be done.[200] Wells claimed his Modern State "neither absorbed nor destroyed individuality" but (citing St. Paul) all were "members of one body."[201] Nonetheless, his Utopia suggests the "horrible theory of the Soul of the Hive" that Chesterton warned about.[202]

Wells' worldview, including his approach to "the Jews," continues to be misunderstood. Like Chesterton he used Jewish characters to exemplify the "un-English" vices of venality and greed but also like Chesterton satirized prejudice and explicitly rejected racial theories. In his satire on dictators *The Holy Terror* (1939) the printer Mr. Abrahams is dubious about providing material for an anti-Semitic fascist group, but his wife asks: "The money's all right?" When he assents, she counsels: "I wouldn't interfere."[203] *The Holy Terror* concerns a "weak snivelling bully who rises to be a world dictator," based on Wells' view of Hitler and Mussolini and of "how personal power and authority could corrupt the soul." Together with his reactions to fascism and Nazism, including his defense of free speech,[204] it earned Wells a place "very near the top" of the Nazis' list of undesirables, to be dealt with after the invasion of Britain.[205] Chesterton and Belloc were not included on this list, but Nancy Astor was, despite being seen as extremely anti-Semitic.[206]

196. Ibid., 324–325.

197. Ibid., 390; "[a]ll that part of man's life and interests has been socialized entirely against his natural disposition in the matter" (ibid., 416).

198. H.G. Wells, *Mankind in the Making* (London: Chapman & Hall Ltd., 1903), 30–31.

199. Ibid., 392.

200. Ibid., 396.

201. H.G. Wells, *The Shape of Things to Come*, op. cit., 416–417; see: 1 Corinthians 12:13.

202. G.K. Chesterton, "The Empire of the Insects," *What's Wrong with the World* (Sandy, Utah: Quiet Vision Publishing, 1910/2003), 112–113.

203. H.G. Wells, *The Holy Terror* (London: Michael Joseph Ltd., 1939), 173.

204. D.C. Smith, *H.G. Wells: Desperately Mortal: A Biography*, op. cit., 341–342.

205. Ibid., 352.

206. Astor, whose "Cliveden Set" had been accused of Nazi sympathies and promoting pro-German sympathies, "reacted with a cry of delight" (Norman Rose, *The Cliveden Set: Portrait of an Exclusive Fraternity* [London: Jonathan Cape, 2000], 207).

Smith quotes *The Holy Terror* on the subject of "twentieth-century Dictators" who "broke out like wasps in a dry summer," citing the passage as a condemnation of dictators:

> Conditions favoured them. A peculiar species they were. A crescendo of scav-
> engers because the unadapted world was rotten with shabby evasions and
> make-believes. It asked for blow-flies and wasps. Not a loyalty, not a religion
> left that was not dead and stinking. These Dictators were master stinks, stinks
> like burning rubber and creosote, in a world of cowardly skunks.[207]

But as Carstall insists, the dictators were not just the inevitable product of a
rotten system, but a "necessary evil"[208] who would clear the ground for the
World State by destroying nationalism, organized religion, and capitalism, so
that even "financiers" and "power politician[s]" would die out.[209]

The Holy Terror charts the rise and fall of a dictator but also sets out Wells'
worldview and hopes for the future, although, with Hitler putting eugenics into
practice, Wells bestows less attention on it than formerly: "[A]part from licens-
ing parenthood and subsidising motherhood" his World State avoided interfering in sexual matters.[210] The Dictator Rudolf ("Rud") Whitlow, in what might
have been a posthumous dig at Chesterton, begins his political career leading
the Common Man's Party, speaking up for "the Common Man everywhere."[211]
Rud's internationalist "Group" met with "astonishingly little resistance. It had
slipped in between right and left with such an air of undogmatic neutrality that
few people realised that its fundamental propositions ploughed deeper than
either reactionary or 'red.'"[212] Rud takes over the Popular Socialist movement
but the "power-snatching, essential rebel . . . instinctive lawless grabber . . .
antisocial egotist" never stands for election, implausibly concealing his true
political stance from the electorate, the ruling classes, and even political opponents,[213] emerging after an inconclusive World War as global ruler. Rud's
worldview, apart from a less ideological, although equally eugenic, state interference in sexual relationships, strongly resembled Wells' worldview, so that the
book initially seems to be a joke against his World State idea, especially as some
of its aspects are treated humorously. Moreover, when the youthful Rud is
approached by two oafish anti-Semitic fascists he says ("when their footsteps

---

207. "This is Chiffan commenting on Rud, and his compadres, just after he has disposed of him"
(D. C. Smith, *H. G. Wells: Desperately Mortal: A Biography*, op. cit., 352); in fact it is "Carstall" recalling
years later (to "Krause") how he killed Rud (H. G. Wells, *The Holy Terror*, op. cit., 439).
208. Ibid., 437.
209. Ibid., 428.
210. Ibid., 357.
211. Ibid., 151.
212. Ibid., 289.
213. Ibid., 388–389.

had died away and the door was safely shut"): "Blaggards... If I was a Jew I'd get a revolver. I'd get a razor like niggers do." But his mind does not "go forward to the time when myriads of such "blaggards" would march at his bidding."[214] When eventually he takes up anti-Semitism and plans a final pogrom,[215] a friend kills him. The book also mentions concentration camps,[216] and Jewish refugees relate tales of persecution.[217]

Rud is mocked in ways that would have enraged the Nazis. Portrayed as indolent and with a Jewish grandmother, he is even likened to Donald Duck.[218] Unlike Hitler, however, his anti-Semitism does not emerge until middle age,[219] reflecting the belief that Hitler simply used anti-Semitism as a political tactic. Furthermore, the World State movement's dictatorial approach hardly supports the view that Wells opposed dictatorship. Despite "The Group's" alleged devotion to the common people Rud's friend, Norvel, remarks: "I don't blame him very much for becoming Dictator of the World . . . but, by God! I feel sick at the crawling of the millions before him." Despite such qualms, he saw himself helping "in the making of a new mankind. . . . [W]e educators and biologists are setting out now to breed and educate a race of gods," and he concludes: "Mankind! Mud! Shall we ever do more than make mud pies out of them?"[220] Sharing Rud's aims, "The Group" only loses confidence in him when he has his oldest friend, Chiffan, murdered. Rud had no original ideas, in fact it is seen as vital that he does not, but his World Government clears away organized religion and other obstacles to the World State.

Wells rejects Rud's solution to the Jewish people—persecution and murder—but includes a joke about Jewish noses and a dig at his former friend Israel Zangwill when Rud's colleague argues: "[Judaism] is just a dwindling cult now of old ladies, old rabbis, sentimentalists, eccentrics, Zangwills, men with caricature profiles which they cannot escape, professional champions, who keep the old Promise alive."[221] Rud's ruthless chief of police Rothberg, despite his Jewish name, is tasked with the pogrom.[222] Hitler began persecuting the Church straight away, and Wells sees Rud's anti-religious persecution as a necessary step to world government. Early in his career Rud abuses Christianity,

214. Ibid., 46–47.
215. Ibid., 419.
216. Ibid., 62.
217. Ibid., 78–79.
218. Ibid., 400; portrayed as impotent (ibid., 380) and prone to temper tantrums, he is nicknamed "The Stink" because as a child he knocked over his chamber pot (ibid., 431).
219. Ibid., 418–419.
220. Ibid., 430–431.
221. Ibid., 420.
222. Ibid., 423; this may have suggested Hitler's henchman Alfred Rosenberg, assumed by many to be Jewish.

telling his colleagues: "Mussolini and Hitler said almost as much—and got away with it." Russia was "no longer a Christian country. That thing's not going on for ever. High time it was wound up . . . the old rubbish has to be cleared away."[223] The youthful Rud is against both pro- and anti-Semitism, advocating Jewish integration: "To hell with all this Jew-consciousness, either way! . . . Smash up the Ghetto and let them run."[224] But as in real life, Jews under threat converted and kept flowing into the "Neo-Christian" movement. Rud thunders: "It's that damned Bible, with its Chosen People poison. Isaiah was the first and the worst of all the Nazis!" He maintains that until the Bible was "stamped out and forgotten," Jews and Christians would "coagulate and re-coagulate about it."[225] This leads to Rud's pogrom, and his sympathetically portrayed colleagues are in agreement with his aims if not his method.[226]

The Holy Terror, like all Wells' non-fiction, reflected his philosophy, and, although Wells differentiates between Rud's anti-Semitism and Hitler's ("It was not the Jewish race [Rud] hated, it was the Jewish idea"),[227] it came to the same thing, as Rud demonstrates: "Why do they go on being Jews at all *now*? . . . All through history the Jew has been hunted like a dog with the Bible tied like an old tin can to his tail." Rud discusses the Jews "with Gentiles who were interested in them," but "most" of these "disliked them," since, "for a modern intelligence to be interested in Jewish particularism without a resentful irritation" was quite unreasonable:

> Gradually the conviction grew upon him that all Jewry constituted a conspiracy, though it was never quite clear in his mind what the conspiracy was about. . . . It was impossible to believe that they were still genuinely worried about the Exodus from Egypt or the Captivity or the destruction of Jerusalem. Yet still they seemed to brood and wail over these things and bear a grudge against the Gentiles on account of them.[228]

Wells disapproves of Rud's pogrom, but believes that the Jews "caused" it by clinging to their identity and exploiting the history of anti-Semitism to deflect criticism.

Although it satirizes dictators in superficial ways, *The Holy Terror* approves of the World State dictatorship, fantasizing about how an English dictator could succeed.[229] Above all it shows the World State emerging from the age of

223. Ibid., 207.
224. Ibid., 178.
225. Ibid., 419.
226. Ibid., 396.
227. Ibid., 422.
228. Ibid., 418–419.
229. For example, by emphasizing common bonds among English speakers and avoiding the wearing of colored shirts (ibid., 49).

dictators, as Carstall opines: "A dictator ... seems to be necessary whenever there is a broad readjustment of human relationships." It was "necessary," he maintained, for "a major power system" to "destroy any minor power system that preceded the readjustment or arose out of it. Hence there must be a dictatorship. But no dictatorship can go on indefinitely." Lenin, he said, "saw far beyond anyone else" these "inevitable phases" following a revolution, but there was "no earthly reason whatever for another Dictator in the world—none. Not for centuries."[230] Dictators were necessary because ordinary men were inadequate for the task of imposing the World State: "[W]e hadn't the courage and honesty. *He* was needed somehow to make it real."[231] In fact Rud rose to power dishonestly, for while the common people wanted "The Group" to bring order out of chaos, "The Group" sees the chaos as bringing about a new world order. Wells' "happy ending" has Carstall killing Rud for the sake of the World State: "it was amazing but true; he has destroyed so much, so many irritating boundaries, so many poisonous traditions, that he has united the world unawares."[232] Initially the book appears to be a warning against the danger of populists, but Rud uses their rhetoric to usher in Wells' internationalist utopia, steering a course between Darwinian "inevitability" politics and the politics of free will—revolution. Rud is manipulated but also manipulating.[233] Ancient institutions crumble and fall at a touch, with "The Group"—all administrators and technocrats—ready to take over the world for its own good, destroying the "irritating boundaries" that Chesterton defended.

In *The Holy Terror*, predicting the future while purporting to record the past, Wells describes how British fascist marches "had a diminishingly irritating effect, in Jewish districts," finally petering out[234] because communists found ridicule a more effective response than "indignation and violence."[235] In fact the fascist marches were curtailed by The Public Order Act (1936), introduced as a response to the violence they provoked. Wells also says that British marines shot American strikers in South Carolina;[236] that Germany and Italy were "just as sick" of their governments as any other country;[237] and that Hitler retired "to some remote hunting-lodge."[238] Air transport led to "the entire world ... com-

230. Ibid., 428–429.

231. Ibid., 440.

232. Ibid., 429–430.

233. Bodisham "nodded approval [of Rud's lecture] ... and tried not to look like a teacher hearing a recitation" (ibid., 244).

234. Ibid., 116.

235. Ibid., 139.

236. Ibid., 134.

237. Ibid., 221–222.

238. Ibid., 241.

ing into step as one community." Mutiny was everywhere, with "clear evidence as early as 1939" that the German army leaders dared not discipline their troops.[239] "The Last War on Earth, the second War to End War" was, Wells says, "a huge, ill-managed tangle of conflicts which began informally and did not so much end as peter out."[240] Once again, with relish Wells recounts how "the masses" met their fate: "[P]eople ran this way and that, clapped on silly gas masks and crowded out inadequate shelters until they were squashed or smashed or suffocated or starved, many millions of living, feeling human beings . . . converted into red pulps and messes."[241] But as Rud tells "The Group," the longer the war lasted, "the better for the New World. From our point of view the war to end war can have no formal end."[242] Finally he is quietly murdered and his body embalmed like Lenin's as an object of secular veneration for the Common Man, his posthumous reputation preserved in hagiographies for children.[243]

The real War did intrude into Wells' last novel *You Can't Be Too Careful*, published in 1941. The usual mix of fact and fiction, prediction and wishful thinking, its hero is another of Wells' "little men." But Edward Albert Tewler remains a little man, failing to break out of his narrow suburban, lower middle class world. He wins the George Cross, but by accident.[244] Like his equally narrow, ignorant, complacent neighbors in Morningside Prospect, Tewler is influenced by the conspiracy theories of Nesta Webster, *The Protocols of the Elders of Zion*, and anti-Bolshevik propaganda,[245] and even sympathizes with Hitler and Mussolini. Wells mocks their anti-Semitism[246] and dismisses their conspiracy theories: "Admittedly the Jews are tactless and vain and clannish, but that after all is the worst that can be said about the worst of them. The most they did was to irritate. The great Jewish conspiracy is and always has been a fantasy." He also rebuts claims that "international finance was essentially Jewish. It is not. It is less so than ever it was." Once again, in his youth, Wells' "specimen Englishman" was "practically unaware of contemporary Jews," thinking that "they were a disagreeable lot of people in the Bible whom even God had had to give up at last, and that had been the end of them." Tewler had "never perceived any distinctive difference" about Jews—if they were "so different you ought to be able

---

239. Ibid., 264–266.
240. Ibid., 268.
241. Ibid., 271.
242. Ibid., 281.
243. Ibid., 446.
244. H. G. Wells, *You Can't Be Too Careful: A Sample of Life 1901–1951* (London: Secker & Warburg, 1941/1941), 255–261.
245. Ibid., 238–239.
246. Ibid., 242.

to tell."[247] Chesterton's fiction reflected his theory of nationality, under which Jews were recognizably different. Wells' fiction reflected his belief in cosmopolitanism, under which Jews were not recognizably different from non-Jews.[248]

Wells reiterated his complaint about the "bright young men of the Armenoid type" who "set up as 'champions' for their 'people,' to revive the sense of being downtrodden if it threatens to wane and insist upon a preferential association. Jew must help Jew." Wells adds that after the Great War, "professional Jewish 'champions' set themselves with particular energy to inflame this racial segregation in every possible way," ignoring "as blatantly as possible" the world state idea. Instead of progressing to "a new world," they "headed their 'people' for Zion." Wells claimed:

> No public man, no writer, no journalist could go anywhere without having the Jewish Problem thrust into his face as though it was the one supreme interest of mankind. He was threatened implicitly or explicitly with boycotts and mischief if he refused his appointed rôle as a Gideonite, a hewer of wood and a drawer of water for the Great Race. The mildest, most broadminded of humanitarians found themselves provoked into saying, 'Oh, *damn* those Jews!'[249]

Wells was impatient for Jewish talents, not least the talent for survival, to infuse the non-Jewish world, which remained stubbornly *Homo Tewler*: "If the Tewlers are timid and disingenuous fools by education and enslavement rather than by birth, there may be hope for them."[250] In Russia, in contrast, the invading Nazis found "for the first time . . . a people who had divested themselves of their Morningside encumbrance." Wells' predictions had failed dismally, but he continued to dismiss the Nazi threat: "Nobody had planned this [war]." There was "no sign in *Mein Kampf* of any realisation on the part of Rudolf Hess and Adolf Hitler that they had fired a limitless mine." They "felt they were brilliant cynical lads who had taken the world by surprise," but "modern warfare took them by surprise. By 1941 they were as helplessly anxious as everybody else to put out the fire again and crawl away with any loot they could lay their hands on."[251]

Having dismissed the Nazi threat, Wells insisted that the "Roman Catholic Church" was "the most evil thing in the whole world." Its "shameless symbol" was "Jesus the Son of Man, drooping, crucified and done for."[252] Having

247. Ibid., 236–238.
248. See Chapter Seven.
249. H.G. Wells, *You Can't Be Too Careful*, op. cit., 237–238; the "Armenoid," a Caucasian sub-race, is found throughout Eurasia, its greatest concentrations in Asia Minor.
250. Ibid., 247.
251. Ibid., 244–245.
252. Ibid., 268.

blamed anti-Semitism on the Jews, Wells blamed anti-Catholic persecution on the Church: "Wherever the Catholic Church has been in complete control of education, the final outcome has been a revolution at once bloodthirsty and blasphemous."[253] Wells' "loyal but anxious publishers" begged him to invest Tewler with "some flash of real nobility," but he refused. Tewler, he said, was "not so much detestable as pitiful," and "to every reader without exception" he said: "This means you.... You are Tewler and I am Tewler."[254] Despite the Nazis' reversal of civilized norms in the trampling of the weak by the strong, Wells ends on a disturbingly Nietzschean note. The human beings of the future, he said, "may be good by our current orientation of things; they may be evil. Why should they not be in the nature of our good and much more than our good—'beyond good and evil'?"[255] In belittling the English and dismissing the Nazi threat, the book could hardly have helped the war effort, and although it rejected conspiracy theories and "Jewish financial power" it continued to blame anti-Jewish persecution on "the Jews." Most importantly Wells failed to face up to the implications of his Utopian World State: it could work with Nazism, fascism, or Bolshevism, but it could never work while the Jews remained Jews.

Wells and "Race"

Cheyette notes Shaw's "ambivalent self-identification with 'the Jew,'" but that Wells "scientifically" applied the "logic" of Shaw's eugenic evolutionary beliefs to project a perfect society in which Jewish "racial difference" was "eliminated." Even though assimilated, in the Wellsian Utopia Jews would still be able to prefigure a "socialist world state." Wells' fiction, unlike his Utopias, "invariably constructed semitic racial difference" as embodying "a disorderly capitalist plutocracy" and, as seen, between the Wars, Shaw and Wells associated Jews with those elements that were holding back society.[256] Cheyette further notes that while both were influenced by Samuel Butler's utopian *Erewhon* (1872), which speculated that the Erewhonians were the ten lost tribes of Israel,[257] *You Can't be Too Careful* reinforced Wells' later view of the selfishness of Zionism in contrast to his earlier, more open stance.[258] In 1906 the *Jewish Chronicle* reported Wells' response to Israel Zangwill's letter to prominent individuals regarding a Jewish homeland: "The [Jewish Territorial Organization] has my sympathy—in

253. Ibid., 278.

254. Ibid., 285–286.

255. Ibid., 293.

256. B. Cheyette, *Constructions of "the Jew" in English literature and society: Racial representations, 1875–1945* (Cambridge: Cambridge University Press, 1997), 95.

257. Ibid., 126.

258. Ibid., 143; see Chapter Five.

the abstract—and the project seems altogether sane and practicable. But it's not my doorstep, and I can offer you neither help nor advice. Your people are rich enough, able enough, and potent enough to save themselves."[259] Much later, Wells displayed increasing impatience with the idea of Jewish "difference" until by the Second World War he could describe the Communist Manifesto of Karl Marx, "son of a rabbi," as "pure Nazi teaching of the 1933–8 vintage."[260]

Wells struggled to harmonize his belief in the equality of Man with the Darwinist view of the inequality of Man. He denied that Jews were in any way special, yet he wanted their superior qualities to enhance the genetic brew of non-Jewish humanity. Chesterton used some of his Jewish characters to illustrate their negative, "foreign" influence on England, as did Wells, and thus both could be seen as using "the Jews" as scapegoats for the ills of English society. In his belief in superior Jewish qualities and in suggesting that they had digressed from more noble pathways, like Shaw and Chesterton, Wells hinted at a Jewish "dual image." But his rejection of religion made him a prisoner of his own universalism, forcing him to reject the notion of a distinctive Jewish people. Ironically, the atheist Wells was advocating the Christian approach, for as St. Paul told the Ephesians, Christ's purpose in "restoring peace" between Jew and Gentile was "to create a single New Man out of the two of them."[261]

Wells and Chesterton

Gilbert Chesterton and his brother Cecil enjoyed playing the riotous games for which Wells was famed, and this side of Wells undoubtedly appealed to Chesterton, whose wife also visited the Wells household.[262] The two writers' early correspondence is full of mutual admiration, though it came to be tinged with mockery on Wells' part ("You write wonderful praise and it leaves me all aquiver").[263] Wells supported *The New Witness* over the Marconi affair, attacked Herbert Samuel "incessantly,"[264] and supplied the *Witness* papers with

259. "'Amen!' Is Mr. Zangwill's laconic comment" (*Jewish Chronicle*, March 30, 1906, 33); see Chapter Seven.

260. H.G. Wells, *The Outlook for Homo Sapiens: An unemotional Statement of the Things that are happening to him now, and of the immediate Possibilities Confronting Him* (London: Secker & Warburg, 1942), 196; in this book, an "amalgamation and modernization" of *The Fate of Homo Sapiens* (1939) and *The New World Order* (1940) Wells stated: "All these considerations, I wrote them in 1939 and I see no reason to amend them" (ibid., 113).

261. Ephesians 2:11–18.

262. Frances "thought Wells was good for Gilbert" because he took him for walks, although Gilbert came to dread the enforced exercise (M. Ward, *Gilbert Keith Chesterton*, op. cit., 376–379).

263. H.G. Wells, Letter (undated), M. Ward, *Gilbert Keith Chesterton*, op. cit., 605.

264. M. Coren, *The Invisible Man: The Life and Liberties of H.G. Wells*, op. cit., 214–215; the leading Fabians, including Cecil Chesterton and the "'semi–detached Fabian' H.G. Wells" supported the

free articles.[265] A political minority, left-wing writers developed a siege mentality and formed defensive alliances. Gilbert asked Wells' help in defending a court case brought by Lever Brothers,[266] and Chesterton and Shaw defended Wells' *Ann Veronica* (1909) against allegations of immorality. Its heroine articulated Wellsian feminism—the need for women's education and employment— but caused scandal because she propositioned her married professor.[267]

In the 1920s, however, with Chesterton's growing advocacy of Distributism, Shaw and Wells "would still write for G.K., but only because he was their friend."[268] Chesterton's friendship with Wells, though "exceedingly cordial," was "occasionally threatened by explosions from Wells. Gilbert's soft answer however invariably turned away wrath." Wells claimed: "No one ... ever had enmity for him except some literary men who did not know him."[269] During the War Wells raged about a *New Witness* review of a friend's book,[270] but later apologized because he knew Chesterton was not responsible for his brother Cecil's comments.[271] Wells knew this because Chesterton had informed him of the review, and, in fact, had apologized first, or at least tried to smooth things over. Chesterton writes:

> Most certainly you have always been a good friend to me. . . . I know enough of your good qualities in other ways to put down everything in your last letter to an emotion of loyalty to another friend. Any quarrel between us will not come from me. . . . Don't you sometimes find it convenient, even in my case, that your friends are less touchy than you are? By all means drop any paper you dislike, though if you do it for every book review you think unfair, I fear your admirable range of modern knowledge will be narrowed.[272]

Boer War (M. Ward, *Gilbert Keith Chesterton*, op. cit., 125); Wells and Cecil contributed to a long debate in the *New Age* about joining political parties (D.C. Smith, *H.G. Wells: Desperately Mortal: A Biography*, op. cit., 119–20).

265. Ibid., 256.

266. In a debate Gilbert had referred to their model industrial town Port Sunlight as "corresponding to a 'slave compound'"; he asked Wells for a "general sociological line of defence" based on the word "slavery," but Lever Brothers dropped the case, accepting his defence that he was not making a slanderous attack, so Wells was not called (M. Ward, *Gilbert Keith Chesterton*, op. cit., 373–376); "Mr. Lever" appears in a Father Brown story as a Jewish hotelier: see Chapter Three.

267. M. Coren, *The Invisible Man: The Life and Liberties of H.G. Wells*, op. cit., 86; Maurice Baring also praised it, comparing the work with Dostoevsky's (D.C. Smith, *H.G. Wells: Desperately Mortal: A Biography*, op. cit., 213).

268. M. Ward, *Gilbert Keith Chesterton*, op. cit., 503–504.

269. Ibid., 376.

270. "The whole outbreak is so envious, so base, so cat-in-the-gutter-spitting-at-the-passer-by, that I will never let the *New Witness* into the house again" (H.G. Wells, Letter [undated], M. Ward, *Gilbert Keith Chesterton*, op. cit., 411); for a full account of this episode see Chapter Six.

271. D.C. Smith, *H.G. Wells: Desperately Mortal: A Biography*, op. cit., 174–175.

272. G.K. Chesterton, Letter (undated), M. Ward, *Gilbert Keith Chesterton*, op. cit., 411–412.

Ward comments: "The others were apt to score off Wells in these exchanges because he lost light-heartedness and became irritable. Even with Gilbert he sometimes broke out, although in a calmer moment he told Shaw that to get angry with Chesterton was an impossibility."[273]

Though firm in his beliefs, Gilbert had a "marvelous ability not to take himself too seriously."[274] Even Wells the escapologist could not escape from the loyalty of Chesterton, and after the latter's death showed more generosity than he did to Shaw: "I never knew anyone so steadily true to form as G.K.C."[275] Loyalty was a defining feature of Chesterton's character, reinforced by the public school ethos that viewed with horror disloyalty to a friend, especially a guilty friend. Chesterton condemned libertarian theories but did not condemn Shaw when his private life did not match up to the Puritanism with which Chesterton was wont to tease him.[276] Shaw's "lapses," such as his philosophy of nudism, "never . . . invalidat[ed] respect or friendship."[277] Nudism was more than a philosophy to Shaw, who posed naked for photographers, but Chesterton claimed Shaw "really hates and despises Bohemianism; in the sense that he hates and despises disorder and uncleanness and irresponsibility."[278] Wells' private life would pose even more of a challenge to Chesterton's loyalty but their friendship survived even that.

Chesterton, Wells, and Shaw were united in their opposition to capitalism, and initially at least their differences went unnoticed by the public, who thought they shared the same philosophy. In fact, each referenced the others in their writings so frequently that their opponents objected: "In *The New Age* Shaw wrote about Belloc and Chesterton and so did Wells, while Chesterton wrote about Wells and Shaw, till the Philistines grew angry, called it self-advertisement and log-rolling and urged that a Bill for the abolition of Shaw and Chesterton should be introduced into Parliament."[279] Chesterton was solidly and unapologetically middle class,[280] while Wells, whose parents had escaped their working class origins by moving to the china shop, had in turn escaped

---

273. Ibid., 410.

274. G.K. Chesterton, *Chesterton on War and Peace: Battling the Ideas and Movements That Led to Nazism and World War II*, Michael W. Perry, ed. (Seattle: Inkling Books, 2008), 381–382, note 91.

275. M. Ward, *Gilbert Keith Chesterton*, op. cit., 435.

276. See: Sally Peters, *Bernard Shaw: The Ascent of the Superman* (Yale University Press: New Haven/London, 1996).

277. G.K. Chesterton, *George Bernard Shaw*, op. cit., 281–282.

278. Ibid., 83.

279. M. Ward, *Gilbert Keith Chesterton*, op. cit., 196–197.

280. Shaw was also middle-class, but at a public lecture a "working-man Socialist" maintained: "'I'll tell you wot the matter is with Mr. Chesterton . . . Mr. Chesterton is *Middle Class*.'" Chesterton at once responded "'clapping his hands and repeating: 'Hear, hear!'" (M. Ward, *Return to Chesterton*, op. cit., 128).

the lower middle classes by achieving literary fame. Chesterton looked to the working classes to overthrow capitalism, but Wells saw revolution coming from people like him: "These are the only brains to which we can look for creative drive." In fact: "For the purposes of revolutionary theory the rest of humanity matters only as the texture of mud matters when we design a steam dredger to keep a channel clear."[281] Wells agreed with Marx on little else except his view that a movement to reconstruct society was unlikely to receive "the immediate enthusiastic support of the majority."[282] Whereas most Marxists, and Chesterton, continued to cherish the hope of a peasants' revolt, Wells' concern was how to create the conditions for a revolution that would usher in his Utopia: "One is forced to admit that in periods of tolerable general prosperity . . . or stabilized repression . . . there is little hope for direct revolutionary effort."[283] There was little hope of revolt from the more comfortable classes, who had most to lose, but also the less comfortable who aspired to climb the capitalist ladders of success. Wells thought Clarence Darrow and his American humanist colleagues were sentimental anarchists for supporting the "imaginary 'little man'" against the monopolists.[284] To Chesterton the "little man" was far from imaginary. He thought that the philosophies of Shaw and Wells represented "not a heaven on earth . . . but a kind of final hell to be avoided, since it banished all freedom and human responsibility."[285]

Wells' non-fiction, which will be fully explored in the next chapter, is crucial to an understanding of his fiction and to his friendship with Chesterton: *Modern Utopia* (1905) projects not a classless society, but a society of new classes, with the "Dull" and "Base" at the bottom.[286] In Chesterton's Distributist utopia there would be a restoration of property to the people at the bottom, thus providing a stable foundation, but *Anticipations* saw the World State as the only viable form of government.[287] In Wells' socialist Utopia failures would be crushed, starved, or overwhelmed, with the help of Nature and an elite class of "Samurai"; inferior races would be exterminated, directly or indirectly; as to the survivors, no aspect of life—marriage, diet, recreation, clothing—would escape the zeal of Wells' controlling classes, a glamorized version of the bureaucratic English middle classes, thinly disguised.[288]

281. H.G. Wells, *Experiment in Autobiography: Discoveries and conclusions of a very ordinary brain (since 1866) Vol. II* (London: Victor Gollancz Ltd., 1934), 735.

282. Ibid., 730.

283. Ibid., 732.

284. Ibid., 787.

285. M. Ward, *Gilbert Keith Chesterton*, op. cit., 196.

286. M. Coren, *The Invisible Man: The Life and Liberties of H.G. Wells*, op. cit., 75–76.

287. Ibid., 71.

288. Ibid., 76–77.

These differences on social policy are important because it was the effect of such philosophies on the family that helped Chesterton revisit his views on the "Jewish question." Wells later explained: "The spreading knowledge of birth-control . . . seemed to justify my contention that love was now to be taken more lightly than it had been in the past. It was to be refreshment and invigoration, as set out quite plainly in my Modern Utopia."[289] The "knowledge of birth-control" had not prevented the appearance of Wells' illegitimate children; therefore it seemed that Chesterton had a better grasp of reality and the nature of man than Wells, who clung to the belief that birth control would solve the problems of "free love." His advocacy of legal abortion subject to woman's choice suggests a belief in real freedom, but since women would be dependent on the state rather than individual men, it meant state control of reproduction, espoused by Wells under Plato's influence, because "[i]n a world where pressure upon the means of subsistence was a normal condition of life, it was necessary to compensate for the removal of traditional sexual restraints"; hence the support in *Anticipations* for "the propaganda of the Neo-Malthusians." Wells said he continued his advocacy "in a period when Neo-Malthusianism was by no means the respectable movement it has since become."[290] In fact the Neo-Malthusian movement was still controversial,[291] but unlike Shaw, who rebuffed the abortion movement,[292] Wells supported abortion, birth control, and euthanasia.[293]

Regarding Neo-Malthusianism, Wells' biographer, David.C. Smith, claims that Wells was "a friend and advocate of this aspect of female emancipation. His stand of course attracted the attention of radical feminists of the time."[294] Contrary to Smith's claims, the vast majority of feminists ignored or actively repudiated the birth control movement[295] for the very reason that Wells' lifestyle

289. H.G. Wells, *Experiment in Autobiography Vol. II*, op. cit., 436.

290. As Plato had found before him, "propagation of more and franker and healthier love-making was not . . . a simple proposition. It carried with it certain qualifying conditions" (ibid., 475).

291. The Neo-Malthusian movement, which arose in the late 19th century, promoted the philosophy of T.R. Malthus, but not his insistence on sexual restraint, arguing that celibacy was physically dangerous and that birth control was the answer to poverty; their campaign failed with the poor because it was perceived as offensive as well as anti-working class; see: R. Soloway, *Birth Control and the Population Question in England 1877–1930* (Chapel Hill: University of North Carolina Press, 1982).

292. G.B. Shaw, *Bernard Shaw: Collected Letters 1926–1950 Vol. IV*, op. cit., 237–238.

293. A. Farmer, *By Their Fruits: Eugenics, Population Control and the Abortion Campaign* (Washington DC: Catholic University of America Press), 259.

294. D.C. Smith, *H.G. Wells: Desperately Mortal: A Biography*, op. cit., 366–367.

295. Smith notes Wells' political differences with the right wing Malthusian C.V. Drysdale (ibid., 365–366); Stella Browne, Drysdale's Malthusian colleague, was an exception to the feminist rule; A. Farmer, *By Their Fruits: Eugenics, Population Control and the Abortion Campaign*, op. cit., 95–100.

illustrated: his first concern was the emancipation of men from the fear of pregnancy.[296] For Wells, abortion was the necessary back-up for contraceptive failure. When his mistress Rebecca West became pregnant, Wells tried to persuade her to abort their child, but she refused.[297] The affair was kept quiet, but in his *Experiment in Autobiography* (1934) he admitted to certain indiscretions, alluded to in his fiction, including going "furtively and discreetly" with a prostitute. In this connection, moreover, he revealed attitudes on race that owed more to exploitation than equality.[298] Soon after marrying he had a brief encounter with another woman: "Sentimentally and 'morally' [a] quite shocking incident to relate [but] in truth . . . the most natural thing in the world." Swiftly estranged from his wife, he "meant to get in all the minor and incidental love adventures" he could.[299]

This was not a provocative novel, or a theory, the kind Chesterton dismissed with the socialist argument that birth control was a right-wing plot to control the numbers of the poor, or the result of philosophical pessimism.[300] But when Chesterton launched an unsparing attack it was on Aldous Huxley's *Brave New World*. His Utopia, Chesterton alleged, was a "horrible human, or inhuman, hive," a "base world, and a filthy world, and a fundamentally unhappy world," although, admittedly "[i]t would need some courage, and even some self-sacri-

---

296. A. Farmer, *Prophets and Priests: The Hidden Face of the Birth Control Movement* (London: The Saint Austin Press, 2002), 18–19. Wells "remained loyal to those who had helped him satisfy his physical wants," supplying material help when asked (D.C. Smith, *H. G. Wells: Desperately Mortal: A Biography*, op. cit., 365).

297. Anthony West, *H. G. Wells: Aspects of a Life* (London: Hutchinson & Co. Ltd., 1984), 19.

298. H. G. Wells, *Experiment in Autobiography Vol. II*, op. cit., 421; according to suppressed material from his autobiography, later published as *H. G. Wells in Love* (1984) he "[o]ccasionally . . . did resort to professionals, but these incidents were very limited in number. There were always younger women about" (D.C. Smith, *H. G. Wells: Desperately Mortal: A Biography*, op. cit., 197); visiting President Roosevelt in 1906, Wells asked to be taken to a "'gay house'": "This was before the moral purgation of Washington. 'White or Coon?' [the cabdriver] said. It seemed to me that I ought to experience the local colour at its intensest. 'Coon,' said I" (H.G. Wells, *H. G. Wells in Love: Postscript to an Experiment in Autobiography*, G.P. Wells, ed. [London: Faber & Faber, 1984], 64–65); the reminiscences were not published in 1934 mainly because "a number of people who were still living . . . were bound to be affected very seriously by a public analysis of the rôles they played in my life" (ibid., 52).

299. H.G. Wells, *Experiment in Autobiography Vol. II*, op. cit., 423–424.

300. Birth Control, supposedly "a social reform that goes along with other social reforms favoured by progressive people," was in fact a "piece of mere pessimism, opposing itself to the more optimistic notion that something can be done for the whole family of man. . . . The old oligarchs would use any tool against the new democrats; and one day it was their dismal good luck to get hold of a tool called Malthus" whose argument was "an argument against all social reform" (G. K. Chesterton, "Social Reform versus Birth Control," *Brave New Family: G.K. Chesterton on Men and Women, Children, Sex, Divorce, Marriage and the Family*, A. de Silva, ed. [San Francisco: Ignatius Press, 1990], 193–194).

fice, to establish anything so utterly disgusting as that."[301] Huxley was describing a "voluntary" Totalitarianism in which people would "love their servitude," and Chesterton believed he was certainly brave in satirizing the Utopias of people like Wells, for in a clever mix of Darwinism and Nietzschean will-to-power, Wells assured his readers that the eugenic future would "happen anyway," while he urged his more committed followers to make it happen. Posing as a disinterested prophet absolved him from criticism for his views. The public thought Wells was seeing into the future when he was describing what he wanted to happen, and through his writings was helping to make happen by destroying what Chesterton saw as society's and democracy's foundation—the family. Huxley supported eugenics and population control,[302] but he pulled aside the veil of ambivalence that encouraged people to believe that Wells was simply predicting what would happen "if things did not change." Chesterton claimed that the "same work" that Huxley described was being accomplished by capitalism, which had "destroyed the Family in the modern world"; it was "being done in other worlds that are not particularly new, and not in the least brave," because there were:

> [P]eople of another sort, much more common and conventional, who are not only working to create such a paradise of cowardice, but who actually try to work for it through a conspiracy of cowards. The attitude of these people towards the Family and the tradition of its Christian virtues is the attitude of men willing to wound and yet afraid to strike; or ready to sap and mine so long as they are not called upon to fire or fight in the open.[303]

And yet capitalism was not deliberately undermining the family, despite collateral damage caused by its pursuit of profit; the deliberate policy Chesterton described was eulogized by Wells in *The Shape of Things to Come*, published a year before Chesterton's attack on Huxley. But Chesterton also referred to "the

301. G.K. Chesterton, "Three Foes of the Family," *The Well and the Shallows* (London: Sheed & Ward, 1935), 147–148 (originally published August 2, 1934); "I would as soon die as live in such a Utopia in a life so dead within"; its citizens would live "without any soul to save, without any honour to defend, without any affection or memory ... seasoned only with their horrible mechanical sexuality, artificially sterilised and isolated from every generous and creative risk or purpose" (G.K. Chesterton, "Queries on Fascism [III]," *G.K.'s Weekly*, July 19, 1934, 312–313).

302. In the 1958 edition Huxley wrote that "babies in bottles and the centralized control of reproduction" were "not perhaps impossible" but that "[f]or practical purposes, genetic standardization may be ruled out" (A. Huxley, *Brave New World Revisited* [New York: Harper Perennial, 1932/2005], 239); "overpopulation" was a grave problem but birth control "must be practiced by countless individuals, from whom it demands more intelligence and will power than most of the world's teeming illiterates possess" (ibid., 241); nonetheless Huxley's book helped deter people from Wells' Utopian ideas (H.G. Wells, *The Outlook for Homo Sapiens*, op. cit., 167).

303. G.K. Chesterton, "Three Foes of the Family," *The Well and the Shallows*, op. cit., 148.

Brave New World which Mr. Aldous Huxley described with detestation" and "the New Utopia which Mr. H. G. Wells described with delight."[304] Wells' Open Conspiracy was meant to rescue humanity from "the net of tradition in which it was entangled,"[305] and he claimed that his "Why not?" campaign had helped release "a generation from restriction."[306] If the family managed to survive capitalism, however, it would be fatally damaged from within as its members asked "why not" adultery, divorce, and cohabitation; and then, "why children." If it came to conspiracies of cowardice, Wells admitted privately that *Anticipations* was "'designed to undermine and destroy the monarch, monogamy and respectability'" although he thought it advisable to "go quietly" at first.[307] Publicly and much later, he admitted that his 1906 plea for family endowments was "advocating . . . what is plainly a correlative of the break-up of the family." While acknowledging that "fatherly influence and . . . eugenics" should be considered when paying family allowances to mothers,[308] the "paradox" of socialism (as he saw it) was in emphasizing economic collectivism but sexual individualism:[309] "[T]o the very great dismay of the strategists and tacticians of the Fabian Society, and to the immense embarrassment of the Labour Party societies, I began to blurt out these ideas and attempt to sexualise socialism."[310] Whether the embarrassment was caused by the ideas themselves or by the implication that people should be treated like commodities, a charge often leveled against capitalism, it led "the wolves to howl after Wells' scalp." He responded: "[T]o say it is my dictum that the ultimate goal of socialism is free love is an outrageous lie."[311]

In contrast to Chesterton's chivalrous approach based on the Judeo-Christian view of the family, the chief role of women in Wells' Utopia was to be promiscuous without endangering the race or increasing the population.[312] In his

---

304. G. K. Chesterton, "When the World Turned Back" (ibid., 33).

305. H. G. Wells, *Experiment in Autobiography Vol. II*, op. cit., 643; *The Open Conspiracy*, revised between 1928 and 1933, was a re-presentation of Wells' World State idea (*The Open Conspiracy and Other Writings* [London: no publisher, 1933]).

306. H. G. Wells, *Experiment in Autobiography Vol. II*, op. cit., 467.

307. Arthur Conan Doyle detested the book (M. Coren, *The Invisible Man: The Life and Liberties of H. G. Wells*, op. cit., 67–68).

308. In "Socialism and the Middle Classes" Wells stated that the institution of marriage was "no more permanent than competitive industrialism"; "Socialism and the Family" was "more discreet" (H. G. Wells, Papers read to the Fabian Society, October 1906, *Industrial Review*, 1906, in H. G. Wells, *Experiment in Autobiography Vol. II*, op. cit., 478–479).

309. Ibid., 470.

310. Ibid., 476–477.

311. *Daily Express*, September 19, 1906, in D. C. Smith, *H. G. Wells: Desperately Mortal: A Biography*, op. cit., 208–209.

312. A considerable proportion of the Modern State "fellowship" was female (H. G. Wells, *The Shape of Things to Come: The Ultimate Revolution*, op. cit., 329).

fiction Wells increasingly blamed Judaism for women being treated like chattels, but his attitude to his own overburdened mother was one of pity tinged with contempt, describing her as "the unpaid servant of everybody."[313] The hero of *In the Days of the Comet* admits subjecting his mother to household drudgery and bad temper: "[W]ith the docility of a good servant, she went from me. Dear heart of submission that the world and I had used so ill!"[314] When a mysterious green vapor from outer space abolishes inconvenient emotions like jealousy, "free love" emerges: he "marries" a young woman then finds he still loves his former fiancée, who still loves him, but also loves another man. But it no longer matters, because in their "changed world love is unstinted; it is a golden net about our globe that nets all humanity together."[315] But free love came at a price for the women in Wells' life. He was unfaithful to both his wives and bullied the second, a "free love" feminist, who became his hostess, manager, and secretary, and even arbitrated between his lovers.[316] She changed her first name to please him[317] and agreed to tolerate his affairs.[318]

In contrast, Chesterton insisted that women were too good to work outside the home,[319] but in real life worked with women (all his secretaries were female, and he worked with his sister-in-law Ada in his journalistic ventures)[320] while warning of the potential exploitation of women in the workplace and the effects on children and on male employment.[321] Even differences in lifestyle

313. H. G. Wells, *Experiment in Autobiography: Discoveries and conclusions of a very ordinary brain (since 1866) Vol. I* (London: Faber & Faber, 1934/1984), 71.

314. H. G. Wells, *In the Days of the Comet* (1906) *The Complete Science Fiction Treasury of H. G. Wells*, op. cit., 761; Michael Foot says the story "painted an unforgettable portrait of the afflictions which had broken his mother" (introduction to H. G. Wells, *The New Machiavelli*, op. cit., xiv).

315. H. G. Wells, *In the Days of the Comet* (1906) *The Complete Science Fiction Treasury of H. G. Wells*, op. cit., 855.

316. M. Coren, *The Invisible Man: The Life and Liberties of H. G. Wells*, op. cit., 85.

317. Born Amy Catherine Robbins she was always called Jane by Wells (ibid., 55).

318. The "compromise" with Jane that "developed after 1900" meant he would have "passades"; not a "real love affair," a "passade" was "a stroke of mutual attraction that may happen to any couple" (H. G. Wells, *Experiment in Autobiography Vol. II*, op. cit., 465).

319. G. K. Chesterton, "The Modern Surrender of Woman," *What's Wrong with the World*, op. cit., 63; "His defense of keeping women in the home was more eloquent than most such arguments, simply because the home seemed to him a very exciting place" (M. Canovan, *G. K. C.: Radical Populist* [New York/London: Harcourt Brace Jovanovich, 1977], 54).

320. M. Ward, *Gilbert Keith Chesterton*, op. cit., 486.

321. G. K. Chesterton, "The Emancipation of Domesticity," *What's Wrong with the World*, op. cit., 54; "I remember my mother, the day that we met, / A thing I shall never entirely forget; / And I toy with the fancy that, young as I am, / I should know her again if we met in a tram / But mother is happy in turning a crank / That increases the balance at somebody's bank; / And I feel satisfaction that mother is free / From the sinister task of attending to me" (G. K. Chesterton, *Songs of Education: III. For the Crèche: Form 8277059, Sub-Section K, The Works of G. K. Chesterton* [Ware, Herts.: Wordsworth Poetry Library, 1995], 76–77).

could not break his and Wells' friendship, but in taking aim at Huxley's *Brave New World* Chesterton remarks, that as to being progressive, if it meant being "pro-Labour or generally pro-proletarian and anti-Capitalist" he had been that all his life, "often much more violently than Mr Wells." But the "Wellsean implication of differences dropping out and converts dropping in, and a floating accretion of different democrats or lovers of liberty" was "a dream." Chesterton agreed with Stalin and Wells that "sweated and starving people" should be "better paid," but the "abysses" between them were "not bridged by that alone, and are not likely to close very soon."[322]

At the root of such differences was religion, which would be a crucial factor in both authors' reappraisal of the "Jewish question." Wells was brought up on the simple anti-Catholicism of his mother but lost his religious belief at a young age, coming under the influence of Neo-Malthusian doctrine, with its emphasis on sex as part of nature, divorced from the social conventions but also from emotions and personal relationships.[323] His evolutionary beliefs were reflected in his intimate relationships, with their power struggles, bullying by the strong and submission of the weak.[324] But his attempts to justify his behavior in his fiction and non-fiction suggest a lingering guilt. He continued to project an image of the God he claimed not to believe in as a vengeful and deceitful potentate—an image shored up by incidents in which he appears to be looking for reasons not to believe. On hearing a Catholic lay preacher he felt "in the presence of a different, if parallel attack" on his "integrity" to that of "the God of Hell in his most Protestant form."[325]

Though attracted to the Catholic Church he refused to believe that anyone could really believe in it, and spent his life fighting against the "incredible and ugly lie" that the Church was "thrusting ... upon the world."[326] On a visit to Rome, like many an insular English person accustomed to the quaint ruins of the Reformation, he seemed struck by the size and scope of something that should have been broken down, outdated, and irrelevant: "Catholicism is something greater in scope and spirit than any nationalist protestantism and immeasurably above such loutish reversions to hate as Hitlerism or the Ku-Klux-Klan. I should even hesitate to call it 'reactionary' without some qualifica-

---

322. G. K. Chesterton, "Queries on Fascism (III)," *G. K.'s Weekly*, July 19, 1934, 312–313.

323. As a youth Wells bought the *Freethinker* and read the *Malthusian* (Wells, H. G., *Experiment in Autobiography Vol. I*, op. cit., 183).

324. M. Coren, *The Invisible Man: The Life and Liberties of H. G. Wells*, op. cit., 166–168.

325. H. G. Wells, *Experiment in Autobiography Vol. I*, op. cit., 164.

326. Wells had either to "come into this immense luminous coop and submit" or must "declare the Catholic Church, the core and substance of Christendom with all its divines, sages, saints and martyrs, with successive thousands of millions of believers, age after age, wrong" (ibid., 164–166).

tion."[327] During the Great War he published *God the Invisible King* (1917), a serious examination of the role of prayer in difficult times. It led to discussions with Israel Zangwill about Zionism and also "stirred up a stew of protest and congratulations" from believers and non-believers. But though he denied being an Atheist, it was a false dawn for those who hoped for a new, religious Wells.[328]

Long before this, however, his science fiction had appealed to Chesterton. *The Time Machine* draws a political lesson from the conditions of the subterranean Morlocks: "Even now, does not an East-end worker live in such artificial conditions as practically to be cut off from the natural surface of the earth?"[329] In *The Island of Dr. Moreau* Prendick concludes: "There is . . . a sense of infinite peace and protection in the glittering hosts of heaven. There it must be, I think, in the vast and eternal laws of matter, and not in the daily cares and sins and troubles of men, that whatever is more than animal within us must find its solace and its hope. I hope, or I could not live."[330] In *The War of the Worlds* the hero kills a cowardly, sniveling curate because his ranting threatens to alert the Martians to their hiding-place, but prays for his missing wife, and when the danger has passed, stands "weeping and praising God upon the summit of Primrose Hill."[331] In Chesterton, Wells saw a side of Christianity that disarmed his criticism, at least temporarily: "If after all my Atheology turns out wrong and your Theology right I feel I shall always be able to pass into Heaven (if I want to) as a friend of G.K.C.'s. Bless you."[332] In his earthly life at any rate, he seems not to have wanted to.[333]

327. "I have lived for many years in open controversy with Catholicism and though, naturally enough, I have sometimes been insulted by indignant zealots, I have found the ordinary Catholic controversialist a fair fighter and a civilized man—worthy of that great cultural system within which such minds as Leonardo and Michael Angelo could develop and find expression.... It is a question too fine for me to discuss whether I am an outright atheist or an extreme heretic on the furthest verge of Christendom—beyond the Aryans, beyond the Manicheans. But certainly I branch from the Catholic stem" (H. G. Wells, *Experiment in Autobiography Vol. II*, op. cit., 574); presumably he meant "Arians."

328. D. C. Smith, *H. G. Wells: Desperately Mortal: A Biography*, op. cit., 230–231; see Chapter Five.

329. H. G. Wells, *The Time Machine* (1895) *The Complete Science Fiction Treasury of H. G. Wells*, op. cit., 36.

330. H. G. Wells, *The Island of Dr. Moreau* (1896), ibid., 156.

331. H. G. Wells, *The War of the Worlds* (1898), ibid., 382.

332. H. G. Wells, Letter, December 10, 1933, M. Ward, *Gilbert Keith Chesterton*, op. cit., 604–605.

333. "The question 'Is this all?' has troubled countless unsatisfied minds throughout the ages, and, at the end of our tether, as it seems, here it is, still baffling but persistent" (H. G. Wells, *The Last Books of H. G. Wells: The Happy Turning and Mind at the End of its Tether*, G. P. Wells, ed. [London: H. G. Wells Society, 1945/1968], 74); Man might assure himself that "presently the old game will be resumed with all its present stresses gone like a dream," but before sufficiently awake to "tell that dream, of his world restored, he will have forgotten it and passed into nothingness forever" (ibid., 76).

Chesterton on Wells

While avoiding *ad hominem* attacks on Wells, Chesterton criticized the moral and philosophical underpinnings of his Utopias as naive in the extreme. In *Heretics* (1905) he challenges the claim that "medical supervision would produce strong and healthy men," since the "first act of the strong and healthy men would be to smash the medical supervision." In Wells' new Utopia "a chief point" would be "disbelief in original sin," but if Wells had "begun with the human soul—that is, if he had begun on himself," original sin would have been "almost the first thing to be believed in"—a "permanent possibility of selfishness" arose from the "mere fact of having a self, and not from any accidents of education or ill-treatment." Wells' mistake was "the weakness of all Utopias . . . that they take the greatest difficulty of man and assume it to be overcome, and then give an elaborate account of the overcoming of the smaller ones."[334] Wells' philosophy had abolished original sin, but his evolutionism emphasized the danger of man's regression to a more primitive state and his Utopias were planned to avoid any chance of sin's recrudescence.

Wells' technocratic solution to increasingly bloody war was the World State. To Chesterton this would be anti-democratic: the "real difficulty of representative government is how to make it representative, even in the smallest of small nationalities, even in the nearest parish council."[335] More fundamentally, Wells' "cosmopolitanism" indicated yet more "indifference to the human psychology" because unless you can "deliberately . . . prevent a thing being good, you cannot prevent it being worth fighting for." Wells' philosophy, in which there was "no being, but a universal becoming" undermined the very idea of philosophy because there were "no secure and reliable ideas upon which we can rest with a final mental satisfaction."[336] Wells' "hostility to the Platonic concept of truth as timeless" made his philosophy "a denial of the very possibility of philosophy."[337] So keen was he to abolish various aspects of reality that he would abolish reality itself.

Chesterton claimed that Wells, like Shaw, was on the side of the Giant rather than Jack, and could not see the paradox that only the weak could be brave; that only those who could be brave could be trusted in times of doubt: "[T]hat sympathy with the small or the defeated . . . with which we Liberals and Nationalists have been often reproached, is not a useless sentimentalism at all, as Mr.

334. G.K. Chesterton, "Mr. H.G. Wells and the Giants," *Heretics* (1905) *G.K. Chesterton Collected Works Vol. I*, op. cit., 76–77.

335. G.K. Chesterton, *Illustrated London News*, June 16, 1928.

336. G.K. Chesterton, *Heretics* (1905) in *G.K. Chesterton Collected Works Vol. I*, op. cit., 77–78.

337. A. Nichols, *G.K. Chesterton, Theologian*, op. cit., 49.

Wells and his friends fancy." Nonetheless, he believed that there was still hope for Wells. In contrast to Shaw, the Superman did not "bulk so large" in Wells' "cosmos."[338]

In the essay "Wells and the World State," in *What I Saw in America* (1922), Chesterton ridicules Wells' suggestion that the airplane would abolish nationalities as well as distance, and that greater closeness would bring greater harmony, as the existence of border warfare demonstrated.[339] Wells simply could not grasp "the question of despotism and democracy. I cannot understand any democrat not seeing the danger of so distant and indirect a system of government."[340] Wells' belief was not in democracy but in bureaucracy. In his sug-gestion of a committee to avoid tyranny, Wells implied that "the committee controlling the planet could meet almost without any one in the chair, certainly without any one on the throne." Internationalism was not necessarily incompatible with democracy "but any combination of the two" would be "a compromise between the two. . . . Given this difficulty about quite direct democracy over large areas, I think the nearest thing to democracy is despotism." Wells' internationalism was another form of imperialism, and that was subject to another influence: "The insufficiency of British Imperialism is that it is British; when it is not merely Jewish."[341] Jews were often regarded as cosmopolitan in outlook owing to their dispersal throughout the nations, but Chesterton's view of Wells as a cosmopolitan meant that he did not associate the idea solely with Jews in claiming that uniting England and America would "create . . . a cosmopolitan political platform . . . above our own heads to shut out the sunlight, on which only usurers and conspirators clad in gold could walk about in the sun."[342]

Despite such criticisms, Chesterton praised Wells "because he filled my youth with the fairy-tales of science, which are so much more delightful when you have really discovered that they are fairy-tales." Wells had also "interpreted the mind of the Englishman . . . turned by modern conditions into what has been called a Little Man" and brought out "in burning colours of reality . . . the fact that even that small man can also be great."[343] Chesterton said he would

---

338. G.K. Chesterton, *Heretics* (1905) *G. K. Chesterton Collected Works Vol. I*, op. cit., 80–82.

339. "We have been congratulating ourselves for centuries on having enjoyed peace because we were cut off from our neighbours. And now they are telling us that we shall only enjoy peace when we are joined up with our neighbours" (G.K. Chesterton, *What I Saw in America* [London: Hodder & Stoughton Ltd., 1922], 235–238).

340. Ibid., 240.

341. Ibid., 242–244; see Chapter Three.

342. In America slavery had been abolished but "commercial slavery" loomed, in the shape of the Servile State (ibid., 250–252).

343. G.K. Chesterton, "On the Fallacy of Eugenics," *Avowals and Denials* (1934), in G.K. Chesterton, *Brave New Family: G.K. Chesterton on Men & Women, Children, Sex, Divorce, Marriage & the Family*, op. cit., 201.

give Wells a medal as "the Eugenist who destroyed Eugenics" because *Mankind in the Making* had said that governing reproduction was an uncertain business.[344] *Mankind in the Making* had claimed that "the only tolerable stuff was the plain and simple squashing of 'Positive Eugenics,'"[345] but Wells' damning of "positive eugenics" was another way of championing negative eugenics, including euthanasia, which he never ceased to expound. Despite this, Chesterton said he would go to his "neglected pauper's grave continuing to praise, honour, and glorify the name of Mr. H.G. Wells," because it was he, rather than "us poor slaves of superstition, who long ago pointed out the gaping and ghastly scientific fallacy in almost all . . . of Eugenics and Heredity."[346] Chesterton concludes: "[T]here seems to be a queer revival of such things, a belated and benighted renascence of these fads I fancied were forgotten," and so it was "well to repeat our unanswered answer to the creed behind such barbarous tricks; for they are not confined to the curious commonwealth of Mr. Hitler."[347] Perhaps linking Hitler to the "revival" of eugenics in England was Chesterton's way of warning an old friend of the dangers of "barbarous tricks."

In his *Autobiography* (1936) Chesterton calls Wells "a sportive but spiritual child of Huxley"[348] who "reacted too swiftly to everything; possibly as a part of the swiftness of his natural genius." Chesterton "never ceased to admire and sympathise," but "[t]o use the name which would probably annoy him most, I think he is a permanent reactionary." Wells always "seemed to be coming from somewhere, rather than going anywhere"; he "always had been a Liberal, or . . . a Fabian, or . . . a friend of Henry James or Bernard Shaw. And he was so often nearly right, that his movements irritated me like the sight of somebody's hat being perpetually washed up by the sea and never touching the shore." Whereas Wells "thought that the object of opening the mind is simply opening the mind," Chesterton was "incurably convinced that the object of opening the mind, as of opening the mouth, is to shut it again on something solid."[349]

In contrast, Shaw, "unlike some whom I have had to consider here," was "seen at his best" when he was "antagonistic." In fact, Shaw was "seen at his best" when he was wrong: "I might also add that he generally is wrong. Or rather, everything is wrong about him except himself."[350] Chesterton had "[i]n

344. G.K. Chesterton, *Eugenics and Other Evils* (London: Cassell & Co., Ltd, 1922), 69–72.

345. H.G. Wells, *Experiment in Autobiography Vol. II*, op. cit., 656.

346. G.K. Chesterton, "On the Fallacy of Eugenics," *Avowals and Denials* (1934), in G.K. Chesterton, *Brave New Family: G.K. Chesterton on Men & Women, Children, Sex, Divorce, Marriage & the Family*, op. cit., 201–202.

347. Ibid., 204.

348. G.K. Chesterton, *Autobiography*, op. cit., 144.

349. Ibid., 229–230.

350. Ibid., 230–231.

most matters" been "rather more in sympathy with Mr. Bernard Shaw than with Mr. H. G. Wells, the other genius of the Fabians, warmly as I admire them both." But Wells' innocent side still appealed. He could understand "larking" much better than Shaw.[351]

Lauer claims Chesterton's biographies were brilliantly intuitive because his understanding of his subjects was based on "his self-understanding."[352] He wrote perceptively about Shaw but not Wells, suggesting that his psyche was a poor guide to the latter. Chesterton felt the romantic attraction of emotional commitment while Wells constantly tried to escape from it. Wells was unable to fully reveal his true personality, so deeply dissimilar to Chesterton's— although some of his more disreputable "larks" made their way into his own fiction—so that Chesterton was unable to read his soul.

The ChesterShaWells and the Chesterbelloc

Chesterton's friendship with Shaw and Wells was influenced by his friendship with the writer Hilaire Belloc, whose approach to the "Jewish question" will be explored in Chapter Six. While Chesterton had "a great esteem" for Wells, his esteem for Shaw was greater.[353] On his part, Wells preferred Chesterton to Belloc. While admiring the latter "beyond measure" Wells said there was "a sort of partisan viciousness about Belloc that bars him from my celestial dreams." Even before their celebrated quarrel Wells felt "the invisible presence of Belloc" hovering somewhere near Chesterton.[354] In 1922 Wells stood as a Liberal MP and the *Chesterbelloc*'s reactions "not only explain why Wells loved Chesterton and hated Belloc; they explain why a great many other people loved the one and heartily disliked the other." Chesterton, while wishing Wells "all possible luck," remarked: "The question is not whether Wells is fit for Parliament, but whether Parliament is fit for Wells. I don't think it is. If he had a good idea, the last place in the world where he would be allowed to talk is the House of Commons. He would do better to go on writing." Belloc, who also had a low opinion of Parliament, commented: "Of the effect of election upon Mr Wells' style I am not competent to pronounce. But in morals, temperament, instruction, and type of oratory, I know him to be admirably suited for the House of Commons." Belloc's quarrel with Wells "was a sundering quarrel indeed."[355] In his autobiography

351. Ibid., 238.
352. Q. Lauer, *G. K. Chesterton: Philosopher without Portfolio*, op. cit., 8.
353. M. Ward, *Gilbert Keith Chesterton*, op. cit., 209.
354. H. G. Wells, the *New Age*, in M. Ward, *Return to Chesterton*, op. cit., 58–59.
355. Robert Speaight, *The Life of Hilaire Belloc* (London: Hollis & Carter, 1957), 397–398.

Wells scarcely mentions his erstwhile friend,[356] although it was not unusual for him to lose friends along the way.[357] Ward noted: "Chesterton . . . speaks of Wells as 'the fairest man in England' but he feels about both him and Shaw a fundamental bleakness in their outlook on humanity. Temperamentally, he sees Shaw as more akin to Belloc, Wells to himself." Chesterton remarked: "Mr. Belloc expresses fiercely and I express gently a respect for mankind. Mr. Shaw expresses fiercely and Mr. Wells expresses gently a contempt for mankind."[358]

Chesterton opposed philosophies that aimed to alter Man to fit his environment, rather than the other way around, and remained grateful for such warning visions as the "inhuman hybrids and half-human experiments" of Wells' *Island of Dr. Moreau*, creatures which could be bred by "a successful class and almost solely in their interests."[359]

His intense loyalty to such fictional exposés and his personal liking were sufficient to overcome any disquiet about Wells' libertarianism, but that libertarianism was underpinned by Wells' view of history. This caused yet more tension between the two friends as Wells and Hilaire Belloc embarked on a long-drawn out war over Wells' *Outline of History*. Belloc accused Wells of failing to mention scientific disagreements about Darwin's theory of evolution. The feud "brought Wells to his knees, and . . . he never fully recovered."[360] Wells approached Chesterton, who declined to interfere. Wells' plea for a truce only encouraged Belloc, who scented victory. A further appeal to Chesterton to "act as an umpire or mediator" provoked Belloc into insisting that he would accept only "contrition and apology."[361] Chesterton avoided taking sides but hosted a victory party for Belloc at his own home.[362] In 1935 he referred obliquely to Wells' role in the controversy.[363] Regarding Shaw's and Wells' argument over vivisection, Chesterton agreed with Shaw's moral view of science, but "refused

---

356. H.G. Wells, *Experiment in Autobiography Vol. II*, op. cit., 823; Wells' son Anthony West described it as "half novel and half what its title claims it to be" (A. West, *H. G. Wells: Aspects of a Life*, op. cit., 132).

357. M. Coren, *The Invisible Man: The Life and Liberties of H. G. Wells*, op. cit., 96–104; Wells fell out most notably with Henry James (D.C. Smith, *H. G. Wells: Desperately Mortal: A Biography*, op. cit., 151–176).

358. G.K. Chesterton, the *New Age*, in M. Ward, *Return to Chesterton*, op. cit., 59.

359. G.K. Chesterton, "The Empire of the Insects," *What's Wrong with the World*, op. cit., 110–111.

360. M. Coren, *The Invisible Man: The Life and Liberties of H. G. Wells*, op. cit., 158.

361. Wells eventually took an "impossible to know exactly" approach to the argument (ibid., 163–167).

362. Ibid., 169.

363. Regarding Sir Arthur Keith's intervention in the controversy Chesterton says he had apparently "never even heard" of an important work to which Belloc had referred: "Reputations are ruined for ever by that sort of thing, when it happens on the Continent" (G.K. Chesterton, *George Bernard Shaw*, op. cit., 284–285).

to give his public backing to either of the champions." He did say, however, that "Shaw was a man who understood and Wells was a man who argued."[364]

Shaw believed that Chesterton's conversion ruled him out as a serious opponent,[365] while Wells maintained that Catholic apologists like Belloc "did not care whether or not they used truth in their work. The infallibility of the Church was enough to cover them."[366] But truth often fell by the wayside in the war against capitalism because of the unwritten rule that allies should not attack each other. In the context of the larger truth, which was the political truth, unanimity mattered more than the exact details of evolution, the religion that underpinned the worldview of both Wells and Shaw. When Chesterton attacked Wells' *Anticipations*, Sidney Webb, though privately agreeing with some of his sentiments said it was "imperative that the overall belief in eugenics not be attacked by fellow radicals."[367] Wells retreated from the bellicose Belloc but advanced against the more conciliatory Chesterton. Wells saw himself as generous and humane, but during the War had to be persuaded to tone down an abusive letter to the *New Statesman* "aimed, not only at the monarchy, but also at 'all the unteachable elderly, all the conservative elements in our intricate and confused national life.'"[368]

A Fictional Friendship?

The Jewish characters and themes in the fiction of Shaw, Wells, and Chesterton reflected their divergent views on the "Jewish question." All admired the "revolutionary Jew" and deplored the "capitalist Jew," but Shaw, initially at least, expressed high hopes of breeding a race of revolutionary Supermen by synthesizing Jew and non-Jew. The unpleasant overtones of Wells' materialistic Jewish characters conveyed his resentment at the Jewish refusal to be "absorbed,"

---

364. M. Coren, *The Invisible Man: The Life and Liberties of H. G. Wells*, op. cit., 180.

365. Of Gilbert's conversion, Shaw remarked: "I believe that you would not have become a professed official Catholic if you did not believe that you believe in transubstantiation; but I find it quite impossible to believe that you believe in transubstantiation any more than, say, Dr. Saleeby does. You will have to go to Confession next Easter" (G. B. Shaw, Letter, February 16, 1923, M. Ward, *Gilbert Keith Chesterton*, op. cit., 490).

366. D. C. Smith, *H. G. Wells: Desperately Mortal: A Biography*, op. cit., 256.

367. M. Coren, *The Invisible Man: The Life and Liberties of H. G. Wells*, op. cit., 69; the Webbs were fervent Darwinists (A. Farmer, *By Their Fruits: Eugenics, Population Control and the Abortion Campaign*, op. cit., 100).

368. Wells asked *New Statesman* editor Kingsley Martin to publish a letter abusing the Monarchy: "After persuading him to change a few unnecessarily violent phrases" Martin published it in December 1944: "Even then, in the twilight of his life, he was as bellicose as ever" (K. Martin, *Sunday Times*, September 25, 1966, quoted in G. P. Wells, introduction to H. G. Wells, *The Last Books of H. G. Wells: The Happy Turning and Mind at the End of its Tether*, op. cit., 15–16); the Royal family's War-time determination to brave the Nazi danger with the British people inspired widespread admiration.

thereby blocking his World State. Chesterton strove to avoid Jewish stereotypes, but in defending Christianity, the nation state, and the common man, he portrayed Jews as foreign and secular. All three were disappointed on the "Jewish question." Shaw's fictional Jew, under the influence of eugenics, went from projecting strength to weakness, from "hero to zero," though he continued to hope for a "synthesis" even between anti-Semitic dictator and persecuted Jew. Wells' fiction revealed his love affair with eugenics and betrayed a growing contempt for Judaism and exasperation with the Jewish people's refusal to transfer their talents from Zionism to his internationalist Utopia. Chesterton, who approved of Jewish "separateness," promoted Zionism for this very reason; his "Jew" began as recognizably faulty and human but under an increasing preoccupation with the "plutocratic Jew" became sinister and inhuman before entering a more positive phase, finally emerging as a victim of the recurring "German problem." Chesterton revisited his "Jewish" themes and rewrote them more sympathetically, while Shaw and Wells continued to propound their Utopias, from which mass extermination was inseparable, seemingly unable to grasp the fact that the Nazis were putting their ideas into practice; their reputations have not suffered as a consequence.

All three writers condemned anti-Semitism, and although their fiction reflected the failure of "the Jews" to accept their worldviews, ultimately, Chesterton, the only one whose philosophy was not built on the disappearance of the Jewish people, offered the most authentic friendship to the Jews. The ChesterShaWells, its three heads arguing incessantly but unwilling or unable to put an end to the friendship, expressed three distinctive philosophical approaches—Distributism, the Life Force, and the socialist World State Utopia. The public lapped up the fiction but rejected the philosophies. But it was these philosophies that influenced the reactions of the three literary giants to the Age of Dictators, as the next chapter shows.

5

Chesterton, Shaw, and Wells:
Literary Giants in the Age of Dictators

THE JEWISH CHARACTERS AND THEMES in the fiction of Chesterton,
Shaw, and Wells reflected their distinctive philosophies as expounded in
their non-fiction. This chapter will examine their philosophies in greater
depth, and the effect they had on their responses to totalitarianism; how those
responses influenced their approach to the "Jewish question"; and whether the
"three giants" deserve to be seen as prophets in the Age of Dictators. "Totalitarianism" was originally used by Benito Mussolini to mean an all-embracing system of government that would cater for all human needs. Though initially
attractive to radicals, as will be seen, it has become associated with repressive
one-party regimes in fascist Italy, Nazi Germany, the communist Soviet Union,
and Eastern Europe.[1] Mindful of the distorting lens of the Holocaust, this chapter will ask whether the three literary giants of the twentieth century deserve to
be seen as political prophets.

Shaw and Fascism

In his mission to make people think, Shaw appeared constantly to change his
political stance. But from the 1930s onwards he described himself as a communist. In 1934 he asserted that "the Parliamentary party system, with its mask of
democracy, liberty, and all the rest of it, must be smashed" and "replaced by a
constitution which will have a good deal in common not only with the Russian
constitution but also with our own municipal government and with the Corporate State of Mussolini and the National Socialist State of Hitler." Shaw even

---

1. "Thanks to work by Hannah Arendt, Zbigniew Brzezinski, and others, [totalitarian has]
become a catchall for brutal, soul-killing, Orwellian regimes. But that's not how the word was originally used or intended. Mussolini himself coined the term to describe a society where everybody
belonged, where everyone was taken care of, where everything was inside the state and nothing was
outside" (J. Goldberg, *Liberal Fascism* [London: Penguin Books], 14).

claimed: "As against our Parliamentary pretences, Communists, Fascists and Nazis have a common cause."[2] Even the Catholic Church, which originally was "democratic to the extent that its aim was to save the souls of all persons without regard to their age, sex, nationality, class, or color" so that "within its fold all souls were equal," did not, Shaw maintained, "draw the ridiculous conclusion that all men and women are equally qualified or equally desirous to legislate, to govern, to administer, to make decisions, to manage public affairs or even their own private affairs."[3]

Beatrice Webb had noted Shaw's "strange admiration for the person who *imposes* his will on others, however ignorant and ugly and even cruel that will may be." As a "young social reformer" he had "hated cruelty and oppression." He had called for freedom and "idealized the rebel." Now he idealized "the dictator, whether he be a Mussolini, a Hitler or a Stalin, or even a faked-up pretence of a dictator like Mosley," anyone whose will could triumph over "the multitude of nonentities."[4] In 1931 Shaw told Joseph Stalin that Winston Churchill "would never be Prime Minister."[5] By the Second World War Shaw had given up predicting world events: "No epoch is intelligible until it is completed and can be seen in the distance as a whole, like a mountain." He also seemed, at long last, to see some good in his adopted country: "[A]s forgetful people who act in the present can master vindictive people who only brood on the past there is much to be said for England's full share of human thoughtlessness. It is sometimes better not to think at all than to think intensely and think wrong."[6] But he feared that under democracy, imperfect men and women were considered "competent to choose any tinker tailor soldier sailor." They had a "dread and hatred of government as such" and would block any government attempt at "collectivizing production." Shaw, who believed in state intervention, proposed waiting for an emergency, when "the very people who dread Government action" would be "the first to run to the Government for a remedy."[7]

During the Great War he saw "moral equivalence" between "German Junk-

---

2. G.B. Shaw, Letter to Christina Walshe, May 30, 1934, G.B. Shaw, *Bernard Shaw: Collected Letters 1926–1950 Vol. IV*, D.H. Laurence, ed. (London: Max Reinhardt, 1988), 373–374.

3. G.B. Shaw, preface to *Plays Extravagant: Too True to be Good* (Harmondsworth, Middx.: Penguin Books Ltd., 1981), 24.

4. B. Webb, quoted in M. Holroyd, *Bernard Shaw Vol. III, 1918–1950: The Lure of Fantasy* (London: Penguin, 1993), 113–114.

5. Stalin, who had a high opinion of Churchill's ability, asked Nancy Astor why he was so anti-Russian and whether he would regain political influence (Maurice Collis, *Nancy Astor* [London: Futura, 1982], 179–180).

6. G.B. Shaw, preface to *Plays Political: Geneva* (Harmondsworth, Middx.: Penguin Books Ltd., 1986), 314.

7. Ibid., 321–323.

ers" and the English nobility;[8] during the Second World War he saw moral equivalence between democracy and the Axis because the Allies were bombing Europe.[9] He insisted that "[i]ncompetent governments" were "the cruellest," and regarding Nazi concentration camps he stated: "Had there been efficient handling of the situation by the authorities (assuming this to have been possible) none of these atrocities would have occurred. They occur in every war when the troops get out of hand."[10] At this time the death penalty for murder was widely accepted, but the Nazis' summary execution of the non-criminal attracted widespread condemnation. Despite this, Shaw advocated that the disabled and recidivist criminals should be put "in the lethal chamber" to "get rid of them." He described lawful imprisonment as "a malicious injury," but "[u]nder no circumstances should they be allowed to expiate their misdeeds by a manufactured penalty," for if there was to be no punishment there could be no forgiveness.[11] The dictators took ideas very similar to his own, such as natural inequality and "might is right," to their logical conclusions. Shaw explained Hitler as "the creature and tool of the plutocracy" but "[p]ower and worship turned [his] head" and he "became the mad Messiah . . . lord of a Chosen Race," while the "Capitalist West . . . shook hands with Stalin and stabbed Hitler in the back." Hitler "put up a tremendous fight" aided by his "fellow adventurers in Italy and Spain," but "the near West rose up against him" joined by "the mighty far West of America." The Fabian Imperialist Shaw advised dictators not to use savagery, although Mussolini had "made it possible for a stranger to travel [to Abyssinia] without being killed by the native Danakils" thereby "rendering the same service to the world" that Britain had rendered ("by the same methods (including poison gas)") in India, Australia, New Zealand and the Scottish highlands. Consequently it was "not for us to throw stones at Musso" who was "scandalously lynched in Milan." Forgetting his self-denying ordinance against prophecy he claimed that as Napoleon had become a national hero so "presently" would Hitler.[12] While acknowledging that no state could achieve "the maximum of beneficence and stability" without democracy and equality, Shaw equated equality with "intermarriageability" because "the

8. G.B. Shaw, "Common Sense About the War" (1914), in G.K. Chesterton, *Chesterton on War and Peace: Battling the Ideas and Movements That Led to Nazism and World War II*, M.W. Perry, ed. (Seattle: Inkling Books, 2008), 424, note 8.

9. G.B. Shaw, preface to *Plays Political: Geneva*, op. cit., 316.

10. Ibid., 326–328.

11. "It would be far more sensible to put up with their vices, as we put up with their illnesses, until they give more trouble than they are worth, at which point we should, with many apologies and expressions of sympathy, and some generosity in complying with their last wishes, then, place them in the lethal chamber and get rid of them" (G.B. Shaw, preface to *Major Barbara, The Bodley Head Bernard Shaw Collected Plays with Prefaces Vol. III* [London: The Bodley Head, 1971], 60–61).

12. G.B. Shaw, preface to *Plays Political: Geneva*, op. cit., 331–332.

greatest genius" cost "no more to feed and clothe and lodge than the narrowest minded duffer."[13]

Shaw's biographer says he "spent much of his life seeking to prove Democracy a fraud": Parliament was a "political madhouse," a "defense" against government. His interest in the great men of history, not despots, but "dedicated to the public weal," sprang from his Irish love of aristocracy, and his statements about fascism were criticisms aimed at the British Government.[14] Regarding Italy's Abyssinian adventure he insisted: "European civilisation must stand solid."[15] Shaw discussed democracy and fascism with the "virulently anti-Semitic" Conservative MP Nancy Astor,[16] and became part of her "Cliveden Set."[17] Shaw, who believed that Hitler and Mussolini would fall if other countries refused to fight, admitted it was a fascist circle, but as a meeting of Left and Right it was part of democracy. In any case, fascism was "an attempt to moralize Capitalism and enrich it at the same time through Fabian State organization." During the 1920s Shaw dismayed younger intellectuals and older Fabians by "championing" Mussolini. Cognizant of the murder of the General-Secretary of the Italian Socialist Party in 1924, and repressive measures thereafter, he claimed that such things always accompanied the struggle for government. Insouciantly, Shaw said he would support Mussolini until things went wrong. Italian exiles might criticize but he refused to interfere in Italy's internal affairs, warning that Britain would deserve a Mussolini if the people were denied socialism. Beatrice Webb thought Shaw had lost sympathy for the underdog.[18]

But, as seen, the underdog was never a fixed concept, and Shaw extolled the Italian dictator when he invaded Abyssinia, seeming to justify Webb's view of his "strong man" obsession.[19] During the War Shaw distanced himself from the British Union of Fascists, especially its anti-Semitism, but campaigned to release British Union of Fascists' leader Sir Oswald Mosley from prison, arguing that people were allowed to read *Mein Kampf* but not Mosley's writ-

---

13. "Equality of income is practicable enough" (ibid., 334–335).

14. G. B. Shaw, *Bernard Shaw: Collected Letters 1926–1950 Vol. IV*, op. cit., 455–456.

15. Charlotte Shaw "furiously" supported Abyssinia, but Shaw believed that, confronted with primitive "testicle hunting Danakil, European civilisation must stand solid"; to support them "out of hostility to Mussolini would be an act of opportunist scoundrelism which would make the European situation very much worse . . . and do no good in the long run to the Danakils" (G. B. Shaw, Letter to Augustin Hamon, January 20, 1936 [ibid., 424–425]).

16. Ibid., 741–742; in one letter, Shaw's secretary Blanche Patch typed "nigger"; Shaw changed it to "negro" (G. B. Shaw, Letter to Augustin Hamon, February 13, 1935 [ibid., 398–400]).

17. M. Holroyd, *Bernard Shaw Vol. III, 1918–1950: The Lure of Fantasy*, op. cit., 102.

18. Ibid., 143–145; in 1942 Shaw said he "became a worshipper of dictators and despaired when they went wrong. But I do not shoot a dictator until he sells out" (G. B. Shaw, Letter to E. Strauss, August 4, 1942, G. B. Shaw, *Bernard Shaw: Collected Letters 1926–1950 Vol. IV*, op. cit., 631–633).

19. M. Holroyd, *Bernard Shaw Vol. III, 1918–1950: The Lure of Fantasy*, op. cit., 145–146.

ings.[20] While Shaw should not be viewed through the lens of the Holocaust, he continued to support fascism when it revealed its true colors, and even during the War he failed to unequivocally condemn it. He took a similar approach to totalitarian communism.

Shaw and Soviet Communism

Shaw's responses to fascism were influenced by his attitudes to capitalism and to the new world power, Soviet Russia. He had supported the original bloodless Russian Revolution, but regarded voting for socialism as the first step. The parliamentary route was a prelude to physical force, and when Lenin overthrew Kerensky[21] Shaw switched his allegiance. As he aged Shaw became more a man of action than of thought—in his thoughts, at any rate.[22] He supported Stalin when he invaded Finland, arguing that England should support the Soviets in case their help was ever needed.[23] This could be seen as prescient but, visiting Russia with the Astors, he became aware of its oppressive nature: "It will not be a long visit; I shall reach these shores again on the 2nd August: that is, if I am not despatched by the Soviet in the opposite direction to Siberia." This was Shaw's sardonic response to what he alleged were press exaggerations of Soviet repression.[24]

But Shaw did witness the Soviets' tendency to conceal problems[25] and, when asked to intercede on behalf of an émigré's wife, Mrs. Krynine, to allow her to go to America, he refused to act. The Astors threatened to challenge the secret police, but the unfortunate woman disappeared while Shaw, true to his policy of non-intervention in foreign affairs, made laudatory speeches to his hosts on the superiority of Russian freedom. Shaw explained that he received several pitiful appeals each year to which he had to harden his heart,[26] seemingly unaware that his own writings inspired such appeals. Addressing the Central Hall of Trade Unions he made light of "famine" and other "scare stories" in the English press and received a "storm of applause." He met Stalin under strict secrecy at the Kremlin.[27] Laurence says the "Soviet experiment . . . won Shaw's complete admiration" but that "he did not blindly give blanket endorsement to

20. Ibid., 113–114.

21. Ibid., 223.

22. Ibid., 224–225.

23. Ibid., 432–433.

24. G. B. Shaw, Letter to Horace Plunkett, July 16, 1931, G. B. Shaw, *Bernard Shaw: Collected Letters 1926–1950 Vol. IV*, D. H. Laurence, ed., op. cit., 242–243.

25. Shaw visited a Soviet prison established to deal with "the menace of wandering hordes of homeless youths" (G. B. Shaw, Letter to Charlotte Shaw, July 23, 1931 [ibid., 248–250]).

26. G. B. Shaw, Letter to Charlotte Shaw, July 24, 1931 (ibid., 250–251).

27. No detailed reports survive and Shaw did not reveal any details to his wife (ibid., 256–259).

its tenets and its methods," and never joined the Communist Party: "[H]ereti-cally he rejected Marxist determinism and the principle of historical necessity." Nonetheless he "turned a blind eye ... to Stalin's abuses," maintaining that "Russian Communism was the greatest political experiment in all history." Shaw had "[f]or half a century ... preached that only by economic salvation does one free the mind and the spirit" and "his firm conviction" was that "Communism alone could eventually accomplish this," since the Russians were "free from the illusion of Democracy." In 1931 he told his Soviet hosts: "[W]e in the West, we who are still playing at Socialism, must follow in your footsteps—whether we will or no."[28]

As with fascism, Shaw used Russian communism as a stick to beat British democracy, but became "one of the chief agents" for Soviet propaganda in Brit-ain. Beatrice Webb could not understand how he could approve of a dictator-ship that "'liquidated' its objectors," but Shaw said Stalin was no worse than the Tsars. As in *Man and Superman*, the "only hope for the world was to change human nature," and Stalin was praised for shaping the "putty" to produce "a different sort of animal"—"Communist Man"[29]—while in Britain Shaw called for free speech and opposed oppression. He did not believe in an individual "life everlasting,"[30] but was drawn toward the Soviet heaven on earth even if many Russians were going through hell to reach it.

He even converted the Webbs. In 1927 Beatrice thought the Russian revolu-tion, especially the British press's portrayal of it, had been "the greatest disaster in the history of the British Labour movement," but after Labour's poor results in the 1931 election she changed her mind.[31] The main problem with the Soviet Union, it seemed, was drawing attention to the problems of communism. The Webbs became Shaw's "pre-eminent converts" and also his evangelists. They took the "Soviet road" along with a swathe of intellectuals to what Beatrice's nephew Malcolm Muggeridge called "Fabian Fairyland." Shaw said he was fighting a hostile press. If he said nine positive things and one negative, the press would concentrate on the negative, so he said ten positive things.[32] Dur-ing their Russian visit, Shaw's praise of "Bolshevist rule, and the compliments which *Pravda* alleged that Lady Astor had paid" raised "a storm of criticism in England," a storm "led" by Chesterton "in an article published two days before their return." Chesterton claimed that Shaw, the "great dissipater of illusions ... had himself become the victim of the illusion," for rather than "the scene of

28. Ibid., 458.
29. M. Holroyd, *Bernard Shaw Vol. III, 1918–1950: The Lure of Fantasy*, op. cit., 248–249.
30. Ibid., 513.
31. Ibid., 248–249.
32. Ibid., 251–253.

a Socialist victory" Russia "was the scene of its defeat. The so-called dictatorship of the proletariat was the negation of the Socialist vision."[33] Winston Churchill said Shaw was "a wealthy and acquisitive capitalist, and a sincere Communist. His spiritual home is Russia."[34]

As Shaw's Life Force became increasingly preoccupied with death, the only question was not whether to kill, but whom to kill, as he constructed yet another false equivalence between the "Russian liquidator" and the British hangman.[35] He was fully cognizant of the Russian "inquisition" the "OGPU" and its forerunner the Tcheka, "a body of well-intentioned amateurs."[36] While opposing the death penalty for murder he approved of "tribunals"—secular inquisitions into whether "Mr. Everyman" was "a creator of social values or a parasitical consumer and destroyer of them." Admittedly, "to blow a man's brains out" because he could not "for the life of him see why he should not employ labor at a profit," or buy and sell commodities, "or speculate in currency values," was "an innovation which should be carried out with the utmost possible delicacy" if public opinion was to be "quite reconciled." "Everyman" should be told: "You must keep a credit balance always at the national bank"; no individual should cost more to keep than he earned. For those "human nuisances," repeat offenders, there should be an "Inquisition always available" to apply the death penalty. Even lynching prompted him to suggest re-examining "our Visions of Judgment," to "see whether we cannot change them from old stories in which we no longer believe . . . to serious and responsible public tribunals."[37] His biographer, Holroyd, claims that in his eighties Shaw "was not the man for such sensitivity or criticism." There was enough appalling misery around without dwelling on it, but this did not prevent him from dwelling on the miseries of Western capitalist democracies. Moscow's absence of social class thrilled him, since social aspiration led the poor to accept inequalities; he called, therefore, for a "science of happiness" to persuade them that riches did not bring joy.[38]

He saw the "atrocities" in the Soviet Union, but chiefly as "unnecessary boulders stopping the passage of fresh ideas in Britain." When Hesketh Pearson included a chapter on the subject in his biography, Shaw "condensed [his] objections into a single paragraph" and "substituted more than 4,000 words of

33. M. Collis, *Nancy Astor*, op. cit., 181.

34. W. S. Churchill, *Sunday Pictorial*, August 16, 1931 (ibid., 182).

35. M. Holroyd, *Bernard Shaw Vol. III, 1918–1950: The Lure of Fantasy*, op. cit., 252–253.

36. "I, an old Irishman, am too used to Coercion Acts, suspension of the Habeas Corpus Act and the like, to have any virtuous indignation left to spare for the blunders and excesses into which the original Tcheka . . . fell before it had learnt the limits of its business by experience" (G. B. Shaw, preface to *Plays Extravagant: The Simpleton of the Unexpected Isles*, op. cit., 137).

37. Ibid., 142–144.

38. M. Holroyd, *Bernard Shaw Vol. III, 1918–1950: The Lure of Fantasy*, op. cit., 254–255.

his own," painting "a harmless yet exhilarating picture of the Soviet political landscape." Like Chesterton,[39] Shaw supported the idea of revolution, but believed that the bloodshed of the French Revolution had made the British more insular. He praised the Soviet Union and dismissed the bloodshed.[40] But the "combatant pacifist"[41] opposed violence between nations and continued to oppose "killing under authority" as long as it was British democratic authority. Shaw's opposition to capitalism and to democracy blinded him to the abuses of fascism and communism.[42]

Shaw and the Nazis

Before the Second World War, Shaw respected and admired Hitler. Germany was "the centre of gravity of the Protestant North"; he joked that Hitler was "the greatest living Tory, and a wonderful preacher of everything that is right and best in Toryism," albeit a failed Messiah. Shaw was not alone in his admiration, but with his "doctrine of the Life Force and of the Superman" it was unsurprising that he would "look favourably upon the social and political experiments practised by the dictators," especially "such moves as Hitler's early nationalisation of the trade unions."[43] Beatrice Webb had seen his approval of fascism as motivated by a desire for order at any price but, unlike the socialists, Chesterton was not surprised by Shaw's later approval of monarchy.[44] Winston Churchill accused Shaw of becoming "airily detached," such that he had "blinded himself to reality" regarding repression in Italy, Germany and the Soviet Union. Shaw "countered" with the French Revolution, "mob violence" and the abuses of democracies. Laurence notes that Shaw's fascist sympathies "eventually waned" because of their "denial of individual responsibility," until "finally" he was "moved to draw the line" on anti-Semitism. The Nazis' "Judophobia" was "'a very malignant disease,' which 'destroyed any credit [they] might have had.'" He summed up their political bankruptcy with: "No program: try a pogrom."[45]

---

39. The Christian belief in free will gave birth to the secular idea of revolution (G. K. Chesterton, "The Eternal Heroism of the Slums," *The Blatchford Controversies* [1904] *G.K. Chesterton Collected Works Vol. I* [San Francisco: Ignatius Press, 1986], 394–395); see Chapter Two.

40. M. Holroyd, *Bernard Shaw Vol. III, 1918–1950: The Lure of Fantasy*, op. cit., 370–371.

41. Ibid., 431.

42. Ibid., 370–371.

43. G. B. Shaw, *Bernard Shaw: Collected Letters 1926–1950 Vol. IV*, op. cit., 456–457.

44. As evinced in *The Apple Cart* (1929) (W.B. Furlong, *Shaw and Chesterton: The Metaphysical Jesters* [London: The Pennsylvania State University Press, 1970], 182–183); see Chapter Four.

45. "[M]ob violence, beatings, torture, castration and other mutilation, culminating in victims being hanged or burned alive" were tolerated as "popular sports" in "'democracies' like the United States" where "many . . . community and national leaders tacitly sanctioned lynchings and the reign

By the late 1930s Shaw was claiming that Hitler had created the "Jewish problem," although "no single nation could tackle this problem with clean hands,"
but added that Hitler "shrinks from the massacre which the logic of his phobia
demands."[46] Despite the Nazi-Soviet pact and Britain declaring war against
Germany, Shaw wrote:

> We should have warned the Poles that we could do nothing to stop the Ger-
> man steamroller, and that they must take it lying down as Chekoslovakia had
> to, until we had brought Hitler to his senses. Fortunately our old pal Stalin
> stepped in at the right moment and took Hitler by the scruff of the neck: a
> masterstroke of foreign policy.[47]

Shaw told Beatrice Webb: "We must not let Adolf give Socialism a bad name.
We are National Socialists, and for Socialism in a single country as against
Trotsky." The objection was not "to German Socialism but to persecution and
bogus Racialism, which are completely foreign to Socialism."[48] As the situation
worsened his levity increased: "I am seriously thinking of writing an open letter
to Hitler, and sending it to The Observer." He had read *Mein Kampf*, "a curious
combination of an extraordinarily penetrating observation and comprehension
of the political and psychological situation with epileptic phobias and conviction of the eugenic value of racial inbreeding and cross breeding." Nonetheless,
Shaw believed that Hitler had "the courage of his conviction to a sublime
height," further remarking: "Altogether a very remarkable fellow this Hitler,
though a doomed Impossibilist."[49]

Shaw's opposition to anti-Semitism but also to the death penalty prompted
his comment, on hearing of German war criminals being lynched at Bergen-
Belsen concentration camp: "I agree, of course: these lynchings are disgusting."[50] He urged the release of prisoners of war but also political prisoners, and

---

of terror imposed on Negroes, Catholics, and Jews by the cross-burning, white-hooded Ku Klux
Klan," and where the president ordered troops to fire on unarmed marchers (G.B. Shaw, *Bernard
Shaw: Collected Letters 1926–1950 Vol. IV*, op. cit., 457).

46. M. Holroyd, *Bernard Shaw Vol. III, 1918–1950: The Lure of Fantasy*, op. cit., 422.

47. G.B. Shaw, Letter to Nancy Astor, September 28, 1939, G. B. Shaw, *Bernard Shaw: Collected
Letters 1926–1950 Vol. IV*, op. cit., 539–540.

48. G.B. Shaw, Letter to Beatrice Webb, June 17, 1940 (ibid., 559–560); H.M. Hyndman formed
and led the National Socialist Party until his death in 1921, after his support for the Great War led to
a split in the British Socialist Party.

49. G.B. Shaw, Letter, November 26, 1942 (ibid., 649–650); *Mein Kampf* was "one of the world's
bibles" that "changed the mind of the reading world" (M. Holroyd, *Bernard Shaw Vol. III, 1918–1950:
The Lure of Fantasy*, op. cit., 403–404).

50. Shaw said the war criminal William Joyce "would have done better to throw over his lawyers
and claim that a man has a human right to choose his side in a war" (G.B. Shaw, Letter to C.H. Norman, September 24, 1945, G.B. Shaw, *Bernard Shaw: Collected Letters 1926–1950 Vol. IV*, op. cit., 752).

the "darker the subject, the more light-hearted grew his tone."[51] His tone darkened when speaking of democracy, however, and he blamed Nazi expansionism on the West:[52] "Leave Germany to itself, and there will be a reaction against Hitlerism."[53] He proposed a ministry of propaganda to redefine words that had acquired unfortunate connotations, like "appeasement, communism, fascism, Hitlerism and National Socialism." Hitlerism was "a government founded on the idolatry of one person laying claim to the world on behalf of Germans as the Chosen Race." The "combatant pacifist" aimed a constant barrage of military advice at the British government, warning against "tit-for-tat bombing."[54] It was Shaw's democratic right to criticize, but such rights were denied in the dictatorships he defended: Nazi Germany and his beloved Soviet Union. Regardless, Shaw continued to be a critic even during a time of extreme national danger.

Shaw and the Jews

Unlike Chesterton, Shaw harbored no reverence for Judaism. In fact, he claimed that one of his plays was "a valuable contribution to the purification of religion from horrible old Jewish superstitions."[55] He told his Jewish-born Austrian translator that although he had defended Mussolini and Hitler from attacks in the British press he had also condemned Hitler's "Judenhetze" ("Jew-baiting") and would not be silenced: "But whatever you say or do, you must be careful not to shew the least sign of being intimidated, or of caring one snap of your fingers what anybody thinks or threatens."[56] While kindly meant, Shaw's advice suggests an inability to grasp the sort of anti-Semitism that could not be lectured away. As seen in Chapter Four, Shaw supported Einstein but also the right of States to weed out "undesirable strains," including Jews. Moreover, when *Geneva* met with Jewish complaints Shaw called one correspondent "the most thoughtless of Sheenies. . . . Can you wonder at Hitler (and now Mussolini) driving out the Jews?" Shaw said that *Geneva* made "ruthless fun of British Cabinet Ministers, of German and Italian Dictators" but when he "dared to

51. M. Holroyd, *Bernard Shaw Vol. III, 1918–1950: The Lure of Fantasy*, op. cit., 483.
52. Ibid., 421.
53. Ibid., 428.
54. Ibid., 430–432.
55. "I was ridiculously surprised at your reception of The Black Girl story" (G. B. Shaw, Letter to Dame Laurentia McLachlan, Stanbrook Abbey, April 12[14], 1932, G. B. Shaw, *Bernard Shaw: Collected Letters 1926–1950 Vol. IV*, op. cit., 344–345); *The black girl in search of God and some lesser tales* (1934) caused a rift with Dame Laurentia and, despite Shaw's insouciant response, he described it as "a most frightfully blasphemous religious story" (Letter to Nancy Astor, April 15, 1932 [ibid., 286]).
56. "You have not analyzed the position because you hate politics, and are quite unaccustomed to and inexpert at the sort of political controversy in which I am as practised as I am in playwriting. You had better keep out of the melee as much as possible" (G. B. Shaw, Letter to Siegfried Trebitsch, May 12–15, 1933 [ibid., 336–337]).

introduce a Jew without holding him up to the admiring worship of the audience as the inheritor of all the virtues and none of the vices of Abraham and Moses, David and Isaiah ... instantly you ... raise a wail of lamentation and complaint and accuse me of being a modern Torquemada."[57]

Nevertheless, he revised the play several times to keep up with Hitler's actions and to mollify Jewish feelings,[58] and in September 1939 declared: "We should, I think, at once announce our intention of lodging a complaint with the International court against Hitler as being unfitted for State control, as he is obsessed by a Jewish complex: that of the Chosen Race, which has led him into wholesale persecution and robbery"; however, he continued: "Nothing should be said about concentration camps, because it was we who invented them."[59] Despite complaints *Geneva* proved popular with British theater-goers who "wanted to see the terrifying spectres of Hitler and Mussolini ridiculed" and "were convinced that this was what they were seeing." Shaw insisted that unpleasant characters must speak for themselves (i.e. with his voice), consequently the play was "equally unpopular with pro- and anti-Nazis" because the laughter was directed equally at all the characters. *Geneva* was aimed at preventing another war,[60] but when war came Shaw said he would "'strive for a British win" like "the rabidest of Jingoes." When the BBC asked him to make a broadcast for foreign listeners he was "as orthodox as he could contrive," and his "Big Idea" was "the need to defeat anti-Semitism." The Government immediately vetoed the broadcast: Minister of Information Duff Cooper believed that "millions of Americans and some other people [believe] that [Hitler's persecution of the Jews] is the only thing he has done right."[61] There was a strong

---

57. G. B. Shaw, Letter to Lawrence Langner, September 20, 1938 (ibid., 510–511).

58. Lawrence Langner pleaded that he wouldn't want "future generations of Jew-baiters" to quote his friend Shaw as an authority for persecuting Jews (M. Holroyd, *Bernard Shaw Vol. III, 1918–1950: The Lure of Fantasy*, op. cit., 406–407).

59. G. B. Shaw, Letter to Nancy Astor, September 9, 1939, G. B. Shaw, *Bernard Shaw: Collected Letters 1926–1950 Vol. IV*, op. cit., 539–540. In the British concentration camps in South Africa, designed to deprive Boer fighters of family support, 26,000 Boer women and children died from hunger and disease, with more than 14,000 black people whose numbers were not tabulated. Lloyd George accused the Conservative government of a policy of extermination, but while the camps never directly exterminated people on national or racial grounds, Imperialist policy had involved the extermination of native peoples (see: S. Lindqvist, *Exterminate all the Brutes* [London: Granta Books, 1997]).

60. Critic Desmond MacCarthy thought "the case for the Jew ought ... to have been vigorously put" (M. Holroyd, *Bernard Shaw Vol. III, 1918–1950: The Lure of Fantasy*, op. cit., 407–408).

61. Ibid., 432–433; Kushner remarks that "the quantity of books depicting the plight of Jewish refugees was itself creating hostile comment, even from liberal elements within British society.... Orwell remarked in 1940 that 'for the time being we have heard enough about the concentration camps and the persecution of the Jews'" (G. Orwell, *Tribune*, August 23, 1940, in T. Kushner, *The Persistence of Prejudice: Antisemitism in British Society during the Second World War* [Manchester: Manchester University Press, 1989], 115).

pro-Arab, anti-Jewish culture in government circles, but while Shaw's idea was laudable it would have given encouragement to those who claimed that the War was being fought "for the Jews."[62] As will be seen, one Jewish-born anti-Nazi stressed the need to defend the West against barbarism. The proposed broadcast implied that if only Hitler dropped his anti-Semitism his approach would be acceptable, as Shaw did in fact believe.

In 1909 he told a Jewish admirer: "My friend Zangwill is also a Zionist, and has greatly interested me in the movement"; but he did not "know why the Jews should be looking for a land of their own. Their dispersion throughout Europe gives them so much power and influence." The Jews played "a big part in all revolutionary movements," and in view of humanity's lack of "strength" and "character" to solve modern problems he believed that "we need a new race, a race of supermen."[63] Shaw also asked whether Chesterton "like Houston Chamberlain" really thought "Jew *qua* Jew a worse man than himself?"[64] Such attacks undoubtedly helped build Shaw's reputation as a "pro-Semite"—and Chesterton's as an anti-Semite. But when a Jewish interviewer asked Shaw if he believed that Jews were the chosen race, Shaw "returned an almost furious answer. 'Certainly not.... It is this monstrous presumption that has always been their ruin, and the fact that it has also been their consolation in captivity and ostracism does not remove it from the category of dangerous paranoic delusions. The Jews are too prone to console themselves by lies: the Psalms are my witness to the truth of this.'"[65]

Chesterton recognized Shaw's relentless consistency, but Jews were encouraged by his positive-sounding pronouncements, only to be rudely rebuffed. Regarding Shaw's portrayal of a Jewish money-lender in *The Apple Cart* (1929), a *Jewish Chronicle* correspondent mused that "Jews were never certain" whether or not Shaw liked them: he spoke "nicely of them" in *Doctor's Dilemma*, and allowed Mendoza in *Man and Superman* to say "a few good words about the Jewish race"; but still there was "the belief that Shaw does not like Jews." Shaw claimed to be "the most modern of the modernists" but he was "still under the influence of Marlowe and Shakespeare" regarding Jews.[66] And yet from 1930

---

62. When Churchill approved bombing raids on Germany accompanied by leaflets warning of the consequences of persecuting Poles and Jews, Sir Charles Portal, Chief of the Air Staff, "warned that any such raids 'avowedly conducted on account of the Jews would be an asset to enemy propaganda'" (Air Ministry papers, 8/433, in M. Gilbert, *Churchill and the Jews* [London: Simon & Schuster Ltd., 2007], 196–197).

63. I. Cohen, "Superman and Jew: Mr. Bernard Shaw and Herr [Reuben] Brainin—A Notable Conversation," *Evening Standard/St. James's Gazette*, reprinted in the *Jewish Chronicle*, February 5, 1909, 20.

64. "The Jewish Spirit: Enlightenment," *Jewish Chronicle*, June 9, 1916, 7.

65. "'G.B.S.' on Jews: Some 'catechised' opinions," *Jewish Chronicle*, December 28, 1928, 16.

66. "'The Apple Cart': Shaw Play Produced in Warsaw," *Jewish Chronicle*, June 21, 1929, 41.

onwards Shaw and Wells, with other literary figures, actively supported campaigns against anti-Semitism, befriending Freud and Einstein on their ejection from Germany.[67] Shaw and Wells became patrons of the International League for Combating Anti-Semitism,[68] but they were just as opposed to Jews singling themselves out as being singled out. Shaw advised those "'who still want to be the chosen race to go to Palestine and stew in their own juice. The rest had better stop being Jews and start being human beings." In response he was accused of not benefitting from his contact with Einstein, "a proud Jew but [also] an ardent Zionist."[69]

Another Jewish journalist reported: "GBS has broken loose again. The sight of a Jewish interviewer acts on him like a red rag on a bull." This was the same GBS who had made "a manly defence of the Jew against the Party whose slogan is: 'No programme; try a pogrom.' But send a Jew to interview him, and out pour jibes and jeers in a cascade of paradoxes whose only saving grace is that they cancel each other out." Shaw, he alleged, had visited Palestine but remained "blind" to the "sacrifices," the "heroism," the "pent-up yearnings, the poetry, the prayers and the prophetic fervour," continuing to insist that "the Jew" was "a most ferocious type and not at all peace-loving." Inadvertently touching on the truth, the journalist concluded: "Does he honestly think that human miseries will be ended by the peopling of the earth with one uniform race of some curious nondescript tint?"[70] Even Shaw's "manly defense" insisted that prejudice could be found "[i]n every country."[71]

In 1933 Nazis "howled down" his plays, "with cries of 'Down with the Jew Shaw'"; but *On the Rocks* "failed in London and earned for its author, justly or not, the rebuke that in championing dictatorship against democracy he was biting the hand that fed him," while in Berlin the same play was greeted with "[g]reat enthusiasm"—there Shaw's "sallies at the expense of Democracy and Parliament were greeted with joyous merriment."[72] A Jewish reviewer said Shaw was so "enamoured" with the "dictatorship idea" that he would put up "two dictators," and ask "the people to choose."[73]

To Shaw, eugenics, like dictators, offered another short-cut to Utopia. In 1934

---

67. Responding to Shaw's speech at a dinner in his honor, Einstein said: "It rejoices me to see before me Bernard Shaw and H. G. Wells, for whose conception of life I have a special feeling of sympathy" ("Prof. Einstein: Guest of Honour ... Distinguished Gathering: Mr. Bernard Shaw on Science and Religion," *Jewish Chronicle*, October 31, 1930, 16).

68. *Jewish Chronicle*, December 12, 1930, 23.

69. "Jewry Week by Week," *Jewish Chronicle*, October 28, 1932, 7.

70. "Jewry week by week: The 'Ferocious Jew,'" *Jewish Chronicle*, February 3, 1933, 8.

71. Letter, "G.B.S. on the Nazis: 'A Mentally Bankrupt Party,'" *Jewish Chronicle*, December 2, 1932, 23.

72. "The Jew Shaw," *Jewish Chronicle*, April 6, 1934, 14–15.

73. "Watchman," "The Applecart: 'On the Rocks,'" *Jewish Chronicle*, December 29, 1933, 9.

a British eugenicist, while ridiculing Nazi anti-Semitism on scientific grounds, said that the "broad outlines" of the Nazi sterilization bill, which legalized sterilization for "aments, the insane, epileptics, the unsocial (criminal), deaf-mutes, and physical weaklings (tubercular)," would "certainly command the assent of all experienced eugenists"; but while nominally "voluntary," sterilization would be "actually press[ed]" on such individuals.[74] Shaw also attacked Nazi anti-Semitism, and approved of eugenics sterilization. In *The Simpleton of the Unexpected Isles* he proposed the breeding of an ideal race. The play was well received in Nazi Germany. As a Jewish reviewer noted, it "amuse[d] Germans very much, for racial purity is a cardinal point of the Nazi programme." The audience, he related, "roared" when "all the worthless people" in the world were "liquidated," a "swift act which took off all stockbrokers, members of Parliament and doctors." One German critic paradoxically insisted that Shaw had "acknowledged the strength and independence of blood and soil, and preaches the ruthless affirmation of life."[75] Another Jewish review saw *Geneva*, which "arraigned the dictators of Europe for their cruelty to the Jews" and their "destruction of all democratic ideals" as "magnificent," but that just as a "determined anti-Semitic drive" was underway in Italy, Shaw was "praising" Mussolini for "his sensible attitudes on this question," and informing Hitler that "they are both descended from Abraham."[76]

Some Jews had taken his compliments seriously while overlooking his criticism,[77] but one *Jewish Chronicle* reader complained of Shaw implicitly equating the "wars of Joshua" with "the crimes of Adolf Hitler," suggesting that "the Nazi race theory sprang from the Jewish belief in the Divine mission of Israel."[78] His "blasphemous reference to the Deity" at a Jewish "brains trust" showed it was "alas, a disgusting feature of our life to be resentful of any criticism if uttered by fellow-Jews, and to swallow with cringing glee any insults hurled against us by

---

74. "Notes of the Quarter [on Nazism]," 1934, *Eugenics Review*, in Lucy Bland, Laura Doan, eds., *Sexology Uncensored: The Documents of Sexual Science* (Cambridge: Polity Press, 1998), 183–184.

75. "New Play Produced in Germany: Shavian Racial Theme Pleases Nazis," *Jewish Chronicle*, April 12, 1935, 20; a eugenic experiment to breed a better race by combining Eastern and Western blood in "group marriage" ends with the human race being "brought to judgment and convicted of having created nothing" and vanishing from the earth (G.B. Shaw, *Plays Extravagant: The Simpleton of the Unexpected Isles*, op. cit.).

76. "The Malvern Festival: Bernard Shaw and the Dictators: Great Possibilities Wasted," *Jewish Chronicle*, August 12, 1938, 30; "[T]he privilege of a famous playwright which secures for him the liberty to bring thinly-veiled living political notorieties on to the stage could have been used to better purpose" ("Shaw's 'Geneva': Dictators Parade at the Saville," ibid., December 2, 1938, 49).

77. A reviewer remarked of *John Bull's Other Island*: "The author's sneer at the patriotic German Jew remains, but we do not make the mistake of regarding Mr. Shaw seriously" (*Jewish Chronicle*, October 8, 1909, 21); see Chapter Four.

78. "Where was their self-respect?" *Jewish Chronicle*, March 17, 1944, 8–9; "Maccabi Brains Trust," (ibid., 15).

non-Jews, especially if these happen to be famous. . . ."[79] A rabbi complained of Shaw making the same claim in *Everybody's Political What's What*. As seen, Chesterton made a similar point about Nazi hubris, but did affirm the right of the Jews to be the Chosen People. The Rev. Dr. Cohen concluded:

> God, in that Book which Shaw calls a 'jumble of savage superstition and obsolete cosmology,' could say to His chosen and beloved Israel, 'Are ye not as the children of the Ethiopian unto me?' If Shaw does not recognise that as the finest exposition of racial equality then I fear his capacity for clear thinking has, in the words of Aboth, 'died and passed away from this world.'[80]

Shaw claimed that he had not visited a synagogue because he did not possess a tall hat, prompting another reader to remark: "[C]learly [he] does not deem us much worth bothering about and has not given much thought to us."[81]

This was despite the evidence of his own writings, and after Shaw's death, a Jewish commentator, Mr. J. Isaacs, continued to reflect the belief that the "greatest journalist of the age" was "not specially interested in Jews. He had many more important things on his mind." He added, insightfully, that "it would be wrong to think that Shaw wrote about Jews for any benefit he intended to them. It was all one-way traffic. He used them for his own purposes as a stick to beat others with, the stupid, the prejudiced, the illogical, the basely conditioned." For Shaw had insisted: "I must . . . disclaim pro-Judaism as energetically as I repudiate anti-Semitism. . . . I am not in favour of the Jews being a separate entity. They should assimilate with the rest of the people among whom they dwell." Still, Isaacs acknowledged, "[n]o man was more easily provoked to flippancy and self-contradiction than Shaw."[82] His Jewish admirers continued to view Shaw as ambivalent and inconsistent, but Shaw's consistent, coherent answer to the "Jewish question" remained the same: the Jewish people should disappear.[83]

Nonetheless, Jewish commentator H. M. Geduld said *Geneva* showed "quite deliberately, how ineffectual is the case of the Jew against merciless totalitarian antisemitism." Shaw "poke[d] fun at the popular form of antisemitism based on ignorance," although the balance was "readjusted . . . by an amusing satirical touch at the expense of proverbial Jewish acquisitiveness." This was Shaw's "spirit of 'fair play,'" which lasted throughout his "long life and which obviously

79. Letter, *Jewish Chronicle*, March 24, 1944, 16–17; an appended Editor's note discussed the responsibilities of the Jewish organizers of the "brains trusts" rather than Shaw's contribution.

80. "Shaw has not even the excuse here of saying something scintillatingly new or brilliantly clever even if, on analysis, it proves to be a lot of rubbish" (Rev. Dr. A. Cohen, "Rehash of an Old Sophistry," *Jewish Chronicle*, December 29, 1944, 12–13).

81. "'G.B.S.' on Jews: Some 'Catechised' Opinions," *Jewish Chronicle*, December 28, 1928, 16.

82. J. Isaacs, "Bernard Shaw and the Jews," *Jewish Chronicle*, November 10, 1950, 12–13.

83. "'G.B.S.' on Jews," *Jewish Chronicle*, December 28, 1928, 6–7.

informed his light dismissal of the atrocities of Belsen and Buchenwald." But although "it must not be overlooked that as early as 1933 he had urged that extermination may become politically expedient," Shaw "nevertheless took the right approach to antisemitism when it was most needed."[84]

Shaw, a secular prophet who failed to recognise that his prophecy had failed to deliver the benefits he had promised, did oppose anti-Semitism, but while advocating a more humane path to Jewish extinction, he continued to accept extermination as a valid political approach if demanded by other countries. He advocated extermination for a number of "worthless" categories, and by ignoring Hitler's eugenics he provided moral support for the Nazi extermination program. David Daiches believed Shaw was "at bottom an irrational optimist" who "was not above talking what he knew to be nonsense if it enabled him to make a rhetorical point." He was a "brilliant debater" who "could wield tremendous power over an audience" but "to read his speeches in cold blood" was "quite another matter." But Daiches added that Shaw should have denounced foreign fascists "as sharply as he denounced them at home," rather than using "Britain's faults to excuse those of others." Furthermore, while attacking Nazi anti-Semitism, Shaw called himself a National Socialist. As Daiches noted, he condemned cruelty but "believed in the extermination of the physically, mentally and morally unfit." He "liked the idea of gas-chambers, boasting that he had thought of the idea before Hitler." Shaw insisted his exterminations would be painless, but "in some of his arguments" Shaw's victims comprised the "whole of the bourgeoisie" who did "not accept his kind of communism." Daiches concluded that it was "impossible to make consistent sense of Shaw's political position."[85]

David Nathan viewed "the great thinker with the razor-sharp mind" as "a great fool when it came to the dictators." Shaw "simply ignored the facts about Hitler, Mussolini and Stalin when they conflicted with his beliefs, among them the notion that a socialist paradise was worth gaining even by way of a path strewn with corpses." Nathan dismissed claims based on his 1932 statement "No program; try a pogrom" that Shaw "started to withdraw his support for fascism on the attendant issue of antisemitism," pointing out that this was "before Hitler became Chancellor." Nathan maintained that Shaw "supported the dictators for many years afterwards," thus to use it as evidence "of a change of mind between 1937 and 1943" was "either extraordinarily careless or a desperate attempt at pumping some blood into the clay feet." Nevertheless, Shaw was "not silent": his plays were heckled in Nazi Germany as pro-Jewish.[86]

84. H.M. Geduld, "Bernard Shaw and the Jews," *Jewish Chronicle*, July 27, 1956, 13.

85. David Daiches, "The Paradox of G.B.S.," review of *Shaw—'The Chucker-out,'* by A. Chappelow, *Jewish Chronicle*, December 12, 1969, ii.

86. David Nathan, "The writer who took dictation," *Jewish Chronicle*, July 8, 1988, 41.

Later, Nathan said Shaw "converted generations of young idealists to social-ism, and then betrayed them by siding with the fascist dictators some of them died fighting." Shaw, he acknowledged, "abhorred the persecution of the Jews and said so often and publicly" but "praised their persecutors and called them supermen because they got things done." Shaw's support for the dictators had "never been a secret," but "the full extent of his commitment to fascist ideas and even Nazi experimentation" was becoming clear: "In 1934 he was convinced that fascism and Nazism were a necessary prelude to the Communism he so devoutly wished to see built in Britain." Although he could show great sensitiv-ity to the plight of individuals, "there was no sensitivity about certain Nazi ideas," and his impartiality meant he could even praise Hitler. In 1926 he had rebuffed a request from the Jewish Drama League, telling Charles Landstone (who later defended him against charges of anti-Semitism): "I cannot pretend to be a Jew. Even my pretensions to be a Christian have been challenged." His "belief in society's eventual perfectability" rendered him "incapable of seeing the depth of the evil to which he gave his weighty support." This "fundamental failure" saw the "great campaigner against oppression, the apostle of liberty, totter into history" with "the ignoble ... seedy revisionists who say the Nazis did not do it." He also "turned a blind eye to Stalin's terror" and the "deaths he excused and the dead he denied number millions."[87]

Though Holocaust influence needs to be kept in mind when viewing Shaw's earlier pronouncements, even after the Holocaust he advocated killing disabled people, despite the fact that the Nazi "euthanasia" program served as a "practice run" for the slaughter of the Jews. In March 1945 he stated:

> [A]s the necessary work of "weeding the garden" becomes better understood, the present restriction of liquidation to murder cases, and the exemption of dangerous lunatics (who should be liquidated as such, crime or no crime), will cease, and must be replaced by state-contrived euthanasia for all idiots and intolerable nuisances, not punitively, but as a necessary stroke of social economy.[88]

Shaw's position on "the Jews" was also unequivocal, although it continued to baffle. His early fiction especially portrayed Jews positively, but he rebuffed Jewish overtures, and though he attacked anti-Semitism he also praised the dic-tators. Under the influence of his philosophy of the Strong Man, Shaw pro-

---

87. D. Nathan, "In praise of the persecutors: David Nathan reveals the fascist blind spot in George Bernard Shaw's socialism," *Jewish Chronicle*, August 5, 1988, iv. Earlier, Nathan alluded to Shaw's pro-Fascist stance (ibid, September 3, 1982, 13).

88. Shaw's letter to the *Times* launched a debate against capital punishment (March 5, 1945, 5, in Brian P. Block, John Hostettler, *Hanging in the Balance: A History of the Abolition of Capital Punish-ment in Britain* [Winchester, Hants.: Waterside Press, 1997], 103).

gressed in the opposite direction to Chesterton: initially viewing the Jewish people as a powerful revolutionary force, he tolerated Jewish aspirations.[89] But as the Jewish people continued to cling to their identity Shaw eventually defended the right of the Nazis to eliminate Jews in their own way. Thus the weaker the Jewish position became, the more Shaw was found on the side of the Giant; even when the Giant was slain he failed to appreciate the true weakness of strength.

The Shaw Test

Unlike Chesterton, Shaw supported the Boer War and opposed the Great War, and although Chesterton was no uncritical patriot, Shaw resembled Canning's "steady patriot of the world alone, / the friend of every country but his own. . . ." Like Chesterton, he used fascism as a stick to beat British democracy but, despite his burst of patriotic fervor during the Second World War, he continued to apply the "Shaw test" to every issue, seeing false moral equivalence between democracies and totalitarian regimes. Shaw, enjoying the democratic freedom to criticize democracy, refused to criticize other countries where dictators suppressed dissent, because his own country was imperfect. Chesterton also complained of the failures of democracy, but his response to the Age of Dictators was to criticize the dictators. In contrast, Shaw, disapproving of extermination for the "wrong" (i.e., non–eugenic) reasons, and reluctant to criticize foreign powers, criticized the lynching of a War criminal at Bergen-Belsen but refused to criticize the concentration camp where the lynching took place. Under the influence of Friedrich Nietzsche, Shaw had transposed the concepts of good and evil, so that killing the weak and promoting the powerful was good. Jews were good, but they were weak; thus he demanded the synthesis of the two "opposing forces," insisting that Nazis divest themselves of anti-Semitism and Jews of their Jewishness to produce his "perfect" human race. Impatient with anything that delayed the coming of the Superman, Shaw viewed anti-Semitism and pro-Semitism as equally irrational, but on that "reasonable" basis he approved the killing of the mentally and physically "unfit"—even allowing that this might include Jews—while excusing and even praising the morally unfit. The only way to avoid the nightmare vision of Shaw turning into a Hitler or a Mussolini was, as Chesterton observed, the smiling figure of Shaw himself.

89. Dr. Max Nordau's criticism was: Shaw said, "based partly on a misunderstanding, which I most deeply regret . . . I am known to be a friend of the Zionists" ("Dr. Nordau and Mr. Bernard Shaw: Mr. Shaw's Reply," *Jewish Chronicle*, May 2, 1930, 30).

Wells and his Worldview

Like Shaw, Wells adapted Darwin's theory to support his political approach. For Wells, immortality did not involve "our egotisms, but convergently and overpoweringly . . . the future of our race."[90] In this evolutionary narrative Man originated in a fetid swamp. There was no Fall, no struggle to return to a Garden of Eden, but a continuous Rise that involved constant struggle and the danger of degeneration, the "fall back" into the swamp. Through Nietzschean "will to power" and a "transvaluation" of Christian values, encouraging the strong and idealistic and curbing the weak and worldly, Man would reach perfection: Eden, but in the far distant future. Despite Wells' rejection of sin, his "heaven" required careful planning to avoid the "mistakes" of the past. *A Modern Utopia*, a mixture of fact and fiction set on a parallel planet, described how humanity could conform itself to his socialist world state,[91] although (notwithstanding his "anti-Christian bias") in Rome he found "something congenial in the far flung cosmopolitanism of the Catholic proposition." Despite its "decaying ancient theologies" and "strong taint of otherworldishness," the Church ("in its own half-hearted fashion") was an "Open Conspiracy to reorganize the whole life of man."[92] Wells thought he recognized a conspiracy parallel to his own, and liked what he saw, except that the power was in God's hands, and the only God Wells knew was a cruel ogre who occasionally punished Man for his actions: "The plain, if inadvertent, evidence of Holy Writ is that from the beginning, God knew he had made a mess of things and set Himself to savage his Creation."[93] A humble self-sacrificing God would be relegated to the bottom layer of Wells' Utopia, and in his fiction and non-fiction Wells assumed god-like powers to "reorganize the whole life of man."

But his non-fiction lacked the irony that redeemed his fiction, revealing a "tendency toward crude, messianic power fantasy." Wells saw most of the world's population as inferior and, as seen, he admitted taking pleasure when composing *The War of the Worlds* in writing about the death and destruction portrayed in the story as happening among his neighbors. It was Wells' mission to re-make Man, but in whose image? Draper comments that "Utopias take

90. H.G. Wells, *Anticipations of the Reaction of Mechanical and Scientific Progress Upon Human Life and Thought* (London: Chapman & Hall, 1901/1902), 318; see Chapter Four.

91. H.G. Wells, *A Modern Utopia* (London: Thomas Nelson & Sons Ltd., 1905/1911), 18; this was not an admission of belief in the Fall.

92. H.G. Wells, *Experiment in Autobiography: Discoveries and conclusions of a very ordinary brain (since 1866) Vol. II* (London: Victor Gollancz Ltd., 1934), 573; see Chapter Four regarding Wells' "Open Conspiracy."

93. H.G. Wells, *The Last Books of H. G. Wells: The Happy Turning and Mind at the End of its Tether,* G. P. Wells, ed. (London: H.G. Wells Society, 1945/1968), 48.

their shape from the prejudices of their authors."[94] Utopias become "I-topias," with the world revolving around the I-topian's ego. *Anticipations* (1901) remained for Wells "the keystone to the main arch of my work"[95] and is more wishful thinking than prophecy. He denied there was a "Rapid Multiplication of the Unfit," but this was because such "organisms" were naturally destined for death.[96] Industrialization produced "this bulky, irremovable excretion . . . these gall stones of vicious, helpless, and pauper masses," which were "an integral part of this physiological process of mechanical progress, as inevitable in the social body as are waste matters and disintegrating cells in the body of an active and healthy man."[97]

Like Shaw he believed parliamentary democracy was based on the inequality of man, which was a very shaky foundation, since "neither men nor their rights" were "identically equal."[98] He foresaw a "scientifically trained middle-class . . . not arising out of the older middle-classes, but replacing them." It would become "*the* State, controlling and restricting very greatly the three non-functional masses."[99] The new world state would arise "peacefully and gradually as a process of change," or by revolution, war, or threat of war.[100] The socialist Wells later speculated, however, on catching "the ear of a prince . . . or invad[ing] and captur[ing] the mind of a multi-millionaire"; in which case the New Republic "might come almost at a stride."[101] With his Darwinian explanation of the origins and development of life combined with Nietzsche's "will to power," Wells constantly stressed that what he "foresaw" was bound to happen, but only if men took action.

Contra claims that such a Utopia would be bland and boring, *Anticipations* asserted that cultures such as the pan-German and pan-Slav movements might survive in dispersed fashion, as would the Jews.[102] There would be no compulsion. The men of the New Republic would form an "informal and open freemasonry" to influence and control government.[103] As for equality: "To give [inferior types] equality is to sink to their level, to protect and cherish them is

94. M. Draper, *H.G. Wells* (London: Macmillan Publishers Ltd., 1987), 60–61.

95. M. Coren, *The Invisible Man: The Life and Liberties of H.G. Wells* (London: Bloomsbury, 1994), 63.

96. H.G. Wells, *Anticipations*, op. cit., 305.

97. Ibid., 81–82.

98. Ibid., 147.

99. Ibid., 152.

100. Ibid., 165.

101. H.G. Wells, *Mankind in the Making* (London: Chapman & Hall Ltd., 1903), 71; while urging a Republic, Wells praises King Edward VII for his "unobtrusive but sterling moral qualities" (ibid., 23).

102. H.G. Wells, *Anticipations*, op. cit., 247–248.

103. Ibid., 278.

to be swamped by their fecundity."[104] But birth control would "check the pro-creation of base and servile types, of fear-driven and cowardly souls." And death control, which would hold no terrors, but would mean "the end of all the pain of life, the end of the bitterness of failure, the merciful obliteration of weak and silly and pointless things." Under the "new ethics," life would be "a privilege and a responsibility, not a sort of night refuge for base spirits." For the "multi-tude of contemptible and silly creatures, fear-driven and helpless and useless, unhappy or hatefully happy in the midst of squalid dishonour, feeble, ugly, inefficient," death would be the "alternative . . . to living full beautiful efficient lives." In Wells' Utopia, the "procreation of children who, by the circumstances of their parentage, *must* be diseased bodily or mentally" would be seen as "absolutely the most loathsome of all conceivable sins." Those with "hideous incurable habits," such as alcoholism, would be treated with "pity and patience" if they agreed not to "propagate," but the men of the New Republic would not "hesitate to kill when that sufferance [was] abused." A plea of insanity would not be a reason for clemency but "an added reason for death," and the New Republicans would not be "squeamish" in inflicting it.[105] Like Chesterton, Wells considered his own ideas "sane," but unlike Chesterton he had a deadly solution for the insane. People who could not "live happily and freely in the world without spoiling the lives of others" would be "better off out of it."[106]

Among the "lower races," "undesirable" human "types" were, he maintained, "quite willing to die out" through the use of birth control because they "multi-ply in sheer ignorance, but they do not desire multiplication even now, and they can easily be made to dread it." There was nothing "edifying" in the "spec-tacle of a mean-spirited, under-sized, diseased little man, quite incapable of earning a decent living even for himself, married to some underfed, ignorant, ill-shaped, plain and diseased little woman, and guilty of the lives of ten or twelve ugly ailing children." Wells was diabetic for many years but believed the future would be planned to avoid "a swelling tide" of such "miserable little lives."[107] He doubted whether old-fashioned "permanent monogamic mar-riage" would survive, foreseeing the rise of "ampler grouping[s]." But he failed to foresee any resultant problems, arguing that an unhappy home was "worse than none for the child." He blamed economic disadvantage for making "wife-hood" the "chief feminine profession,"[108] and the "Christian states" for "slave-breeding"—allowing the poor to multiply recklessly, thus playing into the

104. Ibid., 290.
105. Ibid., 298–300.
106. Ibid., 302.
107. Ibid., 305–307.
108. Ibid., 308–309.

hands of the "sweating employer" by driving down wages. Wells' State would manage all undernourished or neglected children and "enforce their charge upon the parents."[109]

A Modern Utopia (1905) is if possible more terrifying: Wells' future World State would abolish the "last base reason for anyone's servitude or inferiority" by abolishing the laboring class.[110] As to society's "congenital invalids, its idiots and madmen, its drunkards and men of vicious mind, its cruel and furtive souls, its stupid people . . . its lumpish, unteachable and unimaginative people," as well as "the rather spiritless, rather incompetent low-grade man" who tramped the streets looking for work, or worked in sweated trades: "[T]he species must be engaged in eliminating them; there is no escape from that." Nature's way was to "kill the weaker and the sillier, to crush them, to starve them, to overwhelm them," but the enlightened man of the future would prevent births among inferior types and encourage them among the superior.[111] For "evilly diseased births" there would be death, but not for criminals, since Wells could "think of no crime, unless it is reckless begetting or the wilful transmission of contagious disease, for which the bleak terrors, the solitudes and ignominies of the modern prison do not seem outrageously cruel."[112] His Utopia would have "maximum general freedom,"[113] but population control, as "clearly demonstrated by Malthus for all time," was essential.[114] Moreover, to keep track of everyone, "all day and all night for ever a swarm of clerks would go to and fro correcting [the] central register. . . . So the inventory of the State would watch its every man." But this would not be sinister, since there was no need to "assume" that in the future, government would be "necessarily bad, and the individual necessarily good."[115]

In his chapter "Woman in a Modern Utopia"[116] Wells admits that women's freedom would be "not only for woman's sake, but for man's."[117] He advocates sexual freedom but also Malthusian birth control, and State interference in childcare, paid for by parents, although with "sane marriage and birth laws" such interference would be purely temporary and "exceptional,"[118] especially as the State would decide which children to "shelter."[119] State endowment of

109. Ibid., 311.
110. H.G. Wells, *A Modern Utopia*, op. cit., 106.
111. Ibid., 138.
112. Ibid., 148.
113. Ibid., 42.
114. Ibid., 152.
115. Ibid., 164–165.
116. Ibid., 174.
117. Ibid., 185.
118. Ibid., 154.
119. Ibid., 180–181.

motherhood would enable eugenically superior women to have superior children, but with rising living standards there would be only one or two children per family, meaning that the birth rate would be unlikely to rise "very greatly." To Wells, "sound childbearing and rearing" was "a service done, not to a particular man, but to the whole community." Anyone who could not manage on the "minimum wage" would not have children.[120] Wells never discarded his "fascist" approach to the family, under which breeding was a matter for the State, even after real fascism made it a reality.

Far from egalitarian, his Utopia would grade people into creative "Poietic," clever and capable "Kinetic," and "Dull and Base," with various sub-categories.[121] His "nobility," the "Samurai," while open to anyone, would mostly marry among themselves.[122] At the Utopian wedding ceremony each partner, duly licensed for age and health, would receive an index card containing full details of his or her "future mate['s]" age, previous marriages, diseases, offspring, domiciles, public appointments, criminal convictions, and property. This would give the happy couple the chance to change their minds: "Possibly it might be advisable to have a little ceremony for each party, for each in the absence of the other, in which this record could be read over in the presence of witnesses, together with some prescribed form of address of counsel in the matter."[123] Wells would not rule out "multiple" marriage, and[124] while intruding without apology into the lives of the poor, he saw "the adult's private life" as "the entirely private life into which the State may not intrude," providing it did not involve "the protection of the community from inferior births." In a reflection of his own private life, he insisted that a man's infidelity should be a private matter, with State relief only if the woman objected: "The extent of the offence given her is the exact measure of her injury; if she does not mind, nobody minds." The cruel, controlling side of his Utopia was meant to curb the disorder he hated and feared, but which was an inevitable outcome of its libertarianism.[125]

Wells' third Utopian book, *Mankind in the Making* (1903), was even more preoccupied with births,[126] although not in the sense of improving maternity services but in encouraging the "fit" to produce more children: "In that way

---

120. Ibid., 187–188.
121. Ibid., 257–261.
122. Ibid., 283.
123. Ibid., 190–191.
124. His Utopia would not rule out "grouped marriage" between two, three, or more "freely consenting persons" (ibid., 206–207); the Modern Utopia would synthesize all cultures, including polygamous ones (ibid., 209).
125. Ibid., 191–193.
126. H. G. Wells, *Mankind in the Making*, op. cit., 32.

man has risen from the beasts, and in that way men will rise to be over-men."[127] Civilized society had not the "courage" to kill sickly children "outright, quickly, cleanly, and painlessly," or the "heart and courage and ability" to supply their needs. Since "improving the race by selective breeding" was "too remote" (as Chesterton had noted approvingly) they must improve on the "wastage of such births as the world gets to-day."[128] This meant, however, that some people must be "discouraged and prevented from parentage";[129] bad parents whose children were taken away might "be put into celibate labour establishments" if they failed to pay child maintenance, "to work off as much of the debt as they could," until it was "fully discharged."[130]

The existing class system ("Our greatest peers are shareholders . . . equipped by marriage with the wealth of Jews and Americans") would be swept away,[131] but, far from a "homogenous race" there would be a "rich interplay of free, strong, and varied personalities."[132] Wells' I-topia was based on his own personality, on which he based his view of Everyman: "[E]very man who has searched his heart . . . knows himself to be a criminal, just as most men know themselves to be sexually rogues"; moreover, if asked to choose between men with a "bold and enterprising character" who had the courage to commit crime and those afraid to, he preferred "the wicked to the mean." He would "rather trust the future to the former strain than to the latter."[133] Since procreation among the "diseased" was the "nadir of crime," any step "short of torture" was justified to "deter and punish the offender."[134] Even more chillingly, the "people of the Abyss" would be "swept out [of] the rookeries and hiding-places." They "would exist, but they would not multiply—and that is our supreme end. They would be tramping on roads where mendicity laws would prevail, there would be no house-room for them, no squatting-places. The casual wards [of the workhouse] would catch them and register them, and telephone one to the other about them."[135]

Wells' Utopian Socialist World State, predicted to arrive in the 1940s, never materialized, although many of its worst features did, thanks to Stalin and Hitler. Despite this, Wells the open conspirator, on the basis of "they plot, we plan," saw the Catholic Church as a sinister conspiracy. In 1943 published *Crux*

127. Ibid., 39.
128. Ibid., 90–91; see Chapter Four.
129. Ibid., 99.
130. Ibid., 101.
131. Ibid., 255.
132. Ibid., 41.
133. Ibid., 54–55.
134. Ibid., 63–64.
135. Ibid., 110.

Ansata, explaining why Rome had not been bombed. His earlier dismissal of anti-Catholic conspiracy theory forgotten, he claimed Pope Pius XII was "an open ally of the Nazi-Fascist-Shinto Axis since his enthronement" and had "never denounced the abominable aggressions, murder and cruelties they have inflicted upon mankind." Moreover: "[T]he pleas he is now making for peace and forgiveness are manifestly designed to assist the escape of these criminals."[136] In *You Can't Be Too Careful* he had dismissed the Nazi threat, while seeing the Church as the real enemy. Now, his denunciation of Nazism was aimed at the Church.

Wells' last work of non-fiction, *Mind at the end of its Tether* (1945) announced: "Our universe is not merely bankrupt; there remains no dividend at all; it has not simply liquidated; it is going clean out of existence, leaving not a wrack behind."[137] Wells' son George Philip ("Gip") Wells said that when writing this his father had experienced "a recoil from total pessimism," but "presently the recoil spent itself." His father did still hope for the emergence of superior types: "Ordinary men . . . are at the end of their tether. Only a small, highly adaptive minority can possibly survive."[138]

Wells and Fascism

In Wells' evolutionary view of history, nations would come together in a world state, but at the end of the Great War the world was more nationalistic than ever. To Wells, even this "relapse" could be a stage on the way to the World State, but although his own authoritarian approach to the poor was "at once Fascist and Liberal,"[139] he described a meeting of Mosley's Blackshirts as "a

---

136. H.G. Wells, *Crux Ansata: An Indictment of the Roman Catholic Church* (Harmondsworth, Middx.: Penguin Books, 1943), 7. Until the 1960s Pius was regarded as an opponent of Nazism; privately he saved many Jews (see: Pinchas Lapide, *The Last Three Popes and the Jews* [London: Souvenir Press, 1967]); historian Michael Burleigh has traced less favorable attitudes to post-War Italian communist politics ("Dark Enlightenment," More4 TV, January 15, 2006). Wells' biographer sees *Crux Ansata* as a response to "the Church's then-recent manifestations of an increasingly aggressive proselytism under Pius XII," and that Wells' long-standing "anti-Catholicism . . . had been inflamed" by the Belloc controversy"; the book "simply paid all his old debts" (D.C. Smith, *H.G. Wells: Desperately Mortal: A Biography* [New Haven/London: Yale University Press], 457–458). Earlier, Wells said that "the Holy See has recently condemned racialism very clearly and definitely" (H.G. Wells, *The Outlook for Homo Sapiens: An unemotional Statement of the Things that are happening to him now, and of the immediate Possibilities Confronting Him* [London: Secker & Warburg, 1942], 80), and that the Vatican's "relations to fascism" had "always lacked enthusiasm" (ibid., 113).

137. H.G. Wells, *The Last Books of H.G. Wells: The Happy Turning and Mind at the End of its Tether*, op. cit., 77.

138. H.G. Wells, Appendix, ibid., 82–84.

139. A. Maurois, *Prophets and Poets*, trans. Miles, H. (Milton Keynes, Bucks.: Lightning Source UK Ltd., 1935/n.d.), 64.

queer exhibition of futility . . . it would be hard to imagine anything sillier."[140] Mussolini, he said, was a "fantastic renegade from social democracy."[141] But he saw democracy going through a transitional phase. The adversarial parliamentary system "bred such labels as Whig and Tory, Radicals and Conservatives, Labor and Capital, Left and Right, Them and Us." A system in which political parties struggled for votes should have suited the evolutionist approach, but it had not delivered the result Wells wanted. He argued that "the greater part of the voting mass remained marginally literate and effectively innumerate," and although he denied wanting to strip votes from them, "the educated" must "save democracy from itself by becoming a political force." In fact, the masses were not politically uneducated but did not share his political stance, as was their right in a democracy. Wells could no more recognize his own fascist tendencies than could Shaw and the Webbs, but Wells' son Anthony West defended his father from such accusations, arguing that his ideas bore fruit after the War in the United Nations and the European Community.[142]

Although he ridiculed the fascists, in his fiction and non-fiction Wells saw them converting to the world state idea. Arguably, too, his writings encouraged an appeasement mentality against Nazi Germany, but Wells' search for consensus was doomed. He was accused of ignoring the fascist menace, but was convinced that the world state would arise from the wreckage of the coming war.[143] In 1932 he called on progressives to become "liberal fascists" and "enlightened Nazis,"[144] while taking the evolutionary, biological view that real fascism would pass like a fever. But it was infected by the same Nietzschean "will to power" that he espoused and could only be overthrown by force after inflicting immense damage, especially on the types of people he advocated killing.

Wells and Soviet Communism

In contrast, Wells seemed to feel that communism would pass if "left to itself" because he intervened to defend it in 1918 when, in the face of a "great storm of rancour" following the Russians' exit from the Great War, he urged people "to rethink their opposition to the Bolsheviks." Kerensky, "a weak person," had been "overthrown," and Wells "felt that the aims of most liberals in the world continued to coincide with Russian aims; that is, an end to German milita-

---

140. H.G. Wells, *Experiment in Autobiography Vol. II*, op. cit., 782–783.

141. Wells' comment was made during his Australian tour in January 1939 (D.C. Smith, *H.G. Wells: Desperately Mortal: A Biography*, op. cit., 343).

142. A. West, *H.G. Wells: Aspects of a Life* (London: Hutchinson & Co. Ltd., 1984), 115–117.

143. Ibid., 129.

144. H.G. Wells, Address to Young Liberals, Oxford, July 1932 (P. Coupland, "H.G. Wells' Liberal Fascism," *Journal of Contemporary History* 35, no. 4, October 2000, 549, in J. Goldberg, *Liberal Fascism*, op. cit., 21).

rism." He added that the Bolsheviks were "altogether wiser and plainer than our own rulers."[145] Chesterton, who had been "[i]nclined at first to hope for the fruits of democracy from the Russian revolution" was soon "reproached by H.G. Wells for 'dirty' suspiciousness about the Bolshevik leaders and their motives."[146] Later, Chesterton would claim that Russian State communism had become State capitalism. Wells agreed, and said that Russia was "no longer a Communism nor a democratic Socialism" but had "come out of these things as a chick comes out of its egg." It was "a novel experimental state capitalism, growing more scientific in its methods every year."[147] Wells approved the scientific approach, including the suppression of religion, but he "prided himself on not having an overly romantic or sanguine view of this enigmatic country and its band of dedicated revolutionaries." His visit to Russia was not an unbroken round of mutual admiration,[148] but he continued as a supporter, albeit more critically. In 1934 he visited Roosevelt and met Stalin in Moscow:[149] "I disbelieve in [the Bolsheviks'] faith, I ridicule Marx, their prophet, but I understand and respect their spirit."[150]

He was aware of repression, but "[i]t was not merely a question of the loss and misery . . . inflicted upon the Russian people, appalling though that aspect of the matter was." More important was the effect of such "brutalities," which were "inseparable from the execution of these policies" on world opinion, particularly in America.[151]

Wells was concerned that these "unavoidable" Soviet brutalities would prevent closer rapprochement between America and Russia, needed to bring about his world state: "Big business is by no means antipathetic to Communism. The larger big business grows the more it approximates to Collectivism. It is the upper road of the few instead of the lower road of the masses to Collectivism."[152]

Wells said of Stalin that he had "never met a man more candid, fair and honest." It was "to these qualities . . . and to nothing occult and sinister," that the Soviet leader owed his "tremendous undisputed ascendancy in Russia." Wells

145. H.G. Wells, "Mr. Wells and the Bolsheviks: Some Disregarded Aspects," *Daily Mail*, January 15, 1918, in D.C. Smith, *H.G. Wells: Desperately Mortal: A Biography*, op. cit., 235.

146. M. Ward, *Gilbert Keith Chesterton* (New York: Sheed & Ward, 1943), 405.

147. H.G. Wells, *Experiment in Autobiography: Discoveries and conclusions of a very ordinary brain (since 1866) Vol. I* (London: Faber & Faber, 1934/1984), 264–265.

148. Lenin said of Wells: "'Ugh! What a narrow petty bourgeois! Ugh! What a Philistine!'" (M. Coren, *The Invisible Man: The Life and Liberties of H.G. Wells*, op. cit., 175–176).

149. Ibid., 197.

150. H.G. Wells, *Russia in the Shadows* (London: Hodder & Stoughton, 1920), 88.

151. A. West, *H.G. Wells: Aspects of a Life*, op. cit., 134.

152. H.G. Wells, *Russia in the Shadows*, op. cit., 152.

had believed Stalin "might be where he was because men were afraid of him," but it was because "no one is afraid of him and everybody trusts him."[153]

Wells and Nazism

Many saw fascism as a bulwark against communism, but with the rise of Nazism, Sovietism appealed even more strongly to the anti-capitalist Wells, who saw it as a beacon of hope. Like Shaw, however, Wells projected his own views onto the dictators, rationalizing and almost excusing their war-like tendencies. In 1938 he attacked Neville Chamberlain's appeasement of Hitler but claimed that "dictators such as Hitler, Mussolini, and Stalin were forced to make spectacular moves to retain their power."[154] By 1939 he believed that "[i]f the common people of the United Kingdom, the Commonwealth, and the United States could take charge of the situation the trouble might be thwarted." Wells had never seen "the common people" as anything other than an obstacle to progress. Now he argued that the British Parliament "did not want the people in power, as it would mean the end of Hitler, and a social revolution, perhaps even an alliance with Russia." He realized that "war was at hand" and "only a radical reform of government would forestall it."[155]

Wells blamed Britain for this situation, and argued with Shaw and left-winger Harold Laski over who was responsible for the War. The intellectual Left had been in turmoil since Hitler and Stalin signed their non-aggression pact, stalled in their criticism of Nazism by the Man of Steel's about-turn. While the Labour Party joined a war-time coalition government and the trades unions and ordinary socialists supported the war effort, the far-Left spent the early War years sniping at war-time conditions.[156] But when Hitler invaded Russia and Stalin became an ally, communists could support the War with a clear conscience, in defense of the Soviet Union. Wells even urged the United States to enter the War,[157] but supporting his own government was an unnatural and consequently stressful position. Wells, the constant opponent, could not support his country or attack the dictators too wholeheartedly, and solved the problem by attacking the Catholic Church instead.[158]

---

153. However, the "furnishing" of Stalin's mind "stopped at the point reached by Lenin when he reconditioned Marxism"; whenever Wells tried to move him he fell back on Marxist "orthodoxy" (H.G. Wells, *Experiment in Autobiography Vol. II*, op. cit., 805–806).

154. D.C. Smith, *H.G. Wells: Desperately Mortal: A Biography*, op. cit., 341.

155. H.G. Wells, "1939—What Does it Hold?" *News Chronicle*, January 2 & 3, 1939, 2 (ibid., 340).

156. See: Paul Addison, *The Road to 1945: British Politics and the Second World War* (London: Jonathan Cape, 1975).

157. D.C. Smith, *H.G. Wells: Desperately Mortal: A Biography*, op. cit., 452.

158. Ibid., 454–455.

Seen as one of the "first to analyse Fascism and Nazism" his remarks on the "impact of racism" have been regarded as "prescient."[159] And yet the fascists and Nazis achieved power as ruthlessly as the Bolsheviks, killing political opponents—an approach Wells favored, as he also did the killing of the weak and breeding "better" men. Many English eugenicists envied the Nazi eugenics program, and while they too criticized Nazi anti-Semitism, their chief worry was that Hitler would give eugenics a bad name.[160] Michael Coren remarks: "[T]hrough his political writings Wells helped create an intellectual climate in the 1920s and 1930s that—though not leading directly to the social-engineering horrors of Hitler and Stalin—certainly gave credibility to the atrocities of the dictators." Wells "injected permissibility into political eugenics," and "varnished murderous ideas with respect and reputation." The "social engineers" believed that by "exterminating or incarcerating perhaps one half of the world's population the remaining half would enjoy unparalleled benefits. Wells not only went along with this, he encouraged it."[161]

This critique may be seen as influenced by the Holocaust, but in 1941, in his essay *Wells, Hitler and the World State*, George Orwell claimed that Wells' persistent dismissal of the Nazi threat as "spent" represented "the same gospel" as he had been preaching "almost without interruption for the past forty years, always with an air of angry surprise" at those who failed to "grasp anything so obvious." The "main object of English left-wing intellectuals" for the last twenty years had been to destroy patriotism, and "if they had succeeded" they might now be "watching the S.S. men patrolling the London streets." Orwell claimed that Churchill had been more accurate regarding the threat of Bolshevism than Wells, who equated "science with common sense." Germany was "far more scientific than England," but "more barbarous." In fact: "Much of what Wells has imagined and worked for is physically there in Nazi Germany. . . . Science is fighting on the side of superstition."[162]

Wells supported his country in its hour of need but, still dazzled by the ideas that influenced the dictators, gave no sign that his philosophy had been proved disastrously wrong. Rather he showed growing impatience that people still failed to agree with him. In a 1943 radio talk he "discussed the abolition of distance, the tremendous increase in mechanical power, and how these had made it possible and necessary for the new world order to be egalitarian," views cited

159. Ibid., 281.

160. A. Farmer, *By Their Fruits: Eugenics, Population Control and the Abortion Campaign* (Washington D.C.: Catholic University of America Press), 117–118.

161. M. Coren, *The Invisible Man: The Life and Liberties of H. G. Wells*, op. cit., 226.

162. G. Orwell, "Wells, Hitler and the World State," *Horizon*, August 1941, accessed February 15, 2009, http://www.orwell.ru/library/reviews/wells/english/e_whws.

by his biographer as evidence of "the bright and cheerful Wells, saying that all were learning together." He adds that Julian Huxley "thought the talk admirable,"[163] although in 1931 he had discussed employing the "lethal chamber" as a solution to the "problem" of "evil recessives" in *Science of Life* with Wells and his son Gip, and was still advocating eugenics and population control long after the War.[164] In *Mind at the End of Its Tether*, Wells' biographer sees as a sign of "optimistic promise" his reiteration of his old prescription for the human race, under the heading "Adapt or Perish":

> Deliberately planned legislation, food shortages, and such-like economic processes, waves of sentiment for or against maternity, patriotic feeling, or the want of it, the natural disposition of love coupled with a desire to fix a relationship by some permanent common interest, and a pride in physically and mentally well-begotten children, may play incalculable parts in the production of a new humanity, capable of an adaptation to the whirling imperatives about us, sufficient to see out the story of life on earth to its end.[165]

Wells sounds more optimistic in believing that Mankind would survive, but it would be in a radically altered form. He still believed that in order to survive, the human race would have to "perfect" itself by eliminating all perceived weakness, but it would thereby sacrifice its humanity. His failure to even acknowledge that eugenics had led not to the Utopian dream but to a dystopian nightmare, represents a failure of imagination in the most imaginative of authors, fatally damaging his claims to prophet status.

Wells and the Jews

Chesterton had dissected and rejected eugenics in 1920, but somehow Wells' reputation survived the wreckage of a discredited philosophy that depended on the disappearance of a distinctive Jewish people and the murder of millions of others, while Chesterton acquired a reputation for anti-Semitism and small-mindedness.[166] Since the Nazis were anti-Semitic, and communism opposed Nazism, communism has been regarded as pro-Jewish.[167] The same chain of reasoning has meant that the "anti-Semitism" of thinkers like Wells has been

---

163. D.C. Smith, *H.G. Wells: Desperately Mortal: A Biography*, op. cit., 466–467.

164. In the future incest might be encouraged provided there was "no reason to suspect a grave recessive taint"; it might even be made compulsory, "with a prompt resort to the lethal chamber for any undesirable results." A "grim Utopia, no doubt, but in that manner our race might be purged of its evil recessives for ever" (H.G. Wells, J. Huxley, G.P. Wells, *Science of Life* [London: Cassell, 1931], 307).

165. D.C. Smith, *H.G. Wells: Desperately Mortal: A Biography*, op. cit., 476–477.

166. M. Coren, *The Invisible Man: The Life and Liberties of H.G. Wells*, op. cit., 212–213.

167. Goldberg, *Liberal Fascism*, op. cit., 75.

overlooked because they were socialists, while Chesterton—like Wells, an opponent of capitalism—has been positioned on the Right because of his opposition to socialism, and consequently has been regarded as anti-Semitic.[168] Anti-Semitism has been found across the political spectrum, however. The ethnically Jewish Karl Marx, father of communism, condemned Judaism as a religion of hucksters,[169] and Wells, who ridiculed Marx, portrayed Jews as materialistic. Coren says Wells' anti-Semitism "was as constant as it was consistent,"[170] such that Israel Zangwill broke off their friendship.[171] Wells, unlike Chesterton and Belloc, did not know many Jews,[172] and was still attacking Zionism on the brink of the Second World War.[173] Coren also cites the *Jewish Chronicle*'s attack on Wells' reference to the "essential parasitism of the Jewish mycelium upon the social and cultural organisms in which it lives" in *The Anatomy of Frustration*, along with Wells' response—that they had not appreciated his "essential altruism towards their people."[174]

In 1940 Wells asked: "Is this a war to salvage a world manifestly far gone in decay, or is it a vast tragic clearance for a new order? The only answer with hope in it is the latter."[175] This was an echo of *The Holy Terror*, in which Wells' dictator clears away the decayed world order to usher in the World State, before being shot. Wells undoubtedly hoped the Nazis would be cleared away once they had cleared away all the "decay" that was holding back his new world order. One of these things was Jewish particularity, which he blamed for causing anti-Semitism, and when in November 1942 he was "faced with Jan Karski's eye-witness account of Belzec death camp," he asked why "in every country where Jews reside, sooner or later antisemitism emerges."[176] It was not the first

---

168. "As joint figurehead of Distributism with Belloc, Chesterton has been associated with an increasingly entrenched and anti-Semitic 'radical right' after the First World War" (J. Stapleton, *Christianity, Patriotism, and Nationhood: The England of G.K. Chesterton* [Lanham MD/Plymouth, England: Lexington Books, 2009], 183) (citing A. Sykes, *The Radical Right in Britain: Social Imperialism to the BNP* [Basingstoke, Hants.: Macmillan, 2005], 76–77). Despite Fascism's anti-capitalist stance, the *Jewish Chronicle* apologized for a "typographical error" stating that A.K. Chesterton was "the leader of the extreme Left-wing National Front. This, of course, should have read 'Right-wing'" (May 15, 1970, 16–17).

169. K. Marx, *On the Jewish Question* (1844, Paris); see Chapter Two.

170. M. Coren, *The Invisible Man: The Life and Liberties of H.G. Wells*, op. cit., 213.

171. Ibid., 51; 213; 216.

172. Ibid., 213.

173. Ibid., 217.

174. Ibid., 219.

175. H.G. Wells, *The Common Sense of War and Peace: World Revolution or War Unending* (Harmondsworth, Middx.: Penguin Books, 1940), 25.

176. Jan Karski, "The Message that was Delivered, But Not Heard," in M. Littell, R. Libowitz, E.B. Rosen, eds., *The Holocaust Forty Years After* (New York, 1989), 29–35, in B. Cheyette, *Constructions of "the Jew" in English literature and society: Racial representations, 1875–1945* (Cambridge: Cambridge

time Wells had heard such testimony.[177] Judaism was not supposed to be cleared away like this, but his worldview remained unshaken.

Nevertheless, Wells often used scientific terminology regarding groups of people, including "that miscellany of enquiring and experimenting people," the Fabian Society, which "spread like the mycelium of a fungus throughout that organisation."[178] Furthermore, during the Great War Wells "called for restoration of Palestine to the Jews, creating a real Judaea."[179] Wells' autobiography refers to "[m]y friend Philip Guedalla,"[180] and in a situation reminiscent of Chesterton's friendship with the Solomon brothers, Guedalla moved near Wells, helped him with proofreading, and even dedicated a book to him.[181] As a boy, inspired by history, race theories, and Imperialism, Wells commanded imaginary armies, which defeated the "decadent Latin peoples." This "blended very well with the anti-Roman Catholic influence of the 18th-century Protestant training," and his "distrust and hostility . . . remained quite vivid when much else of that teaching had faded." The youthful Wells "had ideas about Aryans extraordinarily like Mr. Hitler's," and in his imagination drove "the inferior breeds into the mountains." His "ultimate triumphs everywhere" in these games "squared accounts with the Jews, against which people I had a subconscious dissatisfaction because of their disproportionate share of Holy Writ. I thought Abraham, Isaac, Moses and David loathsome creatures and fit associates for Our Father [God]." But "unlike Hitler" Wells admitted "no feelings about the contemporary Jew" and his autobiography mentions neither Zangwill nor Zionism. He claimed that as a student he knew several Jews without being "aware of it": "My particular pal, Sidney Bowkett, was I think unconsciously Jewish; the point never arose."[182]

Like his youthful dictator in *The Holy Terror* Wells often rehearsed the theme

---

University Press, 1997), 146–147. In response to such reports Jews and Christians held a public protest meeting on October 29 1942 (M. Gilbert, *Churchill and the Jews*, op. cit., 192). When Karski reported in December 1942 that thousands of Jews had been sent to Belzec, Jewish and Christian leaders urged a public statement by the Allies; simultaneous broadcasts were made from London, Washington, and Moscow on December 17, 1942 (ibid., 195).

177. In 1940 Wells claimed that Lord Halifax cared little for "the hardships of the Jews in the concentration camps" (H.G. Wells, *The Common Sense of War and Peace*, op. cit., 22); in 1942 he said he had heard some cases personally; discussing whether such cruelty was unique to Germans he argued that if it was "innate, then biologically it would an excellent thing to kill all Germans," but concluded that the German was "a being innately as gentle as you and I, only he is inspired by an hysterical desire to be utterly tough" (H.G. Wells, *The Outlook for Homo Sapiens*, op. cit., 108–110).

178. H.G. Wells, *Experiment in Autobiography Vol. II*, op. cit., 607.

179. H.G. Wells, Letter to Holbrook Jackson, late 1916, in D.C. Smith, *H.G. Wells: Desperately Mortal: A Biography*, op. cit., 236–237.

180. H.G. Wells, *Experiment in Autobiography Vol. II*, op. cit., 707.

181. D.C. Smith, *H.G. Wells: Desperately Mortal: A Biography*, op. cit., 400; see Chapter Seven.

182. H.G. Wells, *Experiment in Autobiography Vol. I*, op. cit., 99–100.

of not recognizing Jews among his acquaintance, blaming the Bible and the "separateness" of Jews for creating anti-Semitism. While explicitly rejecting modern racial theories, Wells' fictional Jews were mostly materialistic stereotypes, but he did know real Jews in his youth. He and his friend Walter Low ("tall and dark, not the Jew of convention and caricature, the ambitious and not the acquisitive sort, mysterious and deliberate") "argued endlessly" about "the Jewish question, upon which he sought continually to enlighten me. But I have always refused to be enlightened and sympathetic about the Jewish question. From my cosmopolitan standpoint it is a question that ought not to exist."[183] In line with his conception of Jews as harbingers of his socialist World State, *Russia in the Shadows* (1920) approved of Jewish communists. Many Bolsheviks were Jewish exiles, drawn back from America by the Revolution, but few, he said, had any "strong racial Jewish feeling." They were "not out for Jewry but for a new world." In fact, they had "put most of the Zionist leaders in Russia in prison" and "proscribed the teaching of Hebrew as a 'reactionary' language."[184]

Wells, like Chesterton, did not see himself as anti-Semitic, but Rubinstein describes his views as "notorious," saying that he saw the Jewish people as "an atavistic survival," their Chosen People concept as the cause of recurrent anti-Semitism, and their Zionism as selfishness unworthy of world citizens.[185] Tony Kushner agrees, although "[o]ther 'liberal' socialists, such as . . . Shaw and . . . Orwell, were united with Wells in his opposition to Jewish exclusivity."[186] Wells agreed with Shaw that Hitler had stolen the Chosen Race idea, and valued Jewish qualities highly enough to urge their assimilation. But Hitler was determined that German "blood" would not be so polluted. Under the Nuremberg Laws of 1933 no one with traceable Jewish heritage was safe, and the War demonstrated the Nazis' determination to eliminate Jews wherever they were found. There would be no assimilation. Still Wells believed that if only the Jews would disappear as a people, anti-Semitism would cease. On a simplistic level he was right—no Jews, no anti-Semitism.

The "scientific" Wells rejected anti-Semitism, but also saw religious belief as unscientific and unlike Chesterton ridiculed Jewish beliefs. In *Anticipations* Wells appears ambivalent on the "Jewish question," asking how the New

183. Low and Wells "never quarrelled" but had some "lively passages and if we convinced each other of nothing we considerably instructed each other" (ibid., 353).

184. Lenin the "beloved leader" had "a Tartar type of face and is certainly no Jew" (H. G. Wells, *Russia in the Shadows*, op. cit., 74–75).

185. W. D. Rubinstein, *A History of the Jews in the English-Speaking World: Great Britain* (London: Macmillan Press Ltd., 1996), 220.

186. T. Kushner, *The Persistence of Prejudice: Antisemitism in British Society during the Second World War*, op. cit., 93.

Republic will "tackle that alleged termite in the civilized woodwork, the Jew? Certainly not as races at all" but as "any other man." Wells adds: "If the Jew has a certain incurable tendency to social parasitism, and we make social parasitism impossible, we shall abolish the Jew, and if he has not, there is no need to abolish the Jew." Wells claimed not to understand anti-Semitism, since non-Jews also exhibited negative characteristics.[187] Granted, Jews had asserted their nationality "with a singular tactlessness" but so did the English. Wells saw nothing in their "curious, dispersed nationality to dread or dislike," seeing the Jew as "the mediaeval Liberal" whose "persistent existence had given 'the lie to Catholic pretensions' and now gave it to 'all our yapping nationalisms.'" He saw Jewish dispersion throughout the world as paradigmatic of "the coming of the world-state," but "the Jew" would "probably lose much of his particularism, intermarry with Gentiles," and "in a century or two" would "cease to be ... physically distinct." But Wells concludes by hoping that "much of his moral tradition" would "never die." As for the "swarms of black, and brown, and dirty-white, and yellow people, who do not come into the new needs of efficiency," they would "have to go."[188]

A Modern Utopia is less brutal, but insists that the "unfit" be "weeded out."[189] *The Shape of Things to Come* posits that, thanks to evolution, the descendants of the "shrill, unhappy, swarming, degenerate, under-nourished, under-educated, under-bred and short-lived populations" that had been killed off by "pestilences ... and grimly disciplined by the Tyranny" would become the "finest, handsomest, longest-lived" in the world, bearing "as fine flowers of literary and scientific achievement as any other racial masses."[190] Wells denied that "half-breeds" were "peculiarly evil" and in his explicit rejections of racism came closest to Chesterton's stance.[191] He even claimed his Utopia would include "white and black, brown, red and yellow, all tints of skin, all types of body and character,"[192] but there would be no bent people, no fat, bald, grey, "obviously aged" or sick people.[193] And now he argued that there was "only one sane and logical thing to be done with a really inferior race," which was "to exterminate

---

187. In *Tono-Bungay* the non-Jewish Uncle Ponderevo lacks business ethics, but unlike the Jewish characters is sympathetically portrayed; see Chapter Four.

188. "[T]he world is ... not a charitable institution, and I take it they will have to go.... So far as they fail to develop sane, vigorous, and distinctive personalities for the great world of the future, it is their portion to die out" (H. G. Wells, *Anticipations*, op. cit., 315–317).

189. H. G. Wells, *A Modern Utopia*, op. cit., 316–317.

190. H. G. Wells, *The Shape of Things to Come: The Ultimate Revolution* (London: J.M. Dent, 1933/1999), 403.

191. H. G. Wells, *A Modern Utopia*, op. cit., 322.

192. Ibid., 33.

193. Ibid., 221.

it." He claimed the British had done this by keeping the Fijians in adverse conditions, maintaining: "The extermination need never be discriminatory."[194] Wells also praised the father of eugenics, Sir Francis Galton, and his "really very noble-spirited and high-class scheme" of eugenics mating,[195] and in *The Shape of Things to Come* the World State has a "general plan for the directed evolution of life."[196] But, he argued, Man would no longer be "distressed and driven to cruelty by overcrowding, under-nourishment, infections, mental and physical poisons of every sort."[197] Chesterton would applaud Wells' ridicule of a Jewish skull type in *A Modern Utopia*,[198] which anticipates Jewish qualities (especially their "cosmopolitan" tendencies) being devoted to the World State: "[M]y friend, Moses Cohen, thinks there is much to be said for the Jew."[199] Galton too saw superior qualities in Jews, some of whom adopted the idea as a defense against allegations of their inferiority, possibly leading to expendability.[200]

In *The Shape of Things to Come*, in which Wells attacked the Jewish religion and foretold its end, despite their "obstinate resolve" to remain separate, between 1940 and 2059 "this antiquated and obdurate culture disappeared," along with the Zionist state. "The Jews were not suppressed; there was no extermination."[201] The story's claims of the gentle evolutionary death of religion clashed with its revelation that after the gassing of the pope, the chief Muslim holy places were closed, and Indian religious observances suppressed, along with "the slaughter-houses in which Kosher food was prepared in an antiquated and unpleasant manner." An "Act of Uniformity came into operation everywhere. There was now to be one faith only in the world, the moral expression of

194. H.G. Wells, *A Modern Utopia*, op. cit., 324–325.

195. Galton's graded adolescent intelligences lacked "only the rules for identifying" the above-average (H.G. Wells, *Mankind in the Making*, op. cit., 38).

196. H.G. Wells, *The Shape of Things to Come*, op. cit., 381.

197. Ibid., 384.

198. H.G. Wells, *A Modern Utopia*, op. cit., 318.

199. Ibid., 330–331.

200. J. Jacobs, *Jewish Contributions to Civilization: An Estimate* (Philadelphia: The Jewish Publication Society of America, 1919), 50; Jacobs said Houston Stewart Chamberlain had "pushed the concept of the Chosen Race beyond all bounds"; that the modern notion of the chosen race was that of "Chosen Races," in which every race, with its own special characteristics, could contribute to human achievement (ibid., 51–52); Israel Zangwill, skeptical of racial theories, said that Jacobs, a "disciple" of Francis Galton, measured thousands of Jewish children, concluding that there was a "Jewish type"— but this "type" happened to resemble Zangwill's brother Louis, one of the children studied; Jacobs, keen to emphasize the value of Jews to civilization, claimed that only 13 per cent had "the notorious "Jewish nose"" while nearly 60 per cent had "Greek" noses (I. Zangwill, *The Voice of Jerusalem* [London: Wm. Heinemann, 1920], 339–340). Galton described the eugenicist Harold Laski as ""[s]imply a beautiful youth of the Jewish type,"" while Laski argued against the idea of a specific physical Jewish "type" (Daniel J. Kevles, *In the Name of Eugenics: Genetics and the Uses of Human Heredity* [Harvard University Press, 1985], 86).

201. H.G. Wells, *The Shape of Things to Come*, op. cit., 372–373.

the one world community."[202] After the "Modern World State" emerges, the Jews are told "the truth about their race," and they surrender their education and lifestyle and dissolve their qualities in the human gene pool.[203]

Wells' factual work *The Outline of History* (1920) maintains that the Jews, "a People of Mixed Origin," went to Babylon and "came back with an intense and exclusive national spirit," becoming "convinced at last . . . that they were the chosen people of the one God of all the earth."[204] *The Anatomy of Frustration* (1936) articulates Wells' views on the socialist World State and takes a much harsher line on the Jewish people. Under the heading "Cultural Obsessions," narrator William Burroughs Steele describes his plan of making "a sort of History of Persecution" in which "the persecuted" were "hardly ever . . . completely in the right. They were really destructive or demoralizing. They were really malicious. They were really a threat. They would tolerate no compromise and made the dispute an issue of 'my way or yours.' Something had to be done about them."[205] Wells' narrator insists that although his readers might "repudiate and fight against the clumsy revengefulness, the plunderings, outrages and fantastic intimidations of the Nazi method," it would not "close the Jewish problem," and, as seen, describes the "the essential parasitism of the Jewish mycelium" on the "social and cultural organisms" in which it lived. He further claimed that they had not "faced up to" this "problem."[206] Many Jews had "faced up to" the "Jewish problem" by espousing Zionism, but the book blamed Zionism for Nazi anti-Semitism: "In one surprising passage Steele argues that the German National Socialist movement is essentially Jewish in spirit and origin, it is Bible-born, an imitation of Old Testament nationalism." Wells interpolates insouciantly: "The Jews have been taxed with most sins but never before with begetting the Nazi" before "Steele" further alleges that preserving the Bible "as a book sacred beyond criticism has kept alive a tradition of barbaric cunning and barbaric racialism, generation after generation, to the infinite injury of economic and political life." He concludes: "Why specialize in Erin or Mother India or Palestine, when the whole world is our common inheritance? *Come out of Israel!*"[207]

Travels of a Republican Radical in Search of Hot Water (1939) is even more unsympathetic: "I met a Jewish friend of mine the other day and he asked me,

202. Ibid., 324; see Chapter Four.

203. Ibid., 373.

204. H. G. Wells, *The Outline of History: Being a Plain History of Life and Mankind from Primordial Life to Nineteen-sixty* (London: Cassell, 1920/1961), 265–266.

205. H. G. Wells, *The Anatomy of Frustration: a modern synthesis* (London: The Cresset Press, 1936), 173.

206. Ibid., 178.

207. Ibid., 181–183.

'What is going to happen to the Jews?' I told him I had rather he had asked me . . . 'What is going to happen to mankind?' 'But *my* people—' he began. 'That,' said I, 'is exactly what is the matter with them.'" Wells reiterates his claim that his friend Walter Low "first suggested" that he was "behaving badly to a persecuted race,"[208] and that "he was treated as an outcast, and presently along came Zangwill in a state of racial championship, exacerbating this idea that I was responsible for the Egyptian and Babylonian captivities, the destruction of Jerusalem, the ghettos, auto-da-fés—and generally what was I going to do about it? My disposition was all for letting bygones be bygones." Wells claimed that in England there had been "no social, political or economic discrimination against the Jews for several generations," but there was a "growing irritation at the killing and wounding of British soldiers and Arabs . . . because of this Zionist idea." In his youth, in England and America, "it was possible . . . to answer the Jewish Question with one word, 'Assimilate.' We would declare we had no objection. Wasn't our civilisation good enough for anyone?" But he admitted that in 1939, this response was no longer practical: "Life has very suddenly and swiftly taken on a grimmer face to everyone, but more immediately towards the Jew. The doors to assimilation are being slammed upon him. He is being driven out of countries where he had seemed to be secure. He is no longer free to escape to the countries which tolerate his kind. . . . He is threatened very plainly with a systematic attempt to exterminate him . . . brutally and cruelly."[209]

At last Wells appeared to grasp the seriousness of the Jewish plight; yet his answer was "to modernise," arguing: "No people in the world have caught the fever of irrational nationalism that has been epidemic in the world since 1918, so badly as the Jews," reiterating his belief that "the current Nazi gospel is actually and traceably the Old Testament turned inside out," and, moreover, that it was "one step from the Lutheran Church to the Brown House."[210] The belief, dating back to 1914 and influenced by "third-rate writers such as Gobineau and Stewart Chamberlain" had convinced the Germans that they were "a people of peculiar excellence to dominate the earth."[211]It was, he warned, "quite possible

---

208. "When I was a schoolboy in a London suburb I never heard of the 'Jewish Question.' I realised later that I had Jewish and semi-Jewish school-fellows, but not at the time. They were all one to me. The Jews, I thought, were people in the Bible, and that was that" (H.G. Wells, *Travels of a Republican Radical in Search of Hot Water* [Harmondsworth, Middx.: Penguin, 1939/1947], 53); Low illustrated *The Autocracy of Mr. Parham* (1930); see Chapter Four.

209. Wells claimed that throughout the Great War "Zangwill and the Jewish spokesmen . . . most elaborately and energetically" showed that they "cared not a rap for the troubles and dangers of English, French, Germans, Russians, Americans or of any other people but their own" (ibid., 54–56).

210. Ibid., 58–60.

211. H.G. Wells, "The War of the Mind," 1914 *Illustrated—the Book of the Year: a Record of Notable Achievements and Events*, accessed November 16, 2009, http://www.greatwardifferent.com/Great_War/Bishop/Mind_01.htm.

that the Jewish story" would "end in forcible sterilisation and death." And yet there was "no reason why it should do so," provided that people ceased clinging to "flattering lies, delusions, animosities, mean advantages. The accepted tradition of the Jews is largely nonsense. They are no more a 'pure' race than the English or the Germans or the hundred per cent Americans. There never was a 'Promise'; they were never 'Chosen'; their distinctive observances, their Sabbath, their Passover, their queer calendar, are mere traditional oddities of no present significance whatever." According to Wells, the "only way out from the present human catastrophe . . . for Jew and Gentile alike" was "a worldwide, conscious educational emancipation. In books, universities, colleges, schools, newspapers, plays, assemblies, we want incessant, ruthless truth-telling about these old legends that divide and antagonise and waste us. We want a great massacre of stale beliefs and ancient grievances and claims, if we are to avoid great massacres of human beings."[212] In effect, Wells' response to Nazi persecution was a propaganda campaign telling everyone that the Jews were nobody special—that their belief in being chosen by God was hubristic, delusional, and a downright lie. This was before the Holocaust, but the Jewish people would have been massacred long before a program such as Wells proposed had gained acceptance; but even if it had been put in place, it would have been completely counter-productive.

In *The Outlook for Homo Sapiens* (1942) Wells again warned: "I can see no other destiny for orthodox Judaism and those who are involved in its obloquy, unless that enormous effort to reconstruct human mentality for which I have been pleading arrives in time to arrest their march to destruction."[213] In reality, Judaism and "those involved in its obloquy" were not under equal threat of destruction, but Wells saw the Jewish religion as the more dangerous: "It is this orthodox remnant and its behaviour and influence, the repercussions it evokes and the dangers to which it has exposed the whole Jewish community, which constitute the Jewish problem." Worse, he saw in the "orthodox remnant" a Jewish conspiracy:

> Almost every community with which the orthodox Jews have come into contact has sooner or later developed and acted upon that conspiracy idea. A careful reading of the Bible does nothing to correct it; there indeed you have the conspiracy plain and clear. It is not simply the defensive conspiracy of a nice harmless people anxious to keep up their dear, quaint old customs that we are dealing with. It is an aggressive and vindictive conspiracy. . . . Much of it is ferocious; extraordinarily like the rantings of some Nazi propagandist.

212. H.G. Wells, *Travels of a Republican Radical*, op. cit., 60–62.
213. H.G. Wells, *The Outlook for Homo Sapiens*, op. cit., 88.

> The best the poor Gentile can expect is to play the part of a Gibeonite, a hewer of wood and a drawer of water for the restored elect.[214]

Despite this, like Shaw and Chesterton, Wells was an early critic of Nazi anti-Semitism, actively supporting initiatives against it.[215] He intervened personally to help a German Jewish refugee with naturalization,[216] and at the 1938 Evian Conference advocated help for such individuals.[217] When war began, he called the Nazis "a flight of locusts. . . . One has to kill them or be killed, because reason would be wasted on them."[218] While Shaw campaigned for the release of fascists, Wells campaigned against fascists, traitors and "fifth columnists."[219]

Jews alternately praised and criticized Shaw and Wells as they appeared to lurch from anti-Semitism to pro-Semitism and back again. Reviewing *The Shape of Things to Come* in 1936, "Watchman," writing in the *Jewish Chronicle* thought Wells, "a writer with a very original and independent mind," who had "qualities [that] seem to lead him into strange and unexpected lines of thought about Jews." Notable among these was the idea that anti-Semitism would disappear if Jews abandoned their Jewishness:

> The Nazi indictment of the Jews is swallowed at a gulp. The separate Jewish culture is to be abandoned. Nazism is steeling us 'for finer and broader efforts.' When sufficiently 'steeled' presumably, the racialism of Hitler will be dropped. A Jew will miraculously become a German and a Jewish Paradise will arise on the spree! . . . Mr. Wells should take this stuff to the STUERMER rather than the SPECTATOR.

Wells, the paper continued, had profited from his books and films, but "when some Gentiles make money, the fact has no general significance," but Jews who made money were said to be "animated by a distinctive Jewish tradition." As for his remarks about Jews not being good citizens: "One can only be

---

214. Ibid., 76–77.

215. Responding to calls from French, Polish, and Belgian delegates that German discrimination against Jews, especially writers, be denounced, President H.G. Wells ruled that "politics could not be barred from discussion, since it was a question of the life of humanity," leading to German protests ("Germans Walk out of PEN Club Congress: Resolution of Protest Carried," *Jewish Chronicle*, June 2, 1933, 11).

216. "H.G. Wells on Wholesale Internment," *Jewish Chronicle*, July 5, 1940, 16–17.

217. "Refugees and Evian: Appeal to British Government: "Support Tradition of Humanity," *Jewish Chronicle*, June 24, 1938, 36–37.

218. H.G. Wells, *The Common Sense of War and Peace*, op. cit., 9.

219. "'Doing Goebbels's Work': H.G. Wells Accuses Officials of Treachery: Deliberate Wrecking Alleged," *Jewish Chronicle*, August 2, 1940, 6–7. In a "vigorous article" in the *Sunday Despatch* Wells called for highly placed German sympathizers to be charged ("Mr. Wells Accuses: 'Fifth Column Traitors Must Be Charged,'" ibid., October 25, 1940, 10–11); at a meeting of the National Peace Council, British fascists demanded that Oswald Mosley be allowed to broadcast; Wells remarked: "'He never said anything worth hearing'" (ibid., March 15, 1940, 30–31).

sorry that Mr. Wells should, if only by inference, seem to lend his great and splendid reputation to such stale anti-Jewish stuff. There will be rejoicing in Germany and wherever else life is made hell for the Jewish underdog." Recalling Shaw's tribute to Einstein, "Watchman" concludes: "That man was robbed and driven from his native land by the persons who will now take H.G. Wells to their bosom!"[220]

Wells responded that he had made a "very friendly and helpful criticism of Jewish traditionalism" and was "at least as hostile to isolationist imperialism, German 'Aryanism' and Irish nationalism." He continued: "I ask the Jewish reader . . . just to think *why* his tradition has irritated such diverse peoples as it has done through the ages. I say: 'Let us enquire for a moment if there is just a faint grain of cause why the Nazis, for example, hate you.'" Dismissing Watchman's "hysterics" he demanded: "[A]re we Gentiles never to be allowed to utter any impression of this ancient, narrow and racially egotistical Jewish culture, except in terms of cringing admiration and subservience? Is anyone who is not a complete Jew-worshipper, a hewer of wood and a drawer of water for all and any of the chosen people, to be marked down—and it isn't very nice to be marked down—as an enemy of the Jewish race?" Once again he dismissed "the accepted story of the Origin of the Jews" as "about as credible as Nazi ethnology," insisting that it was "the vast wealth of Semitic ability" that prompted him to "protest against any deliberate attempt to corral it back into a distinctive ghetto (as in Palestine) and divert it from human service to racial boasting, ganging and bickering." He warned that if they rejected "that sort of protest," the Jewish tradition was "past praying for."[221]

Watchman dismissed Wells' claims of Jewish friends as "familiar words, time-honoured protection" that seemed "compatible sometimes with so much hearty dislike of Jews in the mass!" That "form of disclaimer," he warned, had "long ceased to be a passport to Jewish confidence." But he added: "In common with all Jews, I am only too eager to welcome him as a friend. All I ask is that he live up to the part and not seem to talk at times like an enemy!" The Jews, Watchman maintained, stood for "the common brotherhood of men and the common fatherhood of God," while the Nazis were "bitten to the point of insanity with the disease of xenophobia."[222] He did, however, express "admiration" for Wells: "I, for one, and, I imagine many co-religionists with me, do not regard Mr. Wells as a man who has consciously and deliberately set out to

220. *Der Stuermer* was a Nazi publication ("Watchman," "H.G. Wells and the Jews," *Jewish Chronicle*, May 29, 1936, 13–14).

221. "H.G. Wells and the Jews: A Reply to 'Watchman,'" *Jewish Chronicle*, June 12, 1936, 16.

222. "Watchman," "My Reply to H.G. Wells," *Jewish Chronicle*, June 19, 1936, 13; Wells helped organize Freud's eightieth birthday celebrations ("Freud's 80th Birthday: World-wide Tributes," [ibid., May 8, 1936, 39]).

inflame feeling against the Jews."[223] A reader remarked that Wells' condemnations of Nazi anti-Semitism would "hearten those of his admirers" who like him "were shocked and humiliated to find the great champion of Universalism appearing as *advocatus diaboli* for the worst excesses of a crazy nationalism."[224]

In fact Wells' attitude to anti-Jewish persecution had caused controversy since the Tsarist pogroms.[225] In 1914 he had written to the *Daily Chronicle*: "Dear Mr. Zangwill,—and now what is to prevent the Jews having Palestine and restoring a real Judea?" But as the *Jewish Chronicle* remarked in 1936, "a very different" Wells "evolved in later years." This changing attitude was "not peculiar" to Wells, but Nazi anti-Semitism lent added urgency to Jewish hopes of Palestine: "Here, at least, was one solid hope, one consolation, one chance. If it were wrested from Jewry nothing else would remain. . . . The lights would go out."[226] But in spite of Wells' trenchant condemnations of Zionism and belief in a world state, Watchman continued to see him as a Zionist,[227] although one reader interpreted "the real meaning" of Wells' "sneering" question as: "And now what should prevent the Jews clearing out from this country?"[228]

In 1937, in response to the "point-blank question of whether he was an anti-Semite" Wells maintained that he was neither "anti-English . . . nor anti-Semitic," repeating his opposition to Zionism, nationalism and British Imperialism, and "the Jews styling themselves the 'Chosen People,'" an example now being "copied by Hitler."[229] In 1939 a Jewish commentator challenged the thesis of *Adventures of a Republican Radical*: "In Germany they became so Germanized that they completely forgot they were Jews until Hitler came along and reminded them of it. If Mr. Wells is right, then Germany should have been the last place in the world for anti-Semitism to have arisen."[230] Despite "a consider-

223. "Watchman," "The Problem of Defence," *Jewish Chronicle*, July 17, 1936, 13.

224. "Why single out the Jews, as though they were the only or the chief obstacle in the way of the cosmopolitan ideal?" (Leon Simon, Letter, *Jewish Chronicle*, July 17, 1936); members of the Hebrew P.E.N. Club in Jerusalem sent a message of congratulations to a special London P.E.N. Club dinner for Wells' 70th birthday—represented by Simon ("Jewish Tribute to Mr. H.G. Wells," ibid., October 16, 1936, 22–23).

225. Wells "saw 'a thousand and one unnameable iniquities'" in Russia but then "'proceeded to the opposite extreme,'" declaring that he "saw no iniquities in Russia at all. . . . 'I object,' he says, 'that my people should be made to quarrel with the Russian people because there is a feud between the Jews and the Christians'" (*Jewish Chronicle*, March 13, 1914, 10–11).

226. "Zionism's Crisis," *Jewish Chronicle*, August 21, 1936, 11.

227. Wells' remark to Zangwill about Jews claiming Palestine was a "noble question," but it was "a pity" that he had directed the question at Zangwill, President of the Jewish Territorial Organisation, since "Itoism" had "always been considered" by ordinary Jews as "militating against the Jewish national aspirations" (N.S. Burstein, Letter, *Jewish Chronicle*, November 20, 1914, 28–29).

228. Benjamin Grad, Letter, *Jewish Chronicle*, December 18, 1914, 13.

229. "Mr. H.G. Wells Repudiates Anti-Semitism," *Jewish Chronicle*, March 5, 1937, 40–41.

230. Harold Brown, Letter, in H.G. Wells, *Travels of a Republican Radical*, op. cit., 65.

able measure of agreement" with Wells, increasingly, Zionism was the sticking point. He was advised to "make a closer and deeper study of Judaism, of Jews, and, above all, of Zionism in practice in the Zionist colonies in Palestine."[231] Wells' War-time writings were less sympathetically received. The *Jewish Chronicle* noted that in *The Fate of Homo Sapiens*, Wells "naturally fulminate[d]" against everything that divided men, therefore Judaism came in for "unsparing criticism." But while "he disapprove[d] of the persecution of Jews," he found "justification for it." Worse, "the section . . . on 'The Jewish Influence'" could only provide fuel for those who, "quite indifferent to the Chosen People idea," were "endeavouring to keep the fires of anti-Jewish hatred ablaze." Wells would, therefore, "be accessory to 'the ruthless hounding of decent folk into exile'" that he found "so distressing to his spirit."[232] In 1942 *You Can't Be Too Careful* was criticized for describing Jews as having enormous families, being "tactless, vain, and clannish," and for attacking Zionism and Jewish leaders.[233]

But in the same year, Wells' works, along with those of the "redoubtable" Bernard Shaw and all books by Jews, were banned by the Nazis.[234] Wells' rationalization of anti-Semitism, ridicule of Judaism, and Utopian plans for the elimination of the Jewish people faded into the background. The following year, he condemned the "horrible martyrdom of the Jews."[235]

On Wells' death in 1946 the *Jewish Chronicle* remarked that "his thoughts on the Jews were, unfortunately, cast in a conventionally anti-Jewish mould," but his denunciations of "the harsh treatment of individual Jews" and praise for their achievements, even his Jewish friends, were cited in his favor, although "his views on the Jewish people and its survival were not so flattering."[236] In 1973 *Jewish Chronicle* reviewer Chaim Raphael praised a biography of Wells for "analysing the deep conflicts" in his nature, and his interest in "the central problem of the twentieth century—the rise and fall of the notion of perfectibility" as it affected Jews. Raphael notes that Wells "became the world prophet of the twentieth century. Only now, looking back, do we question the solidity or validity of the idea of progress which, in his hands, served to embody a hope that would raise the downtrodden and triumph over the superstitions of the past." Wells' "enthusiasm and gaiety . . . put all readers in his debt" but it "had a certain weakness at the centre, expressed in a kind of irritation when nations

231. "H.G. Wells and the Jews," *Jewish Chronicle*, January 6, 1939, 8.

232. A. Cohen, "Mr. Wells and the Jews: 'The Fate of Homo Sapiens,'" *Jewish Chronicle*, September 29, 1939, 12–13.

233. Dr. Aron Cohen, Letter, *Jewish Chronicle*, May 1, 1942, 16–17.

234. "Banned!" *Jewish Chronicle*, January 16, 1942, 12.

235. *Jewish Chronicle*, October 29, 1943, 6–7.

236. "Mr. Wells and the Jews," *Jewish Chronicle*, August 16, 1946, 6–7.

and individuals refused to comply with the 'progressive' behaviour he called for." In 1933 Wells had "declined to join a committee to combat anti-Semitism" as "a natural reaction to the intense nationalism of the Jews and to the very distinctive role they play in the world of art and business." His view of Nazism as inverted Judaism was "Wells the dogmatic crank, turning history into half-baked ideas in the name of a woolly progressivism." But "if he was cranky, his heart, we are told, was in the right place." And in view of Israel Zangwill's caution about Palestinian Zionism in 1914, "[f]or once . . . Wells was the better prophet."[237]

According to Cheyette, Coren's biography of Wells had been "rightly criticised for its many factual errors and its crudely polemical tone," but "the case against Wells" was "certainly worth examining further." His own supporters had discussed his attitudes for many years, and his "many statements on 'the Jews'" had been documented by the *Jewish Chronicle* "on a regular basis." But against Coren's view of Wells' anti-Semitism as a "peculiar, un-English evil—much worse than that of G.K. Chesterton or Hilaire Belloc," Cheyette insisted that anti-Semitism was part of "British liberal culture." Wells, he added, regarded Gentiles as well as Jews as vulgar and materialistic, and "[s]uch qualifications" were "important," because he "believed, above all, that Jews would become like everyone else over the years and assimilate into the New Republic as world citizens." Zangwill admired Wells' portrayal of the Jewish people in *The Outline of History.* Moreover: "As early as 1939, Wells foresaw the systematic attempt to exterminate European Jews." Although Wells "blamed this on the failure of Germany Jewry to assimilate" he was not alone. In fact, the most "disturbing" thing about Wells' "anti-Semitism" was that it was "commonplace in Britain before the war."[238]

Wells, Shaw, and Chesterton were not remarkable for expressing views on the "Jewish question" but, unusually, all attacked anti-Semitism. Unlike Shaw, however, Wells never revised his works in response to Jewish criticism. Unlike Chesterton, his humor verged on the cruel. His views also influenced public opinion. Kushner notes, regarding War-time "attacks on Jewish exclusivity," that "the ideas of H.G. Wells were often cited." Wells' writings, "right up to his death, reveal a deep antipathy primarily towards Catholicism but also towards Judaism." While he attacked "Nazi antisemitism," he saw it as a "response" to Jewish claims to be "the Chosen race." As a socialist, Wells' influence was "on the wane" by the outbreak of war, but his "attitude to Jews appears to have gained popular

237. Chaim Raphael, "The Time Traveller: The Life of H.G. Wells," *Jewish Chronicle*, July 6, 1973, 19.

238. B. Cheyette, "Who poisoned Wells?" *Jewish Chronicle*, February 5, 1993, vi.

support."[239] His fiction, with its gory descriptions of surprise air attacks, also remained popular, and encouraged panic among the civilian population during the unexpectedly quiet "Phoney War."[240]

Not all Jews appreciated Wells' attacks on religion or royalty,[241] but he was quoted in support of Judaism: "Throughout long ages the Talmud has been a potent factor in the preservation of Judaism and the Jewish people."[242] Jewish sympathy for Wells appeared to survive his denigration of the Jewish Scriptures and the Jewish religion, whereas organized Christianity, with its legacy of religious anti-Semitism, was treated warily by Israel Zangwill and Joseph Jacobs.[243] James Parkes says of Jewish writers' "scathing denunciations" of Christianity: "[W]hat did the Church represent to them, but the body which had persecuted

239. T. Kushner, *The persistence of prejudice: Antisemitism in British society during the Second World War*, op. cit., 93.

240. Following Britain's declaration of war against Germany in September 1939 little happened on the "home front" until May 1940; in stark contrast, the terrifying 1936 film version of Wells' *The Shape of Things to Come* portrayed war breaking out "swift and terrible" with enemy bombers "raining certain death from the skies in the form of gas bombs. With no defence against this new and indiscriminate form of warfare" bodies were "soon piled high in the rubble that was London," a "startling image . . . regarded by many cinema-goers as a dreadful prophecy" (Neil Tweedie, "The day the balloon went up," *Daily Telegraph*, September 3, 2009, 21).

241. "Mr. Wells rejects [the] theology of the Old Testament . . . with almost as much aversion as he shows for the doctrine of the Trinity" ("A Sermon of the Week: 'God the Invisible King,'" *Jewish Chronicle*, October 19, 1917, 13); Wells claimed the Christian God had "little to identify him with that hereditary God of the Jews who became the 'father'" in Christianity; his references to God's "jealousy, his strange preferences, his vindictive Old testament past" would not appeal to Jews (H. G. Wells, *God the Invisible King* [1917], accessed April 21, 2011, http://www.online-literature.com/wellshg/invisible-king/); "Would the Jew be a better citizen if he recited in Synagogue every Sabbath chapters from the works of H. G. Wells instead of Amos and Isaiah?" ("Wells on Jewish Nationalism," *Jewish Chronicle*, January 1, 1937, 22–23); Wells appeared "to delight" in his "rudeness" to the King and the Royal family in *The World of William Clissold* ("About Books: Insulting the King: Mr. Wells' New Book," [ibid., October 6, 1926, 13]).

242. However, a further quote, "The Jew stands for a faith through storm and sun-shine, and so long as he clings to his religion nothing will ever destroy him," contradicted his belief that the Jews would be destroyed if they did "cling to their religion" ("The Talmud in English," *Jewish Chronicle*, March 29, 1935, 10).

243. In Zangwill's poem *The Goyim* "the worst of the *Goyim* are the creatures called Christians" (I. Zangwill, *The Voice of Jerusalem*, op. cit., 311). "One might perhaps convince the Roman Catholic Church that the enemies of the Jews were in reality its own enemies and that the connection of Jews with Freemasonry was not so close as it imagines. But it would be impossible for it to relinquish its old principle of the Church-State without ceasing to be Catholicism"; the Jewish question was firmly linked to the modern spirit's struggle against the "Counter-Revolution," thus the "Jewish defence" must be based on the Jewish contribution to "modern life" (J. Jacobs, *Jewish Contributions to Civilization: An Estimate*, op. cit., 43–44); these included the Jewish Scriptures (ibid., 47); Jacobs said Chesterton "appear[ed] to be prejudiced against the Jews on the general principle that a fine old crusty prejudice is a good old Johnsonian quality" (ibid., 40); Zangwill arranged for Jacobs to meet Chesterton: see Chapter Seven.

their people for centuries?"[244] Despite this, a "Hit back!" campaign proposed by a *Jewish Chronicle* correspondent writing under the name of "Mentor" received little support among readers. Sparked during the Great War by *New Witness* allegations about Sir Alfred Mond's "subterranean plot" to trade with Germany, it accused the *Witness* of a "Catholic plot" against Jews, since Chesterton, at that time the editor, was assumed to be a Catholic, but readers appeared reluctant to jeopardize good relations with the Church.[245]

At the same time, Jewish commentators appeared anxious to demonstrate to forward-thinking individuals like Wells and Shaw that, far from being an irrelevant relic of bygone days, Jews could play a part in their dream of world peace and brotherhood. But just as their existence was threatened, the "great modern thinkers" who had seemed to be travelling in the same direction, went into reverse. Progressives in perpetual motion, they urged the Jews to divest themselves of their Jewishness, to inaugurate the era of secular world peace and brotherhood, but it was their Jewishness that motivated Jews to work for world peace and brotherhood. Reflecting the unchanging reality of the God who told Moses "I am who am," Jews were primarily concerned with "being," In contrast, as Chesterton noted, Wells' philosophy was one of "becoming": the present was already the past, and soon the Jews would cease to be Jews and become world citizens. Beyond that, Shaw envisaged Jew and Nazi merging into his Superman. Shaw and Wells envied what they saw as the Jewish people's strength, disregarding the Biblical lesson that God chose to show His strength, available to all humankind, through a small, weak tribe; and that when they relied on their own strength as a people, or were exiled from the land, the Jews became weak again. The ShaWellian proposal was blasphemous in a Biblical sense, since God had forbidden the Jews from intermarrying with non-Jews, lest they be corrupted, and this may have increased Wells' resentment of their refusal to assimilate.

Ironically, as Jewish commentators struggled to close the ever-widening gap with Wells by presenting the Jewish vision of brotherhood under the Fatherhood of God ("[O]ur goal . . . is that very universalism which Mr. Wells

---

244. J. Parkes, *Antisemitism* (London: Vallentine Mitchell & Co. Ltd., 1963), 72.

245. Regarding "the downright lying of Mr. Chesterton," the "foremost anti-Semites in this country, as in many another land," were those who "religiously look to Rome" ("Mentor," "Hit Back! Hit Back! Hit Back!" *Jewish Chronicle*, October 11, 1918, 7); two readers advised that such attacks be ignored (*Jewish Chronicle*, October 18, 1918, 7; October 25, 1918, 10); another defended the Catholic Church and Cardinal Bourne, as an "an unpretentious Jew, whose admiration for the Roman Catholic Church is equalled by his respect for the Protestant Church of England"; he was ready "to cooperate in any effective 'hit back' movement" but not this one (Sgt. M. Goodenday, War Office, Sudan, Letter [ibid., January 31, 1919, 22–23]; the Editor added that "Mac" "did not, of course . . . denounce all Catholics indiscriminately"; see Chapter Six).

preaches so eloquently") they came closer to Chesterton's position.[246] Some-what earlier, *Jewish Chronicle* contributor "Mentor" echoed Chestertonian logic when he remarked that Wells' solution to war—abolishing the nations—would, by the same "logically flawless" argument mean the abolition of marriage in order to abolish the problems of marriage.[247] Wells, however, wanted to abolish religion as well as marriage, joking that Israel Zangwill "would insist on treat-ing me as a devout Christian. Then he could say: 'But your Saviour was a Jew!' Useless to plead that I was not a Christian."[248]

Zangwill knew this,[249] and challenged him for misreading Judaism in his "noble book" *God the Invisible King*. As to Wells' "finite" God: "[F]orced to choose between God's omnipotence and his own omniscience, Mr. Wells opts for the latter."[250] In *Outline of History*, Zangwill said, Wells used "any old stick" to beat Judaism[251] and displayed an "unconscious prejudice in favour of Chris-tianity."[252] Wells admitted being "greatly attracted by such fine phrases as the Will of God, the Hand of God, the Great Commander. These do most wonder-fully express aspects of this belief I choose to hold." Mostly, it was the power of God that intrigued Wells, but "at times in the silence of the night and in rare lonely moments," he came upon "a sort of communion of myself and some-thing great that is not myself."[253] Wells was attracted to religion, even to the Church, but favored the New Testament over the Old, undoubtedly influenced by evolutionary theories that saw the newest as best and anything old as decay-ing and deserving of death. His concept of a Chosen People was fatally flawed, for as Zangwill remarked: "A 'chosen people' is at bottom . . . only a choosing people. . . . It would have been a monstrous egotism had the Jew said he was to be worshipped; he was merely throbbing with the vital message he had to deliver."[254] Wells projected his resentment of the chosen people idea, itself closely linked to his prejudice against religion, onto the Nazis.

Even in 1942, while condemning Nazi anti-Semitism, Wells made light of Jewish suffering and dismissed Zionism as selfishness, recalling a conference at

---

246. "H. G. Wells and the Jews: 'Practical,'" *Jewish Chronicle*, June 19, 1936, 14; *The New World Order* (later combined with *The Fate of Homo Sapiens* as *The Future of Homo Sapiens*) was described as "a stimulating and sincere book which one hopes will be widely read" ("D. F. K.," "Mr. Wells' Latest New World" (ibid., January 12, 1940, 6–7).

247. "Mentor," "Nationalism and Peace," *Jewish Chronicle*, July 19, 1929, 7.

248. H. G. Wells, *The Outlook for Homo Sapiens*, op. cit., 80–81.

249. I. Zangwill, *The Voice of Jerusalem*, op. cit., 35.

250. Ibid., 49–50.

251. Ibid., 52.

252. Ibid., 55; Wells always referred to Jesus as a Galilean and never a Jew (ibid., 57).

253. H. G. Wells, "On Using the name of God," *First and Last Things* (*The Open Conspiracy and Other Writings*) (London: no publisher, 1933), 133.

254. I. Zangwill, *The Voice of Jerusalem*, op. cit., 34–35.

which Rebecca West, "eminently free from racial prejudices," had "listened with a growing impatience" to Zangwill's "demands" and was "suddenly... inspired" to express "our general impatience. 'Mr. Chairman,' she said, 'should I be in order if I moved a pogrom?'" Wells added that the Jews "dun Jehovah still, at the Wailing Wall and elsewhere, for a Promise he perpetually evades," and were still "dunning the poor old British government for the bright hopefulness of the Balfour Declaration, irrespective of its other quite contradictory entanglements." The Zionists, he concluded, took "no thought for the common dangers and the common welfare of the race. The rest of the world may go hang.... Why should any country want these inassimilable aliens bent on preserving their distinctness?"[255]

Wells in the World of Dictators

Wells wanted to abolish poverty, misery, ignorance, and ugliness, under the teleological Whig view of history that saw the Reformation as the first of a series of reforms on the way to the perfect society. The radical urge to get things done could lead, as Burke remarked, to seeing mere innovation as reform. In Wells' Darwinist view, it was inevitable that the things he foresaw would happen, but in the Darwinist aristocracy some men were cleverer, stronger, and more pro-active than others. The stupid, weak and lazy, provided that they were not kept alive by misguided Christians, would die out through birth control, although the process could be speeded up by killing them.

This conflicted with the Enlightenment belief in the equality of man, but Wells addressed the cognitive dissonance by rearranging mankind into two categories: the progressives and the reactionaries, the free-flowing water and the common clay, the elect and the damned. Wells could not ignore the eugenics paradox that the weak seemed to be surviving and multiplying at a greater rate than the strong, but—having rejected the Biblical view that the meek would inherit the earth and the virtuous would be rewarded by many children[256]— eugenicists took refuge in the scientific explanation that the lowest forms of life tended to rapidly reproduce in swarms.

Shaw and Wells had replaced belief in original sin with belief in the perfectibility of Man, which allowed the potential for improvement, but they equated power with perfection, and weakness with imperfection. They longed for the power to get things done, and envied the totalitarian dictator; but the dictator also had the power to suppress dissent, and in *The Holy Terror* Wells portrays his world state being ushered in by fascist power that clears away the old world

---

255. H.G. Wells, *The Outlook for Homo Sapiens*, op. cit., 80–83.
256. See Psalm 37:11; Genesis 1:22.

order. One of his characters argues that there can be "no right, there can be no truth, there can be no healthy life—without some dissent, without some opposition,"[257] but while purporting to chart the "evolutionary" extinction of dissent and diversity, the book describes "The Group" seeking out dissent and diversity and killing it off.

During the War Wells maintained that the "existence of an opposition" was "fundamental" to democracy, but this opposition provided "the clue to a comparatively peaceful world revolution," offering a path "by which power can be readjusted without killing or cruelty, by stages if necessary." Wells, who had approved Kerensky's deposition by Russian Bolsheviks, saw fighting on the side of democracy as a preliminary to undermining democracy after the War, thereby ushering in the socialist world state.[258] Grassroots opposition to his Utopian ideas was, he claimed, the product of "intense jealousy." It was "an intolerable thought for the greedier sort of mind that there should be any possible life finer than the one they live."[259] Shaw looked forward to phasing out such reactionaries with his democracy of Supermen, while Wells defined his New Man as "Man in Common . . . not a man magnified, but men aggregated, a super-man with larger thoughts and aims, something not so much collective as quintessential." This was "[t]he real Leviathan—not the State, as Hobbes had it, but man's entire achievement."[260]

Wells' "New Man" was really all men singing in unison in praise of the State, all opposition having been silenced. Chesterton warned of the dangerous glamor of the "strong man," and Wells exemplified the dangers. His weakness was in seeing weakness as strength and strength as weakness. He admired lack of self-control and disdained "putting up with things." He believed that the elimination of all "weakness" would strengthen humanity, but the Wellsian vision of a world where technocratic progressives achieve power with little opposition was more fantastic than his science fiction. War was not a sideshow that would peter out, distracting attention while a few experts built a scientific brave new world. Totalitarianism was not the seedbed for a benign world order. With his mistaken analysis of history and current affairs, and with his belief in democracy fatally undermined by his belief in the inequality of Man; with his sympathy for the strong and distaste for the weak, and his belief in the homogeneous New Man existentially challenged by the Jewish people, Wells was an innocent abroad in the world of dictators. Totalitarians were seizing power and putting into practice Wells' merciless Utopia, while he frantically rewrote the

257. H.G. Wells, *The Holy Terror* (London: Michael Joseph Ltd., 1939), 392: see Chapter Four.
258. H.G. Wells, *The Common Sense of War and Peace*, op. cit., 90–91.
259. H.G. Wells, *The Outlook for Homo Sapiens*, op. cit., 166–167.
260. H.G. Wells, *The Holy Terror*, op. cit., 442–443.

future to keep up with them. Meanwhile, Homo Tewler shambled along, unable and unwilling to evolve. Wells approved of the power of the dictators but wished that they could seize it more gradually; that their nationalism could be internationalism; that they could find a more peaceful way of fighting.

Chesterton and the Fascists

Shaw and Wells regarded fascism as an evolutionary stage on the way to something better, but Chesterton has been seen as sympathizing with fascism per se.[261] Regarding claims of his anti-Nazism Cheyette says that Chesterton "defended" Mussolini's fascism in *The Resurrection of Rome* (1930).[262] Post-Holocaust, fascism has come to be "irremediably associated with Nazism,"[263] with the benefit of hindsight being brought to bear on those who praised or defended fascism, or even evinced a love of order, leading to various interwar groups being labeled fascist.[264] Although fascism has been associated with anti-Semitism, some Italian Jews were involved in the early fascist movement;[265] Winston Churchill initially saw Mussolini as a counter-force to communism,[266] but by the 1930s the British Union of Fascists was using violence to intimidate Jews in the East End of London.[267] Chesterton's response to foreign fascism was complex, but the British Union of Fascists, like their Nazi role models, supported compulsory sterilization.[268] This alone would have guaranteed Chesterton's implacable opposition, and he warned those who believed that the State, fascist or socialist, could "do no wrong," that these "most modern governments" would "organize sterilization to-day and may organize infanticide to-morrow."[269] A significant difference between fascism and Nazism was the latter's

261. K.L. Morris, "Fascism and British Catholic Writers 1924–1939," *The Chesterton Review*, XXV (1 & 2), (February/May 1999): 21–51.

262. G.K. Chesterton, *The Resurrection of Rome* (1930), in B. Cheyette, *Constructions of "the Jew" in English literature and society: Racial representations, 1875–1945*, op. cit., 200.

263. P. Hunt, "Who Dared Attack My Chesterton?" *The Chesterton Review*, XXV (1 & 2), (February/May 1999), 60.

264. Martin Blinkhorn, *Fascism and the Right in Europe 1919–1945* (Harlow, England: Pearson Educational Ltd., 2000), 4.

265. D. Stone, *Breeding Superman: Nietzsche, Race and Eugenics in Edwardian and Interwar Britain* (Liverpool: Liverpool University Press, 2002), 25.

266. W.D. Rubinstein, "Winston Churchill and the Jews," *Jewish Historical Studies*, 39 (2004), 172.

267. With Jews fleeing Nazi Germany, signs urging the boycott of German goods were a common sight in London's East End (William J. Fishman, *The Streets of East London*, [London: Duckworth, 1992], 126–129).

268. A. Farmer, *By Their Fruits: Eugenics, Population Control and the Abortion Campaign*, op. cit., 130–131.

269. G.K. Chesterton, "St. Thomas More," *The Well and the Shallows* (London: Sheed and Ward, 1935), 241–242.

"race" obsession,[270] a distinction Chesterton recognized.[271] While he sympathized with the resurgence of nationalism after the Great War, Nazi nationalism was "corrupted by an 'ethnological' type of loyalty." This "tribalism," he argued, represented not true nationalism but "the decay of religion"—Protestantism decayed into "Prussianism."[272]

Chesterton's developing response to the Age of Dictators and its impact on Jews can be traced in *G.K.'s Weekly* from its launch in 1925 until his death in 1936. Neither capitalist nor communist, Chesterton advocated Distributism, his decentralizing alternative based on the small property owner. Chesterton, like Wells, saw fascism as essentially foreign, but like Shaw he argued that foreign countries had a right to choose their own style of government: "If we were Italians, we should probably find ourselves supporting the Popular Party, which has become as much separated from the Fascists as from the Socialists." Socialists, he insisted, were not "fools," but "heretics" who were "completely wrong." Dismissing horrified reactions to intellectuals being "hurled into exile or captivity by the revolutions or restorations of men like Mussolini," he warned instead of Wells' new revolutionary caste, which would suppress civil liberties in a very British coup: "If Bolshevist bureaucracy is the ultimate danger, it is the intellectual who might evolve it out of the existing bureaucracy and that evolution is much more dangerous than revolution."[273] Arguably, England has suffered an "invasion" of European bureaucracy.[274]

Accused of denouncing the Bolshevist and excusing the Blackshirt he insisted: "We do not condemn Communism because it is violent and revolutionary. We condemn Communism because it is false."[275] According to *Sidelights* (1932), revolutions were not always "a bad thing," but "so often burst in the wrong place." The Bolshevist Revolution had "burst" in the towns, forcing land-owning peasants "to become slaves owning no land" because that was "the

270. R. Casillo, *Genealogy of Demons: Anti-Semitism, Fascism, and the Myths of Ezra Pound*, (Evanston, Illinois: Northwestern University Press, 1988), 137; M. Biddiss, "Mind at the end of its tether: political ideology and cultural confusion, 1914–1945," in P. Hayes, ed., *Themes in Modern European History 1890–1945* (London: Routledge, 1992), 281.

271. J.P. Corrin, *G.K. Chesterton and Hilaire Belloc: The Battle Against Modernity* (Athens: Ohio University Press, 1981), 185–186.

272. G.K. Chesterton, *Illustrated London News*, February 10, 1934, 186.

273. G.K. Chesterton, "A Dull Dictator," *G.K.'s Weekly*, November 28, 1925, 250.

274. The British Parliament now mostly rubber-stamps European Union laws; William Pitt the Elder's declaration of 1760, that "[t]he poorest man may in his cottage bid defiance to all the force of the Crown," established around 1300 and reaffirmed in 1604 ("the Englishman's home is his castle") was swept aside in 2007 when powers to enter households were extended, allowing bailiffs to use physical force against householders; see: Christopher Booker, Richard North, *The Great Deception: Can the European Union Survive?* (London: Continuum, 2005).

275. G.K. Chesterton, "Straws in the Wind: Our Critics: The Case Against Mussolini," *G.K.'s Weekly*, March 6, 1926, 618–619.

law of the towns." In "an evil hour, Russia fell under the power, not of a French philosopher, but of a German Jewish economist." Karl Marx was a "typical townsman," as were "most Jewish intellectuals of his type," and "could not understand peasants any more than the present Russian Government."[276] Yet Chesterton did not demonize the Jewish revolutionaries and had "precious little sympathy with the victims" of fascism or Bolshevism: "I do not agree with Bolshevists; but I think that Capitalists have only themselves to thank. I might not agree with Fascists; but I think that Liberal politicians have only themselves to thank. However bad Bolshevism may be it cannot be worse than our plutocracy deserves. It can be an unjust principle and still be a just punishment." And in any case, the newspapers were biased against Catholic countries.[277] Shaw refused to condemn Soviet and Italian repression because of bias in the British press. But Mussolini had censored the Italian press and abolished the right to strike. Despite this, Chesterton likened the English to "pompous and preposterous" Pharisees who excused their "own killing" with "hypocrisy" but lectured men "writhing in mortal combat because they talk of their own killings with candour. That is the exact extent of my uncritical acceptance of Fascism; and it is not strictly speaking an acceptance of Fascism at all."[278]

Later, however, Chesterton met Mussolini in Rome,[279] and when lunching together, "found him full of real friendship for England and remarkably interested in English authors." Shaw and Wells met with Stalin because of their distrust of the capitalist press. Chesterton agreed that "the 'man in the street'" needed to "learn the truth" about famous men.[280] Canovan asks whether Chesterton's "willingness to see some good in Mussolini" was "simply charity toward his Catholic coreligionists, or . . . a natural affinity between his own brand of populism and fascism." But she also comments: "Worst of all—though a trait more associated with the French or German Right than with Mussolini's Fascism—his hostility to both plutocracy and Bolshevism . . . was strongly marked by anti-Semitism."[281] Chesterton was more hostile to Nazism, whose defining feature was race, than to Bolshevism, with its noted Jewish component, and to Italian fascism, which was not markedly anti-Semitic until Germany put pres-

---

276. G. K. Chesterton, *Sidelights on New London and Newer York and Other Essays* (London: Sheed & Ward, 1932), 175–176.

277. He knew "little" about the Italian Government; moreover: "[T]he little I know is probably untrue, for it depends on . . . the English press" (G. K. Chesterton, "Our Critics: the Case Against Mussolini," *G. K.'s Weekly*, March 6, 1926, 618–619).

278. G. K. Chesterton, "The Mystery of Mussolini (II)," *G. K.'s Weekly*, May 1, 1926, 132–133.

279. M. Ward, *Gilbert Keith Chesterton*, op. cit., 579–580.

280. Patrick Braybrooke, *I Remember G. K. Chesterton* (Epsom, Surrey: Dorling & Co., 1938), 74.

281. M. Canovan, *G. K. C.: Radical Populist* (New York/London: Harcourt Brace Jovanovich, 1977) 128–129.

sure on Mussolini.[282] More Jews were rescued from destruction in Italy[283] where, to Nazi frustration, the anti-Jewish drive was less than wholehearted.[284] Unlike Shaw and Wells, Chesterton was attracted to what seemed genuine grassroots politics. In 1930 he discussed Distributism with Mussolini, but, aware that *The Resurrection of Rome* would lead to pro-fascist allegations,[285] a later edition assured readers he was "very far from being what is usually understood as a British Fascist; for many very strong reasons," including his "doubt, as Mussolini himself would doubt, whether Fascism is likely to be British." The "whole political and financial world" had been "goading Fascism into revolt" for fifty years, therefore the book "might rather be called a warning against Fascism, as a wise man of the early eighteenth century might have uttered a warning against the French Revolution." His point was not whether Parliamentarians realised "the Fascist's very real virtues," but that they began to "realise their own vices."[286]

Chesterton saw communism and fascism as offspring of capitalism, but saw capitalism itself as a form of fascism, with rich plutocrats "pulling the strings," and as Canovan notes, with "many another populist, he preferred a popular dictatorship ruling openly."[287] Mussolini remained popular with some Italians, but plutocrats could manipulate one dictator much more easily than pulling the multifarious, tangled strings of a democracy. Communism and fascism both relied on "salvation through strength," and the only way to dismiss a dictator was with force, but Shaw, Wells, and Chesterton were cushioned from the harsh realities of a real dictatorship by the imperfect democracy they criticized. In Chesterton's case, however, his defenses or rationalizations of foreign totalitarianism were really attacks on capitalism.

Unlike Shaw and Wells, Chesterton did not hope to get rid of democracy along with capitalism. Much earlier he maintained: "If civilization really cannot get on with democracy, so much the worse for civilization, not for democracy."[288] True democracy was not consulting "the ordinary citizen" like consulting an Encyclopedia,[289] but Italian fascism was religious, patriotic and family-

282. A. Kolnai, *The War Against the West* (London: Victor Gollancz, 1938), 494–495; M. Gilbert, *The Righteous: The unsung heroes of the Holocaust* (London: Black Swan, 2003), 336.

283. Ibid., 432–433.

284. J. Goebbels, Diary entry, December 13, 1942, in M. Gilbert, *The Holocaust: The Jewish Tragedy* (London: Fontana Press, 1987), 505.

285. G. K. Chesterton, *The Resurrection of Rome* (London: Hodder & Stoughton, 1930), 242.

286. Ibid., 345–346.

287. M. Canovan, *G.K.C.: Radical Populist*, op. cit., 133.

288. G. K. Chesterton, *What's Wrong with the World* (Sandy, Utah: Quiet Vision Publishing, 1910/2003), 45.

289. G. K. Chesterton, "The Thing," *A Miscellany of Men* (Norfolk, VA: IHS Press, 1912/2004), 26.

oriented, whereas democracy had become associated with the opposite world-view.[290] Although his view would later change, in the 1920s his paper was accused of explaining fascism while condemning "Prussianism." His response suggested that the critics had a point: "Italy has dictators because it is wild. Prussia has despots because it is tame." Nevertheless, regarding "the militant threat of modern Italy" Chesterton said he would argue "no further" with a critic: "For a thousand times I do agree."[291] Much later he maintained that Europeans had "rights to be asserted against tyrants," but also "against invaders." Where "these two enthusiasms" coexisted, a dictator would "always be possible." It was nothing to do with "decay." England would be "the last country on earth to have a Dictator" because it was "not sufficiently democratic."[292] Such Shavian arguments, notwithstanding occasional side-swipes at communism,[293] were aimed at his main target, capitalism. Chesterton was "not at all concerned to deify" or "denounce" Mussolini, though he stated that fascism was "in many ways a right reaction against all that intolerable international treason" that had become "part of professional politics." Mussolini was "a real Italian leader," therefore even the "triumph of reaction" was "national." In contrast the plutocracy, epitomized by Jewish industrialist Alfred Mond, was a kind of international fascism, and there was "nothing national about the dictatorship of Mond." Mussolini was unpopular in Britain because the capitalists used Bolshevism as a "Bogey" to frighten the workers, and "the cruel Italian" would deprive them of their sport.[294] In response, Chesterton used Mussolini as a Bogey to frighten the capitalists.

Julia Stapleton says that Chesterton "certainly sympathized with some of the new Fascist movements abroad, particularly in Italy," but was "well removed from both the radical right and the far right in Britain. Against both . . . he retained an unswerving, pre-1914 faith in reason, democracy, and the autonomy of nations in the face of the Fascist threat." She adds that although "[t]hese ideals sat uneasily with his anti-Semitism," they "were not diminished by it."[295] But by 1936 Chesterton was insisting that there was "nothing wrong with democracy" and "nothing wrong with the people ruling, except what is wrong with anybody out of the people ruling," and that was "forgetting that people are

290. G. K. Chesterton, "The Mystery of Mussolini (III)," *G. K.'s Weekly*, May 8, 1926, 147–148.

291. G. K. Chesterton, "The mystery of Mussolini (IV)," *G. K.'s Weekly*, May 29, 1926, 174–175.

292. G. K. Chesterton, "How Dictators Grow," *G. K.'s Weekly*, August 23, 1934, 389.

293. "Oscar Levy is perfectly right in seeing that a Communist is a Christian gone mad" (G. K. Chesterton, "A Word with Dr. Oscar Levy," *G. K.'s Weekly*, October 16, 1926, 72–73).

294. G. K. Chesterton, "Fascism *versus* Folly," *G. K.'s Weekly*, June 25, 1927, 463.

295. G. K. Chesterton, *Illustrated London News*, July 17, 1926, 100; *Illustrated London News*, May 25, 1929, 890, in J. Stapleton, *Christianity, Patriotism, and Nationhood: The England of G. K. Chesterton*, op. cit., 184.

only people. They will make mistakes, as you and I make mistakes." So would "all our superiors, the supermen, the dictators, the makers of modern systems." The "supreme modern mistake," was that "men forgot for a hundred years" that men "are liable to make mistakes."[296]

Chesterton, the Prussian, and the Pacifist

If the press obsession with Mussolini distracted from the "capitalist problem," Chesterton believed it also distracted from a resurgence of "the Prussian problem."[297] Fear of another war drove many to work for peace, blinding them to the danger of "Prussianism" even up until 1939.[298] With exaggerated tales of atrocity from the Great War still fresh, many dismissed reports of Nazi anti-Semitism; and some pacifists were so anxious to avoid war that they also ignored injustice. As Chesterton noted, "most Pacifists do not love their enemies; they only hate their friends for fighting against their enemies.... The kind of Pacifist who told us for the last ten years to be friendly to Germany would never in ten million years become friendly to France.[299]

France and Italy had been England's allies in the Great War. Chesterton believed the Armistice had merely deferred the problem of German aggression, and in the early 1930s repeatedly warned of the German threat, exacerbated by pacifism. Since Frederick the Great (1740–86) transformed it into a formidable military power, Prussia had helped defeat France in 1815, won the Franco-Prussian War, and been the moving force of the Great War. The independent German states had been caught in the strong embrace of "Prussianism," and moulded into the first totalitarian state, under which the workers were kept fit and healthy to man the Prussian war machine. Many socialists, especially the Fabians, admired Prussia's utilitarian welfarism,[300] as did the Liberal Winston Churchill, although he feared German power.[301] To Chesterton, however,

---

296. G. K. Chesterton, *As I Was Saying* (London: Methuen, 1936), 126, in Q. Lauer, *G. K. Chesterton: Philosopher without Portfolio* (New York: Fordham University Press, 1991), 117–118.

297. Much earlier British socialist E. Belfort Bax drew attention to this danger ("The German Situation I," *Justice*, September 30, 1915, 2; "The German Situation II," *Justice*, October 7, 1915, 2, accessed February 1, 2009, http://www.marxists.org/archives).

298. Richard Griffiths, *Fellow Travellers of the Right: British Enthusiasts for Nazi Germany* 1933–9 (London: Constable, 1980), 222–223.

299. G. K. Chesterton, "The Pacifist as Prussianist," *The End of the Armistice* (London: Sheed & Ward, 1940), 207.

300. See: G. Stedman Jones, *Outcast London: A Study in the Relationship between Classes in Victorian Society* (Harmondsworth, Middx.: Penguin Books Ltd., 1976).

301. Churchill visited German labor exchanges and the following year introduced them into Britain to help the long-term unemployed (R. S. Churchill, *Winston S. Churchill Vol. II: Young Statesman* 1901–1914 [London: Wm. Heinemann Ltd., 1967], 312), but also feared the growing power of Germany (Richard Holmes, *In the Footsteps of Churchill* [London: BBC Books, 2005], 78).

"Prussianism" exemplified the Protestant state, seen most clearly in the *Kulturkampf*, a ruthless struggle waged by William I of Prussia and his Iron Chancellor, Prince Otto von Bismarck against the Catholic Church, from 1873 to 1887.[302]

On January 1, 1933, Hitler was appointed German Chancellor, and the Reichstag fire in February provided the pretext for eliminating his communist opponents. On achieving the two-thirds Reichstag majority needed to suspend the constitution, he became dictator of a Germany dominated by the "Prussian" problem, the "wild worship of race." Nationalism might "in rational proportion help stability, and the recognition of traditional frontiers," but the "right name for Race" was "[a]nthropology gone mad." It meant "everlastingly looking for your own countrymen in other people's countries."[303] Nationality had "nothing to do with race," he insisted, but was "the product of the human soul and will."[304] In 1933 Chesterton derided claims that "Hitler's raving appeals to racial pride and hatred and (what is worse) contempt" were simply a ploy "to ensure popularity," that he was cunningly concealing "the tranquil glow of an ideal of international friendship" and feeling "nothing but the charity and humility of a true Catholic towards his fellow-Catholics and ... fellow-creatures." Neither was he a tool of the Prussians: "[A] Dictator is not dictated to." Distinguishing between the "Hitlerite problem" and the "Fascist problem," Chesterton said Hitler had not achieved power by "enunciating a certain theory of the State" or "by any of the very excellent experiments," in which he had "shown the increasing influence of the Distributist State." He had "risen by appealing to racial pride," whose frontiers, in contrast to "normal patriotism and even Jingoism," were "curiously vague and shifting." Hitler's "apologists" defended the "desire to restore order in his own country," but Hitler "went to what would normally be called a foreign country, except that it was linked up by some loose theories about Aryans and Teutons and the heathen worshippers of the Swastika." In that sort of "anthropological atmosphere," what was "his own country? Where *is* the German's Fatherland? Or rather, where is it not?" On this basis, Germany would claim Norfolk and Suffolk and hail Nelson "as a true German hero." Chesterton concluded that if "the old Prussia" was still leading "the Germanies" it would "lead them into war."[305]

During the War, Shaw refused to criticize Nazi concentration camps, citing

302. See: D. Wilson Johnson, *The Peril of Prussianism* (New York/London: G.P. Putnam's Sons, 1917); E.E.Y. Hales, *The Catholic Church in the Modern World* (London: Eyre & Spottiswoode, 1958), 227–242.

303. G.K. Chesterton, "The Heresy of Race," *G.K.'s Weekly*, April 20, 1933, 103–104.

304. G.K. Chesterton, *Heretics* (1905) *G.K. Chesterton Collected Works Vol. I* (San Francisco: Ignatius Press, 1986), 133.

305. G.K. Chesterton, "Who is Dictator?" *G.K.'s Weekly*, May 18, 1933.

British "crimes," but Chesterton argued: "I know it is the custom to equalise all these things, and talk of the pot calling the kettle black"; but someone who had "tried for thirty years to clean the pot" had "the right to call the kettle black, when it is really blacker than the pot. And it is blacker than the pot." The English officer might be "an insolent noodle" with "a class-arrogance that cries to God for vengeance," but unlike the Prussian officer he did not "elbow ladies into the gutter." If he planned to "seize the Dictatorship of the Distributist State," Chesterton said he would appeal "to the fools of England" by a "frenzy of folly" like Hitler's, with things "as nonsensical as the Nordic Race, and about as tenth-rate" as the Swastika. He would then "tell them what fools they were." But to do so would entail having to "crawl on my stomach . . . through all the foulest filth of the world. . . ."[306]

In 1919, Chesterton had described "Prussianism" as a "typically modern combination of moral anarchy with mechanical order" in military but also "mercantile and other social things," arguing that "underselling and freezing out" were not medieval practices: "[N]o modern capitalists made more ruthless use" of such "low trade tricks" than "the German Jews who carried German trade round the world."[307] In 1933, he asserted: "I have been called an Anti-Semite myself and even mistaken for a furious one," insisting that "a non-Christian culture, embedded for ages in what has always been a Christian culture," acted "as an irritant and to some extent as a parasite, because it trades and schemes but does not plough or produce." This was Chesterton recapitulating his thesis that the lack of a homeland "caused" Jewish "faults"—but faults that could be corrected in the right environment. Nevertheless, his main aim was to ridicule British fascists who thought aristocrats were "furiously Anti-Semite," when in fact it was "most outspoken among the working-classes; among the poor; in what are called the masses or the mob." They were not deceived by the "pawn-broker being called Gordon," and "no man in a slum in Poplar" had "any delicacy about noticing the shape of the local money-lender's nose. All the poor in all the pubs talk about Jews as Jews as frankly as any Hitlerites, though perhaps a little more calmly, being English."[308] Not all money-lenders and pawnbrokers

306. G.K. Chesterton, "If it were England," *G.K.'s Weekly*, May 25, 1933.

307. G.K. Chesterton, "Hindenburg and German Guilt," *Illustrated London News*, July 19, 1919, in G.K. Chesterton, *Chesterton on War and Peace: Battling the Ideas and Movements That Led to Nazism and World War II*, op. cit., 377–380); Perry comments: "Chesterton should have pointed out that these 'German Jews' were usually employees of others"; that for "centuries wealthy Europeans used a few Jews to do their dirty work. When a public outcry developed, rage was turned on Jews in general, who had to flee, conveniently allowing the wealthy to get out of their debts to Jewish moneylenders" (ibid., 379 note 88); Chesterton made this point in *A Short History of England* (1917): see Chapter Three.

308. G.K. Chesterton, "The British Fascist," *G.K.'s Weekly*, August 17, 1933, 375–376.

were Jews, and not all poor people were anti-Semitic,[309] but Chesterton added that although he could understand people believing that the "aristocratic state" had brought the country "to ruin," or that the "aristocratic state" was their "only hope of avoiding ruin," if anybody thought that defending such ideas meant following "the antics of foreign fanatics who murder Jews in the street— then I tell him plainly, in crude, coarse, outspoken words, that he is a British Fascist."[310]

The Allure of Fascism

The following year, while admitting that there were "many important points" on which he "strongly sympathise[d] with the Fascists, especially . . . the original Fascists," Chesterton said that their "facile and superficial eloquence" was "not a new creed but an old cant." Their demand for a National Government, an "extreme sort of national unity," only necessary in war-time, would make the state pre-eminent, as in communism.[311] Men, he claimed, still desired political representation: "We cannot compromise on that . . . and we respectfully ask how Fascism stands towards it." So far, there had been no clear answer. But, he added, it was "all to the good" that fascism should "assert the right of central government to override the impudence of individual financiers and economic intriguers," which had happened "again and again in defence of distributed independence." It was "quite as welcome to a Distributist as to any Fascist" that "the king, in order to help the peasant, must be stronger than the usurer or the rack-renter." But if the fascist was right in this, "his soundest idea," he would be "utterly wrong" if he "mixe[d] it up" with "patching up the Capitalist system."[312]

To Chesterton, fascism also exposed the fundamental flaws of Wells' world state philosophy. Wells was "torn apart by two quite contrary ideas": that everyone "must at once . . . pull things together," thus reducing "indefinite chaos to a definite order, on pain of perishing of war or famine"; and "absolutely unlimited liberty, not to say licence." Wells believed in "a movement of men towards agreeing with each other, and especially towards agreeing with him. And he actually does it still, in the darkest hour of the Black Shirt and the Steel Helmet." The fascists were pulling everybody together, whether or not they agreed. Wells believed that "we must not disregard differences or coerce opponents," but if the world was "in mortal peril now, something must be done now"; and

309. The author's mother and aunt went regularly to pawnbrokers in East London in the 1930s without noticing a preponderance of Jews; both worked for Jewish tailoring companies.
310. G.K. Chesterton, "The British Fascist," *G.K.'s Weekly*, August 17, 1933, 375–376.
311. G.K. Chesterton, "Queries on Fascism (I)," *G.K.'s Weekly*, July 5, 1934, 279.
312. G.K. Chesterton, "Queries on Fascism (II)," *G.K.'s Weekly*, July 12, 1934, 295–296.

nothing could be done "except by coercing opponents and disregarding differences. That is the policy of the Fascists."[313]

Wells, convinced of the inevitability of his Utopian idea, believed that it would be ushered in, even by extreme nationalism. He admired the dictators' power and capacity to get things done, but the one thing they would not do was to usher in his Utopia. Chesterton noted similarities between Wells' "Samurai whom he idealised" in his first books and the fascists he denounced in his latest books, but whether fascist, socialist, or communist, all appealed "to the same supreme and sacred authority"—the state. It seemed that the fascist agreed with everybody "except a small group of people who are almost nobody; and that group is our own." The fascist was at least honest in admitting the need for a power struggle, but Distributists objected to the communists and collectivists because "they only salute the State." There was "next to nothing in Communism or Collectivism about the Family or the Faith or the Man." Admittedly, there was "not much more about them in British Fascism," nonetheless: "[O]n many vital matters they tell very vital truths . . . in many fields, which will more and more be battle-fields," they were "fighting on the right side . . . many and perhaps most of them" were "rightly objects of respect and even of enthusiasm." Shaw and Wells looked to "Strong Men" to deliver communism, but some Distributists also envied the power of Dictators to "get something done" about financiers and the family. Despite this, Chesterton concluded: "[I]t seems clear to me that our own cause, however hopeless it may be, cannot with any intellectual integrity look to British Fascism for its hope," for "with all its practical value" fascism had "*not* got a new attitude." It would "give the poor man a better wage or a wiser dole, but not a stake in the country." It might "produce a new Capitalism or a better Communism, but we cannot call it Distributism without denying our nature and our name."[314]

Distributism was concerned with home, family, property, and protecting the weak, but Chesterton came to doubt whether the Strong Man could be trusted with these. His disquisitions on Jack and the Giant prepared him for the threat of Hitler, and in August 1934 he wrote: "[T]he strong man is he who can really face the fact that he is weak." In contrast, being "utterly and unbearably serious about his own superiority" the "Nordic Man, even when he is born as far south as Austria, will never admit that he is weak." Hitler, he said, had a "long career"

---

313. Chesterton had been "pro-Labour or generally pro-proletarian and anti-Capitalist" all his life, "often much more violently" than Wells, but the "Wellsean implication of . . . a floating accretion of different democrats or lovers of liberty" was "a dream. Stalin and Mr. Wells and myself all wanted sweated and starving people better paid but the abysses between . . . us are not bridged by that alone, and are not likely to close very soon" (G. K. Chesterton, "Queries on Fascism [III]," *G. K.'s Weekly*, July 19, 1934, 312–313).

314. G. K. Chesterton, "Queries on Fascism (IV)," *G. K.'s Weekly*, July 26, 1934, 328–329.

as a criminal: "Many gangsters and great criminals have been jailed or hanged because of their vanity...partly wishing to conceal their crime and partly wishing to boast of it." Significantly, "the most unnatural and blood-curdling quality about many of the Nazi actions is the attempt to brag of brutality, in the very act of assuring the world of good intentions.... So Hitler roars through the loudspeaker, 'Give me your children or I will come and take them.'"[315]

Hitler Re-Visited

That same month President von Hindenburg died and Hitler declared himself Führer—supreme leader. In September 1934 Chesterton wrote: "Having spoken so strongly against such weaknesses, and especially the weakness that may exult in wickedness, I may possibly cause some surprise, if I concluded the composite portrait by saying that in certain aspects, and under certain limitations, I do not believe that Hitler is altogether a bad fellow; and that he is almost certainly a much better fellow than the men who are going to use him." This was because Hitler was "not the Dictator." Chesterton explained that "Prussianised Germany" had never repented of the Great War, but "[t]he spirit of barbarism could no longer work through a man like Bismarck, with his cold and automatic monomania," but "through a man like Hitler." With his "sentimentalities, his inconsistencies, his idealism gone wrong, his patchy popular sympathies, his scrappy popular science, born of a litter of pamphlets on anything from Anthropology to Abortion, his flavour of being modern, his suggestion that Fascism is the fashion," he was the ideal choice. Chesterton, "to be fair" to Hitler," said he was "young enough to have heard of some of the things the nineteenth century neglected, such as the virtues of peasants and the vices of usurers." This "hotchpotch of post-war social ideals, fads or follies" had to be "embodied" in someone who appeared "a little more modern than a Potsdam drill-sergeant in a spiked helmet." The "old despotism" needed a "demagogue," but Chesterton now argued that "[i]t was not the Dictator who dictated to the drill-sergeant. It was the drill-sergeant who drilled the Dictator." Hitler, he concluded, was "said to have been a brave soldier in the field, and doubtless lived the hard life of soldiering with firmness, patience and obedience. His drill-sergeant will soon give him his marching orders again."[316]

Chesterton's reference to the "virtues of peasants and the vices of usurers" strikes an ominous note, but he does insist on "certain limitations," and it is doubtful whether any politician who advocated eugenics would receive his approval. In keeping with his philosophy, his main target was not individual

---

315. G.K. Chesterton, "The Gangster," *G.K.'s Weekly*, August 30, 1934, 408–409.
316. G.K. Chesterton, "The Tool," *G.K.'s Weekly*, September 6, 1934, 8–9.

leaders but "Prussianism," the "old despotism," which had already led to what has been regarded as a prequel to the Holocaust: the genocide of black tribes in German South-West African death camps.[317] In his autobiography Chesterton claimed that "Kaiser Bill" was not responsible for the Great War, but was "one of the series of British bogeys like Kruger before or Mussolini afterwards" and that "the evil originally arose with the power of Prussia."[318] The 1934 English edition of *Mein Kampf*, in line with Chesterton's revised opinion of Hitler, conveyed the impression not of a great leader, but a common soldier influenced by a ragbag of ideas and prejudices, especially against Jews, giving vent to them in clumsy prose and at interminable length.[319] Shaw and Wells continued to claim that fascism was a tool of big business until after war broke out. David Goldberg says the idea was "one of the most persistent . . . myths of the past century," although it reflected the views of the intellectual Left rather than the reality of German or Italian big business.[320] Against this view, John Roth and Richard Rubenstein maintain that "German industrialists, military leaders, and right-wing politicians . . . successfully prevailed upon a hesitant" von Hindenburg to appoint Hitler as a puppet chancellor "who in turn would control the labor unions and stem the Communist tide that seemed ready to engulf German society."[321] Ker remarks that "Chesterton, prophetic though he was, certainly underrated Hitler and the Nazis," seeing them as "simply . . . the rag-tag-and-bobtail of the nineteenth-century Prussianism; the camp followers of the far better disciplined army of Bismarck," and "merely a revival" of Bismarck's plan for a Prussian-led Germany aiming to dominate the Catholic Rhineland and Bavaria.[322]

But although Chesterton regarded the Nazis as less disciplined than their Bismarckian predecessors, he saw them as equally dangerous. He described the murder of Austrian leader Engelbert Dollfuss as "the filthy butchery at Vienna," commenting that the Nazi was "swift to shed innocent blood" and had "a cer-

317. See: David Olusoga, Caspar W. Erichsen, *The Kaiser's Holocaust: Germany's Forgotten Genocide* (London: Faber & Faber, 2011).

318. G.K. Chesterton, *Autobiography* (Sevenoaks, Kent: Fisher Press, 1936/1992), 213.

319. The *Times* published extracts in the summer of 1933; an abridged English version was available in October (Introduction to A. Hitler, *Mein Kampf* (London: Pimlico, 1925–26/2001), xlii), in which Hitler lauded the Prussians (ibid., 141; 592), displayed racial anti-Semitism and attacked Judaism (ibid., 138) and the Christian clergy (ibid., 101); none of this would have appealed to Chesterton; however, the Austrian Hitler petitioned the King of Bavaria to join the German army on the outbreak of the Great War, served honorably, was promoted and received the Iron Cross (J. Goldberg, *Liberal Fascism*, op. cit., 65).

320. Ibid., 286–289.

321. Richard L. Rubenstein, John K. Roth, *Approaches to Auschwitz: the Holocaust and its Legacy* (Atlanta, Georgia: John Knox Press, 1987), 103.

322. G.K. Chesterton, *The Well and the Shallows* (1935), *G.K. Chesterton Collected Works Vol. III* (San Francisco: Ignatius Press, 1990), 444; 530–532, in I. Ker, *G.K. Chesterton: A Biography* (Oxford: Oxford University Press, 2011), 713–714.

tain technique in the matter of murdering other people." Hitler, he added, "killed quite a creditable number of people for one week-end holiday," and Dollfuss's assassination showed "some touch of that efficiency, which the Nazis once promised to display in other fields of activity." The Nazi approach bore no relation to the political theory of "the Corporative State; or the Fascist Theory; or the thousand theories, including our own, for improving our ancient civilisation," but was simply "the blow of the barbarian."[323] While it could be argued that Chesterton was merely displaying sympathy for Austria as a Catholic country, he saw Hitler's Austrian Catholic roots as material for satire.[324]

Dollfuss was murdered on July 25, 1934, but in the Plebiscite of August 19, 90 per cent of Austrian votes supported unification with Germany, though they were cast in an atmosphere of violence and intimidation, disappearances and mysterious deaths, the hallmarks of Nazi "political theory." Chesterton's "reassessment" of Hitler was published on September 6, 1934, but his savage indictment of Hitler regarding Dollfuss's murder was made in 1935, and Chesterton continued to warn about racial pride—"Prussianism"—as Nazism's driving force. He saw the chief danger not as disciplined armies confronting each other but barbarism as it affected the weak. On August 10, 1934 in his Introduction to a Friends of Europe pamphlet, *Germany's National Religion*, Chesterton described "the strange staleness which makes the racial religion stink in our nostrils with the odours of decay and as of something dug up when it was dead and buried." He condemned claims that Christian charity caused "national degeneration" by encouraging the care of "the physically weak and infirm," and reiterated his belief in equality, defined as "conscience." This, he insisted, embraced Jews as well as Germans: "Teutons" as well as "various Celts and Slavs and Semitic Arabs."[325] Wells and Shaw attempted to fit the dictators into their worldviews, and Chesterton tried to fit Hitler into his interpretation of German history, yet there was a crucial difference. Wells and Shaw saw the advent of the Strong Man as a hopeful sign; Chesterton did not. In addition, as will be seen, other considerations may have influenced his apparent reassessment of Hitler.

323. G.K. Chesterton, "Austria," *The Well and the Shallows*, op. cit., 250–252.

324. Regarding Chesterton's apparent dismissal of Nazism as the undisciplined heir of Bismarckianism, Ker notes that Chesterton "does not add . . . that Hitler who was soon to annexe Austria into a Greater Germany was himself an Austrian Catholic by birth. Instead, he insists that 'Prussianism' came from Protestantism'" (I. Ker, *G.K. Chesterton: A Biography*, op. cit., 713–714); regarding "the jolly old catchword of calling Hitler a Catholic," Chesterton said: "[T]here are countless Catholics whom I think wrong in politics. But I wonder if it is much truer to call Hitler a Catholic than to call Bertrand Russell an Anglo-Catholic. He was quite probably christened in an Anglican Church" (G.K. Chesterton, "Where is the Paradox?" *The Well and the Shallows*, op. cit., 273).

325. "Since all men, even the rudest, have some rude form of conscience" (G.K. Chesterton, introduction to Friends of Europe pamphlet [London: Friends of Europe, 1934], 1–2); published August 10, 1934, it was one in a series of German publications translated into English.

Chesterton, Churchill, and the Dictators

In July 1932 Winston Churchill warned Parliament about Hitler.[326] He read *Mein Kampf*, and in April 1933 protested Nazi anti-Jewish brutality.[327] And yet, in November 1935, like Chesterton, he appeared not to have reached a final verdict on Hitler. He asked whether Hitler, despite his reputation as a warmonger, "in the full sunlight of worldly triumph, at the head of the great nation he has raised from the dust," would still feel "racked by the hatreds and antagonisms of his desperate struggle," or perhaps he would discard them "like the armour and the cruel weapons of strife under the mellowing influences of success . . . ." Foreign visitors, Churchill averred, had found Hitler "a highly competent, cool, well-informed functionary with an agreeable manner" and the world hoped to find him "a gentler figure in a happier age." Churchill concluded, however, that despite Hitler's "words of reassurance," Germany had rearmed.[328] In September 1937 Churchill "appealed to Hitler to become 'the Hitler of peace.'" It was to be his final appeal.[329]

Italian fascism had, as Chesterton feared, distracted from the threat of "Prussianism," but as Italy menaced Abyssinia, an unsigned leading article in *G.K.'s Weekly* "sparked off a controversy" that raged well beyond Chesterton's death.[330] The tiny populist organization failed to attract popular support but did attract conspiracy theorists.[331] Some were drawn to fascism and Chesterton tried to reconcile opposing factions, but increasingly he saw fascism as Imperialistic: "All my moral instincts are against Imperialism"—it was "bad for the

326. Winston Churchill, Speech to House of Commons, July 11, 1932, W. S. Churchill, *Churchill Speaks: Winston S. Churchill in Peace and War: Collected Speeches, 1897–1963*, R. R. James, ed. (Leics.: Windward, 1981), 549.

327. "[T]his persecution of the Jews . . . distresses everyone who feels that men and women have a right to live in the world where they are born, and have a right to pursue a livelihood which has hitherto been guaranteed them under the public laws of the land of their birth" (Winston Churchill, Speech to House of Commons, April 13, 1933, ibid., 564).

328. W. S. Churchill, "The Truth About Hitler," *Strand* magazine, November 1935, in M. Gilbert, *Churchill and the Jews*, op. cit., 103–105.

329. "'We cannot say that we admire your treatment of the Jews or of the Protestants and Catholics of Germany . . . but these matters, so long as they are confined inside Germany, are not our business.' What mattered was for Germany to give up its desire for conquest" (W. S. Churchill, "Friendship With Germany," *Evening Standard*, September 17, 1937, in M. Gilbert, *Churchill and the Jews*, op. cit., 139); later he stated: "It is a horrible thing that a race of people should be attempted to be blotted out of the society in which they have been born" (W. S. Churchill, Parliamentary Debates, *Hansard*, December 21, 1937, ibid., 140).

330. "Abyssinia," *G.K.'s Weekly*, July 18, 1935, in B. Sewell, *G.K.'s Weekly: An Appraisal* (Maidstone, Kent: The Aylesford Press, 1990), 50–51. Border clashes between Italian troops in Italian Somaliland and Abyssinia in December 1934 led to a League of Nations arms ban on both sides in 1935, in effect aiding Italy, which invaded in October 1935.

331. M. Canovan, *G.K.C.: Radical Populist*, op. cit., 8–9.

soul," hardening the heart "with the running sore and weakness of pride." He was still opposed to the "plutocracy," which was "not a form of government" because it was "formless"; in fact it was not "a democratic state; or a state at all." In contrast, fascism was a state: "But it is not the state I want." Chesterton's "little army was breaking apart at the seams." Chesterton tried to pacify pro- and anti-fascist Distributists as letters raged back and forth, but, unlike his Boer War denunciations of Imperialism, his anti-fascism was more nuanced:[332] "[W]hether fighting in Abyssinia or forcing its way into Westminster," fascism was "a new force." He did not agree with it "in principle," but he did "respect" it compared to "things" that were "in practice much more unprincipled." But "above all," he continued to "disagree" with fascism because it was "travelling only too tamely in the old [path]."[333] Imperialism was one of these "old paths," but, given England's "terrible evils"—"its idiotic diplomacy, its brainless plutocracy, its corrupt incompetent politics"—Distributism was bound "so far in sympathy" to the British fascists. Fascism "was in many ways a reaction" from pacifism and pessimism, and fought "in a manly manner against general scepticism." Furthermore "centralised powers would be taken over with the finest intentions" by his "Fascist friends," although in his youth, Chesterton added, he would have "said the same" of his "Socialist friends." But neither could "substitute for the completion of the common man." If he "must be detached from his legs, he could probably leave them safely in the cloakroom of the Fabian Society or of the Fascist Headquarters. But he would not have them ... in an emergency." Private property and "the family" were "primary," and "until these reappeared as principles, anything called to govern in this distracted age" would take "more and more liberties, and leave less and less liberty." He concluded: "Never before was there the danger of making one man omnipotent when most men are impotent."[334]

The following month Italy invaded Abyssinia with air raids and poison gas and it seemed Chesterton's caution was vindicated, although Italy was part of a Europe-wide effort to restore Germany to the diplomatic fold, and Britain and France feared that too much criticism might push Mussolini into the arms of Hitler.[335] But when Hitler sent troops into the de-militarized Rhineland on March 7, 1936 he repudiated the Treaty of Versailles, signed in 1919 and intended

---

332. J.P. Corrin, *G.K. Chesterton and Hilaire Belloc: The Battle Against Modernity* (Athens: Ohio University Press, 1981), 186–191.

333. G.K. Chesterton, "First Reply to Fascism," *G.K.'s Weekly*, August 29, 1935, 400–401.

334. G.K. Chesterton, "Further Words on Fascism," *G.K.'s Weekly*, September 5, 1935, 416–417.

335. Under the Locarno Treaty Germany, France, Belgium, Britain and Italy pledged themselves to defend any member under attack. Following border clashes Ethiopia appealed to the League of Nations (Italy and Ethiopia were members), but while the League dragged its feet France reached a

to preserve the peace of Europe. On March 19th Chesterton claimed that Hitler had not "invented the racial arrogance now prevalent in Germany." There was nothing new, he claimed, in leading the "tribe" in his "warlike demonstration without warning." This approach dated from Frederick the Great, but he added that "Hitler like Hannibal dedicated himself to his heathen gods" when standing by Frederick's tomb, and Frederick had "shocked his own age by attacking Austria without a declaration of war," just as Hitler broke a treaty "as a preliminary to proposing it." Consequently, there was nothing in Hitler's "own theory or practice to prevent him from invading France and proposing . . . a yet more universal and benevolent scheme of European reconciliation." Months had been wasted "in some newspaper quarrel with Italy" while "all the time Prussianism had increased in prestige and power." Italy had "long sought to expand over less civilized countries," and as an anti-Imperialist, Chesterton felt free to criticize. But all could "quite consistently blame the very special sort of thing that has long threatened Europe from the Prussian heresy poisoning so much of Germany." It was not "an ethical controversy about whether civilized things may more or less control savage things," but "a pressing practical problem, of whether a more savage thing shall control more civilized things. In itself, the idea of our attacking a semi-civilized people is hateful to me." But that problem became "somewhat academic" when "the semi-civilized people" might "be successful in the attack."[336] Shaw regarded the natives of Abyssinia as savage and in need of control, reflecting the elitist Fabian view of non-white races as inferior, but to Chesterton it was the "semi-civilized" Nazis who were out of control.

Hitler, who had not received his "marching orders," is no longer portrayed by Chesterton as a tool of "Prussianism" but as a purveyor of "Prussian heresy," and he regards the Nazis, with their barbaric emphasis on heredity—something he warned about in 1908[337]—as a greater threat to civilization than Italian Imperialism. Crucially, Mussolini had not yet adopted racial laws and it was hoped that Italy might yet join Britain and France against Germany. Churchill also met Mussolini, in 1927,[338] and thought Italy should not be needlessly antagonized, in view of the greater danger from Nazi Germany. The Allies had

---

secret deal with Mussolini under which Italy's Ethiopian action would be ignored in return for support against Germany; Britain made belated attempts to achieve peace, but Italy invaded Abyssinia in October 1935.

336. G. K. Chesterton, "Hitler versus History," *G. K.'s Weekly*, March 19, 1936.

337. G. K. Chesterton, "Humanitarianism and Strength," *All Things Considered* (USA: Feather Tail Press, 1908/2009), 76.

338. Churchill met Mussolini twice; he was received by Pope Pius XI in Rome (W. Churchill, C. Churchill, *Speaking for Themselves: The Personal Letters of Winston and Clementine Churchill*, M. Soames, ed. [London: Doubleday, 1998], 303), and met Pius XII in 1944 (ibid., 501).

barely won the Great War, even with Italy on their side.[339] Churchill adopted the same stance regarding the Spanish Civil War,[340] and continued to hope for an alliance with Italy and the Soviets to the very brink of war with Germany.[341]

But on May 12 Italy renounced its League of Nations membership. Chesterton, forced by critics to defend his use of the word "tribal," reiterated his warning against Germany: "The point of the tribal spirit which haunts and inhabits, but only occasionally drives the Germans," was that it was "a religion of Race." Unlike patriotism, with its "enthusiasm for a flag or a charter or a shrine or an ideal commonwealth," in this religion, each man was "the sacred image which he worships," and his own blood was "the blood of St. Januarius." There was "a tendency for every German, not merely to take Germany seriously, but to take himself seriously; because Germany is not an abstraction but a breed." "Nazi Nationalism," in trying to "preserve the purity of the race" in a continent where all races were "impure," would ignore all frontiers to "follow race wanderings," with a "pack of hounds" trained to "go through all fences," and "trained in a certain spirit" perilous to their neighbors. Other countries, including England, were not immune from such heresies, but the Germans' "tribal or even barbaric spirit" was not "necessarily present in all nations or all nationalists." Consequently, Chesterton was not "merely slinging mud" when he objected to the "ordeal by blood; the blood-test."[342] Tennyson had warned about "false pride in

---

339. Mussolini had "triumphed over the most ancient state in the world," a "lamentable event," but the League must be strengthened and sanctions against Italy opposed (Winston Churchill, Speech, Chingford, May 8, 1936, W.S. Churchill, *Churchill Speaks: Winston S. Churchill in Peace and War: Collected Speeches, 1897–1963*, op. cit., 621–623); he recalled: "Everyone was so anxious for Mussolini's support in dealing with Germany that it was felt undesirable ... to warn him off Abyssinia" (W. S. Churchill, *The Second World War: The Gathering Storm* [London: Cassell & Co. Ltd., 1948], 104–105); while condemning the Abyssinian invasion Churchill believed Mussolini had helped protect Austria against Nazi ambitions; with "the fearful struggle against rearming Nazi Germany ... approaching with inexorable strides" he was "most reluctant to see Italy estranged, and even driven into the opposite camp," which might have led to the League's collapse (ibid., 129–130).

340. Despite Italy's and Germany's assistance to General Franco in the Spanish Civil War, Churchill, more sympathetic to "'the Anti-Red Movement,'" urged "non-intervention," thus alienating until late in 1938 "a substantial number" of left-wingers who sympathized with his anti-Nazi stance: "Yet he consistently reiterated his loathing for all forms of totalitarian government," deploring in a Parliamentary speech the plight of the Spanish people, but counseling against support for either side, warning of Europe's drift toward "some hideous catastrophe" (Winston Churchill, Speech to House of Commons, April 14, 1937, W.S. Churchill, *Churchill Speaks: Winston S. Churchill in Peace and War: Collected Speeches, 1897–1963*, op. cit., 633–636); "[W]ith all the rest they had on their hands the British Government were right to keep out of Spain" (W.S. Churchill, *The Second World War: The Gathering Storm*, op. cit., 167).

341. William Manchester, *The Caged Lion: Winston Spencer Churchill 1932–1940* (London: Cardinal, 1989), 124.

342. G.K. Chesterton, "The Truth About Tribes," *G. K.'s Weekly*, May 21, 1936.

blood and place"; but to Chesterton, pride solely in blood was most dangerous of all, since the believer demanded to be worshipped wherever he went.

Chesterton's last *G.K.'s Weekly* editorial in June 1936 again warns of "nationalism without borders," but also of a French and English "relapse" into insular nationalism. An unpublished version warns that England and France might forget their Great War alliance, and that there was "only one other application of this principle of the Relapse," which threw "some light on the last news from Germany," adding that "for my own part, I fear it is a very bad Relapse indeed."[343] The published version is more urgent. Chesterton, "challenged to defend himself," says that the Abyssinian invasion was "the first catastrophe," which he had "throughout denounced." But although it was a "relapse" into nineteenth century Imperialism, there was "no reason" why it should "bring about a very much bigger catastrophe." Thanks to press exaggeration about Great War atrocities, "thousands of educated Englishmen" would "never again believe a word of such stories against the poor Germans," while the old caricatures of Italy and France had returned with a vengeance. Mussolini, "the very latest British Bogey," was still in the last century in thinking that patriotism meant Imperialism, but Chesterton did not want the British to "relapse into sleep again, and have all these jolly nightmares. I want them to wake up."[344] His waking nightmare was a "relapse" into the nineteenth century, with France the enemy and Prussia the ally. Despite its "relapse" into Imperialism, therefore, he preferred Italy to a racist Germany that recognized no frontiers at all. In fact, Britain recognized Italy's annexation of Ethiopia in 1938, until it openly allied itself with the Axis.[345] In May 1936 Sir Herbert Samuel reported that a "whole generation" of young German Jews were planning to leave because they felt "hopeless."[346] Jews were being detained in Dachau.[347] Chesterton had German contacts closely affected by such developments, but most people had to rely on the newspapers, which might explain his concern about "educated Englishmen" being primed to fear Italy while dismissing German atrocity stories.[348]

343. G. K. Chesterton, "The Relapse," *The End of the Armistice*, op. cit., 151–154.

344. Mussolini had "no motive in the matter" apart from what was "good for Italy"; there were "no Kimberley Mines or Johannesburg Millionaires in Abyssinia," from which politicians "could get any pickings" (G. K. Chesterton, "The Relapse," *G. K.'s Weekly*, June 4, 1936, 185–186).

345. Under Nazi pressure racial laws were passed in 1938; Italy signed a secret military pact with Germany in May 1939, entering the War in June 1940 with an abortive invasion of Southern France; Italy surrendered in September 1943. However, even in fascist Spain a "well-organized underground network to safety" operated for Jewish refugees from France (M. Gilbert, *The Righteous: The unsung heroes of the Holocaust*, op. cit., 336).

346. "The World Refugee Problem: League of Nations Union Conference: 'Plight of One Million Wanderers,'" *Jewish Chronicle*, May 29, 1936, 1.

347. "Forty-four Jews at Dachau: A Continual Terror," *Jewish Chronicle*, April 17, 1936, 12.

348. See Chapter Eight.

In the run-up to the Spanish Civil War a frustrated Chesterton noted that "Liberalism was only opposed to militarists when they were Fascists; and entirely approved of Fascists so long as they were Socialists."[349] Spanish fascists had been "justified in smashing" corrupt politicians linked to secret societies. Nevertheless: "Fascism could never be quite satisfactory; for it did not rest on authority but only on power," and that was "the weakest thing in the world." The fascists claimed they were "the most vigorous and intelligent minority," making fascism a struggle of the "fittest." Chesterton maintained: "I am no Fascist," but added that the March on Rome jolted the socialists out of complacency about "the inevitable proletarian triumph." Chesterton did not like "inevitable triumphs."[350] Unlike Macaulay, he saw revolution as integral to English progress. The danger was in believing that it would happen of itself.

Chesterton's final months were burdened with strife: "[P]ublic controversy did not trouble him," but "he hated any breach of the peace within the ranks of his own small army."[351] In the "violent personal quarrels" about which he was expected to "take sides" he was "bitterly reproached by one for supposedly favouring another."[352] As well as fighting against pacifism and public apathy about Germany, Corrin says he was combating "Latinophile" Distributists who believed the international "Money Power" was forcing Italy into the Abyssinian invasion, and who saw Italy and Germany as possible allies against communism.[353] Ward says that Chesterton "loved Italy—even more than France . . . yet he could not but condemn the invasion of Abyssinia."[354] The attempt to remain loyal to all sides proved exhausting: from 1934 he suffered serious ill health, "overtired and working with the weary insistence that over-fatigue can bring." The Chestertons visited Lourdes, and even at Lisieux he wrote "a pencilled letter, long and almost illegible 'under the shadow of the shrine'—trying to reconcile the disputants with himself and with one another."[355] The inflammatory Abyssinia article appeared during one such absence. Chesterton told Maurice

349. G. K. Chesterton, "The Case of Spain," *The Well and the Shallows*, op. cit., 60–64.

350. G. K. Chesterton, *Autobiography*, op. cit., 303.

351. M. Ward, *Gilbert Keith Chesterton*, op. cit., 647.

352. Ibid., 649.

353. J. P. Corrin, *G. K. Chesterton and Hilaire Belloc: The Battle Against Modernity*, op. cit., 186–188; see Chapter Six.

354. M. Ward, *Gilbert Keith Chesterton*, op. cit., 647.

355. On his recovery from jaundice in 1934 they went to Rome and thence to Sicily but had to return home when he suffered inflammation of the neck and shoulders (ibid., 641); early in 1936 they went to Lourdes and Lisieux, where he seemed better, but on returning home "his mind seemed not to grip as well as usual and he began to fall asleep during his long hours of work"; he was thought to be suffering from heart failure (ibid., 649–650). Chesterton found internal Distributist quarrels "painful"; he "hated rows of any kind, and was not disposed to take sides" (B. Sewell, *My Dear Time's Waste* [Faversham, Kent: St. Albert's Press, 1966], 35).

Reckitt: "'Between ourselves, and without prejudice to anybody, I do think myself that there ought to have been a more definite condemnation of the attack on Abyssinia.'"[356] A planned article on the subject was never written because Chesterton died of heart failure.[357]

Chesterton, Churchill, Pacifism, and the Jews

Churchill continued to tread his unpopular path against appeasement up to and beyond the outbreak of war.[358] As early as June 1932, Chesterton had warned: "The outlook in Europe is dark; and it looks as if the Pacifists will succeed in dragging us all into War."[359] Chesterton insisted that he was no militarist but "a revolutionist," and to "forbid fighting" was to "forbid what our fathers called 'the sacred right of insurrection.'"[360] Most Fabians, as eugenics-influenced Imperialists who saw the non-white races as inferior, opposed the Great War, in which the principal antagonists were Europeans.[361] Many, like Shaw, influenced by eugenics, did not condemn all killing but preferred killing the weak to killing, or being killed by, the strong. The film *All Quiet on the Western Front*[362] acted as a solemn warning of the horrors of war to the younger generation, and during the 1930s "semi-pacifists," influenced by Burke's "concessions of fear," argued that acceding to Hitler's territorial claims would ensure peace. An Oxford Union debate of February 9, 1933 declared "that this House will in no circumstances fight for King and Country." But Hitler was re-arming just as the British appeared to be throwing down their weapons. To Chesterton, the "perils of pacifism" included ignoring "Prussianism" and its "[a]ggression and annexation" of Silesia, Poland, Denmark, and Alsace, which had "proceeded so mechanically, on oiled and silent wheels," that it seemed "quite natu-

356. Chesterton told Maurice Reckitt, whose "distress at the line which the *Weekly* was taking on Abyssinia" was such that he considered leaving the newspaper's board: "The whole thing happened while I was having a holiday" (G.K. Chesterton, Letter, September 19, 1935, M. Ward, *Gilbert Keith Chesterton*, op. cit., 648).

357. B. Sewell, *G.K.'s Weekly: An Appraisal*, op. cit., 50–51.

358. Conservative MPs who criticized the Munich settlement found themselves under pressure, but Churchill's local Conservative chairman staunchly supported him (W.S. Churchill, *The Second World War: The Gathering Storm*, op. cit., 258).

359. G.K. Chesterton, "Third Thoughts Are Best," *G.K.'s Weekly*, June 11, 1932.

360. G.K. Chesterton, "Lawlessness as Law," *Illustrated London News*, October 28, 1916, G.K. Chesterton, *Chesterton on War and Peace: Battling the Ideas and Movements That Led to Nazism and World War II*, op. cit., 212.

361. G.K. Chesterton, *Autobiography*, op. cit., 231–232; G.K. Chesterton, *Chesterton on War and Peace: Battling the Ideas and Movements That Led to Nazism and World War II*, op. cit., 45–46.

362. Based on the book by Erich Maria Remarque, a German Great War veteran, published in 1928 and burned in 1933 by the Nazis, who claimed he was descended from a French Jew and was not a war veteran.

ral and normal" for those not affected, including the British press, which emphasized the threat of Italy but saw China, under attack from Japan, as "volcanic": "[W]here there is order there is peace; and where there is peace there is justice; or if there isn't, it doesn't much matter."[363] This sort of "Darwinist" pacifism, Chesterton maintained, encouraged the "survival of the fiercest." The German and Japanese "Right to Live" was really the "Right to Kill."[364] In 1932 Chesterton predicted the Nazi-Soviet non-aggression pact, signed in 1939, seeing behind Nazi nationalism and Bolshevist internationalism. Both were "of the same stuff," the "old barbarism" united in its "hatred of the Christian civilisation." Prussia had "proved her Paganism once again in the Nazi movement" in "half a hundred heathen fads. But above all in this vital or very deadly fact; that the *Nazi is ready to dally with Communists*." The "Prussian and the Russian," he argued, would "agree about everything; especially about Poland." Chesterton admitted that like all "generalisations about political problems" his own were "patched all over with exceptions and incongruities," but he applied similar generalizations to "usurers," economic forces that he believed were almost as deadly as military forces: "[T]he moment the [Great] War was over, certain forces which . . . are somewhat alien to old Christendom and the Catholic instinct . . . rushed to the help of Prussia." These "usurers" were "all Pro-German; even those innocent usurers who are now rather too bewildered to know whether their complicated and incompetent financial system is usurious or not." The origin of these forces, he alleged, was New York, "especially all that was most cynical and least traditional about New York." These men, "alien to Europe, had therefore a weak favouritism for Prussia . . . they let us in for our biggest financial crash when Prussia flatly refused to pay."[365] Clearly, the "alien forces" did not help Germany much, despite their "pro-Germanism," but Chesterton does not mention Jews, and even says some "usurers" might be innocent. But the following week Chesterton claimed that during the Great War "a Jingo Jew" whose newspaper *Forward* "told Germany to break through Europe as an oak breaks through the thicket, without thought of right or wrong," toward

363. Japan set up the puppet state of Manchukuo in January 1932 after destroying the authority of the Chinese Republic in Manchuria (G. K. Chesterton, "On Cleaning Up," *G. K.'s Weekly*, January 30, 1932).

364. By appeasing the Japanese aggressor the international community reflected Herbert Spencer's "survival of the fittest" idea (G. K. Chesterton, "The Right to Rob," *G. K.'s Weekly*, March 5, 1932).

365. G. K. Chesterton, "Third Thoughts are Best," *G. K.'s Weekly*, June 11, 1932. Heavy War reparations caused massive inflation in Germany, which ceased payments, leading to the reoccupation of the Rhine and the Dawes Plan (1924) under which the American financier J. P. Morgan floated a massive loan on the US stock market. Quickly oversubscribed, it enabled Germany to make payments to Britain and France, helping them to service their enormous American War debts. The loans helped prop up the German economy until 1928, but the Wall Street Crash meant that American loans to Europe dried up; in 1930 the Allies agreed to evacuate the Rhineland.

the end of the War "became a Pacifist. When I think of that particular sort of Jew, I can understand Hitler being an Anti-Semite. But he is none the less a fool to fall back on believing the Jew's first lie, which the Jew himself had to abandon."[366] As will be seen, the subject of pacifism linked to the Great War inevitably invoked the memory of Chesterton's dead brother, but Jewish German patriotism was no "lie." As Einstein remarked of Jewish German Fritz Haber, his "life was the tragedy of the German Jew; the tragedy of unrequited love."[367] It was the carnage of the Great War, not cowardice, that drew Jews and Gentiles to pacifism, but both Jewish and Gentile Germans espoused views ranging from internationalism to extreme nationalism, as did Ernst Lissauer, who wrote the *Hymn of Hate* against England.[368] Nonetheless, although attention to fine detail was not always a prominent feature of Chesterton's journalism, it was always based on truth,[369] and his article about Jewish pacifism referred to real individuals.[370] He calls Hitler a "fool," and, as will be seen, he continued to mock Hitler for his anti-Semitism. His reference to "that particular sort of Jew" distinguishes between Jews, thereby avoiding the pitfall of a "racist" approach. "Jingo Jew," "Jew Imperialist" and "Jew press" were

366. G. K. Chesterton, "One Word More," *G. K.'s Weekly*, June 18, 1932.

367. Despite his contribution during the Great War and Christian conversion, Haber suffered under the Nazi racial laws; seeking work, he moved to England, where he died ("Scientist whose assimilation experiment went badly wrong," *Jewish Chronicle*, April 15, 2011, 47).

368. "You we shall hate with enduring hate; / We shall not forbear from our hate; / Hate on water and hate on land, / hate of the head and hate of the hand, / hate of the hammer and hate of the crown, / Hate of seventy millions pressing down. / We love as one; we hate as one; / We have one foe, and one alone—ENGLAND!" *Hassgesang gegen England* ("Hate song against England") (1914), although not widely popular among German Jews, was distributed in the Germany army, set to music, sung in concerts and taught in schools. Decorated with the Order of the Royal Eagle by the Kaiser, Lissauer died in 1937; Hitler expunged his memory but continued to use his work for propaganda.

369. M. Canovan, *G. K. C.: Radical Populist*, op. cit., 57–58. Ward noted that "Chesterton might commit a hundred inaccuracies and yet get at the heart of his subject in a way that the most painstaking biographer and critic could not emulate"; using news reports to illustrate general principles (M. Ward, *Gilbert Keith Chesterton*, op. cit., 307–308) he claimed an official order decreed that "all little girls should have their hair cut short. I mean, of course, all little girls whose parents were poor" (G.K. Chesterton, *What's Wrong with the World*, op. cit., 120); however, it later transpired that Sir Cyril Burt, the London County Council's education authority's first consultant psychiatrist, was secretly operating on poor "mental deficients"; a quarter died and the survivors showed no improvement; thus Chesterton underestimated the oppression of the poor (M. Canovan, *G. K. C.: Radical Populist*, op. cit., 58–59); see Chapter Two regarding the Mental Deficiency Acts.

370. Revisionist and patriot, Viennese-born Jew Friedrich Stampfer edited the German socialist newspaper *Vorwärts* with other Jewish Social Democratic Party members; at the end of the War some left wing Jews rejected Stampfer's stance—and the extreme revolutionary views of Jewish communist Rosa Luxemburg—supporting instead Jewish Marxist Hugo Hasse, a humanist pacifist (see: P. Pulzer, *Jews and the German State: The Political History of a Minority* [Oxford: Blackwell, 1992]).

common shorthand in political commentary,[371] and Chesterton also referred to "Japanese Jingoes."[372]

But in October 1917, as editor of *The New Witness*, Chesterton claimed that "some Jews in the East End jumped up and began to assault and kill our soldiers for defending our country."[373] Dean Rapp concludes that he "did not really want to understand the patriotic contribution of Jewish soldiers to the British war effort." This complex controversy will be explored in more detail,[374] but earlier, Chesterton observed that Jewish soldiers were not only "heroic among the Jews" but "exceptional ... even among the heroes." Such heroic cases were "not so rare," and he himself had "one such Jewish friend" whose grave had been lately dug behind enemy lines, adding that these "strangers coming from far to fight for us" should be "accorded a double salute."[375] This reflected his theory of nationality, under which Jews could not be true Englishmen. Unlike anti-Semites, however, who believed all Jews were cowards, he insisted that such examples meant that Jews were doubly brave. In his *Autobiography* Chesterton paid tribute to his school-friend, Great War poet Robert Vernède, whose "full promise as a poet he did not keep; because he kept a better one, and is dead on the field of honour."[376] He adds that he would "never have been surprised" if a friend of Vernède's, "the most unselfish man I ever knew in my life, of the sort that is still unsatisfied even with its own unselfishness," had been a conscientious objector," but he "went to the Front in a flash like fire; and had his leg shot off in his first battle."[377]

Chesterton was always careful when writing about Jews to avoid blanket prejudice, and his anti-pacifist warnings of the 1930s avoided blaming the entire Jewish people for inherent cowardice. But by 1934, writing of the Great War, pacifism and pessimism, he appeared to step over the line between Enlightenment rationalism into prejudice:

> If every dirty little Jew pessimist and pervert is within his rights in writing books to prove that all his or my countrymen are cowards, or to dance on the

371. Social Democratic Federation founder H. M. Hyndman condemned the Russian pogroms of 1903 and the Aliens Immigration Bill; however, he blamed the Boer conflict on a "'Jew-Jingo gang' and a 'Jew press'"; Jerome K. Jerome and the anti-Imperialist J. A. Hobson also used such expressions (B. Cheyette, *Constructions of "the Jew" in English literature and society: Racial representations, 1875–1945*, op. cit., 57).

372. G. K. Chesterton, "The Right to Rob," *G. K.'s Weekly*, March 5, 1932.

373. G. K. Chesterton, "The Grand Turk of Tooting," the *New Witness*, October 25, 1917, 610–611.

374. J. K. Prothero, (Ada Chesterton), "The Necessity for a Bomb-Proof Ghetto," the *New Witness*, October 4, 1917, 543, in Dean Rapp, "The Jewish Response to G. K. Chesterton's Antisemitism, 1911–1933," *Patterns of Prejudice*, 24 (2–4), (1990), 75–86; see Chapter Six.

375. G. K. Chesterton, "The Jew and the Journalist," the *New Witness*, October 11, 1917, 563.

376. G. K. Chesterton, *Autobiography*, op. cit., 63.

377. Ibid., 76.

graves of my brethren who died in battle, then I am within my rights in most obstinately refusing to be hustled into a half-built Utopia that does not allow for any private property or any personal God.[378]

Despite appearances, however, in the same year, a German Jewish pacifist sexologist, Magnus Hirschfeld published *The Sexual History of the World War*, which detailed "sensuality in the trenches."[379] Hirschfeld described the Wartime release of sexual restraints, prostitution, the erotic aspects of military drill, venereal diseases, as well as male and female homosexuality, sadism, and rape. Linking these subjects to servicemen would have enraged Chesterton, whose brother perished in the War.[380] Hirschfeld, a homosexual campaigner who made a film, *Different from the Others*, in which he starred, was a moral relativist.[381] His long-standing, vigorous campaign for homosexuality had encouraged perceptions of it as a "Jewish" trait,[382] although others blamed Judaism, with its strict moral code, for encouraging opposition to homosexuality.[383]

Furthermore, on June 28 1934, weeks before Chesterton's condemnation of Hirschfeld, Hitler had ordered the murder of his rival Ernst Rohm and his henchmen. Rohm had remained a revolutionary while Hitler turned increasingly to democratic pathways to power, but the "Rohm purge" also helped Hitler avoid personal entanglement in a growing scandal. Rohm was a notorious sexual deviant, as Arendt[384] and Hirschfeld noted.[385] Hitler claimed a moral purge, but another unsigned editorial in *G.K.'s Weekly* said that "too

---

378. G.K. Chesterton, "Queries on Fascism (III)," *G.K.'s Weekly*, July 19, 1934, 312–313.

379. M. Hirschfeld, *Sexual History of the World War* (New York: Panurge Press, 1934) (published as *Sittengeschichte des Weltkrieges* [Leipzig, 1930]).

380. Hirschfeld "discovered" transvestism and organized the first Congress for Sexual Reform; this led to the formation of the World League for Sexual Reform, which met in London in 1929 (M. Hirschfeld, "Transvestites" [1910], in L. Bland, L. Doan, eds., *Sexology Uncensored: The Documents of Sexual Science*, op. cit., 97–104).

381. "Every people (and every religion) is convinced that its own morals constitute morality in the *objective* sense" (M. Hirschfeld, "Men and Women" [1933], ibid., 227).

382. Hirschfeld's Jewish background "linked the cause of gay rights with Judaism in the minds of many German conservatives at the time" (Richard S. Levy, *Antisemitism: A Historical Encyclopedia of Prejudice and Persecution* [Santa Barbara, CA: ABC-Clio, 2005], 303).

383. The Bible's condemnation of homosexual practice (see: Leviticus 18:22; 20:13) was claimed by one Jewish scholar to have prompted the Nazis' insane hatred of the Jews (S. Igra, *Germany's National Vice* [1945], in S. Lively, *The Poisoned Stream: "Gay" Influence in Human History Vol. I, Germany 1890–1945* [Keizer, Oregon: Founders Publishing Corp., 1997], 12–14); Igra, who fled Germany in 1939, saw Hitler as leading a band of evil men linked by "a common vice" (Igra, S., *Germany's National Vice* [London, 1945], 26), in W. D. Rubinstein, *Genocide: A History* (Harlow, England: Pearson Longman, 2004), 189.

384. H. Arendt, *The Origins of Totalitarianism* (London: Harcourt, Inc., 1994), 407.

385. M. Hirschfeld, "Racism" (1938), in L. Bland, L. Doan, eds., *Sexology Uncensored: The Documents of Sexual Science Sexology Uncensored: The Documents of Sexual Science*, op. cit., 228.

many crimes" had been "dressed up in high-flown sentiments."[386] But the Rohm purge might help explain Chesterton's "composite portrait" of Hitler as a common soldier, presented in September 1934, as well as his continued warnings about "Prussianism," for "Prussianism" was also associated with militaristic homosexuality.[387] In his *Autobiography* Chesterton said that as a youth he "could . . . imagine the worst and wildest disproportions and distortions of more normal passion" but had "never indeed felt the faintest temptation to the particular madness of Wilde."[388]

In fact, Hirschfeld was equally opposed to militaristic "Prussianism," and it has been argued that as well as being Jewish, it was this opposition, and his mass of revealing files about individual Nazis, which led to his persecution.[389] Chesterton may have believed that Hitler, not a Prussian but an Austrian Catholic, the "plain soldier" from those trenches denigrated by the pacifist Hirschfeld, had "dealt with" Nazi sexual deviancy. Opposition to "decadence" fuelled Chesterton's writing from the beginning,[390] and his opposition to pessimism has been seen as the outcome of natural jollity, but he insisted that *The Man Who Was Thursday*, in "resisting the heresy of pessimism," did not imply

386. For example, "the Reichstag Fire, when the mistake was made of leaving the evidence lying about alive to be the subject of a Supreme Court trial" ("Exit the Third Reich," [unsigned], *G.K.'s Weekly*, July 5, 1934, 1–2).

387. Hitler's hero and inspiration was the homosexual "philosopher king" Frederick the Great, whose cult of Prussian militarism and homosexual Teutonic heroes echoed Plato's ideal Republic, modeled on Sparta's aggressive homosexual elite (S. Lively, K. Abrams, *The Pink Swastika: Homosexuality in the Nazi Party* [Sacramento, CA: Veritas Aeterna Press, 2002], 130–131); Greek military tradition encouraged pederasty to promote bravery and morale; Plato's *Republic* proposed a "brutal law" forcing men and women to submit to the sexual demands of soldiers during wartime, to encourage military enthusiasm and valor (Karl R. Popper, *The Open Society and its Enemies Vol. I: The Spell of Plato* [London: Routledge & Kegan Paul, 1945/1977], 150–151).

388. G.K. Chesterton, *Autobiography*, op. cit., 90; he also referred to the "Greek vices, oriental vices, hints of the old horrors of the Semitic demons [which] began to fill the fancies of decaying Rome" (G.K. Chesterton, *The Everlasting Man* [San Francisco: Ignatius Press, 1993], 159).

389. Rohm was "a notorious homosexual who used his party connections to scour the countryside in search of handsome young men of similar tastes" (A.S. Lindemann, *Esau's Tears: Modern Anti-Semitism and the Rise of the Jews* [Cambridge: Cambridge University Press, 1997], 502); however, for many years Hitler ignored Rohm and his exploits, and the "great majority" of the Purge's victims "were not homosexuals" (S. Lively, *The Poisoned Stream: "Gay" Influence in Human History Vol. I, Germany 1890–1945*, op. cit., 95–100); Hirschfeld opposed pederasty and sado-masochism, in contrast to Rohm and his associates who disdained his approach as "effeminate"; his Institute, which contained many files on Nazis undergoing treatment for their sexuality, was attacked by the Nazis in 1933 and his books burned (S. Lively, K. Abrams, *The Pink Swastika: Homosexuality in the Nazi Party*, op. cit., 188).

390. "[W]hen I did begin to write, I was full of a new and fiery resolution to write against the Decadents and the Pessimists who ruled the culture of the age" (G.K. Chesterton, *Autobiography*, op. cit., 92).

support for "the equally morbid and diseased insanity of optimism."[391] Decadence and pessimism were closely linked to eugenics and racism, which implied that poor and non-white people could not help their inferiority. Decadence implied that sexual sin could not be "helped." To Chesterton, nothing could be more pessimistic than the pessimism of decadence.

Most Weimar-era sexual campaigners, such as Hirschfeld, were influenced by Darwinist theories,[392] as were Shaw and Wells.[393] But so were the Nazis. Hitler's philosophy was based on "struggle," and Chesterton's apparent reassessment of Hitler as a "Prussian tool" was merely temporary. Anti-Semitism failed to figure in his "reassessment" and he never ceased warning against the racial religion of "Prussianism." In June 1932 he had called Hitler a fool for believing that Jews could be patriotic, but in October 1932 he condemned the Nazis for attacking Jews, although he also claimed that in late Victorian times "the Jews, and especially the German Jews, were at the very top of their power and influence." He alleged that from the time "they forced the Egyptian War to the time when they forced the South African War, they were imperial and immune. Certainly much more so than they are now." For, he added, the Jews were "now being jumped on very unjustly in Germany itself, and old Victorians like Mr. Belloc and myself, who began in the days of Jewish omnipotence by attacking the Jews, will now probably die defending them."[394] Many anti-capitalists blamed Jewish influence for the Boer War and other conflicts,[395] but rather than powerful Jews driving Imperialism, the situation reflected Chesterton's own historical view of governments seeking Jewish resources and cynically discarding the Jewish people after making them unpopular.[396] Arendt comments: "For a very brief time, there was some truth in Walter Rathenau's remark that 300 men, who all know each other, held the destinies of the world in their hands." Jews, she remarks, were "more deluded by the appearances of [this] golden age of security than any other section of the European peoples. Antisemitism seemed to be a thing

---

391. G. K. Chesterton, "The Man Who Was Thursday," *G.K.C. as M.C.*, J. P. de Fonseka, ed. (London: Methuen & Co. Ltd., 1929), 205.

392. A. Farmer, *By Their Fruits: Eugenics, Population Control and the Abortion Campaign*, 116.

393. However, they never included homosexuality in their Utopias. Shaw referred obliquely to the subject to Nancy Astor whose son had been in prison (G. B. Shaw, Letter, April 15, 1932, G. B. Shaw, *Bernard Shaw: Collected Letters 1926–1950 Vol. IV*, op. cit., 284–286).

394. G. K. Chesterton, "The Backward Bolshie," *G.K.'s Weekly*, October 29, 1932; see Chapter Two.

395. B. Cheyette, *Constructions of "the Jew" in English literature and society: Racial representations, 1875–1945*, op. cit., 57.

396. Financiers, mainly Jews who had fled the Russian pogroms, facilitated the exploitation of South African gold and diamonds; they had useful British banking links but the non-Jewish Cecil Rhodes persuaded Britain that imperialist force was needed to protect such investments; while the Jewish financiers were seen as rootless cosmopolitans, Rhodes was feted as the epitome of a benign and disinterested British imperialism (H. Arendt, *The Origins of Totalitarianism*, op. cit., 200–204).

of the past," but the "growing influence of big business on the state and the state's declining need for Jewish services threatened the Jewish banker with extinction." Consequently, "[m]ore and more Jews left state finance for independent business."[397] Chesterton had seen pride—the "true vanity of vanities"[398]—in the "financial Jew," but now he saw it in Nazi racism, which was persecuting its fallen victim. While justifying his own reading of history, Chesterton's chief aim was to condemn the Nazi attacks. Moreover, his stance went against popular wisdom: the following year, the British ambassador in Berlin regretted that "foreign opinion" had failed to "fully gras[p] the fact that the National-Socialist programme is intensely anti-Jewish."[399]

In a "prophetic speech" in June 1931 Churchill warned against disarmament,[400] and in October and November 1932 he warned against re-arming Germany, "[s]ounding the alarm even before Hitler moved into the chancellery."[401] Hitler had won over 30 per cent of the Presidential vote against Hindenburg in March 1932, but Chesterton had been warning about "Prussianism" and pacifism since January 1932. Furthermore, in March 1933 he wrote that "Hitler seemed intent upon 'setting all Christendom aflame by a raid on Poland.'"[402] The reactions of Churchill and Chesterton to the Nazi threat were remarkably similar. Churchill also warned against Japanese ambitions in China.[403] But they were in a tiny minority.[404] Like Shaw and Wells, David Lloyd George was

397. Ibid., 51.

398. G.K. Chesterton, "The True Vanity of Vanities," *The Apostle and the Wild Ducks, and Other Essays*, D. Collins, ed. (London: Elek, 1975), 12.

399. Documents on British Foreign Policy 1919–1939 (E.L. Woodward, R. Butler, eds., with A. Orne [London, 1952] series 2, vol. IV, nos. 263, 30), in W. Manchester, *The Caged Lion: Winston Spencer Churchill* 1932–1940, op. cit., 89.

400. Winston Churchill, Speech to House of Commons, June 29, 1931, W.S. Churchill, *Churchill Speaks: Winston S. Churchill in Peace and War: Collected Speeches*, 1897–1963, op. cit., 540.

401. *Daily Mail*, October 17, 1932 and *Hansard* November 23, 1932, in W. Manchester, *The Caged Lion: Winston Spencer Churchill* 1932–1940, op. cit., 69.

402. G.K. Chesterton, *All I Survey* (1933) in I. Ker, *G.K. Chesterton: A Biography*, op. cit., 677.

403. Winston Churchill, Speech, Constituency meetings, Loughton and Waltham Abbey, October 26, 1937, W.S. Churchill, *Churchill Speaks: Winston S. Churchill in Peace and War: Collected Speeches*, 1897–1963, op. cit., 637–638. At a discussion on Japan hosted by George Wyndham (who died in 1913) Chesterton said he distrusted Japan because it was "imitating us at our worst" with its "factories and materialism"; what "amused" Churchill "was that as long as Japan was beautiful and polite, people treated it as barbarous," but having "become ugly and vulgar, it was treated with respect"; when someone remarked that although "every man-jack of us . . . seems to hate the Japanese" they were "forbidden to say a word against them in any of the newspapers," Churchill "smiled the inscrutable smile of the statesman" (G.K. Chesterton, *Autobiography*, op. cit., 120–121).

404. In June 1935 Churchill attended a meeting of "Focus," a tiny organization concerned about appeasement of Nazi aggression; six months after Chesterton's death the Anti-Nazi Defence of Freedom and Peace held its "first great rally," in December 1936 (W. Manchester, *The Caged Lion: Winston Spencer Churchill* 1932–1940, op. cit., 219–220).

impressed by Germany's "Strong Man." After visiting Hitler in 1936, the Great War Prime Minister called him "a born leader of men. A magnetic, dynamic personality with a single-minded purpose, a resolute will and a dauntless heart"; he reassured those who feared that Germany had "swung back to its old Imperialist temper" that the "idea of a Germany intimidating Europe with a threat that its irresistible army might march across frontiers forms no part of the new vision."[405] Lloyd George was listened to, while the Nazis' anti-Jewish persecution was rationalized or dismissed.[406] No wonder that in March 1933, Chesterton complained that he and Belloc were "denounced as demented fanatics, who wished to torture Jews in the cells of the Spanish Inquisition," while Hitler, who proposed to "beat and belabour Jews like mules, to treat all Jews as such, at best as beasts of burden and more often as beasts of prey," had "better luck." Chesterton and Belloc "never hinted, or dreamed of hinting, at any mere herd-hatred of this kind." They "never proposed to batter men merely because they were Jews; to hound out or exterminate hundreds and thousands of harmless little fiddlers and schoolmasters and actors and poor students, because they were Jews who were honest enough to keep their Jewish names." Chesterton reiterated his belief that the "financial Jew" was a problem stemming from the lack of a Jewish homeland, but he and Belloc "were never such fools as to think it could be solved by massacre." When Hitler jumped over "all the hedges" and stole "all the horses, good or bad, well-treated or ill-treated," however, most English people tried to "find excuses for him." The Dreyfus affair "may have been a miscarriage of justice" but "at least he was tried for being a traitor and condemned for being a traitor. The ordinary Jew in Germany is not tried at all; and is condemned for being a Jew."[407]

When writing about anti-Jewish persecution, Chesterton's information was accurate and up to date,[408] and in July 1933, he again warned about Nazi anti-Jewish persecution in *The Judaism of Hitler*. Unlike Shaw, who rebuffed Jewish enquiries, the article led to a September 1933 *Jewish Chronicle* interview in which he went even further, saying he was "appalled by the Hitlerite atrocities" carried out on "the most famous scapegoat in European history," and that he and Belloc would "die defending the last Jew in Europe." The "Prussian spirit,"

---

405. D. Lloyd George, "I talked to Hitler," *Daily Express*, November 17, 1936, in J. Remak, ed., *The Nazi Years: A Documentary History* (Prentice-Hall, 1969), accessed April 24, 2009, http://www.cdo jerusalem.org/icons-multimedia/ClientsArea/HoH/LIBARC/ARCHIVE/Chapters/Stabiliz/Foreign/ LloydGeo.html.

406. W. Manchester, *The Caged Lion: Winston Spencer Churchill* 1932–1940, op. cit., 101–102.

407. G. K. Chesterton, "The Horse and the Hedge," *G. K.'s Weekly*, March 30, 1933, 55.

408. After the Nuremberg Laws of 1933 great numbers of Jews, including baptized Jews, were dismissed from the civil service and other professions (M. Gilbert, *The Holocaust: The Jewish Tragedy*, op. cit., 36; 47–48).

with its "arrogance and ... truculence of the self-righteous," was, he warned, "fraught with ... danger to harmless people." In mistreating "harmless, and in scores of cases, valuable and distinguished Jewish citizens of the German Reich," Hitler had "forfeited all claim to the label statesman"; with the opportunity to do "incalculable good" he had done "the worst possible mischief." Chesterton also referred to "the Jewish Spirit," which he saw as "a spirit foreign in Western countries," but the expression was as impersonal as pacifism, pessimism, and Prussianism. More significantly, he refers to the Jewish victims as German citizens.[409] Moreover, as will be seen, true anti-Semites continued to see Jews as all-powerful even under extreme persecution.[410] Months later, in *A Word for the Dictator*, Chesterton includes Jews with French Canadians and Boers as naturalized citizens of foreign extraction.[411]

The *Jewish Chronicle* had believed Chesterton "irrevocably hardened against the Hebrews" but said he had experienced "a violent revulsion of feeling" in response to the "uncivilised atrocities" in Nazi Germany.[412] Despite this, *The Judaism of Hitler* might now be regarded as anti-Semitic, given Chesterton's claim that "Hitlerism" was "almost entirely of Jewish origin." His aim, however, is to satirize Nazism, since he adds: "This truth, if inscribed ... on a large banner and lifted in sight of an excited mob in a modern German town, might or might not have the soothing effect which I desire." Chesterton then uses Hitler's appearance to mock his racial views, saying that he was "very fond of the real Nordic Man, especially when he does really look like a Nordic Man. ... Hitler does not look in the least like a Nordic Man; but that is another question." Unlike Wells, Chesterton does not ridicule the claims of Judaism but taunts the Nazis by insisting that they had borrowed imperialism from the Romans, "the more modern and much more mortally dangerous idea of race" from Gobineau, and "the grand, imperial idea of a Chosen Race ... of a people that is God's favourite and guided by Him," from "the Jews." Furthermore, Chesterton explains that the idea came through "that obscure conspiracy against Christendom, which some of them [Jews] can never abandon ... sometimes ... marked not by obscurity but obscenity." Hirschfeld's "conspiracy" was marked by obscenity but not by obscurity, although, characteristically, Chesterton avoids blaming all Jews. Nonetheless, he also alleges that the German education system "fell into the hands of the Jews," and that their "ideals" were "insinuated" into German culture: "[D]oubtless [they] very often acted, not only as sceptics,

409. G. K. Chesterton, "The Judaism of Hitler," *G. K.'s Weekly*, July 20, 1933, in *End of the Armistice*, op. cit., 92–97; see Chapter Two.

410. See Chapter Six.

411. G. K. Chesterton, "A Word for the Dictator," *G. K.'s Weekly*, November 16, 1933, 167–168.

412. *Jewish Chronicle*, September 22, 1933, 14; see Chapter One.

but as cynics. But, even if they were only pretending to be mystics, they could only pretend to understand one kind of mysticism." Therefore, "German mysticism became more and more like Jewish mysticism," infused with the Chosen People idea. Chesterton concludes that it all began "with the power of the Jews" and had "ended with the persecution of the Jews."[413]

The idea of chosenness held enduring secular appeal,[414] and Hitler had assumed the mantle of Messiah[415] but, as Chesterton himself notes, England absorbed the Chosen People idea through the Protestant Old Testament emphasis,[416] just as Germany did. Chesterton feared that without their religion, Jews would become skeptics, but he also feared that without *their* religion, Christians would become barbarians. He had blamed "Prussianised" Protestantism for the Great War, enabling him to avoid blaming German Catholics in Bavaria and the Rhineland,[417] and now notes the irony of German Protestants trying to destroy what nobody else wanted to "set apart for idolatry," namely, the "ancient story of the Covenant with Israel."[418] Hannah Arendt comments that the "most fateful element in Jewish secularization" was "the concept of chosenness ... being separated from the Messianic hope," since Judaism viewed "these two elements" as "two aspects of God's redemptory plan for mankind." Jewish secularization, she notes:

> [F]inally produced that paradox ... by which Jewish assimilation—in its liquidation of national consciousness, its transformation of a national religion into a confessional denomination, and its meeting of the half-hearted and ambiguous demands of state and society by equally ambiguous devices and psychological tricks—engendered a very real Jewish chauvinism, if by chauvinism we understand the perverted nationalism in which (in the words of Chesterton) 'the individual is himself the thing to be worshipped; the individual is his own ideal and even his own idol.'[419]

413. G.K. Chesterton, "The Judaism of Hitler," *G.K.'s Weekly*, July 20, 1933.

414. For the doctrine of the chosen people "Marx's historical philosophy" substituted "the chosen class, the instrument for the creation of the classless society, and at the same time, the class destined to inherit the earth" (K.R. Popper, *The Open Society and its Enemies Vol. I: The Spell of Plato*, op. cit., 9).

415. "Hence today I believe that I am acting in accordance with the will of the Almighty Creator: *by defending myself against the Jew, I am fighting for the work of the Lord*" (A. Hitler, *Mein Kampf*, op. cit., 60).

416. G.K. Chesterton, *A Short History of England* (1917) *G.K. Chesterton Collected Works Vol. XX* (San Francisco: Ignatius Press, 2001), 536.

417. G.K. Chesterton, *The Barbarism of Berlin* (1914), I. Ker, *G.K. Chesterton: A Biography*, op. cit., 353.

418. G.K. Chesterton, "The Judaism of Hitler," *G.K.'s Weekly*, July 20, 1933.

419. Disraeli was an example of "an English imperialist and a Jewish chauvinist," but his "superstitious belief in blood and race ... carried no suspicion of possible massacres, whether in Africa, Asia, or Europe proper" (H. Arendt, *The Origins of Totalitarianism*, op. cit., 74–75); see Chapter Two.

Chesterton's article *The Judaism of Hitler* concludes: "This is the great Prussian illusion of pride, for which thousands of Jews have recently been rabbled or ruined or driven from their homes." For the many who said the Jews deserved this fate, he added: "I am certainly not enough of an Anti-Semite to say that it served them right."[420] Wells also blamed the Chosen People idea for Nazi persecution—but unlike Chesterton, he believed that the Jewish people's adherence to the idea caused the persecution. Chesterton noted that the English were not immune to the idea, since the Puritans had seen the Spanish Armada's defeat as a sign of their "election."[421] In 1926 he insisted that the only chosen race was the human race.[422] In 1928, he maintained that despite the "defects" of Islam, "any civilised Christian would infinitely prefer the Turks" to "many of the fads of Western Europe" because Islam had "no Chosen Race ... no nonsense about lesser breeds without the law." With "no rant of merely racial superiority," there was only a "brotherhood of men, if it be a brotherhood of Moslems." This, he claimed, was "the whole difference between the Turks and the Prussians."[423] But, as noted in Chapter Two, it was Nazi anti-Semitism that prompted Chesterton to accept the Jews alone as the Chosen People.

The Judaism of Hitler was seen by the *Jewish Chronicle* principally as an attack on Nazism, although it could be argued that Chesterton's anti-Nazism was really a vindication of Italy. But he had warned against racism and the secular Chosen People idea from the beginning of his career. At a time when few people took Nazism seriously and still fewer linked it to anti-Semitism, Chesterton did. The essay was a distillation of the more subtle and gradual change of emphasis in his fiction. Three years after his death the *Jewish Chronicle* warned that pacifism was leading some to accept Nazi anti-Semitism as the price of appeasement.[424]

Chesterton, Race, and Prussia

Churchill, Wells, and Chesterton thought it equitable to criticize Jews as well as non-Jews, and Chesterton avoided criticizing Jews in the mass, although his

420. G.K. Chesterton, "The Judaism of Hitler," *G.K.'s Weekly*, July 20, 1933.

421. G.K. Chesterton, *A Short History of England* (1917) *G.K. Chesterton Collected Works Vol. XX*, op. cit., 536.

422. G.K. Chesterton, *The Catholic Church and Conversion* (San Francisco: Ignatius Press, 1926/2006), 51–52.

423. G.K. Chesterton, *Illustrated London News*, April 11, 1928, 244, in J. Stapleton, *Christianity, Patriotism, and Nationhood: The England of G.K. Chesterton*, op. cit., 187.

424. "The Peace Pledge Union and Fascism: Need for Vigilance: 'Pacifists at the Crossroads': Attempts to Inject Anti-Semitism," *Jewish Chronicle*, August 18, 1939, 24.

generalizations regarding the "Jewish spirit" and "the plutocracy" now sound like blanket criticism. But to Chesterton, such blanket criticism suggested racism—the Nazi approach. In fact, his opposition to racial theories, which alerted him to the dangers of Nazi anti-Semitism, pre-dated his economic theory of Jews. In his 1904 biography of the painter G.F. Watts, one passage recalled his article *Jews Old and New*:[425] "To [Watts and his school], as to the ancient Jews the Spirit of the unity of existence declared in thunder that they should not make any graven image, or have any gods but Him."[426] Regarding "the racial legend about the Watts family," he also warned: "Long before heredity has become a science, it has become a superstition."[427] The English had been attracted to the Chosen People idea, but Chesterton said that the "heresy of a tribal pride . . . took even heavier hold upon the Germans."[428] In 1929 he saw the "good points" of the "German character" as "very good indeed" except where "pickled too long in the Prussian poison."[429] In 1933, noting the effect on German Jews of the Nazis stealing the Chosen People idea, he denounced "Race" as "one huge and howling Heresy" that was "run quite wild and raving: Race and the Pride of Prussia." Chesterton complained that while Hitler was "hounding the Jews like rats," the Nazis own "election" was based on dubious science: "Oh those speeches about Race! Oh, the stewed staleness and stupidity of the brains of a thousand boiled owls, diluted and filtered through the brains of a thousand forgotten Prussian professors! The German is not only a German. He is an Aryan. His heart leaps up when he beholds a Swastika in the sky." But the Jew was "not an Aryan. Most of us imagined that it was enough, for general common sense, that he was a Jew; but, alas, he is a Semite. Show him a Swastika and he remains cold. . . . Must these golden-haired giants (like Mr. Hitler) go on calling on the German God exactly and unalterably as of old?"[430]

The following year Chesterton condemned the "new movement of Prussianism," characterized "by a purely racial persecution of the Jews." He remained skeptical of press reports on Italian fascism, but believed that "Prussian" atrocities were not just "scare headlines," because the Prussian "national note . . . was insolent and pedantic."[431]

425. G.K. Chesterton, *The Speaker*, March 2, 1901, in *The Chesterton Review*, IX (1), February 1983, 601–602; see Chapter Two.

426. G.K. Chesterton, *G.F. Watts* (Whitefish, Montana: Kessinger Publishing, 1904/2000), 16.

427. Ibid., 21–22.

428. G.K. Chesterton, *A Short History of England* (1917) *G.K. Chesterton Collected Works Vol. XX*, op. cit., 536.

429. G.K. Chesterton, "Where is Wotan?" *G.K.'s Weekly*, February 2, 1929, 329.

430. G.K. Chesterton, "The Barbarian as Bore," *G.K.'s Weekly*, April 27, 1933, 119–120.

431. G.K. Chesterton, "Atrocities Again," *G.K.'s Weekly*, March 22, 1934, 39–40.

Slaying the Giant

In 1927 Chesterton warned of the anti-Jewish prejudice involved when the authorities got hold of "the wrong man" and refused to admit it: "[T]he man they get hold of is generally a loose fish, frequently a foreigner, and generally a Jew"—in this case a poor Jew, Oscar Slater. The other "terror" was "judging, by the type rather than the man," the "method of a barbarous sheik or sultan," but also of the "highly modern and scientific criminologist." "Reformers," he said, wanted "preventive legislation or indeterminate sentences" to protect society "from a type," rather than proving a crime "against a person."[432] To Chesterton this was scientific prejudice—literally, in this case, "pre-judging" Jews. But he was suspicious of wealthy Jews, regarding "plutocratic power" as secret fascism. In 1928 he claimed that Mussolini had taken "command" to "get rid of this Parliamentary sham" and that England had "a dictatorship ... as absolute as Mussolini's *only we do not know the name of our dictator.*" This dictator, with "international interests," had, he claimed, "come out into the open" but "[t]rue to the instinct of the Octopus, immediately he hides that name behind another"; but on "the face of the new Mond building" the world could see "the face of Lord Melchett done in stone."[433] Melchett—Alfred Mond—was Jewish, although Chesterton does not mention it. As a Liberal MP he had warned that a return to the Gold Standard would "'enslave' Britain to America," but later joined the Conservatives.[434] Consequently, Mond embodied all Chesterton's preoccupations, but his "name change" was no secret, being the result of his elevation to the peerage. In 1933 Chesterton insisted he and Belloc "never had any quarrel with the non-financial Jews; we had both of us many friends among them"; but "the intermediate commercial position of the Jewish nation created a very real thing called the Jewish Problem";[435] now he was swimming against the tide of non-Jewish opinion, emphasizing the poor Jew, the oppressed Jew, the harmless Jew. Unlike Shaw and Wells, Chesterton cheered Jack instead of the Giant; in the article *The Other Cheek* he applies his sling-shot to the Nazi

432. G. K. Chesterton, "In defence of a Jew," *G. K.'s Weekly*, August 27, 1927, 575; see Chapter Six.

433. G. K. Chesterton, "The New Dictator," *G. K.'s Weekly*, September 1, 1928, 385–386.

434. Sir A. Mond MP, House of Commons debate, April 29, 1925, quoted in M. Gilbert, *Winston S. Churchill Vol. V 1922–1939* (London: Heinemann, 1976); 116; as Liberal MP, Mond held Ministerial office under Lloyd George in 1906, was created baronet in 1910, joined the Conservatives in 1926 and in 1928 received a peerage; in 1926 he merged his chemical company Brunner Mond & Co with similar companies to form the mammoth Imperial Chemical Industries. The *Jewish Chronicle* called for a campaign against *New Witness* anti-Jewish "attacks" against Mond: allegations that he had traded with Germany during the War persisted even after the Director of Public Prosecutions found no offences had been committed ("Mentor," "Hit Back! Hit Back! Hit Back," *Jewish Chronicle*, October 11, 1918, 7).

435. G. K. Chesterton, "The Horse and the Hedge," *G. K.'s Weekly*, March 30, 1933, 55.

Goliath, "Adolf the Aryan." Ridiculing the attempts of New German Protestants to excise all Jewish references from Christianity, he wonders why Nazis should "particularly dislike the Old Testament"; true, it was "full of Jews," but so was the New Testament. And while the Nazi encouraged "clerks and shopkeepers" to murder each other in "a civilized city," he recoiled "in horror from the primitive epic of the Hebrew heroes," who were "fighting for their lives in a desert." This was something that most Christians could "understand and accept," but the Nazi was no "normal Christian."[436] In Chesterton's own fight for the "small man," "the Jew" had been magnified out of proportion, but under the Nazi onslaught he seemed like a rapidly shrinking fallen giant, while the Nazi grew to hideous proportions. One Jewish Christian[437] was inspired to quote Chesterton's *The Ballad of the Battle of Gibeon* as "the first and foremost answer . . . to the manifestations of reactionary Anti-Semitism":

> Now we have said as the thunder says it,
> Something is stronger than strength and slays it.
> Now we have written for all time later,
> Five kings are great, yet a law is greater. . . .[438]

Hitler, Eugenics, and the Family

Closely entwined with racialism and springing from the same evolutionary root, along with decadence and pessimism, was eugenics. All threatened human freedom and free will. In 1927 Chesterton correctly saw eugenics as a form of medical fascism controlling the weak, claiming of the Mental Deficiency Bill: "[W]hen any person for any reason wants to lock up another person, he will not have to prove anything definite, but . . . something that cannot possibly be proved."[439] In 1929 he warned that "Mental deficients" would "be classed . . . and possibly segregated, possibly sterilized; but at all events, placed within a special category in the State." It was the social reformers' "widest and worst assumption" that "the Bureaucracy (for *that* is their State)" had "the right to inspect and segregate the people" to decide who was "capable of citizenship."

---

436. G. K. Chesterton, "The Other Cheek," *End of the Armistice*, op. cit., 87–91. In 1934 the Nazis persecuted the *Bekennende Kirche* (Confessing Church) (see: J. S. Conway, *The Nazi Persecution of the Churches* 1933–1945 [Vancouver: Regent College Publishing, 1968/2001]); Chesterton said "this new Nordic nonsense" had "nothing whatever to do with Protestant theology; or rather to be completely contrary to it. No one is more sincerely glad than we are to know that some of the German Protestants are still most consistent and courageous Christians" (G. K. Chesterton, "The Religion of Fossils," *The Well and the Shallows*, op. cit., 28).

437. A. Kolnai, *The War Against the West*, op. cit., 495.

438. Ibid., 492–493; see Chapter Seven.

439. G. K. Chesterton, "More Mental Deficiency," *G. K.'s Weekly*, April 2, 1927, 319.

But in so doing they overrode "the institution of the family . . . the very foundation of the commonwealth." Moreover, "the next step after the foundation of a caste of Mental Deficients" might be the removal of all human rights, for if they could be sterilized "may they not also be destroyed?" And if one caste could be "formed and recognized, should there not be others?"[440] In Germany, within a few years, mental patients would be sterilized and secretly murdered. The same methods would be used on Jews and other "castes" segregated in the death camps.[441]

In 1930 Chesterton called a proposal to sterilize disabled people on pain of losing state benefits "slavery, no more and no less."[442] In 1936 he said that there was "something almost pathetic in Professor [Julian] Huxley saying, with his own beautiful innocence and sincerity, that Eugenics would now only mean docility in the millions and mastery by the millionaire. Why, what in the world does he imagine that it was ever meant to mean?"[443] Hitler, described as "perhaps the greatest applied eugenist who ever lived" applied eugenics to Jews and others he deemed inferior,[444] but both Left and Right advocated sterilization and extermination for their "castes" of "undesirables." Huxley and other left-wing eugenicists distanced themselves from Nazi anti-Semitism but wanted to apply eugenics to the whole human race.[445]

Long before, Chesterton noted that even worse than "the Communist attacking the family or the Capitalist betraying the family" was the "very astonishing vision of the Hitlerite defending the family." Having made "every family dependent on him and his semi-Socialist State," the Nazis preserved parental authority "by . . . telling all the parents what to do."[446] He insisted that the only protection under socialism or fascism was the much-maligned family, for there would be "rather more personal adaptation in a household than in a concentration

440. G. K. Chesterton, "Mental Deficiency," *G. K.'s Weekly*, June 22, 1929, 225–226.

441. The gas vans used to kill mental patients in Germany were later used in Poland to kill Jews before gas chambers were constructed ("Auschwitz: the Nazis and the Final Solution," BBC2 TV, January 18, 2005).

442. A Modern Churchmen's proposal (G. K. Chesterton, "An Attack from the Altars," *G. K.'s Weekly*, August 30, 1930, G. K. Chesterton, *Brave New Family: G. K. Chesterton on Men & Women, Children, Sex, Divorce, Marriage & the Family*, A. de Silva, ed. [San Francisco: Ignatius Press, 1990], 221).

443. G. K. Chesterton, "End of Eugenics," *G. K.'s Weekly*, March 5, 1936, 380–381.

444. Stephen Trombley, *The Right to Reproduce: A History of Coercive Sterilization* (London: Weidenfeld & Nicolson, 1988), 110.

445. A. Farmer, *By Their Fruits: Eugenics, Population Control and the Abortion Campaign*, op. cit., 134–136; the fertility controls they proposed were supposed to be voluntary, but obtaining authentic consent from those deemed mentally deficient remained problematical.

446. G. K. Chesterton, "Three Foes of the Family," *The Well and the Shallows*, op. cit., 150; originally published August 2, 1934.

camp."[447] His disgust at Nazi anti-Semitism and eugenics, combined with admiration for Jewish family values, lent potency to his change of attitude, demonstrated in his Christmas message of 1935. He said that "We live in a terrible time, of war and rumour of war," and urged that "to make vivid the horrors of destruction and mere disciplined murder we must see them more simply as attacks on the hearth and the human family; and feel about Hitler as men felt about Herod."[448] His *Autobiography* concluded: "Already there hover on the horizon sweeping scourges of sterilisation or social hygiene, applied to everybody and imposed by nobody."[449] "Nobody" was the impersonal bureaucracy, and the "scourge" would be imposed by a state machine from which the Nazis had eliminated free will, leaving the individual cogs to "follow orders."[450]

Prophecy in the Age of Dictators

Faced with poverty and misery, the three giants wanted a clean sweep of society. Shaw wanted a revolution in the nature of Man; Wells, a revolution of technocrats; while only Chesterton wanted a revolution of the masses.[451] Suspicious of minutely-worked-out Utopias that would destroy private life,[452] he believed that revolution was really "Restoration." Only conservative mobs rebelled, and thus revolution was a "return to the past"—a complete turn of the wheel.[453] Shaw and Wells foresaw peaceful and gradual revolutions, but their Utopias grew increasingly ruthless, while Chesterton increasingly desired not a "nasty" revolution but a "Christian Revolution" which, "[l]ike all revolutions . . . must

447. G.K. Chesterton, "St. Thomas More," ibid., 241–242.

448. G.K. Chesterton, *G.K.'s Weekly*, in M. Ward, *Gilbert Keith Chesterton*, op. cit., 637; reprinted as "The Winter Feast" in G.K. Chesterton, *The Apostle and the Wild Ducks and other essays*, op. cit., 42–48).

449. G.K. Chesterton, *Autobiography*, op. cit., 354.

450. See: H. Friedlander, S. Milton, eds., *The Holocaust: Ideology, bureaucracy, and genocide: the San Jose papers* (Millwood, New York: Kraus International Publications, 1980); H. Sherrer, "The Inhumanity of Government Bureaucracies," *The Independent Review*, 5 (2), (Fall 2000), 249–264, accessed May 10, 2011, http://www.independent.org/pdf/tir/tir_05_2_sherrer.pdf.

451. "[H]e was a little hazy as to the exact nature of the revolution he proposed. He certainly hoped to avoid the guillotine!" (M. Ward, *Gilbert Keith Chesterton*, op. cit., 306–307); although in the *New Age* there was "much talk of revolution, and not everybody took the allusions to the guillotine as a joke" (M. Ward, *Return to Chesterton* [London: Sheed & Ward], 58).

452. "The so-called economic freedom which the planners promise us means precisely that we are to be relieved of the necessity of solving our own economic problems and that the bitter choices which this often involves are to be made for us. Since under modern conditions we are for almost everything dependent on means which our fellow men provide, economic planning would involve direction of almost the whole of our life . . . from our primary needs to our relations with our family and friends, from the nature of our work to the use of our leisure" (F.A. Hayek, *The Road to Serfdom* (condensed version) [London: The Institute of Economic Affairs, 1945/2001], 55).

453. G.K. Chesterton, *What's Wrong with the World*, op. cit., 121.

begin in the mind."[454] J. P. Corrin remarks that despite his fictional emphasis on "violence and struggle" Chesterton "probably was never completely serious when arguing for battle in real life,"[455] adding that revolution would require "more than the destruction of capitalism and socialism."[456] Crucially, Chesterton believed that revolution could never be imposed from above. In Shelley and Whitman, the "revolutionary optimists," Chesterton saw as Catholic truth the "universal duty to love men as men."[457] Under Belloc's inspiration he took this "nugget of gold" from the French Revolution's "Declaration of the Rights of Man."[458] When Chesterton attacked the Utopias of Shaw and Wells in *Heretics*, they demanded that he "play fair by setting forth his own Utopia." His response was *Orthodoxy*, which presented orthodox Christianity as a revolutionary force for change.[459]

All three prophesied the downfall of capitalism, revolution, and the emergence of a New Man. But capitalism totters on, England has not yet risen, and the Superman has yet to evolve. Wells and Shaw believed that Soviet repression and starvation were harbingers of better things. Wells predicted "a more or less complete restoration of intellectual liberty in Russia in the next few years."[460] Shaw gave up trying to predict what would happen. None foresaw the fall of communism, and none foresaw the "mixed economy" increasing prosperity for the poor. Chesterton warned against creeping bureaucracy, and foresaw "health and safety" mania.[461] Wells believed that the death of the traditional family would lead to greater harmony. Chesterton's warnings about the negative outcomes of its decline have been vindicated.[462] Wells predicted a sexual revolution underpinned by birth control, but Chesterton predicted that birth control

---

454. M. Ward, *Gilbert Keith Chesterton*, op. cit., 611. Increasingly, he looked for a Distributist revolution (G. K. Chesterton, "The Fear of the Past," *What's Wrong with the World*, op. cit., 12).

455. J. P. Corrin, *G. K. Chesterton and Hilaire Belloc: The Battle Against Modernity*, op. cit., 217.

456. Ibid., 45.

457. G. K. Chesterton, *The Thing* (London: Sheed & Ward, 1929), 30.

458. A. Nichols, *G. K. Chesterton, Theologian* (London: Darton, Longman & Todd Ltd., 2009), 193.

459. M. Ward, *Gilbert Keith Chesterton*, op. cit., 191.

460. H. G. Wells, *The Outlook for Homo Sapiens*, op. cit., 151.

461. The "modern spirit" was "trying to abolish the abuse of things by abolishing the things themselves" (G. K. Chesterton, "The Terror of a Toy," *Fancies versus Fads* [London: Methuen, 1923], 108).

462. By the end of the century the proportion of births outside marriage was 40 per cent; 15 per cent of babies are now born into homes without a resident father; there has been a decline in marriage and, Europe-wide, while 8 per cent of married parents split up by their child's fifth birthday, the figure is 43 per cent for cohabiting couples; this leaves even more children, especially poorer children, in chronic poverty and/or at risk of physical, emotional or sexual abuse (See: The Centre for Family Justice, *Breakthrough Britain, Vol. I, Family Breakdown*, July 2007).

would be used to control the poor, as now happens in population control.[463] Wells' prophesies about devastating military developments have proved more accurate than his rose-tinted views of sexual revolution.[464] He believed the Munich settlement would bring down Chamberlain's government,[465] but also that the dictators would usher in his World State. And if the welfare state accomplished Wells' bureaucratic revolution, Chesterton warned about that too.

All three attacked "inhumane" capitalism, but as Jonah Goldberg notes, Wells' World State was a "progressive" version of "totalitarian temptation," with a "priesthood of experts."[466] With its army of snooping bureaucrats, his Utopia resembled a vast open prison. Shaw and Wells showed mercy to the strong but not the weak and well-behaved. They called for "supermen" and the elimination of "useless lives"; the Nazi "supermen" tried to breed "over-men" and eliminate "under-men," creating not heaven but hell on earth. After his death Chesterton's Distributism inspired the Conservative Party's "property owning democracy" idea, although global capitalism further dispossessed the poor by lending to those who could not repay.[467] The self-employed have been seen as living the Distributist idea.[468]

Shaw and Wells admired fascism and communism, both totalitarian systems of state-worship, and expansionist in their own way.[469] But as Jonah Goldberg remarks: "It is difficult now, in the light of their massive crimes and failures, to remember that both ... were, in their time, utopian visions and the bearers of great hopes."[470] Shaw and Wells saw totalitarianism as a Platonic utopia in

---

463. See: Jacqueline Kasun, *The War against Population: The Economics and Ideology of World Population Control* (San Francisco: Ignatius Press, 1988); George Grant, *Grand Illusions: The Legacy of Planned Parenthood* (Nashville, Tenn.: Cumberland House, 2000).

464. Michael Foot's introduction to *The New Machiavelli* cites Wells' "prophecy" regarding the British withdrawal from India (H.G. Wells, [London: Penguin, 1911/2005], xix).

465. H.G. Wells, "1939—What Does it Hold?" *News Chronicle*, January 3, 1939, 2, in D.C. Smith, *H.G. Wells: Desperately Mortal: A Biography*, op. cit., 340.

466. J. Goldberg, *Liberal Fascism*, op. cit., 392.

467. Phillip Blond, *Red Tory: How the Left and Right Have Broken Britain and How We Can Fix It* (London: Faber & Faber Ltd., 2010), 30–31.

468. See: Christopher Ferrara, *The Church and the Libertarian: A Defense of Catholic Teaching on Man, Authority and the State* (Forest Lake, MN: Remnant Press, 2010).

469. "[I]t is most convenient to think in terms of two [totalitarian groups]: those who believe that the sacred entity of the nation itself requires protection and redemption as a prelude to national expansion and greater influence and power; and those who believe that the human race as a whole needs a single moral and political purpose, and that the greatest contribution the people can make is to become a totalitarian state, with the objective of spreading the great moral purpose to the rest of the world.... The first group we call Fascists, the second ... Communists" (M. Walker, *The National Front* [Glasgow: Fontana/Collins, 1977], 15).

470. Jonah Goldberg, *Liberal Fascism*, op. cit., 7.

which strong medicine was administered to the masses by a wise, all-powerful leader of the intellectual elite, creating a stable, enduring, semi-mystical state—not a democracy, but a reflection of the aristocracy overthrown by the French Revolution.[471] In Plato's Utopia, eugenics was an important feature, but as Karl Popper remarked: "Our dream of heaven cannot be realized on earth," and in trying to "return to a harmonious state of nature" there were no half-measures: "If we turn back, then we must go the whole way—we must return to the beasts."[472] Chesterton warned that "all brave men" were "a little afraid" of the future: the "unreal reformer sees in front of him one certain future, the future of his fad," while the "real reformer sees before him ten or twenty futures among which his country must choose, and may, in some dreadful hour, choose the wrong one."[473]

Despite this, he remained hopeful of mankind, while Shaw and Wells dreamed of "canvas cleaning"—abolishing large portions of mankind.[474] When the Nazis put their ideas into practice, their strong, intelligent Utopian man turned out to be a sadistic bully. As Edmund Burke observed, they were "planning the future by the past," and in their much-admired Soviet Union, when the grand plan failed to feed the people, they eliminated the people, not the plan.[475] Shaw and Wells envied the strength of the Strong Man and advocated the destruction of the weak, while Chesterton advocated strengthening the weak and restraining the Strong Man. But only Chesterton's Utopia did not impose the creator's will on creation.

Goldberg remarks that Wells, "more than anyone else lent romance to the

---

471. Like Plato's Utopia based on the Spartan state, Shaw's and Wells' philosophies included breeding human beings like animals; rule by an "elect"; the State as perfect (self-sufficient) entity, higher than the individual; the common ownership of women and children in the ruling class to promote "union" and avoid disruption; Plato's slave state would abolish class war by giving absolute power to the ruling class; like intelligent dogs they would "shepherd" the lower classes (see: K. R. Popper, *The Open Society and its Enemies Vol. I: The Spell of Plato*, op. cit.).

472. Ibid., 200–201.

473. G. K. Chesterton, *Appreciations and Criticisms of the Works of Charles Dickens* (Thirsk, N. Yorks.: House of Stratus, 2001), 45.

474. Plato's architects of the perfect city had first to "'make their canvas clean'" by banishing all those aged over ten so that children could grow up free from the influence of older people, including their parents (in *Republic*); also by purging dissidents (in *Statesman*); "This is what canvas-cleaning means"—the "artist-politician" has to "eradicate the existing institutions and traditions. He must purify, purge, expel, banish, kill. ('Liquidate' is the terrible modern term for it.)" (K. R. Popper, *The Open Society and its Enemies Vol. I: The Spell of Plato*, op. cit., 166).

475. Economist Friedrich Hayek maintained that a "planned" society would inevitably lead to totalitarianism (F. A. Hayek, *The Road to Serfdom*, op. cit., 61); he also believed that big business would collude with big government against small traders: "Our freedom of choice in a competitive society rests on the fact that, if one person refuses to satisfy our wishes, we can turn to another. But if we face a monopolist we are at his mercy. And an authority directing the whole economic system would be the most powerful monopolist imaginable" (ibid., 53–55).

progressive vision of the future." Shaw, "no doubt because of his pacifist opposition to World War I . . . acquired the reputation of an outspoken individualist and freethinker suspicious of state power and its abuses." But Shaw was totally committed to eugenics,[476] while, as Goldberg points out, Chesterton "was subjected to relentless ridicule and scorn" for opposing "the sophisticated position" of "nearly all 'thinking people'" in Britain and America.[477] Chesterton noted that "the very newest of the intellectuals" had "more in common with some antique authority than with some merely modern rebellion." Some "would set up Dictators to enforce obedience."[478] The "Totalitarian State," he said, was "making a clean sweep of *all* our old notions of liberty." If, for example, he stated that failed democracy was better than successful Dictatorship, Rome's religious authority would not silence him, but the secular authorities of fascism, Bolshevism, and "Hitlerism" "would silence me."[479]

According to Lauer, Chesterton's "prophetic spirit . . . saw the inevitable cruelty (criminality) of totalitarianism."[480] By contrast, Shaw and Wells were attracted to that supreme, neutral entity, the totalitarian state, by its power for doing good—although their idea of good was different to Chesterton's. Ignoring Acton's warning about the corrupting power of power, they believed that so long as absolute power was in the right hands it would be wielded safely. But they saw the right hands as the strongest hands, and although their advocacy of extermination did not cause the Holocaust, they saw the Age of Dictators as an evolutionary stage to their Utopias. Desperately revising their predictions in the light of the latest totalitarian outrage, Shaw and Wells became prophets in reverse. They supported totalitarianism because they saw it implementing some of their cherished ideas, while Chesterton rejected fascism despite its potential for implementing Distributist ideas.

Nonetheless, a true prophet must speak to every age, and a literary giant who fails the anti-Semitism test must fail the prophet test. Notwithstanding Holocaust influence, it took no special powers to foresee the recurrence of anti-Semitism, that most notorious and enduring of hatreds. History showed that distinctive Jews made clearer targets, but despite this Chesterton predicted disaster if they assimilated. Shaw and Wells disagreed, predicting disaster if they did not assimilate, but assimilation did not protect the Marrano Jews of Spain either. While not planning their Utopias principally to eradicate anti-Semitism, all claimed their Utopias were the answer to it. All attacked Nazi anti-Semitism,

476. J. Goldberg, *Liberal Fascism*, op. cit., 249–250.

477. Goldberg describes Chesterton as "[t]he Catholic conservative" (ibid., 257).

478. G. K. Chesterton, "The Last Turn," *The Well and the Shallows*, op. cit., 135.

479. G. K. Chesterton, "The Return of Caesar," ibid., 246–247.

480. G. K. Chesterton, *Fancies versus Fads* (1923), quoted in Q. Lauer, *G.K. Chesterton: Philosopher without Portfolio*, op. cit., 90–91.

but when the Jews failed to spearhead his revolution Shaw transferred his hopes to the Nazis. Wells eventually accepted that Jewish assimilation was not an immediate possibility, but blamed them anyway. When tested by anti-Semitism, their Utopias survived, while many Jews did not.

Shaw distrusted science but trusted eugenics, believing that the Nazis should be able to eliminate their own people according to their own preferences. Wells warned in 1905 against "new arbitrary and unsubstantiated race prejudices" causing "a large proportion of the wars, hardships, and cruelties."[481] But he too advocated eugenics, and while he believed religion was dangerous and should be eliminated he failed to see the danger of the Nazi "race religion" eliminating the Jewish people. Chesterton alone warned that racial and eugenic theories, driving the state and systematized by the state, would lead to the most horrific power abuse.

Criticizing "Jewish money power" inevitably associated Jews with money and power, lending support to racial theory, but Chesterton was careful to attack general concepts—the "Jewish spirit," "Jewish Plutocracy," etc.—rather than attacking the entire Jewish people. He was also careful, when criticizing Jewish behavior, to distinguish between the "guilty" and the "innocent," the rich and the poor, thus avoiding the charge of racism. By advocating political remedies he emphasized that no vice was inherent. Despite this, however, his tendency to associate the failures of capitalism with the vices of Jewish plutocrats helped to sustain negative Jewish stereotypes.

Lauer notes that Chesterton often held "a position to be true" simply because "'ordinary' human beings" consistently believed it was true,[482] but this included the "ordinary man's" anti-Semitism. Joseph Jacobs argued that "Jew-hatred" had "always come from above" and been "kept alive among the people" because it was "supported by the opinions of men whom they respect."[483] If it is impossible to quantify the influence of the three literary giants on popular anti-Semitism, neither should it be discounted. All saw it as irrational, but Chesterton's rational solution—a Jewish homeland—although it did not prevent persecution, at least provided a haven from it. Moreover, when his theory of the powerful Jew was challenged by reality, Chesterton increasingly emphasized Jewish "virtues" against Nazism, thus supplying the positive portraits whose absence suggested anti-Semitism. While Shaw constructed false equivalences to avoid passing moral judgment on the Nazis, and Wells only accepted much

481. H. G. Wells, *A Modern Utopia*, op. cit., 316–317.

482. Chesterton was "completely misinformed with regard to Kant, Hegel, Marx, Kierkegaard, and Nietzsche" but might be seen as "'intuitively rational'—*seeing* connections rather than *deducing* them, even though he constantly speaks of 'deduction' and 'syllogistic reasoning'" (Q. Lauer, *G. K. Chesterton: Philosopher without Portfolio*, op. cit., 10).

483. J. Jacobs, *Jewish Contributions to Civilization: An Estimate*, op. cit., 42.

later that Germany posed a serious threat,[484] Chesterton—the only one who did not live to see the War—responded most realistically to Nazi anti-Semitism.

Wars often spring from seeds sown in past conflicts, which should make them easier to predict, but very few did. According to Ward, Chesterton would be remembered "as a prophet, in an age of false prophets" because he saw the 1918 peace as "only an armistice."[485] He also predicted the Nazi-Soviet pact in 1932, but in 1934 appeared to reassess Hitler, reluctant to see him as a "Superman."[486] In contrast, it was Hitler's Superman potential that led Shaw and Wells to dismiss him as a threat. They were applauded for telling a nervous world what it wanted to hear while Churchill's warnings were derided. Chesterton too conveyed a stark message, but from the grave brought inspiration and comfort to the British people facing the fearful reality of war through his *Ballad of the White Horse*, reasserting freedom against the threat of paganism.[487] If the claim to prophet status in the Age of Dictators is based on correct analysis of power politics and identification of the biggest threat to Britain, to democracy and to civilization, Chesterton's claim surpasses that of Wells and Shaw.

Chesterton: Flawed Prophet in the Age of Dictators?

Shaw and Wells saw the Jews as an existential threat to their Utopias, but Chesterton believed that even if they wanted to they should not disappear; therefore his approach may be seen as equally flawed. But unlike Shaw's Shawtocracy of the Strong Man, and Wells' worldwide expertocracy, Chesterton never abolished free will. When his worldview was largely rejected only Chesterton trusted Man as God trusted Man: enough to accept rejection. Shaw and Wells trusted men but distrusted Man. Chesterton's belief in original sin meant that he trusted Man but distrusted men.

---

484. H.G. Wells, *The Outlook for Homo Sapiens*, op. cit., 113; between the book's writing in 1939 and publication in 1942 the Nazi-Soviet Pact ended with Hitler's invasion of Russia in 1941.

485. G.K. Chesterton, "Open Letter to Lord Reading," *New Witness*, December 13, 1918, in M. Ward, *Gilbert Keith Chesterton*, op. cit., 420–425; Ward's view of his Open Letter as a "prophecy" of the Holocaust is less sound: see Chapter Six.

486. Despotism was "successful" in "very small matters" like taking decisions at social gatherings, but when "all men's souls grow taller in a transfiguring anger or desire, then I am by no means so certain that the great man has been a benefit even when he has appeared"—even Cromwell and Napoleon were not crucial to the movements they led (G.K. Chesterton, "The Duty of the Historian," *The Uses of Diversity* [London: Methuen & Co. Ltd, 1920/1927], 109–110).

487. During the Great War "many soldiers had it with them in the trenches," and in the Second World War, the *Times* reported the fall of Crete followed by Our Lady's words to King Alfred: "I tell you naught for your comfort"; later, when Winston Churchill "spoke of 'the end of the beginning,' the *Times* returned to *The White Horse* and gave the opening of Alfred's speech at Ethandune: 'The high tide!' King Alfred cried. / 'The high tide and the turn!'" (M. Ward, *Gilbert Keith Chesterton*, op. cit., 285–286).

Wells and Shaw foresaw the demise of orthodox religion, making them seem more in tune with post-Holocaust Western culture. But while Chesterton has been suspected of authoritarian leanings, Shaw and Wells were influenced by "will to power" and Darwinism, which were important influences on the Nazis and the Holocaust.[488] As to tolerance, Chesterton debated Shaw and Wells on rational commonsense grounds, while they dismissed his views as dictated by the Pope.[489] Shaw's and Wells' belief, "to eliminate difficulties, eliminate differences," jars with the post-Holocaust emphasis on diversity, which was one of Chesterton's most fundamental and enduring political beliefs. Shaw and Wells, guided by secular philosophy, and in the interests of philanthropy, urged the disappearance of the Jews. By contrast, Chesterton's orthodox religion decreed that God had chosen the Jews from among men—had chosen, in fact, to be a Jew—and he held fervently "that philosophy and philanthropy are truisms in a religion of reasonable men," which "we do most truly owe, under heaven, to a secretive and restless nomadic people; who bestowed on men the supreme and serene blessing of a jealous God."[490]

To Chesterton, if the Jews ceased to exist it would make a difference—not just to him, or to them, but to all humanity—and to God, who when asked His name by Moses simply said that He was the one who existed: "I AM."[491] Chesterton instinctively grasped the ontology of St. Thomas Aquinas—"to be" was better than "not to be." His grandfather's remark that he should thank God even if he were a lost soul was the "thin thread" he clung to under the nihilistic shadow of suicide that blighted his early manhood.[492]

Shaw and Wells, the moderns who rebelled against the Victorian Age, failed to adjust to the age of Dictators, while the "backward-looking" Chesterton was the only one to change with the times. It is impossible to say whether he would have continued to change in response to the War and the Holocaust, but in 1936

488. The Nazis used an "elaborate apparatus of policing and repression" to suppress all opposition in Germany (R. J. Evans, *The Third Reich in Power* 1933–1939 [London: Allen Lane, 2005], 55–66); see also: R. Weikart, *From Darwin to Hitler: Evolutionary Ethics, Eugenics, and Racism in Germany* (Basingstoke, Hants.: Palgrave Macmillan, 2006); N. Goodrick-Clarke, *The Occult Roots of Nazism: Secret Aryan Cults and their Influence on Nazi Ideology* (London: I.B. Tauris, 1992); concentration camps, slave labor and death marches practiced selection of the fittest and the dehumanization of prisoners; Social Darwinism was at the heart of the Wannsee Protocol, drawn up by leading Nazis in January 1942 to discuss the Final Solution (S. J. Gould, *Dinosaur in a Haystack: Reflections in Natural History* [London: Jonathan Cape, 1996], 43–47).

489. Shaw and Wells, "able and indeed brilliant men," showed "not only an amazing degree of ignorance concerning the tenets of Catholicism but also a bland conviction that they knew them well"; however, "even stranger" was "the absence on the Catholic side of any effort to explain to these men the doctrines they misconstrued" (M. Ward, *Gilbert Keith Chesterton*, op. cit., 504).

490. G.K. Chesterton, *The Everlasting Man*, op. cit., 97–98.

491. Exodus 3:14.

492. See Chapter Eight.

he was still "quite certain" that "the evil" responsible for the Great War "originally arose with the power of Prussia."[493] He insisted: "I thought and think . . . Prussian militarism and materialism should not dominate Europe." But regarding the Boer War, he maintained: "I thought and think that Jewish financial power should not dominate England."[494] Nonetheless, he believed that this power had waned since the Boer War, and was still doggedly opposing "Prussianism" and anti-Semitism when he died.

Canovan says that if Chesterton "had lived to see the full development of Nazism—which he detested from the start—and the alliance between Hitler and Mussolini, it is virtually certain that he would have changed his stance again," and that "even the corrupt and ramshackle British parliamentarianism would have seemed worth defending."[495] The 1930s, Stapleton asserts, saw him "warming toward the figure of the gentleman" because in the "absence of a peasantry" he could be an "ally" against the "pseudo-aristocracy" of more modern provenance.[496] His patriotism also underwent a change as he attempted to reconcile England's reluctance to revolt with its "instant resistance to the threat of despotism emanating from abroad."[497] Chesterton had believed that criticizing England was a patriotic duty,[498] but increasingly he would echo Cowper: "England, with all thy faults, I love thee still." He himself marked this change on the King's Silver Jubilee[499] in a year that also saw him change his views of the monarchy—a government strong, as Bagehot saw it, because it was "intelligible." Its German origins had proved an obstacle to Chesterton[500] but now he

493. G. K. Chesterton, *Autobiography*, op. cit., 213.

494. Ibid., 252.

495. M. Canovan, *G. K. C.: Radical Populist*, op. cit., 144–145.

496. G. K. Chesterton, *Illustrated London News*, July 30, 1932, 154, in J. Stapleton, *Christianity, Patriotism, and Nationhood: The England of G. K. Chesterton*, op. cit., 192.

497. G. K. Chesterton, *Illustrated London News*, May 4, 1935, 730, ibid., 188–189; of *The Old Curiosity Shop* Chesterton had remarked: "Kit is meek and Kit is a snob. His natural dignity . . . is partly marred by that instinctive subservience to the employing class which has been the comfortable weakness of the whole English democracy, which has prevented their making any revolution for the last two hundred years" (G. K. Chesterton, *Appreciations and Criticisms of the Works of Charles Dickens*, op. cit., 35.

498. On hearing of Queen Victoria's death, he "wept," and at that "great and serious hour" renewed "private vows of a very real character to do my best for this country of mine which I love with a love passing the love of Jingoes. It is sometimes easy to give one's country blood and easier to give her money. Sometimes the hardest thing of all is to give her truth" (G. K. Chesterton, Letter to Frances Blogg [undated], M. Ward, *Gilbert Keith Chesterton*, op. cit., 144–145).

499. G. K. Chesterton, *Illustrated London News*, May 4, 1935, 730, in J. Stapleton, *Christianity, Patriotism, and Nationhood: The England of G. K. Chesterton*, op. cit., 188–189.

500. G. K. Chesterton, "The Backward Bolshie," *G. K.'s Weekly*, October 29, 1932; however, later he rejected (with many apologies) a Thomas Derrick cartoon depicting Queen Victoria giving her blessing to an "*entente*" with Hitler's Germany (M. Ward, *Return to Chesterton*, op. cit., 54).

praised the King's Christmas radio broadcast for emphasizing the importance of home and family. The King, Chesterton said, plainly saw "the one big British family as a collection of families," with "his Empire as a League of Families, a League of very little nations." As such, it was not "remarkable" that "our King" should speak "in this familiar homely way," something which "a dictator, still less an expert sociologist," could never hope to do. Even "good republicans," he said, would admit that it was "a good thing to have an ordinary man" as their ruler because "ordinary things are the important ones," adding that "you are far more likely to get an ordinary man as your King than as your dictator or your Prime Minister," especially when "[a]t this moment . . . from all sides the rights of the family are threatened with invasion." Men, women and children were "treated, not as members of separate families, not as brothers and sisters in one great family, but as cyphers . . . in a financial statement." To Chesterton it came "with the force of a new revelation" that "our King has spoken this old-fashioned, homely, familiar, human word."[501] He warned that people should not "trust a Monarchy, in the sense of expecting that a monarch will be anything but a man,"[502] but the King, as Chesterton had earlier realised, represented the "'protection of the patient and unrecorded virtues of mankind." He even represented a link to God.[503]

Chesterton had been two steps ahead in foreseeing the "scourges" of the future, but rather than falling silent in response to opposition and general indifference, his disgust at attacks on the family from capitalism, Bolshevism, and fascism reawakened his appreciation of Jewish love of family and lent urgency to his warnings. Guided by his own philosophy, "common sense" told him there was a "Jewish question," and he began to view "family" links between Jews with suspicion, but the "theory of thanks" recalled to him gratitude, "one of the great Jewish virtues." At the end of his life it was these two Jewish virtues that he wished to praise.[504] Unlike Shaw and Wells, who took the family for granted and wished to abolish the Jewish people, Chesterton saw thanks as "the highest form of thought"—"gratitude" was "happiness doubled by wonder"[505]—and he was grateful to the Jewish people for demonstrating how vital

501. G.K. Chesterton, "The Family," *G.K.'s Weekly*, January 3, 1935, in G.K. Chesterton, *Brave New Family: G.K. Chesterton on Men & Women, Children, Sex, Divorce, Marriage & the Family*, op. cit., 266–267.

502. G.K. Chesterton, "When the World Turned Back," *The Well and the Shallows*, op. cit., 34.

503. "[T]here may return to the mystical institution of the Crown, something of that immemorial legend which linked it with religion, and made one baron, alone of all the barony, mysteriously responsible to God for the people" (G.K. Chesterton, *Come to Think of It... A Book of Essays* [Methuen, London, 1930], 242, in A. Nichols, *G.K. Chesterton, Theologian*, op. cit., xvi).

504. G.K. Chesterton, *Autobiography*, op. cit., 72; see Chapter Eight.

505. G.K. Chesterton, *A Short History of England*, op. cit., 59.

the family was in sustaining democracy, just as it was vital in sustaining the Jewish people as a people among many.

None of the three giants were perfect, or a perfect prophet. But the "prophet test" is not a test of perfection. Chesterton admitted he was not perfect: "no merely human being is,"[506] but he was the only giant to reserve a place for the Jewish people. This came to be of crucial importance in the Age of Dictators, when what Shaw and Wells saw as an attraction—the strength of the Strong Man and his capacity to carry out eugenics—was, as Chesterton warned, directed to other categories, most notably the Jews. Far from an historical curiosity, Darwinism is once again influencing the view that certain categories of people are not human and therefore may be killed. Once more, just as anti-Semitism is on the rise, such views are receiving praise rather than condemnation.[507]

Despite their differences on the "Jewish question," Chesterton was intensely loyal to Shaw and Wells as the three friends confronted what they saw as the evils of capitalism. But he was even more loyal to his friend and colleague Hilaire Belloc, whose political position he came increasingly to share, and to his brother Cecil. Sometimes the obverse of loyalty is antagonism to the "outsider" and the *Chesterbelloc* circle's association with anti-Semitism as well as anti-capitalism will be examined in the next chapter.

---

506. Q. Lauer, *G. K. Chesterton: Philosopher without Portfolio*, op. cit., 24.

507. A leading proponent of such views, Atheist Darwinist Peter Singer lost three of his grand-parents to the Holocaust, but believes that newborn babies cannot possess "personhood," therefore disabled babies may be killed if their parents wish it; also that mentally disabled adults are less human than intelligent apes, and so deserve fewer rights; he has been awarded a Companion of the Order of Australia for his "eminent service to philosophy and bioethics" ("Is this really the world's most dangerous man?" *The Jewish Chronicle*, August 17, 2012, 16; see: P. Singer, *Practical Ethics* (Cambridge: Cambridge University Press, 1993); *Writings on an Ethical Life* (London: Fourth Estate, 2001); see Chapter Nine.

6

The Chesterbelloc
and the Jews

Hilaire Belloc

Chesterton met the other half of the *Chesterbelloc*, his closest political associate aside from his brother Cecil,[1] in 1900.[2] Belloc's biographer John Bingham (J.B.) Morton said that Chesterton and Maurice Baring were "no match" for Belloc's "wide range of knowledge" and his "multiple" interests. Belloc's strong "personality" was crucial on "Chesterton's thought," although not his "style." Indeed, "one can trace it in Chesterton's books." On England, and on "international affairs and the Church they usually agreed."[3] Joseph Hilaire Pierre René Belloc (1870–1953) was a popular, versatile, and prolific writer. By nature combative, he waged a long war of attrition against H.G. Wells, although, like Chesterton, he eschewed personal criticism.[4]

According to his sister, Marie Belloc-Lowndes, Belloc's French ancestry was crucial to understanding his character. It would be "impossible," she remarked, to "exaggerate how much Hilaire's French heredity meant to him." It was "a happy day," she recalled, when he received the watch of "his great-uncle, Armand Swanton, one of Napoleon's officers, at the Battle of Waterloo," which had "saved its owner's life by deflecting a bullet."[5] But in his early adulthood, the "tension he felt between his two countries" was "very deep."[6] The Bellocs fled on the last train before the siege of Paris, on the outbreak of the Franco-Prussian War: "born to the sound of the rumble of guns" his mother called him

---

1. I.T. Ker, *The Catholic Revival in English Literature 1845–1961* (Oxford: Gracewing, 2003), 57.

2. I. Ker, *G.K. Chesterton: A Biography* (Oxford: Oxford University Press, 2011), 65.

3. John Bingham Morton, *Hilaire Belloc: A Memoir* (London: Hollis & Carter, 1955), 76.

4. Readers would find none of the "personal descriptions or offensive allusions to private life by which our vulgarians aim at extending their large circulations" (H. Belloc, *A Companion to Wells' 'Outline of History'* [London: Sheed & Ward, 1926], 3–4); see Chapter Five.

5. M. Belloc Lowndes, *The Young Hilaire Belloc* (New York: P.J. Kenedy & Sons, 1956), 75.

6. Ibid., 86.

"Old Thunder."[7] His home wrecked and pillaged by Prussian troops, Belloc felt such injustices deeply, but the English retained the image of Prussian troops helping to defeat Napoleon, and some were thrilled to "discover" common racial origins with Germany in Houston Stewart Chamberlain's *The Foundations of the Nineteenth Century.*

Belloc lived in England but chose to complete his national service in the French military, informing his mother: "I speak English, I wish to write in English ... but I cannot bear the cosmopolitan folly which is destroying the Frank and Gaul in our class."[8] He claimed the army opened his eyes to the "Jewish question," but A. N. Wilson comments: "Some would think it truer to say that it ... closed his mind ... before the Dreyfus affair had ever happened." To the prejudice of the French military was added their suspicion about his "semitic" name. One of Belloc's French ancestors was "a seventeenth-century Nantes wine-merchant" named "Moses Belloc or Bloch," but, as Wilson notes, Belloc would "dismiss" the idea that Moses "might have been Jewish with raucous contempt."[9] With a French father, an English mother, a dash of Irish and possibly Jewish blood, Belloc, Wilfrid Sheed remarks, was the constant "outsider" in both France and England, who "with unconscious irony" claimed Jews were "unassimilable outsiders, and the outsider will always be persecuted."[10] Sympathetic to the Jewish people, he was also antagonistic because he felt that the English were suspicious of Frenchmen while they appeared to welcome Jews. But he too became a perpetual wanderer: an Englishman in France, in Protestant England a French Catholic.

In fact Belloc's life was full of contradictions. Morton remarks that he resented his mother's lost fortune, and enjoyed the hospitality of the rich while satirizing their foibles.[11] Wilson notes that he loved Balliol but felt cheated of an Oxford fellowship and savagely mocked dons and pedants.[12] A romantic

7. J. B. Morton, *Hilaire Belloc: A Memoir*, op. cit., 2–3.

8. Hilaire Belloc, Letter to Bessie Rayner Parkes, 1887, M. Belloc Lowndes, *The Young Hilaire Belloc*, op. cit., 86.

9. Andrew Norman Wilson, *Hilaire Belloc* (London: Hamish Hamilton, 1984), 43–44; when in 1898 Belloc went to Paris to look into the Dreyfus case "it was becoming apparent to most reasonable people that [he] ... was completely innocent" (ibid., 89–90); his doubts about Dreyfus say "the final word on his anti-Semitism: he got it from the French Army Office Corps, the one group whose contribution to his unhappiness he had mysteriously forgiven"; H. G. Wells "claimed to have once surprised Belloc with the question 'Are you one-quarter Jewish or one-eighth?'; to which Belloc answered, 'One-eighth.' But that may just be a story about H. G. Wells" (W. Sheed, "ChesterBelloc and the Jews," *The New York Review of Books*, 17 [3], September 2, 1971). Bloch, a German Baron, features in *Emmanuel Burden* (H. Belloc, *Emmanuel Burden* [London: Methuen & Co., 1904], 188).

10. Wilfrid Sheed, "ChesterBelloc and the Jews," op. cit.

11. J. B. Morton, *Hilaire Belloc: A Memoir*, op. cit., 75.

12. However, Wilson rejects claims that Belloc failed to obtain a fellowship at All Souls' College, Oxford because of his views (A. N. Wilson, *Hilaire Belloc*, op. cit., 61).

who delighted in political muck-raking, he admitted giving up a Parliamentary career, partly due to his disgust with declining political standards, but also to earn money to support his family.[13] Belloc pursued vendettas with relish, but as biographer Robert Speaight recalls, he was personally courteous and hospitable.[14]

Although a Republican Revolutionary, Belloc, John McCarthy notes, eventually warmed toward the monarchy,[15] although Speaight recalls that he believed the French Revolution "had to come . . . otherwise everything would have dried up."[16] According to McCarthy, Belloc, while deeply religious, prided himself on emphasizing Enlightenment reason over superstition.[17] He rejected the pseudo-science of racism but thought along racial lines. While sharing the Leftist belief in Jewish-influenced capitalist conspiracy, in 1924 he rejected Jewish conspiracy theories, telling a Jewish friend that Nesta Webster's *The Cause of the World Unrest* was "a lunatic book. She is one of those people who have got one cause on the brain. It is the good old 'Jewish revolutionary' bogey" and for that "type of unstable mind which cannot rest without morbid imagining," the "conception of a single cause simplifies thought. With this good woman it is the Jews, with some people it is the Jesuits, with others Freemasons and so on. The world is more complex than that." Belloc's Jewish American friend, Major Louis Henry Cohn, despite his German origins volunteered to fight for France in 1914. But as Speaight relates, when Major Cohn hosted a New York lunch for Belloc it was marred by allegations of anti-Semitism.[18] This typified the contradiction that was Belloc, for as Speaight further notes, he was "naturally fond" of

13. "Every day that passes makes me more determined to chuck Westminster; it is too low for words. The position is ridiculous and the expense is damnable. More than that, it cuts into my life, interferes with my earnings, and separates me from my home" (Hilaire Belloc, Letter to J.S. Phillimore, June 12, 1910, H. Belloc, *Letters from Hilaire Belloc*, R. Speaight, ed. [London: Hollis & Carter, 1958], 27).

14. Belloc was "more delicate and more courteous" in person (R. Speaight, *The Property Basket: Recollections of a Divided Life* [London: Collins & Harvill Press, 1970], 377), but Speaight was no "uncritical disciple" (ibid., 369): Belloc "gave his views on pretty well everything" but "however brilliantly expressed" they were "on occasion very unbalanced indeed" (ibid., 371).

15. John P. McCarthy, *Hilaire Belloc: Edwardian Radical* (Indianapolis: Liberty Press, 1978), 334.

16. "If there were to be kings, then they should be seen to govern. He had no sentimental attachment to royalty as such" (R. Speaight, *The Property Basket: Recollections of a Divided Life*, op. cit., 372–373).

17. He saw no fundamental clash between revolutionary theory and the Church (J.P. McCarthy, *Hilaire Belloc: Edwardian Radical*, op. cit., 315–316).

18. Hilaire Belloc, Letter to Maj. Cohn, February 6, 1924, R. Speaight, *The Life of Hilaire Belloc* (London: Hollis & Carter, 1957), 455–456; when Speaight's biography quoted Belloc denouncing Nesta Webster's "anti-semitic book" as "lunatic," it had to be withdrawn while Webster's lawyers argued about a public apology (R. Speaight, *The Property Basket: Recollections of a Divided Life*, op. cit., 373).

Jews, but his "solution for the Jewish problem was rational and relatively humane—a kind of mitigated *apartheid*. The trouble was that he insisted on regarding Jews as problems rather than as people."[19] Typically, too, Belloc also satirized himself: "Heretics all, whoever you be, / In Tarbes or Nîmes, or over the sea, / You never shall have good words from me. / Caritas non conturbat me." The Latin at the end, he adds, was "to show that it was a song connected with the Universal fount and with European culture, and with all that Heresy combats. I then thought what a fine fellow I was, and how pleasant were my friends when I agreed with them."[20]

A "radical-liberal in the tradition of Bright, Cobden, Morley, and the younger Joseph Chamberlain," Belloc's "claim to admiration," according to McCarthy, is "compromised by his sympathy for authoritarianism and his anti-Semitism."[21] An anti-Dreyfusard long after the "heated atmosphere" passed, his politics "duplicated" the late nineteenth-century "left-right ambivalence of French nationalism" of which anti-Semitism was a "particularly unpleasant characteristic." Belloc saw Jewish influence in the "more unpleasant activities of the Edwardian plutocracy, especially in . . . the purchase of government policies and honors" and his "anti-Semitism was closely connected with his hostility to finance capitalism."[22] Speaight agrees that Belloc's "strident, exotic anti-Semitism" left him with a reputation that was "to dog him till the end of his life."[23] The Dreyfus case was emblematic of the increasingly tribal nature of French politics since the Franco-Prussian War. It split France into religious royalist Right and secular Republican Left. The Revolution emancipated Jews,[24] and some blamed them for the negative aspects of industrialization and modernity,[25] although as Parkes says, in reality Jews disapproved of the same things as non-Jews.[26] Edouard Drumont, founder of the Antisemitic League of France, authored *La France Juive* (1886), which argued for the civil exclusion of Jews. His journal *La Libre Parole* became Dreyfus's most strident opponent. The Third Republic's anti-clericalism exacerbated a sense of grievance that led to

19. "A man cannot spread abroad amusing and insulting verses about Sir Alfred Mond or Sir Herbert Samuel and then be surprised that people think he is anti-Semitic" (ibid., 373).

20. "But Catholic men that live upon wine / Are deep in the water, and frank, and fine; / Wherever I travel I find it so, / Benedicamus Domino" (H. Belloc, *The Path to Rome* [London: Geo. Allen & Unwin Ltd., 1902/1936], 165).

21. J. P. McCarthy, *Hilaire Belloc: Edwardian Radical*, op. cit., 15.

22. Ibid., 42.

23. R. Speaight, *The Life of Hilaire Belloc*, op. cit., 97.

24. J. Parkes, *Antisemitism* (London: Vallentine Mitchell & Co. Ltd., 1963), 69.

25. See: A. Toussenel, *Les Juifs, Rois de l'Époque: histoire de la féodalité financière* (Paris, 1847); Roget de Gougenot, *Le Juif, le Judaisme et la Judaisation des Peuples Chrétiens* (Paris, 1869).

26. J. Parkes, *Antisemitism*, op. cit., 23–24.

feverish conspiracy theories about Jews, Freemasons, and Socialists, which survived the Holocaust only to deny it.[27]

By contrast, Belloc and Chesterton, although deeply religious, supported the French Revolution. United in suspicion of Germany, both opposed the Boer War but supported Britain in the Great War—a "crusade against Prussian barbarism."[28] As a Member of Parliament, his sister Marie recalled, Belloc was regarded as having a "bee in his bonnet" for advocating artillery increases to face the German threat.[29] To Marie, Belloc's anti-Dreyfusard stance was a reaction to extreme anti-French, rather than pro-Dreyfus attitudes in England, where Dreyfus lost support for accepting a French pardon. But both she and Belloc regarded Dreyfus as guilty, relying heavily on the honesty of the French officers involved—unlike their family, which was pro-Dreyfus.[30] McCarthy remarks that Belloc's "French connection, especially his French political sentiments" made him "something of an outcast" but "even more distressing" was that "the nation which seemed to evoke the most favorable English attitude was Germany."[31] Chesterton's friend E.C. Bentley recalled that Belloc was "the one person" in Oxford who "declined to assume" that Dreyfus was "a victim of persecution," but that the affair was often used as a stick to beat the French while English anti-Semitism was ignored.[32]

Paradoxically, "pro-Dreyfus" England probably encouraged Belloc's "anti-Semitism," while the Bellocs' Republicanism made them sympathetic to Jewish issues. Hilaire was only two when his father died, and his English mother Bessie Rayner Parkes, female suffrage campaigner and great-granddaughter of Joseph Priestley, was an "English liberal" with many Jewish friends. Belloc's niece Lady Iddesleigh said his mother and sister "expressed extreme shock ... when Belloc

27. Jane N. Brodhead, *The Religious Persecution in France* 1900–1906 (London: Kegan Paul, Trench, Trübner & Co., Ltd., 1907), 11; also influential were Ernest Renan's pseudo-scientific view of Jews as racially inferior and envy of Jewish social and intellectual success, but the Catholic Church, marginalized by the Revolution, tended more and more to conspiracy theories involving Protestants, Jews and Freemasons (Paul Johnson, *A History of the Jews* [London: Weidenfeld & Nicolson, 1987], 380–384); see Chapter Nine.

28. J.P. McCarthy, *Hilaire Belloc: Edwardian Radical*, op. cit., 318.

29. M. Belloc Lowndes, *The Young Hilaire Belloc*, op. cit., 164.

30. Ibid., 129–130.

31. J.P. McCarthy, *Hilaire Belloc: Edwardian Radical*, op. cit., 42.

32. "I could understand, later on, how excessively irritating the universal British attitude towards this matter must have been to a man who knew much more about France, and especially the French Army, than any of us did. We were in the right, no doubt; but it is curious to recall how we insisted on making another country's business our own to the extent that we all did." Later, "under the Dictatorships," worse things happened "without my countrymen being united in a continuing, deafening chorus of horror and denunciation" (E.C. Bentley, *Those Days* [London: Constable & Co. Ltd., 1940], 87–88).

let fall vigorously anti-Jewish sentiments."[33] Bessie was "displeased by the anti-Jewish tone" of some *Eye Witness* articles, forcing Belloc to defend himself.[34] When Emile Zola, the Dreyfus campaigner "was obliged to leave France" he was "well-received" by Bessie and Marie, but Belloc would "never admit" to being wrong about Dreyfus.[35]

A prolific and successful writer of fiction and biography, Marie mixed with literary, political and establishment figures, especially the Asquiths.[36] Friendly with H.G. Wells, she remained close to Belloc,[37] and had many Jewish friends, including Sir Philip Sassoon and the Hon. Mrs. Charles de Rothschild.[38] She lectured to Jewish groups and the *Jewish Chronicle* reviewed her work favorably.[39] In 1939 she noted that Margot Asquith changed her pro-German stance because of Hitler's "persecution of the Jews."[40] Though prescient in warning that England's lack of a common religion or philosophy would cause problems,[41] in contrast to his poetry,[42] Belloc's other works, McCarthy says, fell out of favour, owing to their "elements of authoritarianism and anti-Semitism."[43] A frequent visitor to Cliveden, "and for a time a close friend" of wealthy Nancy Astor, her biographer Norman Rose remarks that "for all his undoubted gifts" Belloc "was seriously flawed. A zealous Catholic, moved by a deep vein of hysterical anti-Semitism, he allowed his bigotry conspicuous, and continuous display. Nancy finally concluded that having two manias, 'against the Jews and the rich, I had to give him up.'"[44] But—unlike Belloc, who dismissed such claims—

---

33. Lady Iddesleigh, Letter to Marie Belloc Lowndes, in A.N. Wilson, *Hilaire Belloc*, op. cit., 44.

34. Ibid., 187.

35. Ibid., 89–90.

36. M. Belloc Lowndes, *Diaries of Marie Belloc Lowndes 1911–1947*, S. Lowndes, ed. (London: Chatto & Windus, 1971), 49.

37. "I sat next H.G. Wells at lunch on Tuesday. He said that like me, he did not think the war would be long. He is *very* shrewd. I have known him about 40 years!" (Marie Belloc Lowndes, Letter to Susan Lowndes, October 7, 1939 [ibid., 182–183]).

38. Ibid., 49.

39. *Jewish Chronicle*, October 1, 1920, 30–31; January 7, 1921, 30. *Marrying London* described a Jewish wedding, "perhaps the most picturesque of marriage ceremonies" ("Books and Bookmen," ibid., October 25, 1901, 31).

40. Margot "was what used to be called pro-German, for she was passionately in favour of doing everything possible to restore Germany to her old place in Europe after the First War"; however, "[t]he persecution of the Jews . . . completely altered Margot's view of the nation to which she had been so devoted" (M. Belloc Lowndes, *Diaries of Marie Belloc Lowndes 1911–1947*, op. cit., 182).

41. H. Belloc, "The Death of the Middle Class," *Fortnightly Review* 151 (March 1939): 267–275, in J.P. McCarthy, *Hilaire Belloc: Edwardian Radical*, op. cit., 338.

42. Belloc's verse was "constantly quoted" in Parliament, the *Times*, and in speeches (Marie Belloc Lowndes, Letter to Susan Lowndes Marques, August 12, 1944, in M. Belloc Lowndes, *Diaries of Marie Belloc Lowndes 1911–1947*, op. cit., 250–251).

43. J.P. McCarthy, *Hilaire Belloc: Edwardian Radical*, op. cit., 339.

44. Norman Rose, *The Cliveden Set: Portrait of an Exclusive Fraternity* (London: J. Cape, 2000), 39.

Astor alleged the American press was controlled by Jews, and Cliveden was suspected of Nazi sympathies.[45] It was Belloc who severed the friendship when Christian Scientist Nancy tried to turn his daughters against Catholicism after his wife's death.[46] But as Christopher Sykes notes, on hearing of his "wretchedness" after his son Peter's death during the War, Nancy kindly invited Belloc to Cliveden, the rupture apparently healed.[47]

The Fiction of Belloc

Cheyette remarks that "[t]o his detriment" Chesterton's *The Man Who Knew Too Much* appeared "unduly influenced" by the emphasis on "all-powerful Jewish plutocrats" in Belloc's "Barnett" books. [48] Corrin maintains: "Chesterton's late-blooming anti-Semitism can be attributed to Belloc," and had "a deleterious effect on his reputation."[49] Turnbull describes Belloc as "that pathological anti-Semite."[50] He adds that Chesterton, "to a lesser extent" campaigned "against the corrupting influence of Jews in public life," promoting "the myth of Jewish conspiracy" with Belloc, who, he says, "advocated a form of *apartheid* and stripping of Jews' civil rights, and endorsed emigration to Palestine."[51]

Chesterton's Zionism will be explored in the next chapter, but his views on "Jewish finance" were mainly confined to his "middle period" in *The Man Who Knew Too Much*, while Belloc's fiction was dominated by such themes. In *Emmanuel Burden* (1904), Belloc, Corrin says, "angrily dramatized" his "repugnance" at the activities of mainly Jewish "financial wire-pullers" who were "purchasing favors of British politicians." I. Z. Barnet is portrayed as "a corpulent Jewish financier with a dark complexion and a foreign accent" who snares politicians in a web of intrigue to promote his exploitation of African natural

45. Ibid., 181; she was overjoyed to learn that the Nazis had added her name to their Black List (ibid., 207); Cliveden Set member Bernard Shaw, "an implacable Marxist Communist for nearly sixty years," defended it by citing their eclectic political views (G. B. Shaw, interview in *Liberty*, April 1939 [ibid., 202–203]). Astor said the Germans were "quite right to rearm" because they were surrounded by hostile Roman Catholic powers (Christopher Sykes, *Nancy: The Life of Lady Astor* [London: Collins, 1972], 382).

46. Ibid., 178; she became obsessed less with "the supposed Jewish menace as the so-called Catholic threat. Her hardline anti-Catholicism smacked of genuine bigotry" (N. Rose, *The Cliveden Set: Portrait of an Exclusive Fraternity*, op. cit., 469–70).

47. C. Sykes, *Nancy: The Life of Lady Astor*, op. cit., 441–443.

48. B. Cheyette, *Constructions of "the Jew" in English Literature and Society: Racial Representations, 1875–1945* (Cambridge: Cambridge University Press, 1995), 197.

49. J. P. Corrin, *G. K. Chesterton and Hilaire Belloc: The Battle Against Modernity* (Athens, OH/London: Ohio University Press, 1981), 213 note 3.

50. M. J. Turnbull, *Victims or Villains: Jewish Images in Classic English Detective Fiction* (Bowling Green, Ohio: Bowling Green State University Popular Press, 1998), 19.

51. Ibid., 25–26.

resources. Belloc denied anti-Semitism, however, amending the manuscript in deference to his publisher.[52] McCarthy says that his anti-Semitism, although "more theoretical than personal," was "undisguised," especially in his novels and "occasionally" in his poetry."[53] In fact it was thinly disguised. *Emmanuel Burden*'s non-Jewish narrator, while praising Barnett, "inadvertently" draws attention to his origins and dubious dealings: "His birth was a continual drawback: the change of name necessary to his career in England was another" and the "slight accent" that Barnett "retained throughout his career"[54] is actually guttural German.[55] A banking experiment collapses after "a venomous article, inspired perhaps wholly by political hatred," hinted that "interest already paid could only come out of the new capital daily furnished to the concern"—an "abominable insinuation."[56] English merchant Charles Abbott typifies, the narrator adds, "men who hate the successful or the rich." Their hatred was "not quite dishonest," although "wildly unjust":

> They see conspiracies upon every side, they scowl at every new fortune, but they do so in good faith, for they are haunted by a nightmare of Cosmopolitan finance—pitiless, destructive of all natural ideals, obscene, and eating out the heart of our European tradition. I need hardly say that this kind of hatred was roused against Mr. Barnett.[57]

According to Wilson, Belloc's "tone of blanket irony" satisfied his publishers.[58] Mr. Capes the money-lender is not Jewish and Chesterton's caricature is John Bullish.[59] But Belloc's broker is called Zimmer, and while Barnett is one negative portrayal among many, Abbott, the sole honest character, describes him as "a greasy German Jew"—although the narrator deplores his "shameful words."[60] Like Wells, but unlike Chesterton, Belloc makes little attempt to humanize the characters that articulate his political worldview. Barnett has a "full pendulous" nose,[61] but the tone lacks Wells' revulsion, and nearly all Chesterton's caricatures sport comical noses.

---

52. J.P. Corrin, *G.K. Chesterton and Hilaire Belloc: The Battle Against Modernity* (Athens, OH/London: Ohio University Press, 1981), 23–24.

53. J.P. McCarthy, *Hilaire Belloc: Edwardian Radical*, op. cit., 261.

54. H. Belloc, *Emmanuel Burden*, op. cit., 68–69.

55. Ibid., 209.

56. Ibid., 70–71.

57. Ibid., 89.

58. A.N. Wilson, *Hilaire Belloc* (London, 1984), 128, in B. Cheyette, *Constructions of "the Jew" in English Literature and Society: Racial Representations, 1875–1945*, op. cit., 160.

59. H. Belloc, *Emmanuel Burden*, op. cit., 34.

60. Ibid., 275–276.

61. Ibid., 66.

In *Mr. Clutterbuck's Election* (1908), Barnett, still lisping, is now Duke of Battersea. Foreign and Jewish-sounding names abound, including the anti-Semitic Bill Bailey's manservant. Belloc's eponymous Gentile hero makes his fortune in the Boer War and enters Parliament as Sir Percy Clutterbuck. He innocently enquires about the Duke's "vulgar" nickname, "Peabody Yid,"[62] but eventually the sympathetic old Duke is revealed as a ruthless puppet-master, manipulating people and politics. Eccentric Bill Bailey, "a peculiarly ambiguous figure,"[63] goes "mad upon the Hebrew race," seeing them "everywhere" and "all in conspiracy."[64] He subscribes to "absurd foreign papers" that "dripped" with an "anti-Semitic virus"[65] and sends £25 to a "Jew-baiting organisation in Vienna; a foul gang of which he knew nothing whatsoever save that he had read its address in one of those vile Continental rags from which he derived so many of his prejudices."[66] Bailey's eyes held "that strange and dangerous power which the demagogue has commanded in all ages" but to Clutterbuck's "untutored mind" it is "a glance of singular fascination."[67] Bailey writes Clutterbuck's speeches "with the irresponsibility of a boy," a "mood ... dangerous in a man."[68] Despite this, his fantasies turn out to be fact, and even his young relative has Jewish antecedents.[69] Belloc satirizes Bailey, but also satirizes the English who view Belloc as anti-Semitic: Bailey is not so irrational after all, because, like Belloc, he did not believe "the conspiracy was conscious," and "discreetly dropped" claims that the press was "subsidised by a mysterious gang of foreign financiers" because he found them "untenable."[70]

A Change in the Cabinet (1909) warns that Bill Bailey will come into the story, yet he never does.[71] Rising politician Sir Charles Repton, closely linked to the Van Huren Company, "master of this Cabinet and the last,"[72] suffers from "Caryll's Ganglia," largely afflicting the "money-lender, the solicitor and the politician." It causes the sufferer to lie habitually, but when the condition is accidentally reversed Repton blurts out the truth about high finance. Barnett

62. H. Belloc, *Mr. Clutterbuck's Election* (www.forgottenbooks.org: n.d.), 222; characters with names suggestive of Jewish origins include Zachary, Bill Bailey's manservant; also Baron de Czernwitz, Sir Henry Nathan, Mr. Sachs, Natty Timpson, Isaacs, Ernest Meyer, and Lady Steyning.

63. B. Cheyette, *Constructions of "the Jew" in English Literature and Society: Racial Representations, 1875–1945*, op. cit., 168.

64. H. Belloc, *Mr. Clutterbuck's Election*, op. cit., 214.

65. Ibid., 216.

66. Ibid., 301.

67. Ibid., 209.

68. Ibid., 260.

69. Ibid., 243.

70. Ibid., 213–214.

71. H. Belloc, *A Change in the Cabinet* (London: Methuen & Co. Ltd., 1915), 18.

72. Ibid., 74.

remains in the background,[73] but he and Bailey reappear in *Pongo and the Bull* (1910). Set in 1925, the cozy arrangement between Prime Minister "Dolly" and leader of the Opposition "Pongo" ends happily when they dissolve Parliament against the Duke of Battersea's wishes. Dolly is "shocked" by the expression on the face of "the old man" whom he had "often ridiculed": those who witnessed it were "constrained to remember" and "to hate . . . in silence."[74] In a Wellsian description, Barnett, with his "thick lips" and "thick nostrils," brings down his "fat hand at the conclusion of each objection, crushing an invisible something." Dolly watches as Barnett's "fat mouth greased on."[75] The overweight Duke gloats over obtaining a valuable long-term commercial concession in famine-stricken India. Having "got his grip on the relief works," his "old usurer's heart continued to be glad within him." This made up for past insults,[76] but in a scene loaded with religious significance Dolly is forced to "taste in his heart things that Englishmen of his generation had never yet tasted, and the bitterness of a certain cup. Leaders of every other people in Christendom save his had drunk deep of that cup at one time or another. He was being bullied: his country was being bullied by the money-lenders." A "certain hand" had "held the stem of the chalice: it had been forced to his lips and he had sipped it—the savour of it was terrible!" Dolly had seen England "as the ally and even the contemptible ally of the forces . . . now opposed to him." He "had watched with indifference the intermarriage of the great families with these swine," and even had a Jewish wife, but now he "was almost a fanatic."[77] With echoes of *Dracula*[78] Barnett lies awake "feeding internally and nourishing his soul upon Dolly and the Indian Loan. He held Dolly between his spatulated forefinger and his gross thumb. But . . . he did not understand blood which was not his own, nor what sympathies might arise between men of one race and one society."[79] Had he been "of Dolly's race he might have understood . . . but he wasn't."[80]

But Belloc continues that, as was "often the case with men of the Duke of Battersea's kind," he "respected Dolly for having thrashed him soundly"— unlike financial rivals Smith, Fischer & Co., whose "commission rankled . . . for three long years," after which, Belloc concludes: "I am exceedingly glad to say

73. Ibid., 239.

74. H. Belloc, *Pongo and the Bull* (London: Constable & Co. Ltd., 1910), 70–71.

75. Ibid., 73–74.

76. Ibid., 77.

77. Ibid., 79–80.

78. B. Cheyette, *Constructions of "the Jew" in English Literature and Society: Racial Representations, 1875–1945*, op. cit., 170.

79. H. Belloc, *Pongo and the Bull*, op. cit., 94.

80. Ibid., 75.

the Duke of Battersea, having lost a good deal of money, died."[81] Cheyette notes that Belloc's "ironic narrator" no longer acts as mediator,[82] but sees Belloc's Gentile "usurers" Smith and Fischer as more acceptable,[83] although "Fischer" suggests Bellocian irony. Belloc explains the Duke's fall in terms of "the inevitable decline of a cyclical 'Jewish financial power'" peaking at the beginning of the century, resulting in "an "anti-Semitic" backlash" with "the exposure of its worst excesses."[84] In 1916 Belloc maintained that the "simple solution of absorption neither has nor can succeed. There is some fate against it. After every great period of financial power in the hands of a few Jews (the mass of the nation is absurdly poor), that power wanes and then there is no check upon the bad passions which the friction between the races allows."[85] Chesterton made a similar point in the early 1930s, but in the context of attacking Nazi anti-Semitism, not justifying it as a "backlash." Cheyette says that although the "rational" anti-Semitism of the Barnett novels has been seen as "anticipating" the Marconi affair, in fact, the Marconi affair was the outcome of Belloc's view on the "Jewish question."[86]

Anti-Semites would scarcely approve of Belloc satirizing their obsession but it also made his own approach appear more reasonable. Nonetheless, a crudely drawn "thriller" would have been more effective in stirring violent anti-Semitism than Belloc's civilized style, slow pace and attempt at nuance. He satirized paranoid anti-Semitism but also the hypocrisy of the Gentile "wire-pullers" who exploited people they privately despised, as when Dolly's friend, Mary Smith, socializes with Barnett but privately refers to him as "the old Yid."[87] Even on its own fantastic terms, however, the credibility of Belloc's fiction is strained by his overarching theme: Mary Smith is related to every public figure, and controls everything that Barnett does not. Dolly refuses to read newspapers he finds offensive and,[88] though Prime Minister for many years, seeks her advice on how to dissolve Parliament. She advises a sham attack on Pongo.[89] Dolly misses a vital appointment with Mary's American uncle to discuss the

81. Ibid., 305.

82. B. Cheyette, *Constructions of "the Jew" in English Literature and Society: Racial Representations, 1875–1945*, op. cit., 169.

83. Ibid., 171.

84. Ibid., 176.

85. Hilaire Belloc, Letter to Maurice Baring, January 1, 1916, R. Speaight, *The Life of Hilaire Belloc*, op. cit., 453.

86. B. Cheyette, *Constructions of "the Jew" in English Literature and Society: Racial Representations, 1875–1945*, op. cit., 172.

87. H. Belloc, *A Change in the Cabinet*, op. cit., 63.

88. H. Belloc, *Pongo and the Bull*, op. cit., 181–182.

89. Ibid., 247.

nation's financial security due to chronic indolence.[90] Barnett's circle appears supernaturally all-knowing.[91] When Pongo, unavoidably detained by the eponymous bull, fails to appear at the rigged Parliamentary debate, Dolly collapses, since Pongo has no Deputy, an even more unlikely scenario.[92]

In *The Mercy of Allah* (1922) a Muslim merchant relates how he became a multi-millionaire—a combination of brilliance and unscrupulousness—but Belloc's publisher "thought the merchant was Jewish" and advertised the fact: "Belloc was enraged and made them retract."[93] Speaight claims: "The Islamic setting deceived no one." Belloc, he says, was angry because the publisher had "allowed the Semitic cat to get out of its bag."[94] Belloc had been so successful at conveying "anti-Semitism" cloaked in irony that when he wanted to change the subject, readers "saw Jews everywhere." In fact the book's setting perfectly serves its theme, the introduction of the Servile State,[95] illustrated by the merchant's boast: "I paid for a law which compelled all slaves to insure and so was certain of a fixed revenue in this kind."[96] *Mr. Petre* (1925), set in 1953, is also concerned with finance and politics, but offers a more balanced treatment of Jews, although it contains echoes of the Marconi affair: J.K. Petre loses his memory but finds a talent for making money. Gentiles—even his bank manager, a "fine old English gentleman"—exploit this talent.[97] When the implicitly Jewish Henry Trefusis issues debentures in a self-aggrandizing scheme, the public seized upon them "very willingly as cows galloping into a new pasture."[98] Once again Belloc satirizes conspiracy theorists but once again the "fantastic fools" are right, although the libel laws help to conceal the "truth" about "well-established people."[99] His brother Charles, a politician, although feeling "a very honourable scruple" about involving himself in Henry's business

90. Ibid., 105.

91. Ibid., 73.

92. Ibid., 295; Barnett "stifled" the press "insult" he suffered regarding the Anapootra ruby mines affair, but with great "difficulty" (ibid., 78).

93. H. Belloc, *Belloc: A Biographical Anthology*, H. Van Thal, J. Soames Nickerson, eds. (London: George Allen & Unwin Ltd., 1970), 210.

94. R. Speaight, *The Life of Hilaire Belloc*, op. cit., 474.

95. Belloc outlined his fears about the negative moral effects on the population of introducing a welfare state in *The Servile State* (London: Constable & Co., Ltd., 1912/1950). He saw such "ostensibly reformist legislation" as Lloyd George's National Insurance Act of 1911 as benefiting capitalism and leading to this "servile state" (H. Belloc, "The Prevention of Destitution," *The New Age*, April 14, 1910, 556 [J.P. McCarthy, *Hilaire Belloc: Edwardian Radical*, op. cit., 286–287]; see also Chapter Two).

96. H. Belloc, *The Mercy of Allah* (London: Chatto & Windus, 1922/1973), 304.

97. H. Belloc, *Mr. Petre: a Novel* (London: Arrowsmith, 1925), 86; 141–142.

98. Ibid., 196.

99. Ibid., 131–132.

affairs, leaves it to his most intimate Cabinet colleagues.[100] Henry wants a monopoly of power generation, but, unable to buy up the "Tidal Power" areas, rather than leave them to "dangerous competitors" he would "kill them, as railways had killed canals."[101]

Petre is urged by his greedy Gentile stockbrokers to "swallow up" Henry Trefusis, but feels a "recurrent spasm of disgust." Trefusis presses on: "One scheme was wrecked? He would build a vaster one," catching "the fool public with debentures: they should buy the tides for him and yet leave him master," providing "wide support for his raid upon the wealth of England."[102] Like the Duke of Battersea, Trefusis felt it was "worth being thrashed at such a price. He would be delighted to take a second thrashing on such terms."[103] At Petre's office, "[t]he air of the place, the face of Trefusis, the talk of lesser men ruined and of the innocent caught unaware, of guttersnipes suddenly enriched, poisoned him out of all measure. It was perhaps the heat," but later the "face of Trefusis began to haunt him unpleasantly." Echoing "Barnett" themes, Henry Trefusis, the "Dark Spirit," possesses "brilliant dark eyes and [a] raven beak."[104] Petre is haunted by a "Daemon" tormenting him with his own greed and guilt"; he suffers terrible dreams and "during the day, a savour of what was vampire-like and snake-like in the vices of the modern market fastened on him within. His soul was in hell."[105]

Nonetheless, Belloc describes the Trefusis brothers, sons of a "Hamburg merchant" who arrived in England "in early youth," as "men of genius."[106] He also satirizes praise of "the Nordic Race" in the Duke's newspaper.[107] There is no Bill Bailey and no explicitly Jewish characters. The implicit Jews, aside from the Trefusis brothers, are neutral, positive, or ambivalent.[108] There are no insulting nicknames, and Jews are not "behind" everything. In fact Belloc's plutocratic Australian Duke, with his coarse, controlling ways, his "flabby-fleshed" face and his "flair for any weakness in others, and his rapid clutch at money,"

---

100. Ibid., 161.

101. Ibid., 164.

102. Ibid., 194–195.

103. Despite his "stage-villain face" there was "little of the Pun-d'Onor ("Point of honour" or "self respect") about Trefusis" (ibid., 199–200).

104. Ibid., 214–215.

105. Ibid., 202–203.

106. Chesterton's two almost identical figures have dark curly hair, large noses, and self-satisfied expressions (ibid., 158–159).

107. Ibid., 135.

108. For example, Mr. Petre's lawyer is Jacob King, and the clever private detective he hires to investigate his own history, Jos Daniels, discovers Mr. Petre's true identity.

could be seen as "balancing" Barnett.[109] The Gentile stockbroker "John Charlbury" has "cunning little piggy eyes,"[110] while Charles Trefusis scarcely features and Henry fades out, his improbable financial naivety exploited by Gentile stockbrokers "Blake and Blake," who entrap him into buying up Petre's shares.[111] Most remarkably, like Chesterton, Belloc allows Henry to "explain" his motivation: "Let 'em attack. He had it all now—his own thing—and no one could undo it"; he would "become sole Master again of the thing he had made."[112] Belloc writes that the "image of Mr. Trefusis rose in [Petre's] mind and nauseated him," although "[d]oubtless had he met the Great Organiser," his memory recovered, "he would have respected him as highly as did . . . all our business world"; but they met "in days of mental torture and warping" when "the picture was distorted."[113] Petre discards most of his fortune: "He had given the slip to that incredible world of shuffling and of falsehood," of "vain gambling and snatching and open robbery,"[114] but although he is tormented by what remains, and thinking about giving it away, he is "still thinking."[115]

Mr. Petre's Gentile characters outdo his Jewish creations in greed and avarice, but Belloc's overarching message is that by 1953 England will be thoroughly "Judaized." By contrast, as seen, Chesterton's "Moses Gould" illustrated his belief that if secularized Jews behaved badly, it was because they had seen no good Gentile role-models; far from the English becoming Judaized, the Jews were becoming "Englishified." In Belloc's England of 1979, in *But soft—we are observed!* (1928), bribery and corruption are rife. Britain is ruled by a Coalition, with a female Prime Minister and Foreign Secretary, civil liberties are curtailed, and spies are everywhere. But Belloc "explodes" the conspiracy. There are no Jewish themes or characters, explicit or disguised, and the threat emanates from the Islamic Council.[116] In *The Missing Masterpiece* (1929), set in the corrupt, contemporary art world, the greedy English are suspicious of foreigners, but "Delgairn" "cannot resist the charm" of the "'Italian' Signor Alessandria,"—although he had met "such a profile . . . often enough in England."[117] The main players in this murky world, Sir Hugh Bensington, Henri Caen, and Signor Alessandria, enjoy "the inestimable advantage of acquaintance with the German tongue,"[118] but

109. Ibid., 59–60.
110. Ibid., 105.
111. "I don't understand these things. What's to be done?" (ibid., 208).
112. Ibid., 215–216; see Chapter Three.
113. Ibid., 291.
114. Ibid., 271.
115. Ibid., 310.
116. H. Belloc, *But soft—we are observed!* (London: Arrowsmith, 1928/1930).
117. H. Belloc, *The Missing Masterpiece: a Novel* (London: Arrowsmith, 1929), 158–159.
118. Ibid., 32; 136–137.

their origins, footloose tendencies and linguistic abilities suggest they are Jewish.[119] Chesterton's caricatures, all equally absurd, support the implication.[120]

But the snobbish and gullible English lap up modern race theories. The only explicit Jewish reference is to Paris landlords, but it is their non-Jewish agent, "that abominable monster the Bourgeois," who is "off to suck more blood."[121] This might suggest a "Jews behind everything (bad)" theme or, like Chesterton, an attempt to "balance" bad Jews with bad Gentiles; or a Bellocian ironic reversal, with the implicitly Jewish characters illustrating the English admiration of Germany. The implicitly Jewish Sir Hugh Bensington[122] threatens and bribes foreign dealers whose positions are more precarious, aware of "the advantages of living in England after being born in Cologne, compared with living in France after being born in Vienna."[123] His rivals are "card-indexed" and he keeps "a whole dossier of their movements and their little adventures: all they had done throughout their interesting lives";[124] the banks, the police, and "all those . . . who have an interest in watching our affairs" do the same.[125] Bensington rigs the art market[126] but does not plan world domination or conspire with other Jews. Each seeks his own advantage.[127]

In *The Man Who Made Gold* (1930), set in corrupt and greedy England, "respectable" Gentiles break the law and oppress the poor, while people disap-

119. The French M. Machabée has a "brother, Charles Grant McCabe of Chicago" (ibid., 41); Henri Caen of Paris was "born in Vienna, where his parents happened to be residing at the time"; Signor Carlo Alessandria's parents were "of doubtful origin" but German was their "common language" (ibid., 136–137); Verecundia, fifteenth Marchioness of Norbolt (twenty-first Countess of Pulborough, thirty-third Baroness Workup of Northumberland) did not speak German but "derived, as her name implies, from the exotic regions. She was mainly of the Blood indeed . . . of the Nordic breed and of the island race, for all she knew or I know or anyone else knows. For her late father's name—or that by which he had been last known in life—was Wugg." Her mother's origins were "forgotten" but from the daughter's appearance, "the forgotten lady must have had in her some rich southern strain"; her father made his fortune in the Pacific islands "when he was passing under the name of Wonks," although some old friends "gave him another name sounding more like Malchedo" (ibid., 77).

120. "Verecundia" is dark-haired, imperious, with a hooked nose (ibid., 78); "Signor Alessandria" has dark slicked-back hair, a hooked nose and a superior smile, although he could be Italian or Maltese, as claimed (ibid., 159).

121. Ibid., 15–17.

122. He was "born at Cologne, where his parents happened to be resident" (ibid., 32).

123. Ibid., 179–181.

124. Ibid., 177, 219.

125. Ibid., 141.

126. Ibid., 34–35.

127. These art dealers were unknown to the general public but their names were "household words with the powerful groups which buy pictures"; the pictures were sold on, "bought again by friends in connection with the Government for permanent exhibition in the Great Galleries of Europe" (ibid., 137–138).

pear on trumped-up charges.[128] There are no Jewish characters, explicit or implicit,[129] until the final page, when the international committee dealing with the problems—and advantages—of making gold includes M. de Caen from France, Herr von Kuhn from Germany, Senor Coheno from Spain, and Signor Cuneo from Italy, while the Soviets are "unofficially but effectively represented by Commissar Kahn."[130] Chesterton's thesis about an informal conspiracy between communist and capitalist Jews was tentative and temporary, and his fiction recovered from the conspiracy-fixated *The Man Who Knew Too Much*, whereas, over time, Belloc's fiction reflected an ever-deeper belief in a Jewish conspiracy.

But Belloc's next and final political novel, *The Post-Master General* (1932), although continuing his "Barnett" theme, represents a change in direction. Cheyette says Belloc "rewrote 'Marconi'" to represent such political dealings as "now the norm"[131] and yet, rather than becoming more explicit, or more conspiracy-minded, in response to increasing British anti-Semitism Belloc portrays a Jewish financier putting his influence to good purpose: saving his Gentile friend the Post Master General. The serious tone compares favorably with his earlier spite masquerading as *faux* innocence. *Mr. Petre*'s tentative "explanation" of Jewish motivation is expanded with references to persecution: "That dreadful day and night of the Pogrom . . . had both seared and branded him" with its "horrid cruelty which had stabbed his soul."[132] Religion is reverently handled: the Jewish brothers converse "in the ancient tongue: 'Blessed be God.'"[133] While Wells' fiction allowed readers to project vices such as greed onto "the Jews,"[134] and respectable Golden Age characters are often driven to crime by pitiless moneylenders, Belloc portrayed the English as growing ever greedier and more venial, although his prompt and trenchant protests about Nazi anti-Semitism at around the same time as *The Post-Master General* suggest a genuine change of direction on the "Jewish question." But the cleverly cloaked anti-Semitism that dominated Belloc's earlier fiction ensured that when he at last assumed a serious tone he was not taken seriously by Jews. *The Postmaster-General* was dismissed by Myer Jack Landa, who saw the character of Arthur

---

128. H. Belloc, *The Man Who Made Gold* (London: Arrowsmith, 1930), 179.

129. The "powerful Mrs. Meyer" merely forces the main character to act in her amateur theatricals (ibid., 186); Chesterton was involved in amateur theatricals with his Jewish friends: see Chapter Eight.

130. All variations on "Cohen" (ibid., 296).

131. B. Cheyette, *Constructions of "the Jew" in English Literature and Society: Racial Representations, 1875–1945*, op. cit., 178.

132. H. Belloc, *The Postmaster-General* (London: Arrowsmith, 1932), 156.

133. Ibid., 235.

134. J. Parkes, *Antisemitism*, op. cit., 10.

Lawson "né Aaron Levina" as "patronisingly introduced as a pogrom victim for Belloc's literary pogrom and his apotheosis into the master-mind millionaire, who pulls the strings behind."[135] Ironically, Belloc's fiction, unmistakable in its meaning at the time, now appears more acceptable than that of Chesterton's growing but subtly expressed pro-Semitism.

Belloc and Chesterton

Cheyette says Chesterton, unlike Belloc, was unable to sustain the "extreme contradictions" of his "Janus-faced view of the world."[136] Maisie Ward reveals that Belloc had been "prejudiced" against Chesterton before their first meeting, believing him to be Jewish.[137] They were brought together, through the Liberal *Speaker*, against the Boer War's "immoral abuse of the English fighting forces and national treasure for the benefit of alien financiers." McCarthy notes that they "very rapidly . . . developed a rapport,"[138] seeing themselves in the tradition of Bright, Cobden, and Gladstone in emphasizing "democracy, international morality, and humanitarianism."[139] Liberal theorist J. A. Hobson saw Imperialism benefiting vested interests at the behest of the great financial houses: "United by the strongest bonds of organization, always in closest and quickest touch with one another, situated in the very heart of the business capital of every state, controlled, so far as Europe is concerned, chiefly by men of a single and peculiar race, who have behind them many centuries of financial experience, they are in a unique position to control the policy of nations."[140] Belloc sympathized with the "zeal for social reconstruction" of the "new Liberals" and their attacks on the inequalities of Edwardian society.[141] He "enthusiastically approved" the 1909 Liberal Budget,[142] but he became suspicious of

135. Myer Jack Landa, "Books and Bookmen: Pogrom and the Pen," *Jewish Chronicle*, July 22, 1932, 18–19.

136. B. Cheyette, *Constructions of "the Jew" in English Literature and Society: Racial Representations, 1875–1945*, op. cit., 179.

137. Lucian Oldershaw for "some time" attempted to get the *Speaker* group to read Chesterton but "in vain": F. Y. Eccles "declared the handwriting was that of a Jew" and "prejudiced Belloc, says Oldershaw, against reading 'anything written by my Jew friend'" (M. Ward, *Gilbert Keith Chesterton* [New York: Sheed & Ward, 1943], 127).

138. J. P. McCarthy, *Hilaire Belloc: Edwardian Radical*, op. cit., 58.

139. Ibid., 206.

140. J. A. Hobson, *Imperialism: A Study* (London, 1902/1938), 56–59 (ibid., 60–61). He was echoed by political scientist, historian, jurist, and sociologist Moisey Ostrogorsky, member of the Russian Duma who developed a theory of political party allegiance as akin to religion (M. Ostrogorsky, *Democracy and the Organization of Political Parties* [New York, 1902]), ibid., 171; Ostrogorsky, son of a Jewish teacher, influenced the British Left including Robert Blatchford and his *Clarion* Fellowship (ibid., 252).

141. Ibid., 215.

142. Ibid., 221.

"new Liberals" like Asquith and Lloyd George and their "top-down" reforms, especially the 1911 Insurance Act,[143] seeing its compulsory provisions as leading to a Bismarckian "servile state."[144]

Belloc's analysis was shared by many on the Left. George Lansbury, writing in the *Eye Witness*, called for the destruction of "the party system,"[145] while some guild socialists shared Belloc's "distrust for parliamentary politics and ameliorative welfare legislation" because it tended "to postpone the drive for worker control."[146] *Emmanuel Burden*, first published in the *Speaker*, portrays Barnett and his Gentile dupes betraying Mr. Abbott's English business values— (free trade, the gold standard, and suspicion of foreigners)—reflecting left-wing views of political elitism,[147] but Belloc's opposition to socialism and support for small ownership was influenced by Cardinal Manning, friend of the poor and Irish Catholics.[148] Belloc's "almost isolated position . . . in British thought" was shaped by "Victorian radicalism" and religion—specifically the Papal encyclical *Rerum Novarum* (1891) which condemned unrestrained capitalism but also the collectivist's centralization of responsibility and antagonism to individual property. While deploring state intervention in the family it approved intervention to improve workers' conditions and prevent injustice,[149] an approach more characteristic of the British Left than Wells' sexual collectivism—holding "all wives in common."[150] Since the time of William Cobbett many anti-capitalists, notably the architect A. W. N. Pugin, William Morris's pre-Raphaelite art movement, and critic John Ruskin, reacting against industrialization, the loss of craftsmanship and rural culture, found inspiration in the Middle Ages. Morris inspired Robert Blatchford, and in 1893 Chesterton briefly but "enthusiastically embraced the Socialism of Blatchford's *Merrie England*" as "essentially Christian."[151] G.D.H. Cole became interested in guild

143. Ibid., 229–230.

144. Ibid., 256; the scheme was paid for by the poor, including domestic servants, who did not need it (ibid., 243–244).

145. G. Lansbury, November 23, 1911, 721 (ibid., 254).

146. Ibid., 202.

147. "At Mr. Harbury's dinner, half academic and half political, Cosmo [Burden] met a group of those men who principally direct our State and its great destinies" (H. Belloc, *Emmanuel Burden*, op. cit., 49).

148. J.P. McCarthy, *Hilaire Belloc: Edwardian Radical*, op. cit., 118.

149. Ibid., 266–269; *Rerum Novarum*, which made no mention of Jews, condemned "devouring usury" and also socialism for "exciting the envy of the poor toward the rich"; workers' associations were supported, but abolishing private property was "injurious" to workers; conferred by natural law, it could not be abolished by the State (Pope Leo XIII, *Rerum Novarum* ["On the Condition of the Working Classes"], May 15, 1891).

150. H.G. Wells, *New Worlds for Old* (New York, 1907), in J.P. McCarthy, *Hilaire Belloc: Edwardian Radical*, op. cit., 275–276; see Chapter Five.

151. I. Ker, *G.K. Chesterton: A Biography*, op. cit., 24; see Chapter Eight.

Socialism, and in 1906 the architect A.J. Penty, with A.R. Orage of *The New Age*, formed the Guilds Restoration League.[152]

Belloc's view of history was not unique either, but akin to Cobbett's radical Toryism: they opposed the "Whig" view that everything had improved since the Reformation. Populist by temperament, they were suspicious of "finance" and government acting together in their mutual interest, against the people. The Conservative Disraeli described the Reformation plunder of the Church,[153] as did "Liberal Tory" Winston Churchill.[154] Christian Socialist historian R. H. Tawney's *Religion and the Rise of Capitalism* (1926) explored the negative effect of capitalism on Christianity. Herbert Butterfield wrote his definitive *The Whig Interpretation of History* in 1931. *Emmanuel Burden* was dedicated to anti-Whig historian and Liberal politician H.A.L. Fisher. In 1926 Lloyd George, "long-standing" supporter of "rural radicalism," founded the Land and Nation League.[155] Clearly the *Chesterbelloc*'s Medieval inspiration was far from unusual, although their Medieval "solution" to the "Jewish problem" was atypical. But their interest in the Middle Age was not confined to the "Jewish question." McCarthy argues that "contrary to what might have been expected of an ardent medievalist," Belloc did not envisage "the first experimental nucleus of small landowners ... to consist of agricultural holders."[156] Chesterton's supposed promotion of the Middle Ages was equally non-prescriptive because rather than a program of action it was really a defense of a much-maligned era that had become synonymous with ignorance and squalor.[157]

Whereas others on the Left saw the Middle Ages as vindicating their anti-capitalist stance and as a kind of proto-socialism, McCarthy notes Chesterton's and Belloc's practically identical commitment to "widespread property ownership as a solution for the social crisis of industrial capitalism."[158] Belloc's defense of the Middle Ages was crucial to his historical view of Catholicism as the European faith,[159] and Cecil Chesterton claimed, contra Shaw, that Belloc was Chesterton's major political influence; that from the beginning the two were intellectually and temperamentally in accord; and that Belloc's views "had already ... solidified round the iron framework of Catholic dogma" while Gil-

152. J.P. McCarthy, *Hilaire Belloc: Edwardian Radical*, op. cit., 299.

153. Ibid., 322–323.

154. W.S. Churchill, *A History of the English-Speaking Peoples* (London: Cassell, 2003), 255.

155. P. Adelman, *The Decline of the Liberal Party 1910–1931* (London: Longman, 1995), 54.

156. H. Belloc, "Reformation: III—The Restoration of Property," *Oxford & Cambridge Review* 24, October 1912, 57, in J.P. McCarthy, *Hilaire Belloc: Edwardian Radical*, op. cit., 305–306.

157. See Chapter Seven.

158. J.P. McCarthy, *Hilaire Belloc: Edwardian Radical*, op. cit., 272–273.

159. Belloc's "idea that the protectionist guilds, with their small parcels of wealth, could have financed industrial development is somewhat fanciful" (J. Newham, "Hilaire Belloc and the attack on liberal economics," *Catholic Life*, February 2013, 50).

bert's were still forming.[160] Chesterton especially "relied on" Belloc's historical knowledge,[161] to the extent that sometimes "Chesterton simply was echoing Belloc, as when he described a Europe he hardly knew or dilated on history of which he had read very little."[162]

Chesterton's view of English literature, of which Belloc admitted ignorance, remained unchanged, but he embraced Belloc's views on socialism and property, while delivering the half-French Belloc's view of English history in his own way. Ward believed Chesterton "preferred the attitude of a disciple," listening to Belloc and, regarding history, his "tendency was simply to make an act of faith in Belloc." Most importantly, Chesterton learned "a certain realism about politics—which meant a certain cynicism about politicians." Belloc's influence on Chesterton's Distributism was, she adds, "[f]ar more valuable" than his influence on the "Jewish question."[163] Belloc's religion played a crucial role in Chesterton's politics, but as Wilson notes, by the time of the latter's conversion in 1922 their friendship "had slightly cooled," and guests "were amazed" that Belloc did not attend Chesterton's reception into the Church.[164]

As will be seen, Chesterton's loyalty to Belloc would conflict with his loyalty to the Jews.[165] According to Sheed, however, shifting blame for Chesterton's "anti-Semitism . . . bothers in its own way"—why did "a thinker of visibly painful independence, an arguing machine . . . swallow the Belloc line, even under stress?" Belloc's age, French background, and military training inspired trust on issues such as Dreyfus, and he also filled a void after Cecil's death. Chesterton, Sheed maintains, embraced "certain Bellocian positions out of simple loyalty, and with less of his early scepticism (he had always feared that his hairshirt itch to question everything might lead to madness; Belloc's affirmations were an antidote)." Sheed adds, however, that anti-Semitism was "a small part of the package," and "small to vanishing as his mind regained its strength," although Chesterton "would have picked Belloc's general philosophy to pieces in five minutes if it hadn't paralleled some thought-out position of his own." But there were differences in Chesterton's stance, glimpsed in his choice of words and his fiction. Moreover, no one ever mentioned Chesterton's "subtle, personal" influ-

---

160. Cecil Chesterton, *G. K. Chesterton. A Criticism* (London, 1908), in B. Sewell, *Cecil Chesterton* (Whitefriars, Kent: St. Albert's Press, 1975), 100.

161. A. Nichols, *G. K. Chesterton, Theologian* (London: Darton, Longman & Todd Ltd., 2009), 18.

162. M. Ward, *Return to Chesterton* (London: Sheed & Ward, 1952), 60.

163. M. Ward, *Gilbert Keith Chesterton*, op. cit., 129–134.

164. "[A]s they looked at their watches in puzzlement, there was no Belloc. Nor did he ever offer apology or explanation for his absence" (A. N. Wilson, "Forgotten Champion of The Catholic Thing" (edited version of essay in *English Catholic Heroes*, J. Jolliffe, ed. [Leominster, Herefordshire: Gracewing Publishing, 2008], quoted in the *Catholic Herald*, September 19, 2008, 8); see Chapter Eight.

165. See Chapter Seven.

ence on Belloc. This included "raising his friend's spirits, sharpening his comic gifts, maintaining a schoolboy atmosphere." In fact, it was "easy to forget how funny [Belloc] usually was about it, even on the attack." This was "the strongest link between him and Chesterton, not any kind of prejudice." As to their grasp of reality, it did not "compare so hopelessly with Shaw and Wells on Hitler and Mussolini (as to Adolf, the ChesterBelloc at least knew a bounder when it saw one)."[166]

Belloc's Non-fiction

In his travelogue *The Path to Rome* (1902) Belloc asks a French shopkeeper if there is "any anti-Semitism" in his town. The shopkeeper replies that it flourishes despite the absence of Jews,[167] and Belloc claims that in England "Lord Saxonthorpe (whose real name is Haupstein) now plans our policy."[168] *The Old Road* (1904), which described the Winchester Hebrew settlement, was sympathetically received by Jews,[169] and Belloc frequently lectured to Jewish groups where, ironically, his views on "race" found most favor. At the East London Synagogue he stated that the "motive-force" of national development was its religion or philosophy more than "its racial instincts—much more the attitude of its mind than its physical characteristics." This thesis, Belloc said, was easier to sustain regarding the mixed-race French or Irish, but with Jews "there was the majesty of the race expressed." But, he added, "many modern Jews thought it did not matter whether they kept their religion sacred as long as they preserved their race intact." The Chairman was "largely in agreement," but said "it was a great and pleasant surprise to . . . a Jewish religious worker, to find this self-same thesis expounded so eloquently by a distinguished member of another faith."[170] In 1908 a Jewish commentator remarked that Jewish "coward-

---

166. Chesterton's godson, and the son of his biographer Maisie Ward and her husband Frank Sheed, Wilfrid Sheed said Chesterton's "anti-Semitism (which he preferred to call Zionism—i.e., get them out of here) differed from Belloc's in quality and stress," but both "would have been horrified" to find Jews "being liquidated in Prussian gas chambers; both, in fact, hated Germany, and only distrusted Jews. . . . [T]hey thought (with Rothschilds on the brain) that the Jews might some day sell England out to relatives in Prussia" (W. Sheed, "ChesterBelloc and the Jews," op. cit.); see Chapter Seven.

167. The shopkeeper added: "'For my part I am a liberal, and would have each go his own way: the Catholic to his Mass, the Jew to his Sacrifice'"; Belloc could not "imagine" what "the Jews sacrificed in this remote borough," despite having "a great many" Jews among his friends (H. Belloc, *The Path to Rome*, op. cit., 86–87).

168. Ibid., 317.

169. *Jewish Chronicle*, November 10, 1905, 17.

170. H. Belloc, "The influence of race and Philosophy upon Civilisation" ("Race and Religion," *Jewish Chronicle*, May 25, 1906, 36); Belloc lectured at the Beth Hamidrash, Mulberry Street (ibid., February 8, 1907, 4–5), and at the Jewish Institute on "Anti-Semitism" (ibid., March 6, 1908, 19).

ice and indifference ... may manifest themselves in the changing or inversion of names" and that *Mr. Clutterbuck's Election* had "a good deal to say about this, and says it well."[171] Belloc continued to lecture to Jewish groups,[172] but when he stood for Parliament a *Jewish Chronicle* reader warned that he was "an enemy of Jews as Jews—in other words, an anti-Semite ... avowed and unashamed ... expressing his sentiments in the usual language of the anti-Semite." Jews did not "wish the foul poison of Continental anti-Semitism introduced in the British body politic," since "corruption once introduced spreads and the end of the mischief cannot be foreseen."[173] But he was accused by another reader of playing party politics.[174]

Belloc responded to a Jewish enquirer: "[A]ny Jew writing to me, as you have had the courtesy to do, deserves a clear reply from me in return." He explained that since 1898 he had become increasingly interested in the "Jewish question," and meant to write a book on it. He had "a dislike—a profound dislike—of international finance," which was "in the nature of things largely Jewish," but the "cosmopolitan organization of that power" was "big with danger to the Jew" as well as the "alien" race with whom he resided. Belloc feared there might be "an explosion" and "the solution" would "have to be found (ultimately) in some form of special privilege for the Jews accompanied by special representation." Assimilation would fail—as Zangwill, "a real patriot," agreed—and led to "hiding and changing Jewish names; pretending that such and such prominent men" were not Jewish. He detested such stratagems, which were "mean and dangerous to both Jew and non-Jew." If this made him "an anti-Semite" he "must bear the reproach of it." But if it meant that he "would injure or hate a Jew simply because he was a Jew," it was "too ridiculous to be considered." He had "hosts of intimate friends ... wholly or partially Jewish by race," who discussed with him what he believed was "the only final solution of a pressing danger."[175] Belloc, like Chesterton and Wells, rejected "race" theories, believing that Jewish "vices" were caused by historical sociological pressures, but Belloc

171. *Jewish Chronicle*, October 2, 1908, 20–21.

172. On "The Expulsion of the Jews from England in 1290" at the Jewish Institute (*Jewish Chronicle*, April 2, 1909, 11).

173. "[A]nti-Jewish prejudice" seemed to be "spreading among Liberals"—the Chancellor of the Exchequer had attacked "Jewish opponents on racial ... not political lines" ("Mac," Letter, "Jews and the General Election," *Jewish Chronicle*, January 7, 1910, 16).

174. Labour MP Philip Snowden's House of Commons "outburst" on "'the Jewish gang of vampires'" who "'arranged the South African War'" ("Mac," Letter, "Jews and the General Election," *Jewish Chronicle*, January 7, 1910, 16), according to another reader was simply "a little oratorical display," typical of socialists and not to be taken "seriously"; like Belloc, Lloyd George had "publicly repudiated that charge," but he would have ignored the matter if "Mac" had only criticized Belloc (M. Wolfsohn, Letter, ibid., January 10, 1910, 26).

175. Meyer Horewitz, Letter, *Jewish Chronicle*, January 10, 1910, 27.

saw racial mixing as culturally deleterious and through his fiction promoted the view that Jews would remain Jews while the English became more "Jewish."

Belloc's historical works had enjoyed a favorable Jewish reception, but by 1910 the *Jewish Chronicle* said he was suffering from "an obsession" about "the power, or alleged power, of the Jew."[176] One reader accused him of stirring animosity between Catholics and Jews for political reasons.[177] Another urged "hitting our attacker a considerably harder blow." It was time, he said, "to squelch, by home thrusts and hard facts, this incipient attempt to found an anti-Semitic party in English politics," adding that the Dreyfus affair, the "prime flower of Jesuit teaching and plotting," was proof of a worldwide Catholic conspiracy.[178] Shortly after, the paper interviewed Belloc, praising "the delights of this attractive author's writings" but noting the "impression" that he was "decidedly unfriendly towards our people." Belloc responded that he was "ever willing" to address Jewish literary institutions but restated his views on assimilation causing "friction" because "the interests of the two races, their ideals, their psychology" were "different." Interestingly, given his own heritage, he claimed "the Jew" was "always possessed—consciously or unconsciously—of his Jewishness," and that this was "as true of the man of almost remote Jewish descent as it is of the regular synagogue attendant. He cannot get away from his ancestry and this

176. Despite Belloc's "fantastic" claims, the "all-powerful" Jews were unable stop the Aliens Act "or to bring about its amendment" ("Mr. Belloc and the Jews," *Jewish Chronicle*, February 25, 1910, 8).

177. It was "extraordinary" for a Liberal to attack "a much smaller denomination," who like Roman Catholics had "suffered a great deal from misrepresentation"; Oswald Simon said that "good feeling" and "sympathy" had "long subsisted" between the Catholic and Jewish communities, and Cardinal Manning had been his "friend and counselor" and that of his "co-religionists" in the "struggle against persecution abroad"; Manning's "successors and his clergy generally" had followed his example. No "high political aim" could be achieved through "sectarian animosities and the kindling of ill-will." Belloc regretted giving "pain," but the "Anglo-Judaic plutocracy" was "a fact"—the "command of European finances" was "mainly in the power of a race alien to Europeans"; he opposed restrictions on the Jewish religion, but the Catholic Church was "the permanent and necessary religion of Europe"—the "accident" that it had "long been in a minority" in Britain left him "quite indifferent." Simon replied that he was descended from "Spanish Jews who were burnt and otherwise driven from their native land" despite having lived there "long before the Catholic Church was established." Belloc agreed to publish their exchange: "We Catholics never hide" ("Mr. Belloc, MP, and an 'Anglo-Judaic Plutocracy,'" *Jewish Chronicle*, March 11, 1910, 14); see Chapter Five.

178. Catholics "as a body" had shown little support toward the Jews "during the Dreyfus affair"; as to the "Anglo-Judaic plutocracy," Belloc's true allegiance was to "his Pope, an Italian . . . whose church, moreover, has in all times aimed at gaining control, not only of souls, but of all the vital forces of a State." In Britain, "the balance of power" was "held by the Irish Party, in other words, by Roman Catholics." Belloc claimed that Catholics "never hide," but in "notorious cases," Jewish children were removed from their parents "and hidden away, first in one place, then in another"; in "convents or monasteries . . . all statistics as to births, deaths, etc., which take place behind their secretive prison-like walls" were hidden. The editor interpolated that he could "appreciate and sympathise" this response to Belloc's "nonsenses" but Mr. Emanuel took him "a good deal too much *aux grand serieux*" (F. L. Emanuel, Letter, *Jewish Chronicle*, March 18, 1910, 15).

makes him quite different from his neighbours." There was "nothing peculiar or uncivic," he maintained, about Jews rallying to a Jewish defendant, but he objected "most strongly" to "the vast international influence" of "cosmopolitan financiers." It was not about "personal character," but about their "remaining practically unrestrained by all patriotic ties." He had "never joked at a man's religious belief or customs," and never would restrict the Jewish religion. "Jewish finance" was far less influential than fifty years previously, but as in 14th century Spain Jews should "take warning," because: "The nations rose against the Jews who had acquired power and the reaction was terrible." They must "beware lest history, in accordance with her practice repeat herself." He insisted that he did not "speak in a hostile spirit" but "the Roman system of privilege . . . a private law," would restore Jews to their pre-Expulsion status, although "all suggestions of such magnitude," especially historical ones, "must be merely vague adumbrations." His "medieval solution" was not, he maintained, "originally a method of persecution," but admitted that "when the Jews became impoverished it was used as such."[179]

Once again Belloc's claims were met with allegations of a "Catholic conspiracy"[180] and while another reader praised him as "a writer of striking ability"— especially for his *French Revolution*—he alleged that Belloc embraced the racial theory of Houston Stewart Chamberlain, and that the *Eye Witness* "charged itself to propagate, to arouse, to disseminate an anti-Jewish policy," in the belief that a large Jewish community was "inimical to the interests of Great Britain."[181] Despite this, Belloc continued to claim Jewish friendships, and with an apparent lack of irony, lectured Jewish groups on the "very disturbing" increase of "professed" anti-Semites. Many people, he warned, pretended not to be but "were not always successful in hiding it. It came out sooner or later." But he also distanced himself from the *Witness*, now edited by Cecil.[182] Belloc rejected

---

179. "The Jewish Question: Interview for the Jewish Chronicle with Mr. Hilaire Belloc, M.P.," *Jewish Chronicle*, August 12, 1910, 14; a reader complained about publicizing Belloc's "prejudiced crudities" but the editor said it was akin to giving "free ventilation . . . to disease germs" ("K.M.," Letter, ibid., August 19, 1910, 10–13).

180. The "menace to the peace of the world and the liberty of mankind" was "in that unscrupulous international secret society known as the Jesuits"; their "twin maxims" were "the end justifies the means and that the killing of a heretic is no crime"; they were responsible for "90 per cent" of wars, "the sworn foe of freedom" and the "staunch upholder of oppression" ("Mac," Letter, *Jewish Chronicle*, September 9, 1910, 16).

181. "Mentor," "The Disliker of the Jew: Draining off the Virus," *Jewish Chronicle*, March 22, 1912, 12–13.

182. Anybody "could abuse the Jew; that was an easy matter, especially when the Jew was not there." The anti-Semite attacked Jews "irrationally," whereas Belloc "feared" the Jewish "powerful, almost too powerful, grasp of the springs of the economic situation"; however, he "desired to explode the popular fallacy held by so many anti-Semites, that the Jews as a whole were the most wealthy race

racial and Jewish conspiracy theories along with claims that Jews controlled the press, insisting that they were "scapegoated" in affairs like "Dreyfus," and Jewish groups continued to issue lecture invitations at least until 1921.[183] Some Jews even agreed with his view of Jewish "separateness,"[184] but as Wilson remarks: "Jews are allowed to distinguish themselves; but it is embarrassing if the Gentiles do so."[185]

The Great War led to increased anti-Semitism, especially as many Jews were of German background. Jewish links to Bolshevism led to further tensions when Russia withdrew from the war. Interest in Zionism grew, and in 1919, speaking to the London University Zionist Society at the Jews' College, Belloc appeared to soften his earlier line. While he still "firmly believed" the only solution to anti-Semitism was the "open recognition" of difference between "the two races," it was "not in the sense . . . of isolation or exile." He sympathized with the belief that the "the wanderings of the Jews" would cease, but not while people believed the "palpable and even foolish falsehood that Jews were not a separate and distinct nation." Some applauded, but M. J. Landa, an "old opponent," responded to Belloc's claim that small Jewish communities were never attacked with the word "Limerick." Landa said that Belloc, with his solemn warnings, was "like the fat boy in 'Pickwick'" trying "to make their flesh creep"—although "he had not succeeded."[186]

---

in the world. They were not"; if Jews thought there was no anti-Semitism, "[h]e knew better." His audience thought that "the Church was in no little degree responsible" for that "evil," and Belloc "the greatest anti-Semite" in the country ("'The Anti-Semite': Mr. Hilaire Belloc defines the Term," *Jewish Chronicle*, December 13, 1912, 25).

183. "We are glad to see that Mr. Hilaire Belloc . . . repudiated the silly anti-Semitic myth of a Jewish-controlled Press"; however, his "suggestion that the detachment of the Jew enabled him to take up a brief for any cause that was going did less than justice to the Jewish newspaperman" ("Jews and the Press," *Jewish Chronicle*, December 9, 1910, 8); Belloc lectured to the Jews' Free School Old Boys Club on the economist David Ricardo (ibid., December 23, 1921, 34–35).

184. "Now the political Zionist must accept Mr. Belloc's thesis. The present writer does so unhesitatingly" (Emanuel Sternheim, *Jewish Chronicle*, December 9, 1910, 8).

185. A. N. Wilson, *Hilaire Belloc*, op. cit., 259.

186. Belloc believed "the possibility of praising the Jews was evident to anyone who considered the problem. But the Jews as a race were accused of things which as a race they did not suffer from"; they did not "understand" the "friction" they caused because they did not feel about non-Jews the same as non-Jews felt about them. Jews were "never persecuted" until they were poor and "in a great mass." He called a request for more detail "purely controversial" and denied that "the national solution would lead to pogroms in England—isolated outbreaks, perhaps"—and "more knowledge" would not help when it involved "anything alien. . . ." ("Mr. Hilaire Belloc on the Jewish Problem," *Jewish Chronicle*, December 5, 1919, 26–27). Landa's "pugnacity . . . came out especially when he took up the cudgels against antisemitism and antisemites"; on one occasion, Belloc agreed to lecture on the "Jewish Problem" but was "worried about this Landa, who followed him around wherever he was speaking to attack him" (Joseph Leftwich, ibid., March 1, 1974, 14). The "Limerick Boycott," also called the "Limerick Pogrom" was an economic boycott of the tiny Jewish community in Limerick,

The Party System (1911), by Belloc and Cecil Chesterton, claimed the House of Lords' "normal and shameful method" was to recruit men who "made their fortunes...in commerce or by money-lending."[187] They alleged that widespread anger against using Chinese labor in the South African gold mines sprang from "the desire to chastise" South African Jews, who, for monetary gain, had deliberately encouraged popular support for the Boer War. Both front bench leaders had "consulted with the South African Jews" about their needs, the answer being cheap, docile labor. In the future, Belloc and Chesterton warned, "the Duke of Battersea...a money dealer of sorts, born Heaven knows where" might decide he needed to legally control the working classes for the same reasons,[188] although they acknowledged that Fabian socialists favored a similar policy.[189] They believed that the political system depended on "letting the moneylender, Mr. Judaeus, suck dry the resources of such and such an Oriental district," controlled by the crooked politician's "colleague and first cousin."[190]

Belloc, according to McCarthy, saw the "new Liberalism" of Asquith, Lloyd George, and Winston Churchill as serving the interests of capitalist plutocrats, but their 1909 Budget, including a new land tax to benefit the poor from the unearned income of the rich, was "entirely in accord with the decades-old radical agitation, in which Belloc himself had taken part."[191] Belloc saw the hand of plutocracy in the House of Lords stalemate over the Liberal Budget, and while the front benches did sometimes collude to their mutual benefit, party politics was a much more complex affair.[192] Finance was involved in politics, but it did not direct it, as Belloc and Cecil insisted.[193] The country was ruled by a small, interrelated governing class—itself unhealthy for democracy—but there was no deliberate conspiracy to corrupt politics.[194] Politicians sometimes agreed for

---

Ireland, instigated in 1904 by Father John Creagh, and lasting for two years. The boycott, accompanied by assaults and harassment, led to five out of 31 Jewish families leaving Limerick (Dermot Keogh, *Jews in Twentieth-Century Ireland* (Cork University Press: Cork, 1998).

187. H. Belloc, C. Chesterton, *The Party System* (London: Stephen Swift, 1911), 29; each "wrote one half," just as "the Hail Mary was written half by the Church and half by St. Gabriel" (Hilaire Belloc, Letter to George Wyndham, December 27, 1910, R. Speaight, *The Life of Hilaire Belloc*, op. cit., 301).

188. H. Belloc, C. Chesterton, *The Party System*, op. cit., 74–76.

189. "Mrs. Webb's policy" of "imprisoning working men in compounds until they consent to work for the rich" (ibid., 137) was the 'carrot and stick' approach of her nephew William Beveridge, Welfare State architect and President of the Board of Trade who thought vagrants "should be detained in penal colonies." (P. Addison, *Churchill on the Home Front 1900–1955* [London: J. Cape, 1992], 123).

190. H. Belloc, C. Chesterton, *The Party System*, op. cit., 163.

191. J.P. McCarthy, *Hilaire Belloc: Edwardian Radical*, op. cit., 138.

192. Asquith obtained the guarantees Belloc wanted, creating new peers to circumvent Tory opposition to the Liberal Budget, but they would come into force "only after another election had returned a Liberal majority" (J.P. McCarthy, *Hilaire Belloc: Edwardian Radical*, op. cit., 152–153).

193. Ibid., 183–184.

194. S. Low, *The Governance of England* (New York, 1913), 185–189 (ibid., 186–187).

ignoble reasons, but they would not risk parties or careers, as Belloc suggested.[195] Proposals for coalitions tended to founder on political differences,[196] and if Lloyd George's impatience with such differences prompted him to seek a coalition, dissatisfaction with democracy made Belloc "more sympathetic to authoritarianism."[197] Far from Liberals and Tories being in cahoots, as Ward remarks, the Conservative opposition helped expose "Marconi."[198] Paul Adelman notes that some did begin to view Lloyd George as "unscrupulous and insincere, lacking any sound consistent political principles" while his "cavalier attitude towards the 'sale of honours'" and his "Lloyd George fund" appeared "to debase still further the standards of public life," leading to his eventual downfall.[199] But Belloc claimed that the upper classes opposed free trade in their own interests, although as McCarthy notes, "most outspoken free traders were Conservatives of ancient and prestigious lineage, like Winston Churchill and Lord Hugh Cecil, or Whigs, like the Duke of Devonshire," whereas "protectionists" were often nouveau riche, middle-class, or even radicals.[200] Furthermore, Lord Robert Cecil deplored the sale of peerages because he "resented the pollution of the hereditary aristocracy."[201] Belloc believed that a "newer privileged class, the plutocracy which financed the parties" had taken over the Edwardian Liberals, but as McCarthy remarks, "[i]t did not occur to him" that the "democratic masses" had "lost interest in the radical causes" or that the Liberal government was more in touch with the electorate than he.[202] While the *Chesterbelloc* saw the nascent welfare state as a disturbing erosion of freedom, to the poor it signaled security.[203] Unlike *The Party System*, his collaboration with Cecil, Belloc's own work, *The Servile State* (1912), contains no references to

195. Parliamentary Debates (House of Commons), 5th series, 20 (November 18, 1910), 101 (ibid., 154); increasing ministerial control of Parliament resulted from "impersonal developments" linked to changes in government's "role and functions" more than "conspiratorial" efforts of a "ruling elite" (ibid., 168–169).

196. For example, Lloyd George's proposed political coalition, prompted by the (Tory-dominated) House of Lords' frustration of the Liberal Budget (ibid., 197).

197. Ibid., 199.

198. A Conservative asked questions in the House of Commons; some young Conservatives paid for Cecil Chesterton's defense costs; the Parliamentary inquiry's Conservative members tried to discover the truth; the leading Conservative Commissioner Lord Cecil issued a restrained but damning report, rejected by the Liberal majority (M. Ward, *Gilbert Keith Chesterton*, op. cit., 356–357).

199. Paul Adelman, *The Decline of the Liberal Party 1910–1931*, op. cit., 32.

200. J. P. McCarthy, *Hilaire Belloc: Edwardian Radical*, op. cit., 85–86.

201. Ibid., 179–182.

202. Ibid., 135.

203. Unexpectedly large numbers claiming old age pensions suggested that "the stigma of destitution" and the "harsh deterrence principle" of the old Poor Law relief had "inhibited the really deserving aged poor from seeking assistance" (M. Bruce, *The Coming of the Welfare State* [London, 1966], 155; ibid., 218).

Jews.[204] Extremely influential, it warned not against socialism but against a Bismarckian welfare state under which the poor would be socially secure but permanently dispossessed.[205] *Europe and the Faith* (1920) briefly recapitulates Belloc's view of the Jewish role in capitalism's development, its beginnings in England "powerfully supported by the Jewish financial communities in the principal towns."[206] But his chief concern was Europe's progressive loss of Christian faith, dating from the Reformation: "Europe will return to the Faith, or she will perish. The Faith is Europe. And Europe is the Faith."[207]

The Jews (1922), Belloc's most controversial work, attacked anti-Semitism, stoked by "the sudden appearance of Jewish Bolshevism," but also blamed Jews for labeling as anti-Semitic anyone who attempted to discuss the "Jewish question."[208] Belloc castigates those who "would not look at the evidence against Dreyfus" because he was Jewish, but also those who "would not listen to the strong evidence" in his favor, insisting that all Dreyfusards were "dupes or knaves." Belloc said that the "mere fact that the Jews exist, let alone that they are powerful, poisons life for such a man."[209] But he complained of the "folly" of "the Jewish weapon of secrecy," which led such men to trawl through "the ramifications of anonymous finance" until they caught the "Jew who was behind the great industrial insurance schemes, the Jew who was behind such and such a metal monopoly, the Jew who was behind such and such a news agency, the Jew who financed such and such a politician." This "exposure" grew daily, and when publicly known, there would be "no answer to it."[210] Belloc drew "a definite line" between "the Anti-Semite" and those "attempting to solve the Jewish problem"; between those motivated by peace and those motivated by "antagonism"; between those whose object was "action against the Jew" and those who sought a "settlement."[211] Belloc warned: "Unfortunately we now know that he *can* do something. The Anti-Semite can persecute, he can attack. With a sufficient force behind him he can destroy."[212]

After the War Belloc rejected isolation or exile for Jews, returning to his earlier proposal, although he described it not as "segregation (which has a bad connotation)," but "*recognition*." Under this system, he said, Jews would "openly

204. H. Belloc, *The Servile State* (London: Constable & Co. Ltd., 1912/1950).

205. J.P. McCarthy, *Hilaire Belloc: Edwardian Radical*, op. cit., 288–289.

206. H. Belloc, *Europe and the Faith* (London: Constable & Co. Ltd., 1924), 296; the Jews of Spain were "allies" of the "Mohammedans" (Ibid., 248).

207. Ibid., 331.

208. H. Belloc, *The Jews* (Suffolk, England: Bloomfield Books, 1922/1983), 160–163.

209. Ibid., 149.

210. Ibid., 153.

211. Ibid., 155.

212. Ibid., 158.

recognize their wholly separate nationality and we on ours shall equally recognize that separate nationality, treat it without reserve as an alien thing, and respect it as a province of society outside our own."[213]

McCarthy says Belloc "would have regarded the creation of a distinct Jewish national state as quite logical,"[214] but at best he was a lukewarm Zionist. In 1910 he saw Zionism as "the view of the Jewish patriot—of the type of Zangwill" but did not "care to express a view on it" since only Jews were "qualified to do so." But "with hesitation," and "little qualified" as he was "to judge," he thought the idea "quite impracticable." Jews were "too much a part of Europe ever to be satisfied and successful" outside of Europe. Moreover, the very Jews who were "most firmly fixed among the other nations" were "the chief causes of the problem." If they could be absorbed, like the Huguenots, by their "alien surroundings," the "Jewish problem" would "in course of time solve itself. But this they cannot or will not do, and if I were a Jew, I should certainly not desire the absorption of my race."[215] After the Balfour Declaration Belloc had reminded Zionists that they "could not with justice speak of a Jewish State," and did not have any "territory, or responsible government, or centre, to which they might appeal."[216] In *The Jews* Belloc's fears of a Palestinian homeland emerged. He said it "could never have crossed [Balfour's] mind" that "a Jew governing Golgotha might be a source of serious irritation to important opponents," since Christian pilgrims would have to seek permission from "a local Jewish authority." He reiterated the sentiment in 1937.[217] Belloc admitted that Jewish settlers had bought their land and increased its value "immensely," not "merely by the pressure of millions of money," but by their "organizing power and . . . industry." It was "true, as the Zionist complains, that he took nothing from Palestine, but hugely added to what he had found there." Nevertheless, he said that "Islam hates and despises the Jew" and British policy "was to thrust an increasing body of Jews under the protection of British power, into the flesh of Islam."[218]

But, he added, this could not "be undone." If the British cut their losses "by abandoning the Jews to their fate," they would "certainly be destroyed by the surrounding power of Islam." In 1922 he had asked whether "Jews throughout the world" would be regarded as citizens of the projected Jewish state, or "regis-

213. Ibid., 5.

214. J. P. McCarthy, *Hilaire Belloc: Edwardian Radical*, op. cit., 339.

215. "The Jewish Question: Interview for the Jewish Chronicle with Mr. Hilaire Belloc, M.P.," *Jewish Chronicle*, August 12, 1910, 14.

216. H. Belloc, Address to the London University Zionist Society at the Jews' College ("Mr. Hilaire Belloc on the Jewish Problem," *Jewish Chronicle*, December 5, 1919, 26–27).

217. H. Belloc, *The Jews*, op. cit., l.

218. Ibid., lii.

tered as such," without their consent.[219] In 1937 he saw a "full immediate solution of the problem" as "impossible," since, as everyone knew, Britain had
"promised the Arabs their country if they would help us against the Turks."[220] In
fact, the British had established Transjordan, Lebanon, Syria, and Iraq while the
Jews awaited their promised homeland, but Belloc said that "it was not until the
new Prussian policy, attacking the Jewish race as a whole, was launched that
Zionism entered what may be called 'the acute phase.'" Only with the Arab
revolt of 1935–1936, he claimed, did "the West in general and England in particular" begin to "understand how serious the business was," but if the "Jewish question" was not settled "in justice and peace," the Gentile, not the Jew, would be to
blame.[221]

Belloc insisted that there was "grave and glaring injustice in the Nazi policy
against the Jews," which could not "solve any problem."[222] In confiscating Jewish property and depriving Jews of their livelihood the Nazis were committing
theft and breaking contracts.[223] But, he added, the "worst weakness of the
whole attack" was that it had "no philosophy behind it, or at least no philosophy of general application and of ascertainable principle."[224] Chesterton, as
seen, described the Nazi "philosophy" as "racial vanity gone mad," and Belloc
was underlining the view that this approach disqualified them from any claim
to be considered a civilized government, concluding: "But for my part, I say,
'Peace be to Israel.'"[225]

The Jews illustrates the contradictions of Belloc's philosophy on the "Jewish
question." He believed in a distinctive Jewish nationality but his support for
Zionism was halfhearted. He warned about anti-Semitism but also about the
"financial Jew." He satirized the anti-Semite's obsession while claiming that he
merely drew attention to the negative effect of Jews on Gentiles in order to prevent anti-Semitism. He failed to acknowledge in 1937 that the Nazi policy of
Jewish "recognition," similar to his own approach, had led to harassment and
violence for Jews rather than a more harmonious society.

Israel Zangwill accused Belloc of alleging that Jews hid their identity
"in order to carry on a secret Jewish plot."[226] Louis Golding maintained:
"In England Mr. Belloc is a professional Frenchman, in France a professional

219. Ibid., 232.
220. Ibid., liv–lv.
221. Ibid., xxv.
222. Ibid., xl.
223. Ibid., xlii.
224. Ibid., xlv.
225. Ibid., 308.
226. I. Zangwill, Speech, *Jewish Chronicle*, August 4, 1922, 26.

Englishman. In both . . . he is a professional anti-Semite."[227] Abandoning caution, the *Jewish Chronicle* savaged *The Jews*: Belloc's "exploit" would "not stop at the Jews," who were "an element that baulks and restrains the Romish Church from rolling back the thoughts and minds of medieval barbarism, if the school . . . for which [he] writes ever has its way." The paper alleged that Jews might be "irreligious and unobservant as Jews," but "the mere fact" of their existence was an "offence" to "the exponents of the Christianity for which Mr. Belloc writes. . . . Eliminate Jews, degrade Jews, belittle Jews, and the Romish Church as envisaged by Mr. Belloc has disposed of a check to its ambitions." The book was presented as a "friendly act towards Jews" because Belloc knew that anti-Semitism was a "vulgar thing" and, "having been very freely indulged in of late," had "grossly nauseated the true Christian"—a type much more numerous than Belloc's audience. The threat he posed seemed small, but "gangrene," which appeared "in a very small portion of the . . . body," if ignored, was "surely fatal." Belloc's "lying pen" had concluded by wishing peace to Israel, but this was dismissed as "humbug," as was his dedication to his Jewish secretary. His self-portrayal as a friend of the Jews was seen as mere "Jesuistry." As for his warning against anti-Semitism: "To provoke further animosity against the Jews, to propagate a deeper prejudice against them, to fix upon them allegations which are groundless, and statements for which there is no warrant, and all of it done under the cloak of a professed friendship for the Jewish people—ugh! it is sickening." Belloc, the paper concluded, "would be as ruthless in his search for Jewish origin," as "meticulous in his quest for the least drop of Jewish blood" as "that servant of his Church, Torquemada." This was no longer a "Jewish question" but a "Christian question."[228] A reader said Belloc was "more dangerous than most anti-Semites because he pretended to be a

---

227. L. Golding, "A Rationale of Anti-Semitism," *Jewish Chronicle*, September 23, 1921, ii.

228. "What is this Christian Question? It is the problem of what to do with or for those who profess to call themselves Christian, and who yet neglect the very first principles of the faith to which they nominally adhere and the doctrines of its great founder"; mostly, Jews changed their names because of "increasing prejudice" and the "blind hatred and fanaticism" that had "its roots in the Christian Question"; and it was not only "Jewish ideals and Jewish aspirations and Jewish ideas that these recidivists would crush or drown in chaos, disorder, and bloodshed" but "every liberal idea, every liberal movement, every liberal thought that animates the heart of any man anywhere" ("Mentor," "The Christian Question," *Jewish Chronicle*, March 31, 1922, 11–13); "Mr. Belloc thinks that to call a Jew an Englishman is an absurdity and really a contradiction in terms" ("Mr. Belloc's Book," ibid, April 7, 1922, 7–8). Belloc should have heeded the Sermon on the Mount—although, unlike him, "the bulk of the German anti-Semites, the supporters of the *Voelkische Partei*, who proudly proclaim themselves heathens" saw the Sermon as "too Jewish" and believed "the mark of the true Teuton" was to "hate his enemy" ("The Letters of Benammi, CCCLIIL: 'Love Your Enemies,'" ibid., August 13, 1926, 12).

friend."[229] Belloc, meanwhile, appeared unaware that people who take pains to list a friend's supposed faults seldom retain that friendship for long.

Jewish critics warned of Belloc provoking a return to historical Christian anti-Semitism, but although his and Chesterton's writings bolstered the confidence of the Catholic community,[230] there was no rush to religious anti-Semitism. Catholic-Jewish relations had been forged by common experience of prejudice and neither community wished to sacrifice a positive relationship.[231] Belloc continued to be seen as anti-Semitic, to the extent that his opinion was cited against Jewish conspiracy theories promoted by *The Morning Post.* The *Jewish Chronicle* said that Belloc, who could not "be regarded as an enemy of anti-Semitism," agreed with the view that Jews had no "serious connection with the French Revolution."[232] But the paper praised Dean Inge of St Paul's "scathing criticism" of *The Jews,*[233] and also Lady Astor, who proclaimed her Zionism and denounced Belloc as "simply a maniac regarding the Jews." She said she admired people who had "inspiration" and were "religious. Maybe that is why I admire the Jews." She recalled once telling Arthur Balfour that she "did not like the Jews. I had never met them. When I became acquainted with Dr. Weizmann, it was the first time that I had actually met a real, genuine Jew," adding that Weizmann was "a splendid man." In fact, Astor had "met a real Jew" before Weizmann,[234] whom, according to her biographer, she publicly embarrassed.[235] With a well-deserved reputation for anti-Semitism, she exemplified the tendency to denounce anti-Semitism in opponents, often using the opportunity to

---

229. "Mr. Belloc's Anti-Semitism: Address by Mr. Israel Cohen," *Jewish Chronicle,* May 19, 1922, 30); Herman Cohen suggested an inquiry into *The Jews* but some at the *Spectator* suggested that Belloc chair it ("The 'Spectator' and the Jews: Proposed Committee of Enquiry!" ibid, May 12, 1922, 12).

230. W. Sheed, "ChesterBelloc and the Jews," op. cit.

231. A Jewish obituary to Cardinal Bourne praised his 1913 letter condemning claims of Jewish ritual sacrifice, written in response to the Chief Rabbi's appeal; also his 1906 condemnation of "anti-Jewish atrocities in Russia"; he had criticized the establishment of the Jewish national home in Palestine, but "spoke 'without the smallest anti-Jewish prejudice,'" thus: "We prefer . . . to forget that attack . . . and to remember only the qualities of a great man and a splendid religious leader" (*Jewish Chronicle,* January 4, 1935, in Thomas Moloney, *Westminster, Whitehall and the Vatican: The Role of Cardinal Hinsley 1935–43* [Tunbridge Wells, Kent: Burns & Oates, 1985], 208).

232. "Unjust and Unfair Charges," *Jewish Chronicle,* August 6, 1920, 12.

233. Catholics were "far more troublesome citizens than the Jews," who had "on the whole, a rather high level of intelligence" ("Dean Inge on 'The Jews': Mr. Belloc's Book: A Scathing Criticism," *Jewish Chronicle,* May 5, 1922, 21).

234. There was not much anti-Semitism in England, and "the late Mr. Aaronson, the agronomist . . . was a very fine man . . . who often visited her home" (Lady Astor, Interview, New York *Jewish Daily News* in "Lady Astor on Zionism and Mr. Belloc: Appreciation of Dr. Weizmann," *Jewish Chronicle,* May 12, 1922, 21).

235. N. Rose, *The Cliveden Set: Portrait of an Exclusive Fraternity,* op. cit., 184.

attack Catholics.[236] As the *Jewish Chronicle* reported, it soon became apparent that Inge's remarks were "palpably influenced as much by his dislike of Roman Catholicism (to which creed Mr. Belloc subscribes) as by his regard for Jews, or his appreciation of Judaism."[237] The Dean had also remarked that "the Jews had better build their Holy City and Temple in New York, where there were enough Jews and plenty of Gentiles to fleece." In response to Israel Zangwill's rebuke he claimed to have been joking, but as Jewish critics pointed out, the "gloomy Dean" was not usually regarded as "jocose." Nonetheless, Zangwill said they should remember Inge's criticism against "the Belloc Book," whose "hilariousness . . . was unsuspected even by the author. On the whole, they were in the Dean's debt, and it was safer that Jews should owe to Christians than they to us." While singling out Chesterton regarding anti-Semitism,[238] Zangwill claimed that "few countries in the world" were "free from the virus" although there had been "some disquiet" since the War regarding the "Bolshevist Bogey," mainly because Jews were "foreigners. Bolshevism is foreign. Therefore Jews are Bolshevists."[239]

Bernard Shaw claimed the "persecution complex, which makes the Jews of the Continent so sensitive," had "no *raison d'être* in England." He claimed Belloc was "[t]he nearest imitation of an anti-Semite among our public men," and in comparison, Shaw himself would be a "pro-Jew, if such a classification existed in England." But compared with Urbain Gohier, Belloc was "a modern

---

236. During the Great War at a dinner party Nancy warned her guests against being charmed by Weizmann: "'He's a great charmer. He will convert you to his point of view. He is the only decent Jew I have ever met.' Stunned into dead silence, the embarrassed guests looked down at their plates, at a loss how to react. It was a pattern to be repeated many times"; she also alleged the American press was controlled by Jews: in New York in 1937 she complained to reporters of "the appalling anti-German propaganda here"—if "the Jews" were behind it they had "gone too far. And it will react on them" (ibid., 181–184); Astor sometimes "expressed herself in deplorable terms that carried a clear anti-Semitic ring. Did this signify genuine intolerance or was it merely another manifestation of Nancy's celebrated lack of tact? Most likely a mixture of both" (ibid., 39–41).

237. *Jewish Chronicle*, June 23, 1922, 7; "the Dean was not the man who would have defended the Jews had he not seen the opportunity for taking the offensive against a prominent Catholic like Mr. Belloc" by perpetrating "'a harmless joke' with Jews and Catholics as his subject." ("A Harmless Joke," ibid., May 22, 1925, 7–8).

238. "Napoleon and Palestine: Mr. Philip Guedalla's Arthur Davis Memorial Lecture: Mr. Lloyd George on Zionism," *Jewish Chronicle*, May 29, 1925, 17; Dean Inge "not being devoid of conscience, had "empowered" Zangwill to express "regret for his frivolous remark," so it remained to be seen whether Chesterton, who had complained that "the Jews had allowed a Protestant to insult them, whereas they had raged against Mr. Belloc and his book," would "meet the situation with candour, with verbal contortions, or with silence" ("Mr. Israel Zangwill on 'Jewish Influence': Reply to Allegation in 'Church Times,'" ibid., June 19, 1925, 11).

239. I. Zangwill, Interview, "Anti-Semitism in England," *Jewish Chronicle*, April 23, 1926, 16.

Maccabean." Despite this, he concluded that "anyone in England" could see that Shaw was "on the side of the Jews" just as Belloc was "against them."[240]

In *The Cruise of the Nona* (1925) Belloc could "pretend to no certain conclusion" about Dreyfus, nor could anyone not present in court or familiar with the documentation. He was certain, however, that the case caused "four years of war" because it "destroyed the French Intelligence Bureau and so permitted the German surprise on Mons and Charleroi."[241] Even his admirers acknowledge that "[o]ne of Belloc's perpetual itches was 'the Jewish problem'" but it was "more a Belloc problem, for it gained him the tag of being an anti-semite." This led Belloc to "prove that he had no quarrel with Jewry," prompting him to write *The Jews*.[242] Jews continued to notice his historical works,[243] and, although, unlike Chesterton, he was appalled by the idea of Jews controlling the holy places,[244] the *Jewish Chronicle* looked more favorably on *The Battle Ground* (1936). The paper said the book contained "fierce anti-Jewish bias (clearly, as now appears, religious in origin)" but also asserted Jewish "contempt for social inequality... a hatred of it." Belloc had remarked that the Jewish millionaire did not "mistake his wealth for excellence," nor did "his fellow-Jews think him the greater for it, but only more fortunate." To Belloc's "main contention" that the Jews, notwithstanding their "strong spiritual motive," could not "maintain themselves in Palestine" without help from "a great European power" because of Muslim "hostility," the paper insisted: "[A] Jewish Palestine [had] existed before in the midst of a hostile world. *Pace* Mr. Belloc, it could exist again."[245] Characteristically, *The Battle Ground* was respectful to Judaism, but in a significant departure, it also affirmed Jewish claims to Palestine.[246] Belloc also affirmed the Jewish claim to be the Chosen Race, maintaining that of "all historical facts proceeding from antiquity" Israel was "alone... permanent and

240. G. B. Shaw, Letter, *Jewish Chronicle*, February 12, 1923, 16–17; Urbain Gohier (born Degoulet, pen-name Blümchen Isaac), a pro-military, pro-monarchist, left-wing, Vichy supporter and Malthusian pro-fascist, was preoccupied with "Judeo-Bolshevik" conspiracies and circulated the *Protocols of the Elders of Zion*.

241. H. Belloc, *The Cruise of the Nona* (Harmondsworth, Middx.: Penguin Books Ltd., 1925/1958), 158–159.

242. H. Belloc, *Belloc: A Biographical Anthology*, op. cit., 196.

243. Belloc's book on Cromwell made no reference to his readmission of the Jews to England: "Mr. Belloc's views on the subject, one would have anticipated, would have been more exciting [than John Buchan's], if less conventional" ("Notes on Books and Authors," *Jewish Chronicle*, November 2, 1934, 22).

244. J. P. Corrin, *G. K. Chesterton and Hilaire Belloc: The Battle Against Modernity*, op. cit., 67.

245. C. Roth, "Palestine in History: 'The Battle Ground,'" *Jewish Chronicle*, April 3, 1936, 29.

246. "Of the wandering tribes" entering South Syria in the 12th century B.C., "one group was to prove of the last importance—to Europe and therefore to the world... 'Bene Israel': that is, the descendants (or 'children') of Israel: twelve closely connected clans called after the twelve sons of Jacob" (H. Belloc, *The Battle Ground* [London: Cassell & Company Ltd., 1936], 81).

alone always provocative." It had "endured" and had "every mark of enduring to the end."[247] Contra the *Jewish Chronicle*'s reference to the book's hostility to Jewish "revolutionary tendencies," *The Battle Ground* viewed them as evidence of a "profound, active and undying passion for equality ... in the presence of an alien society," which led the "'least aristocratic' of the peoples" to "protest against a hierarchy of rank in the structure of any society which at the worst oppressed, or at the best was alien to them." Hence the Jew had "always been a revolutionary" and had "suffered and triumphed in that capacity." It was "not for nothing" that the modern-day "revolutionary prophet" was "a Mordecai, for Mordecai is the real Jewish name concealed under the pseudonym of Marx." Belloc's approval of Jewish "revolutionary tendencies"[248] was in spite of his suspicion of Bolshevism, while Chesterton, Shaw, and Wells, who also approved of Jewish revolutionary tendencies as the obverse of their hostility to Jewish capitalism, were more sympathetic to Bolshevism per se.[249]

The Crusades (1937) contains few Jewish references and similarly strives for balance,[250] but *The Jews* sealed Belloc's reputation as an anti-Semite. This was despite the 1937 edition's attacks on Nazi anti-Semitism, and the *Jewish Chronicle*'s own report of August 1933 noting an article by a "gentleman" who was "Catholic by faith," of whom there had been "good reason for Jews to criticise," but which made "a sane and heartening presentation of the case against the German persecution." It praised his "emphatic declaration" that he could not see how any Catholic could "support or condone" what had happened, and his "denunciation of Hitlerist oppression as "definitely opposed to good morals" under which innocent Jews had "been reduced ... through no fault of their own and merely by accident of birth, to penury at a moment's notice. 'How,' he asks, 'can that possibly be excused?'" Belloc referred to "a number of German Jewish friends, men of the highest distinction in the world of intellect" who had lost everything, describing the crime against them as "abominable and barefaced robbery." He had, the paper said, "utter[ed] a powerful protest" against those who kept silent "in the presence of 'flagrant injustice.' 'They themselves will be poisoned,' he exclaims, 'if they do not protest, for it is their duty to pro-

247. Ibid., 83–84; Belloc does not blame Jews for the Crucifixion (ibid., 267) and gives a balanced but gloomy assessment of Jewish Palestine (ibid., 352–353).

248. Ibid., 134–135.

249. Marx repudiated his Jewish background, blamed capitalism on Judaism and tried to "solve his own Jewish problem (and that of so many of his disciples) by slaying capitalism" (Y. Slezkine, *The Jewish Century* [Princeton/Oxford: Princeton University Press, 2004], 60); see Chapter Five.

250. Predominantly German Crusaders massacred Jews of the Rhine "by way of a send off, storming or failing to storm the palaces of the bishops who would protect such victims, murdering in particular the Chief Rabbi of Mayence to prove their contempt for the special protection of him by the great lay rulers" (H. Belloc, *The Crusades: The World's Debate* [1937/1992], 20).

test.'"[251] The paper even defended Belloc against *The Record*'s accusations of widespread "Germany-baiting," insisting that there was "nothing" of that in his "Catholic conscience," only "a warning note of alarm. Reasonable men" could decide whether Belloc or the *Record* was "the better friend of the world, or even, in the long run, of Germany herself."[252] But a Jewish commentator writing as "Benammi" claimed Belloc was "inclined to accept" *The Protocols of the Elders of Zion*, constructing upon them "a theory of hatred." While praising the *Church Times* for denouncing anti-Semitism, Bennami said "[t]he problem of anti-Semitism" was not "a Jewish problem" but "a Christian problem."[253] This was in spite of *The Jews* emphasizing the need to "take the Jew in his right proportions, rid our mind of exaggeration in his regard—especially of the conception of some inhuman ability capable of conducting a plot of diabolical ingenuity and magnitude,"[254] and insisting that the idea of the Russian Revolution as the culmination of "a vast age-long plot," would "not hold water."[255]

Nonetheless, Belloc's biographer believed that he harbored fascist sympathies, and that although he "always cherished the original democratic dream," and "would have hated fascism if he had been obliged to live under it," he "seemed to think that, on the whole, fascism was a good thing for foreigners."[256] In 1936 British fascists cited *The Jews* in support of anti-Semitism,[257] and although this was nothing to do with Belloc, in the same year he "visited the Spanish Civil War battlefields . . . quite obviously he was pro-Franco," and interviewed the dictator.[258] Despite this, the *Jewish Chronicle* reported in 1936 that Belloc helped arrange the tenth anniversary commemoration for Israel Zangwill with "distinguished" friends including Shaw.[259] In 1938 the paper noted: "Writing in the little anti-Semitic *Weekly Review* for December 1, Mr. Hilaire Belloc denounces the bestial torture and murder of Jews by Nazis at Sachsenhausen, reported in the *News Chronicle*. 'If it is true,' he declares, 'the

---

251. "Hilaire Belloc Speaks Out," *Jewish Chronicle*, August 4, 1933, 6; the Bishop of Gloucester's "eminently correct" condemnation of Nazi anti-Jewish persecution was marred by his "lusty castigation" of German Jews as a "not altogether . . . pleasant element"—"How different a conclusion from that of Mr. Hilaire Belloc" ("Jewry: Week by Week," ibid, August 11, 1933, 5).

252. "Jewry: week by week. A Spoiled 'Record,'" *Jewish Chronicle*, September 1, 1933, 8.

253. [Mortimer Epstein] Benammi, "The Letters of Benammi, No. 745: Common-Sense About the Jews," *Jewish Chronicle*, February 16, 1934, 23.

254. H. Belloc, *The Jews*, op. cit., 266–267.

255. Ibid., 168.

256. R. Speaight, *The Property Basket: Recollections of a Divided Life*, op. cit., 372–373.

257. Addressing a fascist meeting, Raven Thomson said it "foretold these popular risings" against Jews (*Jewish Chronicle*, July 31, 1936, 22–23).

258. H. Belloc, *Belloc: A Biographical Anthology*, op. cit., 378.

259. L. G. Bowman, "The Humour of Israel Zangwill," *Jewish Chronicle*, October 23, 1936, 16; Belloc sent a tribute to Zangwill's Memorial meeting along with Chaim Weizmann, J. B. Priestley and Dr. Stephen Wise ("In Memory of Zangwill: Impressive Meeting at Kingsway Hall: Tributes to a Great

atrocity is on a scale and of a kind unparalleled in what has hitherto been the civilised Europe of to-day.'" It adds that Belloc was "careful ... and rightly so, to condition his denunciation upon the accuracy or otherwise of the newspaper report."[260] In 1940 Belloc was listed on the Council of the Polish Relief Fund in a *Jewish Chronicle* appeal for Jews who had suffered under Nazi occupation, along with Chesterton's friend Father Martindale, Douglas Woodruff, the Archbishop of Canterbury, the Cardinal Archbishop of Westminster, and the Duke of Norfolk.[261]

Belloc's *The Catholic and the War* (1940) again insisted that those who dismissed the "Jewish question" helped exacerbate it, but also that Nazi Germany had "treated its Jewish subjects with a contempt for justice which even if there had been no other action of the kind in other departments would be a sufficient warranty for determining its elimination from Europe." He argued that "the Jew" was morally equal to other human beings, a responsible creature of God, "suffering from original sin, with no inherent vices," and with a "full claim not only to justice but to charity." Cruelty to Jews, he maintained, was "as odious as cruelty to any human being, whether that cruelty be moral in the form of insult, or physical." There was "no special duty to Jews more than our duty to them as human beings and our fellowship with them in the common dominion of God," but while not "bound to go out on crusade to rescue Jews ... any more than ... Japanese or Irishmen," Catholics were "bound to consider" Jewish claims to "general justice and the amenities as well as the just rules of our civilisation." Belloc remarked that Germans viewed the persecution as "the most popular" Nazi action and "unfortunately" it was "almost equally popular" with non-Germans: "You may hear men saying on every side: 'However, there is one thing I do agree with and that is the way they have settled the Jews.'" This response was "directly immoral," and the "more danger" of its increase, the more necessity for "denouncing it. The action of the enemy towards the Jewish race" was "in morals intolerable." Contracts had been broken, careers destroyed, and Jews "treated with the most hideous and disgusting cruelty." This "crudity" was "the mark of barbarism" typical of "the Prussian." Belloc warned that if the Nazis went "unpunished (and only defeat in war can punish them)," Europe's decline would "proceed to catastrophe." He concluded that tales of Nazis atrocities in Poland—"[w]holesale killing, wholesale looting,

Jew: Distinguished Speakers," ibid, October 30, 1936, 14–15); during the War a reader maintained that Belloc, "by no means a friend of our people, felt compelled to state that: 'Jews as a mass are a poor race, because money-making was not their principle object. This is the truth. Even Shylock himself preferred a pound of inedible flesh to thrice his 3,000 ducats'" (A. Solomons, Letter, "Jews and the Money Danger," ibid., February 14, 1941, 18–19).

260. "Horror—and Humbug," *Jewish Chronicle*, December 9, 1938, 8.

261. *Jewish Chronicle*, September 20, 1940, 6–7.

wholesale enslavement," the "regular accompaniments of Prussian war"—showed them as "beyond the pale. The only excuse offered for them is that, perhaps, they have been exaggerated in the telling," but of their "general horror" there was "no doubt."[262]

The Private Belloc and the Jews

While not dominated by Jewish issues, Belloc's correspondence[263] offers insights into his approach to the "Jewish question." In 1924 he had described Nesta Webster's *The Cause of the World Unrest* as a "lunatic book," but in 1906, during his parliamentary election campaign, he told Chesterton: "It is huge fun. I am now out against all Vermin: Notably South African Jews. The Devil is let loose: let all men beware."[264] He asked Maurice Baring about a book on "the Jewish Massacres," which explained "why the Jews / Are massacred in Russia, of which land / We here in England cannot understand."[265] Belloc did not concentrate on the Jewish background of individuals, even when referring to the Isaacs brothers and the Marconi affair,[266] but in 1915 he wrote: "[I]f the German Empire is badly beaten the big financial and Jewish force in modern Germany, which is enormous, will desert the Hohenzollerns. *They would prefer a divided Germany.*"[267] When *The Jews* was unkindly received by the Jews, Belloc sought advice from a non-Jewish friend on "the bad reception of my Jew Book. . . . It saddens me: for if the Jews don't accept a just solution in time they are doomed to a renewal of misery."[268] But he believed that the "thoroughly despised . . . oppressive and dreadfully corrupt" European parliamentary system was "in practice" governed "by a few rich men with an absurd preponderance of financial backing and largely Jewish power. That can't last."[269]

These privately expressed beliefs agreed with his public statements, but the latter were expressed with deadly seriousness, while Belloc's correspondence

262. Prussia joined hands "spiritually with her Communist ally," and the "emotion aroused by the bestial degradation of humanity" would be "enough to justify every effort" to destroy the German Government; but there was "no need to single out the abominable treatment of the Jewish race"—it was "part of a general attitude" for which they "must be called to account"; the "only moral agency" capable of this was the Catholic Church's "moral theory" (H. Belloc, *The Catholic and the War* [London: Burns Oates, 1940], 28–31).

263. Few letters in Speaight's collection are reproduced in full (H. Belloc, *Letters from Hilaire Belloc*, op. cit., x).

264. H. Belloc, Postcard to G. K. Chesterton, 1906, M. Ward, *Gilbert Keith Chesterton*, op. cit., 288.

265. H. Belloc, Letter to Maurice Baring, January 20, 1907, H. Belloc, *Letters from Hilaire Belloc*, op. cit., 10–11.

266. H. Belloc, Letter to Maurice Baring, 1913, ibid., 53–54.

267. H. Belloc, Letter to J. S. Phillimore, January 21, 1915, ibid., 67.

268. H. Belloc, Letter to Mrs. Reginald Balfour, February 24, 1922, ibid., 115–116.

269. H. Belloc, Letter to Mrs. Reginald Balfour, June 28, 1922, ibid., 122.

satirized everything, including the Jews and his obsession with them. But he also attacked Nazi anti-Semitism, and his black humor was not necessarily indicative of hatred: he was very fond of children, but they met horrible fates in his poems.[270] He made fun of the rich and of Americans,[271] and told "the dons" and the wealthy: "Remember that you will shortly die."[272] Belloc satirized all of these when sailing to New York in 1937: "Talking of Yids the swarm of Yids on board this sparsely populated craft is extraordinary: there are hardly 100 people on board and at least 81 are incredible: monsters of the deep." They formed "the bulk" of north transatlantic travel, but would not "take German boats, they crowd into French, Dutch and English." Of the American passengers, Belloc claimed: "Americans are vocally and loudly and simply and in child-like fashion Jew-haters. So I live in hopes of an explosion before we reach the beatitudes of New York. Wouldn't it be amusing if this next outburst of blind rage against the poor old Jews were to blow up in New York?" His sardonic humor was also directed at the "Oxford dons," "still reeling under the blow of their beloved Prussia having attacked Israel," suggesting that "if their Anglo-Saxons (as they call the Yankees) were to follow up they would think the world had come to an end. If or when the New Yorkites rise against the Jews there will be a pogrom: for the Americans yield to none in promiscuous violence and bloodletting."[273]

But in 1923, visiting America, Belloc had defended Jews: "The Jew question is a fearful bore over here. Those who know I have written a book on it take it for granted that I am in approval of a general massacre." This, he remarked, showed "the usual extreme confusion Americans reach when they have worked themselves up on the matter," but that "the very much smaller number" who had "*actually read* my book, disagree with its judicial tone: they want blood and thunder." Most had not read it, however: "[I]n Toronto and Montreal, Buffalo, New York, Pittsburg, Boston, everywhere rave and howl against the Jews. It may or may not come to an outbreak—on the whole I think not—but it makes the life of the mass of Jews here—who are poor—very hard." The law was biased against them, and they were "insulted in public and refused entry to Clubs and even hotels and in general made to feel that they are enemies. What a life! Fancy some wretched man coming with his family from, say, Poland, and landing into this!" He claimed that the American, with "no tradition or habit in the matter . . . never appreciates complexity," merely feeling "the racial friction"

270. "Do let me tell you again how much I think London . . . is of advantage to one's own life and to (much more) children" (H. Belloc, Letter to Mrs. Katharine Asquith, December 28, 1920, ibid., 146–147).

271. J.B. Morton, *Hilaire Belloc: A Memoir*, op. cit., 137.

272. H. Belloc, *Advice to the Rich* (1926), H. Belloc, *Belloc: A Biographical Anthology*, op. cit., 270.

273. H. Belloc, Letter to Katharine Asquith, February 5, 1937, A.N. Wilson, *Hilaire Belloc*, op. cit., 344–345.

and reacting with "violent revulsion."[274] Belloc prided himself on his Jewish friendships, dedicating *The Jews* to Ruby Goldsmith, his secretary since 1908, but described it as his "admirable yid book." Belloc was personally courteous, but Wilson suggests he "was protesting too much" and that the Jewish issue "interested him to the point of obsession."[275] Nonetheless, his old age was not spent "shuffling about in a state of permanent disgruntlement with the Jews, or the Rich, or the Dons."[276]

It provoked Belloc's ire to be singled out as anti-Semitic when, as he satirically remarked in 1932, the press were so "happy" about Hitler's election: "[T]he party for immediate action, of which the wretched Hitler is a figure head and the clever Yid Rosenberg the manager, has had not only a notable success but a big promise for the future." Rosenberg was not Jewish,[277] and although Chesterton came to see Hitler as a tool of capitalism and the "Prussians," he did not portray him as being manipulated by Jews. In 1935 Belloc reported that "The Jews" were "becoming masters" of the Holy Land, "and that means great trouble for the future.... I came in by way of Nazareth, which is a cool, delightful little town and happily full of Catholicism. The Protestant flood of money and the Jewish intrusion seem to have spared it."[278] Wilson says that on the "Zionist question" it "has perhaps taken longer for the power of Belloc's prophecies to be seen." His stance would seem "almost comically, medievally superstitious" to non-Catholics, but as *The Jews* made clear, "[i]t was, quite simply, that no good would come of handing over the Holy Places to the Jews," which he saw as the "most perilous of all the results of Zionism."[279] Still, Belloc called Hitler "that lachrymose windbag"[280] and despite his fear of communism opposed him when many regarded Germany as "the bulwark against Russia and Marxism." According to Morton, during the War he was barely able to restrain himself

274. H. Belloc, Letter to Mrs. Reginald Balfour, March 17, 1923, R. Speaight, *The Life of Hilaire Belloc*, op. cit., 454–455.

275. A.N. Wilson, *Hilaire Belloc*, op. cit., 188; "Belloc's 'admirable Yid book'" would "go unread today"; it was "too upsetting"; however, it contained "two very chilling prophecies. The antagonism between Israel and Europe would lead ... to greater and more hideous persecution of European Jewry"; the "more paradoxical" prophecy was that "a Zionist movement would exacerbate anti-Jewish feeling in Europe"—the "persecutors would, for the first time in history, be able to say, 'Go back to your own country,'" making things worse for "the poor Jews left behind" (ibid., 259–260).

276. Ibid., 373; although he couldn't get over Oxford's refusal to grant him a fellowship, and of "the 'professional politicians'" (J.B. Morton, *Hilaire Belloc: A Memoir*, op. cit., 173), in old age and with memory failing, rather than becoming more impatient "[t]he reverse happened" (ibid., 175).

277. H. Belloc, Letter to Duff Cooper, March 14, 1932, H. Belloc, *Letters from Hilaire Belloc*, op. cit., 227–228; see Chapter Five.

278. H. Belloc, Letter to Mrs. Reginald Balfour, May 4, 1935, ibid., 250–251.

279. H. Belloc, *The Jews* (1922/1937), 244, in A.N. Wilson, *Hilaire Belloc*, op. cit., 260.

280. H. Belloc, Letter to Lady Phipps, March 16, 1936, H. Belloc, *Letters from Hilaire Belloc*, R. Speaight, ed. (London: Hollis & Carter, 1958), 255–256.

when "some highly intelligent" lunch partners began praising the Germans, implying that "their gifts of organization and administration fitted them to rule Europe."[281] Like Chesterton, Belloc believed that Germany and Russia were "equally determined to destroy the moral code of Christian domination, and to subjugate by armed force whatever should oppose them."[282] Chesterton in 1934 had appeared reluctant to believe Hitler a Superman, and in 1940 Belloc claimed he was "not remarkable . . . save as a commentary on the wretched half-baked Germans, full of virtue, kindly and child-like, but damnably immature." Hitler told they were "demi-gods," and they allowed him to treat them as "slaves."[283]

It could be argued that Belloc's real animus was against Germany rather than anti-Semitism, and that Belloc—and Chesterton—attacked German anti-Semitism while refraining from criticizing French anti-Semitism regarding Dreyfus. Much earlier, both linked their dislike of Germany to what they saw as Jewish influence. But both protested Nazi anti-Semitism at a time when many prominent people not only sympathized with Germany but blamed "the Jews" for anti-Semitism and even for the War.[284] The *Chesterbelloc*'s Francophilia was certainly piqued by the lack of English reaction to Hitler's anti-Semitism, in stark contrast to the storm of anti-French feeling surrounding Dreyfus. Nonetheless, Chesterton did not defend French anti-Semitism, and called Edouard Drumont a "ferocious Anti-Semite."[285] Belloc was accused of concealing his true attitudes to Jews, but in attacking Nazi anti-Semitism he was merely following his "rational" approach to the "Jewish question," which involved argument and persuasion, not violence.

But Belloc did believe in the influence of "race" on culture,[286] and it is possible that the *Chesterbelloc*, by discussing the "Jewish question," became a tool of Hitler. The German dictator admitted that anti-Semitism was "beyond all ques-

---

281. J. B. Morton, *Hilaire Belloc: A Memoir*, op. cit., 163.

282. Ibid., 158.

283. H. Belloc, Letter to Evan Charteris, February 3, 1940, ibid., 287–288.

284. Founded in September 1935, the Anglo-German Fellowship favored increasing commerce between the two countries; members included Bank of England Governor Montague Norman and *Times* editor Geoffrey Dawson; its chairman Lord Mount Temple resigned after Kristallnacht in November 1938; see: A. Liaquat, *Lords of Finance: the Bankers who broke the World* (London: Wm. Heinemann, 2009).

285. Divorced people demanding re-marriage in church were comparable to "some ferocious Anti-Semite like M. Drumont" being "buried as a Jew with all the rites of the Synagogue" (G.K. Chesterton, "The Tragedies of Marriage," G.K. Chesterton, *Brave New Family: G.K. Chesterton on Men & Women, Children, Sex, Divorce, Marriage & the Family*, A. de Silva, ed. [San Francisco: Ignatius Press, 1990], 226).

286. Recruiting white men "not corrupted by Levantine or negro blood" could make for a "good" Belgian army providing "instruction" was "sufficient" and "the discipline strict" (H. Belloc, Letter to Major-General Guy Dawnay, May 23, 1939, H. Belloc, *Letters from Hilaire Belloc*, op. cit., 276–277).

tion the most important weapon" in his "propaganda arsenal," to be "exported" to "all countries" in order to undermine them,[287] although, as robust critics of Nazi anti-Semitism and defenders of Jews Chesterton and Belloc would be viewed as "Jew-lackeys."[288] But Belloc expressed his views unrestrainedly in private,[289] insisting that because discussing "Jewish power" provoked "violent emotion" it was "essential to avoid anything like the suspicion of fanaticism. It destroys all one's case and weakens all one's efforts."[290] This might suggest that his restraint was merely strategic. Moreover, he appeared to approve of Franco, whose campaign Hitler supported. And yet Spain remained neutral during the War and even offered a haven for persecuted Jews.[291] If Belloc was concealing his "true colors" he concealed them even more effectively in the age of Dictators, ignoring the opportunities offered by fascism and anti-Semitism for "dealing thoroughly" with the "Jewish question." Unlike Lord Rosebery, Belloc spoke respectfully of the Jewish religion[292] although he was less sensitive to Catholics, who expected pietism but were "often disappointed" because he "was more likely to shock them by a jovially disrespectful way of talking about religious matters."[293] Such factors suggest that Belloc's restraint on the "Jewish question" was not meant to conceal a private agenda, but sprang from a desire not to jeopardize his "rational" approach by public displays of irrationality.

The Legacy of Belloc

Belloc's *Jewish Chronicle* obituary in 1953 stated: "He wrote that the Jews were a separate nationality and should be treated as such and segregated from general society as they were in the medieval Church-State." While correctly citing *The Jews*' rejection of Jewish conspiracy theories, and that Bolshevism was not a Jewish plot,[294] the paper quotes: "There is no doubt that the Nazi attack was

---

287. "My Jews are a valuable hostage given to me by the democracies. Antisemitic propaganda in all countries is an almost indispensable medium for the extension of our political campaign" (H. Rauschning, *Hitler Speaks* (1939, 223), in J. Parkes, *Antisemitism*, op. cit., 88.

288. Ibid., 95.

289. At Maurice Baring's flat Belloc "discoursed" with "indescribable gusto and vehemence" of the Catholic Church, the Chanson de Roland, Ronsard and the Pyrenees and "the Jewish Peril" (R. Speaight, *The Life of Hilaire Belloc*, op. cit., 111).

290. H. Belloc, Letter to Maurice Baring, August 27, 1913, ibid., 363.

291. There were also "well-organized" escape routes for Jews (M. Gilbert, *The Righteous: The unsung heroes of the Holocaust* [London: Black Swan, 2003], 336).

292. The Liberals were sitting "with the fly-blown phylacteries of obsolete policies bound round their foreheads" and "mumbling their incantations to themselves" while the world was "marching and revolving" (Lord Rosebery, Speech, *Rosebery*, R. R. James, ed. [New York, 1963], 425–426, in J.P. McCarthy, *Hilaire Belloc: Edwardian Radical*, op. cit., 71).

293. J.B. Morton, *Hilaire Belloc: A Memoir*, op. cit., 13.

294. H. Belloc, *The Jews*, op. cit., xv.

sincere.... But can it be fruitful?" The obituary writer acknowledged that he "vigorously condemned the German atrocities on a number of occasions." But, once again quoting from *The Jews*: "[H]e insisted that 'this shock has cleared the air ... no one is now afraid to discuss the Jewish question as they used to be.'" The paper overlooked Belloc's satirical approach, as well as his rejection of Nazism, which emerged at the conclusion of the passage.[295] The obituary quotes from 1939: "This country ... is, more than any other, involved in the consequence of the [Jewish] problem, both because we are regarded as protectors of the Jews and because the Jews have played so much greater a part in our life ... and are now the most powerful single influence therein." But the paper also quoted *The Battle Ground* regarding the unassuming Jewish millionaire who was seen as fortunate rather than superior by his fellow-Jews. The paper also claimed that Belloc wrote "'How odd of God To choose The Jews.'"[296] Although Belloc was innocent of the rhyme, a reader swiftly supplied Humbert Wolfe's "rejoinder" about preferring the devil to a Jew,[297] thus adding to an historical legacy of misunderstanding and simple error built on his marked preoccupation with the "Jewish question."

Belloc, Max Beloff recalled, turned "the 'Marconi scandal' into a Dreyfus case in reverse."[298] He was seen by Robert Nunes Carvalho as one of a group of "antisemites" who "[n]ever before or since in British history have ... been so respectable or so well led. And never have they been so misled." The anti-Semitic obsession "ruined some very good literary reputations." Belloc's story was "the strangest and saddest of them all," although the Marconi campaign also included Conservatives Leo Maxse and Rudyard Kipling. He added that it was "as great a pity that G. K. Chesterton's love for his brother Cecil should have

---

295. "The Late Mr. Belloc," *Jewish Chronicle*, July 24, 1953, 16–17; "Let us begin by remarking that this shock has cleared the air. That is the effect of most shocks. They get rid of humbug. It is perhaps their chief advantage, and often their only one. ... It is indeed true that since the violent attack on the Jewish race by the Prussian Government through wholesale spoliation, the destruction of their professional careers in Germany, the extraordinary restrictions upon intercourse and, most extravagant of all, the declaration of Jewish blood up to and including the last generation but one—all these things have cleared the air. ... A murder may have some lasting political result if you can ensure the continuance of its effect by the continued prosperity of the murderer. But injustice of this kind cannot solve any problem, and there is grave and glaring injustice in the Nazi policy against the Jews, for these two simple reasons ... first, that justice concerns the individual soul, not a type or race. Secondly, that you cannot justly destroy a bilateral agreement by a unilateral declaration" (H. Belloc, August 1937 introduction to *The Jews*, op. cit., xl–xlii).

296. "The Late Mr. Belloc," *Jewish Chronicle*, July 24, 1953, 16–17; H. Belloc, *The Battle Ground*, op. cit., 134.

297. *Jewish Chronicle*, July 31, 1953, 12–13; "Here lies Hilaire Belloc, who / Preferred the devil to a Jew. / Now he has his chance to choose / Between the devil and the Jews" (Humbert Wolfe, *Lampoons* [London: Ernest Benn Ltd., 1925], 69); see Chapter Eight.

298. Max Beloff, "From the Other Side," *Jewish Chronicle*, January 27, 1956, 28–29.

led him to write 'The Sign of the World's End.'"[299] Chesterton and Belloc were seen by Lord Hailsham as influencing younger generations toward anti-Semitism,[300] compared unfavorably to T. S. Eliot,[301] and described by one *Jewish Chronicle* reader as "a pro-fascist antisemite."[302] In the 1980s a racist campaign donated a copy of *The Jews* ("by the late antisemite, pro-fascist author Hilaire Belloc") to a public library.[303] By the end of the twentieth century, English anti-Semitism had faded into history, and Chaim Bermant suggested that "[t]he term antisemite should be used with a certain amount of care," applied "to someone, like, say, Hilaire Belloc who actually hated Jews and derived joy from their misfortunes."[304]

Cheyette's more nuanced literary study was seen by Clive Sinclair as presenting Belloc, Chesterton, Wells, Shaw and others "not as fellow travellers of the Final Solution, but as self-hating crypto-Jews—or better, self-hating scripto-Jews."[305] Geoffrey Wheatcroft, Gentile author of *From the Suburb to Zion*, said of *The Jews*: "This book, odiously anti-Semitic by the standards of 1922, let alone now, is dedicated to 'Miss Ruby Goldsmith, the best and most intimate of our Jewish friends,' taking 'some of my best friends' beyond parody."[306] Zangwill said it was "rather curious" that prominent anti-Semites were "ready to concede" the "many fine characters among the Jews," had Jewish acquaintances "whom they thoroughly appreciate[d]," and even liked the Jews they knew, but "illogically enough" believed that the ones they did not know harbored "every bad quality"; even Belloc "has or had a Jewish Secretary."[307]

Summarizing *The Jews*, Julius says that after Emancipation Jews "infiltrated everywhere, sometimes in close alliance with Freemasonry, which the Jews had

299. Robert Nunes Carvalho, "The Marconi Affair," *Jewish Chronicle*, October 26, 1962, 22–23.

300. "[Lord] Hailsham on Antisemitism," *Jewish Chronicle*, December 7, 1962, 8–9.

301. "Eliot: forget the pain, think only of the pleasure," *Jewish Chronicle*, 19, 1988, 22.

302. J. Garnel, Letter, *Jewish Chronicle*, August 26, 1988, 22.

303. *The Servile State* would not be displayed at Barnet Library but would be available on request ("[National Front] book accepted," *Jewish Chronicle*, May 26, 1989, 1). In the 1890s Belloc wrote enthusiastically from the United States: "There is *no lower class*—absolutely none. No difference in tone can be distinguished between the address of a Negro servant and of a friend—both are polite to a degree" (M. Belloc Lowndes, *The Young Hilaire Belloc*, op. cit., 101).

304. Chaim Bermant, "On the other hand," *Jewish Chronicle*, August 24, 1990, 20; Rudyard Kipling "never descended to the depths" of Belloc or Chesterton, "but, unlike them, he was not a Catholic" (C. Bermant, "Kipling the Poet," ibid., March 25, 1994, 33). The *Jewish Chronicle* remarked that many "distinguished non-Jewish writers" had "aired their views" in its pages, "including the odd figure, such as Hilaire Belloc," whose opinions could "hardly be said to be friendly" ("Still Growing Strong," *Jewish Chronicle*, November 11, 2001, 29).

305. Clive Sinclair, "Created in Whose Image?" *Jewish Chronicle*, January 21, 1994, 29.

306. G. Wheatcroft, *Jewish Chronicle*, July 5, 1996, 25.

307. I. Zangwill, Interview, "Anti-Semitism in England," *Jewish Chronicle*, April 23, 1926, 16.

inaugurated and whose ritual is Jewish in character."[308] Belloc's terminology ("They entered the Parliaments everywhere, the English Peerage as well, and the Universities in very large numbers. A Jew became Prime Minister of Great Britain, another, a principal leader of the Italian resurrection; another led the opposition to Napoleon III. They were present in increasing numbers in the chief institutions of every country") reflects his and Chesterton's self-consciously rational attempt to avoid words like "infiltration"—itself a euphemism for "Jews getting in everywhere." It could be argued that this was simply semantics—that their real meaning was identical to the irrational anti-Semite's but delivered in more measured tones. Nonetheless, Belloc continues: "It is an illusion to believe that all this great change was Jewish in origin. The Jew did not create it, he floated upon it, but it worked manifestly to his advantage." But he adds: "The Jews intermarried everywhere with the leading families"; "Strains of them were even present in the reigning families."[309] Belloc also alleged that in Britain, "[s]pecially Jewish institutions, such as Freemasonry (which the Jews had inaugurated as a sort of bridge between themselves and their hosts in the seventeenth century)" were "particularly strong," leading to "a political tradition ... ultimately to prove of great importance" in which foreign powers saw Britain "as the official protector of the Jews in other countries," expected to "interfere" whenever Jews were persecuted "in the East of Christendom," and to support "Jewish financial energies throughout the world," receiving "in return the benefit of that connection." Belloc praised Jewish abilities but failed to see a community motivated by religion and supported by strong families, their linguistic talents stimulated by the Hebrew tongue, and with the "outsider's" ability to see opportunities. Instead, like the Egyptian Pharaoh he feared their success, although, unlike Chesterton, without foreseeing the "happy ending" of the Promised Land. Jewish alliances among the "great territorial English families" were, he insisted, so numerous that those without Jewish blood were "the exception." In some, "the name was still an English name and the traditions those of a purely English lineage of the long past," but "the physique and character had become wholly Jewish." This was more redolent of his anti-Semitic creation Bill Bailey than his self-consciously rational approach.[310] Cheyette says that in *The Jews* Belloc asked "in his 'balanced' fashion" about the Nazis' sincerity in attacking the Jews, that doubtless they felt "provoked," and asked whether it could be "fruitful," adding: "The attack made upon the Jews is neither thor-

308. H. Belloc, *The Jews* (London, 1922), 47; 223, in A. Julius, *Trials of the Diaspora: A History of Anti-Semitism in England* (Oxford: Oxford University Press, 2010), 404.

309. H. Belloc, *The Jews*, op. cit., 47–48.

310. Ibid., 223–224; "The institution of Freemasonry (with which they are so closely allied and all the ritual of which is Jewish in character) increased very rapidly and very greatly" (ibid., 47).

ough nor final." Cheyette states that Belloc would "reinforce this point" by saying that "'the Nazi attack upon the Jewish race . . . [is] not thorough, not final, but incomplete, and I think soon to prove abortive.'" Cheyette criticizes Wilson for seeing Belloc's words as prophetic when his "criticisms of the Nazi's lack of 'thoroughness' in succumbing temporarily to violent anti-Semitic emotion could not have been further from the prophetic mark."[311] But in the same place Belloc insists: "I say this apart from the fact that Israel is eternal, and Nazidom most certainly not eternal. The policy has missed its mark, on lower grounds . . . because it has not dared to be thorough and has not had the competence to be well thought out."[312] As noted earlier in this chapter, Belloc continued by saying that there was "grave and glaring injustice" in the Nazi policy, and that it could not solve any problem. Rather than chastising them for not being "sufficiently thorough," he is satirizing them for failing even on their own "lower grounds." As seen, later he maintained that its treatment of Jews disqualified Nazi Germany from claims to be a civilized nation, and was sufficient grounds for its "elimination from Europe."

Nonetheless, also contra the "prophetic" view, Cheyette cites Belloc proposing his "apartheid system of 'Privilege'—or separate 'Jewish' and 'Christian' development" in Europe as "a more lasting and reasonable 'solution' to the 'Jewish question.'"[313] Belloc, even while attacking the Nazis' policy of "recognition," did indeed continue to believe that this approach would work if carried out calmly and with justice.

Cheyette also notes, however, that Belloc distanced himself from the "fanatical anti-Semitism" of Frank Hugh O'Donnell and Cecil Chesterton, telling Maurice Baring that the impression of "fanaticism" should be avoided because it was counter-productive, and that this suggests Belloc really was "Janus-faced."[314] But the fact that he did not exploit anti-Bolshevik anti-Semitism, despite his lack of sympathy with Bolshevism, and failed to make common cause with British fascism (although he sympathized with foreign fascism), suggests that Belloc was sincere though self-deluded. Moreover, unlike O'Donnell and Cecil Chesterton, Belloc took time to debate with Jewish audiences, appearing genuinely disappointed when *The Jews* met with all-too-predictable results.

311. H. Belloc, *The Jews* (1937), in B. Cheyette, *Constructions of "the Jew" in English Literature and Society: Racial Representations, 1875–1945*, op. cit., 178–179; H. Belloc, *The Jews*, op. cit., xl, xliii.

312. Ibid., xliii–xliv.

313. B. Cheyette, *Constructions of "the Jew" in English Literature and Society: Racial Representations, 1875–1945*, op. cit., 178–179.

314. H. Belloc, Letter to Maurice Baring, 27 August 1913, H. Belloc, *Letters from Hilaire Belloc* (London, 1958), 363, ibid., 174–175. Frank Hugh O'Donnell had been an Irish Nationalist Member of Parliament.

But Julius cites Andrew Sharf's claim that in November 1938 Belloc asked "sceptical questions" about press reports of a particularly "brutal" act of Nazi anti-Jewish violence; the story was not "'impossible,'" but "how do we know for certain? If it is false, how can we believe anything that the anti-Nazi side had to say? We must 'bolt out the truth.'" Julius adds that according to Sharf, Belloc demanded more evidence, but when after several weeks none was forthcoming, insisted that "the bulk of readers should be 'chary of accepting such stories in the future.'"[315] As seen, the *Jewish Chronicle* praised Belloc's attacks on Nazi anti-Semitism, while commending his caution. And as Sharf notes, "the word 'atrocity'" proved an "obstacle" to conveying the seriousness of the Jewish plight. First used by Prime Minister William Gladstone to describe the Turkish crushing of the Bulgarian revolt, his "allegations deservedly left British journalists with the impression that the word 'atrocity' applied to a story was an imputation on its authenticity." In 1933—the same year the *Chesterbelloc* attacked the Nazis' anti-Jewish persecution—Sir Harold Nicolson praised a Jewish pamphlet for avoiding long lists of Nazi atrocities, which produced "lassitude, rather than indignation," while publications like Israel Cohen's "with calm logic, exposed their stupidity."[316] Three years later Beverley Nichols claimed "Jewish atrocity stories" had been "wildly exaggerated."[317]

Sharf quotes Belloc more fully:

> [T]o those who know the Prussian spirit and its traditions, the horrible picture presented here is not impossible . . . on the other hand . . . the story is at least exceptional. Is it true or false? . . . At the moment of writing this, no evidence has appeared beyond the bare statement of fact in the *News Chronicle*: with ample dates and figures it is true, but no names. We know nothing of the victims, nor anything of the eyewitness who brought over or sent this tremendous and decisive revelation of Nazi methods. . . . It won't do.

Belloc insisted that if the *News Chronicle* failed to "make its story good or takes refuge in silence," it would be concluded that "a vicious falsehood, dangerous to the conduct of the state, has been forged and uttered"; but he added that if the Nazis could not or did not "meet the indictment," they would "stand condemned," and that the *Chronicle* could not, "obviously, hand over its informant to vengeance by giving his or her name."[318] But yet another enquiry from

315. Andrew Sharf, *The British Press and Jews under Nazi Rule* (London, 1964), 81–84, in A. Julius, *Trials of the Diaspora: A History of Anti-Semitism in England*, op. cit., 404.

316. Sir Harold Nicholson, *Daily Telegraph*, August 25, 1933, in A. Sharf, *The British Press and Jews under Nazi Rule* (London: Oxford University Press, 1964), 71–72.

317. Beverley Nichols, *Manchester Sunday Chronicle*, September 13, 1936, ibid., 79.

318. H. Belloc, *Weekly Review*, December 1, 1938, ibid., 82.

Belloc prompted "the short and obvious editorial comment" that the report came from a reliable source "which clearly could not be divulged," moreover, "there had been no denial in Germany."[319] Belloc continued to query the account although as Sharf comments, *Time and Tide* "expressed what must have been the opinion of the vast majority": the Sachsenhausen atrocity was "a characteristic scene."[320] That the public might dismiss yet another undocumented "atrocity story" is perhaps the only risk that could justify Belloc's pedantry, but after being among the first to condemn the Nazi atrocities, he was undoubtedly piqued at the newspapers' belated interest. Moreover, his initial, almost kneejerk reaction was to believe the stories rather than dismiss them, as many continued to do. In fact, even the Government failed to condemn the atrocities.[321]

Of Belloc's persistent questioning, Julius remarks: "This established the methods of denial that later generations of Holocaust deniers would adopt."[322] Belloc never denied earlier pogroms, and never denied the reality of the Holocaust. Moreover, few, if any, Holocaust deniers also attack Nazi anti-Semitism. Julius notes Shaw's praise of Houston Stewart Chamberlain's *Foundations of the Nineteenth Century* but says "he deprecated the extravagance of its anti-Semitism," that he argued against claims of a "battle between the Teuton and Chaos," seeing "the enemy" not as "the Jew but the British greengrocer, with his 'short round skull', his militarism and his mediocrity."[323] But as Cheyette notes, increasingly, Shaw excluded the Jewish people from his worldview while admiring the Dictators. As to Wells, Julius places him in the category of intellectuals who disliked both Jews and anti-Semitism, "something of an English cultural reflex"[324]—the "anti-anti-Semite" category, in which Wells occupied "a distinctive place." This category could also, however, include Belloc and Chesterton, and Julius further claims that Wells' approach was "radically incoherent" because he included all ideas about Jews in his works, including the "antagonistic," and was unable to get these "miscellaneous views . . . to cohere."[325] In fact, Wells' view of the "Jewish question" was perfectly coherent: the failure of the Jewish people to disappear not only prevented the advent of the socialist World State but also caused anti-Semitism.

319. H. Belloc, *News Chronicle*, December 21, 1938, ibid., 83.

320. *Time and Tide*, November 26, 1938, ibid., 84.

321. H. Belloc, *Weekly Review*, February 16, 1939, ibid., 83–84.

322. A. Julius, *Trials of the Diaspora: A History of Anti-Semitism in England*, op. cit., 404.

323. G. B. Shaw, *Fabian News*, in G. G. Field, *Evangelist of Race* (New York, 1981), 464–465, cited in ibid., 396; see Chapters Four and Five.

324. Ibid., 418.

325. Ibid., 420–421; the "Lichtensteins" in *Tono-Bungay* "speak for nothing more than 'a disorderly instinct of acquisition'" (ibid., 221–222).

Belloc: Anti-Semite or Anti-Anti-Semite?

Belloc is remembered mostly for humor and anti-Semitism although, in public at least, he refused to joke about the "Jewish question." Ironically, among Jews he continued to amuse,[326] and the "How odd of God to choose the Jews" rhyme, "originally uttered in a jocular spirit and never intended to be committed to cold print," was later correctly assigned by a *Jewish Chronicle* reader to pro-Semite W. N. Ewer.[327] In fact, the myth had been scotched by Belloc's biographer, who records that when Belloc heard it he said: "'That's not the way I write.' But people continue to attribute it to him, probably because of the false idea that he was what is called 'anti-Semitic.' He liked or disliked a Jew as he liked or disliked any other man, and he wrote a book called *The Jews*, which those who called him an 'anti-Semite' should have taken the trouble to read."[328] In fact the book sealed Belloc's reputation in that respect, and the rhyme continued to be seen as anti-Semitic not least because of its Bellocian associations.[329]

The *Jewish Chronicle* did not react to *A Companion to Mr. Wells' Outline of History* (1926) in which Belloc, unlike Wells, affirmed the uniqueness of the Jewish religion in history.[330] Both rejected modern race theories, but while Wells defined the Jews by religion (which he believed they could abandon as a human construct) Belloc defined them as a distinct "race and nation."[331] Belloc's approach to the "Jewish question" rested on his reading of history.[332] A Jewish Holy Land was a provocation to Islam and Islam was a continuing threat

326. Belloc's "alphabet" was performed to music (*Jewish Chronicle*, January 24, 1964, 32–33); a children's poetry prize was awarded for reciting *Charles Augustus Fortescue* (ibid., May 22, 1981, 26); Sir Jack Jacob's entry in *Who's Who* made, "as Belloc might have put it, 'one gasp and stretch one's eyes'"—although in this case it was true (ibid., July 31, 1981, 15); "[w]ith apologies to Hilaire Belloc" Cyril Davidson recited: "The chief defect of Henry Mandels / Was chewing up old Chanucah candles" ("Junior Chronicle: The dreadful tale of Henry Mandels," ibid., December 1, 1995, 19).

327. H. Soref, Letter, *Jewish Chronicle*, September 19, 1958, 27.

328. J. B. Morton, *Hilaire Belloc: A Memoir*, op. cit., 7.

329. G. Alexander, Letter, *Jewish Chronicle*, January 4, 2002, 23; "Israel Zangwill retorted to Hilaire Belloc… 'How odd, Hilaire, / That you should dare / To urge or prod / The choice of God'" (Mrs. J. DelMonte, Letter, ibid., January 18, 2002, 26); however, journalist W. N. "Trilby" Ewer wrote it after a guest at the Savage Club asked whether there was any anti-Semitism there: Jewish pianist Benno Moiseiwitsch "snarled back: 'Only amongst the Jews'" (R. Harris, Letter, ibid., January 11, 2003, 25); further stanzas were provided (Mrs. E. S. Weiss, Letter, ibid.).

330. "One body of Men—the ancient Jews—did indeed say that their God was the only true God and the Universal God. But they were unique in this" (H. Belloc, *A Companion to Wells' 'Outline of History,'* op. cit., 39).

331. Wells claimed the Jews were "not a race but a religion," but "when a Jew comes into the room, everybody knows that he is a Jew, and nobody either knows or cares what his religion may be" (ibid., 59).

332. "The Jews were expelled from England because they had become poor" (H. Belloc, *A History of England: Volume II: Catholic England: The Early Middle Ages A.D.* 1066–1348 [London: Methuen &

to Christianity.[333] He saw it as his mission to prevent the recurrence of violent eruptions, arguing that name-changes led to anti-Semitism, but Jews who did not change their names, like the Isaacs brothers, were also vulnerable.[334] Despite this, Belloc claimed that "recognition" of Jews would prevent pogroms, and that Jews should not become too wealthy and powerful because, historically, they suffered when they lost power. But in Russia, where they were compelled to live separately and remained poor, they were even more vulnerable to pogroms. No wonder that his solution to anti-Semitism—"civic separation"— confirmed Jewish suspicions that he was a rabid anti-Semite.[335] Jewish emancipation was a product of secularism, not Christianity, which Jews associated with repression. Belloc's deadly seriousness, rather than allaying such fears, made him seem more dangerous.[336] Corrin says Belloc believed that while people might openly demand a despot, money was a secret, evil power, and opposed everything he saw as opposing the Church, including Jews and capitalism.[337] Despite this, as seen, Belloc failed to exploit anti-Semitism, continuing to propound the same vague proposals for Jewish separateness while attacking anti-Semitism. If his vagueness was a cunning disguise for a detailed plan of persecution, he never unveiled it later, when anti-Semitism was more prevalent,

---

Co. Ltd., 1927], 356), but as "the chief dealers" in 1279, a mutilation of the coinage meant they were "naturally the chief victims, and something like three hundred men and women were put to death. The tragedy was not confined to the Jews . . . but the Jews bore the whole brunt of this dreadful business"; most would not "abandon" their faith, the "very badge of nationhood," the Jew's "pride, and his cement," but "in any community actively united by another religion" he could not "freely mix"; later the Jews were "exiled" (ibid., 358–359).

333. *The Jews* ends with a warning about "the immemorial debate, still unconcluded, between Islam and Christendom and the Beni-Israel. But for my part, I say, 'Peace be to Israel'" (H. Belloc, *The Jews*, op. cit., 307–308).

334. Regarding his "celebrated tirade: 'Men whose race is universally known will unblushingly adopt a false name as a mask. . . . This is particularly the case with the great financial families," he was "wrong"—and "if, as Belloc suggested, it was intended for self-protection, it did not always work" (C. Bermant, "What's in a name?" *Jewish Chronicle*, June 9, 1978, viii).

335. His "inhumanly impracticable and absurdly quixotic" proposals, "used in times of feudalism," would leave Jews "ethnically free but socially bound" (J. Berman, Letter, *Jewish Chronicle*, August 19, 1910, 10–13).

336. When men like Belloc, "not moved by fanaticism or narrow-mindedness, but from conviction," spoke of the impossibility of Jews assimilating, they did "a far deeper injury . . . than the rabid reviler or the persecutor of the Jewish religion" (C. A. Toledano, Letter, ibid., August 19, 1910, 10–13); having attended one of his lectures, a reader claimed that the Catholic Belloc "sighs for the good old times of the Spanish Inquisition," but as "a disciple of Carlyle" who, it was "well known, nursed some prejudices against the Jews," Belloc's "antagonism" was "directed only against the wealthy Jews" in "sedulous imitation"; although an "anti-Semite," he had determined to be "discreet," but unlike the anti-Semite who believed that Jews "should assimilate" and thus "disappear from the face of the earth," Belloc "had "no objection to our existence" (G. Coutts Lewis, Letter, ibid., August 26, 1910, 12).

337. J. P. Corrin, *G. K. Chesterton and Hilaire Belloc: The Battle Against Modernity*, op. cit., 21–22.

and if he appealed to anti-Semites they were the sort that did not mind being ridiculed.

In public at least Belloc refrained from making anti-Semitic remarks, but while claiming to oppose capitalism *per se* he singled out Jewish financiers. The Rothschilds, a family of international bankers, did anger some left-wing Jews,[338] but, as one of them pointed out, if such influence was "bad in itself, then the true and honest reformer should condemn it for itself,"—it was "the *Jewish* cosmopolitan financial influence," he said, that annoyed Belloc. Therefore he had "no place amongst honest reformers, and must be classed among anti-Semites—pure and simple."[339] Belloc saw the "Jewish problem" from a historical perspective but his own historical perspective underpinned his belief that Jews had always been a problem, and would always be—especially in the Holy Land. In the wake of the 1911 South Wales riots, it seemed disingenuous to warn about people ignoring anti-Semitism, but Belloc claimed: "Not one educated man in a hundred" had "any appreciation of the past history of all this," making it "so difficult to give an effective warning." He "especially" blamed those "in England and France" who said "the vilest things about the Jews behind their backs, never make a real friend of a Jew, gloat over their misfortunes," but accepted their hospitality and pretended "to mix with them as though there were no racial or cultural problem at all."[340] Belloc satirized this phenomenon in his novels, while people like F. Hugh O'Donnell mainly appeared concerned to protect Gentiles from Jews.

Notwithstanding his private jokes and the friction generated by his attempts to avoid friction between Jew and Gentile, Belloc's dogged persistence with his thesis, despite its failure to gain Jewish acceptance, suggests he genuinely believed he was not an anti-Semite. Whether a sincere but deluded anti-Semite is less dangerous than a cynic exploiting anti-Semitism for political ends is open to debate. But Belloc's self-image, shaped by the French Revolution, with its commitment to liberty, equality, and fraternity, clashed with the "Medieval Catholic" Belloc on the "Jewish question." His solution to this "question" was shaped by the latter, but while the "Medieval" Belloc refused to admit that his scheme of marking out Jews as different was being pursued with disastrous

---

338. A.S. Lindemann, *Esau's Tears: Modern Anti-Semitism and the Rise of the Jews* (Cambridge: Cambridge University Press, 1997), 202.

339. It was because Belloc was "not of the 'rabid order'" that he was "most dangerous"; his "animosity" was "confined only to the Jewish cosmopolitan financiers," thus it deserved "serious criticism"; moreover, to warn Jews "against acquiring wealth in a lawful way," lest they "arouse the jealousy" of their "Christian neighbours" was to "plant anti-Semitism in England" (J. Finn, Letter, *Jewish Chronicle*, August 19, 1910, 10–11).

340. H. Belloc, Letter to Maurice Baring, January 1, 1916, R. Speaight, *The Life of Hilaire Belloc*, op. cit., 453–454.

results by the Nazis, it was the "revolutionary" Belloc that responded to Nazism.

The Chesterbelloc

While less critical of Chesterton, Julius,[341] quoting from his *Short History of England,* makes a point applicable to Belloc as well: "This 'mutual charge of tyranny . . . is the Semitic trouble in all times.' It is a nicely balanced formula, one that appeals to a kind of fair-to-both-sides . . . sentiment, but it does not quite survive the paragraph, because Chesterton adds that when Edward 'flung the alien financiers out of the land,' he was both 'knight errant' and 'tender father of his people.'" Chesterton and Belloc did address "both sides" of the "Jewish question," i.e., Jews and anti-Semites, and Chesterton's nuance is evident in the full quote: "[I]t was when Edward, breaking the rule by which the rulers had hitherto fostered their bankers' wealth, flung the alien financiers out of the land, that *his people probably saw him* most plainly at once as a knight errant and a tender father of his people."(added emphasis)[342] Chesterton's careful phrasing highlights his sympathies for the common folk but also for suffering Jews.

Despite differences of emphasis the *Chesterbelloc* held many beliefs in common, which included, Corrin says, the common man's desire for "the Distributist alternative to the Servile State." In view of "the real possibility of a totalitarian alliance" between capitalist and socialist, Belloc in particular was "swayed" in the direction of small ownership by *Rerum Novarum.*[343] Both, according to William Oddie, approved the French Revolution as a corrective to unjust distribution of power, but Chesterton's approval pre-dated Belloc's, and Chesterton was more committed to socialism than he later admitted.[344] But any tension in the *Chesterbelloc* showed itself in divergent styles, reflecting, as Corrin remarks, very different temperaments: Chesterton was "humble in combat, overflowing in friendliness and almost childlike in humor," while Belloc was "vain, bitingly cynical and cantankerous in political debate."[345] Belloc, Morton recalls, was "a loyal friend and a dangerous enemy." His "life was ruled by certain iron convictions," and he saw it as "his duty to bear witness to the truth, not hesitatingly or quietly, but with enthusiasm, and in the face of the world." Belloc's "campaigns isolated him and destroyed his peace of mind," but "he struck no noble attitude," complaining "incessantly in a humorous manner

341. A. Julius, *Trials of the Diaspora: A History of Anti-Semitism in England,* op. cit., 202–203.

342. G.K. Chesterton, *A Short History of England* (London, 1917), 108–109, ibid., 422.

343. J.P. Corrin, *G.K. Chesterton and Hilaire Belloc: The Battle Against Modernity,* op. cit., 44.

344. W. Oddie, *Chesterton and the Romance of Orthodoxy: the Making of GKC, 1874–1908* (Oxford: Oxford University Press, 2008), 97–98; see Chapter Five.

345. J.P. Corrin, *G.K. Chesterton and Hilaire Belloc: The Battle Against Modernity,* op. cit., 27.

which endeared him to a large circle of friends." Although "aggressive both by temperament and by the conditions of the time in which he lived," his battles were "also the outcome of a planned strategy."[346] Belloc, like Shaw, chose his ground carefully, and his combativeness increased with age, as he told George Wyndham: "The older one grows the more the regrets and responsibilities and worries keep up. The only way out is to pick out things for attack and fight them. Then when one dies one has had exercise and one is properly tired and one can rest." But he continued: "I don't know what to pick out next. I am tired of Jews and as for the Rich, I determined last Thursday to become one myself, so I must give up abusing them. I think I'll have a shot at the Atheists. They have not been beaten up for a long time."[347] Belloc wrote that there was "nothing worth the wear of winning, but laughter and the love of friends,"[348] and eschewed personal criticism, but lost many friends, including Wells.[349] Morton says that Chesterton was "easy-going, Belloc was not," and "this difference in their natures . . . made Chesterton deplore what he called the 'sundering quality' in Belloc's quarrels. When Belloc quarrelled it was no sham fight. It was battle, and he struck to kill, because, as he said, without battle there is no victory on this earth." But Chesterton "admired immensely" Belloc's "pugnacity" and having led a "sedentary life," responded "with all his heart to the man of action, the rider of horses, the soldier, the sailor, the walker."[350]

Whether or not they agreed on quarrelling they differed on the significance of the Dreyfus case.[351] Notwithstanding subtle differences in their writings on the "Jewish question," Belloc "modified" Chesterton's attitude to the Dreyfus affair.[352] Even so, for Chesterton, the Marconi case remained pivotal. Belloc saw the Dreyfus affair revealing the same decay in France as "Marconi" did in England, under its alleged Jewish-influenced plutocracy, but many of Chesterton's references to the "Jewish question"—even to Marconi—almost immediately wander off the point. Like Belloc he highlighted evil in order to highlight what was good, maintaining: "What is wrong is that we do not ask what is right."[353] Belloc needed to attack, but Chesterton's attacks were really defenses:

346. J. B. Morton, *Hilaire Belloc: A Memoir*, op. cit., 16.

347. H. Belloc, Letter to George Wyndham, April 22, 1911, H. Belloc, *Letters from Hilaire Belloc*, op. cit., 39–40.

348. H. Belloc, *Dedicatory Ode*.

349. Wells, who had supported the *Witness* throughout the Marconi affair, was "stung" by Belloc's attacks (D. C. Smith, *H. G. Wells: Desperately Mortal: A Biography* [New Haven/London: Yale University Press, 1986], 256); see Chapters Four and Five.

350. J. B. Morton, *Hilaire Belloc: A Memoir*, op. cit., 77.

351. A. N. Wilson, *Hilaire Belloc*, op. cit., 98.

352. M. Ward, *Gilbert Keith Chesterton*, op. cit., 129–134.

353. G. K. Chesterton, *What's Wrong with the World* (Sandy, Utah: Quiet Vision Publishing, 1910/2003), 3.

"To love anything is to see it . . . under lowering skies of danger," and loyalty implied "loyalty in misfortune."[354] Belloc "knew remorse" over his "frequent failures to restrain himself" from being "vindictive in a moment of victory," and brooded over the dangers of "making uncharitable judgments,"[355] but despite such qualms acquired a reputation for anti-Semitism. Some of this reputation was in turn acquired by Chesterton thanks to the political journalism through which their names became inextricably linked.

The Chesterbelloc and the Witness

Although Chesterton and Belloc were drawn together in opposition to the Boer War, Cecil Chesterton was a "Tory democrat," and at that time pro-War.[356] But after 1910 Cecil and Belloc "became fast friends."[357] Speaight blames much of Belloc's "Jewish power" preoccupation on Cecil. Their friendship "cost Belloc several years of embittering controversy. Such controversy, with its technique of direct personal attack, is dangerous for the soul." It was unwise for someone who disliked Lloyd George or Sir Alfred Mond as much as Belloc did "to think of them too much. But Belloc thought about them incessantly." Belloc's "admirers" thought Cecil a bad influence, although Speaight acknowledges that "with or without" Cecil, Belloc "would never have sat quietly" at home.[358] Nonetheless, regarding the Marconi campaign, Belloc did attempt to restrain Cecil, insisting:

> [T]he detestation of the Jewish cosmopolitan influence, especially through finance, is one thing, and one may be right or wrong in feeling that detestation or in the degree to which one admits it; but mere anti-Semitism and a mere attack on a Jew because he is a Jew is quite another matter, and I told him repeatedly that I thought the things he allowed [F. Hugh] O'Donnell to publish were unwise and deplorable.[359]

Cecil did not share Belloc's emphasis on the need for restraint or, like Belloc, show signs of agonizing over his failures. His mother's favoritism may have contributed to his outspokenness.[360] Cecil and Gilbert argued incessantly, entirely without rancor, and Gilbert's indulgence of Cecil's headstrong determi-

---

354. G. K. Chesterton, "Thoughts Around Koepenick," *All Things Considered* (USA: Feather Tail Press, 1908/2009), 49.

355. J. B. Morton, *Hilaire Belloc: A Memoir*, op. cit., 130.

356. M. Ward, *Gilbert Keith Chesterton*, op. cit., 125; B. Sewell, *Cecil Chesterton*, op. cit., 20.

357. J. P. Corrin, *G. K. Chesterton and Hilaire Belloc: The Battle Against Modernity*, op. cit., 38.

358. R. Speaight, *The Life of Hilaire Belloc*, op. cit., 299.

359. H. Belloc, Letter to Maurice Baring, February 21, 1913, ibid., 311.

360. Mrs. Chesterton was "said to have considered" Cecil as "intellectually Gilbert's superior, at least in their younger days" (B. Sewell, *Cecil Chesterton*, op. cit., 2).

nation to take part in adult debate may have contributed to his lack of self-control.[361] Their older sister Beatrice died two years before Cecil's birth in 1879, and Gilbert felt intensely protective of his young brother, although it was the mild and dreamy Gilbert who was more in need of protection. Even he admitted that Cecil was "in his public relations . . . supremely pugnacious and provocative."[362] Cecil's biographer Brocard Sewell says that Jewish writer Leonard Woolf, a fellow pupil at St Paul's School, remembered Cecil as differing from Gilbert in his "fanatical intolerance . . . fertilized, not by profound convictions, but by personal animosities."[363] Sewell adds that the brothers "seem to have acquired the elements of their attitude to the Jews" at school. There was "no need to put the blame on Hilaire Belloc, whom they did not know until much later."[364]

In fact Cecil's youth, like Gilbert's, was marked by intense pro-Semitism. He joined Gilbert's Junior Debating Club, with its large Jewish membership, but "unlike his brother" seemed to have made "no close friendships," mainly because for all his efforts, Gilbert's friends never took to the little brother who showed no reverence for their friend.[365] Cecil's boyhood letters to Gilbert are peppered with references to the latter's Jewish friends Maurice Solomon and Leonard Magnus, and in 1896 the teenage Cecil wrote to Maurice about another of Gilbert's friends: "I have written to d'Avigdor a very silly letter and sent him my address; remind him to write to me if he has time as I want so much to hear from him."[366] Cecil's youthful poem *To the Jews* is as pro-Semitic as Gilbert's early verse, if more vehement:

> Oh people bespitten and rifled
> Of the fruits that were gotten by toil,
> Have revenge upon those who have trifled
> With you, come down to your spoil.
> Ye are firm in your faith that we scoff at,
> Ye are strong in your hope that we scorn,
> While our angels are cast into Tophet
> Our creed is outworn.[367]

361. Their boyhood was "one long argument" (G. K. Chesterton, *Autobiography* [Sevenoaks, Kent: Fisher Press, 1936/1992], 167).

362. Ibid., 38.

363. B. Sewell, *Cecil Chesterton*, op. cit., 104. Leonard was married to Virginia Woolf,

364. Ibid., 73.

365. Ibid., 4; M. Ward, *Gilbert Keith Chesterton*, op. cit., 27; Gilbert's friend Digby D'Avigdor recalled Cecil's "filthy" appearance (M. Ward, *Return to Chesterton*, op. cit., 14).

366. B. Sewell, *Cecil Chesterton*, op. cit., 6–7. The d'Avigdor brothers Waldo and Digby were friends of Gilbert, although Sewell does not identify the brother to whom Cecil wrote; see Chapter Eight.

367. Ibid., 5.

A qualified surveyor, Cecil became a struggling journalist,[368] but there was "an element of ruthless antagonism towards his opponents, real or imagined," and "even Cecil's closest friends suffered at times from his aggressiveness."[369] His "vendetta" against their friend, Liberal MP Charles Masterman, was "one of the rare occasions" on which Gilbert disagreed with Cecil and Belloc.[370] Cecil rejected his family's Liberalism, influenced by Fabian socialist Hubert Bland,[371] and was elected to the Fabian Executive in 1904, sitting on various committees with Shaw and Wells.[372] While embracing many *Chesterbelloc* ideals, Cecil ridiculed their "peasant Utopia" in the *New Age* magazine.[373] His outspokenness soon caused friction among the Fabians, and Shaw's attempts to defend him failed.[374] He also alienated many in the Christian Socialist Union.[375] While still disagreeing on Distributism, however, under Belloc's and Gilbert's influence his "faith in Socialism weakened" until eventually he "abandoned it altogether."[376]

Cecil's *Gladstonian Ghosts* (1905) warns fellow socialists not to be fooled by the "ghost" of the reformist Gladstone, since the Liberal Party's Nonconformist agenda was based on a fossilized Calvinism manifesting itself in opposition to Catholic ritual, an established church, and popular pastimes like horse-racing, public houses, and music halls.[377] Furthermore, Lord Randolph Churchill's "great Tory revival" had ended in "fashionable incompetence above, and frivolous Jingoism . . . below," with "the wires being pulled vigorously . . . by the unclean hands of Hebrew finance—a sight that would have made Churchill sick at heart."[378] This did not reflect Churchill's views,[379] and although such references were few and not all negative,[380] Cecil warned: "[O]ne of these days our Hebrew masters will say to us: 'Very well. You object to conditions; you shall

---

368. He never claimed an allowance from their father but borrowed small sums from Gilbert (ibid., 8–9).

369. Ibid., 104.

370. Gilbert did not differ from his predecessors Cecil and Belloc on politics and social reform, but when he took over at the *New Witness* "the attacks on Masterman ceased" (M. Ward, *Gilbert Keith Chesterton*, op. cit., 327).

371. B. Sewell, *Cecil Chesterton*, op. cit., 20.

372. Ibid., 19.

373. M. Ward, *Gilbert Keith Chesterton*, op. cit., 225–226.

374. B. Sewell, *Cecil Chesterton*, op. cit., 21–22.

375. Ibid., 24.

376. Ibid., 29.

377. C. Chesterton, *Gladstonian Ghosts* (London: S.C. Brown Langham & Co. Ltd., 1905), 30–31.

378. Ibid., 17.

379. M. Gilbert, *Churchill and the Jews* (London: Pocket Books, 2008), 1.

380. Disraeli's "quick Hebraic imagination and insight" helped him grasp social problems (C. Chesterton, *Gladstonian Ghosts*, op. cit., 47–48).

have none. We will import Chinamen freely and without restriction'"; these would "supplant white men," not only in the mines, but in every South African industry.[381] The "anti-Semitic" aspects of the anti-Boer War campaign chimed with Cecil's anti-capitalism and anti-Liberalism, but he saw the Tories as "less positively dangerous" because "the very cloudiness of their political outlook" made them "to a great extent amenable to skilful and systematic pressure from general reformers."[382]

In *G. K. Chesterton: A Criticism* (published anonymously in 1908) Cecil states: "The idea that brains were any part of the make-up of a gentleman was never dreamed of in Europe until our rulers fell into the hands of Hebrew moneylenders, who, having brains and not being gentlemen, read into the European idea of aristocracy an intellectualism quite alien to its traditions."[383] Cecil's style was reminiscent of Gilbert's but on the "Jewish question" his attempts at humor were less good-humored. *The Party System*, written with Belloc, contained few comments about Jews, all of them incidental, in contrast to his own works. McCarthy sees Cecil as "much more combative and pugnacious" than Gilbert, making him a "logical, if not prudent, partner for the argumentative Belloc." But unlike Belloc "whose views sprang from a long-range philosophy and historical position, the younger Chesterton had more of a journalistic approach ... without concern for overall conceptual consistency."[384] More positively, Cecil shared Gilbert's and Belloc's commitment to individual freedom. His chapter on "Democracy and the Great State" in Wells' *Socialism and the Great State* (1912) refused to bind the future because "[e]very democrat ... if his democratic faith be genuine" wanted the people to "have, not the form of government *he* likes, but the form of government they themselves like." Although Cecil might think of a "very ingenious" proposal, "the ultimate decision" was for his fellow-citizens.[385]

The chapter contained no Jewish references, but after the Marconi affair, Cecil set out his views on the "Jewish question." Rejecting anti-Semitism—defined as violent persecution of Jews—he emphasized the need to confront the issue in order to avert a "dangerous explosion" caused by "friction." A "revolt" was "even now preparing," which would harm "thousands of honest

381. "The Fetish of Free Trade," ibid., 107.

382. Ibid., 16–17.

383. Anon. (C. Chesterton), *G. K. Chesterton: A Criticism* (London: Alston Rivers Ltd., 1908), 5; Frances told Ward that they "suspected Cecil" because "many of Gilbert's" opinions were criticized from Cecil's "angle" (M. Ward, *Gilbert Keith Chesterton*, op. cit., 192).

384. J. P. McCarthy, *Hilaire Belloc: Edwardian Radical*, op. cit., 163.

385. C. Chesterton, "Democracy and the Great State," in H. G. Wells, ed., *Socialism and the Great State* (New York, 1912), 218, accessed December 2, 2009, http://www.openlibrary.org/b/OL7187395M/Socialism_and_the_great_state.

Jews up and down the country" including "wretched immigrants in the East End of London." Absorption had failed, Cecil claimed, and expulsion would be "unjust" and "hopelessly impracticable," consequently he recommended "Recognition of Jewish Nationality," involving a measure of self-government, "some exemptions," "probably some special representation in Parliament" but "exclusion from certain national responsibilities and functions." In this he echoed Belloc, and like Belloc he declined to elaborate, pleading lack of space. As Chapter Seven shows, Gilbert espoused such a policy after Cecil's death.

Like Gilbert, Cecil denied that "financial Jews" were typical and praised Jewish virtues, especially gratitude and family life. His tone, however, is qualitatively different to Belloc's and Gilbert's. He describes Jewish generosity as "admirable even in its childlike and innocent ostentation." He links Jewish "public self-effacement" to "secret arrogance." Disraeli, he says, "would have sunk England under the sea rather than that harm should come to the House of Israel." He insisted that Jews had become "more powerful than ever": they had a "grip over finance" and the press, as well as "the machinery of Government," using their "new power as they had used the old, for purposes sometimes personal, sometimes racial, or cosmopolitan." Cecil acknowledged that fears of anti-Semitism motivated the "ostrich-like policy" of Jews "pretending not to be there," but they made their presence felt "by some financial coup or some Ministerial scandal or some betrayal of the national interest to a cosmopolitan intrigue."[386]

Unsurprisingly, Cecil was accused of anti-Semitism. The Rev. Morris Joseph alleged that, "[a]dopting the favourite device of his school" Cecil used "the shortcomings of the few" to smear the many, citing their "want of patriotism." He would make Jews "aliens, pariahs," but nobody wanted to be "known as a fanatic, or to be regarded as irrational," and so, "[m]asquerading as a protector of the Jews" Cecil stoked "anti-Jewish feeling," making it "all but impossible" for them to remain in England. While opposing "Jew-baiting" he offered "covert incitements to it." He would not put Jews "on the rack, or engineer pogroms," but favored "systematic detraction and studied misrepresentation." And allied with Cecil was "a group of writers, all intent upon the same campaign of persistent defamation and dangerous incitement." Their "motto," the Rev. Joseph concluded, was "*Judaei ad leones!*"[387]

---

386. C. Chesterton, "Israel a Nation," *The British Review*, May 1913, 161–169; see Chapter Seven.

387. "Jews to the lions!"; "Mr. Cecil Chesterton [was] found guilty the other day of criminal libel. The judge held that he was actuated by 'Invincible ignorance and racial prejudice,' judicial terms which the Daily News bluntly translated by 'anti-Semitic.'" ("'Anti-Semitic Tendencies in England': Striking Address by the Rev. Morris Joseph," *Jewish Chronicle*, July 4, 1913, 16–17).

Like Gilbert, Cecil was a Zionist: "I should regard any Englishman who obstructed the efforts of patriotic Jews to re-establish a Jewish fatherland as an enemy not less to his own people than to Israel." Zionism had "no keener friend," but Cecil added that "the kind of Jew who prefers the fleshpots of Egypt to the glories of Zion" had "taught his fellow-countrymen" to regard him as an anti-Semite.[388]

Sewell describes Cecil's Great War pamphlet *The Prussian Hath Said in his Heart* (1914) as "less subtle" than Gilbert's *The Crimes of England* (1915),[389] although it contains no aspersions on Jewish patriotism.[390] But his posthumously published *A History of the United States* (1919), with a generous introduction by Gilbert,[391] states: "The problem of the Jew exists in America as elsewhere—perhaps more formidably than elsewhere"—"not because Jews, as such" were "worse than other people: only idiots are Anti-Semites in that sense"—but because, uniquely, America lived "by its power of absorption," and "the Jew" was "a singularly unabsorbable person." "The Jew," he continued, possessed "an intense nationalism . . . that transcends and indeed ignores frontiers" but was "often consciously and almost always subconsciously hostile" to the "nationalism of European peoples." In a variety of ways, Cecil alleged, he tended "to act as a solvent of such nationalism," for example, in "[c]osmopolitan finance." Like Gilbert, Cecil saw "cosmopolitan revolutionary idealism" as "more morally sympathetic," but as "not much less dangerous" to American nationalism. The American socialist and anarchist movements, although divided in philosophy, were "much more akin in temper" than in Europe, and were "almost wholly Jewish, both in origin and leadership," and since America's entry into the War, in contrast to most European socialist parties, they showed themselves "violently anti-national and what we now call 'Bolshevist.'"[392] In a chapter entitled "The Black Terror" while striving for balance, Cecil appeared to embrace racist fears.[393]

---

388. "A Melting Pot Correspondence," *Jewish Chronicle*, March 20, 1914, 26–27; according to a reader, Cecil supported Zionism as "the only relieving feature in the satanic nature of the Jew" (I. Rothfield, Letter, ibid., January 23, 1914, 33).

389. B. Sewell, *Cecil Chesterton*, op. cit., 84.

390. C. Chesterton, *The Prussian Hath Said in his Heart* (London: Chapman & Hall Ltd., 1914).

391. Cecil "died in a French military hospital of the effects of exposure in the last fierce fighting that broke the Prussian power over Christendom; fighting for which he had volunteered after being invalided home" (C. Chesterton, *A History of the United States* [London: Chatto & Windus, 1919], vii); among the Fabians he was "above all things, a democrat as well as a Socialist," but "began to feel as if he were the only Socialist who was also a democrat" (ibid., viii–ix).

392. Ibid., 232–233.

393. It was "very far" from his purpose to "write contemptuously of the Negroes"—there was "something very beautiful about a love of freedom wholly independent of experience and deriving solely from the just instinct of the human soul"; and "if, as some Southerners said" they saw freedom

Cecil and the Witness

The *Eye Witness* was launched in 1911 with Belloc as editor and Cecil as his assistant, contributing articles on politics and economics, many of them defending socialism against Distributism.[394] In November 1912 Cecil rescued the failing newspaper with financial assistance from his father. As editor of the *New Witness*, one of his chief aims was "the detection and exposure of political corruption," but as Sewell records, "his targets were not always well chosen, nor were his words always well weighed. The facts, or alleged facts, that he aimed to expose were not always sufficiently verified." With little access to political information and gossip—Belloc was no longer in Parliament—and unable to pay for research, "[s]ometimes he drew his bow at a venture, acting on insufficient evidence, or on surmise" and regarding the Marconi trial, "this was to prove his undoing."[395] Sewell praised Cecil's "direct and powerful intelligence" and "pungent and telling prose-style," but said he lacked "the subtlety and paradoxical charm of G.K., or the massive knowledge of Belloc."[396] Many of Belloc's distinguished contributors departed, "antagonised by the new editor's fierce polemics and by his anti-semitism."[397] Ward remarks that it was "only too easy to get angry" with Cecil "as he appeared in the New Witness," but that there was a "curious . . . contrast between the genial personality so loved by his friends" and the "waspishness" of his newspaper.[398]

The *New Witness* League, formed by the paper's readers, "did great service in exposing the totalitarian overtones" of the eugenicist birth control campaign, with its "implicit racism and proposals for mandatory sterilization and even outright elimination of the poor and mentally deficient" but even this, Corrin remarks, was "marred by crude anti-Semitism." The paper claimed that the eugenics campaign was "supported by Jewish financiers who, along with the Germans, hoped to decrease British population and deliberately sap the foun-

---

as freedom from work, the "right to be idle if and when you choose without reason given or permission sought" was "the essential difference between freedom and slavery"; it said "much for the essential kindliness of the African race" that freedom brought "no massacres and deliberate cruelties were rare. On the other hand, the animal nature of the Negro was strong, and outrages on white women became appallingly frequent and were perpetuated with complete impunity. Every white family had to live in something like a constant state of siege." The Ku Klux Klan's origins were "justified by the only thing that can justify secret societies—gross tyranny and the denial of plain human rights," but "[u]nfortunately" people got used to "the irregular execution of Negroes," leading to "'lynchings'" for which there was no "defence" (ibid., 220– 223).

394. B. Sewell, *Cecil Chesterton*, op. cit., 27.

395. Ibid., 42.

396. Ibid., 93.

397. B. Sewell, *My Dear Time's Waste* (Faversham, Kent: St. Albert's Press, 1966), 24.

398. M. Ward, *Gilbert Keith Chesterton*, op. cit., 410; see Chapters Four and Five.

dations of common morality by destroying the home."[399] The truth was more mundane, however: some Jews did support eugenics, but they rejected religion, as did the Gentile eugenicists.[400] In contrast, the English Chief Rabbi Joseph Hertz was a prominent member of the League of National Life, along with many Christians.[401]

Cecil's increasingly negative view of the "Jewish question" culminated in 1912 in the "Marconi affair." This political scandal, involving corruption and nepotism, shocked the British public and ended in a famous court case, which was marked by accusations of anti-Semitism against its chief exposer, Cecil, but also Belloc and Gilbert. The Liberal Government had awarded the Marconi Company a contract to provide a chain of radio stations throughout the British Empire. Godfrey Isaacs, managing director of Marconi and of the American Marconi Company, had bought up the tangible assets of his liquidated American rival, the United Wireless Company. He then sold American Marconi shares to his brother Rufus, Liberal Attorney-General, and another brother, Harry, knowing the price would soar when the radio station contract became known. Rufus sold some shares to Lloyd George, Chancellor of the Exchequer, and Chief Whip Lord Murray, Master of Elibank, who disposed of some at considerable profit. No money changed hands but the transactions occurred before American Marconi authorized the issue of new capital and before Parliament ratified the Marconi contract. The Ministers involved, including Herbert Samuel, when called before a parliamentary investigation committee, denied speculation but failed to mention American Marconi. The Liberal-dominated committee duly exonerated the Liberal politicians.

Ward says Gilbert, "not . . . an investigator of political scandals," trusted in Cecil and Belloc. Cecil "certainly said more than he knew and possibly more than was true,"[402] but as Corrin notes, he was "perfectly willing to flirt with libel" in "an honest attempt to get what he called 'truth' into the spotlight." The "struggle to expose the culpability of those involved," he adds, was "a watershed in the history of ChesterBellocian journalism," with the scandal offering "final proof of the venal and plutocratic character of British politics."[403] Some aspects of the affair's aftermath suggested an element of truth in their analysis, but as

---

399. "Comments of the Week," *New Witness*, October 4, 1918, in J. P. Corrin, *G. K. Chesterton and Hilaire Belloc: The Battle Against Modernity*, op. cit., 53–54; see Chapter Two.

400. The Modern Churchmen's Union supported all eugenics measures, but was unrepresentative of mainstream Christian opinion (A. Farmer, *By Their Fruits: Eugenics, Population Control and the Abortion Campaign* [Washington DC: Catholic University of America Press, 2008], 140).

401. Ibid., 138–142.

402. M. Ward, *Gilbert Keith Chesterton*, op. cit., 362.

403. J. P. Corrin, *G. K. Chesterton and Hilaire Belloc: The Battle Against Modernity*, op. cit., 55–56.

one press baron demonstrated, there was no carefully orchestrated plot involving politics, capitalism and the news media.[404] Cecil tried to provoke Godfrey
Isaacs by publicizing his poor business record, and when finally a libel action
was brought against the *Witness*, he refused to divulge the names of individual
authors.[405] Even earlier, as Ward notes, the *Outlook* was "attacking vigorously,"
and the *Witness* could not prove deliberate corruption—it was a case of
"striking . . . in the dark." While considering Cecil's claims "exaggerated" Ward
applauded his "courage," preferring "the immoderate man who said more than
he knew to the careful men who said so much less." At Cecil's trial Gilbert said
he envied his brother the dignity of his position.[406] The politicians kept everyone, including Parliament, in the dark, while enriching themselves with privileged information, but, contra the *Chesterbelloc*'s claims of political collusion,
the "party system," in the shape of the Conservative opposition, helped uncover
the truth.[407] Frances Donaldson, chronicler of the Marconi affair, viewed the
response of Cecil Chesterton's circle to the Marconi case as "the strangest
thing." They saw it as a victory, despite him losing and being fined £100. They
did not "seem even to have understood that he withdrew."[408] But it had
exposed what the *Chesterbelloc* saw as the bigger truth: the corrupt nature of
politics.

They saw the scandal as laying bare the machinations of "Jewish finance,"
and the trial judge suggested that Cecil "and possibly" his supporters were
influenced partly "by racial prejudice." They were also, he said, "partly blind to
business matters," leading to "the extraordinary series of libels" on Godfrey
Isaacs.[409] Donaldson said it was "seldom seriously questioned that Belloc was
instinctively anti-Jewish," which was "an ugly and a stupid thing." Belloc was
"far too intelligent and far too noble to be satisfied with the position himself."
He often refuted the accusation and "no doubt strove to obtain objectivity,"
saying that he "could think of no one less Jewish" than Lloyd George. Nonetheless, as she notes, initially neither he nor Cecil "knew anything about Lloyd
George"—he was simply "thrown in for luck." Originally their targets were
Rufus Isaacs and Herbert Samuel, both Jewish. It was "generally agreed" that

404. Lord Northcliffe warned that his newspapers would not hold back relevant information
despite his sympathies: "Your Marconi friends stage-manage their affair most damnably" (Lord
Northcliffe, Letter to W. S. Churchill, April 11, 1913, *Winston S. Churchill, Companion Vol. II Part 3,
1911–1914*, R. S. Churchill, ed. [London: Heinemann Ltd., 1969], 1740).

405. M. Ward, *Gilbert Keith Chesterton*, op. cit., 350.

406. Ibid., 354–355.

407. Ibid., 358.

408. Frances Donaldson, *The Marconi Scandal* (London: Rupert Hart-Davies, 1962), 188.

409. B. Sewell, *Cecil Chesterton*, op. cit., 69.

Cecil was "a bad influence on Belloc."[410] As his biographer points out, at his trial Cecil maintained: "I have not the slightest prejudice against the Jews as a people; but I do think Jewish finance is a dangerous thing, and should be curbed."[411] Donaldson says Cecil's supporters insisted he was "in private life of a kindly nature" and bore "no personal ill-will towards the men whom he harried publicly," but the "bland impertinence of this particular tribute to him seems to have occurred to none of his friends." Cecil could be "better understood," she maintained, once it was "realised that to the reckless courage, the dislike of Jews and politicians, the duty he shared with Belloc to clean up public life" was added "a passion for argument." Cecil was "good-tempered though relentless," and had "the weakness of the born debater: he treated all men as equals, even those who were less robust and of inferior forensic talent. He hit hard, but he expected to be hit hard in return."[412]

That Cecil's "opponents" did nothing for a long time only emboldened him. His "vindictive" campaign against C.F.G. Masterman, said by Sewell to have ended his political career,[413] may have encouraged him. Attacking someone who offers only letters of complaint can engender feelings of invincibility. As Donaldson notes, even when the *Witness* hired "sandwich-men" to parade outside Godfrey Isaacs's office "with placards advertising his 'ghastly [business] failures'" the Isaacs seemed reluctant to "hit back." Godfrey was not such a commercial failure as the *Chesterbelloc* alleged,[414] although as Parkes points out, anti-capitalists would not see that as proof of honesty.[415] Donaldson says that in contrast to his disapproval of the Masterman campaign, Gilbert swal-

---

410. F. Donaldson, *The Marconi Scandal*, op. cit., 70; "anti-Jewish feeling was quite common" but "as an intellectual attitude" was "already disapproved"; however, England had "never been hysterical about her Jews in the manner of many continental countries" because they had "not been sufficiently numerous or powerful" (ibid., 48–49).

411. B. Sewell, *Cecil Chesterton*, op. cit., 64.

412. F. Donaldson, *The Marconi Scandal*, op. cit., 70–71.

413. There was "little doubt" that the *New Witness* and the League for Clean Government "were largely responsible" for Masterman's three successive electoral defeats and "the ending of his public life" (B. Sewell, *My Dear Time's Waste*, op. cit., 27–28).

414. Herbert Samuel cautioned "against suing the *Eye-Witness* for libel," fearing it would "increase its notoriety" and create "adverse publicity" for "the Jewish community"; Prime Minister Asquith thought the newspaper too small and unimportant to worry about; only when the affair became a *cause célèbre* did Godfrey Isaacs decide to sue (J.P. Corrin, *G.K. Chesterton and Hilaire Belloc: The Battle Against Modernity*, op. cit., 58–59). Isaacs, concerned that Marconi had paid no dividend since its inception in 1897, sued the United Wireless Company for patent infringement, bankrupting it; Marconi America became the world's largest radio company and Marconi shares rose in April 1912; later it was claimed that he had unwisely invested Marconi assets, and in November 1924 he resigned from the board (*Oxford Dictionary of National Biography*).

415. J. Parkes, *Antisemitism*, op. cit., 12.

lowed possible misgivings,[416] but when the "all-powerful Jewish plutocracy" eventually "hit back" in the shape of a minor court case, Cecil was unprepared. Unable to substantiate his paper's specific claims, Cecil backed down. Donaldson remarks: "[H]is courage seems excitable, reckless, unequal, the courage of a delinquent child." Worse, "[m]en whose lives and careers were at all other times distinguished by courtesy, goodwill and intellectual integrity seem to have taken leave of their senses." In her view, no case was "more striking" than Gilbert's: he "was and remained all his life obsessed by the case." While not personally involved in exposing the scandal, Gilbert "took his views" from his brother, remaining "to the end of his life convinced that Cecil had been the champion of public morals against corrupt and evil men." This, she says, "led him to the most astonishing excesses." His Open Letter to Rufus Isaacs (later Lord Reading) was "written in a spirit of self-righteousness and with an ironic assumption of charity masking a hatred and contempt for which it would not be necessary to be a Christian to be ashamed."[417]

Corrin says that "Marconi" "transformed the ChesterBelloc's latent anti-Semitism into a more conspicuous feature of their journalism." From its beginnings, the New Witness "continually emphasized that the Isaacs brothers and Samuel were Jews who had close links with their brothers in international finance." Their journals remained "hostile to 'international Jewry,'" although under Cecil the New Witness was "rampantly anti-Semitic. Regular Jew-baiting was generally the forte of F. Hugh O'Donnell."[418] Most damaging, Corrin notes, were the claims of Charles Granville. Associated with the Eye-Witness from June to September 1912, Granville claimed to be a mere "figurehead," since Cecil wrote all the articles, but that he was "more than any man, in a position to reveal the real motive of the articles and the instigators of them. I am, in short, in a position to unmask a conspiracy as dangerous to England as the anti-Dreyfus agitation was to France." He had been "in constant warfare" with Belloc and Cecil regarding "their attacks on Jews qua Jews," and that the earlier articles were written "without data. The origin of the whole thing was . . . an attitude of mind." There was also "a certain animosity" to Lloyd George because of his insurance scheme.[419] Granville had been sole proprietor of Stephen Swift &

---

416. F. Donaldson, The Marconi Scandal, op. cit., 64–66.

417. Ibid., 188–189.

418. J. P. Corrin, G. K. Chesterton and Hilaire Belloc: The Battle Against Modernity, op. cit., 62.

419. "The Marconi Inquiry: 'An Anti-Jewish Conspiracy': Remarkable Statements," Jewish Chronicle, April 25, 1913, 8; the Daily News and Leader said that the Witness motives were "anti-Semitism and antagonism to the Government"; there were "good and bad Jews" as well as "good and bad Gentiles" and "good and bad Teutons and Latins"; Jews should "have justice on their individual merits" but there should be no "jihad against Jews in the interests of Rome" ("The Chesterton Case," ibid., June 13, 1913, 10–11).

Co., owners of several periodicals, including the *Witness,* until its financial collapse in September 1912. As Donaldson reveals, at the time of the Marconi trial Granville was on bail for fraud, and was charged with bigamy and obtaining money under false pretenses. An undischarged bankrupt, he had absconded to Tangier with £2,000, and was "slightly incoherent" in giving evidence.[420] The *Jewish Chronicle* reported that at the Marconi Inquiry, Belloc's rebuttals of "anti-Semitism" charges were met with laughter; he claimed to be motivated by "honest indignation and the earnest desire to criticise thoroughly—I will go further, and say expose—a dangerous piece of public policy." While he had many Jewish friends, "the Jewish element was a large one in cosmopolitan finance." Yet he claimed never to have written "one word—I will not say sneer—of hatred or evil jest against the great mass of the Jewish race which is poor and oppressed."[421]

The *Jewish Chronicle* remarked that, "[f]ortunately," Granville's accusations had been "pointedly contradicted" by Belloc, but that he admitted "a qualified anti-Semitism," and although he aimed at Jewish financiers, "the Jewish pedlar" would "be hit," for of all "the enemies which an individual or a race has to meet," there was "none so insidious as a vague and malicious phrase."[422] Laurie Magnus, a Unionist parliamentary candidate, called the Marconi politicians "a curious and unprepossessing crew," but condemned anti-Semitism: he was a Jew and "proud of it." Doubtless "a certain number" of wealthy Jews were "connected with finance"—"he did not happen to be one"—but people would always be envious of wealth, "however honestly acquired." Ironically echoing Belloc, he added that most Jews were "persecuted or driven out [of Europe] because of their poverty and because of their poverty they were true to their religion." Trying to "stir up" anti-Semitism against "poor refugees was a very cruel and dastardly, as well as a dangerous, thing."[423]

Unlike Belloc, the "anti-Semite" claimed that all Jews were rich and grasping, and among Gentiles the Marconi affair increased suspicions of Jewish influence on public life. Among Jews it increased fears of anti-Semitism: Israel Zangwill

420. Granville had also owned the *Oxford and Cambridge Review, Rhythm,* the *Onlooker,* and the *Free Woman* (F. Donaldson, *The Marconi Scandal,* op. cit., 161–163); Belloc said Cecil had been editor since his departure—Granville was "the proprietor" (ibid., 166).

421. Belloc had "heard, on authority" that an unnamed man in public life "had through inside knowledge been able to multiply by three" his Marconi investments, and in an unrelated article had used the information to "illustrate" what it had "proved to be true": wealthy men could "increase their wealth perpetually while the small investor was heavily handicapped"; far from being anti-Semitic, he had "frequently lost time and money in addressing audiences of Jews—always poor Jews" ("The Marconi Inquiry. The Alleged 'Anti-Jewish Conspiracy.' Mr. Hilaire Belloc's Explanation," *Jewish Chronicle,* May 2, 1913, 10–11).

422. *Jewish Chronicle,* May 2, 1913, 8–9.

423. *Jewish Chronicle,* May 2, 1913, 10–11.

accused the *Witness* of blaming Jew as well as Gentile for Russian pogroms: "[t]hough you detest the pogrom, and fear it may break out even in England." Cecil's responses suggest a game of attack and retreat rather than Belloc's and Gilbert's sincere dialogues with Jewish critics.[424] During the Great War, with Jews accused of divided loyalties, one *Jewish Chronicle* reviewer said the *New Witness* should be called "*The False Witness*," and that its "conductors," who were "understood to be Roman Catholics" should "recapitulate its contents in the confessional."[425] Cecil had converted to Catholicism while awaiting the "Marconi" trial,[426] influenced, Ker says, by Belloc's wife[427] and, doubtless, Belloc himself. Gilbert was not yet a Catholic, and Ward remarks: "It was a pity that Cecil Chesterton's rather fierce way of handling such matters as race questions got fathered onto Gilbert."[428] But even with Gilbert as editor, the *Witness* alleged that Alfred Mond maintained a "subterranean labyrinth of Jewish communications" between England and Germany[429] and in 1920 the *Jewish Chronicle* angrily refuted *Witness* allegations that it had published the names of German Jews killed in the War.[430]

Much later, Ward attempted to explain the *New Witness* stance, saying that people usually referred to it as "a religious prejudice." Jews did indeed fear a "Christian" campaign to return them to "Medieval" status, but Ward insisted that the *Witness* denied religious prejudice "not always patiently but with unvarying clarity." They also denied racial prejudice, and although "this . . . was true only of some of the staff," their "only prejudice was against the pretence that a Jew was an Englishman." It was "undeniable," she added, that there were Rothschilds in Paris, London, and Berlin "all related and conducting an international family banking business."[431] As Parkes pointed out, however, although the Rothschilds' financial power was "great," their political power was not as great as their critics supposed, because each branch of the family adopted the

424. The *Witness* had alleged that Zangwill's play *The War God* aimed to teach Jews to abandon their nationality, and that the Russians, a "naturally kindly people" were "led to perpetrate atrocities" ("A Melting Pot Correspondence," *Jewish Chronicle*, March 20, 1914, 26–27).

425. "Book Reviews: 'The War for the World': Israel Zangwill's struggle for Zionism," *Jewish Chronicle*, July 21, 1916, 22–23; the *Witness* continued to cause concern on this issue (ibid., February 8, 1918, 18).

426. "[O]ne day Cecil left the office for a few hours to be received into the Catholic Church" (Mrs. C. Chesterton, *The Chestertons* [London: Chapman & Hall Ltd., 1941], 97); Cecil was baptized at the Brompton Oratory on June 7, 1912 by Father Sebastian Bowden (B. Sewell, *Cecil Chesterton*, op. cit., 43).

427. I. Ker, *G. K. Chesterton: A Biography*, op. cit., 314.

428. M. Ward, *Return to Chesterton*, op. cit., 115.

429. *Jewish Chronicle*, October 4, 1918.

430. "Nailing a Lie," *Jewish Chronicle*, September 10, 1920, 8–9.

431. M. Ward, *Gilbert Keith Chesterton*, op. cit., 415–416.

prevailing attitude of the nation where it resided, attitudes which "were often at variance with each other."[432] Ward emphasized that many Jews had "died gallantly" in both Wars, and "[v]ery many" were patriotic for England—and America, and Germany, and "no doubt" this made "the problem more acute." But "any discussion" was "nonsense" if it omitted this "certain fact. There are Jews patriotic first for the country they live in, the country that gave them home and citizenship," but "others who feel that Jewry is their *patria.*" Consequently: "A Jew might not be specially pro-German in feeling, yet his actions might help Germany by being pro-Jewish. International Jewish trading *was* trading with the enemy." Moreover, "international finance was getting nervous over the continuance of the war as a menace to its own future," desiring "a peace that should still leave it in possession in this country—and in Germany." Chesterton, she maintained, "was passionately determined to cast it out." Still "obsessed" by the Marconi affair, "the surrender of English politics to the money power seemed to him to represent as great a danger for the future as Prussianism. For a moment the two dangers were the one danger."[433]

When Cecil enlisted in September 1916, Gilbert stepped in at the *New Witness*, despite his heavy work load. His "war effort" would be fighting profiteering and cowardice. Valor ranked high in his list of virtues. Always humble, he humbled himself still further before Cecil's superior brand of bravery: "[T]hough I can never be so good as my brother, I will see if I can be better than myself."[434] Dale Ahlquist says that the "anti-Semitic writers who had previously contributed articles no longer appeared in the paper,"[435] but as Ward notes, the brothers were artists rather than managers or businessmen,[436] and suspicion of profit-making and political disillusionment primed them to see collusion in politics and finance. Armed with conviction rather than hard facts, emboldened rather than deterred by "Marconi," Gilbert took up Cecil's mantle. *Ad hominen* attacks were out of the question, but Liberal politician and wealthy industrialist Sir Alfred Mond of the Mond Nickel Company personified the plutocracy, justifying attacks on him. His "foreignness" provided an added incentive, which the Distributist League delighted in exploiting.[437]

---

432. J. Parkes, *Antisemitism*, op. cit., 72.

433. M. Ward, *Gilbert Keith Chesterton*, op. cit., 415–416.

434. Ibid., 431.

435. D. Ahlquist, "The Marconi Scandal," *Gilbert Magazine*, 12 (2 & 3), (November/December 2008): 28, accessed May 19, 2011, http://www.209.236.72.127/wordpress/wp-content/uploads/2010/12/gilbert_12.2_5.pdf.

436. M. Ward, *Return to Chesterton*, op. cit., 215.

437. A song by C.T.B. Donkin, published in *G.K.'s Weekly*, was popular at Distributist League meetings: "My name it is Alfred und English I vos, / I lof my dear gountry where I am der Boss; / Perhaps you don't know it, but still on der whole / In merry old England I geep der gontrol. (Chorus) Oi

To Gilbert it was "a sacred trust to carry on his brother's work" and when the Armistice came and Cecil did not return, Ward says "the trust remained. Cecil's hopes and ambitions must not be allowed to perish simply because Cecil had perished."[438] Nonetheless, Gilbert "got far less fun out of making these attacks. Still less had he the recklessness that made Cecil indifferent even to the charge of inaccuracy." Gilbert "had no fear of a lawsuit when he was certain of his facts," but admitted having "one fear only," the fear "'of being answered.'" Ward claims that "Marconi" induced caution in people like Mond: instead of "answering" Gilbert's attacks, in 1919 he brought a libel case against "a pair of cranks," Frazer and Beamish, who displayed a placard in a back-street window calling him a "traitor" for "trad[ing] with the enemy." Damages of five thousand pounds indicated "some measure of the risk G. K. took in making exactly the same attacks," although "G.K.'s immense popularity made such an attack a still more doubtful move."[439] As Parkes noted, those who attacked the "underdog" could get "immense satisfaction" by "inventing immeasurable power in the objects of their hatred," thus "endowing themselves with tremendous courage in daring to express their hostility."[440] A Jewish industrialist may have seemed like Goliath but he risked bad publicity if he chose to retaliate against "David."

Gilbert did admit a fear of "hurting or distressing his friends," a special danger for someone editing a paper "so controversial," whose friends "were also opponents in politics or religion." When H. G. Wells was offended by the *Witness*, Chesterton explained his "very difficult position," for many things appeared "with which I wholly disagree."[441] It was "physically impossible" for him to edit it when he needed his earnings from paid journalism to support the

---

yoi, vot a game, vot a business too, / Dey call me a German, dey say I'm a Jew, / But ach! I vos English, I tell you dis much, / I vos Alfred der Great mit der Yiddisher touch!" Once, in Cardiff, Mond had the "audacity" to speak of "We Welshmen!"; much later, a song like *Alfred the Great* would be seen as anti-Semitic, but in combating "every form of racial discrimination and hatred" the "risk" was "not being able to denounce certain people for what they do, because of what they are"; Mond was "attacked by Distributists for his actions, not for his race . . . a Jew from Germany who claims to be a Welshman can hardly be expected not to be reminded of his origins" (B. Sewell, *My Dear Time's Waste*, op. cit., 43); see Chapter Five.

438. M. Ward, *Return to Chesterton*, op. cit., 213. Gilbert's "brother had plunged into the fray with that very political paper the *New Witness*." Cecil's death "left it in Gilbert's hands. He felt the task to be a sacred legacy" and when it failed, "his one thought was how to start it again" (ibid, 487); Gilbert said Cecil asked him to edit the paper "until he returned. But I went on editing it; because he did not return" (ibid, 264).

439. M. Ward, *Gilbert Keith Chesterton*, op. cit., 431–432; Beamish founded an anti-Semitic group, The Britons.

440. J. Parkes, *Antisemitism*, op. cit., 17.

441. G. K. Chesterton, Letter to H. G. Wells, M. Ward, *Gilbert Keith Chesterton*, op. cit., 433–434.

paper, and to leave "a little over to give it from time to time." While praising the "loyalty and capacity" of William R. Titterton, he could not "oversee everything" and neither could he resign "without dropping as you truly said, the work of a great man who is gone; and who, I feel, would wish me to continue it." As Robert Louis Stevenson said of "marriage and its duties: 'There is no refuge for you; not even suicide.'"[442] When the *Witness* failed, Gilbert felt he couldn't allow Cecil's paper, which stood for "all he believed in, go," without doing everything possible to save it, but the anxiety was so great it interfered with his thoughts of religious conversion:[443] "I have again been torn in pieces by the wars of the *New Witness*."[444]

Gilbert's "sacred trust" became bound up with Cecil's Marconi campaign, magnifying its significance in retrospect. He recalled in his *Autobiography*: "It is the fashion to divide recent history into Pre-War and Post-War conditions. I believe it is almost as essential to divide them into the Pre-Marconi and Post-Marconi days." Marconi led "the ordinary English citizen" to lose "his invincible ignorance; or, in ordinary language, his innocence."[445] Bernard Shaw saw Marconi as "a silly business," an "attempt to show that there was nothing to choose between a Modern Cabinet Minister and Titus Oates,"[446] but, as Corrin notes, it remained "of monumental importance" in the "hardening" of Chesterton's politics.[447] Had Cecil survived, Marconi might never have loomed so large, as Gilbert's poem *Human Nature: or Marconi Memories*, suggests. It contains no reference to Jewish issues,[448] and *Song of Cosmopolitan Courage*, also written in 1913, was satirical rather than savage: "I brought a libel action, / For the Times had called me 'thief,' / Against a paper in Bordeaux, / A paper called *Le Juif. . . .*"[449] Even in 1913 Gilbert said he could forgive the "public swindling" of the Isaacs brothers and Herbert Samuel, while warning that the "philanthropic tyranny" of the Mental Deficiency Bill would mean that "every man

---

442. G. K. Chesterton, Letter to William R. Titterton, ibid., 434–435.

443. G. K. Chesterton, Letter to Father Ronald Knox (undated), ibid., 459–460.

444. G. K. Chesterton, Letter to Father Ronald Knox (undated), ibid., 463–464.

445. G. K. Chesterton, *Autobiography*, op. cit., 205.

446. G. B. Shaw, "Wireless Indignation," *The New Statesman*, April 12, 1914, in B. Sewell, *Cecil Chesterton*, op. cit., 69.

447. J. P. Corrin, *G. K. Chesterton and Hilaire Belloc: The Battle Against Modernity*, op. cit., 56.

448. It does however mention "statesmen" going "to South America," an allusion to the Master of Elibank (G. K. Chesterton, "Human Nature: or Marconi Memories from our 'Simplified Psychology for Statesmen' series," *G. K. Chesterton Collected Works Vol. X Collected Poetry Part I* [San Francisco: Ignatius Press, 1994], 394–395).

449. In suing a foreign newspaper, *Le Matin*, for publishing a story on the Marconi affair, Herbert Samuel and Rufus Isaacs were able to avoid telling the whole truth about their involvement (G. K. Chesterton, *Song of Cosmopolitan Courage*, New Witness, I, 1913, 655, in M. Ward, *Gilbert Keith Chesterton*, op. cit., 343–344); the poem "drew attention even more effectively to the other strange aspect of the case" (F. Donaldson, *The Marconi Scandal*, op. cit., 98).

convicted of three small crimes" could be imprisoned for crimes not yet committed. Steered through Parliament by Jewish Liberal MP Herbert Samuel, it was "the unpardonable sin."[450] The following year, Chesterton responded to Shaw's comment that, like Houston Stewart Chamberlain, he thought "Jew qua Jew" was "a worse man than himself" by saying that he knew "individual Jews" who were "much better" than he, but that "the Jew was distrusted in the Middle Ages . . . for initiating international intrigues of the Marconi type." The *Jewish Chronicle* said that Chesterton's "childish babbling" should not be treated with "disdain, contempt and silence"—it was their "duty as a matter of public obligation to enlighten him"—though it mattered "very little" what he thought.[451] But in 1917, in *Utopia of Usurers,* Chesterton described the Marconi affair as a "conspiracy of a very few millionaires," adding that there was "no man in the street who could not understand (and like) Rufus Isaacs as a Jew better than he [could] possibly like him as a British statesman."[452]

But after Cecil's death, Marconi was carved on Gilbert's personal war memorial, the blame for the *Witness* burden transferred from Cecil to the Marconi ministers. For a time Gilbert seemed to succumb to "Jewish conspiracy" fever. Sheed blamed Gilbert's brain illness of 1914 on anxiety about the Marconi court case and "his loutish younger brother . . . whose death was such a brutal turning point in his life."[453] Having endured the stress of the Marconi court case and his brain illness, followed by responsibility for the *New Witness,* Cecil's death came as a terrible blow just as he was expected to resume the editor's chair at the end of a terrible war in which millions died. Much later, Gilbert acknowledged that Cecil's death motivated his Open Letter to Rufus Isaacs.[454] The Letter began by saying that the work Cecil "put first he did before he died. The work which he put second, but very near to the other, he left for us to do. There are many of us who will abandon many other things, and recognize no greater duty than to do it." Ward believed Gilbert incapable of bitterness, but with "profound and burning indignation" he "thought of his fellow Englishmen who had fought and died—and then looked up and saw 'Marconi George' and 'Marconi Isaacs,' still rulers of the fate of his country."[455] The career of neither politician suffered:

450. G.K. Chesterton, "The Intolerable Thing," *Daily Herald*, March 29, 1913, in *Gilbert Magazine*, 14 (8), (July/August 2011): 8–9.

451. "Mentor," "The Jewish Spirit: Enlightenment for Mr. G.K. Chesterton," *Jewish Chronicle*, June 9, 1916, 7.

452. G.K. Chesterton, "The Tyranny of Bad Journalism," *Utopia of Usurers* (Norfolk VA: IHS Press, 1917/2002), 107–110; see Chapter Two.

453. W. Sheed, "ChesterBelloc and the Jews," op. cit.

454. G.K. Chesterton, *Autobiography*, op. cit., 265.

455. M. Ward, *Gilbert Keith Chesterton*, op. cit., 420–421.

Lloyd George became Prime Minister, while Isaacs, as Lord Reading, became Lord Chief Justice and later Viceroy of India.[456] Gilbert's Open Letter, coinciding with Reading's appointment as American Ambassador, was published in the same *New Witness* edition as his elegy on Cecil's passing.[457] Cecil died of kidney disease in a French hospital in December 1918, following a long march, but Gilbert described him dying "in the trenches to which he had freely gone." Denying that he wrote with "personal acrimony," his jocularity, employed as an offensive rather than defensive weapon, sounds very like Cecil's when addressed to Lord Reading: "It would be irrational to ask you for sympathy; but I am sincerely moved to offer it. You are far more unhappy; for your brother is still alive." This appalling sentiment arose from contemplating the fallen Cecil against Lord Reading's continued rise in politics, and the threat to England partly from "certain men of the tribe of Isaacs" who "kept their own strange private loyalty." Gilbert insisted that there was no "question of disliking any race" or "even . . . of disliking any individual"—but told Lord Reading that this raised "in some strange fashion, the question of loving you. Has it ever occurred to you how much a good citizen would have to love you in order to tolerate you?" Was England, Gilbert demanded, to lose the War after all—could anyone doubt "the Jewish International" was "unsympathetic" to Poland's national claim, and did "the chief Marconi Minister" have "the serious impudence" to call the *Chesterbelloc* anti-Semites because they were not so "extravagantly fond of one particular Jew as to endure this for him alone?" The *Chesterbelloc* circle was certainly "not Pro-Semite in that peculiar and personal fashion." Gilbert said he had made "many attempts . . . to imagine and allow for an alien psychology," but if Reading and "far worthier" Jews were wise, they would not "dismiss as Anti-Semitism" what might be "the last serious attempt to sympathise with Semitism." While adding that he allowed for Reading's position "more than most men allow for it; more, most assuredly, than most men *will* allow for it in the darker days that yet may come," it was "utterly false" to claim that Gilbert, "or a better man . . . whose work I now inherit, desired this disaster for you and yours." He wished Reading "no such ghastly retribution," concluding: "Daniel son of Isaac. Go in peace; but go."[458]

Ahlquist says the Letter "may have been the most uncharacteristic thing he

456. Ibid., 356.

457. F. Donaldson, *The Marconi Scandal*, op. cit., 189.

458. "[T]he spirit of prophecy was upon Chesterton after a truly dark and deep fashion. Yet even he did not guess that the retribution he feared would fall, not upon that 'tribe of Isaacs' . . . but upon the unfortunate Jewish people as a whole, from the German nation that Isaacs had gone to Paris to protect" (G. K. Chesterton, "Open Letter to Lord Reading," *New Witness*, December 13, 1918, in M. Ward, *Gilbert Keith Chesterton*, op. cit., 420–425).

ever wrote, in tone if not in substance."[459] Chesterton's *Elegy in a Country Churchyard* echoed these bitter sentiments: "And they that rule in England, / In stately conclave met, / Alas, alas for England / They have no graves as yet . . . ."[460] For once the Imperialist agreed with the anti-Imperialist, as Rudyard Kipling's poem to Reading concluded: "Stand up, stand up, Gehazi, / Draw close thy robe and go / Gehazi, judge in Israel. / A leper white as snow!"[461] In 1919 Chesterton again warned that Polish interests would be sacrificed to Germany's "by the most secret of all secret diplomacy," and would be given "by German Jews to other German Jews." All such "international adventurers" would "find themselves floating on the top of any tide that drowned the nations," not caring "what nations they drown."[462] Sheed claims the "Zionist" chapter in *The New Jerusalem*, published the following year, was "almost written in his brother's voice," with its "brutal swagger."[463]

Gilbert wrote no comparable indictment of Lloyd George, though he rose to even greater heights than Reading. But by the time he wrote his *Autobiography* both Isaacs brothers were dead and Gilbert's view of them had mellowed. Cecil had risen even higher in his estimation: "[A]lone of all the men of our time," he "possessed the two kinds of courage that have nourished the nation; the courage of the forum and the field."[464] Cecil certainly possessed physical courage, since despite his weakness he had volunteered for military service, and yet his "courage of the forum" had failed when he retreated from the Marconi court case. In 1915 he suffered a strange repeat of this in America, where he had been invited by pro-British groups to lecture on the Allied cause. In a debate with pro-German George Sylvester Viereck, editor of *The Fatherland*,[465] Viereck asked whether the *New Witness* had called for certain prominent Jews to be "sent to a concentration camp and put to some useful occupation, like wood-chopping, so as to do for the first time an honest day's work?" Cecil's biogra-

---

459. D. Ahlquist, "The Marconi Scandal," *Gilbert Magazine*, 12 (2 & 3), (November/December 2008): 28, accessed May 19, 2011, http://www.209.236.72.127/wordpress/wp-content/uploads/2010/12/gilbert_12.2_5.pdf.

460. M. Ward, *Gilbert Keith Chesterton*, op. cit., 420–421.

461. Ibid., 361–362.

462. G. K. Chesterton, *New Witness*, April 1919, ibid., 428–429; some Polish Jews were Polish nationalists, but "[t]hese particular Poles" were "anti-Polish Jews," i.e., of German extraction (G. K. Chesterton, "Polish Nationalism," *Illustrated London News*, January 11, 1919, in G. K. Chesterton, *Chesterton on War and Peace: Battling the Ideas and Movements That Led to Nazism and World War II*, M.W. Perry, ed. [Seattle: Inkling Books, 2008], 338–343; "Poland and Peace-Mongers," *Illustrated London News*, January 18, 1919, [ibid., 343–348]); see: *Mission of the United States to Poland: Henry Morganthau, Sr., Report* (1919).

463. W. Sheed, "ChesterBelloc and the Jews," op. cit.

464. G. K. Chesterton, *Autobiography*, op. cit., 265; Godfrey Isaacs died in 1925, Rufus in 1935.

465. B. Sewell, *Cecil Chesterton*, op. cit., 84–86.

pher said he gave a "gallant and forceful reply," reminding Viereck that they were "not debating the Jewish problem."[466] But in the published account Cecil merely answers: "Yes, I did." Viereck again quoted Cecil as saying: "Unfortunately, the many virtues of the Jewish race do not include tact and delicacy in dealing with Europeans ... their manner is often insolent and offensive. To give Jews the control over our honored Belgian guests, is an outrage ... not put upon them by the will of the English people, but by the stupidity of a Jewish financier who has been allowed to worm himself into the Ministry." Viereck challenged Cecil: "Did you or did you not write this because two Jewish women were placed on the Belgian Relief Committee in London?" To hisses, Cecil responded: "I did." Viereck later became a Nazi apologist, however,[467] and just as Cecil had taken responsibility for the Marconi articles, as will be seen, he may have accepted Viereck's charges to protect the individual responsible for these offensive remarks.

Gilbert's *Autobiography* confirms that the Marconi affair only became a significant influence on his views of the "Jewish question" after Cecil's death, but he maintained that in private Cecil had been "always more ready to excuse the Jews than the Gentiles." It was "another of the legends about the Marconi Case" that it was "an attack on Jews."[468] But he adds that Cecil's death did indeed lead to his Open Letter "upon the memories of our great Marconi quarrel"—an "odd reaction" that he could not "altogether explain."[469] The Letter's hint at "Jewish conspiracy" could be linked to the *New Witness* staff's reaction to Cecil's death. Sewell relates that although he had endured "two years' active service" in "atrocious conditions in Flanders" that "weakened his physical resistance ... this natural explanation ... was not accepted." Cecil's colleagues argued that he had been "passed as medically fit" for the march, despite bad weather and ill health, therefore "someone on the Government had given instructions that something of this kind should be done when a suitable opportunity occurred."[470] Having regarded the Marconi court withdrawal as a victory for Cecil, the *Witness* circle now saw that victory as so crushing that he had fallen victim to State assassination. In fact, Cecil, who had enlisted for active

---

466. Ibid., 88–89.

467. *Debate between George Sylvester Viereck Editor of 'The Fatherland' New York and Cecil Chesterton Editor of the New Witness London* (New York: The Fatherland Corporation, 1915), 18–19, accessed December 7, 2009, http://www.archive.org/stream/debatebetweengeooovier#page/n5mode/2up. Indicted in 1941 for violating the Foreign Agents Registration Act, Viereck was imprisoned from 1942 to 1947.

468. G.K. Chesterton, *Autobiography*, op. cit., 211.

469. Ibid., 265.

470. Sewell "first heard this story in 1928 in the offices of *G.K.'s Weekly*"; it seemed "unlikely," but could anyone who knew "anything of the secret scandals of British politics" say it was "impossible?" (B. Sewell, *My Dear Time's Waste*, op. cit., 28).

service despite unfitness, showed his courage in refusing to be exempted from the rigors of army life.[471] But if Gilbert succumbed to the *Witness* circle's paranoia the mood did not endure, as his *Autobiography* reveals: "Whatever Godfrey Isaacs was really like, he is dead now; and I certainly am not going back to dig up the poor fellow's defunct companies." Gilbert even saw "a curious and ironic conclusion" to the saga: "[F]or many years after my brother received the Last Sacraments and died in a hospital in France, his old enemy Godfrey Isaacs, died very shortly after having been converted to the same universal Catholic Church. No one would have rejoiced more than my brother; or with less bitterness or with more simplicity. It is the only reconciliation; and it can reconcile anybody. *Requiescant in pace.*"[472]

Stapleton says that the "bitterness and disappointment Chesterton may have felt" with the English and their rulers after the War "was short-lived" and once more he was "overcome by admiration of his fellow countrymen in refusing to submit to the forces of Prussian darkness in 1914."[473] His warnings about the Armistice were prescient and he continued to oppose "Prussianism," but Gilbert's characteristic desire for reconciliation reasserted itself: Godfrey had converted to Catholicism on his marriage in 1897,[474] but it pleased Gilbert to transform the Marconi affair into a tragedy of two pairs of brothers in which Rufus Isaacs "had in truth acted throughout from those deep domestic loyalties that were my own tragedy in that hour."[475] He thus projected onto Rufus his own loyalty to Cecil despite private misgivings. While it could be argued that Gilbert's failure to restrain Cecil showed that he shared his anti-Semitism, nobody was less suited to asserting authority than Chesterton, and Cecil's undoubted courage in enlisting bestowed a virtuous gloss on his earlier, reckless act.

Corrin agrees that while "Dreyfus" was "the catalyst for Belloc's anti-Semit-

---

471. Cecil was graded Class C but sent to France on active service (M. Ward, *Gilbert Keith Chesterton*, op. cit., 407); "twice sent home on sick leave," in 1918 he was "discharged from active service" with a septic hand; after promising that he would not return to the Front, he wrote his wife "that for the first and only time in their long association he had broken his word to her. The position of the British army in France was desperate; manpower was short; and his Colonel had asked him to return"; Cecil "felt that he could not refuse" (B. Sewell, *Cecil Chesterton*, op. cit., 94).

472. G. K. Chesterton, *Autobiography*, op. cit., 211.

473. J. Stapleton, *Christianity, Patriotism, and Nationhood: The England of G. K. Chesterton* (Lanham MD/Plymouth, England: Lexington Books, 2009), 188.

474. Godfrey "left the Jewish faith, and adopted Roman Catholicism on his marriage" (*Jewish Chronicle*, April 24, 1925, 11) to Leah Felicitie Seta, possibly a Jewish convert, in Paris in 1892. When Rufus Isaacs received the freedom of the City of London, Leah attended the Lord Mayor's banquet with the Chief Rabbi, Lord and Lady Swaythling, Sir Alfred and Lady Mond, Sir Edward and Lady Stern, Mr. and Mrs. Harry Isaacs and the Earl of Oxford and Asquith (ibid., June 11, 1926, 13).

475. G. K. Chesterton, *Autobiography*, op. cit., 265.

ism," "Marconi," which "impugned his brother's personal honor" seemed to have "triggered G.K.'s hostility." Despite this, he was "never as rancorous as Cecil or as obsessive as Belloc."[476] Thereafter, Corrin says, Gilbert's "rare personal attacks were reserved for the Jews, politicians and moneyed groups who were either directly involved in the Marconi incident or had supported the Liberal government during the parliamentary investigation." This "change in G.K.C.'s gentle style appeared immediately after his brother's conviction" and in the following months "his writing became more recklessly violent than at any period in his career."[477] According to Ward, taking over the *New Witness* "after the long repose of his illness" Gilbert appeared "like a giant refreshed and ready to run his course."[478] Cecil's death gave Gilbert moral permission, at least temporarily, to take up Cecil's other legacy, on the "Jewish question." Wilson describes Cecil as "spittingly, uncontrollably anti-semitic" and that in Cecil, Belloc found "his hostility to the Jews mirrored, distorted and magnified to an almost grotesque degree."[479] Cecil's biographer said his "anti-Semitism" was undeniable, "though he denied it himself with perfect sincerity,"[480] but he praises the *Witness'* defense of a poor Jew convicted of murder on dubious evidence. In this instance, however, Cecil claimed Dreyfus "was able to enlist on his behalf the influence of the rich Jewish political families" and "the resources of the Hebrew money power," eventually leading, "after many vicissitudes," to a free pardon, while poor Stinie Morrison had none of his advantages.[481] *New Witness* supporters, including Belloc and E.S.P. Haynes, protested at Cecil's anti-Jewish attacks—but although such defenses were not characteristic of anti-Semites, neither were they free of anti-Semitism. It was Gentile support for Dreyfus—notably that of Emile Zola—that finally obtained justice. Furthermore, the Jewish community did support Morrison.[482] Gilbert would later refer to "very rich" Dreyfus when supporting another poor Jew, Oscar Slater.[483] Cecil began as a fervent "pro-Semite" but his increasingly negative view of the "Jewish question" even outstripped Belloc's. Cecil's death briefly though seriously unbalanced Gilbert's own approach. Ward even suggests that loyalty to Cecil shortened Gilbert's life. He grew old too soon, "straining his heart with

476. J.P. Corrin, *G.K. Chesterton and Hilaire Belloc: The Battle Against Modernity*, op. cit., 66.

477. Ibid., 61.

478. M. Ward, *Gilbert Keith Chesterton*, op. cit., 403.

479. A.N. Wilson, Hilaire Belloc, op. cit., 184.

480. B. Sewell, *Cecil Chesterton*, op. cit., 105.

481. Ibid., 80.

482. Ibid., 106; the detective involved in the Morrison case recalled: "Ample funds for his defense were forthcoming—I believe provided by prominent members of the Jewish community" (F. Porter Wensley, *Forty Years of Scotland Yard: A Record of a Lifetime's Service in the Criminal Investigation Department* [USA: Kessinger Publishing, 2005], 131).

483. G.K. Chesterton, "In defence of a Jew," *G.K.'s Weekly*, August 27, 1927, 575; see Chapter Five.

work crushingly heavy," remarking that "if there was a single altar for that supreme sacrifice it was no other than the altar of Cecil's memory."[484]

Ada Chesterton

Cecil's wife Ada, a published author when they met at a debate in 1901,[485] was a feminist, "hard-bitten," hard-drinking journalist.[486] Known as "Keith," she wrote as J. K. Prothero for the *New Witness* and *G. K.'s Weekly*. For her work with homeless women she was awarded an OBE in 1938. Cecil proposed to the much older Ada many times but they married just before he went overseas to war in 1917. In 1942 she followed his example in becoming a Catholic.[487] Ada, the *New Witness* assistant editor during the Marconi affair, was described by Donaldson as a "strange but influential figure" who "must have had great influence" on Cecil, and "[a]t least once . . . used it recklessly."[488] Like the rest of the *Witness* circle, she adds, Ada saw the Marconi trial as a triumph for Cecil, "a blow . . . struck for public morals" of which they had "boasted . . . ever since."[489]

Ada wrote romantic fiction, and Donaldson describes her memoir *The Chestertons* as "written in seedily romantic clichés . . . betray[ing] vanity and malice."[490] Rather than revealing family secrets, the book suggests ambivalence toward Gilbert's fame and dislike of his wife.[491] *The Chestertons* was comprehensively rebutted by Ward,[492] and Donaldson questioned its veracity.[493] According to Cecil's biographer, Ada was "unfair" to Frances Chesterton and

484. M. Ward, *Gilbert Keith Chesterton*, op. cit., 668.

485. At "The Moderns" debating club (B. Sewell, *Cecil Chesterton*, op. cit., 29).

486. I. Ker, *G. K. Chesterton: A Biography*, op. cit., 79.

487. "He was so wistful, so indomitable that somehow I could not refuse. . . . [W]hen I said 'yes' there came into his eyes a look of such adoration, such unfathomable joy that I felt suddenly, strangely humbled" (Mrs. C. Chesterton, *The Chestertons*, op. cit., 166–168). Born into a journalistic family, Ada Elizabeth Jones (1869–1962) began as a Fleet Street reporter aged 16, writing fiction and non-fiction as Sheridan Jones, J.K. Prothero, and Margaret Hamilton. She married Cecil on June 9, 1917. Her research into homelessness for the *Daily Express* was published as *In Darkest London* (1926), followed by *Women of the Underworld* (1928) and *I Lived in a Slum* (1936). She became a Catholic in 1942 (*Oxford Dictionary of National Biography*).

488. F. Donaldson, *The Marconi Scandal*, op. cit., 72.

489. Ibid., 188.

490. Ibid., 72.

491. "She had never had to earn her living in the ordinary strenuous sense, and her experience of employment had been confined to the secretaryship of a society called, I think, 'The Parents' Reform League,' or something of that kind" (Mrs. Chesterton, *The Chestertons*, op. cit., 26); Gilbert recalled that Frances had "worked very hard as secretary of an educational society in London" (G.K. Chesterton, *Autobiography*, op. cit., 154–155).

492. M. Ward, *Gilbert Keith Chesterton*, op. cit., 662–668.

493. "Her account of the Marconi case is inaccurate and its value lies only in the picture she gives of the fervour with which she and Chesterton approached their task" (F. Donaldson, *The Marconi Scandal*, op. cit., 72).

"unreliable" about Gilbert. He says that her memory was "often at fault" (she was "over seventy when she wrote it"). Still, he adds, the book was a valuable source of information on Cecil since Gilbert had destroyed Cecil's youthful writings, and the Blitz destroyed other papers.[494] It also throws light on Cecil's posthumous influence on Gilbert, who warned Ada that the *Witness* "must end." She recalled: "[E]ven then he was striving to break from certain old influences." The paper had been "the expression of Cecil's forceful personality," but under Gilbert, "the family journal gradually dimmed its torch and lost that challenge which had been the trumpet call of the lesser brother's crusade." Having "followed Cecil to the Editorial chair" as well as "the political arena," Gilbert was "standing on the brink of the Church his brother had already entered." When he came to launch his own paper, Ada said, "Gilbert perhaps felt that, if I still worked side by side with him, Cecil's ideals rather than his own must inevitably have been pushed to the front."[495] Dale Stone comments: "It must have taken incredible courage" for Gilbert "to summon Ada" to impart the bad news: "[I]nevitably she took it badly."[496] Ward says Ada was not a Catholic or a Distributist "and her political outlook was entirely different from Gilbert's." His "intense dislike of having to tell Mrs. Cecil" may have delayed his new paper's launch almost as much as money worries.[497]

In fact, Gilbert asked Belloc to edit the *Witness* not least because of the "somewhat delicate personal situation" that needed to be tackled first. But, he added, he had "brought it off once before" and believed that "if necessary" he could "do it again." Ker says this may refer to the previous year when he became editor and "persuad[ed]" Ada to "relinquish, at least temporarily, the assistant editorship."[498] He told Belloc: "[A]part from my sympathy for her, [Ada] is not and never has been a person I could treat like an ordinary subordinate on what was, after all, my brother's paper ... If it were a property, she would be the heiress." He had to "get her consent in a free and friendly fashion," and if Belloc could help the paper financially, it would seem natural for him to want to run it. He thought that he and Belloc "could make it" the sort of paper that England needed,[499] although Chesterton saw himself as suited to editing as he was to "tight-rope dancing." While he and Belloc did not agree on everything, Chesterton believed that the paper "would be 'better without any intervention by

494. B. Sewell, *Cecil Chesterton*, op. cit., xi–xii.

495. Mrs. C. Chesterton, *The Chestertons*, op. cit., 262–263.

496. A. Dale Stone, *Outline of Sanity: A Biography of G.K. Chesterton* (Bloomington, Indiana: iUniverse.com, 2005), 245.

497. M. Ward, *Gilbert Keith Chesterton*, op. cit., 491–492.

498. G.K. Chesterton, Letter to Hilaire Belloc, April 22, 1919, John J. Burns Library, in I. Ker, *G.K. Chesterton: A Biography*, op. cit., 395.

499. G.K. Chesterton, Letter to Hilaire Belloc, May 3, 1919, John J. Burns Library (ibid., 395–396).

other influences Cecil left on it." But "private relations" were "more important than public" and Gilbert refused to "go out in a sort of stink" over poor treatment, especially of his sister-in-law: "Those nearest to our nearest may not happen to be the people who would have been our chief chosen friends" but "they must be our friends"—if not, memories were "wounded and life made very ugly." Gilbert's "great respect" for Ada's "real loyalty to the cause" and "great regard for her many good qualities," meant having to "protect not only her interest but her feelings." If she were offered the job of drama critic it would "rule out all political intervention," and Belloc would have "the ordinary right to oversee or end the experiment."[500] Gilbert later reported: "The obstacle has removed herself with a gesture of considerable generosity." He felt "under an obligation" to Ada for "the tone" she had taken. She was "a curious and in some ways a very fine character," but she was "not the sub-editor for the *NW*."[501]

Belloc never took over, but as drama critic Ada continued to cause problems for *G.K.'s Weekly*. Zangwill, author of the play *We Moderns,* complained of "Mr. J.K. Prothero's" comment that "more than one of his admirers cherishes the hope that Mr. Zangwill will go back to his race for inspiration." Also that he "corruptly" wrote plays for money. Chesterton appended an emollient note to the letter: "We appreciate v. highly the compliment of a letter from Mr. Zangwill; the points raised are not within our immediate department."[502] This recalled the time Chesterton had soothed Wells over a *Witness* review of his friend Ford Madox Hueffer's *Zeppelin Nights* (1915). Ward deleted the reviewer's name in her biography, but Wells told Chesterton: "Some disgusting little greaser named Prothero"—probably "a dirty minded priest or some such unclean thing"—had been "allowed to insult old F.M.H. in a series of letters that make me ashamed of my species."[503] "J.K. Prothero" had claimed the book

500. G.K. Chesterton, Letter to Hilaire Belloc, August 25, 1919, John J. Burns Library 396–397).

501. G.K. Chesterton, Letter to Hilaire Belloc, undated, John J. Burns Library (ibid., 397).

502. "If Mr. Prothero was able to write plays he too would write them for money" (J. Leftwich, *Israel Zangwill* [London: James Clarke & Co., 1957], 116–117); *We Moderns*, performed in London in July 1924, was reviewed in a specimen copy of *G.K.'s Weekly*, which began publication in 1925 (M. Ward, *Gilbert Keith Chesterton*, op. cit., 490). Later, Zangwill referred to "Mr. J.K. Prothero's not unkindly notice of my comedy" and offered Chesterton tickets "for yourself and friends" (I. Zangwill, Letter to G.K. Chesterton, July 21, 1925 [Chesterton Collection, British Library, 73230]); see Chapter Seven.

503. M. Ward, *Gilbert Keith Chesterton* (London, 1944), 350, corrected from BL Add. MS 73199, folio 26 with "Prothero" restored, in I. Ker, *G.K. Chesterton: A Biography*, op. cit., 370. Wells complained to Gilbert although Cecil was editor, saying that Hueffer was "serving his country" rather than "pleading his age and his fat and taking refuge from service in a greasy obesity as your brother has done" (H.G. Wells, Letter to G.K. Chesterton, M. Ward, *Gilbert Keith Chesterton*, op. cit., 411); later Wells told Gilbert that he "let fly at the most sensitive part of the New Witness constellation, the only part about whose soul I care" (H.G. Wells, Letter to G.K. Chesterton, ibid., 412–413); see Chapter Four.

showed "Hueffer's lack of patriotism" by portraying Londoners "cowering in terror in their cellars," while "[t]he only panic was in the 'foreign' parts of London, particularly Whitechapel, which were 'inhabited by non-Europeans.'" Furthermore, that Hueffer was "not exactly of pure European extraction, and this book is certain to confirm such impression."[504] A *Witness* reader complained that there was "no reason" to "go out of your way to insult Mr. Hueffer," who was a Catholic, "by calling him a Jew and a coward."[505] Ada "retorted . . . that, because Hueffer had converted to Catholicism, that did not mean that 'he ceases to be a Jew.'"[506] Chesterton told Wells that while often disagreeing with "Prothero's" criticisms he regarded the controversy as "a point of taste." Ker links this response to "Marconi," which, apparently, "justified any lapses of 'good taste.'"[507] As Editor the following year, 1917, Chesterton apologized for "Prothero's" offensive comments about Jews[508] in her article *The Necessity for a Bomb-Proof Ghetto*, where she alleged that East End Jews hysterically trampled other people when seeking shelter during an air raid. Chesterton described Ada as his "able" colleague but also praised Jewish courage, attempting to pacify both parties, although the controversy reemerged after the War.[509] The strain on Chesterton's loyalty caused by being caught between Jewish and Gentile friends[510] will be explored in Chapter Eight. He praised Ada in his *Autobiography*[511] and generously remembered her and her charities in his will, but as Ward notes, Ada failed to mention this in her memoir.[512]

The Chestertons, which appeared in 1941, recalls how the League for Clean Government brought together "all kinds of warring factions in a common cause. Tories, Socialists, Atheists, Liberals, Catholics and Jews eagerly joined,

504. *New Witness*, January 6, 1916, in I. Ker, *G. K. Chesterton: A Biography*, op. cit., 369.

505. *New Witness*, January 13, 1916, ibid.

506. *New Witness*, January 20, 1916, ibid. Ford's German antecedents were Catholics, but he "converted . . . as a teenager, encouraged by some of his relatives but also in reaction against the 'militant atheism and anarchism' of his English cousins," his mother being the daughter of Pre-Raphaelite painter Ford Madox Brown (Jonathan Newham, "Catholic Writers at War: Tolkien, Ford and Leighton," *Catholic Life*, April/May 2015, 18).

507. G. K. Chesterton, Letter to H. G. Wells, M. Ward, *Gilbert Keith Chesterton* (London, 1944), 351–352, text corrected from BL Add. MS 73199, folio 27–28 (ibid., 371–372).

508. *New Witness*, October 11, 1917, in D. Rapp, "The Jewish Response to G. K. Chesterton's Antisemitism, 1911–1933," *Patterns of Prejudice*, 24 (2–4), (1990): 82–83; see Chapters One and Five.

509. J. K. Prothero, (Ada Chesterton), "The Necessity for a Bomb-Proof Ghetto," the *New Witness*, October 4, 1917, 543; *New Witness*, September 3, 1920, 350; September 17, 1920, 375–376, ibid., 81.

510. G. K. Chesterton, "The Jew and the Journalist," *New Witness*, October 11, 1917, 563; see Chapter Five.

511. It was a "great honour to be connected" to the "brilliant" Ada, who might "without exaggeration" be called "the Queen of Fleet Street"; homeless women found "real hospitality" in her Cecil Houses (G. K. Chesterton, *Autobiography*, op. cit., 190–191).

512. "Appendix C: *The Chestertons*," M. Ward, *Gilbert Keith Chesterton*, op. cit., 668.

rallying to Cecil's leadership. He had the rare gift of binding alien opinions to his own."[513] The Jewish Zionist Dr. Eder, Ada says, was a "close adherent . . . a most valued supporter of the League and always ready to champion the poor against injustice—and the rich."[514] But the League debated "the Party System, the Money Power and the Jewish Problem." It was resurrected as the *New Witness* League in 1918,[515] but "Gilbert had not the particular qualities necessary to make such a challenging body a success."[516] Cecil, Ada says, spent his Sunday mornings "pleasantly" with a Jewish friend in army camp, both unable to get to a place of worship,[517] but recalled that on first meeting Cecil, Gilbert said seven tobacconists in Kensington High Street were "very sad because they earn very little." Cecil interjected that there were "only five," and one belonged to "Salmon and Gluckstein, a combination which suggests many things, but hardly sorrow at small earnings." Gilbert "smiled serenely" and called the intervention "materialistic cavilling."[518] Ada gives the impression that it was Gilbert, rather than Cecil and herself, who harbored extremist tendencies, claiming that Gilbert had "a growing admiration for Mussolini." Recalling his "passionate pro-Boer days" spent protesting "vehemently against the violation of a weaker country's independence," she had expected "a flaming denunciation of Imperialist aims against the simple Abyssinian. But the voice of the defender of small people was silent."[519]

Ada did not recall, however, that as Gilbert was struggling to pacify warring Distributists on the issue, she was revealing her own ambivalence about Hitler in *Sickle or Swastika?* (1935). In this work she claimed that posterity "must, I think, agree as to his original sincerity." When Hitler was elected Chancellor, "the regeneration of the national spirit was so direct and overwhelming that a general feeling of relief ran through Western Europe."[520] This "regeneration of the national spirit" filled Chesterton with dread rather than relief, but Ada went beyond reporting German responses to sharing them. At a Nazi rally in Berlin she saw "something truly terrifying" in the crowd's "abasement," offering up "their souls and bodies at the altar of their faith." To Ada, "Hitler worship" was "a variant of the Mahommedan religion in which God is Germany, Hitler his prophet." Nevertheless, she joined with those making the "Hitler salute" even

---

513. Mrs. C. Chesterton, *The Chestertons*, op. cit., 113–114.

514. Ibid., 118–119.

515. J. P. Corrin, *G. K. Chesterton and Hilaire Belloc: The Battle Against Modernity*, op. cit., 54.

516. Mrs. C. Chesterton, *The Chestertons*, op. cit., 127.

517. This ended when "the Catholic" was ordered to clean the latrines and "the Jew" to scrub the kitchen floor: "The reason for the discrimination remained a mystery" (ibid., 197).

518. Ibid., 2–3.

519. Ibid., 297–298.

520. Mrs. C. Chesterton, *Sickle or Swastika?* (London: Stanley Paul & Co. Ltd., 1935), 9.

while acknowledging that opponents were "put to the stick—the lethal alternative that serves the rank and file."[521] Ada's concern for women's employment eclipsed concerns about the "ejectment of Jewish doctors" from hospitals and clinics: "The Nazi reaction to feminine status" was "from every angle . . . reactionary."[522] Ordinary Germans, she said, "regarded Hitler as the common man *in excelsis*," but communists or their families would disappear, sometimes fatally beaten in the sinister Brown Houses, sometimes removed to concentration camps. She adds, however, that "[f]ear, as in most cases of cruelty" was "obviously an actuating cause of Nazi barbarism." People grumbled about Jews "who stopped fair play for small shopkeepers; the Jews who maintained the high price of food," and Ada blamed "Nazi propaganda" for influencing the unemployed, who, once in the Nazi ranks could proclaim the hatred "which those in regular situations did not share." Those attempting to leave the country had to surrender their money, and Ada's homeless "friends under the arches" told her "of Jews who had lost their homes and their work and like pariah dogs only ventured out at night to rake the gutters or beg assistance from their Gentile friends." But it was dangerous to help "a starving Jew."[523] Ada "ran into an old little Jew in the Friedrichstrasse" who "tremblingly extended his open palm towards me apprehensively glancing around," looking "very ill, dreadfully hungry and horribly afraid. Feeling at the moment that he and I might both be beaten, I gave him a trifle and realised that I was in a very mad world." Those who were not with Hitler were against him "and must be exterminated."[524]

As Chesterton and Belloc had protested earlier, Ada describes Jews being "turned out of professions and schools," banned from public entertainments and "routed from commerce." Big stores were forced to "shed" their Jewish employees, but despite noting all this, she adds: "[T]he old Hebrew control of finance remain[ed] unshaken," observing that not only were the banks "under Jewish control," but "quite seventy per cent" of the workers were "non-Christian. It amazed me to find in the Dresden Bank, and others equally influential, cashier after cashier palpably Semitic. I asked the reason for this seeming tolerance repeatedly, but the question remained unanswered. 'The Leader does his best,' was as far as I could get; 'we must be patient.'" Ada commented that "the non-Aryan grip remains, nor does it seem likely that even the most rigorous baiting and denunciation will loosen it." An American businessman told her: "Germany cannot get rid of Jewish finance, any more than Great Britain,

---

521. Ibid., 25–26.
522. In state departments women could be employed only in subordinate positions (ibid., 13).
523. Ibid., 30–33.
524. Ibid., 35.

France or Italy. The whole business is too international." Despite noting that "Jew hunting, even in the most impossible places, [was] perpetual,"[525] Ada thought anti-Jewish policies should be applied more rigorously and even drew attention to those not yet ruined. *The Chestertons'* emphasis on Gilbert's response to fascism was ironic, given that her own attitude to the "non-Aryan grip" on Germany reflected those non-Germans who, as Belloc complained, sympathized with Hitler's anti-Jewish policy—except that Ada believed Hitler was not doing enough.

Chesterton said Ada had "sympathy with Communists, as I have, and perhaps points of agreement I have not,"[526] and *Sickle or Swastika?* described "the frenzied acclamation" greeting Hitler, but "the adoration of Lenin in the U.S.S.R."[527] Ada praised the "Communist miracle." Four years earlier, she said, Russia had been living on bread and tea,[528] but now there was "caviare, roast chicken, bortsch and lobster, ice-cream and every kind of salad . . . wine and vodka flowed like the Volga."[529] Moreover, at a writers' dinner at Maxim Gorky's mansion"[530] it "lent a special delight to the feast to feel" that such "delicacies" could be shared by all. Life, she said, was "not only good but inexpensive."[531] She did note the public humiliation of rent defaulters,[532] and "undesirables" rounded up to show that crime had fallen.[533] Starving old peasants were squeezed out of their crumbling properties while money was lavished on the "show piece" collective farms.[534] Some Russians went hungry, and "in extreme cases, half starve[d]." But for British newspapers to portray these "unhappy products of a system into which they cannot fit" as typical country-dwellers was "to fail utterly, and often wilfully, to apprehend the actual facts." Inadvertently summing up the ghastly truth, Ada insisted: "[T]hey represent a single and rapidly dwindling class."[535] Like other left-wing visitors anxious to defend communism, Ada overlooked or excused repression. Unable to speak Russian, like them she believed the official narrative.[536]

---

525. Ibid., 37–38.
526. G.K. Chesterton, *Autobiography*, op. cit., 191.
527. Mrs. C. Chesterton, *Sickle or Swastika?* op. cit., 13.
528. Ibid., 175.
529. Ibid., 191.
530. Ibid., 186.
531. Ibid., 191.
532. Ibid., 219.
533. Ibid., 233.
534. Ibid., 248.
535. Ibid., 259.
536. An old woman spoke "at length, and I should say eloquently" while Ada "listened uncomprehending but with respect" (ibid., 231).

Despite urging even more rigorous anti-Jewish measures in Germany, and with her provocative writings about Jews cloaked in anonymity, Ada lectured to Jewish groups,[537] and took an interest in Jewish charities.[538] Jews generously supported her work with homeless women.[539] In the same year that *Sickle or Swastika?* was published, Ada joined J.B. Priestley and other notables on an inquiry into the plight of Jewish refugees in Nazi Germany.[540]

G. K.'s Weekly *and the Distributists*

According to Ward, Chesterton "would never, he once said, have turned of his own accord to politics," and that arguably "it would have been better if he never had." But although Gilbert saw *New Witness* as a "sacred legacy,"[541] according to Ker, he was "much more open" than was Cecil to contributions from outside their "small circle."[542] After prizing Ada from her influential position he restarted it under his own name.[543] Distributist, and "Catholic (although not exclusively) in religion," it was "in that sense" a "continuation of Cecil's paper," but, Ker remarks, it was "also funny in a Chestertonian way."[544] It was to be "a different kind of paper ... one marked by humour above all," not something associated with the "combative" Cecil.[545] Ker adds that it would be "important personally" as an outlet for Chesterton, because, apart from his *Illustrated London News* column, which "had to steer clear largely of politics and religion," he

537. To the West London Synagogue Association on "Russia To-day" (*Jewish Chronicle*, March 3, 1933, 10–11); on "Young China and New Japan" (ibid, January 18, 1935, 10–11).

538. Ada spoke at the new Jewish Day Nursery in Kensington, London (*Jewish Chronicle*, July 22, 1938, 12–13); she unveiled the foundation plaque at the Cecil Residential (Grannies) Club, accompanied by Vice-President of Cecil Houses Major Brunel Cohen, and his wife (ibid., November 1951, 18–19).

539. Miss Annie Wolff left £150 to Ada's Women's Public Lodging House Fund (*Jewish Chronicle*, October 20, 1933, 14–15); Maj. Cohen presided over a meeting in support of the Cecil Houses for homeless women, resulting in "[v]ery substantial donations" (ibid., November 23, 1934, 26–27); it was "a source of pride to the Jewish Community" that the meeting took place in Sir Philip Sassoon's house, and that Major Cohen became Hon. Treasurer. Chief Rabbi Dr J.H. Hertz showed "a keen interest in the work" (ibid., May 31, 1935, 22); Major Cohen presided at the laying of the foundation stone of the new Cecil Club for Girls in London; the Chief Rabbi spoke of the "appalling condition of Jewish refugees" (ibid., June 16, 1939, 44).

540. "Nazi Terrorism Condemned," *Jewish Chronicle*, July 12, 1935, 15; Ada attended the first meeting of the Terror Against Refugees Commission, to "ascertain and publicise the truth" about the recent "killings and kidnappings of refugees" in Europe (ibid., July 19, 1935, 17).

541. M. Ward, *Gilbert Keith Chesterton*, op. cit., 487.

542. I. Ker, *G. K. Chesterton: A Biography*, op. cit., 375.

543. Something that Shaw advised against (G. B. Shaw, Letter to G.K. Chesterton, February 11, 1923, M. Ward, *Gilbert Keith Chesterton*, op. cit., 487).

544. I.T. Ker, *The Catholic Revival in English Literature 1845–1961*, op. cit., 513.

545. Ibid., 497.

"no longer had any access to the press,"[546] ever since he had savaged the Liberal papers in the wake of Cecil's Marconi campaign.[547]

Obliged to subsidize the new paper from his earnings, besides contributing articles, once again he left the day-to-day running to others. If any problems arose he poured oil on troubled waters. As Ward notes: "[T]here was one thing he could not bear—quarrels on the Board or on the staff and above all the suggestion that he should adjudicate." The sub-editor had "great difficulty" getting him to read and select contributions, which were "uneven in quality." Leading columns and "Notes of the Week" were "weak imitations" of his or Belloc's work, and although at first Chesterton wrote all the latter, his assistant editor W.R. Titterton's soon resembled them so closely it was difficult to tell them apart.[548]

Chesterton's reluctance to impose his authority could, as seen, lead to problems, not least regarding the "Jewish question," and Titterton, Gilbert's biographer and "most loyal supporter," although an "excellent journalist" and fierce anti-eugenicist, later founded *The Englishman*, which was dedicated to the "bit of truth" that "England should be governed by Englishmen and all alien influences suppressed, beginning with . . . Scots, Jews, Welshmen, and Irishmen, all of whom were to be deported."[549]

If this was meant tongue-in-cheek, earlier, Shaw had advised Chesterton that his new periodical should "drop" the "pseudo race feuds" because he could not "compete with the Morning Post," which gave "the real thing in its succulent savagery" while Chesterton could only give "a 'wouldn't hurt a fly' affectation of it."[550] George Macdonald described *G.K.'s Weekly* as "not anti-Semitic as compared with its predecessors,"[551] and although not entirely free of Jewish references the tone was markedly different. The *Jewish Chronicle* appeared to ignore it, unlike the *New Witness*, although it claimed: "Mr Chesterton told us recently that in a final analysis his complaint against the Jews is that they are not mem-

---

546. Ibid., 593.

547. Chesterton resigned from the *Daily News* after his satirical "A Song of Strange Drinks" appeared in the *New Witness*, January 23, 1913; *Daily News* owner George Cadbury, scion of the "cocoa" family, was a leading Liberal supporter (I. Ker, *G.K. Chesterton: A Biography*, op. cit., 2011, 326).

548. Staff member Miss Dunham recalled Chesterton as "so kind": he "never got angry" and "never minded being interrupted" (M. Ward, *Gilbert Keith Chesterton*, op. cit., 493–495).

549. William R. Titterton, *G.K. Chesterton: A Portrait* (London, 1936), 138, in J. P. Corrin, *G.K. Chesterton and Hilaire Belloc: The Battle Against Modernity*, op. cit., 90.

550. G. B. Shaw, Letter, February 16, 1923, M. Ward, *Gilbert Keith Chesterton*, op. cit., 489; Ker corrects the text from the original letter (BL Add. MS 73198, fo. 89, I. Ker, *G.K. Chesterton: A Biography*, op. cit., 496–497).

551. George Macdonald, "A response to Owen Edwards," *Chesterton Review*, 6 (1), (Fall-Winter 1979–80): 91–95.

bers of the Catholic Church."[552] The new paper reflected Chesterton's view that modern race theories were bunkum, and that the Jewish religion and poor Jews should be defended, but wealthy Jews could, via international capitalism, financially "invade" sovereign nations to the detriment especially of the poor. Nationalism was "moral and just" when a nation prioritized the rights of its families, and "only immoral" when it meant "a vainglorious insistence upon looking for new worlds to conquer, whether by force of arms, 'economic pressure' or market-juggling."[553] In *Sidelights* (1932) Chesterton claimed that the "perilous power and opportunity" of "wealth and worldly success" had passed from the British Empire to the United States, but that Imperialism was still Imperialism even when advanced by "economic pressure or snobbish fashion rather than by conquest." Chesterton had "more respect" for the Empire spread by fighting than by finance, but in "both cases," the "worst things" were spread.[554] He added that because America happened to be "the *pied a terre* of the wandering international financer," the Union Jack had been dipped in surrender to the Stars and Stripes "out of respect for the sort of Jew who cannot get into any club in New York."[555]

When attacking Nazi anti-Semitism in 1933 he said he never had a quarrel with "non-financial Jews," explaining that the "intermediate commercial position" of the "Jewish nation" caused the "Jewish problem."[556] But the origins of Jewish financiers were not always mentioned,[557] and in 1925 Chesterton maintained: "The Jews are a great reality; and if they are hated, that hatred is a reality. But who in the world ever hated Semites?" Race theory was, he insisted, all speculation, invented "to provide politicians with the excuses of poltroons." Rather than saying he "distrusted the Irish" a man would say he "distrusted the Celts." The Englishman "who thought it a little vulgar to boast of being an Englishman would boast of being an Anglo-Saxon" while the man who knew it was "a little provocative and preposterous to talk about the superiority of the Germans would talk learnedly about the superiority of the Teutons." People "who felt annoyed with Jews pretended that their Aryan instincts quivered with

552. "Why Don't You Like Us?" *Jewish Chronicle*, July 24, 1925, 5.

553. "True Nationalism," (unsigned), *G.K.'s Weekly*, July 13, 1933; "Invasion may be a sword; but peaceful penetration is a poison.... To attack the culture is to attack the country... from within" (G.K. Chesterton, *Illustrated London News*, April 9, 1927).

554. G.K. Chesterton, *Sidelights on New London and Newer York and Other Essays* (London: Sheed & Ward, 1932), 164.

555. G.K. Chesterton, "Exodus from Europe," *G.K.'s Weekly*, December 28, 1929, 247.

556. G.K. Chesterton, "Straws in the Wind: The Horse and the Hedge," *G.K.'s Weekly*, March 30, 1933, 55; see Chapter Five.

557. Even Sir Alfred Mond, criticized along with other millionaires (G.K. Chesterton, "A Point of Delicacy," *G.K.'s Weekly*, July 2, 1927, 475).

some racial repulsion at the sight of certain types of skull or skin supposed to be Semitic." Jews, he added, could be "liked and disliked and pitied and reverenced and scorned and hated," but "[i]f we hated them, we should not pretend to be hating something else. As a matter of fact we do not hate them, either in a personal or a tribal sense." They were, he concluded, "what we have always called them, a problem; but never so much of a problem as when they themselves deny that there is any problem."[558] But even Zangwill agreed: "Hilaire Belloc, in his book *The Jews*, said rightly that the Jewish problem 'cannot be avoided. It must be met.'"[559]

More positively, *G.K.'s Weekly* followed the *Witness* tradition in defending a poor woman prosecuted for slamming the door on a government official because the milk was boiling over.[560] Chesterton argued that "welfare" considerations were used to justify intrusion into the poor family: "No man is innocent until he has proved his innocence"; parental authority was "set aside"; the "sanctity of the home" was "invaded."[561] His defense of the family was bound up with his defense of democracy. Compulsory education might lead to "a State power that could bring up the whole population as British Fascists or Bolshevists."[562] A "free state," he argued, was "made of families," and there was "no right so real as the right to open and shut a door . . . the roof-tree is the tree of liberty."[563] If, as claimed, there was "a large class of mentally deficient persons" who would "breed, increase, and corrupt the whole community with their own taint," and if the world was producing "an increasing number of victims," then "we must change the world."[564] In April 1934, before Chesterton's "reassessment" of Hitler as a tool of capitalism, the paper claimed the Nazis "were thrown into power rather unexpectedly as the result of an agreement concluded by financial, industrial, and agrarian groups . . . determined to exploit their own interest under the forms of a new regime." This "compromise" might "go down to history as Adolf Hitler's fatal blunder." Granted, it was "probably his only means of achieving power, and he may have meant to outwit in his own time the forces controlling him," although "[t]he idealists of the movement were immediately warned off" when they attempted to help "the small man" by controlling the banks, or interfering with big business. But the "doctrinaires" insisted on "eugenic legislation, racial persecution, a pagan attack upon Chris-

558. G.K. Chesterton, "On Being Called 'Anti-Semite,'" *G.K.'s Weekly*, April 18, 1925, 78.

559. I. Zangwill, *The Voice of Jerusalem* (London: Wm. Heinemann, 1920), 161.

560. "[S]he saved the milk; but had to pay £3 in fines for the milk she managed to save" (G.K. Chesterton, "The Song of Deborah," *G.K.'s Weekly*, January 12, 1929, 281).

561. G.K. Chesterton, "State and Family," *G.K.'s Weekly*, March 28, 1935, 33.

562. G.K. Chesterton, "A Note on Novelists," *G.K.'s Weekly*, April 13, 1929, 68.

563. G.K. Chesterton, "A Debate on Degeneracy," *G.K.'s Weekly*, April 4, 1925, 27.

564. G.K. Chesterton, "Mental Deficiency," *G.K.'s Weekly*, June 22, 1929, 226.

tianity and an extreme theory of political uniformity."[565] There was no mention, however, of the "Jewish capitalist" in discussing the rise of Hitler, a claim which would have been comparable to claiming that "the Jews" were trying to engineer a war. Hitler believed in the existence of the "Jewish money power" and that "the slow disappearance of the right of private property, and the gradual transference of the entire economy to the ownership of stock companies" was "[a] grave economic symptom of decay."[566] However, he also blamed Germany's Great War defeat on "the Jews," along with every negative feature of German life.[567]

Chesterton ridiculed claims that Jews had engineered Germany's defeat. Now he rejected the totalitarian approach, preferring to "rely on the strength of [the Distributist] case and on the fairness and judgment of our countrymen," a case "so strong indeed that we can afford to work and to wait another while." With his belief in human dignity, he remained confident that "those who are consciously and unconsciously one with us" were "in no danger at any time either of practising the goose step or walking rough-shod over the rights, feelings or bodies of others." The latter approach was "peculiar to those who invest the state—an abstract conception—with the dignity that a rational philosophy must reserve for the individual."[568] Corrin believed the Distributists "generally approved of Mussolini's politics . . . almost to a man" but "opposed fascist authoritarianism for Britain," seeing it as "alien to the nation's long tradition of aristocratic tolerance and geniality." Despite the British fascists' attempts to woo them, "virtually all" Distributists had "nothing but contempt for Nazism." Chesterton, and "even Belloc, the irrepressible anti-Dreyfusard" were among the first to "condemn Hitler's persecution of the Jews." The *Chesterbelloc* "hated Hitlerism because they thought it was Prussianism in its last and most virulent stage of madness." Chesterton's view of Hitler as merely "the puppet of the Junker drillmasters" was taken from Belloc. Nonetheless, Corrin argued, they were prescient in distinguishing between fascism, an over-zealous patriotism that recognized boundaries even in over-stepping them, and the racist Pan-German movement: "Chesterton had discovered very early that Hitler's funny crooked cross represented something quite different from Mussolini's bundle of fasces." The latter represented "the glory of an empire which once had really existed, whereas the swastika represented something the world had never known."[569] As early as 1915, Chesterton noted that the Germans had done what

---

565. G. K. Chesterton, "German Conflict," *G. K.'s Weekly*, April 12, 1934, 81.

566. A. Hitler, *Mein Kampf* (London: Pimlico, 1925–26/2001), 214.

567. Ibid., 210.

568. G. K. Chesterton, "The Goose Step," *G. K.'s Weekly*, June 14, 1934, 226.

569. G. K. Chesterton, "The Tool," *G. K.'s Weekly*, September 6, 1934, in J. P. Corrin, *G. K. Chesterton and Hilaire Belloc: The Battle Against Modernity*, op. cit., 183–185.

he had "described as a wild fancy in the *Flying Inn*; combined the Cross and the Crescent in one ornamental symbol."[570]

Brocard Sewell, who praised Oswald Mosley, worked on *G.K.'s Weekly* and later claimed anti-Semitism charges were "unjust," unless it meant "as so many people seem to nowadays . . . any criticism of any Jewish person for anything whatsoever." A "reasonable definition," he maintained, was "the use and fostering of words and actions with the deliberate intention of subjecting Jews to hostility, contempt, or violence." In those days, he claimed, such things "were not taken amiss," and Chesterton "was not censured by either Jews or others." But it had to be "admitted that sometimes things were said or written that would not be said, or at least would be said differently, today."[571]

After GKC

The more serious and confrontational style of Cecil's *New Witness* can be seen in his "defense" of Rufus Isaacs: "He is an alien, a nomad, an Asiatic, the heir of a religious and racial tradition wholly alien from ours. He is amongst us: he is not of us."[572] Under Gilbert, *G.K.'s Weekly* attracted less Jewish criticism, and after his death Corrin notes that the paper lurched towards fascism, asserting that "the powers of monopoly capitalism, spearheaded by Jewish Wall Street

---

570. G.K. Chesterton, Letter to E.C. Bentley, July 20, 1915, M. Ward, *Gilbert Keith Chesterton*, op. cit., 398–399); in the *Flying Inn* "Dr Moole" suggests "some sort of double emblem" for St Paul's Cathedral, "combining cross and crescent" in G.K. Chesterton, *The Flying Inn* (Harmondsworth, Middx.: Penguin, 1914/1958), 38.

571. B. Sewell, *G.K.'s Weekly: An Appraisal* (Maidstone, Kent: The Aylesford Press, 1990), 52–53. Michael Seymour Sewell (religious name Brocard) (1912–2000) converted to Catholicism in 1931 and became a Carmelite friar, writer and publisher. He joined *G.K.'s Weekly* in 1928 but in the 1960s, in contrast to Chesterton, publicly criticized Church teaching on contraception (B. Sewell, *The Habit of a Lifetime: An Autobiography* [Padstow, Cornwall: Tabb House, 1992], 144–147). Described as "a former Distributist League and [British Union of Fascists] member" (Stephen Dorril, *Black Shirt: Sir Oswald Mosley and British Fascism* [London: Viking, 2006], 387), he recalls that Distributist Herbert Shove "joined Sir Oswald Mosley's British Fascists—something he very much disliked to be reminded of later on" (B. Sewell, *My Dear Time's Waste*, op. cit., 74). *The Alternative* (1947) and *Europe: Faith and Plan* (1958) showed what Mosley could have achieved "had he chosen letters and not politics"; a "humane" and "greatly misunderstood man," Mosley was "partly . . . to blame," because of "his ideas on the 'race' question—especially as expounded by his more extreme followers"; Sewell knew Mosley "a good many years" and praises his "magnanimity and lack of bitterness towards his opponents," his "absolute fearlessness"—the "marks of a great man" (ibid., 138–139); they last met shortly before Mosley's death, at the launch of Lady Diana Mosley's biography of the Duchess of Windsor; he and Lady Mosley remained friends (B. Sewell, *The Habit of a Lifetime: An Autobiography*, op. cit., 141).

572. C. Chesterton, "For the Defense," *Eye-Witness*, July 4, 1912, in J.P. Corrin, *G.K. Chesterton and Hilaire Belloc: The Battle Against Modernity*, op. cit., 58.

financiers," posed "a far greater threat than international Bolshevism." Chesterton, although seeing communism as "a practical threat" in Poland, regarded it as a reaction against capitalism and a "bogey" used by "various schools of fascists" to "alarm the people," while "unbridled capitalism" was "the real enemy." The paper's foreign policy, Corrin remarks, was probably Belloc's, since, "unlike Chesterton," Belloc "was generally considered something of an authority on continental politics." Chesterton's "basic approach" to international affairs, "although more temperate, seems to have been molded by Belloc's opinions." But Corrin adds that "[c]ontrary to general belief, G.K. was not always an enthusiastic supporter of Mussolini and Italian Fascism." Chesterton was a "voice of moderation and common sense," and after his death Distributism grew "more sanguine about dictatorship and fascism as useful expedients against . . . international Bolshevism."[573]

According to Corrin, both Belloc and Chesterton saw that the fascist "ideology which had sprung from the soil of Italy in response to peculiar needs, had nothing to offer the British,"[574] but Abyssinia and Chesterton's death proved "a watershed" for Distributism. After 1936, Corrin says, it "shifted further to the right," with "many of Chesterton's ideals . . . thoughtlessly cast by the wayside. In a sense, the Distributist circle lost its sanity after Chesterton's passing," plunging ever deeper into a welter of conspiracy theories linking politics to finance.[575] In June 1936, Corrin comments, the paper (named the *Weekly Review* from March 1938) "assumed a palpably pro-fascist outlook. Its editors generally lauded Mussolini and ignored Hitler's excesses," emphasizing "the far worse danger of international Bolshevism." Many contributors left, and Belloc himself warned of a "group of men . . . Cosmopolitan and largely Jewish, with the Jewish intensity of purpose—whether humanistic, and Messianic or devoted to power of vengeance—the Jewish ability to act in secret, the Jewish indifference to property and national ideals, the fierce Jewish sense of justice and, above all, the Jewish tenacity." There had been "much exaggeration of the Jewish element in Bolshevism," but "no exaggeration of that element, however crude" was "so

---

573. Ibid., 172–174.

574. Ibid., 183.

575. Some Distributists created a "storm" because they felt the Abyssinian invasion had not been denounced, but "Latinophiles" believed "international moneylenders" were trying to force France and Italy off the gold standard, an "elaborate conspiracy of the 'Money Power'"—those "faceless Wall Street bankers" who had rigged Germany's reparations to "drain" Britain, Italy, and France" and wanted Europe's chief economies "completely dependent upon American finance" so as to "monopolize the world's wealth"; the Abyssinian war was a bid for economic freedom: Britain, France, Poland, and Italy should make common cause against America, Germany, and Russia (ibid., 186–188); see Chapter Five.

inept as to affect ignorance of it: for it colours the whole affair."[576] The paper urged the British government to support Franco in the Spanish Civil War and in 1937 "proposed . . . an alliance with Hitler against the Soviet Union."[577] Many old Distributists saw the paper's direction as "completely contrary" to Chesterton's ideals.[578] His death "seriously weakened" Distributism. He alone, Corrin concludes, was "capable of holding the factions together."[579]

Much earlier, McCarthy says that under Belloc, the *New Witness* approach to Imperialism reflected the French nationalist critique of the Panama Canal Company scandals of the 1890s, as "a form of profiteering against the public good by a handful of cosmopolitan financiers who were, in significant numbers, Jewish."[580] By 1939, lack of funds forced Belloc to abandon day-to-day control. He complained that "hosts of second-rate cranks" were willing to "write their fingers to the bone for nothing" but saw "everything quite out of proportion," especially when they were "on the right side." Many others, agreeing "on one point or another," were "shocked by the rest of the points."[581] Wilson notes that "[b]y the time it was publishing articles by such fascists as A.K. Chesterton (G.K.'s cousin)" urging a British alliance with Franco and Hitler against Bolshevism, Belloc "was once more on the high seas" to New York for another lecture tour.[582] Belloc continued to ridicule "race" theories and, while criticizing others' "extreme views" saw his own as reasonable.[583] Corrin says that after 1936, he began "to describe Hitler as a manifestation of 'revived monarchialism,'" and Nazism "like Italian Fascism" as an "authoritarian movement" defending "Europe's common culture against atheist Bolshevik revolution," albeit a "German monarchical impulse function[ing] through the activities of a fantastic Teutonic clique." It was "barbaric, whereas the new Italian monarchy was homogenous in its religion and far more cultural," living as

576. H. Belloc, "Moscow," *G.K.'s Weekly*, August 13, 1936, ibid., 191; his "commentaries on Italy and Spain were outrageous at times," as when he insisted that "Mussolini's fascist dictatorship not only saved Italy from communism but European civilization as well" (H. Belloc, "Mussolini and the Guild," June 15, 1939, ibid., 233).

577. Ibid., 194.

578. Ibid., 196.

579. Ibid., 210.

580. J.P. McCarthy, *Hilaire Belloc: Edwardian Radical*, op. cit., 261.

581. H. Belloc, Letter to Lady Phipps, June 27, 1939, R. Speaight, *The Life of Hilaire Belloc*, op. cit., 483; Belloc continued to try to raise money, advising "from time to time, especially as to what not to put in," because there was "always a danger in sheets of this kind that they will become cranky and, what is worse, indulge in personal attack for the fun of the thing without a clear object" (H. Belloc, Letter to Major-General Guy Dawnay, November 9, 1938, H. Belloc, *Letters from Hilaire Belloc*, op. cit., 271–273).

582. A.N. Wilson, *Hilaire Belloc*, op. cit., 344.

583. For example, the pose of Danes and Swedes as "a conquering Race, or Races" (H. Belloc, Letter to Duff Cooper, July 9, 1938, H. Belloc, *Letters from Hilaire Belloc*, op. cit., 270–271).

it did "in the memory of classical Rome."[584] Corrin comments: "In the end, the Distributists fell victim to that sin of exaggeration which Chesterton had once called heresy. They stretched a portion of Catholic truth out of its proper and well-balanced perspective." The "Latinophiles" were "guilty of . . . that heretical oversimplification of one complex of ideas (Bolshevism, Jewish finance, and Catholicism as culture) at the expense of the intricate whole." With Chesterton's death, the Distributist movement "lost its balance."[585]

In 1930 *G. K.'s Weekly* had condemned the Nazis' "wish to punish the Jews for not being Nordic." If Hitler believed, as he "undoubtedly" did, that the press, "banking, art, etc" were "dominated by a thoroughly corrupt and decadent spirit," he was "clearly justified in attacking the leaders in these spheres, Jew or Gentile." But "to attack an otherwise harmless and decent Jew (and it is the harmless and decent Jews who suffer worst in a pogrom) on purely ethnological grounds" was "so old-fashioned! If these Bavarian Nordics object to non-Nordic domination, why not start with the Prussians!"[586] Some Nazi measures might be seen as fulfilling the Distributist agenda, but "real Distributism," the paper insisted, was "the only practical politics."[587] After the Rohm Purge it commented that "[f]ear" was "the order of the day, not only for the Jews and the Marxists but for the Aryans of the Swastika as well." It was, the paper concluded, "the end of Nazi Germany."[588]

The Mystery of the Chesterbelloc

Chesterton and Belloc came from pro-Semitic backgrounds, but with their anti-capitalist emphasis on "Jewish finance" they acquired a lasting reputation for anti-Semitism, despite their strong anti-Nazi stance and refusal to exploit fascist anti-Semitism.

John Coates argues: "[N]o one could or should attempt to deny that there are passages in Chesterton's writings which are painful to read, expressions of a crude anti-Jewish feeling, not very numerous indeed, but bewildering in a mind generally notably humane and sophisticated." Yet: "So admirable and attractive is Chesterton that there is a strong temptation to gloss the subject

---

584. H. Belloc, "Another Five Facts," *G. K.'s Weekly*, September 27, 1936; "The Breach," *G. K.'s Weekly*, September 23, 1937; "The Two Monarchies," *Weekly Review*, August 25, 1938, in J. P. Corrin, *G. K. Chesterton and Hilaire Belloc: The Battle Against Modernity*, op. cit., 194–195.

585. Ibid., 210–211.

586. "Notes of the Week," (unsigned), *G. K.'s Weekly*, September 27, 1930, 34–35.

587. "Hitler as Distributist," *G. K.'s Weekly*, June 8, 1933, 209–210.

588. "Exit the Third Reich," *G. K.'s Weekly*, July 5, 1934, 273–274.

over."[589] While Gilbert's humorous approach meant that he was taken less seriously than Cecil and Belloc, he did use humor in his paradoxes as a shortcut to the truth.[590] Nonetheless, like Chaucer, he used "flippancy to avoid an argument" rather than to "provoke it."[591]

A courteous listener as well as a great talker, Chesterton preferred political argument to personal quarrel. Often he would smooth over disagreements and soothe hurt feelings caused by less sensitive colleagues: "'I am,' he said, 'like a little child in this, that I can never understand how people I like so much can possibly dislike each other.'"[592] The death of the pugnacious Cecil, to whom he was deeply loyal, rather than the Marconi affair, proved to be the catalyst for Gilbert's more pessimistic approach to the "Jewish question." Arguably, Cecil's posthumous influence on Gilbert was greater than his living influence, but despite the desire to carry on Cecil's legacy, *G. K.'s Weekly* was not, as its name implied, Cecil's *Witness* resurrected.

The paper caused less offence among Jews, and after Gilbert's death it moved closer to fascism. Although greatly influenced by Belloc, Chesterton's attempts to reconcile opposites that do not attract showed that he was undoubtedly a moderating influence on Belloc, especially with regards to the "Jewish question." That moderating influence can be seen in Chesterton's Zionism, which sprang from yet another loyalty, which will be explored in the next chapter.

589. Chesterton's utterances, like many "jocular references to Jews in popular literature," sound "far worse after the horrors of Hitler's final solution"; nonetheless, in his criticisms of Rufus Isaacs, "or the Rand millionaires whom he and Belloc thought, not entirely without justification, had helped to cause the Boer War," Chesterton was "thoughtless in his choice of language" (J. D. Coates, *Chesterton and the Edwardian Cultural Crisis* [Hull: Hull University Press, 1984], 14–15).

590. A. Nichols, *G. K. Chesterton, Theologian*, op. cit., 105.

591. G. K. Chesterton, *Chaucer: A Study* (1932), *G. K. Chesterton Collected Works Vol. XVIII* (San Francisco, 1991), 309–310, in J. Stapleton, *Christianity, Patriotism, and Nationhood: The England of G. K. Chesterton*, op. cit., 191.

592. At a Distributist meeting Chesterton "compared himself to the little child in those stories of quarrels between husband and wife," who "comes in and restores unity" (M. Ward, *Return to Chesterton*, op. cit., 211).

7

Chesterton and the Zionist Dream

CHESTERTON'S ZIONISM was once seen as proof against allegations of anti-Semitism,[1] but with the motivations of non-Jewish Zionists under increasing scrutiny, more recently he has been regarded as a proto-Nazi and even compared to Hitler.[2] Turnbull says that Belloc, "and to a lesser extent G. K. Chesterton . . . campaigned against the corrupting influence of Jews in public life, promoted the myth of Jewish conspiracy to achieve world domination, advocated a form of *apartheid* and stripping of Jews' civil rights, and endorsed emigration to Palestine."[3] This chapter will study Chesterton's Zionism as it developed throughout his career, in order to determine whether it should be seen as evidence of pro- or anti-Semitism.

In the early 1890s Chesterton wrote: "No Christian ought to be an Anti-Semite. But every Christian ought to be a Zionist."[4] In 1911, he defended Lord Swaythling for leaving his money to his children providing they followed the Jewish religion. The resulting *Jewish Chronicle* interview revealed a far more complex philosophy on the "Jewish question" that closely resembled Belloc's. Regarding his claim that there was "a problem, and, above all, a Peril, in the international and largely secret power of the great Jewish houses" they expressed "surprise" that he was "afflicted with such a bogey." Chesterton "humbly pleaded" that he could "only look at things" as they were: it was this "métier in life" that got him "into no end of troubles." The "problem" was great Jewish banking houses wielding international "secret" power. The fact that it was Jewish power made "all the difference." International Jewish labor organi-

---

1. K. Whitehorn, "The Return of G. K. Chesterton," 1974, in D. Conlon, ed., *G. K. Chesterton: A Half Century of Views* (Oxford: Oxford University Press, 1987), 305–309.

2. G. Kaufman, "Chesterton's final solution," *Times Educational Supplement*, January 2, 1998; see Chapter One.

3. M. J. Turnbull, *Victims or Villains: Jewish Images in Classic English Detective Fiction* (Bowling Green, Ohio: Bowling Green State University Popular Press, 1998), 25–26.

4. D. Collins, ed., "Extracts from note-book (about 1893. G. K. C. aged 19)," *The Tablet*, April 4, 1953, in W. Oddie, *Chesterton and the Romance of Orthodoxy: The Making of GKC 1874–1908* (Oxford: Oxford University Press, 2008), 109 note 55.

zation was "just as much a problem and a peril." It was not the Jewish religion, he insisted, but, historically, they were "a separate people with a separate tradition." Admittedly they called themselves Englishmen, were "patriotic and loyal," held land and gave "liberally to English institutions." They subsidized party funds, entered Parliament, entertained, hunted, shot, and so on; nonetheless, "the Jew" was "not an Englishman, because his nationality is not English. They are something different, and in many ways very much better. Still, being better, they cannot be the same." He believed that they were "allied, and rightly and justifiably, to their own people of their own race" who were not English "even in point of citizenship," in Germany, Russia, France, and throughout the world. Jews had no "exclusive right" to be "monopolists and wire-pullers" but the *Nation* had been "horribly inconsistent" in rebuking a Jew, not for "doing the most un-Jewish things according to the Old Testament as so many non-Jews do the most un-Christian according to the New Testament," but for keeping his religion: "I am no anti-Semite. I respect and have the deepest regard for Jews, for their wonderful history, for their wonderful faith, and for the remarkably fine qualities, mental and moral, which the Jew evinces in his national state." But, Chesterton added, he could not "stand the Jew who, having struck oil, oils himself all over." He was "only a little more repugnant ... than the non-Jew who does likewise, because he is a Jew with infinitely finer potentialities." Likewise, a "Jewish capitalist" was "different from an ordinary capitalist," who was "restrained by nationality." The English capitalist was "tied to England ... by something more than his land, by association with his past." Echoing Belloc, Chesterton warned that England was "in danger of a real smash-up, of a great national disaster," and that "our wealthy people" would "remain here and bear the burden of the nation's sorrow. The Jews won't, and we can't expect them to." They were "born civilised" and there was no "no yokel type." They would leave "as they did when Spain ceased to be a first-class power." Chesterton added: "I know what you are thinking of; they were made to leave, and, therefore, as a fact they did leave," but weakened countries were "naturally prone to look with suspicion and even honest fear upon any elements that make for national disintegration." The interviewer protested that Chesterton opposed assimilation but saw "the Jew ... as a national danger" because he did not assimilate: "[U]nless, perhaps, he is always and everywhere ground down by poverty. Must, then, the Jew always be burnt?"

Chesterton agreed that this would be the case—but only "until he finds himself! Till the Jew discovers he is of a separate race, with a history of his own." His future could only be "worthy" if he made it "his own," rather than depending on the Gentile. This would mean recognizing "the necessity for a habitat, a centrum, wherein he can develop that which he now lacks, nationality. You see I am not an anti-Semite. I am a Zionist." To confuse the two was "arrant nonsense," like calling a man "anxious for the preservation" of the English race's "supremacy" an "Anglo-phobe." The "average Englishman" did not dislike foreigners if they were "the real thing. It is the sham they object to." Some did object to foreigner qua foreigner; but Chesterton maintained that a "territorial patriotism" to channel Jewish creative energies would "put an end to the eternal entanglement of mutual wrong of which he is the unhappy cause between himself and the nations among whom he lives." He acknowledged that Palestine could not absorb all the Jews, and all would not go; but it would "absorb all the Judaism," so that, worldwide, Jews could "quite safely and conscientiously, without, I should think, any disloyalty, allow themselves to be absorbed." With the "continuity of the race, its traditions and its history" thus "secured" by the pioneers, "it would not matter" if "the rest" were "lost. Nay, I think it might be an advantage." By "lost" Chesterton meant intermarriage, but, he said, people need not "bother their heads about 'solving' questions," doing everything at once or by any "preconceived, definite, set, plan"; the "most and best" they could do was to "put it upon lines whereby it will have the best opportunity of solving itself." Zionism was "the right line," and Jews who were "anxious to see the Jewish question solved should do their utmost to shunt it on that line." Otherwise, he concluded, Jewish millionaires, although "very few" in number, would be "too safe and the Jewish pedlar too harassed." History would repeat itself because it would have "nothing but the same material to work upon."[5]

In echoing Jewish Zionists, Chesterton was building on his earlier position, but his remarks suggested the anti-Semitic view that Jews were unpatriotic, clannish, and materialistic. Extreme anti-Semites did not espouse Zionism, but neither did most Jews. Chesterton told one complainant that his *Nation* letter about Swaythling "was not an attack on Judaism, but a defence of it." Portrayals of him "as a black persecutor and slanderer of Israel" were "highly comic" to those who knew him or his "social circle." He said he was not going to persecute Jews, but would "go on talking about them" as "freely" as he would about Germany or Japan—about "their dangers, defects, or neglected merits." Thus he would "say that a group of financial Jews urged on the African war, because they did: I heard them doing it," but he would also say that he "heard many of the equally unmistakable artistic and Bohemian Jews denounce the war fiercely." Asking why "the Jews" should be "the only people who refuse to be talked about intelligently," he implored the Rev. Morris Joseph "in all

5. "G.K.C.: Interview for the Jewish Chronicle with Mr. G.K. Chesterton," *Jewish Chronicle*, April 28, 1911, 18; G.K. Chesterton, Letter to the *Nation*, March 18, 1911, in Sr. M. Loyola, "Chesterton and the Mystery of Israel," *The Chesterton Review* XIII, (2), (1987); "I don't mind how fiercely you fight for the pedlar" (G.K. Chesterton, Letter to Leslie Claude Greenberg, April 26, 1911, BL MSS Add. 73237, fo. 109, W. Oddie, "The Philosemitism of G.K. Chesterton," in W. Oddie, ed., *The Holiness of G.K. Chesterton* [Leominster, Herefordshire: Gracewing, 2010], 134); see Chapter Two.

amicability . . . to overcome the morbid sensitiveness that makes him cry out so wildly at criticism."[6]

Chesterton socialized with liberal Jews rather than "financial Jews," but he did emphasize Jewish virtues. He complained, however, that the Rev. Joseph would allow "no third course between seeking his life and denying his existence," alleging that the rabbi could "only imagine two things: the curse that drives forth all Jews like devils, or the platitude that says that everybody is pretty much alike." All races or religions consisted of "very varied groups and types of unique individuals," but people were "pretty much alike." That was "a dogma of religion," but history was about "tracing in what ways they are different . . . not only in persons, but in peoples and parties." Although, he said, "it would be absurd to talk about Mr. Zangwill as a moneylender or Sir Rufus Isaacs as a pawnbroker," it would be "more absurd to pretend that a solitary Jew only 'happens' to be a moneylender or a pawnbroker, as a Scotchman might happen to be a postman." The type had been "traced to the misconduct of Gentiles," but to say that there was "no Jewish problem" was "practically to say that there is no Jewish people." Uniquely, Israel, "a nation without a country," produced "peculiar results, good and bad." In "pious" Jews it produced "great strictness in keeping the ritual and guarding the pedigree; lest the nomad nation be swallowed up"; but in the "cynical" it produced "not devotion to the nomad nation, but an indifference to all the other land-tied nations. Having themselves no flag or frontier, it is not shocking to them to suppress a frontier or betray a flag." Chesterton "never said" that no one wanted the South African war "besides the Jewish financial group"; rather: "I said, and I say, that this group wanted it for particular reasons and in a particular spirit: the reasons were international finance: the spirit was a contempt for nationality." He had "merely explained that spirit, and (to that extent) excused it"; but regarding Swaythling's will, "all I emphasised, and all I primarily cared about" was that the Jews' "own loyalty to blood and doctrine, can now be derided as superstitious," while "their indifference to the loyalties of others" could "be praised as the flower of progress."[7]

Chesterton made a point of blaming Gentile influence for "Jewish vices," and believed "truth telling" did not mean "telling all the nice stories about the

---

6. The "upshot" of Joseph's "liberalising" was that "the good Jew on the steps of the synagogue" could "still be pelted" but the "bad Jew on the steps of the Stock Exchange must not even be criticized"; newspapers might "print a joke about a Jew in church putting on his hat," an "ancient, sincere and native custom," but few would "print a joke about a Jew in Westminster Abbey putting on a kind of feudal and chivalric crown" that he had "purchased by a greasy political job"; however, neither was it permissible to "insult America by discussing trusts, or France by discussing dueling" (G.K. Chesterton, Letter, *Jewish Chronicle*, June 16, 1911, 38–41).

7. G.K. Chesterton, Letter, *Jewish Chronicle*, June 30, 1911, 18–19.

Scotch, and all the nasty stories about the Irish";[8] but, especially after Cecil's death, he increasingly emphasized the "vices." Nonetheless, he continued to offer "rational" explanations for those "vices," and to see Zionism as the "rational" solution. Struggling to throw off the "Judas" label, the majority of Jews disagreed with that solution, which would, they argued, mean accepting the anti-Semite's view of them as greedy and disloyal.[9] But in August 1911 the first anti-Jewish riots occurred in modern Britain.[10] This coincided with increased Jewish enthusiasm for Zionism. When in November Chesterton addressed the West End Jewish Literary Society his Zionism was criticized by a *Jewish Chronicle* reader, but another maintained that "Mr. Kisch entirely misrepresents what Mr. Chesterton said," pointing out that if Chesterton was "reactionary" for believing in nationality, Jews were "the most reactionary people in the world." Far from seeing Zionism as a "possible danger to the British Empire," Chesterton "saw a source of demoralisation in those rich cynical Jews" who had "no enthusiasm for any ideal." The reader agreed with Chesterton's doubt that the loyalties of individuals with "two nationalities" could survive "any testing crisis," concluding that they should "welcome all critics" who helped "clear away the endless humbug" of those who believed in Jewish nationality but did not want "self-government."[11]

Another reader said it was "not in the least surprising" that the lecture had "proved so unpalatable," because when someone of Chesterton's "logical cast of mind" told them that "good Jews" could not be "patriotic Englishmen" it was "not unnatural" that they "should kick." Jewish patriotism, he maintained, was "simply a cloak" he assumed "to please the Englishman"; such a Jew was "suspect," and he knew it, but hoped that Gentile suspicions would be "drowned" in the patriotic "noise," and so became "more vulgarly loud in his profession of patriotism." Jews "of the younger generation," who found the Zionist question "more acute and insistent than ever," were, he said, "being coerced and intimidated" by Gentile society into "a profession of patriotism, which . . . must always be viewed with distrust." This was being accomplished "not through . . . physical force" but "the more subtle and insidious compulsion of a tyrannous

---

8. G.K. Chesterton, "The Boy," *All Things Considered* (USA: Feather Tail Press, 1908/2009), 53.

9. A. Julius, *Trials of the Diaspora: A History of Anti-Semitism in England* (Oxford: Oxford University Press, 2010), 292–293.

10. Jewish shops were targeted in Tredegar, South Wales during industrial unrest (M. Gilbert, *Churchill and the Jews* [London: Pocket Books, 2008], 19–20).

11. "The Jewish Position: What Mr. Chesterton said," A.D. Lewis, Letter, *Jewish Chronicle*, December 8, 1911, 38–39; "The Poor were nice and the rich were nasty," A. Kisch, Letter, *Jewish Chronicle*, December 1, 1911, 20–21; "the reporter in large letters made a headline: 'Mr. Chesterton said that speaking generally, as with most other communities, THE POOR JEWS WERE NICE AND THE RICH WERE NASTY'" (M. Ward, *Gilbert Keith Chesterton* [New York: Sheed & Ward, 1943], 264).

public opinion." The more English Jews became, the less Jewish they became; those who pretended they could be "patriotic Englishmen and good Jews" were "simply living lies."[12]

Another Zionist, Joseph Cowen, disagreed with the implication of "some speakers that evening," that "an anti-Semitic wave, or more Bellocs, or an addition of Chestertons" could provide "an impetus" to Zionism.[13] As seen, Chesterton's reputation as an anti-Semite[14] suffered even more from his editorship of the *New Witness* during the Great War.[15] Despite this, in 1919 the English Zionist Federation solicited his signature, along with over 200 "prominent non-Jews," to combat fears stirred by the Balfour Declaration that Christian shrines in the Holy Land would be controlled by "those who were not Christians."[16] But *The New Jerusalem* (1920) proved controversial, and he admitted that the *Daily Telegraph* did not publish the chapter, "The Problem of Zionism."[17] His American tour, he said, was "besieged by Rabbis lamenting my 'prejudice'" regarding "some studies on Palestine,"[18] adding that if the rabbis had "read all the chapters on the Jews" and believed "they constituted fanaticism," the fanaticism was "on their side."[19] Chesterton's wife noted that at Boston they were

12. B. Felz, Letter, *Jewish Chronicle*, December 8, 1911, 38–39.

13. "Zionism: The Effect of the Balkan War," J. Cowen, Report, *Jewish Chronicle*, December 20, 1912, 38–39.

14. Pan-German and French Nationalist "super-patriotism" were linked with English "neo-Conservatives" Belloc, Chesterton "and other anti-Semites," whose patriotism implied not so much love of their "countries and peoples, as HATRED AGAINST THE OTHER GROUPS" ("Abroad and the Colonies: 'America First': The Movement and the Jews," *Jewish Chronicle*, December 17, 1915, 10–11); Chesterton was compared to Houston Stewart Chamberlain ("Mentor," "The Jewish Spirit: Enlightenment for Mr. G.K. Chesterton," *Jewish Chronicle*, June 9, 1916, 7).

15. A common soldier's tribute to Captain Frank W. Haldenstein, recently killed, was "more valuable as propaganda than anything likely to be fulminated against our friend Chesterton—that half genius, half devil (*pace* Kipling) and his like" (F.S. Franklin, Letter, *Jewish Chronicle*, November 9, 1917, 18); "anti-Nationalists" were "living in a fool's paradise" if they thought that "men like Belloc, Chesterton, and Leo Maxse" cared "one jot for their protestations" of Englishness: "their Jewishness is all they will recognise" (Rev. A. Cohen, Letter, *Jewish Chronicle*, October 12, 1917, 17); the *Morning Post*, the *New Witness*, Leo Maxse and Chesterton all attacked Jewish "civil and political status" ("Diarist," *Jewish Chronicle*, December 14, 1917, 5); however, a Judaism hostile or indifferent to the possession of the Holy Land would be "a paradox, wilder even than any yet conceived by Chesterton!" (*Jewish Chronicle*, January 4, 1918, 14).

16. "The Petition to the Peace Conference," *Jewish Chronicle*, March 14, 1919, 18–19.

17. Owing to "[a] difference of opinion" with that newspaper's "politics" in G.K. Chesterton, Preface to *The New Jerusalem* (1920), *G.K. Chesterton Collected Works Vol. XX* (San Francisco: Ignatius Press, 2001), 191; Chesterton told Maurice Baring that the book was to be "not political but romantic and religious" (M. Ward, *Gilbert Keith Chesterton*, op. cit., 441–443).

18. G.K. Chesterton, *What I Saw in America* (London: Hodder & Stoughton Ltd., 1922), 140–141.

19. Chesterton Collection, BL Add. MS 73402, fo. 32, I. Ker, *G.K. Chesterton: A Biography* (Oxford: Oxford University Press, 2011), 447.

"[a]gain assaulted by a wailing crowd of journalists."[20] Chesterton was "not a little hurt and puzzled about their unreasonable attitude" because he had "honestly tried to be objective, fair, and understanding, but they won't see that."[21] His response was reminiscent of Belloc's reaction to the reception of his "Jew book."

Wells' anti-Zionism was influenced by his universalism. Chesterton's Zionism was influenced by his nationalism, although the equally nationalistic Belloc was lukewarm and saw Palestinian Zionism especially as a problem. In 1919, Chesterton advocated Irish autonomy, adding: "Many of us hope to see a Jewish commonwealth reconstituted in Palestine."[22] In 1933 he expressed the belief that "the credential of antiquity in terms of both borders and cultural identity" was an "essential" qualification for "independent nationhood." Without "one or both of these factors, the claim to nationhood was not only false but dangerous, too."[23] He criticized Jewish Poles who opposed Polish independence based on the right of the national majority to self-determination.[24] Zionism satisfied Chesterton's first two criteria, but was not favored by the Jewish majority. Furthermore, Palestinian Jews were still a minority in a predominately Muslim region. Nonetheless, while ruling out the pan-German approach of claiming territory on a racial basis, Chesterton supported Zionism. What might be "criticised" in *The New Jerusalem* "as Anti-Semitism," he said, was "only the negative side of Zionism." Thus "[f]or the sake of convenience" he would begin "by stating it in terms of the universal popular impression," which some called "a popular prejudice." Dismissing "[t]he usual arguments about religious persecution and racial hatred" causing anti-Semitism, he offered Zionism "whether . . . right or wrong" as "a real and reasonable answer both to Anti-Semitism and to the charge of Anti-Semitism."[25] This was to be Chesterton's answer to anti-Semite and to Jew.

He was attempting "to do justice in a very difficult problem," but admitted that on re-reading the work, he was "far from satisfied" that he had kept "the proper proportions." His "first impressions" were written in Palestine "where

20. Frances Chesterton, "American Diary," G.K. Chesterton Library (ibid., 436).

21. Cyril Clemens, *Chesterton as seen by his Contemporaries* (New York, 1969), 87–88 (ibid., 447).

22. G.K. Chesterton, *Irish Impressions* (1919) *G.K. Chesterton Collected Works Vol. XX* (San Francisco: Ignatius Press, 2001), 135–136.

23. G.K. Chesterton, *Illustrated London News*, July 8, 1933, in J. Stapleton, *Christianity, Patriotism, and Nationhood: The England of G.K. Chesterton* (Lanham MD/Plymouth, England: Lexington Books, 2009), 187.

24. G.K. Chesterton, "Victory Will Efface All," *Illustrated London News*, December 7, 1918, G.K. Chesterton, *Chesterton on War and Peace: Battling the Ideas and Movements That Led to Nazism and World War II*, M.W. Perry, ed. (Seattle: Inkling Books, 2008), 325 note 81; see Chapter Six.

25. G.K. Chesterton, *The New Jerusalem* (1920), *G.K. Chesterton Collected Works Vol. XX*, op. cit., 404–405.

everybody recognises the Jew as something quite distinct from the Englishman or the European; and where his unpopularity even moved me in the direction of his defence." It had come as "something of a shock" to "return to a conventional atmosphere" in which Jewish "unpopularity" was "still actually denied or described as mere persecution."[26] If this suggests that Jewish "unpopularity" provoked attacks, he did not alter his "first impression," insisting that the worst problem was to deny the problem, for which Zionism offered "a diagnosis and a remedy." As a patriot he sympathized with the man whose heart was set "on a particular home or shrine," for to be "locked out" was to be "locked in. The narrowest possible prison for him is the whole world."[27] It was unfair, he maintained, that Judas the faithless disciple was remembered more than the faithful Jude; a man could "betray like Judas Iscariot in another man's house" but not "fight like Judas Maccabeus for another man's temple." As yet, Palestine had no "patriotism to be betrayed"—but it had Arabs and Syrians, "a peasantry to be oppressed."[28] His solution was Swiss-style self-governing cantons, cited as Chaim Weizmann's idea. Sinanoglou notes that *The New Jerusalem* was "one of the earliest British publications to mention partition," although the suggestion came "[i]n the midst of anti-Semitic musings on the plight of 'the Jew,'" inspiring Chesterton with "the idea of creating Jewish cantons *outside* of Palestine as well" because it could not accommodate all Jews.[29] She adds that "[n]early a decade later . . . *Palestine Weekly* vaguely mentioned a scheme to carve 'out of the Holy Land a special *enclave* which should be wholly Jewish.'"[30] But as Howard M. Sachar notes, in 1947 a British partition proposal was "immediately denounced" by the Arabs, who wanted the whole territory, while the Jews were "appalled by the cantonal plan and rejected it outright."[31]

Chesterton was "moved in the direction of defending the Jews" by the Arab riots he witnessed in Jerusalem: "[I] have seen with my own eyes wild mobs marching through a great city, raving not only against Jews, but against the English for identifying themselves with the Jews."[32] His wife also recorded the

---

26. Ibid., 191.

27. Ibid., 404–405.

28. Ibid., 408–409.

29. P. Sinanoglou, "British Plans for the Partition of Palestine, 1929–1938," *The Historical Journal*, 52 (1), (2009): 136, Cambridge University Press, accessed July 3, 2009, http://journals.cambridge.org.

30. "Zionism: a critical phase," *Palestine Weekly*, February 17, 1928 (ibid.).

31. H.M. Sachar, *A History of Israel: From the Rise of Zionism to Our Time* (New York: Alfred A. Knopf, 2007), 276.

32. "I have seen an Englishman arriving in Jerusalem with somebody he had been taught to regard as his fellow countryman and political colleague, and received as if he had come arm-in-arm with a flaming dragon" (G.K. Chesterton, *The New Jerusalem* [1920], *G.K. Chesterton Collected Works Vol. XX*, op. cit., 393); this was a period of growing Arab unrest and attacks on Jews (H.M. Sachar, *A History of Israel: From the Rise of Zionism to Our Time*, op. cit., 123).

riots.[33] While continuing to advocate Zionism, he did question the practicalities, raising the question of whether he promoted Zionism regardless of its dangers to Jews. He did appear to project onto the rioters his own opposition to Herbert Samuel's appointment as Palestine's High Commissioner, but he was not alone in fearing it might be counterproductive to select a Jewish Zionist before Britain obtained League of Nations approval for the Palestinian Mandate.[34] Neither was Chesterton alone in regarding General Allenby's entry into Jerusalem in 1917, liberating it from Turkish rule, as the completion of the Crusaders' campaign against Islam.[35] He said this not out of "hostility to the religion of Mohammed," but while "fully conscious" of its "many values and virtues," pointed out that Islam was the invader, and "Christendom...the thing invaded."[36] During the Great War the *Chesterbelloc* had linked Jews to Germany. Now, ahead of Churchill, who would link militant Islam to Nazism in the 1930s, Chesterton linked Islam to Germany because of its "barbarism." He noted that centuries after the Crusades, "the Sultan of the Moslems riding on his Arab steed...fell finally with that other half-heathen power in the north, with which he had made an alliance against the remains of Roman and Byzantine culture. He fell because barbarism cannot stand."[37]

Chesterton's poem *Lepanto* (1911) commemorated the historic Catholic defeat of Turkey in 1571, and the Great War German-Turkish alliance "intensified his enmity still further." *The Flying Inn* (1914) ends with a Turkish invasion and portrays the cultural threat of Islam. This, Stapleton notes, was a threat to which

33. The Chestertons were in Jerusalem from January 26 to March 30, 1920. Frances's diary for February 27, 1920 records "the great demonstration and protest against the Jews by the Christian and Mohomedan inhabitants of Jerusalem"; the "manifesto" was "fiery enough" but the demonstrators "fairly peaceful"; on March 8, "at the Damascus Gate I got into the crowd that was having another anti-Jew demonstration. Rather excited. The leader had two drawn curved swords which he flourished about a great deal"; they both saw the procession again outside the Jaffa Gate and "listened to the speeches—no untoward incident occurred (as might easily have happened) though three Jews got their hats knocked off." The following day, at the "Wailing Place" they saw an old Jew pelted with chestnuts (Frances Chesterton, Diaries, Chesterton Collection, British Library [D. Conlon, personal communication]).

34. The Mandate allowed the British to administer the territory pending the creation of a state. General Allenby, who liberated Jerusalem from the Turks in 1917, claimed the appointment was technically illegal, since no peace treaty had been signed with Turkey, thus it violated military law and the Hague Convention; however, Samuel proved a popular appointment; his concern about being seen as partisan meant he avoided favoring the Zionist side, but "far from placating Arab nationalism... these conciliatory gestures apparently encouraged it" (H.M. Sachar, *A History of Israel from the Rise of Zionism to Our Time*, op. cit., 124–125).

35. G.K. Chesterton, *The New Jerusalem* (1920), *G.K. Chesterton Collected Works Vol. XX*, op. cit., 390–391; I. Ker, *G.K. Chesterton: A Biography*, op. cit., 407–408.

36. G.K. Chesterton, *The New Jerusalem* (1920), *G.K. Chesterton Collected Works Vol. XX*, op. cit., 209.

37. Ibid., 390.

England had been "especially vulnerable," in Chesterton's eyes, ever since the Reformation. He believed that if England ignored the Turkish threat, then Islam, having "entered through the door opened by Puritanism" could "invade" England culturally, eradicating "those interlocking remnants of Christianity, nationhood, and patriotism upon which individual liberty in this life and salvation in the next depended."[38] Some English people, he said, were attracted to what they saw as a simpler religion, but: "The complex God of the Athanasian Creed" was "far less likely to gather the mystery and cruelty of a Sultan than the lonely god of Omar or Mahomet." The "triple enigma" of the Trinity was "as comforting as wine and open as an English fireside," while the god who was "a mere awful unity" was "not only a king but an Eastern king." And "out of the desert, from the dry places and the dreadful suns," the "cruel children of the lonely God" were advancing. With "scimitar in hand," they "laid waste the world," for it was "not well for God to be alone."[39] The desert was in "the nature of all this outer nomadic anarchy." It was "capable sooner or later of tearing anything and everything to pieces." Having "no instinct of preservation or of the permanent needs of men," where it passed, "the ruins remain ruins and are not renewed."[40] The "man of the desert" tended to "simplify too much, and to take his first truth for the last truth." Chesterton allowed that there was a "considerable deposit of common sense" in the "Moslem character," the "first fact" of which was "the common bond of men." But there was "also a deep and most dangerous potentiality of fanaticism," because the "fanatic of the desert" took "his faith as a fact . . . not even as a truth in our more transcendental sense."[41] The "real mistake of the Moslems" was not "any particular or passing persecution of Christians" but in their belief that they had "a simpler and saner sort of Christianity." Unfortunately, "many modern Christians" agreed, and since it appeared "self-evident, to Moslems as to Bolshevists, that their simple creed was suited to everybody," they wished, in their "sweeping fashion to impose it on everybody."[42]

Judaism was not a Trinitarian religion either but, as seen, Chesterton praised "the survival of the blinding simplification of existence" caused by the impact of the "enormous philosophic truth" of "the unity of creation." In addition to Islam's recognition of "the equality of men," or at least the "equality of Moslems," however, he praised the Muslim for not desiring to "complicate his con-

---

38. J. Stapleton, *Christianity, Patriotism, and Nationhood: The England of G.K. Chesterton*, op. cit., 172–174.

39. G.K. Chesterton, *Orthodoxy* (1908) *G.K. Chesterton Collected Works, Vol. I* (San Francisco: Ignatius Press, 1986), 340.

40. G.K. Chesterton, *The New Jerusalem* (1920), *G.K. Chesterton Collected Works Vol. XX*, op. cit., 205.

41. Ibid., 212–213.

42. Ibid., 387.

science with any sham science about races." In this, he had "something like an intellectual advantage over the Jew," who was "generally so much his intellectual superior; and even in some ways his spiritual superior." The Jew had "far more moral imagination and sympathy with the subtler ideals of the soul,"[43] but also the "mere family pride" of race that "flatter[ed] every member of the family." "Racial pride" had produced "the arrogance of the Germans," and was "capable of producing a much subtler kind of arrogance in the Jews." In contrast, the "more savage man of the desert" was free from that "particular sort of self-deception." If he did not consider someone as a Muslim, he would "consider him as a man. At the price of something like barbarism" he had "at least been saved from ethnology." But if Islam "admirably" asserted the equality of men, it was "the equality of males."[44] Later Chesterton would reassert his belief in the Jews' claim to be the Chosen People, and his caveat about Islamic "equality" was all too true for minorities in Islamic countries.[45]

Chesterton also approved of the fact that Judaism, like Christianity respected the sanctity of "place": "The mystery of locality, with all its hold on the human heart, was as much present in the most ethereal things of Christendom as it was absent from the most practical things of Islam." The Muslim "had his own holy places," but he "never felt about them as Westerns can feel about a field or a roof-tree," thinking of the "the holiness as holy, not of the places as places. The austerity which forbade him imagery, the wandering war that forbade him rest, shut him off from all that was breaking out and blossoming in our local patriotisms." This desert-influenced, austere outlook had "given the Turks an empire without ever giving them a nation."[46]

The Palestine tour left Chesterton less sanguine about Zionism. The "exasperations," he said, came "chiefly from the two great Semitic traditions of monotheism." In Jerusalem, one day "a wild Jewish proclamation" would be circulated, "denouncing disloyal Jews who refuse the teaching [of] Hebrew; telling doctors to let them die and hospitals to let them rot," which rang with "the old unmistakable and awful accent that bade men dash their children against the stones." Then the city "would be placarded with posters printed in Damascus, telling the Jews who looked to Palestine for a national home that they should

43. Ibid., 213; see Chapter Five.
44. Ibid., 214.
45. The two "well-established" myths of Jewish and Christian "Dhimmi" status under Islam were of "complete equality" and servitude and humiliation, but "the historic truth" was "somewhere in the middle"; however, until modern times, in Islamic societies there was no view of Jews representing a cosmic evil, comparable to that of Christianity (B. Lewis, "The New Anti-Semitism," *The American Scholar*, 75 (1), (Winter 2006): 25–36, accessed June 27, 2011, http://www.hnn.us/blogs/entries/21832.html.
46. G.K. Chesterton, *A Short History of England* (London: Chatto & Windus, 1917), 64–65.

find it a national cemetery." These cries clashed "like the clash of those two crooked eastern swords, that crossed and recrossed and revolved like blazing wheels, in the vanguard of the marching mob." Since one group was threatening its own people while the second group was threatening the first, this might be seen as a false equivalence, but Chesterton heard a "voice not of my reason but rather sounding heavily in my heart ... repeating sentences like pessimistic proverbs. There is no place for the Temple of Solomon but on the ruins of the Mosque of Omar. There is no place for the nation of the Jews but in the country of the Arabs." In the "same narrow space and in the same dark hour" Chesterton "heard Islam crying from the turret and Israel wailing at the wall."[47] The Arab riots confirmed his worst fears of militant Islam, but he continued to support Palestinian Zionism while becoming less certain of the form it should take.

The Chestertons met many Jews during their two months' stay in Palestine. Frances Chesterton recorded several meetings with their old friend David Eder and his wife. They met Chaim Weizmann and even Herbert Samuel, visited Jewish establishments, and enjoyed sampling the alcoholic produce on a tour of the rural Jewish "colonies."[48] Chesterton praised Weizmann as a sincere Zionist who did not "desire to enter Palestine like a Junker or drive thousands of Arabs forcibly out of the land," but added that Weizmann and his associates needed to "disprove" such allegations.[49] Chesterton's ideal Palestine had to be better than other nations, just as Jewish capitalists had to meet a higher standard than Gentile capitalists. In fact Palestine embraced collectivism and cooperation,[50] as the Chestertons discovered. Gilbert admitted that no one seeing a Jewish rural settlement like Rishon, could "doubt" that some Jews were "sincerely filled with the vision of sitting under their own vine and fig-tree," but that it was "first necessary to grow the fig-tree and the vine." Flourishing Rishon had been financed by a French de Rothschild,[51] but to Chesterton the Jewish homeland would be

47. G. K. Chesterton, *The New Jerusalem* (1920), *G. K. Chesterton Collected Works Vol. XX*, op. cit., 288–289.

48. On their way home the Chestertons sailed on the same ship leaving from Alexandria as Herbert Samuel (I. Ker, *G. K. Chesterton: A Biography*, op. cit., 415); they met him in Palestine (Frances Chesterton, Diaries, Chesterton Collection, British Library [D. Conlon, personal communication]).

49. G. K. Chesterton, *The New Jerusalem* (1920), *G. K. Chesterton Collected Works Vol. XX*, op. cit., 410–411.

50. For example Tel Aviv (H. M. Sachar, *A History of Israel from the Rise of Zionism to Our Time*, op. cit., 78–79); this approach inspired "the young visionaries" of Rishon LeZion, which the Chestertons visited (ibid., 29).

51. The French Baron Edmond Benjamin James de Rothschild (1845–1934), a leading supporter of the Zionist movement and generous benefactor to Palestinian Zionism, financed Rishon LeZion, the first settlement, which the Chestertons visited on March 10, 1920; Frances referred to "Edmund de Rothschild" as a great benefactor and capitalist of the colony (Frances Chesterton, Diaries, Chesterton Collection, British Library [D. Conlon, personal communication]).

successful only when it was unsuccessful: "when the Jews in it are scavengers, when the Jews in it are sweeps, when they are dockers and ditchers and porters and hodmen."[52] Chesterton never gave his Jewish characters manual occupations, reflecting his view that exiled Jews were ill-adapted to manual labor, itself an echo of Jewish Zionist arguments: "Jews do not generally work on the land, or in any of the handicrafts that are akin to the land; but the Zionists reply that this is because it can never really be their own land."[53] While insisting that Jews must not use cheap Arab labor to do the manual work, he added that it was "our whole complaint against the Jew that he does not till the soil or toil with the spade," and thus it was "very hard on him to refuse him" when he said: "Give me a soil and I will till it; give me a spade and I will use it." Warning of the peasant's "general impression of a business pressure from the more brutal and businesslike type of Jew, which arouses very violent and very just indignation," he advocated what he described as Weizmann's "commonwealth of cantons after the manner of Switzerland" for both Jews and Arabs—if he "correctly represent[ed] Dr. Weizmann's meaning." Weizmann does not mention the idea in his memoirs,[54] but may have spoken of it when he met the Chestertons on their tour. It was discussed by Zionists, as will be seen. To Chesterton the idea "clearly involve[d] the abandonment of the solidarity of Palestine, and tolerate[d] the idea of groups of Jews being separated from each other by populations of a different type." Moreover, if the notion was "considered admissible" it seemed "capable of considerable extension." There might also be "Jewish cantons outside Palestine . . . in suitable and selected places in adjacent parts or in many other parts of the world." These "might be affiliated to some official centre in Palestine, or even in Jerusalem," where there would be "some great religious headquarters," although if he were a Jew he "would build the Temple without bothering about the site" chiefly because the old site would "raise a Holy War from Morocco to the marches of China." Chesterton's proposals for "something like a Jewish territorial scheme" or for "some such extension of the definition of Zionism" were aimed at solving its "greatest difficulty," the "resettling" of a "sufficient number of so large a race on so small a land." Permitting "Jews to be scattered no longer as individuals but as groups" appealed to Chesterton because of the medieval associations, but, he insisted, "the Semitic problem" was not, as some alleged, "a brief medieval insanity."[55]

52. G. K. Chesterton, *The New Jerusalem* (1920), *G. K. Chesterton Collected Works Vol. XX*, op. cit., 412–413.

53. Ibid., 406; see Chapter Three.

54. Ibid., 414–416; see: Chaim Weizmann, *Trial and Error: The Autobiography of Chaim Weizmann* (London: Hamish Hamilton, 1949).

55. G. K. Chesterton, *The New Jerusalem* (1920), *G. K. Chesterton Collected Works Vol. XX*, op. cit., 418.

Chesterton's Zionism was consonant with his belief that Jews could change, and that the patriotic Jews in the Bible were not myths. His enthusiasm for the canton idea also originated with Jewish Zionists, but, inevitably, the idea recalls the Warsaw Ghetto imposed by the Nazis. Chesterton was clearly motivated partly by his concern for Jewish security, but although in big cities "voluntary" ghettos—the "Latin quarter," the "Chinese quarter," and the "Italian quarter"— offered security to ethnic minorities, the "medieval" Jewish model was problematic. The Russian Pale of Settlement acted as a more recent warning against "separate living," but Chesterton believed that if such communities were "affiliated to some official centre in Palestine or Jerusalem" it would enhance Jewish security, at least in theory. But he also maintained: "[I]f the advantage of the ideal to the Jews is to gain the promised land, the advantage to the Gentiles is to get rid of the Jewish problem." As seen, the "Jewish problem," which referred to violence against Jews, was more of a problem to Jews than Gentiles, but Chesterton would "leave as few Jews as possible in other established nations," in Jewish "enclaves" with "a special position best described as privilege." Echoing Belloc and Cecil, these "enclaves" would offer "special laws and exemptions," including being excused from conscription, which was "a gross injustice in their case." Jews would be treated with respect, but treated as foreigners, as the exemption from conscription implied. Chesterton would bestow "the same privileged position to all Jews everywhere" if Zionists failed "the only true and the only tolerable test"—if they "failed as peasants" but "succeeded as capitalists."[56] One Zionist reader of the *Jewish Chronicle* believed that a Jewish state would clear up any fears about patriotism regarding Jews who remained in England since they would have made a deliberate choice.[57] But Belloc believed that the very Jews who were the problem would not want to go to a Jewish homeland. The canton idea suggests they might be "encouraged" to go by being stripped of their citizenship.

Chesterton's view of "successful" Zionism—defined by its lack of economic success—was based on his belief, against historical evidence, that there would be no "friction" between poor Jews and equally poor Gentiles. But "plutocratic" Jews would be unlikely to move to Chesterton's "ideal" Palestine if they were unable to achieve economic success, although he may have believed that once their origins were marked out, they would become sufficiently poor to want to go there. Few comfortably circumstanced Jews would be attracted to a peasant existence otherwise. Chesterton saw Zionism as a "rational cause and cure" for the "Jewish problem,"[58] but apart from the injustice of encouraging the depar-

56. Ibid., 416–417.

57. Rev. A. Cohen, Letter, *Jewish Chronicle*, October 12, 1917, 17.

58. G. K. Chesterton, *The New Jerusalem* (1920), *G. K. Chesterton Collected Works Vol. XX*, op. cit., 418.

ture of Jews by withdrawing their civil rights, his solution appears as irrational as it was impractical. The strain of trying to promote "Judas Maccabeus" against the anti-Semite's "Judas Iscariot" was beginning to tell. His "cantons" echoed Belloc's equally vague idea for small Jewish settlements with special (i.e. different) civic status, suggesting that Chesterton was applying a sympathetic gloss to an unsympathetic solution. Doubtless it represented an intellectual compromise between his optimism and Belloc's pessimism: initially embracing Zionism as fitting his patriotic worldview, with "Marconi" refracted through the death of Cecil he had gone to Palestine as a final attempt to save his waning enthusiasm. Once there, he was shaken by Arab hostility, and his "mystical Zionism" prevailed over Belloc's cynicism. Moreover, his security concerns were genuine. In addition to the Jewish communities affiliated to a center in Palestine, he believed "the lands of the Moslem and the Jew" should remain under the "general suzerainty of Christendom" because "[t]he European can do justice to the Jew; but it must be the European who does it."[59]

And yet, as Ker notes, his assimilated Jewish friends "would have had no desire whatever to wear Arab dress, as Chesterton would have known very well."[60] In reality, as Michael Stanislawski comments, "[m]ost Jews described (or decried) as assimilated or as believing in Jewish assimilation by no means advocated Jewish self-obliteration."[61] Even if they wished to "lose" themselves in English culture, they did not wish to be "lost," but neither, as Chesterton's nephew Patrick Braybrooke remarked about Belloc's "nonsense" of an idea, did they wish to be marked out or kept separate with "barbed wired so that none should escape." Chesterton had joked about Jews in public office wearing Arab dress,[62] but Braybrooke, who believed that Belloc saw "in the Jews the gravest national menace" and viewed them "as a cancer eating into the body," saw Chesterton's chief preoccupation not as the "Jewish question" but issues like divorce and birth control.[63]

Before the Marconi affair and Cecil's death, Chesterton argued that such Jews might be "safely absorbed," and that any distinctive characteristics would be "lost" in the Gentile population, but after Cecil's death he embraced a canton idea similar to Belloc's. Belloc's idea was based on his belief in the deleteri-

59. Ibid., 417.

60. I. Ker, *G.K. Chesterton: A Biography*, op. cit., 423.

61. Michael Stanislawski, *Zionism and the Fin de Siècle: Cosmopolitanism and Nationalism from Nordau to Jabotinsky* (Berkeley: University of California Press, 2001), 9.

62. Braybrooke, *Some Thoughts on Hilaire Belloc: Ten Studies* (London: Drane's, 1923), 27–29, California Digital Library, accessed February 7, 2013, http://www.archive.org/details/somethoughtsonhioobrayrich; see Chapter One.

63. Ibid., 21.

ous cultural effects of "race mixing" that he promulgated in his novels. Unlike Chesterton, who believed that negative Jewish characteristics were "copied" from the English, Belloc believed that such negative characteristics were innate, and far from being "lost," would "infect" the English until the whole population "became Jewish." Belloc refused to acknowledge his Jewish ancestry and Chesterton never alluded to it, despite his belief in Jewish "difference," which he claimed was based on ordinary people's perceptions. A "crowd on a racecourse" was not "poisoned by medieval theology," and "navvies in a Mile End pub" were not "misled by the ethnology of Gobineau or Max Muller." Nor was "a mob of little boys fresh from the cricket field or the tuck shop . . . troubled about Marxian economics or international finance." But they all recognized "Jews as Jews" and schoolboys "recognised them, not with any great hostility except in patches, but with the integration of instinct." They saw "not Semites or Schismatics or capitalists or revolutionists, but foreigners; only foreigners that were not called foreigners." This recognition did not, he said, "prevent friendship and affection, especially in my own case; but then it never has prevented it in the case of ordinary foreigners."[64] Chesterton claimed that his belief in Jewish/Gentile "difference" was not a negative but a positive belief, for "[d]ivision and variety" were "essential to praise; division and variety *are* what is right with the world." There was "nothing specially right about mere contact and coalescence." Rather, "blending . . . men and women, nations and nations" was "truly a return to the chaos and unconsciousness that were before the world was made."[65] "Difference" was crucial to Chesterton's theory of nationalism, and the fact that, as he noted, Jews remained "different" in America, proved his case for nationalism as well as for Zionism.[66]

This position also held contradictions, however, and, despite inter-communal "friction," he did not advocate "enclaves" for Scottish and Irish Americans. As Ker notes, "it might well look as though he was discriminating against the Jews—which he was, of course, because of their perceived cosmopolitanism and involvement in international finance, something that could not be said of Irish Catholics."[67] Sidestepping the "race" question, Chesterton insisted that "the nature of the Jewish problem" was that "the Jew . . . came from the East,"[68]

64. G. K. Chesterton, *Autobiography* (Sevenoaks, Kent: Fisher Press, 1936/1992), 73–74.

65. G. K. Chesterton, "What is Right With the World," *T.P.'s Weekly*, 1910, G. K. Chesterton, *The Apostle and the Wild Ducks and other essays*, D. Collins, ed. (London: Paul Elek, 1975), 166–167.

66. D. Ahlquist, "'I Am Fond of Jews': In Defense of Chesterton," *Gilbert Magazine*, 12 (2 & 3), (November/December 2008): 25, accessed May 19, 2011, http://www.209.236.72.127/wordpress/wp-content/uploads/2010/12/gilbert_12.2_5.pdf.

67. I. Ker, *G. K. Chesterton: A Biography* (Oxford: Oxford University Press, 2011), op. cit., 423–424.

68. G. K. Chesterton, *The New Jerusalem* (1920), *G. K. Chesterton Collected Works Vol. XX*, op. cit., 395.

but so did the Chinese, whose rights he defended. His Jewish enclave idea clashed with his commitment to equality, but his religious belief in the "difference" and "specialness" of Jews, and his defense of the Medieval Church convinced him that Jewish attempts to assimilate were doomed, and that Jews would be safer living in communities.

According to Chesterton's worldview, Jews should be allowed to defend themselves, a necessity if they were to be exempted from conscription, something that would enrage anti-Semites, confirming their view of Jews as cowardly and disloyal. Chesterton, in contrast, praised the bravery of Jews, and his emphasis on the right to self-defense highlights his concerns about Jewish security, because in his "even-handed" approach he insisted that Gentiles should be protected against Jews, maintaining that it was absurd to speak about Jews always as the oppressed, never as oppressors.[69] But in *The New Jerusalem* he complained that "the Jews in the West" did not "seem so much concerned" with asking, as he had done "however tentatively," whether "a larger and less local colonial development might really transfer the bulk of Israel to a more independent basis, as simply to demand that Jews shall continue to control other nations as well as their own." It might be advantageous for England "to take risks to settle the Jewish problem," but not to "take risks merely to unsettle the Arab problem, and leave the Jewish problem unsolved."[70] This reflects the early stance of Theodor Herzl, founding father of modern Zionism: "The Jewish question persists wherever Jews live in perceptible numbers"; where it did not exist, it was "carried by Jews in the course of their migrations. We naturally move to those places where we are not persecuted, and there our presence produces persecution." This was so in "every country," and would endure "until the Jewish question finds a solution on a political basis." Herzl maintained that the "unfortunate Jews" were "carrying the seeds of Anti-Semitism into England" as they had "already introduced it into America."[71] There was a fine line between being influenced by such views and using them to bolster a pre-existing anti-Jewish stance. But while he was influenced by Max Nordau and Weizmann Chesterton was also influenced by Israel Zangwill, whose Jewish Territorial Organization, established in 1905 in response to Russian pogroms, was prepared to accept a homeland in East Africa rather than Palestine, demanding: "Are we literally to re-create Palestine and then to be told it belongs to the ignorant half-nomadic tribes who have planted their tent-poles or their hovels?"

---

69. See Chapter Two.

70. G. K. Chesterton, *The New Jerusalem* (1920), *G. K. Chesterton Collected Works Vol. XX*, op. cit., 191–192.

71. T. Herzl, *Der Judenstaat* [The Jewish State], (1896), Jewish Virtual Library, accessed June 16, 2011, http://www.jewishvirtuallibrary.org/jsource/Zionism/herzl2b.html.

Zangwill did not hesitate to ridicule other Jewish Zionists, saying that his "friend, Dr. Nordau" was "loyally striving to cover over the inadequacy of the Zionist solution to the problems of the Diaspora," pretending that the "millions whom Palestine cannot possibly receive, will become Palestinian subjects. As if any country would tolerate masses of pseudo-citizens, or as if any sane man would risk himself or his children to such a status!" Even "[m]ore nebulously," he said, Weizmann suggested that Palestine, like Ancient Greece, would "throw its protection over the Diaspora."[72] This was the view of Chesterton, who was influenced by Weizmann but also by Zangwill, who was also accused of impracticability. But the eminently practical Beatrice Webb was less sympathetic to Zionism than Chesterton. After meeting Chaim Weizmann in the late 1920s she remained indifferent, "comment[ing] only: 'I can't understand why the Jews make such a fuss over a few dozen of their people killed in Palestine. As many are killed every week in London in traffic accidents, and no one pays any attention.'" Her husband Lord Passfield, then Colonial Secretary "bluntly declared himself opposed to mass Jewish immigration into Palestine."[73]

That Chesterton's motivation in proposing a "larger and less local colonial development" was partly motivated by concerns about Jewish security is supported by his prompt and robust condemnations of Nazi anti-Jewish violence. Moreover, remarkably in view of his anti-Imperialist stance, he proposed a "Jewish empire" centered on Jerusalem. His Zionism satisfied his worldview and reconciled conflicting loyalties, but was also symptomatic of contradictory feelings about Jews. In 1913 he admitted: "I think they are a human triumph, a national danger, an intellectual inspiration, and a frightful nuisance." Jews, he said, "attract me, they puzzle me; I find myself forever fitting theories to them."[74] The enduring riddle of "the Jew" was a challenge to what Sheed called Chesterton's "hairshirt itch to question," but also his perpetual tendency to argue, even with himself. The argument, however, appeared to be shut down at the point at which Chesterton decided that Zionism met the needs of both Jew and Gentile. As an Englishman who prided himself on his impartial attachment to justice he proceeded to try to convince both "sides." The Balfour Declaration transformed Zionism into an achievable aim, but also provoked opposition

72. "Zangwill on Weizmann," *Jewish Chronicle*, February 27, 1920, 28; however, Zangwill insisted that the Balfour Declaration was not simply "a war manoeuvre, but sincerely meant to solve the Jewish problem" by establishing "a Jewish State" ("The Jewish World Position: Mr. Zangwill's Address to the American Jewish Congress: 'Watchman, What of the Night?'" *Jewish Chronicle*, October 18, 1923, 18–19).

73. H. M. Sachar, *A History of Israel from the Rise of Zionism to Our Time*, op. cit., 174.

74. G. K. Chesterton, *Illustrated London News*, July 19, 1913, in *Gilbert Magazine*, 12 (2 & 3), (November/December 2008): 8, accessed May 19, 2011, http://www.209.236.72.127/wordpress/wp-content/uploads/2010/12/gilbert_12.2_5.pdf.

from Palestinian Muslims, and under Cecil's posthumous influence and Belloc's historical view, the canton idea shut down the argument once again.[75] That this influence was temporary can be gauged by the fact that Chesterton did not continue to raise the "canton" aspect of his Zionism.[76]

And if the canton idea was vague, it was characteristic of Chesterton's political approach, even regarding Distributism. He argued: "We certainly should not say that the meaning of a peasant state is that all people are peasants. We should mean that it had the general character of a peasant state; that the land was largely held in that fashion and the law generally directed in that spirit."[77] Shaw's and Wells' solutions to the "Jewish problem" were characterized by obsessive, excessive detail but were crucial to the nature and function of their Utopias. More importantly, the ShaWellian Utopia depended on compulsion, while in contrast, no one would be "hustled" into Chesterton's "half-built peasantocracy." As seen, his primary concern was to defend the idea of the Middle Ages rather than to impose a minutely worked-out scheme.[78] He and Belloc tried to "convert" Jewish audiences to their philosophy with "rational" arguments. Clearly the Jews influenced Chesterton more than Chesterton influenced the Jews.

In contrast, anti-Semites like Adolf Hitler blamed "the Jews" not only for Germany's problems but also the world's problems. Driving them out of Germany, he believed, would simply export the problem elsewhere, giving them a further incentive to plot against him. During the War he began the systematic extermination of German and Polish Jewry, demanding the surrender of Jews from his allies in Eastern Europe, in Italy and Vichy France. The 1942 Wannsee Conference set the seal on Jewish genocide. Many assumed Hitler was using anti-Semitism as a political tactic, as in the Russian pogroms, but he wanted a *Judenrein* ("Jew-free") world: convinced that Jews were "behind" Germany's Great War humiliation, he became convinced that by "defeating" them he would win the second Great War.[79] To Hitler, Zionism was anathema: "[A]ll they want is a central organisation for their international world swindle,

---

75. "[I]t is perfectly evident that Chesterton desires for the Jew the dignity of being a separate nation" (P. Braybrooke, *Gilbert Keith Chesterton* (London: Chelsea Publishing Company, 1922), 65.

76. In a debate, Chesterton argued that the Reformers succeeded in creating a narrower religion than Medieval Catholicism: "religious liberty . . . created their social slavery" (G. K. Chesterton, *The Superstitions of the Sceptic* [Cambridge: W. Heffer & Sons Ltd., 1925], 9); Cambridge historian G. G. Coulton, a critic, alleged that the pre-Reformation Church saw dancers as "worse than the Jews; for these shrank from crucifying Christ on a feast-day" while dancers chose feast days for dancing (ibid., 23).

77. G. K. Chesterton, "On a Sense of Proportion," *The Outline of Sanity* (London: Methuen & Co. Ltd., 1926), 57.

78. See Chapter Six.

79. M. Gilbert, *The Holocaust: The Jewish Tragedy* (London: Fontana Press, 1987), 280–285.

endowed with its own sovereign rights and removed from the intervention of other states: a haven for convicted scoundrels and a university for budding crooks."[80] He even claimed that Zionism converted him to anti-Semitism.[81] Whatever the truth of this claim,[82] Hitler saw the Jewish people as an existential threat and opposed the idea of a Jewish homeland in Palestine or anywhere else.

Chesterton, unlike Shaw and Wells, never advocated mass killing, but it has been argued that he wanted to clear out Jews from England—that his Zionism resembled Hitler's.[83] But if the aim was to leave Jews vulnerable to Arab attacks in Palestine, Weizmann and Nordau canvassed similar ideas without apparent security concerns, thus it seems unlikely. While this tentative conclusion need not "close down" discussion of Chesterton's motivations, narrowly "anti-Semitic" interpretations of his Zionism tend to be as labyrinthine as the anti-Semite's view of Jewish conspiracy and similarly verge on the paranoid. Moreover, regarding Chesterton's motivations, while Shaw and Wells ignored compulsory sterilization in Germany because it agreed with their worldviews, when Hitler's anti-Jewish attacks highlighted the dangers of Jewish "separation," Chesterton swiftly and trenchantly protested and continued to advocate Zionism without, however, adverting to the enclave idea.

That idea was influenced by Belloc, but Palestinian Zionism, Stapleton notes, reflected Chesterton's theory of the "sanctity of place" as a focus for loyalty "in accordance with his Christian belief in a God who . . . had revealed Himself to fallen man as the source of all goodness."[84] Chesterton's "Zionist" chapter concludes by "shutting down" his private argument with Belloc's pessimism, in favor of the Jews: "[I]n the fine phrase of an English priest, in many ways more anti-Semitic than I: 'The people that remembers has a right.' The very worst of the Jews, as well as the very best, do in some sense remember. They lie, they swindle, they betray, they oppress; but they remember." While the "unheroic" had "the heroic memory," the "heroic people" had "no memory." This countered Belloc's claim that the "worst of the Jews" would not go to Palestine, because "in some sense," Chesterton believed, they "remembered." And if "the worst" could be "redeemed" by Zionism, it ruled out "racial" anti-Semitism—in fact, as will be seen, he believed that Zionism disproved racist theory. Chesterton privileged the "unheroic" Jews' mystical claim to the Holy Land over the

80. A. Hitler, *Mein Kampf* (London: Pimlico, 1925–26/2001), 294.

81. Ibid., 52–53.

82. He claimed not to have developed anti-Semitism until later in life but "youthful contemporaries" recalled the opposite (J. Goldberg, *Liberal Fascism: The Secret History of the Left from Mussolini to the Politics of Meaning* [London: Penguin Books], 62).

83. G. Kaufman, "Chesterton's final solution," op. cit.; see Chapter One.

84. J. Stapleton, *Christianity, Patriotism, and Nationhood: The England of G.K. Chesterton*, op. cit., 216–217.

"sophistry" of "some Anti-Semites" who said that "the Jews" had "no more right there than the Jebusites," for if any "heroic" Jebusites existed, they were Jebusites "without knowing it"—they did not "remember."[85] Crucially, it was for Jewish Zionists to decide on a solution rather than for Gentiles to impose one: "We know that there is a Jewish problem; we only hope that there is a Jewish solution. If there is not, there is no other." Zionism might fail but if "the Jew" could not "be at ease in Zion," Gentiles could "never again" believe that he was at ease "out of Zion." The Gentile could "only salute as it passes that restless and mysterious figure, knowing at last that there must be in him something mystical as well as mysterious; that whether in the sense of the sorrows of Christ or of the sorrows of Cain, he must pass by, for he belongs to God."[86]

Notwithstanding the problematic albeit alliterative reference to Cain, this conclusion, as well as expressing opposition to ShaWellian homogenized humanity, supported Chesterton's mystical religious beliefs: "the Jew" was different—special—because he "belonged to God." Whereas Belloc warned that Jews would assimilate, with dire consequences for the "English character," Chesterton feared Jewish assimilation for a much deeper reason, which emerged with his emerging religious belief: if Jews did assimilate, it would show that they were not, after all, "different" and "special." Furthermore, because of this "specialness," Jews must be allowed to "pass by," a warning against harassment that throws more light on the motivation behind the "enclave" idea. Moreover, as with his ideas on women, capitalism, and "Medievalism," theory was at variance with practice. Content to champion what he saw as the right approach, he left the details to the only ones who wanted to make the idea work: Zionists, some of whose number guided him in Palestine and influenced *The New Jerusalem*.

The Jews and Chesterton's Zionism

Jews had always been interested in Gentiles, and in 1910 the *Jewish Chronicle* cited Chesterton on the question of Robert Browning's possible Jewish descent.[87] The quest for common ground led one reader to feel "insult[ed]" at suggestions that he kept "company" with such "anti-Semites," maintaining: "No one is wholly bad, and even they are sane and sensible enough, even brilliant, on some other topics." Clearly unaware of Chesterton's revolutionary sympathies, he concluded that if it came to a choice "between an excess or abuse of patriotism which may spell chauvinism, and an excess or abuse of radico-socialism which spells revolution, anarchism and atheism, by all means let us have the

---

85. G.K. Chesterton, *The New Jerusalem* (1920), *G.K. Chesterton Collected Works Vol. XX*, op. cit., 416.

86. Ibid., 418.

87. *Jewish Chronicle*, August 19, 1910, 15.

former."[88] Shaw had joked that "the number of Jews" who would buy Chesterton's new paper just to see what he said about them would not be sufficient to keep it going,[89] but, as seen, Jewish commentators were swift to respond to Gentile views on the "Jewish question." The *Jewish Chronicle* sought interviews with Belloc and Chesterton, although they were less successful with Shaw.

But despite a growing Jewish interest in Zionism, and the fact that Jewish Zionists actively solicited the support of Gentiles like Chesterton, *The New Jerusalem* was virtually ignored by Jewish commentators, who appeared to view both Chesterton and Belloc as irredeemably anti-Semitic.[90] As Braybrooke remarked: "I am not sure that the Jews will be flattered to be told that Chesterton thinks they are worthy of being a nation; it is slightly patronizing."[91]

Regarding the Jewish canton idea, Ker says they "would simply create the kind of ghetto that had facilitated the persecution of Jews," although this could not have been his aim, "which sounds perfectly sincere even if quite impractical—or worse."[92] Rapp cites "specific evidence" that Chesterton's comments caused "pain amongst Anglo-Jews," claiming, "*contra* Chesterton's 'ardent apologists,'"[93] that Leopold Greenberg, editor of the *Jewish Chronicle* and *Jewish World* "ignored" Chesterton's Zionism, "unimpressed by his kind remarks" about Jewry, and that Greenberg "probably" suspected that "they derived from either self-deception" or the "desire to make his antisemitism more palatable to British society, which disliked publicly vocal antisemitism even when sharing its sentiments."[94]

Nonetheless, while Gentile Zionism did not necessarily signal pro-Semitism, as some presumed,[95] being Jewish by no means signaled pro-Zionism. Many feared it would confirm allegations of Jewish disloyalty, and it therefore became a source of deep division among Jews at the beginning of the twentieth century.[96] Hitler's all-embracing anti-Semitism encouraged post-Holocaust views

88. F. L. Emanuel, Letter, *Jewish Chronicle*, January 30, 1914, 24–25.

89. G. B. Shaw, Letter to G. K. Chesterton, February 16, 1923, M. Ward, *Gilbert Keith Chesterton*, op. cit., 488.

90. Belloc or Chesterton should be sent a booklet to enlighten anti-Semites (*Jewish Chronicle*, April 20, 1923, 8); "with his usual bitter anti-Semitism" Chesterton upbraided Dickens for creating the "good Jew" Riah to atone for Fagin (*Jewish Chronicle*, December 28, 1923, VII); unlike Shaw and Wells it was useless to engage with Chesterton and Belloc ("Why Don't You Like Us?" *Jewish Chronicle*, July 24, 1925, 5); see Chapter Three.

91. P. Braybrooke, *Gilbert Keith Chesterton*, op. cit., 67.

92. I. Ker, *G. K. Chesterton: A Biography*, op. cit., 421.

93. D. Rapp, "The Jewish Response to G. K. Chesterton's Antisemitism, 1911–1933," *Patterns of Prejudice*, 24 (2–4), (1990): 76.

94. Ibid., 84.

95. K. Whitehorn, "The Return of G. K. Chesterton," 1974, in D. Conlon, ed., *G. K. Chesterton: A Half Century of Views*, op. cit., 308.

96. Louis Jacobs, *The Jewish Religion: A Companion* (Oxford: Oxford University Press, 1995), 626.

of a united Jewry,[97] but after Jewish emancipation many Jews emphasized Jewish "difference" and diversity.[98] Some embraced this position for religious reasons, while[99] others, like Chesterton's Jewish friends, feared that assimilation would jeopardize their "Jewishness" before a Jewish state could be established.[100] Many Zionists were on the Left, while the militant Jabotinsky was right-wing;[101] Weizmann wanted a Palestinian homeland, but was vociferously opposed by Zangwill's Jewish Territorialist Organization.[102] In 1911 the *Jewish Chronicle* remarked of Chesterton's Zionism that "Jewish nationalism as an ideal" was "best when employed for internal consumption."[103] Leopold Greenberg, a committed Zionist who acted as Theodor Herzl's envoy and negotiated on his behalf,[104] may have been sensitive to Gentiles exploiting an idea that remained sensitive among Jews.[105] Visiting London in 1896, Theodor Herzl met a cool reception from wealthy Jews although poor Jews were more enthusiastic.[106] The Balfour Declaration was delayed because the British Cabinet had wrongly assumed that it was a Jewish objective.[107] Cheyette suggests that Greenberg ignored *The New Jerusalem* because of its perceived anti-Semitism,[108] and in fact, in 1920 the *Jewish Chronicle* commented that the book's "Jew-hatred" was "so manifestly evident in portions . . . as rather to disgust the fair-minded reader."[109] Zionist Philip Guedalla was unimpressed by some of Chesterton's more flippant suggestions such as the "portable Ark" and allowing Jews any

97. J. Sacks, *Faith in the Future* (London: Darton, Longman & Todd, 1995), 45.

98. S. Almog, *Zionism and History: The Rise of a New Jewish Consciousness* (New York: St. Martin's Press, 1987), 9.

99. M. N. Kertzer, *What is a Jew?* (New York: Touchstone, 1996), 114–115.

100. L. A. Hetzler, "Chesterton's Political Views, 1892–1914," *The Chesterton Review*, VII (2), (1981): 132.

101. D. J. Goldberg, *To the Promised Land: A History of Zionist Thought* (London: Penguin, 1996), 180–181; however, Stanislawski argues that Jabotinsky was no fascist (M. Stanislawski, *Zionism and the Fin de Siècle: Cosmopolitanism and Nationalism from Nordau to Jabotinsky*, op. cit., 209).

102. L. Jacobs, *The Jewish Religion: A Companion*, op. cit., 621; see: M. Stanislawski, *Zionism and the Fin de Siècle: Cosmopolitanism and Nationalism from Nordau to Jabotinsky*, op. cit.

103. "Mentor," "G. K. C. 'Peril,'" May 5, 1911, 7.

104. David Vital, *Zionism: the Formative Years* (Oxford: Clarendon Press, 1982), 149; 151; 449.

105. W. D. Rubinstein, *A History of the Jews in the English-Speaking World: Great Britain*, op. cit., 172–173.

106. D. J. Goldberg, *To the Promised Land: A History of Zionist Thought*, op. cit., 46; some religious Jews feared a Zionist state would be a cultural rather than political entity, thus usurping the Divine prerogative (Jehuda Reinharz, *Chaim Weizmann: The Making of a Zionist Leader* [Oxford: Oxford University Press, 1985], 71–72).

107. Joan Comay, ed., *Who's Who in Jewish History after the period of the Old Testament* (London: Routledge, 1995), 378.

108. B. Cheyette, *Constructions of the Jew in English Literature and Society: Racial Representations 1875–1945* (Cambridge: Cambridge University Press, 1995), 203.

109. *Jewish Chronicle*, September 3, 1920, 28–29.

freedom, including preaching in St Paul's Cathedral, as long as they wore Arab dress.[110] Believing that Chesterton wished to see Jews "branded in every possible way as foreigners." Guedalla, who despite his Zionism was an admirer of anti-nationalist H.G. Wells, concluded ominously: "It is an impertinence to praise for mere writing one of the most attractive conjurers with English prose, and it is evidence of dullness to disregard the bitter cry of a humorist asking to be taken seriously. But next time Mr. Chesterton will ask in vain."[111]

Cheyette argues that "Jewish racial difference" was "central" to Chesterton's Zionism;[112] citing *The New Jerusalem*, he notes Chesterton's belief that "Jews could never become 'Englishmen'":

> Patriotism is not merely dying for the nation. It is dying with the nation. It is regarding the fatherland not merely as a real resting-place like an inn, but as a final resting place, like a house or* a grave. Even the most Jingo of the Jews do not feel like this about their adopted country; and I doubt if the most intelligent of the Jews would pretend that they did. Even if we can bring ourselves to believe that Disraeli lived for England, we cannot think that he would have died for** her. If England had sunk in the Atlantic he would not have sunk with her, but easily floated over to America to stand for the Presidency.[113]

But Chesterton's claim was based on nationality, not race; in fact, he believed race theory, "[t]hat nonsense," had "received its death-blow with Zionism. As certainly as the Great War killed the old talk about Teutonism, the Jewish experiment in Jerusalem has killed the old talk about Semitism."[114] It is possible, however, that Chesterton's "nationalist" approach to the Jews was merely disguised racism. In *The New Jerusalem* he also maintains:

> [W]ith all their fine apprehensions, the Jews suffer from one heavy calamity; that of being a Chosen Race. It is the vice of any patriotism or religion depending on race that the individual is himself the thing to be worshipped; the individual is his own ideal, and even his own idol. This fancy was fatal to the Germans; it is fatal to the Anglo-Saxons, whenever any of them forswear the glorious name of Englishmen and Americans to fall into that forlorn description.[115]

110. G.K. Chesterton, *The New Jerusalem* (1920), *G.K. Chesterton Collected Works Vol. XX*, op. cit., 397; see Chapter One.

111. P. Guedalla, "Childe Chesterton," *The Zionist Review*, March 1921, 1990, 199–200.

112. B. Cheyette, *Constructions of the Jew in English Literature and Society: Racial Representations 1875–1945*, op. cit., 184.

113. G.K. Chesterton, *The New Jerusalem* (1920), 284–285 (ibid., 203); *"even" in original; **"with" in original; Disraeli, not American-born, could not have become President; see Chapters Two and Five.

114. G.K. Chesterton, "On being called 'Anti-Semite,'" *G.K.'s Weekly*, April 18, 1925, 78.

115. G.K. Chesterton, *The New Jerusalem* (1920), *G.K. Chesterton Collected Works Vol. XX*, op. cit., 213–214.

Chesterton's earlier, mystical view of Jews as the Chosen Race endured, although he now saw it as a "heavy calamity" for them. Nonetheless, despite fearing that secularized Jews would turn to self-worship, he did not object to Zionists "worshipping" the Jewish homeland. Guedalla continued to attack his canton idea, warning of "Chestertonism and Chestertonian anti-Semitism."[116] Louis Golding thought Chesterton's final "peroration" with its "mystical Jew" read "very prettily" but formed just another "sub-section" of anti-Semitism.[117] But Chesterton saw Zionists, like the French Revolutionaries and Irish rebels, as role-models for the non-revolutionary English, and continued to speak to Jewish societies. At the Ghetto Social Circle in November 1921 he lectured on "the strong nationalistic tendencies of the present time . . . more pronounced than in the days of his youth"; he warned that Wells' world state "would kill liberty rather than procure it"; that Bolshevism had proved "a failure," and that other forces, like "disarmament, which were working for internationalism" were not strong enough "to conquer the nationalistic feeling." To Chesterton, this was a positive development, and he urged Jews to "cultivate their Nationalism" and "acquire a territory for themselves . . . therefore he was a Zionist."[118]

With Zionism gradually gaining respectability among Jews, the view of Chesterton as a confirmed anti-Semite appeared to soften, and the following year, his article on the late Alfred Harmsworth, Lord Northcliffe, who had been "hostile" to Zionism, and had changed his mind too late, was described in the *Jewish Chronicle* as being "valued, not merely because of its inherent interest and the wisdom of its theme," but because of the author's remarks about "the duty of making up our minds. Most people who talk about making up their minds simply mean neglecting their minds and following their wishes or their whims."[119] Similar approval was expressed for his *New Witness* remarks about *Daily Express* proprietor Lord Beaverbrook. Chesterton was reported as saying that in pursuing commercial interests, he had "shed the mantle of pro-Germanism in favour of Arab protection," and should be compared unfavorably to Northcliffe who "came to see the error of his ways."[120] Zionist views of Chesterton remained conflicted, however. In 1923 one campaigner complained of attempts to "disparage the Zionist ideal by representing it as the offspring of

116. "At the Oxford Adler Society Meeting," *Jewish Chronicle*, February 18, 1921, 24.

117. L. Golding, "A Rationale of Anti-Semitism," *Jewish Chronicle*, September 23, 1921, II.

118. *Jewish Chronicle*, November 11, 1921, 38–39.

119. "Mentor," "A Word of Mr. Chesterton's," *Jewish Chronicle*, August 25, 1922, 9.

120. However, if Palestinian Jews uncovered a proposal "worthy" of his consideration, Beaverbrook would "review the situation, and incidentally extend his operations in the East" (G. K. Chesterton, *New Witness*, quoted in "Chesterton on Beaverbrook: A scathing criticism," *Jewish Chronicle*, March 23, 1923, 38–39; 40–41).

anti-Semitism," claiming that Chesterton and other anti-Semites "attack[ed] Zionism and anti-Zionism with equal fury."[121]

As seen, *The New Jerusalem* emphasized Chesterton's fears that Zionism would fail his "capitalism" test, and in 1925 *G.K.'s Weekly* warned: "[I]t is exactly because we have been Zionists, because in a sense we are still Zionists, that we lament with a great lamentation over Zionism." The "world as a whole" had "some persecution to apologise for" and the "Jews as a whole" had "some usury and similar things to apologise for," but, as this stemmed from the lack of a Jewish homeland, he had "hoped that the Jews would really settle down on the land and work on it and become a normal nation again." But, he explained: "The blow that destroyed our own Zionism was the Ruthenberg Concession"—ever since "that monstrous thing was started it was quite obvious that the financial Jews and their backers were going to do in Palestine what they do everywhere else." He was "entirely in favour of Israel being a nation" but "very decidedly not in favour of Israel being an aristocracy."[122] It was the Zionists' socialist and co-operative approach that encouraged Chesterton's support for the Palestinian homeland, but as *The New Jerusalem* declared, "the most serious point" against the project was that "the millionaires" were "for it."[123] Such millionaires were in a minority,[124] but the incident demonstrated that his belief in the Jewish homeland as a non-capitalist enterprise, even if impractical, was sincere. He continued to lecture to Jewish groups,[125] and later events showed that even the Rutenberg Concession did not "destroy" Chesterton's Zionism. He did, however, appear more uncertain that the Jewish homeland should be in Palestine. In 1927 he told a Polish-Jewish newspaper that he was accused of anti-Semitism for discussing the "Jewish question," but that he had written a book about his Palestine visit advocating a Jewish homeland "somewhere" as the only way to solve the problem. While mentioning Chesterton's denials of anti-Semitism, the *Jewish Chronicle* headlined its report "Mr. Chesterton's Anti-Semitism: A Three-Canton Pales-

---

121. "A Zionist Correspondent," "Zionism and Anti-Semitism," *Jewish Chronicle*, July 20, 1923, 28–29.

122. "The Tragedy of a Zionist," (unsigned), *G.K.'s Weekly*, May 2, 1925, 126; Russian Jewish engineer Pinchas Rutenberg obtained a concession for the first electric power station in Tel Aviv and subsequently built power stations in Haifa and Tiberias; private Jewish capital established a salt works, a large flour mill, and an oil and soap factory, later a cement factory and several textile plants (H.M. Sachar, *A History of Israel from the Rise of Zionism to our Time*, op. cit., 155).

123. G.K. Chesterton, *The New Jerusalem* (1920), *G.K. Chesterton Collected Works Vol. XX*, op. cit., 284–285.

124. Sir Moses Montefiore (1784–1885) and Lord Nathaniel Mayer de Rothschild (1840–1915) were generous patrons of Palestinian Zionism; see: H. M. Sachar, *A History of Israel: From the Rise of Zionism to our Time*, op. cit.; D.J. Goldberg, *To the Promised Land: A History of Zionist Thought*, op. cit.

125. He lectured to the Jewish Old Boys' Club in the Mile End Road, London (*Jewish Chronicle*, February 4, 1927, 14–15).

tine?"[126] The following year, Joseph Tunkel, editor of the Warsaw Yiddish *Der Moment* and a "great admirer" of Dickens, Heine, and Shaw, praised Chesterton as "the greatest living writer of humour."[127] In 1929 Chesterton explained to a Jewish enquirer that he was still uncertain about a Jewish homeland in Palestine:

> The view I have always taken is that if possible it would be better for Jews to form self-governing societies of their own. As to its possibility or the form it should take, I have grown more and more doubtful. The particular case of Palestine is unfortunately very difficult and I think in practice rather unsatisfactory not so much by fault of the Jews but by the presence of other people. On the whole I think Zionism gives Israel too little rather than too much national independence. I have often wondered whether the experiment could be made somewhere else.[128]

The letter tends to confirm that Chesterton's growing uncertainty about a Palestinian homeland was linked to the violent reaction of "other people," as he witnessed during his visit. Despite his gloomy prognostications, his Zionism survived, and in 1930, through "Simon," the patriotic Jewish banker in *The Loyal Traitor*, he reiterated his view that "Jewish vices" were caused by the lack of a homeland.[129]

He told Maurice Baring, who helped facilitate his visit,[130] that he had "another motive" for wanting to go to Palestine, which was "much stronger than the desire to write the book," although he thought he "could do it in the right way and, what matters more, on the right side."[131] The "right side" was the Zionist side. He also wanted to avoid the English winter because of his wife's health,[132] but there was yet another motive. As Ward "learned later," the Jerusalem visit was "a determining factor in Gilbert's conversion. Many people both in and outside the Church had been wondering what had so long delayed him."[133] After the visit he thanked Baring for having such a "wonderful time,"[134] and

---

126. "[W]ith anti-Semitism as such I have nothing at all to do. The anti-Semitism of the Morning Post is the anti-Semitism of ignoramuses and fools" (*Nasz Przeglad*, quoted in *Jewish Chronicle*, May 20, 1927, 24).

127. "Jews and Humour: 'Der Tunkeler' in Interview," *Jewish Chronicle*, March 2, 1928, 30–31.

128. Wallach's letter has not survived; Chesterton's reply was signed by his secretary who added: "Mr. Chesterton is too pressed for time just at present to do more than give a general answer to the many questions you have asked" (G. K. Chesterton, Letter to Sidney Wallach, January 3, 1929 [Chesterton Collection, British Library, 73241]).

129. See Chapter Three.

130. M. Ward, *Gilbert Keith Chesterton*, op. cit., 439; see Chapter Eight.

131. G. K. Chesterton, Letter to Maurice Baring, [undated, 1919] (ibid., 442).

132. G. K. Chesterton, Letter to Hilaire Belloc, November 13, [1919], John J. Burns Library, in I. Ker, *G. K. Chesterton: A Biography*, op. cit., 407.

133. M. Ward, *Gilbert Keith Chesterton*, op. cit., 444; see Chapter Eight.

134. G. K. Chesterton, Letter to Maurice Baring (undated) (ibid., 446–447); see Chapter Eight.

only abandoned a further visit in 1934 due to his serious illness at Syracuse.[135] Chesterton's *Autobiography* recalled seeing "the fanatical Arabs come up from the desert to attack the Jews in Jerusalem,"[136] but despite saying that there was "no need to recur ... to Palestinian politics," he added that "[o]ne incident" stood out in his memory "for some strange reason." When "wandering about in the wilderness in a car with a zealous little Zionist," his guide "seemed at first almost monomaniac." Yet Chesterton "came to sympathise with his romance; and when he said, 'It's a lovely land; I should like to put the Song of Solomon in my pocket and wander about,' I knew that, Jew or Gentile, mad or sane, we two were of the same sort." And as his Zionist friend read from the Song of Solomon, "[t]he air was full of poetry; and not without irony."[137]

Chesterton's Jewish Zionist Friends

As seen, although initially the Zionist idea attracted few Jewish supporters, Chesterton was an enthusiastic Zionist; and although his Zionism was seen by Jewish critics as evidence of anti-Semitism, his ideas reflected some of the views of the movement's founder, Theodor Herzl, as well as his Jewish Zionist friends, who eagerly sought the support of prominent Gentiles as well as Jews. One of these friends was the charismatic Chaim Weizmann (1874–1952). The first President of Israel, Weizmann, born in a Jewish "Shtetl" in the Russian Pale of Settlement, influenced several high-profile British politicians toward Zionism, including Arthur Balfour, Herbert Samuel, and David Lloyd George—he even charmed Nancy Astor.[138] Weizmann makes no mention of Chesterton or "cantons" in his autobiography, but he did express several ideas that found their way into *The New Jerusalem*, for example, that Zionism must be based on Palestine, as anything else would be "a form of idolatry"; that Jews had "never forsaken" its memory; that no other land would command the loyalty and energy of Jews, essential for nation-building.[139] Chesterton could have been echoing Weizmann's view of "indifference or hostility" to Zionism among wealthy English Jews,[140] and the Zionist also complained that "[t]he assimilationist handful of upper-class British Jews ... aware that the Zionist cause was making great headway in Government circles and in general public opinion" tried to obstruct the Balfour Declaration in 1917.[141]

135. Ibid., 641.
136. G.K. Chesterton, *Autobiography*, op. cit., 50.
137. Ibid., 318–319.
138. See Chapter Six.
139. C. Weizmann, *Trial and Error: The Autobiography of Chaim Weizmann*, op. cit., 143.
140. Ibid., 150.
141. Ibid., 252.

Israel Zangwill (1864–1926) was not, as seen, afraid to criticize Chesterton regarding anti-Semitism, or on his Zionist views. Regarded as a "Jewish Dickens," he won popular acclaim for *King of Schnorrers* and *Children of the Ghetto*. His play *The Melting Pot* lent its name to a vision of America as a nation forged out of many nationalities, although his biographer Joseph Leftwich claimed some Jews did not like Zangwill's emphasis on poor Jewish communities because they were embarrassed about anything "Jewish."[142] As Joseph Pearce notes, Zangwill was a friend of Chesterton's,[143] but according to Leftwich, he "fought against [the] Chestertonian conception that 'Jews,' as he put it, 'form an alien section of the nation.'" However, he added: "But I knew the Chestertons and Belloc, and they were certainly not 'Fascists.' Nor was their anti-Semitism of the murderous Hitlerist type. I accept their assurance that they would never have persecuted Jews."[144] Leftwich's biography mentions Chesterton as a friend and admirer[145] and refers to *G.K.'s Weekly*'s praise for Zangwill's clear ideal of Zionism.[146] Zangwill's other non-Jewish friends included Lloyd George, Winston Churchill, Bernard Shaw, Jerome K. Jerome, and even H.G. Wells, who said Zangwill's involvement in Zionism was a sign of selfishness.[147]

Chesterton praised "great Jews like Zangwill,"[148] but Zangwill severely criticized *The New Jerusalem*. In *The Voice of Jerusalem* (1920), he remarked of Jewish history that "[w]e shall yet hear that it was their ghoulish insistence on salvation by blood that made the Jews the odium of the human race. Possibly it is Mr. Chesterton who will formulate that indictment."[149] Continuing in satirical vein, Zangwill wrote:

> Of course the Jews ruined Germany, both by overturning the Kaiser and through the Kaiser himself being a Jew. Mr. Chesterton, writing of the Irish, caustically remarks that, having for centuries been accused of religious fanaticism, they cannot now be indicted for its antithesis. Yet in Mr. Chesterton's

142. J. Leftwich, *Israel Zangwill* (London: James Clarke & Co., 1957), 41.

143. Joseph Pearce, *Wisdom and Innocence: A Life of GKC* (London: Hodder & Stoughton, 1997), 446.

144. Chesterton died before Zangwill's memorial meeting in 1936, but Belloc, "very proud and honoured," joined the memorial committee; once, they had met "fairly often" and "never lost touch"—Belloc had "the greatest admiration" for the "sincerity" and "integrity" of the "remarkable writer." When in 1952 the Israel Zangwill Fellowship, planning another memorial, approached Belloc, his son-in-law Reginald Jebb replied that he was no longer able to write letters, and no longer active in public affairs, but "his name could be used on the list of the sponsoring committee" (J. Leftwich, Letter, *Sunday Times*, August 18, 1957).

145. J. Leftwich, *Israel Zangwill*, op. cit., 33.

146. Ibid., 79.

147. See Chapter Five.

148. J. Leftwich, *Israel Zangwill*, op. cit., 124–125.

149. I. Zangwill, *The Voice of Jerusalem* (London: Wm. Heinemann, 1920), 38.

own organisation, The New Witness, the most paradoxical accusations against the Jew find Christian hospitality.[150]

Chesterton, who maintained a reverent attitude to Jewish religion, and ridiculed claims that "the Jews" had lost Germany the Great War,[151] did not take offence when Zangwill introduced Joseph Jacobs to him, saying that Jacobs wished "to study the new anti-Semitic wing of English letters, which had grown up so oddly during his residence in America." Jacobs persuaded Zangwill to arrange a meeting with Chesterton, which took place at the Cheshire Cheese pub, where "the duel of Aryan and Semite came off without casualties" because Zangwill had "prudently" ensured a supply of alcohol. The meeting was their first, thus it was not a complete failure,[152] despite Zangwill's view that Jacobs's reconstruction of the London Jewish community of 1290 was authentic "if only from its substantial accordance with the Ghetto projected anew by the Belloc-Chestertonian school."[153] Zangwill was the archetypal "Jewish friend," and the *Jewish Chronicle* noted that of "three celebrated contemporary anti-Semites," French statesman Georges Clemenceau "sported a Jewish secretary," and Belloc and Chesterton were "always boasting of the number of their Jewish friends."[154]

Public pronouncements notwithstanding, the friendships seemed genuine: Zangwill complained to *G.K.'s Weekly* about J.K. Prothero's review of his play *We Moderns* in 1925, but privately offered tickets to Chesterton and his friends. With the rise of Nazism, the *Chesterbelloc*'s "religious" outlook, and "solution" to the "Jewish question," now equated with Hitler's, seemed less important than their rejection of racial anti-Semitism. Leftwich quotes Zangwill regarding *The Jews* where Belloc "rightly" said that the "Jewish problem" could not be avoided but must be met:

> How did he as a Roman Catholic meet it? Speaking of 'the sharp distinction between the Jew and ourselves,' he said: 'The Rationalist would say that this distinction was racial, and that it only found religious expression on account of its racial quality. His opponent would say that the origin of the quarrel was mainly ... a difference in religious tradition which formed the contrast between the Jew and Christendom.'

Leftwich adds that when Belloc "spoke of inter-marriage, he spoke of it as

150. Ibid., 181.

151. See Chapter Three.

152. I. Zangwill, *The Voice of Jerusalem*, op. cit., 336–337.

153. Ibid., 339.

154. "'The Voice of Jerusalem': Semites and Anti-Semites: Mr. Zangwill reviews his reviewers," *Jewish Chronicle*, February 4, 1921, 18–19.

'marriage between Christian and Jew,' not 'English and Jew.'"[155] Zangwill lambasted Chesterton and Belloc, but also poured scorned on Weizmann's ideas. As Weizmann's biographer Jehuda Reinharz noted, Zangwill worked with Weizmann despite their "deep-seated differences" regarding Zionism,[156] and Zangwill raised laughter in his Jewish audience by describing Weizmann asking "anxiously" whether the Jewish people would rise when the Shofar was sounded, while he himself had "sounded only a penny whistle . . . with a frightened quaver at that." Like Chesterton, Zangwill was anxious about Arab claims on Palestine, although he was less optimistic.[157] It was the more conciliatory Weizmann who eventually won the day, while Zangwill's Jewish Territorialists lost impetus after the Balfour Declaration in 1917 and disbanded in 1925. In 1923 Zangwill called the "Jewish National Home" in Palestine "as little Jewish or National or a Home as any other part of the Diaspora." Nonetheless, with Chestertonian echoes he urged Jews: "[F]or God's sake stand openly and assertively for something worth dying for, so that if die you must, you go down, flag in hand. In that struggle for your own ideal, you will not only find death worth the dying, but life worth the living."[158] Zangwill's obituary noted that if he did "give vent occasionally to pessimistic outbursts of the destiny of our people, it was because he was moved by an over-zealous and restless desire to see the Jewish problem solved . . . speedily in our days."[159]

Zangwill's cousin and friend Dr. Montague David Eder,[160] described by Ada Chesterton as "one of the first and most fiery Zionists," after the Great War "left his London practice and took an orange farm in Palestine" where the Chestertons visited him. Ada said Eder "resolutely . . . flung himself on to the land, cultivating the soil side by side with Jewish and Arab workers."[161] The *Chesterbelloc*'s policy of criticizing wealthy Jews but defending poor Jews[162] meant that the radical Eder was closer to Chesterton than was Zangwill. In *The New Age* Eder attacked "the Rothschilds and other rich Jews as enemies to the cause of Juda."[163] Despite this, his biographer Joseph Burton Hobman described the

---

155. J. Leftwich, *Israel Zangwill*, op. cit., 160–161; see Chapter Six.

156. J. Reinharz, *Chaim Weizmann: The Making of a Zionist Leader*, op. cit., 189.

157. Weizmann "tells us that he has never asked for a Jewish State, first of all because we would not have got it, secondly because if we did get it, we could not govern it" ("Zangwill on Weizmann," *Jewish Chronicle*, February 27, 1920, 28).

158. *Jewish Chronicle*, October 18, 1923, 18–19.

159. Raphael Nelson, *Jewish Chronicle*, August 6, 1926, 16–21.

160. J. Leftwich, *Israel Zangwill*, op. cit., 78.

161. Mrs. C. Chesterton, *The Chestertons* (London: Chapman & Hall Ltd., 1941), 119.

162. "Do not, they said, look for traitors and spies among waiters and small traders—look up, not down" (M. Ward, *Gilbert Keith Chesterton*, op. cit., 414–415).

163. M. Ward, *Return to Chesterton* (London: Sheed & Ward, 1952), 57.

socialist Eder as "no slave of collectivist or communist clichés," being "too human to contemplate without repugnance the sacrifice of individual men and women to such an abstraction as the State."[164] Initially, Eder embraced the approach that the *Chesterbelloc* feared would lead to the death of nationalism for everyone except Jews: a "new world order in which differences of race and creed would, like class distinctions, lose their significance, and Jews would be admitted without question to equality with the rest of mankind." At that time, Eder did not regard Zionism as "a solution of the Jewish problem" but was "well aware that there was a problem to be solved."[165] He also believed Palestine had enough "black-coated workers" and needed more peasants.[166] Eder complained of wealthy Jews' failure to support Zionism,[167] but Chesterton praised Eder in *The New Jerusalem* as one of a "small group" of Zionist pioneers, including Weizmann, who favored "this nationalist ideal when all the international Jewish millionaires were against it."[168]

Eder and Chesterton were also united in opposition to eugenics, although Hobman described the campaign as one of Eder's "most successful [and] single-handed efforts to keep individual liberty free from the invasion of bureaucratic interference." Eder, he claimed, "initiated and led" the 1912 campaign against the Mental Deficiency Bill, and "aroused popular opinion to its dangers...in the *Nation*, the *Eye-Witness*, the *Westminster Gazette* and the *Daily Herald*." When this "project reappeared in the guise of voluntary sterilization," Eder saw "his fears justified that sterilisation might be invoked on political, religious and racial grounds." Hobman notes that these were "the very grounds" on which it "appeared ... under the Hitler regime at the expense of Jewish and democratic victims of the Nazi doctrine of blood and race."[169] As seen, the same fears animated Chesterton and the *Witness* circle, and Belloc thought one of Eder's letters "admirable."[170] *The New Jerusalem* expressed Chesterton's gratitude and "respect" for Eder: the "humour and human sympathy of a Jewish doctor was very welcome to us when we were accused of being Anti-Semites." Dr. Eder was asked "for his own views on the Jewish problem. We found he was then a very strong Zionist." Chesterton added that Eder's

---

164. David Eder, *David Eder: Memoirs of a modern pioneer*, Joseph Burton Hobman, ed. (London: Victor Gollancz, 1945), 87.

165. Ibid., 134.

166. Ibid., 161; Eder said "experience had shown" that "Jews were suited to agricultural work" ("The Eder-Brodetsky Controversy," *Jewish Chronicle*, August 7, 1931, 14).

167. D. Eder, *David Eder: Memoirs of a modern pioneer*, op. cit., 182.

168. G.K. Chesterton, *The New Jerusalem* (1920), *G.K. Chesterton Collected Works Vol. XX*, op. cit., 284–285.

169. D. Eder, *David Eder: Memoirs of a modern pioneer*, op. cit., 81–82.

170. Ibid., 84.

"only defect . . . as a mere detail of portraiture," was "a certain excessive vigi-lance and jealousy and pertinacity in the wrong place," which sometimes made "the genuine Zionists unpopular with the English, who themselves suffer unpopularity for supporting them." This helps to explain Chesterton's policy of addressing the English anti-Semite, because, he says, although he himself was "called an Anti-Semite," there were "periods" when he was "almost the only Pro-Semite in the company." Undeterred, he "went about pointing out what was really to be said for Zionism, to people who were represented by the Arabs as mere slaves of the Zionists."[171]

In contrast, Eder's close friend and patient D.H. Lawrence challenged Eder's plans to visit Palestine as part of the Zionist Commission, asking: "Why do you go with the Jews? They will only be a mill-stone round your neck. Best cease to be a Jew, and let Jewry disappear."[172] Later, Lawrence begged Eder to take him to Palestine, despite his "horror of the dreadful hosts of people, 'with noses,' as your Sister said."[173] Eder, formerly a Harley Street psychiatrist and "contributor to Cecil Chesterton's *New Witness*" also acted as the Chestertons' guide in Pales-tine.[174] Zionism was unpopular in Britain, but even more so in the Soviet Union which, although officially tolerating Zionists, forbade them to organize, campaign, or communicate with Zionists elsewhere. Describing his visit to the country, Eder saw the "chief obstacle to Zionist work" as the "Commissariat for Jewish Affairs," headed by "assimilated Jews, thoroughly indifferent, if not hos-tile, to Jewish national strivings." He told the *Jewish Chronicle* that they vented their "spite" after many electoral defeats "at the hands of the Zionists," portray-ing them as "counter-revolutionaries"—charges he said were "entirely false" and "based on manufactured information." Eder acknowledged, however, that anti-Semitism and discrimination had disappeared, although in the Ukraine "complete anarchy" reigned.[175] Zionism challenged the official portrait of a workers' paradise, where, like the Hebrew slaves in Egypt, Jews were well-treated but not allowed to leave, although, like many left-wing Jewish Zionists, Eder's nationalism triumphed over his internationalism.[176] In addition to his

---

171. G.K. Chesterton, *The New Jerusalem* (1920), *G.K. Chesterton Collected Works Vol. XX*, op. cit., 284–285.

172. D.H. Lawrence, Letter to David Eder, August 25, 1917, D. Eder, *David Eder: Memoirs of a modern pioneer*, op. cit., 119.

173. D.H. Lawrence, Letter to David Eder, 1919 (ibid., 121).

174. B. Sewell, *G.K.'s Weekly: An Appraisal* (Maidstone, Kent: The Aylesford Press, 1990), 53.

175. There were Yiddish papers but "no Jewish papers *per se*"; the "entire press" was "in the hands of the Government" ("Zionism and Soviet Russia: Interview for the *Jewish Chronicle* with Dr. M.D. Eder," *Jewish Chronicle*, March 11, 1921, 18).

176. M. Stanislawski, *Zionism and the Fin de Siècle: Cosmopolitanism and Nationalism from Nor-dau to Jabotinsky*, op. cit., 246.

Zionist work he responded tirelessly to calls for help; he died shortly before Chesterton, similarly worn out.[177]

The New Jerusalem echoed the ideas of Chesterton's Jewish Zionist friends, but it was scarcely noticed by the *Jewish Chronicle*, although Chesterton was not completely ignored.[178] In 1925, the *Jewish Chronicle* correspondent "Mentor," who during the Great War had advocated a "Hit Back!" campaign against the *New Witness*, used Chesterton's reputation for anti-Semitism to refute allegations that Stinie Morrison had received a "persistent and noisy . . . organised backing among his co-religionists." "Mentor" claimed that "one of the most persistent, I will not say noisy, of those who thought the verdict in the Morrison case was wrong, and said so, was none other than Mr. G. K. Chesterton!" No one, he added, would "suppose he of all men was influenced by or co-operated with Jewish influence."[179] With Sir Arthur Conan Doyle Chesterton was cited by a *Jewish Chronicle* reader as a defender of Oscar Slater.[180] As with Belloc, an "anti-Semite" was a much more valuable witness for the defense. Palestinian Zionists, however, showed more positive views of Chesterton: in 1921 a wine advertisement from a colony praised in *The New Jerusalem* quoted Chesterton in an advertisement.[181] The winery manager of Rishon LeZion, second oldest Zionist colony in Palestine told a *Jewish Chronicle* interviewer that a few weeks previously, in the very chair in which he was sitting, "sat . . . the English writer, Mr. Chesterton . . . . I told him all about our work here, and asked him if he would like any further information." Chesterton, however, "replied that he was not interested in collecting facts," prompting the interviewer to respond: "That's just the pity of it . . . Chesterton always ignores the facts, except when he perverts them, and is thus able to give free rein to his anti-Semitic prejudices."[182] Despite this, the advertisements continued. Palwin, as the distribution center for Palestine's Associated Winegrowers, with all profits funding

177. "He has gone as he would have wished; in harness, a soldier, not of lost causes, but of freedom, a warrior of mankind whose lance had never broken, whose sword had never rusted. Truly, a Prince in Israel has fallen" (*Jewish Chronicle*, April 3, 1936, 12); a young Zionist training farm set up in Eder's memory emphasized "constructive work" and "achievement" ("The Palestine Movement: English Chalutzim for Palestine: First Batch from Kentish Training Farm: An Answer to Arab Terrorism," *Jewish Chronicle*, August 28, 1936, 20).

178. His views on divorce were cited (*Jewish Chronicle*, December 28, 1923, IV).

179. "Mentor," *Jewish Chronicle*, May 15, 1925, 11.

180. "A Barrister-at-law," Letter, *Jewish Chronicle*, October 28, 1927, 34–35; 43; see Chapters Five and Six.

181. "Mr. Philip Guedalla once wrote of a fellow wit: 'Mr. Chesterton is perpetually slapping the universe on the back and asking it to have another drink'" ("Palwin" advertisement, *Jewish Chronicle*, December 18, 1925, 21); "Don't believe in anything," Chesterton once wrote to a child friend, "that can't be told in coloured pictures"—although this was the "very antithesis" of Jewish doctrine (January 7, 1927, ibid., 34–35).

182. *Jewish Chronicle*, February 25, 1921, II.

further colonization work, served as an example of the approach favored by Chesterton.

Despite Chesterton's sensational anti-Nazi interview in 1933 and later condemnations of Nazi anti-Semitism, the *Jewish Chronicle* mentioned his introduction to the Friends of Europe booklet *Germany's National Religion*, characterizing that religion as "race," without further comment.[183] Chesterton's later poems ridiculing Hitler and other Nazis were overlooked: "Hitlerites may explain how Race can teach / Imperfect wits to make a Perfect Speech, / But all who know what crowns our mortal dream / Will own that Goering is a Perfect Scream."[184] A more somber poem reads: "And if he seeks the Dark Lady, / Judith or Sheba's Queens, / The public power may shoot him dead / By very private means. . . ."[185] In contrast to Shaw, Wells, and Belloc, there was no *Jewish Chronicle* obituary of Chesterton.

His poetry and fiction still inspired Jewish readers,[186] and posthumous references reflected his humorous side,[187] but such aspects, along with his anti-Nazism, were overshadowed by the Jewish enclave idea. In 1951 it was summed up in the *Jewish Chronicle* as the "neo-medieval day-dreams of such eccentrics as Mr. Belloc and the late Mr. Chesterton."[188] In 1956, in the same paper, Wolf Mankowitz cited Chesterton as proof against Zangwill's belief that education would eradicate racial prejudice, although "Chesterton's sheer ignorance of what a Jew was like" was "an indication of the educational necessity of Zang-

183. *Jewish Chronicle*, August 10, 1934, 13; see Chapter Five.

184. "If any other witness moves or speaks, / The Court-House rings with long protracted shrieks; / Three sounds, mysterious to the racial stranger, / Impress an Aryan people with the danger / Of interrupting strong and silent men / Just at the psychological moment when / They are, for Reich, Race, Goering and Gore, / Having hysterics on the Court-House floor: / Howl at us, black and purple in the face, / To note the calm of the Germanic race" (G. K. Chesterton, "Perfection," *G.K.'s Weekly*, 1933, *G. K. Chesterton Collected Works Vol. X Collected Poetry Part I* (San Francisco: Ignatius Press, 1994), 405.

185. G. K. Chesterton, "Gentlemen prefer Blondes," *G.K.'s Weekly*, 1934 (ibid., 392).

186. A verse from Chesterton's poetry, "and Birmingham grew so big, so big" was "vividly in my head as I trudged through the metropolis, suburbs and environs" of the Royal Academy's annual exhibition ("Art Notes: A Very Dull Royal Academy," *Jewish Chronicle*, May 7, 1937, 60–61); a terrorist incident in Palestine recalled a Father Brown story in which a General ordered a battle to conceal a murder ("Land of Israel News: The Massacre at Haifa: Civil Administration still whitewashing: Need for Martial Law: Terrorism by a Handful," *Jewish Chronicle*, July 15, 1938, 22–23).

187. "G. K. Chesterton . . . complained in his acutely ironical manner: 'The trouble is that you Jews are born civilised'" (*Jewish Chronicle*, April 10, 1942, 8–9); as Chesterton remarked about Dickens and *Pickwick Papers*, "Zangwill was still in a youthful whirl" when he wrote *Children of the Ghetto* (*Jewish Chronicle*, September 25, 1942, 13); "acting on G. K. Chesterton's principle, will not one of our communal leaders inaugurate a Club of Jewish Queer Trades, and seek a place for it on the Board of Deputies?" (D. Massel, Letter, *Jewish Chronicle*, May 12, 1950, 17).

188. "Galut Nationalism," *Jewish Chronicle*, October 5, 1951, 15.

will's work." Continuing in savage vein, Mankowitz alleged that "your bluff Chesterton, rolling in what he calls his 'innocence'" had "no wish to disburden himself of his prejudices." Moses Gould, with his "Negro vitality and vulgarity" showed that "Chestertonian Jews speak stage cockney, are dressed like race-course touts, and are not Christian." Although "never vulgar enough to state it in bold terms" Chesterton believed that "Negro and Jew" were "members of inferior races, celebrants of degenerate cultures." Admittedly, Chesterton's "beery afflatus never lifted him to Dr. Alfred Rosenberg's pinnacle of distaste," but the "burbling Gargantua of the suburbs ... felt a chronic distaste" and, "alas for the efforts of the most earnest educationists!" he "had a taste for his distaste." The same distaste in the "actually ignorant masses" made it possible "for some Manalive to occasionally take hold of their impeccable noses and lead them to the great allegorical practical joke of a necktie party or a pogrom or a gas-chamber." Worse: "The dead nigger in the wood-pile, the good Jew who is a dead Jew," were "helped to their inheritance by all those who, like Chesterton, preserve their irrational distaste like a valuable snobbism." Mankowitz concluded that Zangwill's "pasteboard, two-dimensional" characters in *The King of Schnorrers* would not have harmed "even Chesterton in the slightest way."[189] But, like Zangwill's "King of Schnorrers," Moses Gould was a likeable character in a humorous work, a light-hearted, non-threatening antidote to the "sinister Jew,"[190] with layers of meaning that would remain hidden to post-Holocaust eyes.

The following year, Belloc and Chesterton were remembered by one Jewish writer as literary anti-Semites,[191] and the "Belloc-Chesterton attitude" was blamed by R.N. Carvalho for negatively influencing a generation with "the myth of 'International Jewry.'"[192] In 1961, the positive views of Chesterton expressed by his contemporary Rabbi Stephen Wise, which will be discussed later in this chapter, were dismissed in the *Jewish Chronicle* by Ben Azad: "Rabbi Wise must have suffered from the selective forgetfulness which afflicts so many Jews. Together with Belloc, Chesterton conducted what was almost a *jihad* against Jewry," believing that Jews could be patriotic "only for their race ...

189. Wolf Mankowitz, "The Case of Zangwill v. Chesterton," *Jewish Chronicle*, March 16, 1956, i–ii.

190. I. Zangwill, *The King of Schnorrers* (New York: Dover Publications Inc., 1894/1965).

191. In a debate it was argued that the works of writers like "Belloc, Chesterton, and Dorothy L. Sayers" although "not open examples of anti-Semitism," nonetheless included "numerous and potent 'sly digs' against the Jews"; in opposition, it was claimed that "Jewish villains in drama were often depicted, not with any antisemitic intent," but to paint "a picturesque theatrical figure" ("Antisemitism in Literature: Ignorance or Prejudice?" *Jewish Chronicle*, September 27, 1957, 10).

192. R.N. Carvalho, Review of "In the City. Georgian Afternoon, By L.E. Jones," *Jewish Chronicle*, May 30, 1958, 22.

even after thousands of Jews gave their lives on both sides in the first World War." Such strong "prejudice" required "more than mere facts to dismiss it." In Chesterton's case, he concluded, "it could not have been exorcised with bell, book, and candle."[193] In 1968 the paper recalled the *New Witness* claim about Sir Alfred Mond maintaining an Anglo-German "subterranean labyrinth of Jewish communications."[194] In 1971 Somerset Maugham's Jewish money-lender in *Lady Frederick* (1907) was dismissed as an Edwardian stereotype while Belloc and Chesterton were described as "malicious exceptions" in a generally pro-Semitic milieu.[195]

By 1986 Chesterton's Zionism was regarded as a dangerous mask. Chaim Bermant remarked: "One hears a great deal about anti-Zionism being used as a cover for antisemitism. What was far more insidious was the use of pro-Zionism as an apology for anti-Semitism." Chesterton, Bermant claimed, "was not even sincere," having "hardly a good word to say for the Zionist settlements." Moreover, his anti-Nazism was "mere rhetorical flourish. The man was a humbug." While "he and Belloc had considerable vision and warned of the dangers facing world Jewry . . . one has the unhappy feeling that they viewed them with relish rather than foreboding." Although Chesterton "was, or claimed to be, critical of Hitler," Hitler "ascribed the decline of Germany to the same cause."[196] In 1989, however, *Jewish Chronicle* reviewer Stephen Medcalf took Chesterton's anti-Nazism seriously and regarded his Zionism as sincere if misguided.[197] Writing in the same paper, Cheyette said of the "devout" Chesterton's "Little

193. "Ben Azad," *Jewish Chronicle*, June 23, 1961, 19.

194. *Jewish Chronicle*, October 4, 1918 ("A Cruel Insult," ibid., October 4, 1968, 20–21); see Chapter Six.

195. At a time when Edward VIII, "always short of money," was friendly with "the leading Jewish financiers," the situation was "accepted" by most English writers with "amused toleration" (C. Landstone, "Stage Jews," *Jewish Chronicle*, July 2, 1971, ii–iv).

196. Chesterton "was among the first antisemites to be a Zionist, but he was not the last," although he had "many redeeming qualities both as an individual and a writer" and there were "still many pleasures to be had from his work"; Ffinch's biography did not "try to apologise for his subject's antisemitic attitudes" but was "clearly appalled by them"; nonetheless, he seemed to "venerate him as a prophet, a sage and a man. Not every Jewish reader" would "share his veneration" (C. Bermant, "Humbug from ChesterBelloc," Review of Michael Ffinch, *G. K. Chesterton* [1986], *Jewish Chronicle*, September 12, 1986, 16).

197. Coren spoke "ill" of Chesterton's Zionism because in others it had been "a cloak for anti-Semitism," but it was "a straightforward transposition" of his stance on India, which inspired Gandhi: "[M]istaken, perhaps, romantically reactionary perhaps, but nothing to do with being against Jews"; however, "the crucial point" in judging whether, pre-1933, "coarse, casual or frivolous remarks" had "anything to do with genuine anti-Semitism" was their authors' attitude to Nazism, and Coren emphasized that Chesterton "was among the first . . . to understand and attack Nazism," especially regarding the Jews (Stephen Medcalf, "Deciding whether GK was OK to the Jews," Review of M. Coren, *Gilbert: The Man Who Was G. K. Chesterton* [1990], *Jewish Chronicle*, February 17, 1989, 24).

Englandism" that he was "extremely suspicious of the growth of the secular world," and while this was "understandable," he "tended to blame European Jewry" for the "worst excesses ... of democracy, industrialisation and finance capitalism." His anti-Semitism, however, was "more complex." It was "very different from Belloc's" and needed to be understood as part of "his distinctive Anglo-Catholic notions of religious orthodoxy." *The Duel of Doctor Hirsch*, along with the "crude, schoolboy prejudice" of *The Flying Inn*, showed that Chesterton's Zionism was "a 'narrow-minded' orthodoxy which would neutralise the assimilated, 'broad-minded' Jew." In seeing Lord Swaythling as "the perfect example of an 'orthodox' Jew of religious virtue," Chesterton was "a fundamentalist before our present age of fundamentalism." Cheyette further claimed that in blaming "broad-minded' Jews for causing anti-Semitism," Chesterton was "an unlikely bedfellow of Jewish fundamentalists" who as "strictly Orthodox rabbis" blamed the Holocaust on "the sinful acculturation of European Jewry." He concluded that just as Israeli Chief Rabbis sometimes attributed "national disasters to the sins of the secular majority," Chesterton "condemned assimilated Jews for causing their own downfall."[198]

In 1998, as seen, Member of Parliament Gerald Kaufman selectively quoted *The New Jerusalem*, and mistook Chesterton's defense of Dreyfus as demonstrating a belief that Jews were "horrible" even when they went to Palestine and ruled themselves, concluding that his Zionism should be equated with Hitler's approach.[199] Although Kaufman's own stance on Israel has been seen as problematic,[200] the *Jewish Chronicle* said Kaufman "sought to demonstrate" that anti-Semitism was "central" to Chesterton's "thinking and work" and that he "proclaimed his anti-Semitism on numerous occasions"—possibly a "kind of double bluff" intended to disguise the fact that he was "not an anti-Semite." But, although "undoubtedly a Zionist," Chesterton was "profoundly anti-Semitic." On Kaufman's evidence, the *Jewish Chronicle* stated, the "case [was]

---

198. "Chesterton Assessed by Bryan Cheyette: 'Saint or sinner?'" *Jewish Chronicle*, September 1, 1995, viii.

199. G. Kaufman, "Chesterton's Final Solution," op. cit.; see Chapter One.

200. In a House of Commons debate Kaufman claimed Israel's government "ruthlessly and cynically" exploited gentile guilt over the Holocaust to justify the "murder of Palestinians" (G. Alderman, "The Jews who wish others dead," *Jewish Chronicle*, January 1, 2009, 27); following an Israeli military claim that 500 killed in the Gazan incursion were militants he remarked: "That was the reply of a Nazi. I suppose that the Jews fighting for their lives in the Warsaw ghetto could have been dismissed as militants" (*Jewish Chronicle*, January 23, 2009, 7); "the veteran Labour MP" said that "wealthy Tory donor" Lord Ashcroft "owned one part of the party and 'Jewish millionaires' the other," drawing "condemnation from all sides of politics, and the Jewish press" ("Tories 'too close to Israel' jibe" (*Daily Telegraph*, March 31, 2010, 1).

made."[201] In 2003 a reader wrongly attributed the "How odd of God to choose the Jews" verse to "the anti-Jewish" Chesterton.[202] The verse, as seen, was also wrongly attributed to Belloc.

Despite criticism, condemnation, and confusion, since his death Chesterton has been cited by Jews, including the Chief Rabbi, in a neutral or even positive context.[203] And despite increasingly negative views of Chesterton's Zionism, after the Holocaust, his support for a Jewish homeland in the Holy Land became the mainstream Jewish position. As we will see, however, as the Palestinian cause came to the fore, Zionism would once again become controversial among Jews as well as Gentiles.[204]

Gentile Zionism: Winston Churchill

Like Chesterton, Winston Churchill saw himself as a pro-Semite. Churchill's official biographer comments: "This was true: he was both a friend in their hours of need, and a friend in deed."[205] But Churchill's Zionism, like Chester-

---

201. *Jewish Chronicle*, November 14, 1997, 8.

202. S. Goldstein, Letter, *Jewish Chronicle*, January 11, 2003, 25; see Chapters Six and Eight.

203. "G.K. Chesterton once said that America was the only nation built on an idea. He was, of course, wrong. Biblical Israel was based on an idea . . . : that every individual is in the image of God" (Chief Rabbi Dr J. Sacks, "The JC Essay: Israel needs a more idealistic society," *Jewish Chronicle*, February 8, 2008, 24); the Jewish Maccabi Games had "a press office which moved from place to place like Chesterton's 'Flying Inn'" (B. Glanville, *Jewish Chronicle*, August 28, 1959, 10); Professor J.L. Talmon cited Chesterton in comparing the Kibbutzim to Medieval monasticism: "[N]othing fails like success" ("Heart-searching Reflections," *Jewish Chronicle*, October 2, 1959, 26–27); his "melancholy reflection" was quoted: "Can you tell me, in a world that is flagrant with the failures of civilisations, what there is particularly immortal about yours?" (H. Harris, "Melancholy Musings," *Jewish Chronicle*, April 5, 1963, 32–33); Chesterton "would have been horrified to know that the water *did* get into the wine!" (M. Bourne, "Pack up your Troubles," *Jewish Chronicle*, October 16, 1964, iv–v); an "admirable" short story collection featured Chesterton, Balzac, Wodehouse, Muriel Spark and Graham Greene ("Clerical tales. Best Stories of Church and Clergy," *Jewish Chronicle*, May 20, 1966, 26–27); theologian Louis Jacobs remarked: "Chesterton correctly observed that God is not the chief character in the Bible: He is the only character" (*Jewish Chronicle*, September 12, 1969, 42–43); the creator of a Rabbi detective was "alas, no Chesterton" (*Jewish Chronicle*, August 4, 1972, 9); Chesterton believed "solemnity flows out of men naturally; but laughter is a leap. It is easy to be heavy: hard to be light. Satan fell by the force of gravity. It has the same effect on a soufflé" (M. Watkins, *Jewish Chronicle*, July 16, 1971, x–xi); Chesterton saw golf as "an expensive way of playing marbles" (M. Angel, "A win for women golfers," *Jewish Chronicle*, June 9, 2006, I); his "old cliché" was quoted: "[W]hen people stop believing in God they don't believe in something, they believe in anything" (M. Shaviv, "Global Warming? I'm a heretic," *Jewish Chronicle*, July 13, 2007, 31).

204. For the Jewish anti-Zionist case, see: Yakov Rabkin, *A Threat from Within: A Century of Jewish Opposition to Zionism* (London: Zed Books Ltd, 2006); Anne Karpf et al., eds., *A Time to Speak Out: Independent Jewish Voices On Israel, Zionism and Jewish Identity* (London: Verso Books, 2008); see Chapter Nine.

205. M. Gilbert, *Churchill and the Jews*, op. cit., xvi.

ton's, met with Jewish suspicion,[206] and his support for Palestinian Zionism rather than Territorialism cost him his Manchester parliamentary seat.[207] In 1932 Churchill asked Hitler's friend Ernst Hanfstaengl: "Why is your chief so violent about the Jews? I can quite understand being angry with Jews who have done wrong or who are against the country, and I understand resisting them if they try to monopolise power in any walk of life; but what is the sense of being against a man simply because of his birth? How can any man help how he is born?" This outburst lost him the chance of meeting Hitler.[208] Churchill's "rational" approach to the "Jewish question" echoed Chesterton's, and as Richard Holmes remarks, Churchill, as "one of Britain's most forthright" Zionists, "often wrote about Jews using terms that jar on modern sensibility. Such language was considered unremarkable at the time."[209] A Zionist since 1908,[210] as a Liberal, Churchill supported the "Marconi" Ministers,[211] and also flirted with eugenics.[212] Chesterton grudgingly praised Churchill,[213] but politically, Chesterton's view on the "Jewish question" was almost the exact reverse, since he had "much more sympathy" with the "revolutionary" Jew than the "plutocratic" Jew. To Chesterton, "the new Anti-Semitism" was "merely Anti-Socialism."[214] In contrast, Churchill was disturbed by left-wing Jews, and regarded the clash between Bolshevist and Zionist as pivotal for the Jewish people. While approving of religious and patriotic Jews, and "very helpful" Zionists, he saw "International Jews" as part of a "sinister confederacy" that had forsaken their ancestral religion for Atheism; even worse, their attraction to Bolshevism was

206. *Jewish Chronicle*, February 13, 1920.

207. M. Gilbert, *Churchill and the Jews*, op. cit., 17–18.

208. W. S. Churchill, *The Second World War: The Gathering Storm* (London: Cassell & Co. Ltd., 1948), 65.

209. Richard Holmes, *In the Footsteps of Churchill* (London: BBC Books, 2005), 191.

210. W. Manchester, *The Caged Lion: Winston Spencer Churchill 1932–1940* (London: Cardinal, 1989), 102.

211. F. Donaldson, *The Marconi Scandal* (London: Rupert Hart-Davis, 1962), 158–159; see Chapter Six.

212. See: M. Gilbert, "Churchill and Eugenics," The Churchill Centre and Museum (London), May 31, 2009, accessed April 25, 2011, http://www.winstonchurchill.org/support/the-chill-centre/publications/finest-hour-online/594-chuchill-and-eugenics. Churchill never joined the Eugenics Society (A. Farmer, "Churchill and Eugenics" [2009, unpublished]).

213. G. K. Chesterton, "The Churchills," *G. K.'s Weekly*, February 21, 1935, in B. Sewell, *G. K.'s Weekly: An Appraisal*, op. cit., 46–47.

214. Although there were "good, honourable and magnanimous Jews of every type and rank" he had "more respect" for the Israelite leading "some sort of revolt, however narrow and anarchic, against the oppression of the poor" than the Israelite "safe at the head of a great money-lending business oppressing the poor"; he wished "the rich aliens" rather than "the poor aliens" had been "excluded" (G. K. Chesterton, *The New Jerusalem* [1920], *G. K. Chesterton Collected Works Vol. XX*, op. cit., 394).

aiding the Soviets' reign of terror.[215] At a time when Jewish conspiracy theory was extremely popular, Chesterton and Churchill appeared briefly to take it seriously.

Like Chesterton, Churchill insisted that the Jewish people's "abnormal history" explained their "vices"; so did the great Christian opponent of anti-Semitism James Parkes.[216] In 1911, as Home Secretary Churchill dealt robustly with the South Wales riots when Jewish shops were attacked, acquiring an enduring reputation among opponents for harshness.[217] He attracted similar criticism for his response to the Sidney Street siege anarchists, but refused to emphasize their Jewish origins.[218] After Jerusalem was taken from the Turks he was involved in the historic Balfour Declaration.[219]

In 1911 Chesterton's approach was summed up as seeing the poor Jews as nice and the rich as nasty,[220] and in 1920, Churchill invoked a similar "dual image" of "the Jew" in an article headlined "Good and Bad Jews." He described Jews as acting out the conflict between good and evil, exemplifying the "dual nature of mankind." He argued, "that this same astounding race" could be "producing another system of morals and philosophy, as malevolent as Christianity was benevolent"—Bolshevism. It was "as if the gospel of Christ and the gospel of Antichrist were destined to originate among the same people; and that this mystic and mysterious race had been chosen for the supreme manifestations, both of the divine and the diabolical." Like Chesterton, Churchill's "dual image" was religiously influenced; like Chesterton, too, he rejected a racial view, maintaining that there were good, bad and indifferent men in every country and every race, including Jews.[221] He too was influenced by Chaim

215. Churchill's call for Jews to choose Zionism over Bolshevism has been seen as "a powerful attack on the very heart of anti-Semitic rhetoric" (W. S. Churchill, "Zionism vs. Bolshevism: A Struggle for the Soul of the Jewish People," *Illustrated Sunday Herald*, February 8, 1920, 5, in G. K. Chesterton, *Chesterton on War and Peace: Battling the Ideas and Movements That Led to Nazism and World War II*, op. cit., 344–345).

216. J. Parkes, *Antisemitism* (London: Vallentine Mitchell & Co. Ltd., 1963), 122.

217. Ibid., 10.

218. P. Addison, *Churchill on the Home Front* 1900–1955 (London: Jonathan Cape, 1992), 128. When Eastern European revolutionaries attempted to burgle a jeweler's shop in East London, and shot at policemen, killing two, Churchill refused fire brigade access to the burning building, deeming it too risky; two bodies were found in the ruins (W. L. S. Churchill, sworn testimony, January 18th, 1911, Inquest Pamphlet on Sidney Street Case, W. S. Churchill, *Winston S. Churchill Vol. II Part 2* 1907–1911, R. S. Churchill, ed. [London: Heinemann, 1969], 1242–1244); he refused to "brand the general alien population of the country with the crimes of this particular tribe of criminals" (W. S. Churchill, Memorandum to the King, January 6, 1911, in ibid., 1239).

219. M. Gilbert, *Churchill and the Jews*, op. cit., 27.

220. M. Ward, *Gilbert Keith Chesterton*, op. cit., 264.

221. W. S. Churchill, "Zionism vs. Bolshevism: A Struggle for the Soul of the Jewish People," *Illustrated Sunday Herald*, February 8, 1920, 5; M. Gilbert, *Churchill and the Jews*, op. cit., 38–39.

Weizmann, seeing Zionism as the solution to the "Jewish problem." Unlike Chesterton, he remained undeterred by practical obstacles, acknowledging that although Palestine was "far too small to accommodate more than a fraction of the Jewish race, nor do the majority of national [assimilated] Jews wish to go there," if a Jewish homeland were established "in our own lifetime by the banks of the Jordan . . . under the protection of the British Crown . . . an event would have occurred in the history of the world which would, from *every point of view*, be beneficial, and would be especially in harmony with the truest interests of the British Empire."(Emphasis added)[222] This hinted at Chesterton's view that Zionism would benefit both Jew and Gentile. Both saw a problem in only a minority of Jews, but as Richard Holmes comments, Churchill "saw the Jewish homeland as a poultice to draw the poison distilled into an admirable race by the evil inflicted on them by others."[223] Like Chesterton, Churchill wanted Jews to prepare for agricultural life and visited Rishon LeZion; but unlike Chesterton, Churchill feared the Zionist experiment would turn out not to be capitalist but Bolshevist.[224]

Unlike Chesterton, Churchill could offer official support to the experiment and, despite widespread opposition to the Balfour Declaration—including from the Archbishop of Canterbury—and increasing Arab violence leading to restrictions on Jews purchasing Palestinian land, he defended the Declaration not only as an ideal but "an obligation, made in wartime to enlist the aid of Jews all over the world."[225] Chesterton's Zionism wavered over the Rutenberg Concession, and Churchill warned that at a time of high British unemployment, Rutenberg's plan to buy hydro-electric machinery for his project from Germany would damage British support for Zionism. Parliament was becoming more sympathetic to the Arab cause,[226] but Churchill likened Weizmann to an Old Testament prophet. He too was fascinated by Jewish history and the Jewish role in civilization, monotheism, and ethics.[227] Churchill opposed Goebbels but also Trotsky for their persecution of opinions and race.[228] After the German anti-Jewish pogrom of November 1938, "Kristallnacht," and with violence afflicting Palestine he insisted that Jews and Arabs had "a right to dwell in the land that the Lord hath given them."[229] Like Chesterton he visited Palestine and in 1934 witnessed increasing Arab attacks incited by the Mufti of Jerusalem.

222. Ibid., 41–42.
223. Richard Holmes, *In the Footsteps of Churchill*, op. cit., 192.
224. M. Gilbert, *Churchill and the Jews*, op. cit., 64.
225. Ibid., 69–70.
226. Ibid., 76–77.
227. Ibid., 95.
228. Ibid., 136.
229. Ibid., 149.

While not ignoring the dangers of two communities claiming the same land, he believed the British should keep their pledge to the Jews. Speaking in the House of Commons on Nazi/Arab links and the violent intimidation of poor Arabs, he maintained that Palestine was Jewish before Islam swept in.[230] He also held similar views to Chesterton on the negative effects of Islam as a religion.[231]

Despite his defense of Liberal allies Lloyd George and Rufus Isaacs in the Marconi affair,[232] Churchill was criticized by the *Jewish Chronicle* for his "Good and Bad Jews" article: it was "one thing . . . for a newspaper, for its own purpose, to propagate . . . the fiction of Bolshevism being a Jewish movement" but a much "graver matter" when the idea received "high official sanction." Now, "every Pogromist . . . in Eastern Europe" could "quote the British War-Secretary for a vile campaign." Having "lost his seat for the strongly Jewish constituency in Manchester," Churchill had "raised a cheap laugh by ignorantly—or maliciously—referring to Bela Kun as Bela Cohen." Béla Kun and other prominent Bolshevists were of Jewish background, although they had rejected the religion,[233] but the *Jewish Chronicle* claimed that Churchill's article was really saying: "You Jews have made the Bolshevist movement. If you do not want to be robbed and massacred, shout your hatred of it from the house-tops." Churchill, "a prominent British statesman," in "inviting his victims to confess to a merely imaginary crime" had "adopted the hoary tactics of hooligan anti-Semites." Like the *Chesterbelloc*, Churchill praised Jews, but his description of them as "the most formidable race" did not redeem a "most reckless and scandalous campaign," which was not made "more tolerable by fantastic flattery"—indeed, "very much the reverse. We can dispense with Mr. Churchill's double-edged appreciation in return for some approach to justice in the handling of matters

230. Ibid., 102, 109, 115–116. The Grand Mufti was appointed by Herbert Samuel because, after the First World War the British government held the League of Nations Mandate for Palestine; however, with the rise of Arab nations and anti-Jewish violence, not least from that stirred by al-Husayni, delayed inaugurating the promised Jewish state (H.M. Sachar, *A History of Israel: From the Rise of Zionism to our Time*, op. cit., 174).

231. Based on his army service in the Sudan he saw Islam as encouraging a superstitious outlook and "degraded sensualism" (W. Churchill, *The River War* [1899], in M. Gilbert, *Churchill and the Jews*, op. cit., 53), while the austere Wahabi Islam tended to kill anyone who differed (ibid., p. 68).

232. R. Jenkins, *Churchill* (London: Pan Books, 2002), 223–228.

233. "Churchill and the Jew—Bolshevist Lie," *Jewish Chronicle*, January 9, 1920, 8–9; Béla Kun, born Béla Kohn to a lapsed Jewish father and lapsed Protestant mother, changed his name to Magyar Kun and led the brief Hungarian Bolshevist revolution in 1919; he repudiated all religion (Y. Slezkine, *The Jewish Century* [Princeton, NJ: Princeton University Press, 2004], 178). "Jews were at times attracted in disproportionate numbers" to communism, which "promised an escape" into a "new world" from minority life, with its "ethnic, religious, and socioeconomic boundaries" in J. Frankel, ed., *Dark Times, Dire Decisions: Jews and Communism* (Oxford: The Avraham Harman Institute of Contemporary Jewry, The Hebrew University of Jerusalem/Oxford University Press, 2004), 4; see Chapters Two and Three.

which involve the lives and the honour of millions of men, women, and children." His remarks "smack[ed] . . . of the political huckstering" of which Churchill was "a past master." Overlooking the existential conflict between Bolshevism and Zionism that Dr. Eder had noted, the paper concluded that such claims, in setting up a false rivalry between Bolshevism and Zionism, showed that their proponents were "not the friends of Zionism that they pretend to be."[234]

As with Chesterton, Churchill's Zionism, survived a crisis of confidence, but despite the *Jewish Chronicle*'s fears, the latter's "pro-Semitism" was not governed merely by political calculations, surviving the loss of the Manchester seat.[235] Like Chesterton, Churchill's private correspondence and conversation showed no sign of anti-Semitism, rather, he rebuked a friend for anti-Semitic remarks.[236] Churchill, like Chesterton, faced opposition to his Zionist beliefs, but unlike Chesterton he received Jewish tributes for his fidelity to the cause.[237]

Gentile Zionism: Josiah Wedgwood

Like Chesterton but unlike Churchill, Josiah Wedgwood (1872–1943), of the famous china family, a Liberal and later Labour MP, was an anti-eugenicist. The elitist Fabians Beatrice and Sidney Webb, who were also eugenicists, "were very much opposed" to Wedgwood's support for "Jews and Zionism," and Beatrice called him a "fanatical believer in crude political democracy on a strictly numerical basis."[238] As Lord Passfield, Sidney, a member of Ramsay MacDonald's government, issued a White Paper in 1930 aimed at appeasing Arab hostility. In contrast, Churchill called it a "retrograde step,"[239] and Wedgwood, a particular friend of Weizmann's, believed Palestinian Jews should be armed. A supporter of the militant right-wing Jabotinsky, Wedgwood's fervent advocacy scared many Jewish Zionists,[240] and yet they continued to accept his support. Even the anti-Imperialist Chesterton proposed a Jewish "empire," with a self-governing Jerusalem as its center, and Wedgwood envisaged a self-ruled Jewish

234. "Mr. Churchill, Zionism, and the Jews," *Jewish Chronicle*, February 13, 1920, 8–9.

235. Churchill joined the Liberal opposition and spoke against the Conservatives' Aliens Bill (M. Gilbert, *Churchill and the Jews*, op. cit., 9); re-elected for Dundee he strove to mitigate the Liberals' own Alien Bill's impact on Jews (ibid., 16). He later returned to the Conservatives but maintained friendly links with the Jewish community.

236. Ibid., 5–6, 265; see Chapter Eight.

237. Ibid., 306.

238. B. Webb, *The Diary of Beatrice Webb: Vol. 4, 1924–43* (London, 1985), 201, in C. Bloom, "Josiah Wedgwood and Palestine," *Jewish Historical Studies: Transactions of the Jewish Historical Society of England*, 42, (2009): 150.

239. M. Gilbert, *Churchill and the Jews*, op. cit., 93.

240. C. Bloom, "Josiah Wedgwood and Palestine," op. cit., 152.

state as a British Crown Colony, promoting the idea through his Seventh Dominion League. It received little government support and a mixed reception among Jewish Zionists, but, like Chesterton, Wedgwood believed the Jews would fight for their own homeland,[241] challenging them to "demonstrate their ability to be good producers of food, not just good middlemen."[242] Despite such caveats, as the *Jewish Chronicle* reported, Zionists "loudly cheered" Wedgwood when he said that "the national spirit was the self-respect of the people," insisting that the more a man "was possessed by that national spirit the better citizen was he in the country of his adoption." This was a version of the Chesterton/Churchill view that a Jewish homeland would absorb the patriotism of worldwide Jewry, neutralizing what they saw as Jewish vices. Moreover, Wedgwood bluntly warned of the "dangers against which the Jews must guard themselves," such as assisting Germany by falling under its cultural influence. A further fear (groundless, he asserted) was of being forced to go to a Jewish homeland. In *Chesterbellocian* vein he urged: "The Jews must again become a proud people, and when a Jew was asked whether he *was* a Jew he must be able to reply proudly: 'Yes, I am a Jew. Palestine is my country, Jerusalem the capital, and the Lion of Judah is my flag.'"[243] One Jewish commentator agreed that some Jews hid their identities out of fear of anti-Semitism and were "extremely proud" when somebody told them: "You are not a bit like other Jews," leading them to "positively preen."[244]

Like Chesterton, Wedgwood visited Palestine and wrote a book about it. But according to a *Jewish Chronicle* interview, Wedgwood's Zionism was "not of the ordinary sentimental or abstract nature," since his knowledge of Palestinian affairs was "exhaustive." He said the British Administration in Palestine was prejudiced against Jews, and that most Britons opposed Zionism.[245] Wedgwood's Zionism, unlike Chesterton's, was received enthusiastically by Jews, despite many similarities. But unlike Chesterton (and like Churchill), he only hinted at its benefits to Gentiles. On his death in 1943 the *Jewish Chronicle* reproduced Churchill's tribute to Wedgwood,[246] commenting: "The passing of Lord Wedgwood must evoke, in any Jewish publication, something far deeper than the conventional terms of mourning, for in him Jewry has lost a friend of unique and superlative open-heartedness and fidelity. In foul weather and in

---

241. Ibid., 168.

242. Ibid., 153.

243. "Meeting at Queen's Hall: Commander Wedgwood, MP," *Jewish Chronicle*, October 26, 1917.

244. *Jewish Chronicle*, October 23, 1925, 20.

245. "Palestine as the Seventh Dominion. By Col. The Rt. Hon. Josiah C. Wedgwood, DSO, MP," Interview, *Jewish Chronicle*, February 15, 1929, 21.

246. "The Late Lord Wedgwood: Mr. Churchill's Classic Tribute," *Jewish Chronicle*, July 30, 1943, 4–5.

fair, his fervour for the cause of justice, and therefore for the Jewish cause in its widest sense, remained staunch and steadfast."[247]

Of the three Gentile Zionists, Wedgwood's Jewish reception was the most favorable, at a time when many Jews did not support Zionism and were suspicious of Gentiles who did. Weizmann's biographer noted that even Arthur Balfour, whose Declaration formed the basis of the Jewish homeland in Palestine, appeared ambivalent to the Jewish people, believing it was right to keep out "doubtful" Jewish immigrants.[248] Most Gentiles also opposed a Jewish homeland, and Gentile Zionists honed their arguments accordingly, as Chesterton did most explicitly in *The New Jerusalem*. All advised Jewish Zionists on the "correct" approach. More significant than a totally "pure" Zionism that would resonate with post-Holocaust generations, however, is the fact that, unlike convinced anti-Semites, Chesterton, Churchill, Wedgwood, and Balfour all reserved a place for Jews in the world, as well as their respective worldviews.

Zionism and Anti-Semitism in the Age of Chesterton

In 1912, with racial anti-Semitism beginning to cause concern, the *Jewish Chronicle* commented that as "Englishmen equally as Jews," they resented "those modern abnormalities" like Arnold White, Hilaire Belloc, and Chesterton, "who, in the name of England," preached "retrograde doctrine on RACE approximation."[249] It accused the Conservative *Morning Post* of "seeking to fill its columns in view of the approaching dull season by serving up a re-hash of the old anti-alien articles, which even the less dignified newspapers long since discarded as threadbare and exhausted." The *Jewish Chronicle* asserted that "poking fun at 'Judah'" and using "Isaiah" and other "defamatory epithets" had "an aged and musty smell about them," implying that "'good' English blood" was "being replaced by 'bad.'" During the Great War the *Morning Post* highlighted the role of German Jews.[250] Chesterton praised the paper's interest in the Liberal Party's Marconi scandal,[251] and after the War, while denying anti-

---

247. "The End of a Noble Life," *Jewish Chronicle*, July 30, 1943, 8–9.

248. J. Reinharz, *Chaim Weizmann: The Making of a Zionist Leader*, op. cit., 274.

249. "Mentor," "A Crisis of Unrest: The Place of the Jew," *Jewish Chronicle*, March 8, 1912, 14–15.

250. "The Morning Post Again," *Jewish Chronicle*, July 18, 1913, 10–11; were the Jews, alone of all German citizens, expected to "play the traitor to their country?" (*Jewish Chronicle*, November 13, 1914, 8).

251. Allegations by the *Morning Post* and Leo Maxse of the *National Review* against Lord Murray of Elibank were investigated by the second Marconi inquiry (F. Donaldson, *The Marconi Scandal*, op. cit., 232–235). "I have a respect for the 'Morning Post' for its courage about political corruption and cosmopolitan conspiracies, in spite of deep disagreement on other very vital things" in G. K. Chesterton, "On Being an Old Bean," *Fancies Versus Fads* (London: Methuen & Co. Ltd., 1923), 55; Chesterton also described non-Jews like H. G. Wells as "cosmopolitan": see Chapter Five.

Semitism, the *Post* singled out "Marconi Minister" Lord Reading for criticism.[252]

After the Russian Revolution, the *Morning Post* frequently emphasized the "Jewishness" of the Bolshevist movement, prompting ten prominent British Jews to write to them disavowing Bolshevism.[253] The paper also alleged that "a mob of hooligan and revolutionary Jews from the East End" caused a riot by exploiting for political ends a deputation of unemployed ex-Servicemen pleading for government assistance.[254] One of their leading articles claimed the *Jewish World* had acknowledged that Russian Jews "were responsible for Bolshevism" and that British Jews were "bent on fostering revolution now."[255] In the same year as Chesterton's *The New Jerusalem*, the *Jewish Chronicle* complained that a series of *Morning Post* articles entitled "The Jewish Peril" was "redolent" with "venomous hate," and attempted to show that the Balfour Declaration was "a dangerous error." This sort of anti-Semitism was aimed at keeping Jews "in subjection, moral, physical, intellectual, and economic." The anti-Semite, knowing what the "National Home" meant to the Jewish people, wanted to keep them "scattered and oppressed," therefore the *Post* had portrayed the Declaration as "a rope around [the] neck" of the British administration in Palestine, and "dished up these blood-curdling stories of Moslem revolt and Arab resentment" to "frighten the British public against dealing generously and in large-minded measure with the Jewish trouble."[256] When the *Morning Post* brought a libel case against Lord Alfred Douglas for inventing "vile slanders . . . to make money," which involved claims that some Syrian Jews indulged in "ritual murders" and that Winston Churchill had been "bought" by "the Jews," the

---

252. "The 'Morning Post' in Defence," *Jewish Chronicle*, March 21, 1919, 5.

253. Major Lionel de Rothschild and nine others implied that the *Jewish Chronicle* and *Jewish World* had supported and disseminated Bolshevism, a "malicious" allegation; the Jewish papers had ignored the *Post*'s "formal invitation" to "disavow Bolshevism," because it would "would stamp the Bolshevist creed as something especially Jewish . . . which Jews as such had special cause to repudiate"; the ten had walked into the "carefully-laid trap" of "this anti-Semitic organ" ("Treachery—or Folly," *Jewish Chronicle*, April 25, 1919, 4–5); the *Post* subsequently claimed that the Jewish papers "continued, sometimes by threatening, sometimes by whining, wheedling, imploring" to try to "extract" an "apology or recantation" from the ten (*Jewish Chronicle*, March 12, 1920, 22).

254. "The Lying Post," *Jewish Chronicle*, October 22, 1920, 5; it also alleged that the Labour Party was "pro-German, pro-Jewish, pro-Bolshevist, pro-every enemy of their country" ("The 'Morning Post' Apologises," *Jewish Chronicle*, November 24, 1922, 8).

255. "The 'Morning Post': Our contemporary breaks out again," *Jewish Chronicle*, April 15, 1921, 33; the *Daily Sketch* demanded: "What in the name of the table of shew-bread have the British Jews got to bolsh over? Nothing! If they take my tip they will not only refrain from bolshing, but, for the honour of Jewry, push all known bolshers out of the synagogue" (*Jewish Chronicle*, May 2, 1919, 18–19).

256. *Jewish Chronicle*, November 5, 1920, 8.

Jewish Chronicle noted with irony the *Post*'s publication of Nesta Webster's writings, and its own "bitter and virulent statements about the Jews."[257]

The *Morning Post*'s conservative ally, *National Review* editor Leo Maxse, also attacked the "Marconi ministers."[258] A *Jewish Chronicle* reader said that an earlier Maxse article, "The Jew and His Destiny," published "at a time when the blood of Jews and Christians was flowing in streams in Russia," was "cruel and dangerous" because the worst anti-Jewish persecutions were "heralded by written or verbal accusations." While educated people knew these claims were baseless, they inflamed the mob with "prejudices and mistaken views of their own interests." In fact, "barbarous" Russian anti-Semitism was strengthened by "more restrained manifestations" in "civilised parts of Europe."[259] The *Jewish Chronicle* remarked that Jewish anxiety increased when intelligent men like Maxse and the *Witness* papers started an anti-Jewish campaign.[260] According to the paper's "Diarist," the "Maxse maxim" was always the "International Jew": "[S]ynonymous with high finance," he was supposed to be "conspiring in every country at once to conclude a peace by negotiation," but he was "most powerful" in Germany. Maxse suggested that "German-Jewish" organizations, representing "this alleged combination of Press and finance in the hands of his "International Jew" were "the chief danger to modern Europe," concluding that the "poor man" was "ridden by a monster of his own creation."[261] The paper further maintained that the "log-rolling" of the *National Review* and *Morning Post* was motivated by a shared interest in anti-Semitism.[262]

Maxse protested at being "violently assailed in the Jewish Press for expressing distrust of Jews" but it was not "Jews qua Jews" who provoked the *National Review*'s "uneasiness," but Jews "of Germanic origin, most of whom were decidedly pro-German before the war"; such Jews were "not suitable confidants of responsible statesmen."[263] Others, including the *Chesterbelloc*, similarly claimed that they targeted only a certain section of Jews, but the sum of all these attacks meant that Jews were attacked from all sides. A *Jewish Chronicle* reader mused: "I do not know whether Mr. Maxse is an honest thinker," but he

257. "Libel Action Against the 'Morning Post': Lord Alfred Douglas as Plaintiff: Calumnies Against Jews: Verdict for Plaintiff: Damages: One farthing," *Jewish Chronicle*, July 20, 1923, 32–33.

258. M. Ward, *Gilbert Keith Chesterton*, op. cit., 342–343; F. Donaldson, *The Marconi Scandal*, op. cit., 99; see Chapter Six.

259. *Jewish Chronicle*, November 17, 1905, 16–17.

260. *Jewish Chronicle*, July 6, 1917, 12–13.

261. *Jewish Chronicle*, August 3, 1917, 6–7.

262. Maxse's "chief contribution to international politics" was his "scare about the 'International Jew'"; doubtless this "folly" recommended him to the *Post*, formerly "a conscientious newspaper" (*Jewish Chronicle*, August 10, 1917, 10–11).

263. L. J. Maxse, *National Review*, September 1917, quoted in *Jewish Chronicle*, September 7, 1917, 8–9.

was "not an honest writer. To attack the Jews when one does not mean the Jews is not honesty but dishonesty."[264] By 1925 the *Jewish Chronicle* had become cynical about the disclaimers of those discussing the "Jewish question." When Tory Home Secretary Sir William Joynson-Hicks ("Jix") assured a Jewish deputation "that he was not an anti-Semite," the paper received his "repudiation" with "gratification." It added, however, that anti-Semitism was "a complaint" of which the "afflicted" were "quite unconscious": Hilaire Belloc resented being seen as an anti-Semite "as earnestly as Mr. Chesterton and the editor of the Morning Post," but even Torquemada claimed to be a friend of the Jews.[265]

It has been alleged that Chesterton used Zionism as a cover for anti-Semitism, but Maxse was not a Zionist; neither were British Union of Fascists Oswald Mosley and A. K. Chesterton,[266] or the Militant Christian Patriots, who gave subscribers copies of *The Protocols of the Elders of Zion*.[267] Belloc rejected Zionism, according to Wilson on political grounds,[268] and the BUF opposed Jewish settlement on any occupied land, including Palestine.[269] Mosley suggested "the Jews be transported to one of the 'many waste places on earth'" where they would "escape" the "curse of no nationality." Palestine was not an option, since it was the Arabs' home, and Britain should not do injustice to "the Arab ally."[270] Henry Hamilton Beamish proposed the Jews should be sent to Madagascar.[271] The "vehemently antisemitic" Nesta Webster[272] in her *Morning Post* series on the *Protocols*[273] saw Zionism as the most likely source of the "Bolshevik conspiracy": the *Protocols* conspiracy, she said, had "not been proved," and did "*not*

264. "Another Diarist," Letter, *Jewish Chronicle*, October 12, 1917, p. 12.

265. *Jewish Chronicle*, February 13, 1925, 26–27.

266. R. Griffiths, *Patriotism Perverted* (London, 1998), 47; 87, in A. Julius, *Trials of the Diaspora: A History of Anti-Semitism in England*, op. cit., 308–309.

267. R. Griffiths, *Patriotism Perverted* (London, 1998), 39–41 (ibid., 307).

268. A. N. Wilson, *Hilaire Belloc* (London: Hamish Hamilton, 1984), 260–261.

269. G. C. Lebzelter, *Political Anti-Semitism in England* 1918–1939 (London: Macmillan Press Ltd., 1978), 97.

270. O. Mosley, "Tomorrow We Live" (pamphlet), reprinted in O. Mosley, *My Answer* (London, 1946), 109, in A. Julius, *Trials of the Diaspora: A History of Anti-Semitism in England*, op. cit., 308–309; Mosley's opposition dated to the early 1920s (S. Dorril, *Blackshirt* [London: Viking, 2006], 65).

271. H. Blume, "A Study of anti-Semitic groups in Britain 1918–1940," D.Phil thesis, (unpublished), University of Sussex, 1971, 73, in A. Julius, *Trials of the Diaspora: A History of Anti-Semitism in England*, op. cit., 308–309.

272. D. Stone, *Breeding Superman: Nietzsche, Race and Eugenics in Edwardian and Interwar Britain* (Liverpool: Liverpool University Press, 2002), 47.

273. First published in the Russian Empire in 1903 and publicized in Henry Ford's series of newspaper articles, "The International Jew: the World's Problem," the *Times* exposed the book as a forgery in 1921, but many still believed it to be genuine: see: N. Cohn, *Warrant for Genocide: The myth of the Jewish world-conspiracy and the Protocols of the Elders of Zion* (London: Eyre & Spottiswoode, 1967).

provide the whole key to the mystery,"[274] but the *Protocols* were "genuine and what they pretend to be," or "these advocates put forward by the Jews" had "some interest in concealing the activities of Secret Societies in the past." But while saying that it was "not clearly proved" that Jews were involved in their origins,[275] the "Jewish agitator" was "the tsetse fly carrying the poison germ of Bolshevism from the breeding-ground of Germany." German atheism and Jewish "antagonism to Christianity" had "combined to form the great anti-religious force" that was "making itself felt in the world."[276] While admitting that it was "apostate Jews" who had "thrown themselves into the revolutionary movement,"[277] it was clear that "the Jews were mainly responsible" for capitalism.[278] In 1938 she proposed sending the "whole Jewish race" to the "'vast unpeopled spaces of Soviet Russia'" where they would enjoy "'the government of pro-Semitic rulers.'"[279]

Linking Jews to Germany recalled the *Chesterbelloc* approach, but such pronouncements, rather than encouraging them to become more outspoken, appeared to act as a check. Chesterton especially began to travel in the opposite direction as anti-Semitism became more prevalent in England. Anti-Zionism was certainly more characteristic of anti-Semites than pro-Zionism, and rose with the rise of Arab unrest; as seen, Hitler claimed that Zionism had converted him to anti-Semitism, reflecting the belief of anti-Semites that wherever they went, Jews would be a problem.

Despite seeing Chesterton as anti-Semitic the *Jewish Chronicle* did not highlight his relationship with his South African second cousin Arthur Kenneth Chesterton (1899–1973) even though during the 1930s the latter was biographer and right-hand man of British Union of Fascists leader Sir Oswald Mosley.[280] Mosley was a former Labour MP, and A. K. Chesterton, like Gilbert Chesterton, had had socialist leanings.[281] David Baker, A. K. Chesterton's biographer, while exonerating Gilbert Chesterton from fascist or Nazi sympathies and from "biological racism," claims there were "many similarities" with A. K. Chesterton's "fascist attacks on the Jews, although expressed in more restrained language."[282]

---

274. N.H. Webster, *World Revolution: The Plot Against Civilization* (London: Constable & Co. Ltd., 1921), 296.

275. Ibid., 305–306.

276. Ibid., 309–310.

277. Ibid., 312.

278. Ibid., 94.

279. N. Webster, Letter to the *Patriot*, in A. Julius, *Trials of the Diaspora: A History of Anti-Semitism in England*, op. cit., 310.

280. See: A.K. Chesterton, *Oswald Mosley: Portrait of a Leader* (London: Action Press, 1937).

281. M. Walker, *The National Front* (Glasgow: Fontana/Collins, 1977), 29.

282. David Baker, *Ideology of Obsession: A.K. Chesterton and British Fascism* (London: Tauris Academic Studies, 1996), 149–151.

Baker cites some "particularly nasty examples" of A.K. Chesterton's British Union of Fascists writings, including references to "a gang of greasy gesticulating Jews . . . this alien rabble," the "Judaic-Bolshevik Soviet slave-state," and a reference to Jews as "blood-cousins of the maggot and the leech." In *The Apotheosis of the Jew* A.K. Chesterton claimed that "the entire tragedy of the Jew" was "due to his devastating sense of inferiority." This "terrible knowledge," he alleged, "aroused in him a compensatory itch to dominate the world," and he would not "fail to conquer" if the "inevitable arrogance" resulting from "his half success" did not supervene.[283] Baker compares A.K. Chesterton favorably with the Fascist William Joyce ("Lord Haw Haw") executed after the War for broadcasting from Germany,[284] although A.K. Chesterton complained in *Portrait of a Leader* that Mosley was not anti-Semitic enough.[285] As *Blackshirt* editor, A.K. Chesterton told a fascist rally that it was "very easy to come down here and abuse the Jews" but that they needed a "constructive policy," although if it should come "to a fight between the Jewish people and the British people," the latter would not "be destroyed."[286]

In contrast to G.K. Chesterton and Hilaire Belloc, fascism encouraged A.K. Chesterton to more extreme anti-Semitism. The *Jewish Chronicle* reported that in 1939, the latter gave "[t]he wildest speech" to a "delighted" public meeting, "mainly middle class," by "speaking (in Oxford tones) of 'greasy little Jew-boy pornographers.'"[287] Earlier, the paper had reported that in the fascist publication *Action* he wrote that "poetic justice" would "overtake" Sigmund Freud *"and that he will himself be psycho-analysed by Herr Himmler."* As to Pavlov and other German Jewish scientists, "they would put all such in a concentration camp."[288] In contrast, G.K. Chesterton attacked Nazi anti-Semitism, complimented Jews on their superiority and blamed their perceived shortcomings on lack of a territory, something in which his second cousin was not interested. But like many accused of anti-Semitism A.K. Chesterton really did have a Jew-

283. A.K. Chesterton, *British Union Quarterly*, April–June 1937, 45–54 (ibid., 141).

284. Ibid., 182.

285. *Jewish Chronicle*, August 13, 1937, 13; later, however, he refuted Mosley's "repeated claim that his only pre-war quarrel with the Jews was that they were 'pushing this country into war with Germany'"—Mosley's "memory 'must obligingly have failed him'": he had not curbed anti-Semitism in BUF publications and no editor was ever sacked (*Jewish Chronicle*, October 8, 1971, 8–9); as a League of Empire Loyalist A.K. Chesterton visited Apartheid South Africa with the Union Movement's Sir Oswald Mosley and the South African Society's Blyth Thompson (*Jewish Chronicle*, February 7, 1964, 44).

286. *Jewish Chronicle*, September 10, 1937, 20–21.

287. *Jewish Chronicle*, June 2, 1939, 20–21. He was bound over to keep the peace for 12 months after posting bills reading "Mosley Will Win" and the fascist sign at the London house of Lord Melchett (Alfred Mond) (*Jewish Chronicle*, October 15, 1937, 18–19).

288. *Jewish Chronicle*, March 25, 1938, 46.

ish friend—Zangwill's biographer Joseph Leftwich, who, as Baker relates, wrote to him, "impressed by the non-anti-Semitic aspects" of his Fascism.[289] The opportunities for comparison that this friendship offered might explain Leftwich's defense of G.K. Chesterton and Hilaire Belloc. After the War, Leftwich and A.K. Chesterton published *The Tragedy of Anti-Semitism* in which, the *Jewish Chronicle* said, the latter quoted "the same rubbish" as the *Protocols of the Elders of Zion* "in no less erudite terms. Mr. Leftwich undoubtedly has all the answers; but Mr. Chesterton does not accept them. One cannot penetrate into such minds."[290] The belief that rational argument could influence anti-Semites was no longer tenable. Denials of anti-Semitism and claims of Jewish friends were treated with skepticism.[291] In 1965 A.K. Chesterton published *New Unhappy Lords*, its title taken from his second cousin's poem *The Secret People* (1907). But—notwithstanding a "cringing Jew"—the poem's "unhappy lords" with "bright dead alien eyes" are bureaucrats, who, like the Fabians, are alienated from their traditions.[292]

While A.K. Chesterton's emphasis on patriotism, the "International Money Power" and the "unifying context of Christendom"[293] suggests a worldview similar to Gilbert Chesterton's, in *The New Unhappy Lords* A.K. Chesterton failed to condemn Hitler. Moreover, he really believed in Jewish conspiracy. Because of its secrecy, it was "not often possible to bring against it a direct case, as distinct from a case based on circumstantial evidence," but since this conspiracy had been "active for many years" there were "bound to be occasions when it reveal[ed] its existence." Every twist and turn of history, however unlikely, was seen as "circumstantial evidence." In fact, it placed an even greater "strain on credulity" to suppose that such "multitudinous events" had not been "deliberately contrived."[294] Using milder language than formerly he claimed that Winston Churchill and his anti-appeasers were in a secret cabal against Hitler, with businessman and Zionist Israel Moses Sieff "representing the inter-

289. D. Baker, *Ideology of Obsession: A.K. Chesterton and British Fascism*, op. cit., 140–141.

290. *Jewish Chronicle*, February 24, 1950, 12–13.

291. A.K. Chesterton "disclaimed allegations of anti-Semitism" but was contradicted by his "veiled innuendoes in print," his "public utterances" and "association with persons and groups dedicated to fomenting racial ill-feeling" (*Jewish Chronicle*, September 7, 1973, 42–43).

292. "They have given us into the hand of new unhappy lords, / Lords without anger and honour, who dare not carry their swords. / They fight by shuffling papers; they have bright dead alien eyes; / They look at our labour and laughter as a tired man looks at flies. / And the load of their loveless pity is worse than the ancient wrongs, / Their doors are shut in the evening; / and they know no songs" in G.K. Chesterton, *The Secret People*, *The Works of G.K. Chesterton* (Ware, Herts.: Wordsworth Poetry Library, 1995), 133; see Chapter Eight.

293. A.K. Chesterton, *The New Unhappy Lords: An Exposure of Power Politics* (Hants.: Candour Publishing Co., 1965/1972), 12.

294. Ibid., 9.

ests of International finance."[295] The attack on Pearl Harbor, he alleged, was engineered to get the Unite States into the war.[296] He wanted black Britons repatriated "whence they came, with generous help," warning of the effects of "interbreeding,"[297] for, despite allusions to Christianity, he believed black people were genetically inferior. If given the vote in their own countries (like South Africa), they would "take over," although national administration was "beyond the reach of the African mind."[298] He saw the introduction of blacks into "white" countries as yet another outcome of Jewish world conspiracy, which would result in "the mongrelization of mankind," and "hordes of unhappy half-castes."[299]

A.K. Chesterton admitted that Hitler's racial policy was "anti-Jewish" but merely complained that it had fuelled calls for "all racial concepts ... to be eradicated" throughout the world—"except among the Jews," who possessed the "mysterious power to mould public opinion, decide public attitudes and set intellectual fashions."[300] Hitler alleged that stationing black troops on the Rhine promoted "contamination" of German "blood," blaming the French and the "ice-cold calculation" of the Jews who planned to undermine "the white race ... through infection with lower humanity."[301] But, post-War, A.K. Chesterton said that the "vast majority" of Jews were "law-abiding citizens leading highly respectable lives," who were "well-disposed and kindly towards their neighbours" and accepted their "social customs." This sounds more *Chesterbellocian,* and he added that to "visit upon the mass of Jews opprobrium, or worse," because of the actions of a few was "not only unfair but infamous"— although they "formed the hard core" of Russian Bolshevism and were "identified with Communist movements in every other country." No Zionist, he viewed the creation of Israel as demonstrating "the reality of Jewish power." Moreover, Zionism had "ambitions far beyond the creation of a Jewish State," and if left to its own devices, it would take over Africa, ultimately creating a World State. Possibly this was the "secret final objective" of Zionism, but in any case, "World Jewry" was "the most powerful single force on earth," and therefore "all the major policies" that had been "ruthlessly pursued through the last several decades must have had the stamp of Jewish approval." While it was "ludicrous" to blame Jews "for the destruction, or near destruction, of Christendom and the Western world," it would be "equally ludicrous" to deny Jewish

295. Ibid., 24.
296. Ibid., 26.
297. Ibid., 169–170.
298. Ibid., 134–136.
299. Ibid., 171.
300. Ibid., 221–222.
301. A. Hitler, *Mein Kampf,* op. cit., 569.

involvement, especially where it was "admitted." The solution, he maintained, was to "put things to rights," not via "'hate campaigns' (which in any case play into Jewish hands)" but by making "a determined stand for our own legitimate and distinctive interests."[302]

A.K. Chesterton did not suggest, in line with their alleged power to control world events, that Jews engineered the Holocaust but, unlike Gilbert Chesterton, he exploited anti-Semitism to further the cause of fascism, and later saw the Jewish state as further evidence of the all-powerful Jew, a stepping stone to world domination. But while Mosley was imprisoned for his fascist involvement, AKC fought against Hitler, and, post-War, admitted the defeat of fascism.[303] With his "passionate anti-Nazism and pro-Empire stance" he became "the respectable head who appealed to ultra right-wing Monday Club activists of the Tory Party," although his League of Empire Loyalists, founded in 1953, later merged with other groups to form the racist National Front, aimed at combating non-white immigration.[304] G.K. Chesterton and A.K. Chesterton did share a deep patriotism but it took them in different directions, not least because although A.K. Chesterton wrote to his second cousin inviting him to an anti-Semitic collaboration, as he later recalled with bitterness, Gilbert ignored the invitation.[305]

The Holocaust and Chesterton's Zionism

During the War, Ward mentioned the *Chesterbelloc*'s "strange crank" about the Jews, although, sadly, they were not so "strange" in this respect. But Ward also cites Chesterton's Zionism, his tour of Palestine and friendship with his Jewish guide.[306] She also includes Rabbi Stephen Wise's posthumous tribute: "Indeed I was a warm admirer of Gilbert Chesterton. Apart from his delightful art and his genius in many directions, he was . . . a great religionist. He as Catholic, I as Jew, could not have seen eye to eye with each other, and he might have added 'particularly seeing that you are cross-eyed'; but I deeply respected him. When Hitlerism came, he was one of the first to speak out with all the directness and frankness of a great and unabashed spirit. Blessings to his memory!"[307] His tribute was later dismissed, along with Chesterton's humorous approach, under

---

302. A.K. Chesterton, *The New Unhappy Lords: An Exposure of Power Politics*, op. cit., 211–217.

303. A.K. Chesterton, September 6, 1947, *London Tidings*, in S. Dorril, *Blackshirt: Sir Oswald Mosley and British Fascism* (London: Viking, 2006), 445.

304. Ibid., 636.

305. D. Baker, *Ideology of Obsession: A. K. Chesterton and British Fascism*, op. cit., 87.

306. M. Ward, *Gilbert Keith Chesterton*, op. cit., 414–415; see Chapter One.

307. Rabbi Stephen Wise, Letter to Cyril Clemens, September 8, 1937 (ibid., 264–265).

the influence of the Holocaust. In 1962 the *Jewish Chronicle* reported Sir Henry d'Avigdor-Goldsmid's view that "[s]ince the full story of Nazism had become known" the "Belloc-Chesterton-type antisemitic jokes" were out of favor since it "was no longer a joking matter."[308] In 2010 Julius asked "Are philo-Semites irrational enemies of the Jews?" Many, he said, displayed "a philo-Semitism of mixed signals. Ostensible compliments can be covert disparagements, and a glorification of Jews can pass suddenly into a neurotic anti-Semitism." Some were keen to "reform" Jews by making them more like themselves, frequently conceding "too much of the anti-Semite's case." While acknowledging that "[m]ost personal friendships suffer from certain ambiguities—how could a friendship towards an entire nation ever be simple?" he claimed that such individuals "[a]t the very least," could harbor "a preoccupation with 'Jewishness' unwelcome in its intensity, its singularity of focus"—possibly the result "of some ulterior motive" such as disparaging "one class of Jews by appearing to praise another . . . *or* to convert Jews or otherwise detach them from their given allegiances, *or* to restate the anti-Semite's case against the Jews as parasitic, money-minded, lacking elevated feelings," at the same time "purporting to excuse these vices by reference to 'two thousand years of persecution.'"[309]

Chesterton and Belloc, Shaw and Wells, Wedgwood and Churchill praised Jews as well as criticizing them, but Julius further maintained that "to speak well of Jews" could mean "esteeming them for capabilities they neither possess nor wish to possess," quoting Winston Churchill: "Some people like Jews and some do not. But no thoughtful man can deny the fact that they are beyond question the most formidable and the most remarkable race which has ever appeared in the world."[310] This was an outlook "many anti-Semites embrace and *ex*-anti-Semites will often retain." This "misconception" could "only with difficulty comprise the premise for philo-Semitism," since Jews were "*not* collectively formidable," but "weak, divided, heterogeneous." Julius argued that Jews achieved nationhood only with difficulty, and had not achieved Jewish security worldwide. Moreover, there was "something dubious" in issuing "*any* general statement about Jews—however favourable." Such statements could only "simplify and therefore misrepresent the diversity of actual Jews," thus doing "each one of them a distinct injustice—though we may acknowledge that false esteem is not the most burdensome of injustices." Citing Paul Lawrence's "pose of the disappointed friend," which claimed to be philo-Semitic "the better to deliver an attack upon Jews," Julius claims that Jews feel "*resentful*" to find

---

308. He regarded it as "inconceivable" that a "man of letters" like Rudyard Kipling did not wish to read a book if it was "pro-Yid" (*Jewish Chronicle*, September 7, 1962, 10–11).

309. A. Julius, *Trials of the Diaspora: A History of Anti-Semitism in England*, op. cit., 40.

310. G. Wheatcroft, *The Controversy of Zion* (1996), xi (ibid., 41).

themselves "the object of pity": tolerance was "an inferior version of respect," pity "an inferior version of compassion."[311]

Chesterton, Belloc, Shaw, Wells, Wedgwood, and Churchill praised Jews, and respected them enough to engage with them. None escaped Jewish criticism, but, as seen, in the 1930s such "critical friends" were regarded as more valuable witnesses than those who offered unalloyed praise. In his *Autobiography*, Chesterton said that during his youth he "held by instinct" what he held "by knowledge now," that the "right way" was "to be interested in Jews as Jews; and then to bring into greater prominence the very much neglected Jewish virtues, which are the complement and sometimes even the cause of what the world feels to be the Jewish faults."[312] In contrast, convinced anti-Semites never praised Jews, never "explained" Jews and, since they saw all Jews as bad, were never "disappointed." Moreover, they saw the Jewish people's survival not as commendable proof of their staying power but as a challenge demanding a more permanent solution. The threat posed by critical "friends" paled beside the racially influenced Hitler, who viewed them as a monolithic threat that must be exterminated down to the last unborn child—his "Final Solution." This sort of anti-Semite more closely resembles Julius's description of the individual whose "enmity does *not* derive from opposition to any genuine Jewish project or stance," but "from imaginary grievances, imputed to an imaginary collective entity," "the Jews" or "Judaism."[313] Such an "irrational enemy," Julius says, condemned "imaginary Jewish crimes" such as "the killing of Gentile children" or "world domination."[314]

Chesterton and Belloc derided such beliefs. Yet Kushner claims that "an organised tradition, from the 'ChesterBelloc' circle in the Edwardian period to the Mosleyites in the 1930s," demanded the "reversal" of Jewish rights.[315] It "was the radical right—the ChesterBelloc school and Leo Maxse's *National Review*" that "believed a Jewish conspiracy was at work" in the Marconi affair.[316] But while explaining left-wing anti-Semitism as stemming from anti-capitalism, Kushner acknowledges the problem of categorizing the *Witness* circle's politics.[317] Noting that not all anti-Semites wanted to expel Jews, he says that "extremist sup-

---

311. P. Lawrence, *German Question/Jewish Question* (1990), 6 (ibid., p. 41).

312. G. K. Chesterton, *Autobiography*, op. cit., 71–73; see Chapter Eight.

313. A. Julius, *Trials of the Diaspora: A History of Anti-Semitism in England*, op. cit., p. 4.

314. Ibid., 10–11.

315. T. Kushner, *The persistence of prejudice: Antisemitism in British Society during the Second World War* (Manchester: Manchester University Press, 1989), 9; fascism was "following in the path of the ChesterBelloc circle"; Brooks, the editor of fascist journal *Truth*, in "Belloc's footsteps . . . saw the solution in terms of a form of apartheid" (ibid., p. 81).

316. Ibid., 12.

317. Ibid., 96; "Attempts to draw a clear political spectrum from right to left" were "always fraught with danger"; anti-Semitism, "most readily identified with the extreme right," was not

port for 'Zionism'... did not apply to Palestine." Although, "[p]aradoxically," such people were "race conscious to a high degree, they still championed the Arab cause."[318]

Such views did not apply to Chesterton, and Rubinstein claims that "the well-known 'cultural anti-semites' of the Edwardian period—Chesterton, Kipling, even Maxse and Belloc—invariably turn out, on closer inspection, to be as sensitive to Jewish suffering as they were hostile." Those that lived to see Hitler "were, almost always, repelled by Hitler and publicly disassociated themselves from him."[319] He points to "a populist anti-semitic tradition" dating from Cobbett's time or even earlier, which persisted "especially among self-educated 'auto-didacts' as so many radical leaders of the time were." Constructing their philosophies "from whatever intellectual straw they could find," these populists "differed significantly" from "right-wing" "anti-semites" because unlike political conservatives they were critical of capitalism.[320] The latter, as seen, worried more about Bolshevist Jews.[321] Chesterton, Rubinstein says, had "numerous Jewish friends" at St Paul's School, but was "converted" to anti-Semitism by "his close friend" Belloc. Chesterton "peppered" his stories "with the mindless Jewish stereotypical characters of the period" and the periodicals with which he was linked "of course attacked Jewish 'plutocrats.'" Yet he acknowledges the difficulty of categorizing "his attitude toward the Jews with precision"; it was a "curious mixture of Christian (i.e., Catholic) patriot and English patriot," which saw Jews as "undesirable because they were neither."[322] Belloc's position, he adds, was similarly "complex." Despite uttering anti-Semitic remarks in private, Belloc appeared genuinely upset that people should think him an anti-Semite, believing that "[t]he Jewish nation ought to be recognized as a nation in some way or another, with all the advantages and disadvantages that follow from the recognition of any truth."[323] Rubinstein cites Canovan on the dangers of hindsight in judging such individuals—advice

"absent from liberal and socialist circles," and it was "difficult to subsume the antipathy of Jewish power" from "the ChesterBelloc circle or the British Union of Fascists under the category of conservatism" (ibid., p. 79).

318. Ibid., 42–43.

319. W. D. Rubinstein, *A History of the Jews in the English-Speaking World: Great Britain*, op. cit., 34.

320. Ibid., 113.

321. "Jews were 'good' when constructively engaged in the building up of Palestine, but 'bad' when associated ... with Bolshevism"; some saw Jews as "good" when helping to build the British economy, but worried about the "social and cultural threat they apparently posed" (H. Defries, *Conservative Party Attitudes to Jews* [London: Frank Cass, 2001], vii).

322. W. D. Rubinstein, *A History of the Jews in the English-Speaking World: Great Britain*, op. cit., 114–115.

323. H. Belloc, Letter to Maurice Baring, January 1, 1916 (ibid., 137).

"many of today's commentators on pre-Nazi British anti-semitism would do well to heed."[324] He further notes that, largely because of their Catholicism, Italians were also seen as a threat to "Britishness"—the conversion of "hundreds of well-born Englishmen" to the Catholic Church "was viewed by many as a serious national threat."[325]

Rubinstein sees Winston Churchill's 1920 foray into the "Jewish question" as demonstrating his prescience, and that his views overlapped with Jewish Zionists Herzl, Jabotinsky, and Weizmann: "While most anti-semites of this period were certainly also anti-Zionists," Churchill, who cited *New Witness* conspiracy theories, offered an "encomium to Zionism" that showed that "for some far-sighted conservatives the opposite was true."[326] Rubinstein adds that although not easy to quantify, in Britain, "levels of personal anti-semitism were extremely low," and in the inter-War period were "decreasing rather than increasing."[327] In fact, he sees Chesterton's 1933 attack on Nazi anti-Semitism as part of a "groundswell of reaction of abhorrence" that "does not appear to have been properly noted by previous historians."[328] Hitler's anti-Semitism, he says, broke the rules of civilized behavior, especially the anti-Semitism of polite society.[329] He concludes that, paradoxically, while the British Left "by definition and a priori" supported "persecuted Jews" against anti-Semites, the materialist outlook of Marxists prevented them from understanding Nazi anti-Semitism.[330]

This outlook was shared by Shaw and Wells, who were also beguiled by the "Strong Man" idea. Chesterton said in 1933 that St. Thomas Aquinas was "very much of a Liberal compared with the most modern of all moderns; for they are nearly all of them turning into Fascists and Hitlerites."[331] Richard Griffiths says many British people who were "otherwise fairly anti-Semitic" were shocked by the Nazis.[332] Stone notes that some attempted to play down or excuse Nazi anti-Semitism,[333] that many "'well-meaning' liberal writers" couldn't really

324. M. Canovan, *G. K. Chesterton: Radical Populist* (New York, 1977), 137–140 (ibid., 115).

325. Ibid., 140–142.

326. Ibid., 472, 212–213.

327. Ibid., 288.

328. Ibid., 297–298.

329. Ibid., 319.

330. Ibid., 322.

331. Aquinas "preferred the sort of decisions that are reached by deliberation rather than despotic action" (G. K. Chesterton, *St. Thomas Aquinas* [1933], *St. Thomas of Aquinas; St. Francis of Assisi* [San Francisco: Ignatius Press, 2002], 172).

332. R. Griffiths, *Fellow travellers of the right: British enthusiasts for Nazi Germany 1933–9* (Oxford, 1983), 65, in D. Stone, *Breeding Superman: Nietzsche, Race and Eugenics in Edwardian and Interwar Britain*, op. cit., 83.

333. Ibid., 89.

understand Nazi anti-Semitism, and that even those disgusted by Hitler's measures could still retain "stereotypical images of Jews."[334] Rather than trying to decide whether "complex writers" including Belloc and Chesterton were fascists, Stone looked at the development of their thinking from the rise of Nazism,[335] although Chesterton's case was "quite unequivocal. He was from the start fiercely opposed to Nazism and 'the toppling simplifications of the Totalitarian State'"; he was "more positively predisposed towards Italian and Spanish fascism," but "[b]oth positions were, of course, intimately connected with his Catholicism." His anti-Nazism did not, however, settle "the question of his anti-Semitism or of his support for Franco or Mussolini—expressed regularly in *G.K.'s Weekly*,"[336] and Aurel Kolnai's obituary to Chesterton "tackled this issue head on," praising his "rejection of Nazism but admitting his admiration for Italian Fascism."[337]

Chesterton died before the Spanish Civil War, and like Churchill saw Nazi Germany as a greater threat than Italy. Kolnai supported Chesterton on eugenics,[338] and made no mention of his views on fascism in *The War Against the West* (1938). In fact, he based his anti-Nazism on Chesterton's writings: under the heading "The Meaning of Anti-Judaism" he quotes Houston Stewart Chamberlain ("The Jews are ... the unique example of a purely parasitic product of decay"); Alfred Rosenberg ("Their essential activity is a carping at all manifestations of the Aryan soul"), and Adolf Hitler ("The Jews are carrying out a deliberate attempt to lower the racial level of non-Jewish mankind... They brought the Negroes into the Rhineland .... For hours the black-haired young Jew, with satanic joy in his face, lies in wait for the guileless Aryan girl whom he taints with his blood, thereby stealing her from her people."). Against these Kolnai cites Victor Hugo, and Chesterton's *The Ballad of the Battle of Gibeon*.[339] On "Prussianism" Kolnai quotes from Chesterton's *The Queen of Seven Swords*: "And I knew what Spirit had passed who is vast beyond meaning or measure, / The blank in the brain of the whirlwind, the hollow, the hungry

334. Ibid., 110.

335. "[A] rather fruitless debate" involving "a struggle for reputations between their detractors and their epigones" (ibid, 122–123). Orwell noted that currency reformers and fascists tended to write in the same papers (G. Orwell, "London Letter to Partisan Review," *Partisan Review*, March–April 1942, G. Orwell, *George Orwell Collected Essays Vol.2, 1940–43*, S. Orwell, I. Angus, eds. [Harmondsworth, Middx.: Penguin Books, 1970], 211).

336. G.K. Chesterton, "The Return of Caesar," *G.K.'s Weekly*, July 27, 1933, reprinted in the *Chesterton Review XXV*, (1999): 17, cited in D. Stone, *Breeding Superman: Nietzsche, Race and Eugenics in Edwardian and Interwar Britain*, op. cit., 129.

337. Aural Kolnai, *Der Christliche Ständestaat* [*The Christian Standard*], June 28, 1936, 619–621 (ibid., 220).

338. A. Kolnai, *The War Against the West* (London: Victor Gollancz Ltd., 1938), 482.

339. Ibid., 492–493; see Chapter Five.

thing, / The Nothing that swells and desires, the void that devours and dismembers, / In the hearts of barbarian armies or the idle hours of a King. . . ." He also quotes Cecil Chesterton's *The Prussian hath said in his Heart*: "Prussia is hardly to be called a nation. It is rather an institution animated by a certain spirit, and a certain creed"—the 'creed' being Atheism.[340]

Although of Jewish extraction, Kolnai believed Nazi Germany should be judged "above all by its negation of mankind and its intrinsic enmity to Western democratic society, and not by its special ill-will against Jews." But people "must also refuse to be blind to the symbolic purport of the Nazi discrimination against Jews," and to "bear witness to the peculiar barbarism of the Nürnberg legislation and the mentality underlying it"—a mentality "wholly in tune with the general line of fascism" but also with the "undeniable novelty" of racism.[341]

Chesterton's Zionism in Perspective

The *Chesterbelloc* opposed the internationalist approach of Shaw and Wells which, while appearing to rule out anti-Semitism, could not accommodate Jewish national aspirations. But Stapleton argues that if Chesterton's ideal of "English authenticity" was "not quite defined by anti-Semitism" it was "certainly colored by it."[342] Even his praise for Lord Swaythling's will, she says, was "marred by sweeping generalizations about the inability of the Jews to integrate into the nations in which they settled." But he also refused to accept as genuine the patriotism of Gentile Imperialists Kipling and Lord Milner.[343] Chesterton accused Israel Zangwill of "betray[ing] his own roots by inventing the specious idea of 'the melting pot,'"[344] and awarded double praise to patriotic English Jews precisely because in his view their loyalty was not natural. But, as seen, he called the internationalist Wells a "cosmopolitan."[345] As Stapleton notes, Chesterton viewed patriotism, like marriage, as "based on ties of loyalty that were incapable of being transferred elsewhere in the event of . . . breakdown." Patriotism could not be transferred from one country to another, whether exile was "voluntary or coerced,"[346] but like his injunctions against name-changes this "hit Jews harder

340. Ibid., 528–529.

341. Ibid., 495.

342. J. Stapleton, *Christianity, Patriotism, and Nationhood: The England of G.K. Chesterton*, op. cit., 127.

343. Ibid., 143–144.

344. G.K. Chesterton, "The Higher Realism," *Daily News*, April 27, 1912 (ibid., 142).

345. See Chapter Four.

346. G.K. Chesterton, *The Superstition of Divorce* (1920), G.K. Chesterton, *Collected Works IV* (San Francisco, 1987), 279–280, in J. Stapleton, *Christianity, Patriotism, and Nationhood: The England of G.K. Chesterton*, op. cit., 144.

than any other people, of which Chesterton was surely aware." His definition would see many Jewish refugees "condemned to the lowly status that he described elsewhere as 'mere citizenship' rather than being eligible for the higher status of patriot."[347] Although he criticized Jewish MPs for supporting the 1905 Aliens Act that "denied poor, oppressed Jews in Europe an English refuge" he "could see no further than 'greed' as their own motive for settling in Britain."[348] Stapleton concludes that "in his anti-Semitism" Chesterton "betrayed both his country and himself," becoming "the model of the 'inauthenticity' he so despised," since anti-Semitism was so "un-English."[349]

In 1904, Chesterton's "The Patriotic Idea" portrayed Jews like Alfred Beit and Disraeli as "foreign," but also the German Lord Milner,[350] as well as Imperialists like Kruger and Rhodes—not because of their "blood" but their "un-English" mindset. Rhodes's worst influence, he claimed, was not on "colonial politicians, whom he understood," but "on English gentlemen, whom he could not understand."[351] In Chesterton's view, the gravest threats to England stemmed from "remoteness, from unreality," especially the remoteness of wealth from its producers, from distant wars, and "from the wild use of statistics, from the crude use of names, from the investor and the theorist, and the absentee landlord."[352] Small nations, he said, were seen as "dead or destined to die," but it was the empires that crumbled. Cosmopolitans like Wells saw small nations evolving into federations and federations evolving into world government, and would, therefore, deny nationhood to the Irish, the Poles, and the Zionists. Chesterton defended patriotism against the charge that it caused nation to consume nation, arguing that although some Christian nations had been "swallowed," none, notably Ireland and Poland, had "ever been digested"[353] because of their authentic culture. Imperialists claimed that conquering other countries enriched English culture, but the English were only interested in the cultures of countries they had not been able to conquer, like France. The English "knew so much about German mythology and nothing about Irish mythology" because "[t]he Irish would not sing to us any more than the Jews, as described in their stern and splendid psalm, would sing to the Babylonians."[354] The real danger

347. G.K. Chesterton, *A Short History of England* (1917), in *G.K. Chesterton Collected Works XX* (San Francisco, 2001), 502 (ibid., 144).

348. G.K. Chesterton, *Illustrated London News*, March 20, 1909, 408 (ibid., 143).

349. Ibid., 201.

350. G.K. Chesterton, "The Patriotic Idea," *England: a Nation, Being the papers of the Patriots' Club* in L. Oldershaw, ed. (1904), G.K. Chesterton, *G.K. Chesterton Collected Works, Vol. XX* (San Francisco: Ignatius Press, 2001), 601–603.

351. Ibid., 616–617.

352. Ibid., 614.

353. Ibid., 606–608.

354. Ibid., 610.

was not patriotism but cosmopolitanism and Imperialism. To Chesterton they were the same "disease," and the only "cure" was small nations.[355]

Chesterton included the Jewish people in his pantheon of small nations, alongside the Poles, the Irish, and the Boers. The Boers, he said, were fighting against the sort of Englishmen that the Imperialists were too embarrassed to acknowledge: "[T]he people the Boers called Outlanders were often people whom the British would call Outsiders. Their names were symbolic as their noses." But, he added, that when "an Englishman named Edgar" was murdered, "no portrait . . . was published" because "he was entirely black. Other portraits were published; other Outlanders were paraded and they were of other tints and shades."[356] Furthermore, Chesterton inspired Gandhi with his warning that Internationalism was merely Imperialism in disguise since it was "the imposition of one ideal of one sect on the vital varieties of men."[357] He claimed to respect Indian culture while Imperialists despised it: "[W]hen poor Robert Clive stood with the pistol in his hand, and asked himself the value of life and death, he might have learnt from some ragged fakir, whom he treated as dirt, a pessimism infinitely deeper and more rational than his own."[358]

Chesterton: pro-Zionist or anti-Semite?

In Chesterton's patriotic worldview the Jewish people, equally with Poles and Irish, deserved their own nation, and the rationale of his speculation that Jews might be accommodated in special "enclaves" was the opposite of Belloc's. Belloc believed that wealthy Jews would not want to go to Palestine, while Chesterton's "capitalism test" sprang from his fear that they would want to go there, leaving poor Jews behind in the Diaspora, in need of the protection that he believed the "enclaves" could offer. His insistence that Jews should not be molested, that his proposed Jewish "enclaves" should be affiliated to a Jewish center in Palestine, and that Palestine should remain under Christian Europe's protective umbrella suggests that he was partly motivated by fears for Jewish security. Crucially, however, he insisted that the Jews alone should determine their own course. As with democracy, he believed in trusting those most closely affected to sort out the details for themselves.

355. Ibid., 615.
356. G.K. Chesterton, *Autobiography*, op. cit., 112.
357. G.K. Chesterton, "Our Notebook," *Illustrated London News*, June 17, 1922, 890, in G.K. Chesterton, *Chesterton on War and Peace: Battling the Ideas and Movements That Led to Nazism and World War II*, op. cit., 410; "The principal weakness of Indian Nationalism seems to be that it is not very Indian and not very national" in G.K. Chesterton, *Illustrated London News*, September 18, 1909 (ibid., 409); "I, for one, was led by Mr. Chesterton's article to all these reflections and I place them before readers" (Mahatma Gandhi, *Indian Opinion*, January 8, 1910 [ibid.]).
358. G.K. Chesterton, "The Patriotic Idea," op. cit., 611–612.

Zionism satisfied Chesterton's debt of honor to his own patriotic beliefs and his loyalty to Jews as well as Gentiles, especially Cecil and Belloc. Deriding racial theories that implied all Jews were bad—or, for that matter, good—and the determinism that implied that they could not change, Chesterton argued that thwarted patriotism could explain Jewish "vices." Nonetheless, in spite of condemning "racism" the *Chesterbelloc's* focus on "Jewish finance" projected a view closely resembling the prejudice they formally rejected.

While Chesterton's Zionism has been seen by supporters as evidence of pro-Semitism, and by critics as evidence of anti-Semitism, in reality he was seeking an intellectual Shavian synthesis of the two. The anti-Semitic argument was strengthened by Cecil's death, but eventually pro-Semitism prevailed, albeit with subtle modifications. But if most convinced anti-Semites were not Zionists, neither were most Jews, even though Jewish Zionists actively sought Gentile support. Yet while Churchill and Wedgwood were remembered as friends of the Jews, Chesterton, whose Zionism was influenced by Herzl, Zangwill, Weizmann, and Eder, would be categorized as an anti-Semite, leading in turn to his categorization as right-wing. The largely negative Jewish response to Chesterton was undoubtedly the result of the enclave idea: to Jews it signaled religiously motivated anti-Semitism, the Middle Ages, and the ultra-zealous Pope Pius V (1566–72), who believed that Jews were "guilty of magic, witchcraft and usury," and revived the Rome ghetto and the yellow star.[359]

These perceptions were strengthened by Chesterton's association with Belloc, suggesting a concerted campaign to roll back the equality of the modern era. Yet although on the surface their "solutions" to the "Jewish question" seemed practically identical, beneath Belloc's structure Chesterton built his own foundation, reflecting his own philosophy. This satisfied his loyalty to Belloc and to his own worldview, which was partly based on loyalty to the Jews. Thus he could see the "enclaves" not as ghettoes but as refuges, a typically English idea of the home as fortress and sanctuary, influenced by anxieties about anti-Jewish violence and his romantic theory of "place" as a focus for loyalty. Influenced by his most enduring loyalty to the mystical Old Testament Jew, Chesterton's Zionism was also shaped by the fears induced by Bellocian skepticism; more fundamentally, it satisfied his own need to believe that both Jews and their critics were right.

If Chesterton's political Zionism was inextricably linked to his religion, his view of democracy was religious and highly romantic. Many saw democracies as "dull, drifting things," but he insisted: "A people is a soul," and a soul was "something that can sin and that can sacrifice itself. A people can commit theft; a people can confess theft; a people can repent of theft. That is the idea of the

---

359. J. Watkins, "Pope Pius V," *Catholic Life*, February 2013, 2–4.

republic." A people could do "heroic deeds"—could "commit crimes; the French people did both in the Revolution"; the Irish people had "done both in their much purer and more honourable progress." But a people could also "have adventures, as Israel did crawling through the desert to the promised land."[360] In supporting the Jewish people's claim to nationhood, he attributed to them the same potential for good and evil as other peoples. To Chesterton, democracy was the "soul of the people"—the collective will, a product of the mind but also an act of faith; it had nothing to do with the unthinking "soul of the hive." Fascists forced people to agree with them; communists, while pretending that people agreed with them, did the same. Chesterton wanted people to agree with him of their own free will, and trusted the will of the people. But his canton idea suggested that he did not trust them with the safety of the Jews.

Chesterton said Shaw's Utopian proposals had to be read with the smiling figure of Shaw in mind; perhaps the same could be said of the "combative and charitable" Chesterton.[361] His Zionism was an attempt to reconcile his two loves, England and the Jews. He feared for both because of their imperfections, therefore he criticized them in their own defense. This gained him the reputation of an anti-Semite among Jews, but some were won over by closer acquaintance: he really did have Jewish friends, and these, together with the influence of his parents, his wife, and Gentile friends, will be examined in the next chapter along with his poetry and his other profound influence, religion.

360. G.K. Chesterton, "The Field of Blood," *Alarms and Discursions* (London: Methuen & Co. Ltd., 1910/1939), 163–164.

361. W. Oddie, ed., introduction to *The Holiness of G.K. Chesterton*, op. cit., 10.

8

Chesterton's Best Friends

B y THE 1920s Jews were becoming skeptical of "Jewish friend" defenses offered by those accused of anti-Semitism, but the old cliché was a truism: the Chestertons, Hilaire Belloc, H.G. Wells, and D.H. Lawrence did have Jewish friends—even the fascist A.K. Chesterton could claim the friendship of Joseph Leftwich, a critic of anti-Semitism. This did not mean that these Gentiles were pro-Semitic, but neither does it explain their Jewish friends. Chesterton and Belloc believed that lecturing Jews on their perceived virtues and vices would help them recognize the "Jewish problem." The Jews disagreed, but continued to invite such addresses; apparently, Jew and Gentile shared the view that "the other" was not so other that they were unable to change their minds. Arguably, the Jewish influence on the *Chesterbelloc* was greater than the *Chesterbelloc*'s influence on the Jews.

The New Jerusalem appeared to seal Chesterton's reputation for anti-Semitism, and although *G.K.'s Weekly* attracted less controversy than the *New Witness*, his reputation would put off some Jews from closer acquaintance. Much older Jewish friendships endured, however, and Ward claimed that accusations of anti-Semitism were "often made half in play: very few people entertained it seriously, least of all his oldest group of friends."[1] Chesterton, who in his *Autobiography* described himself as a "ProSemite,"[2] said that one of his oldest Jewish friends, Lawrence Solomon, "happened to have all the Jewish virtues, and also all the others there are."[3] Chesterton met Lawrence's brother, Maurice, the "strange swarthy little creature," when he saved him from being bullied. The adult Maurice, he said, "had a sort of permanent fountain of thanks for that trifling incident, which was quite embarrassing." Chesterton, tall for his age, escaped bullying, but recalled that "[o]ddly enough" he had acquired "the

---

1. M. Ward, *Return to Chesterton* (London: Sheed & Ward, 1952), 115.
2. G.K. Chesterton, *Autobiography* (Sevenoaks, Kent: Fisher Press, 1936/1992), 71–72.
3. Ibid., 74.

name of an Anti-Semite," although from his "first days at school" he "very largely had the name of a ProSemite." His "many" lifelong Jewish friendships had never been "disturbed by differences upon the political or social problem." He did not disclose whether these friends discussed the enclave idea, and although he said the right approach to the "political and social problem" was to praise the "very much neglected Jewish virtues," the "complement and sometimes even the cause of what the world feels to be the Jewish faults," that approach was seldom evident when discussing "Jewish plutocrats."

Nonetheless, Chesterton explained that "what the world feels to be" the faults of those "plutocrats" sprang from the "virtues" he observed in his Jewish friends. These "Jewish virtues" were "gratitude" and a "strong family bond," admirable qualities, since the latter "was not merely disguised but denied among most normal schoolboys." He continued: "Doubtless, I came to know the Jews because in this sense they were a little abnormal, as I was then becoming a little abnormal myself. Yet there is nothing I have come to count more normal, and nothing I desire more to restore to its normal place, than those two things; the family and the theory of thanks." In these virtues he had come to see "the origin and even the justification of much of the Anti-Semitic criticism from without." It was "often the very loyalty of the Jewish family" that appeared as "disloyalty to the Christian state." Furthermore, "it was partly what I admired in private friends, especially in two brothers named Solomon, which I came ultimately to denounce in political enemies, in two brothers named Isaacs." In his conclusion he resisted the temptation to perfect the paradox by matching "good" with its antithesis: "The first were good by every standard, the second vulnerable even by their own standard: and yet they had the same virtue."[4] And Chesterton admitted being governed by the same law that governed all men—"loyalties."[5]

His own conflicting loyalties—to the Jewish people, and to Belloc and Cecil, but also to the poor, whom he saw as suffering under "the plutocracy"—had tested him sorely, but he was "not at all ashamed of having asked Aryans to have more patience with Jews or for having asked Anglo-Saxons to have more patience with Jew-baiters."[6] Given his ridicule of racism—the "Aryan" preoccupation—the terminology is satirical, but as well as "explaining" alleged Jewish "vices" to the "Aryans," he also asked "Anglo-Saxons" to "have more patience with Jew-baiters" by putting the arguments of the "man in the street"—more frank than Belloc and Cecil—alongside the "pro-Semite's." But he was a restraining influence on Belloc, and, by removing Ada from her position of

4. Ibid., 71–73; see Chapters Five and Six.
5. G.K. Chesterton, *Daily News*, August 27, 1904.
6. G.K. Chesterton, *Autobiography*, op. cit., 71–73.

influence, ensured that "Cecil's" re-launched paper was his own in style and emphasis.

Clearly Chesterton wished to set the record straight for posterity; yet, beneath the characteristic desire for "reconciliation" there is a certain lack of empathy for the Jewish friends he praises. Much earlier he had argued: "Some excellent Jews suffer from a sad fallacy: they think it glorious to be a Jew, and yet they think it insulting to be called one."[7] He should perhaps have been more sensitive to his "excellent" friends' legitimate desire to "blend in." They largely shared his anti-capitalist views but, as with the enclave idea, he does not say whether he discussed his "Jewish difference" theory with them. Anxious to avoid the controversy he so hated in personal relationships, perhaps he derived too high a degree of comfort and affirmation from his Jewish friendships but, clearly, he greatly valued them, and despite conflicting interests never discarded a friendship. When asked about "the old set" he was "acutely conscious of having belonged to a large number of old sets."[8]

Family and Childhood Influences

The Chestertons' choice of St Paul's School, with its large complement of Jewish pupils, for their sons' education is hardly suggestive of anti-Jewish sentiment. Cecil Chesterton said their mother "always judged opinions by the people, not people by their opinions." Crucially, she allowed her sons freedom of thought [9] and would be warmly remembered by Gilbert's Jewish friends. Gilbert cherished early memories of his older sister Beatrice—the adored "Birdie"—who died aged eight,[10] and when Cecil was born, Gilbert became devoted to his little brother. At nine, Gilbert showed poetic promise but also the nonconformist's religious and political bias: "Drive the trembling Papists backwards / Drive away the Tory's hord / Let them tell thier hous of villains / They have felt the Campbell's sword" (*sic*).[11] This bias persisted into young

7. G.K. Chesterton, *Illustrated London News*, November 28, 1908, in *Gilbert Magazine*, 12 (2 & 3), (November/December 2008): 58, accessed May 19, 2011, http://www.209.236.72.127/wordpress/wp-content/uploads/2010/12/gilbert_12.2_5.pdf.

8. G.K. Chesterton, *Autobiography*, op. cit., 312; "Gilbert was a very faithful friend: it would be hard to find a broken friendship in his life" (M. Ward, *Gilbert Keith Chesterton* [New York: Sheed & Ward, 1943], 327).

9. Ibid., 466.

10. G.K. Chesterton, *Autobiography*, op. cit., 32.

11. A. Mackey, *G.K. Chesterton: A Prophet for the 21ˢᵗ Century* (Kempston, Bedford: A. Mackey, 2008), 5–6; "Thank God we have no creed now/ Of rule or right divine / To make us cringe to a villain / Who comes of an ancient line" (G.K. Chesterton, [*Blood*], 1886–1888, G.K. Chesterton, *G.K. Chesterton Collected Works Vol. X: Collected Poetry Part II*, D.J. Conlon, ed. [San Francisco: Ignatius Press, 2008], 3–5); Gilbert's father Edward "[i]n several of his letters" mentioned the Catholic Church,

adulthood,[12] along with deep reverence for the Old Testament Jew: Moses was
"[t]he man who gave to the nations / The ten great words of God."[13] Chesterton praised "the noble Hebrew" as "no dead mouth of the divine,/ Not a common mind selected by a deity descending, / But a climber crowned with glory,
by a bright rewarding sign." With their "[w]ild instinct" and "mortal passion"
the Jews were "[m]en . . . in sin and virtue," but they heard "with human ears,
the voices in the lowest deep of conscience" and saw "with human eyes the
glimmer of a life beyond the tomb." As to their spiritual legacy:

> . . . the Holy Volume, where their human words are treasured,
> Let it be our lamp and comfort as a thing inspired indeed,
> As the words of old-world spirits that had grasped the thought of Godhead,
> And who spoke with human passion, utterance of their human need.[14]

Throughout his life Chesterton recorded his thoughts and ideas in note-
books, in the 1890s revealing hatred for the oppression of poor Jews in Russia in
a passionate attack on the seduction of a young Jewish girl by a Christian.[15] In
1891 in the school magazine he co-founded, *The Debater*, and in a series of fictional letters he asked: "What do you think of the persecution of the Jews in
Russia? It has, at least . . . restored my belief in the Devil. . . . I am going to Russia, I think the most godless, hell-darkened place I can think of, to see if I
can't . . . help the Hebrews . . . or do something else that will be for the good of
humanity."[16] In 1899 he wrote *To a Certain Nation*, later misconstrued as an
anti-Jewish tirade, condemning France's treatment of Dreyfus. It concludes:
"Thou hast a right to rule thyself. . . . To crown these clumsy liars; ay, and we /
Who knew thee once, we have a right to weep."[17] He praised Colonel Georges
Picquart, imprisoned for exposing the truth of the affair: "He was brave in the
world's old fashion / And he walked to the world's old song / That a host is a
heap of weapons / And only a man is strong."[18] But in his 1905 edition of *The*

"certainly with no dislike"; he once heard Cardinal Manning preach, and "much admired" the sermon,
noting "no distinctively Roman Catholic doctrine" (M. Ward, *Gilbert Keith Chesterton*, op. cit., 6).

12. "With the bishop's popish crozier and the tyrant's iron rod / We will match angels, warriors of
the everlasting God" (G. K. Chesterton, [*Marston Moor*], ca. 1890 (ibid.); "Dark were the walls as
books on dusty shelves / Where war and love and tears and laughter cease, / Crypts where the sexless
slanderers of themselves, / Eat darkly the forbidden fruit of peace" (G. K. Chesterton, *A Nunnery*,
mid-1890s [ibid., 185]).

13. G. K. Chesterton, [*Moses in Egypt*], ca. 1890 (ibid., 53–54).

14. G. K. Chesterton, *Verbal Inspiration*, ca. 1889 (ibid., 28–29).

15. W. Oddie, "The Philosemitism of G. K. Chesterton," in W. Oddie, ed., *The Holiness of G. K.
Chesterton* (Leominster, Herefordshire: Gracewing, 2010), 127.

16. G. K. Chesterton, *The Debater*, iii, 11, 29 (ibid., 128).

17. G. K. Chesterton, *To a Certain Nation*, *The Speaker*, January 7, 1899, in G. K. Chesterton, *G. K.
Chesterton Collected Works Vol. X: Collected Poetry Part II*, op. cit., 290–291.

18. G. K. Chesterton, *Picquart*, late 1890s (ibid., 292–293).

Wild Knight collection he admitted reluctance to alter early poems even though they contained "innumerable examples of what I now see to be errors of opinion." Some verses he could not "take so seriously" but "[t]he man who wrote them was honest; and he had the same basic views as myself."[19] While not revising *To a Certain Nation*, in a reprint he admitted being unable to reach a "final conclusion about the proper verdict on the individual," blaming his "difficulty" on "the acrid and irrational unanimity of the English Press," concluding that "there may have been a fog of injustice in the French courts; I know that there was a fog of injustice in the English newspapers."[20] From that time Chesterton, whose mother was of French Swiss stock and who never lost his admiration for the French Revolution[21] moved closer to the position of the half-French Belloc. At the end of his life Chesterton maintained: "Dreyfus may have been innocent, but Dreyfusards were not always innocent; even when they were editors."[22] In 1907 his verse suggested an about-face on Jews, the Catholic Church, the Reformation, and the Stuart kings. Now, "the shaven men" are "quaint and kind"; the "King as they killed him" had a face that was "proud and pale." Bureaucracy also emerges as a threat:

> Our patch of glory ended; we never heard guns again.
> But the squire seemed struck in the saddle; he was foolish, as if in pain.
> He leaned on a staggering lawyer, he clutched a cringing Jew,
> He was stricken; it may be, after all, he was stricken at Waterloo.
> Or perhaps the shades of the shaven men, whose spoil is in his house,
> Come back in shining shapes at last to spoil his last carouse.[23]

His hatred of Imperialism and the Boer War, seen as the result of pressure from "Jewish finance" coalesced in a poem of 1907:

> So Cecil Rhodes has gone to Hell,
> —Not there by faithful Beit forsook—
> Eckstein's feeling far from well,
> And Goldtmann is not yet a Duke:
> They lent their aid when England shook,
> At five per cent or even ten,
> Yet Death and Shame their shades rebuke:
> Where are the Empire's choicest men?
> And Kipling's skull's an empty shell

19. G.K. Chesterton, *The Wild Knight* (1905), in D. J. Conlon, introduction to ibid., x.

20. Ibid., 290–291.

21. M. Ward, *Gilbert Keith Chesterton*, op. cit., 4.

22. G.K. Chesterton, *Autobiography*, op. cit., 321–322.

23. G.K. Chesterton, *The Secret People* (*The Neolith*, 1907), G.K. Chesterton, *The Works of G.K. Chesterton* (Ware, Herts.: Wordsworth Poetry Library, 1995), 131–133; see Chapter Seven.

> Just haunted by his bleating spook,
> Who brought such aid to . . . Israel.[24]

This was critical of non-Jews as well as Jews, but three years later:

> They bargain till they can afford
> To sit and make the money fly,
> They like to give out of a hoard
> And—if the interest is high—
> They like to lend it. And they cry
> Whenever customers refuse:
> "I'm persecuted. Hi! Hi! Hi!"
> Such are the customs of the Jews.

The poem reflected popular perceptions of Jews as money-grubbing, selfish liars who equated criticism with persecution, although it did defend Jewish religious practices:

> They put on hats to praise The Lord,
> They bleed their meat till it is dry,
> They scorn the Ploughshare and the Sword,
> And pass the Pig severely by;
> Nor do I see a reason why
> They should not do so if they choose. . . .

But Jews are also portrayed as foreigners pulling multifarious strings:

> They also are a German Spy—
> Such are the customs of the Jews. . .
> Lord Rothschild ruled the Gare du Nord,
> King Solomon the Genii,
> [Herbert] Samuel, the Education Board,
> And Joseph, Egypt's corn-supply.
> [Salomon] Reinarch remodels history,
> And Baron Reuter alters news,
> And Bloch was pained that people die.
> Such are the customs of the Jews.[25]

In 1911, at a time of anti-Semitic violence in Wales, Chesterton wrote:

---

24. G. K. Chesterton, *Lines Suitable to a Lady's Album*, 1907, G. K. Chesterton, *G. K. Chesterton Collected Works Vol. X: Collected Poetry Part II*, op. cit., 398–399; dedicated to C. F. G. Masterman's wife Lucy; "Beit" was probably mining magnate Alfred Beit, seen by the ChesterBelloc as responsible for the Boer War; Hermann Ludwig Eckstein and Marcus Goldman were wealthy Jewish associates of the Beits (ibid.).

25. G. K. Chesterton, *Ballade of an Interesting People*, ca. 1910 (ibid., 416–417).

> A helpless marquess has a bill to meet,
> A helpful Jew will lend him half a ton;
> The Jew would like to conquer Watling Street,
> Constantinople, Cairo and Canton....[26]

Also in 1911:

> In English country houses crammed with Jews,
> Men still will study, spell, perpend and pore
> And read the *Illustrated London News.*
> Our fathers read it at the earlier date
> And twirled the funny whiskers that they wore
> Ere little Levy got his first estate
> Or Madame [Adelina] Patti got her first encore.[27]

But only a minority of poems contained Jewish references; in the same year, one on Imperialism does not mention Jews.[28] Later poems contain occasional tangential, humorous references to Jewish individuals, for example, in a poem about a book he forgot to return:

> O you that measure all things long,
> Long views, long credit and long sight,
> Cyrano's nose, [Marie] Corelli's tongue,
> The pedigree of Otto Beit....[29]

By the 1930s, as well as satirizing Nazism, he had turned his sights on Atheism ("Prince, they've abolished God in Muscovy; / You think that you are safe. That is not so. / Much greater things than you are doomed to die: / They're cutting down the trees in Cheyne Row");[30] libertarianism ("*I'm getting rather tired of D. H. Lawrence*");[31] pessimists, social workers, and "damned Theosophists."[32] This broadly reflects the trajectory of his approach to the "Jewish question" in his fiction and non-fiction, but his Old Testament reverence endured. His Jewish friends brought alive the Bible for Chesterton, representing the "Jewish virtues" that he saw as the origin of the "Jewish vices."

---

26. G. K. Chesterton, *Ballade of an Optimist* [I], ca. 1911 (ibid., 427–428).

27. G. K. Chesterton, *Ballade of a Periodical, Illustrated London News,* 1911 (ibid., 433–434).

28. G. K. Chesterton, *Ballade of an Empire Builder,* ca. 1911 (ibid., 426–427).

29. German born financier Sir Otto Beit became a naturalized Briton in 1888 (G. K. Chesterton, *Ballade of an Old Man* [ibid., 462–463]).

30. G. K. Chesterton, M. Baring, *Ballade of Devastation, The Times,* February 17, 1932 (ibid., 474–475).

31. G. K. Chesterton, Refrain, *Ballade of a Morbid Modern (after reading many reminiscences),* *G. K.'s Weekly,* November 9, 1933 (ibid., 477).

32. G. K. Chesterton, *Ballade of Ephemeral Controversy,* n.d. (ibid., 479).

Chesterton's School Friends

The ancient St Paul's public school, where the Chesterton brothers were day pupils, produced many distinguished pupils both Jewish and Gentile.[33] Here the teenaged Gilbert founded the Junior Debating Club from which sprang several life-long friendships. Gentile members included Arthur and Frederick Salter, E.C. Fordham, B.N. Langdon-Davies, Lucien Oldershaw, and E.C. Bentley. Half the JDC was Jewish;[34] members continued to meet well into old age, and Chesterton continued to commemorate them in poetry.[35] Despite founding a debating society "Chesterton's platform manner was, of course, bad. He never took the trouble to learn public speaking."[36] The mildness of his manner did nothing to quell the endemic disorder of the Club. A literary circle dedicated to the romantic ideal—"[k]nights of [an] eccentric round table"[37]—it formed an outlet for Chesterton's creativity, including his illustrations for a series of "modern dress" Shakespeare plays with "Shylock as an aged Hebrew vendor of dilapidated vesture, with a tiara of hats."[38] The little band of brothers included Jewish brothers Maurice and Laurence Solomon, and Digby and Waldo d'Avigdor; also Robert Vérnède, Hubert Arthur Sams, and Leonard Magnus. The Solomons appear in Chesterton's verse,[39] and an epistolary outpouring to wife-to-be Frances described "Vernède with an Oriental and inscrutable placidity varied every now and then with dazzling agility and Meredithian humour"; apparently, Waldo d'Avigdor "mask[ed] with complete fashionable triviality a Hebraic immutability of passion tried in a more ironical and bitter service than his Father Jacob"; Lawrence and Maurice Solomon showed "another side of the same people, the love of home, the love of children, the meek and malicious humour, the tranquil service of a law."[40]

Waldo d'Avigdor kept up a "warm correspondence" with Chesterton for many years. Preserved by a Canadian descendant, it included a letter in which

33. F.R. Salter, *St. Paul's School* 1909–1959 (London: Arthur Barker Ltd., 1959), 198; distinguished Jewish pupils included Norman Bentwich, Attorney-General of Palestine (ibid., 30), the Great War poet Robert Vernède (ibid., 190) and publisher Victor Gollancz (ibid., 192–194).

34. M. Ward, *Return to Chesterton*, op. cit., 115; D. Conlon, "The Junior Debating Club," G.K. Chesterton, *Basil Howe: A Story of Young Love* (London: New City, 1893–4/2001), 24–25.

35. See: G.K. Chesterton, *G.K. Chesterton Collected Works Vol. X Collected Poetry Part I* (San Francisco: Ignatius Press, 1994).

36. M. Ward, *Return to Chesterton*, op. cit., 224.

37. G.K. Chesterton, Letter to Frances Blogg, M. Ward, *Gilbert Keith Chesterton*, op. cit., 103.

38. Ibid., 28.

39. G.K. Chesterton, *To L. Solomon, Esq., J.D.C.* (Dedication from *Prince Wild-Fire*, c. 1892), G.K. Chesterton, *G.K. Chesterton Collected Works Vol. X: Collected Poetry Part II*, op. cit., 130; "God prosper long our noble [Junior Debating] club, / Our lives and safeties all, / A woeful muddle once there did / At Solomon's befall" (G.K. Chesterton, *Chevy Chase or the Hunting of Rudyard Kipling* [ibid., 113]).

40. M. Ward, *Gilbert Keith Chesterton*, op. cit., 103.

Chesterton and Waldo wrote alternate sentences.[41] He also corresponded with Maurice Solomon ("Grey");[42] they remained life-long friends,[43] and Maurice's younger brother Lawrence, who became Professor of Latin at University College, also remained close friends—he and his wife came to live near the Chestertons at Beaconsfield.[44] Chesterton stayed in London studying art when most of his friends went up to Oxford, and it became a period of mental turmoil.[45] On receiving a photograph frame for his 21st birthday, he told E.C. Bentley that he would "get Grey to give me a photograph of him to put into it." Apparently the Solomons had confided some anxieties about Leonard Magnus, but had come "to some hopeful conclusions": Magnus was "all right. As for Lawrence and Grey, if there is anything righter than all right, they are that."[46] Digby d'Avigdor "felt it a real honour to be Gilbert's friend";[47] Lawrence Solomon recalled "how happy" Chesterton's conversion to Catholicism had made him, seeming to "bring him increased strength of character."[48] Chesterton recollected Robert Ernest Vernède (1875–1917) as having an "oval, almost Japanese face," glimpsed "in some of the Southern French blood of which he came." He praised the Great War poet for his "noble invocation to the English Sea, which multitudes must still remember," before dying "on the field of honour."[49] Chesterton emphasized Vernède's patriotism and his French "blood," but in the same memoir, insisted that Jews were foreign, although praising the Jew one knows while criticizing the one does not know is paradigmatic of the prejudice that Chesterton rejected.

Despite being briefly tempted, Chesterton also rejected Jewish conspiracy theories, perhaps influenced by the elaborately plotted stories that he and his school friends wove to show what was really happening behind the banal façade of school life: a diminutive elderly master, they suggested, was actually a clockwork figure wound up every morning and supported on either side by two much taller masters. E.C. Bentley, Chesterton recalled, "had and has a natural

41. A. Mackey, *G.K. Chesterton: A Prophet for the 21st Century*, op. cit., 24.

42. M. Ward, *Gilbert Keith Chesterton*, op. cit., 52.

43. Ibid., 264.

44. M. Ward, *Return to Chesterton*, op. cit., 115.

45. M. Ward, *Gilbert Keith Chesterton*, op. cit., 43–45.

46. G.K. Chesterton, Letter to E.C Bentley (ibid., 57).

47. D'Avigdor's school friends "would ask him often, 'Why do you go about with that awful fellow Chesterton?'" but "[t]here was no half-way house with G.K. I used to wonder why he was decent to me" (M. Ward, *Return to Chesterton*, op. cit., 14.

48. M. Ward, *Gilbert Keith Chesterton*, op. cit., 477.

49. G.K. Chesterton, *Autobiography*, op. cit., 63. "God grant to us the old Armada weather, / The winds that rip, the heavens that stoop and lour— / Not till the Sea and England sink together, / shall they be masters! Let them boast that hour!" (R. Vernède, *England to the Sea, War poems and other verses* [1917]); see Chapter Five.

talent for these elaborate strategic maps of nonsense, or the suggestion of such preposterous plots." On hearing a solemn old master crack his first and only jest, Bentley surmised that he had intrigued with the High Master of Peterhouse, Cambridge to obtain a Fellowship for a St Paul's master, so that he could joke about it being a case of "robbing Paul to pay Peter."[50]

The JDC's June 1894 collaborative literary project *Our Future Prospects*[51] was more serious. Featuring members under their own names, it predicted (accurately) that Hubert Sams would be knighted;[52] Vernède is described as "the rising poet and littérateur";[53] and Digby d'Avigdor is "an officer in the Carbiniers."[54] Lawrence Solomon makes more than one appearance[55] and Maurice Solomon a disappearance, cast away on a desert island and never rescued. A "small dark lad, with curly black hair and large grey eyes," Maurice is a "rising mathematician [who] never protruded (*sic*) his specialty in conversation, being able and pleased to talk of other things." Asked by Lawrence for his wish, Bentley replies: "I wish Maurice was here." Chesterton, "speaking for the first time," responds: "Wherever he is . . . he will think of us, as we of him. We have found friends very true to us so far and we need not doubt."[56] In Chesterton's earliest novel *Basil Howe*, Vernède appears as a "mild dark young gentleman" called Valentine Amiens,[57] a "slim . . . languid young man, with a youthful oval face and a quaint setting of his dark eyes that gave him that half-Chinese look that some French lads exhibit." Despite this he is "in many respects as English by habits and opinions as any Englishman that despised everything he didn't know," and Valentine and his sisters are described as "sweet-tempered and pure-minded people."[58]

In *Basil Howe* the Jewish characters articulate familiar Chestertonian themes: "Valentine" discourses on the modern treatment—or mistreatment—of women: "The Alruna wives of our teutonic ancestors and the mothers in Israel of Semitic moralism were alike in this that they were great through goodness: and the combination of the two produced the Queen of Love and Beauty of mediaeval chivalry."[59] The late Middle Ages, he agrees, was "an agreeable time," defending the idea with explicitly Christian terms interlaced with Old Testa-

50. G.K. Chesterton, *Autobiography*, op. cit., 59–60.

51. Chesterton "acted as a clearing house by making good copies, adding illustrations and then passing on the narrative" (D.J. Conlon, introduction to *Basil Howe*, op. cit., 13).

52. D.J. Conlon, "The Junior Debating Club" (ibid., 24–25).

53. G.K. Chesterton, "Our Future Prospects" (ibid., 26, 32, 33, 34).

54. Ibid., 35.

55. Ibid., 45, 50–51, 56, 57, 58.

56. Ibid., 51–55.

57. G.K. Chesterton, *Basil Howe: A Story of Young Love* (London: New City, 1893–4/2001), 123; 20.

58. Ibid., 125–126.

59. Ibid., 128.

ment imagery: "[T]he spiritual passions . . . gleamed in every knight's dreams as the burning blood of the Holy Grail." There were "bad men and good men" in that age, not "pessimists and optimists and altruists and individualists."[60] Valentine declares that "the worship of the weak" entered into mediaeval history, adding: "I need not tell you where I think that element came from . . . or remind you whose symbol, the symbol of sorrow, simplicity and sacrifice, the crusader wore on his shoulder"; moreover, "God forbid that I should think a man cannot be chivalrous today, or that romance lies in pennons and morions wherever there are men in Israel who have not bowed the knee to Baal."[61]

The romance of Medieval chivalry notwithstanding, JDC meetings became so boisterous that Hubert Sams received a "gentle rebuke" from "our one and only G.K.C.";[62] but despite the famous bun battles, he recalled that Chesterton's parents made them "very welcome" at his "own hospitable house in Warwick Gardens"; all remembered "the kindness of the gracious lady, his mother" whose death "fill[ed] us with sympathy for her distinguished son."[63] Sams looked forward to attending another JDC reunion with all the old members, with Chesterton in the "capacious" chair.[64] He describes E.C. Bentley's *Trent's Last Case* as the "best detective story" he had read,[65] and his memoir, which does not mention anti-Semitism, does not refer to its "raving crowd of Jews."[66]

But Dudley Barker claims: "In a few of even [his] early letters emerges the anti-Semitism with which Chesterton would later be charged and of which, in spite of his protests along lines that were to become catastrophically familiar, he cannot be acquitted." Barker says that while claiming "indignantly" that "some of his best friends were Jews," in one of his schoolboy letters to Bentley, Chesterton discusses the Solomon brothers:

> I may remark that the children of Israel have not gone unto Horeb, neither unto Sittim, but unto the land that is called Shropshire they went, and abode therein. And they came unto a city, even unto the city that is called Shrewsbury, and there they builded themselves an home, where they might abide. And their home was in the land that was called Castle Street and their home was the 25th tabernacle in that land.

Barker adds: "The letter was, of course, facetious. But the feeling was there," citing a second letter, "evidently arranging some Christmas party or gathering."

---

60. Ibid., 131–132.

61. Ibid., 135.

62. Herbert A. Sams, *Pauline and Old Pauline, 1884–1931* (Cambridge: privately published, 1933), 46.

63. Ibid., 48–49.

64. Mrs. Chesterton was present and Mrs. Vernède represented "our war hero R.E.V." (ibid., 58).

65. Ibid., 51.

66. See Chapter Three.

It begins: "No Jews; that is, if I except the elder tribe coming over on Sunday to take me to see Oldershaw . . . I tried an experiment with Lawrence on Friday night, to see if he would accept on its real ground of friendliness our semitic jocularity; so I took the bull by the horns and said that 'I would walk with him to the gates of the Ghetto.' As he laughed with apparent amusement and even M.S. [Maurice Solomon] betrayed a favouring smile, I don't think we need fear the misunderstanding which, I must say, would be imminent in the case of less sensible and well-feeling pagans."[67] Chesterton found a constant source of amusement in the juxtaposition of Old Testament drama and suburban English banality, but showed sensitivity to the feelings of his Jewish friends by not making jokes in front of them without "permission." The injunction against Jews, at variance with his other correspondence, while possibly explicable in the context of a specifically Christian celebration, suggests other influences at work, although he had not yet attended the University of Belloc. Clearly, the "elder tribe" had passed Chesterton's jocular "test," and since he continued to socialize with Jews and make new Jewish friends, such mild allusions did not appear to repel such friendships. Their approval was important to Chesterton, not so much in order to pretend to others that he was not anti-Semitic, but to prove it to himself. Their friendship gave him "permission" to joke about Jewish issues in his writing, although Jewish jokes can sound unfriendly when told by Gentile friends.

Chesterton's Gentile Friends

According to Ward, among Chesterton's mature, non-political, non-Jewish friendships, "quiet-voiced men stood high," including Max Beerbohm, Jack Phillimore, Monsignor Knox and Father O'Connor, Maurice Baring, as well as "his own father": all represented "a certain spaciousness and leisureliness which was what he asked of friendship."[68] Beerbohm was sensitive to causing offence with his caricatures, but disliked Kipling for his Imperialist stance and portrayed Lloyd George as shifty. He caricatured King Edward VII as consorting with wealthy Jews, and Baron Henri de Rothschild as "One of Fortune's Favourites." Although married to Jewish actress Florence Kahn, Beerbohm was not Jewish (as some speculated) but claimed he would like to have been.[69] Chesterton thought Beerbohm "a remarkably humble man . . . more modest and realistic about himself than about anything else," although "more sceptical about

67. G.K. Chesterton, Letter to E.C. Bentley, (undated), D. Barker, *GKC: A biography* (London: Constable, 1973), 36–37.

68. M. Ward, *Gilbert Keith Chesterton*, op. cit., 269.

69. K. Baker, "The Monstrous Max," *The Spectator*, October 25, 1997.

everything" than Chesterton. He did not, however, "indulge in the base idolatry of believing in himself," on which point Chesterton wished that he himself were "so good a Christian."[70] Their "instant liking grew into a warm friendship."[71] It was at Beerbohm's villa, on their return from Rome in 1930, that the Chestertons met the fascist Ezra Pound, who was "full of a financial scheme . . . to save the world." Pound told Chesterton's secretary Dorothy Collins that it had "the active support of Beerbohm," but "[o]n being told of this, Beerbohm commented: 'Am I? One has only to smile, look pleasant and avoid an argument, to be accused of supporting something one knows nothing about.'"[72]

One of his targets, Maurice Baring (1874–1945) was pleased by Beerbohm's caricatures; from the wealthy banking family, Baring's Francophilia was influenced by his French governess, and by Belloc, whom he encountered at Oxford.[73] He also fell in love with Russia and its people, and in 1904 resigned from the Foreign Office to become the *Morning Post*'s war correspondent in Manchuria, later their special correspondent in St Petersburg. His novels about the late Victorian governing elite were praised as minor masterpieces. Baring's, Belloc's, and Chesterton's "love of literature, love of Europe, a common view of the philosophy of history and of life," was reflected in Gunn's famous portrait. Frances Chesterton "often said that of all her husband's friends she thought there was none he loved better than Maurice Baring." In 1909, their correspondence touched on Baring's conversion to Catholicism, which had led to "*Space and freedom.*"[74] Chesterton sought Baring's advice regarding his own conversion[75] and was reassured by his lack of pressure, finding Baring and Father Ronald Knox, of all his friends, to be most helpful in this regard.[76]

But according to Donald Barr, "a group of [Catholic] converts" including Gilbert and Cecil, Baring and E.C. Bentley "all . . . apparently developed the habit of sneering at Jews."[77] Baring's friendship with Belloc, love of France and Russia, and work for the controversial *Morning Post* would seem to support this thesis; moreover, in *The Man Who Knew Too Much*, Chesterton placed his most savage fictional diatribes about Jewish financial and political manipulation on the lips of "Horne Fisher," said to be based on Baring.[78] Considering how Bar-

70. G.K. Chesterton, *Autobiography*, op. cit., 95–96.

71. M. Ward, *Gilbert Keith Chesterton*, op. cit., 153–154.

72. J. Sullivan, ed., *G.K. Chesterton: A Centenary Appraisal* (London, 1974), 163–164, in I. Ker, *G.K. Chesterton: A Biography* (Oxford: Oxford University Press, 2011), 608–609; see Chapter Three.

73. R. Las Vergnas, *Chesterton, Belloc, Baring* (London: Sheed & Ward, 1938), 90–93.

74. M. Ward, *Gilbert Keith Chesterton*, op. cit., 475–477.

75. Ibid., 451–452.

76. Ibid., 455–457.

77. Donald Barr, introduction to G.K. Chesterton, *G.K. Chesterton Collected Works Vol. VIII*, G. Marlin, ed. (San Francisco: Ignatius Press, 2000), 41.

78. M. Ward, *Gilbert Keith Chesterton*, op. cit., 440.

ing helped Chesterton visit Palestine,[79] Fisher's bitter condemnations of "Jewish wire pulling" seem particularly ironic: Maurice was the younger son of the first Lord Revelstoke, and the Baring family "like the Rothschilds" was "prominent in international finance." He himself recalled that its members made "careers in public affairs," and he "grew up in a world of great country houses, and town houses in London ... of opulence in the externals of life; of casual and habitual contact with royalty and its fringes." Their "rigid adherence to a code of manners ... seemed at times a conspiracy to maintain the visible structure of the upper class at the expense of individuals," both within and without.[80]

Rubinstein notes that Baring, although seen as an anti-Semite, reacted strongly to anti-Semitism in 1938, rebuking Enid Bagnold, author of *National Velvet*.[81] His association with the *Chesterbelloc* probably encouraged views of him as anti-Semitic, compounded by his love of pranks: as a young diplomat in France at the time of "Dreyfus," bemusement vied with amusement: "The infallibility of the Pope is a difficult doctrine for some people; but the infallibility of seven officers! Good gracious!"[82] Passionate pro-Dreyfusards prompted him, while dining with "an academician," to talk about "the Affaire Dreyfus," plunging him "once more into that luring whirlpool." He emerged "an uncompromising anti-Dreyfusard; which I have long suspected that I was."[83] The affair split France in two, leaving few aspects of French life untouched. As Anatole France noted of Sarah Bernhardt's play *L'Aiglon*: "Unfortunately it has been made a political question, and as the Anti-Dreyfusards have adopted it, the Dreyfusards feel obliged ... to say that it is worthless."[84] Baring retained the detached air of the amused Englishman for whom "Dreyfus" was far from a defining issue. Winston Churchill's secretary Edward Marsh recalled that his old friend Baring, a notorious joker, "could be provoking to foreigners," and "in a pause after a long discussion of the Dreyfus case with Anatole France, said

79. Maurice Baring had a contact on General Allenby's staff and "the general himself" said he would be "delighted to welcome the Chestertons in Jerusalem and afford them every facility" (M. Ffinch, *G.K. Chesterton* [London, 1986], 257–258, in I. Ker, *G.K. Chesterton: A Biography*, op. cit., 407–408); E.C. Bentley "almost certainly" suggested to the *Daily Telegraph* that Gilbert be commissioned to write a series of articles on the Holy Land, to be made into a book (ibid., 407–408); see Chapter Seven.

80. M. Baring, *Maurice Baring Restored: Selections from his Work*, P. Horgan, ed. (London: Wm. Heinemann Ltd., 1970), 1.

81. W.D. Rubinstein, *A History of the Jews in the English-Speaking World: Great Britain* (London: Macmillan Press Ltd., 1996), 302.

82. M. Baring, Letter to Mrs. Cornish, March 4, 1899, M. Baring, *Maurice Baring: a postscript (with some letters and verse)*, L. Lovat, ed. (London: Hollis & Carter, 1947), 36–37.

83. M. Baring, Letter to Mrs. Cornish, November 1, 1899 (ibid., 37–38).

84. M. Baring, Letter to Mrs. Cornish, March 23, 1900 (ibid., 42–43).

pensively: 'Si, après tout, Dreyfus était coupable.' For a moment Anatole France was quite nonplussed; and then he burst out laughing."[85] But Marsh maintained that "at the General Resurrection Maurice Baring, of all men now living, will be the most warmly greeted by the greatest number and variety of his fellow-creatures from every country and continent, and from every walk of life."[86]

Baring made the perfect confidante for Belloc, who peppered his letters with remarks about Jews; Baring did not.[87] His "genius" was for the "difficult art of friendship,"[88] and like Chesterton he never seemed to fall out with any of his eclectic groups of friends. He knew Belloc before Chesterton but was also good friends with Beerbohm, and the friend and biographer of Jewish actress Sarah Bernhardt.[89] Baring's writings do not reinforce views of him as an anti-Semite. In *Nero Interviewed* (1910), one in a series of parodies of great historical figures, the Roman Emperor defends his persecution of Christians and Jews in accents of injured righteousness.[90] *The Stoic's Daughter* (1911) mocks anti-Semitic paranoia: when the eponymous heroine converts to Christianity a character remarks: "She must have been got hold of by the Jews"; another responds: "They are terribly cunning; and people say they're everywhere, and yet one doesn't see them."[91]

In Baring's story, *The Pogrom* (1922), distraught Russian Jews beg a Countess for help: "*They* were coming from Kiev by train."[92] In another short story, according to Baring, based on fact, a child believed to be the Antichrist is sacrificed by peasants; a railway guard "bewailed [to him] the blindness of . . . the peasants of Russian villages, who, as he wisely said, had so much kindness in their hearts, but were often led through their ignorance to do dreadful deeds."[93] Belloc's biographer describes Baring, with his love of literature and music as "the most spontaneously international person" who "made nonsense of exclusiveness. Perhaps this was why politics were among the few things in which he took no interest."[94] The *Jewish Chronicle* responded positively to Baring, quoting his *Morning Post* report of a railway journey from Moscow to St Petersburg

85. E. Marsh, *A Number of People: A Book of Reminiscences* (London: Wm. Heinemann Ltd./ Hamish Hamilton Ltd., 1939), 71–72.

86. Ibid., 65.

87. M. Baring, *Maurice Baring: a postscript (with some letters and verse)*, op. cit., 50–56; see Chapter Six.

88. M. Baring, *Maurice Baring Restored: Selections from his Work*, op. cit., 10.

89. M. Baring, *Sarah Bernhardt* (London: Peter Davies Ltd., 1933).

90. M. Baring, *Maurice Baring Restored: Selections from his Work*, op. cit., 184.

91. M. Baring, *Diminutive Dramas* (1911), ibid., 208.

92. M. Baring, *The Puppet Show of Memory* (1922), ibid., 263.

93. Ibid., 253.

94. R. Speaight, *The Property Basket: Recollections of a Divided Life* (London: Collins & Harvill Press, 1970), 160.

in which a priest, a tradesman, and a peasant discuss the pernicious activities of a certain monk and priests who played "an abominable part" in the anti-Jewish pogroms—"worse than murderers," they "stirred up the peasants' blood, and they went to kill the Jews." According to the priest "the universal dominion of the Jews was at hand," because the Jews were "cunning," taking advantage of the Russians being "in a ditch," and saying to them: "Pull us out." The tradesman retorted that "we ought to put up a gold statue to the Jews for pulling us out of the ditch. Look at the time of the pogroms, the rich Russians ran away, but the richest Jews stayed behind."[95]

The *Jewish Chronicle* saw Baring's *Morning Post* "pogrom" report as of "immense importance," providing "a clear idea of the Jewish question and its possible solution."[96] His *Russian Essays and Stories*, the paper remarked, were "wonderful sketches," and *Pogrom* showed "far more than many a . . . reasoned essay . . . the inner springs of the anti-Jewish movement in Russia." In *Anti-Semitism in Russia* Baring had argued "forcibly" that "neither the pogrom movement nor anything else" in Russia in recent years had resulted from "one policy conceived by one master-mind and executed by well-trained and per-fectly organised instruments."[97] Baring suffered his final debilitating illness sto-ically, sustained by his quiet faith. His family's legacy to Jewish-Christian relations was a positive one.[98]

Edmund Clerihew Bentley (1875–1956) invented the eponymous "clerihew," reflecting the JDC style of humor: "Sir Christopher Wren/ Said, 'I am going to dine with some men, / If anybody calls, / Say I'm designing St. Paul's." Chester-ton, who also wrote clerihews, called Bentley his "first and in every sense origi-nal friend,"[99] and in their youthful correspondence, revealed to Bentley the depth of his depression.[100] In *Those Days* Bentley says that Chesterton had "the extraordinary power—of which he was and always remained quite uncon-scious—of inspiring affection and trust in all who had to do with him."[101] One of the peaceable Chesterton's "most keenly felt of pleasures," he recalled, was to

95. "Voces Populi in Russia," *Jewish Chronicle*, August 17, 1906, 34.

96. *Jewish Chronicle*, October 11, 1907, 12–13.

97. "[A]s Mr. Baring notes, anti-Semitism in Russia is, to a very considerable extent, artificial. It is most prevalent among those who have never met a Jew" ("A.M.H.," "Anti-Semitism in Russia," *Jewish Chronicle*, December 4, 1908, 24). His "delicate study" of Sarah Bernhardt was praised (ibid, November 24, 1933, 17).

98. Baring's cousin, Anne Cecilia Baring, a "staunch Catholic with a deep love of Israel and things Jewish and an honours degree in biblical studies" in 1978 was appointed Education officer of the Council of Christians and Jews (*Jewish Chronicle*, July 14, 1978, 19).

99. G.K. Chesterton, *Autobiography*, op. cit., p. 63.

100. M. Ward, *Gilbert Keith Chesterton*, op. cit., 49.

101. E.C. Bentley, *Those Days* (London: Constable & Co. Ltd., 1940), 45.

hold "vigorous and long-sustained arguments with anyone who would take up the cudgels." If no friend was available, there was always "one antagonist who was spoiling for a fight"—Cecil, whose death "was the end of extraordinary talents which had already begun to make their mark, and between whom and G.K.C. there existed the deepest of brotherly attachments."[102]

Bentley wrote for the Conservative *Daily Telegraph* for many years but also for *The Speaker*, having caught his Liberal politics from Chesterton. But as he recalled, even earlier he had, "like many children, a hatred of oppression ... objecting to others being bullied as much as I objected to being bullied myself."[103] The Tories, he believed, were anti-working class[104] but the "intellectual Liberals" could be unbearably nagging;[105] a "good many" English liberals "would attach themselves to one or another of the peoples who were struggling to be free." Some, like Shaw's Liberal in *John Bull's Other Island* were "devoted to the Irish: some would make a pet of this or that people oppressed or persecuted by the Turks." Their devotion was often "very real and self-sacrificing," and they insisted that their chosen underdogs "were people to be admired and loved as well as supported in their fight for liberty"—hopefully "they also felt, deeper down," that "a race of unendurable Yahoos had just as much right to its freedom as any other, if it had the qualities of a nation."[106] Written at the beginning of the Second World War *Those Days* recalls Bentley's "great friend Robert Vernède, one of us in the J.D.C., who died in the [Great] War," whose poetic talent was "unsuspected by most of his schoolfellows, and hardly believed by himself."[107] Bentley also mentions Harold Wiener, fervent Zionist and later a "leading spirit in the Jewish National Home in Palestine ... murdered by an Arab at the gates of Jerusalem."[108]

Bentley, one of the anti-Boer War *Speaker* crowd, who knew Belloc before Chesterton[109] also recalled with amusement two elderly South African Jewish millionaires, "each of whom had apparently been trying to swindle the other in a highly complicated business transaction." Each "suffered from a rather treacherous memory when business facts were in question," and "each happened, by a coincidence, to be liable to brief fits of deafness."[110] But in his *Preface* Bentley

102. Ibid., 48.
103. Ibid., 191.
104. Ibid., 192.
105. Ibid., 201.
106. Ibid., 171–172; see Chapter Two.
107. Ibid., 67.
108. Ibid., 129.
109. G.K. Chesterton, *Autobiography*, op. cit., 298.
110. E.C. Bentley, *Those Days*, op. cit., 134.

apologizes for not writing enough about "the dreadful and benighted hell of the Third Reich"; while initially not thinking "so ill of Hitler" and Nazi Germany, "[w]ho could have imagined the reality in its fullness?" In fact he has much to say on the subject: the "devils' carnival of slaughter, destruction, plunder and enslavement in Poland" was "not the usual non-combatants' gossip about 'atrocities'" but "simple witnessed fact."[111] He says that a "frenzied hatred of Jews" was taught in German classrooms by "unknown men" who had "taken the places of those professors who mysteriously disappeared at one time and another, or went mad, or committed suicide."[112] The majority of Germans, he believed, submitted out of fear to "a body of pseudo-scientific racial rubbish" that was "beneath the contempt of every disciplined mind," and carried on, or "countenance[ed], a racial persecution" that derived its "effectiveness from a love of cruelty for its own sake."[113] The work of "that profoundly interesting mental case Houston Stewart Chamberlain" had "a considerable share, we are told, of the responsibility for producing Adolf Hitler."[114]

Much earlier Bentley met the German Count Reventlow who "ranked highest among the fanatically Anglophobe journalists who were preparing the way for 1914." This "courteous and agreeable" "Bill Bailey" was able to "enlighten" Bentley about how "the Jews were gathering all the realities of power into their hands for the purposes of their vast international conspiracy against the Aryan race." Reventlow's book, *Der Gotha der Juden*, "set forth the family history of all the leading Jews and crypto-Jews in Europe," and included "a section showing that the Harmsworths were indubitably among the children of Israel." The Northcliffe family's genealogical tree was "too idiotic to seem worth trying to bear in mind."[115] Bentley's schoolboy theory about the elderly schoolmaster whose labyrinthine scheming enabled him to tell his one and only joke paled beside this febrile populist version of the "who benefits?" school of politics, in which a "crime"—the poverty of the many, the wealth of the few—the degeneration of society—war and peace—was traced back to a handful of "international" Jewish "wire-pullers." As seen in Chapter Three, *Trent's Last Case*, seen as endorsing myths of Jewish conspiracy theory, in fact mocked such beliefs by trailing an isolated "red herring," as did Chesterton and others.

Post-Holocaust, the JDC-style schoolboy humor may lack appeal but in the context of violent and irrational hatred against Jews it is likely that such satires

111. Ibid., viii–ix.
112. Ibid., xiii–xiv.
113. Ibid., 13–14.
114. Ibid., 170; see Chapters Five and Seven.
115. Ibid., 300–301.

on anti-Semitism were taken as intended. Chesterton believed that the English "had no religion left except their sense of humour,"[116] and if patriotism is the last refuge of the scoundrel, humor is the last refuge of the English patriot, in the sense that poking fun at foreigners and those seen as different, like Jews, was not the precursor of violence but a substitute for it, a way of defusing tense social situations, of lancing the swelling boil of aggression. In fact, humor could be a meeting point between English Jews and Gentiles, since Jewish humor was in many respects similar. Chesterton's changing view of Dreyfus could be seen as a response to English anti-French feeling, and his Francophilia has been blamed for his anti-Semitism,[117] but, while Baring joked about the Dreyfus case, Chesterton never did, and regarded the notorious Édouard Drumont as an anti-Semite.[118] Bentley's and Chesterton's fulsome praise of Jewish friends, condemnations of anti-Semitism, and ridicule of anti-Semites and Jewish conspiracy theories, could be seen as serving to assuage uneasy consciences, their jokes meant to deflect charges of anti-Semitism. Yet such an approach was not normally associated with anti-Semites, and it is clear that some Jews appreciated their work and reciprocated the admiration.

The Beaconsfield Friendships

The phrase "Some of my best friends are Jews," so often flourished in response to accusations of anti-Semitism and eventually dismissed by Jewish commentators, was more than a cliché.[119] Jews mixed with anti-Semites—and so did pro-Semites: Winston Churchill and Bernard Shaw were regular visitors to the Astors at Cliveden, although the "Cliveden Set" was suspected of pro-German sympathies; Nancy Astor socialized with Chaim Weizmann; Joseph Leftwich was friends with A.K. Chesterton. The fruitless search for the "authentic" pro-Semite simply highlights the fact that most Gentiles both praised and criticized Jews—and Jews returned the compliment: Israel Zangwill did not hesitate to

---

116. The English tendency was to use "humour somewhat defiantly as a smoke-screen," as with the "trench" humor of "Tommies" in the face of death, which Gilbert so much admired (M. Ward, *Gilbert Keith Chesterton*, op. cit., 397–398).

117. A review of *Autobiography* (1936) saw Gilbert emulating the French "yellow press" (Anon. [D.L. Murray], "G.K. Chesterton: Child and Man," *Times Literary Supplement*, November 7, 1936, 893–894, in J. Stapleton, *Christianity, Patriotism, and Nationhood: The England of G.K. Chesterton* (Lanham MD/Plymouth, England: Lexington Books, 2009), 200–201.

118. G.K. Chesterton, "The Tragedies of Marriage," G.K. Chesterton, *Brave New Family: G.K. Chesterton on Men & Women, Children, Sex, Divorce, Marriage & the Family*, A. de Silva, ed. (San Francisco: Ignatius Press, 1990), 226; see Chapter Seven.

119. George Watson, *Politics and Literature in Modern Britain* (London: The Macmillan Press Ltd., 1977), 64.

ridicule either Chesterton or his Zionist colleague Chaim Weizmann. Chesterton, however, never ridiculed his friends, Jewish or Gentile. He even dedicated *The Innocence of Father Brown* (1911), which included *The Queer Feet*, to Waldo D'Avigdor and his wife.[120] At Beaconsfield, the Chestertons asked a friend of the Solomon brothers, Mrs. Meredith, to be their secretary. She "demurred at first," telling Chesterton, "'I can't spell and only the Post Office can read my writing.' Gilbert said, 'You seem to be the very person for me.'"[121]

At Beaconsfield, where the Chestertons moved in 1909, they made many Jewish friends, but even earlier they became close friends with the Steinthals of Yorkshire, at whose home they met the inspiration for Father Brown, Father John O'Connor. The friendship ripened on many visits to the Steinthal home,[122] where the Chestertons socialized with many other assimilated Jews of German origin.[123] In his memoir O'Connor praised the couple:

> The master of the house came home from business, a man in ten thousand for charm and integrity, as we often proved in small things and in great. Francis Steinthal, Bradford born, of Frankfort ancestry and the Israel of God. I speak with strong persuasion, for once, at his table, when we were drifting into mischievous merriment at the expense of one of the neighbours, nothing spiteful, but of the horseplay order, he pulled us all up sharp with a 'Now, none of that'. We felt safe in his shadow ever after.[124]

Mrs. Steinthal helped the Chestertons with amateur theatricals,[125] and Chesterton wrote a poem, *The Queen of the Green Elves*, for Mr. Steinthal,[126] and for his fiftieth birthday, *Titania's Prophecy*.[127]

At Beaconsfield they befriended Jewish couple Frank and Margaret Halford, although Mrs. Halford had been put off by his reputation as an anti-Semite: "I wasn't really 'afraid' of my own welcome—but though I had for years been an enthralled admirer of G.K.'s, I'd have foregone the pleasure of a personal friendship, if his true attitude (which is exactly what you describe) had not

---

120. See Chapter Three.

121. M. Ward, *Return to Chesterton*, op. cit., 133.

122. M. Ward, *Gilbert Keith Chesterton*, op. cit., 252.

123. Presumably they were baptized Christians since the house was dedicated to "The Beloved Disciple" (Julia Smith, *The Elusive Father Brown: The Life of Mgr. John O'Connor* [Leominster, Herefordshire: Gracewing, 2010], 40).

124. Ibid., 31–32.

125. John O'Connor, *Father Brown on Chesterton* (London: Frederick Muller Ltd., 1937), 79. Chesterton mentions Mrs. Steinthal's theory of Greek sculpture depicting emotions like fear (G.K. Chesterton, Letter to Frances Blogg, postmarked October 26, 1899, M. Ward, *Return to Chesterton*, op. cit., 46–47).

126. D. Conlon, Letter, *Jewish Chronicle*, December 12, 1997, 25.

127. A. Mackey, Letter, *Jewish Chronicle*, December 19, 1997, 23.

become so manifest."[128] The couples exchanged gifts, and Mrs. Halford continued an admirer, retaining many relics of their association.[129]

The Poetry of Humbert Wolfe

The poet and civil servant Humbert Wolfe (1885–1940), perhaps the most interesting of Chesterton's Jewish friends, illustrates the experience of many Jews during the best and worst of times for English Jewry. Chesterton's fictional Jews and philosophy of the Jewish people echo certain aspects of his life. In 1925 Wolfe included Chesterton in a series of lampoons:

> Here lies Mr. Chesterton,
> who to heaven might have gone,
> but didn't, when he heard the news
> that the place was run by Jews.[130]

Ward comments: "I cannot help thinking that the ease with which the word 'Jew' can be used in rhymes was both a gift for those who wanted to attack him and a pitfall for Gilbert himself."[131] Wolfe records that he was of German Jewish and Italian Jewish parentage, born "Wolff,"[132] possessing the "natural honey-pallor of the Jewish child," the depth of his "velvet brown" eyes "accentuated by the nose already curvedly asserting its Eastern origin."[133] As "a small Jew-boy" he says that he dreamed of having "the abundant golden locks" of Little Lord Fauntleroy.[134] "Berto" grew into a handsome man with a curved nose although a caricature by his Jewish friend David Low depicts him with a hooked nose.[135] His comfortably-off family belonged to Bradford's German-Jewish wool-trade community, but Wolfe longed for acceptance by Gentile society; negative experiences of synagogue ("shul") and his family's weak attachment to religion led him to sneak into church. He attended grammar school, won an Oxford scholarship,[136] and was elected to the Athenaeum club,

128. M. Ward, *Return to Chesterton*, op. cit., 115–117.

129. Gilbert wrote from America to thank Mrs. Halford and other neighbors for their gifts (ibid., 116–120); he told a friend, Claire Nicholl, that Mrs. Halford was "'good: she shines'" (ibid., 258), and dedicated a Christmas play to the Halfords (*The Historic play of the fight between King and the Turkish Knight* [sic], 1920s, [Chesterton Collection, British Library]).

130. H. Wolfe, *Lampoons* (London: Ernest Benn Ltd., 1925), 57.

131. M. Ward, *Return to Chesterton*, op. cit., 115.

132. H. Wolfe, *Now a Stranger* (London: Cassell & Company Ltd., 1933), 3.

133. Ibid., 19.

134. Ibid., 25.

135. Philip Bagguley, *Harlequin in Whitehall: A Life of Humbert Wolfe* (London: Nyala Publishing, 1997), 335.

136. Ibid., 8–9.

his supporters including *The Thirty-Nine Steps* author John Buchan, and Max Beerbohm.[137]

Critics said Wolfe's memoir, *The Upward Anguish* (1938), was the product of a frustrated story-teller who had "novelized" his past, and although not completely unreliable, Wolfe's colorful and minutely detailed reminiscences suggest an element of truth in the charge;[138] in fact, his "budding journalistic career was abruptly terminated" after he embroidered his theater reviews with "pen-pictures of people in the audience," prompting a reader to praise his "psychic powers," since two of them "been dead for some time."[139] J. B. Priestley said Wolfe's recollections of anti-Semitism were influenced by his reaction to Nazism, although Nazism possibly revived and sharpened memories that might otherwise have been discarded.[140] Wolfe said the peerage was "stiff with enno-bled Israelites," including Lord Swaythling and the Marquis of Reading (Rufus Isaacs), both criticized by Chesterton, but he attacked English anti-Semitism with characteristic humor:

> It is the common belief that there is no anti-Semitism in the British Isles. The French may banish a Dreyfus to Devil's Island on the ground that, if he is not a traitor, he is at any rate a Jew, a practically synonymous term; the Germans may advertise seaside resorts as "Judenrein"; the Hungarians may observe "It's a fine day, let's go out and kill something . . . a rabbit or a Jew"; the Rou-manians may quietly beat the Israelites on the head, urging, with force, that whatever else they are, they are not Roumanians. . . . But, as all the world knows, it is different in England. The immortal Dizzy—who almost made the Conservative Party think, was a Prime Minister and a Jew.

Wolfe recalled running the gauntlet of small boys on his weekly visit to the humble Bradford synagogue,[141] and a farmer pursuing their family with the taunt: "Oo killed Christ?"[142] The grown-up Wolfe noticed a more subtle anti-Semitism: the social exclusion of Jews, mild in comparison to the Continent where "to be one of a beleaguered garrison in a world of declared enemies may be a gallant adventure"—but with a fatal outcome: "This form of almost auto-matic anti-Semitism is the most destructive of spiritual integrity"; it was impossible, he said, to "argue with a community who do not like raw ham nor dispute with an inborn distaste for Jews. The fact that the easy-going and good-humoured English couldn't be bothered to carry the thing to extremes, made it

---

137. Ibid., 281.

138. Ibid., 11; see: H. Wolfe, *The Upward Anguish* (London: Cassell & Company Ltd., 1938).

139. P. Bagguley, *Harlequin in Whitehall: A Life of Humbert Wolfe*, op. cit., 115–116.

140. Ibid., p. 21.

141. H. Wolfe, *Now a Stranger* (ibid., 116–118).

142. Ibid., 105.

all the more difficult." In contrast, to be "feared for their cunning with money, hated for their usury, and detested for their religion's sake"—celebrating that religion "in the teeth of possible and often horrible death"—did not, at least, "inspire a faint and prevailing sense of shame."[143] Was it "surprising that, instead of standing on their Jewry as upon a point of honour, some, if not many, were ashamed of it?" Some Zionists made this claim, and Wolfe, who was "bitterly ashamed of it," converted to Christianity. He claimed that Jewish women "contrived . . . to develop an English complexion. They could not alter the shape of their noses, but that proudly curved organ looked out from their pink and white faces like a hawk balanced on a rose-bush."

Chesterton joked about flamboyant Jewish sartorial tastes, and in response Wolfe joked that Jewish women "consented to abandon their natural good taste in dress, and to wear the drab and clumsy apparel habitual among their Christian neighbours." They also "educated their children in the English virtues—reticence, sportsmanship and inattention to thought. In spite of all this, or perhaps a little because of all this, they remained outside."[144] Wolfe had a beloved German Jewish nurse[145] but, as Chesterton noted, during the Great War a German name became a liability: "new English names flowered on Jewish stems to the extent that a revenant could recognize nothing but the noses."[146]

Berto internalized the "supreme fault": that of "'being born a Jew.' Suffer the little Jewish children to come unto Him, and His followers will promptly stone them!"[147] *Now a Stranger* (1933) expresses his estrangement from his youthful self but also his estrangement from general responses to Nazi anti-Jewish persecution; he converted to Christianity on his marriage but his feeling of difference persisted all his life. Fascinated with the pantomime,[148] the enigmatic Wolfe wrote an "epitaph" for himself:

> Now it is time to sleep.
> I only ask
> to be allowed to keep
> unpierced the mask,
> behind whose close
> and changing covers
> I hid myself from foes
> and lovers.[149]

143. Ibid., 125.
144. Ibid., 126–127.
145. Ibid., 26.
146. Ibid., 129.
147. Ibid., 131.
148. P. Bagguley, *Harlequin in Whitehall: A Life of Humbert Wolfe*, op. cit., 2.
149. H. Wolfe, *Epitaph* (ibid., 380).

Some aspects of Wolfe's recollections are reflected in Chesterton's Jewish portrayals, alleged to be stereotypes, including the red hair of his mother; a friend's lisp;[150] the "deep and guttural voice" of a neighbor;[151] the "guttural voice" and "thin German accent" of their rabbi, who lived "next door to the . . . prosperous pawnbroker of the community."[152] Berto would become acutely aware of his community's "foreignness," and its suspicion of "higher learning,"[153] which he embodied as an assimilated, second-generation Jew; but also that his roots were in "trade," rated as lower in the English class system. Many in the community, including his own family, changed their names.[154] The Great War saw anti-Germanism, anti-Semitism, and "column-dodging" accusations.[155] Spy mania reached such a pitch that Wolfe's sick mother was thrown out of a boarding house on the South Coast, recalling Chesterton's tale of spy mania and anti-Semitism on the South coast, *A Tall Story*.[156]

Although not a regular church-goer, like Chesterton he was intensely spiritual and religious themes haunted his poetry—in fact, Wolfe was criticized for it.[157] Fascinated by the Jewishness of Jesus, he did not shy away from the Crucifixion ("the first Jew, the only Jew, that was by Jews betrayed")[158] but (as in *Exodus*) without rejecting his Jewish roots.[159] Unafraid of proclaiming his origins and of alluding to anti-Jewish prejudice and persecution, he was equally sensitive to the sufferings of others. In a poem addressed to Rudyard Kipling, "the politician of force, the first of the Nazis,"[160] he asks:

> [W]ho shall save the driven beast
> when the waters disappear
> and the sun smokes in the East?
> Darkness and shame and a dead negro slave,
> whose withered fingers, as he crumbles, scorch,
> but out of the shame, the darkness, and the grave
> (witness oh crucified!) the torch.[161]

---

150. H. Wolfe, *Now a Stranger*, op. cit., 105–106; see Chapter Three.

151. Ibid., 45.

152. Ibid., 122–123.

153. P. Baguley, *Harlequin in Whitehall: A Life of Humbert Wolfe*, op. cit., 93.

154. Ibid., 132; his friends the Rothenstein brothers later became "Rutherston" (ibid., p. 85).

155. Ibid., 137.

156. Ibid., 139; see Chapter Three.

157. Ibid., 145.

158. H. Wolfe, *A Chant (To be intoned on the Day of Judgment)*, *Out of Great Tribulation—New Poems* (London: Victor Gollancz Ltd., 1939), 18.

159. Ibid., 60.

160. H. Wolfe, *The Upward Anguish*, op. cit., 116–117.

161. H. Wolfe, *The Negro Slave, Out of Great Tribulation—New Poems*, op. cit., 19.

Criticized for his conventional style, and stung by Siegfried Sassoon's satire—his own weapon but wielded less kindly—sales suffered as the "new poetry," "neo-brutalism," rejected romance, patriotism, and rhetorical flourishes.[162] In the culture war between social progressive and conservative, Wolfe, like Chesterton, was not "for Bloomsbury," although his own private life was not entirely blameless.[163] Never part of the "Metropolitan literary clique" he refused to stoop to personal abuse; like Chesterton he appealed to the ordinary reader but as his popularity rose his critical standing fell.[164] Beginning with his extraordinary *Christ at Oberammergau*, from 1933 onwards Wolfe emphasized the Nazi threat to Jews, to peace, and to Western Christian values.[165] With Chesterton and Kolnai he saw Nazism as the age-old conflict between Paganism and Christianity; only the power of Christ could reach out to mankind—unlike Nazism, which was a religion of "race."[166]

Wolfe felt strongly about anti-Semitism, but like a true Englishman, responded with humor. As in his lampoon of Chesterton he satirized "Jewishness" as well as anti-Semitism: "To pummel a Jew, who, by reason of his historical position, has always one hand tied behind his back, even if the other is in your pocket, is a queer way of exhibiting your strength."[167] *Lampoons* also contained an "epitaph" for Belloc:

> Here lies Hilaire Belloc, who
> Preferred the devil to a Jew.
> Now he has his chance to choose
> Between the devil and the Jews.[168]

Wolfe does not include Belloc with "The Poets," but regarding Chesterton:

> Through him, who loved the meanest thing,
> with wonder touched the least,
> this blade of grass becomes a king,
> and all the dust a priest.[169]

While dissenting from Chesterton's and Belloc's opinions on Jews Wolfe felt that "an ounce of clean hatred" was "worth a ton of impertinent indulgence"; therefore he "rejoice[d] in such stuff" as Chesterton's "Two straight lines / Can't

---

162. P. Bagguley, *Harlequin in Whitehall: A Life of Humbert Wolfe*, op. cit., 308–309.

163. Wolfe had a long-term relationship with Pamela Frankau; his marriage eventually foundered (ibid., 305).

164. Ibid., 312–313.

165. "[P]robably" originating in a German holiday in 1930, it involved "Christ Himself coming to play the part and being crucified" (ibid., 334).

166. Ibid., 343–344.

167. H. Wolfe, *Lampoons*, op. cit., vii.

168. Ibid., 69.

169. Ibid., 97.

enclose a space, / But they can enclose a corner / to support the Chosen Race."[170] Similarly, he preferred Belloc's savage satire on "Jewish finance" and the Boer War: "We also know the sacred height / Upon Tugela side, / Where those three hundred fought with Beit, / and fair young Wernher died":

> The little empty homes forlorn,
> The ruined synagogues that mourn,
> In Frankfort and Berlin;
> We knew them when the peace was torn—
> We of a nobler lineage born—
> And now by all the gods of scorn
> We mean to rub them in.[171]

Wolfe was undoubtedly influenced by his admiration for Chesterton's poetry. In *Notes on English Verse Satire* (1929) he claimed Chesterton was "unrivalled in our age, or, had he but written more, in any age save by Dryden himself." Chesterton was "paradoxical, because he dislike[d] rich men for being poor, poor men for being rich, sin for being virtuous, and virtue for being sinful"; but that meant that Chesterton disliked, and "had the searching genius to detect, not only conscious but unconscious hypocrisy, which is the more deadly because the more difficult to recognize." While not adverting to his own criticism Wolfe remarked: "It is objected against [Chesterton] as against Mr. Belloc that he has directed an undue share of his hatred to the address of the Jews"; but in Chesterton's case, the "anger" was "not racial nor even primarily religious" being "excited by that aspect of commercial Judaism which is a symbol of the universal disease in the soul of the huckster." There was "enough of the schoolboy in every abundant genius to betray him into scrawling transitory abuse on the blackboard," as Chesterton had done. But "even his anti-Semitism" was largely "a denunciation not of an ignorant mob that chose Barabbas nearly 2000 years ago, but of a whole world that continues to make that choice daily." Wolfe quoted Chesterton's savage satire *The English Graves*:

> Their dead are marked on English stone, their loves on English trees,
> How little is the prize they win, how mean a coin for these—
> How small a shrivelled laurel-leaf lies crumpled here and curled:
> They died to save their country and they only saved the world.[172]

---

170. Ibid., vi; G. K. Chesterton, *Songs of Education: V. The Higher Mathematics, Form 339125, Sub-Section M,* 1920, G. K. Chesterton, *The Works of G. K. Chesterton,* (op. cit., 78–79); "corner" refers to "cornering" markets.

171. H. Wolfe, *Lampoons,* op. cit., vi–vii; H. Belloc, *Verses to a Lord who, in the House of Lords, said that those who opposed the South African adventure confused soldiers with money-grubbers* (*Verses,* 1910).

172. H. Wolfe, *Notes on English Verse Satire* (London: The Hogarth Press, 1929), 146–150; G. K. Chesterton, *The English Graves,* G. K. Chesterton, *The Works of G. K. Chesterton,* op. cit., 60.

What ameliorated the offence in Wolfe's eyes was that Chesterton's "anti-Semitism" was not religious or racial but political; he saw it as a sign of "unmeasured love"—"the other side of his hatred." Belloc should have been "the greater of the two," and it was "difficult to say" why he was not. Perhaps Belloc knew "far more of contemporary life than the most innocent soul that ever wrote a detective story," and it was "precisely that knowledge which constitutes Mr. Belloc's weakness." But if Belloc did not "reach the height of unbridled genius" he could "hold his own with all but the greatest."[173] Complaints about Belloc's "excessive preoccupation with Jews" were, Wolfe acknowledged, "perhaps better justified" than in Chesterton's case; Belloc's "hatred" often had "the appearance of malice." But in the case of *Tugela Side*, "when the Jews symbolize something rotten as, for example, the Boer War, he rides clean over the personal into the abiding. . . . Mr. Chesterton and Mr. Belloc point the way to a new Augustan age of satire."[174]

Wolfe's nuanced view of Chesterton—and to a lesser extent Belloc—was influenced by certain shared attitudes, among them, ironically, patriotism: on Wells, he wrote: "After having given birth/ to a new heaven and a new earth, / thinking out new sorts of Hells, / here lies Mr. H.G. Wells."[175] While in Bellocian vein: "Bloomsbury and Maynard Keynes / Confident that art and brains / end with them (and Maynard Keynes) / the school of Bloomsbury lies here, / greeting the unseen with a sneer."[176] A Conservative who considered entering Parliament, Wolfe did not share Chesterton's politics,[177] but satirized "The Atheist Orator"[178] and even "The City Financier."[179] As his biographer Philip Bagguley notes, Wolfe's *Lampoons* were mild, as though he were "afraid to strike . . . almost unwilling to wound; and lest his targets should be hurt by these far from caustic portraits, he closes the gallery with a set of admiring epitaphs."[180] These included one on Chesterton; much earlier he had written the harsher (and arguably superior) *Shylock Reasons with Mr. Chesterton*:

> Jew-baiting still! Two thousand years are run
> And still, it seems, good Master Chesterton,

173. H. Wolfe, *Notes on English Verse Satire*, op. cit., 150–151.

174. Ibid., 153.

175. H. Wolfe, *Lampoons*, op. cit., 23.

176. Ibid., 65.

177. P. Bagguley, *Harlequin in Whitehall: A Life of Humbert Wolfe*, op. cit., 77.

178. Ibid., 194.

179. H. Wolfe, *Thrushes* (Kensington Gardens, 1924), P. Bagguley, *Harlequin in Whitehall: A Life of Humbert Wolfe*, op. cit., 192.

180. Bagguley mentions the *Lampoons* criticism of Chesterton and Belloc but not Wolfe's friendship with Chesterton (P. Bagguley, *Harlequin in Whitehall: A Life of Humbert Wolfe*, op. cit., 215).

Nothing's abated of the old offence.
Changing its shape, it never changes tense.
Other things were, this only was and is,
And whether Judas murder with a kiss,
Or Shylock catch a Christian with a gin,
All all's the same—the first enormous sin
Traps Judas in the moneylender's mesh
And cuts from Jesus' side the pound of flesh…
That is the tale. But mark, the moon in heaven
Is hid with clouds. This little time was given
To peace and to remembering one another
Who might have been (God knows) brother with brother.
But since 'tis over and the peace is done
Shylock returns and with him Mr. Chesterton.[181]

Somewhere along the line there had been a change of heart, for Chesterton's "epitaph" reads:

When all was still, save for the evil pealing
of crooked chimes that on the midnight slurred
the raven musics of the Satyrs reeling
out of the pit, his cap and bells were heard.

Like a great wind, after a night of thunder
he rocked the sodden marshes of the soul,
and ripped the mists of cowardice asunder
with laughter vivid as an aureole.

He does not need to knock against the gate,
whose every action like a prayer ascended,
and beat upon the panels. Trumpets, wait
for a hushed instant! We loved him. It is ended.[182]

In the interval between the two poems Wolfe had met Chesterton: early in 1924, having received no reply to an earlier letter, Wolfe sent him some poetry and suggested a meeting.[183] A few years later, he sent more poetry: "[W]on't

---

181. H. Wolfe, *Shylock Reasons with Mr. Chesterton and other poems* (Oxford: Basil Blackwell, 1920), Canadian Libraries Internet Archive, accessed May 4, 2008, http://www.ia331337.us.archive. org/1/items/shylockreasonswi00wolfuoft/shylockreasonswi00wolfuoft.pdf.

182. H. Wolfe, *Out of Great Tribulation—New Poems*, op. cit., 199.

183. Wolfe, "quite certain" that Gilbert's "silence" was "due to some cause" that he "couldn't control," suggested meeting at the Chandos pub in Chandos Street, at the corner of St Martin's Lane (H. Wolfe, Letter to G. K. Chesterton, March 17, 1924 [Chesterton Collection, British Library, 73241]); a "cordial relationship" developed (H. Wolfe, Letter, November 2, 1928, J. Pearce, *Wisdom and Innocence: A Life of GKC* [London: Hodder & Stoughton, 1997], 448–449).

you let us have a meal together sometimes? I should so like it."[184] The following year he wrote: "I suppose that it's hopeless to try to lure you up to town for dinner?" He suggested the Cafe Royal: "I should so like to see you again."[185] Shortly after, for Chesterton's "private amusement; at least I hope it may amuse you," he sent *Rule Britannia*, more extreme than Chesterton's much earlier works:

> Frankau! Thank God thou'rt living at this hour.
> Business hath need of thee and thy sleek pen,
> which, dipped in equal parts of grease and flour,
> strikes for the right—at six per cent or ten.
> This world is too much with us. Thou hast power
> to pick it up and hand it back again,
> thou Hotspur of finance, thou Bank's Glendower,
> a country fit for English businessmen.
> Continue, Gilbert! As dost rightly say
> (lest we unhappily should not detect or
> give thee full credit) in thy modest way
> thou art Britain's Governing Director.
> Rule Britannia! While Frankau rules the waves
> Stockbrokers never shall be slaves.

Wolfe concluded by saying that "it would be more than charming" if he "could sometime have another glimpse" of Chesterton.[186] The following year brought more lunch engagements, and the correspondence continued, with Wolfe using the formal "Dear Mr. Chesterton."[187] Thanking Chesterton for the good opinion of his poetry and for a "charming letter," Wolfe enclosed a further poem, *The Great War*; he was "delighted" with Chesterton's views "particularly at this moment when Bloomsbury has turned en masse to assault me for it. But Bloomsbury sounds very far away and very gnat-like while your letter is as loud and cheerful as a bee."[188] Ward said Chesterton found it impossible to hate individuals—only groups, such as the rich, but that if he knew someone in that group, he would instantly make an exception of them.[189] This may suggest prejudice but, as Chapter Seven found, he did not respond to his relative A.K. Chesterton's invitation to an anti-Semitic collaboration. In contrast—despite being an indifferent correspondent—he did respond to Jews he had never met, including Wolfe.

184. H. Wolfe, Letter to G.K. Chesterton, January 16, 1927 (Chesterton Collection, British Library, 73241).

185. H. Wolfe, Letter to G.K. Chesterton, July 10, 1928 (ibid.).

186. H. Wolfe, Letter to G.K. Chesterton, November 2, 1928 (ibid.).

187. H. Wolfe, Letter to G.K. Chesterton, July 30, 1929; August 1, 1929 (ibid.).

188. H. Wolfe, Letter to G.K. Chesterton, 1929 (ibid.).

189. M. Ward, *Gilbert Keith Chesterton*, op. cit., 610.

Braybrooke notes that while other great men could dissemble, "one thing" was "characteristic of Chesterton"—he was "always . . . genuinely pleased to see you." He had a "wonderful laugh" and a laugh "cannot pretend. We can pretend to like; we can pretend to be pleased; we can pretend to listen; we can't pretend to laugh."[190] Whereas Shaw's approach was characterized by "satire and contempt" Chesterton proceeded "by originality and good nature, except on the question of divorce," which made him "very angry."[191]

The *Jewish Chronicle* praised *Shylock Reasons with Mr. Chesterton* but *Now a Stranger* was received with less favor. Regarding Wolfe's claim that violent anti-Semitism led to more pride in Jewishness: "I have no patience with Mr. Wolfe's plea. It implies a Jewish loyalty feeble and flabby, and incapable of real shame— the shame of capitulation to miserable prejudice and of betraying a heroic past."[192] Much later, under the pseudonym "Oistrous," Wolfe published *Truffle Eater—Pretty Stories and Funny Pictures* (1933), described by Bagguley as "probably the first English verse satire on Nazism." Featuring "Shock-Troop-Headed Adolf, Cruel Heines, Goebbels and the Matches (resulting in the Reichstag fire), The Inky Boys, the Boy who went out to Burn the Books, Little Cock-a-Snook," some pieces concentrated on Nazi anti-Semitism, but "the work as a whole ha[d] a more than narrowly Jewish focus"; its "significance" lay more "in its date and its mere existence."[193] Regarding Britain's official acceptance of Jewish "aliens," the civil servant Wolfe "put it bluntly: policy was 'not to vary the aliens administration in favour of or against refugees.'"[194]

Wolfe was aware that organized, racial Nazi anti-Semitism was even more dangerous than "ad hoc" Continental anti-Semitism, and that neither equated with the English covert sneer and social exclusion; but he also knew "he was inexplicably excluded from the ranks he aspired to."[195] He preferred open criticism that he could repel. Perhaps, when he met Chesterton, he was heartened to find that the "rabid anti-Semite" had an explicit philosophy on the "Jewish question" that could be debated, unlike those who, motivated solely by innate distaste, sneered at Jews behind their backs and excluded them from their "inner circle"; in contrast, Chesterton actually made him welcome.

190. P. Braybrooke, *Gilbert Keith Chesterton* (London: Chelsea Publishing Company, 1922), 66–67.

191. Ibid., 76.

192. "Mentor," "Another Human Document," *Jewish Chronicle*, March 17, 1933, 12–13.

193. "Peter and the Wolfe: a gadfly on Goering: Philip Bagguley recalls the author of a spirited lampoon on the Nazis," *Jewish Chronicle*, September 11, 1998, viii.

194. T. Kushner, "Alien nation," *Jewish Chronicle*, April 1, 2005, 28.

195. "Poetic and Prosaic Love," Margot Strickland, Review, *Jewish Chronicle*, July 11, 1997, 30.

Frances Chesterton

Chesterton met Frances Blogg, four years his senior, in 1896; they married in 1901.[196] What drew the chivalrous but impractical Chesterton to Frances was the need to protect and cherish her, although they ended up protecting and cherishing each other.[197] It was through Frances's work for the Parents' National Educational Union that Chesterton met their Jewish friends the Steinthals.[198] A devout Anglo-Catholic,[199] Frances's opinion was greatly valued by Chesterton, and one of her "proudest days" was hearing him preach at St Paul's, Covent Garden for the Christian Social Union.[200] Chesterton dedicated *The Ballad of the White Horse* (1911) to Frances: "Therefore I bring these rhymes to you/Who brought the cross to me";[201] Ward says that as "one of the good who mysteriously suffer" she gave him his "first respect for sacramental Christianity";[202] but as Chesterton revealed to Maurice Baring, her own beliefs made his conversion to Catholicism a delicate business: he owed it to Frances, to whom he owed "much" of his faith, the "decent chance" to defend her own: "If her side can convince me, they have a right to do so; if not, I shall go hot and strong to convince her." He was concerned that a too "Bellocian" approach would scare her,[203] but as Ward relates, when Father John O'Connor explained Chesterton's fears to his wife, Frances said she would be "infinitely relieved" by his conversion, adding: "You cannot imagine how it fidgets Gilbert to have anything on his mind"—the last three months had been "exceptionally trying"; she would be "only too glad to come with him, if God in His mercy would show the way clear," but he had "not made it clear enough to me to justify such a step."[204] In fact, as Ward notes, Frances had been aware of Chesterton's wishes

196. I. Ker, *G.K. Chesterton: A Biography*, op. cit., 43; Frances was born on June 28, 1870.

197. M. Ward, *Gilbert Keith Chesterton*, op. cit., 533.

198. J. Smith, *The Elusive Father Brown: The Life of Mgr. John O'Connor*, op. cit., p. 40.

199. Regarding the proposed Beaconsfield War memorial, Frances, "then an ardent Anglo-Catholic," caused local consternation by observing, "with an appearance of dreamy rapture, 'Oh, yes! How beautiful! A lamp continually burning before the Cross!'" (ibid., 248) The 1881 Census lists Frances as a pupil boarder at 10 Fitzroy Square, Middlesex.

200. "*Vox populi vox Dei*. A crammed church—he was very eloquent and restrained" (F. Chesterton, Diary entry, March 16th [1904–5], M. Ward, *Gilbert Keith Chesterton*, op. cit., 160); the series of sermons was published as *Preachers from the Pew*.

201. G.K. Chesterton, *The Works of G.K. Chesterton*, op. cit., 164.

202. M. Ward, *Gilbert Keith Chesterton*, op. cit., 460.

203. G.K. Chesterton, Letter to Maurice Baring, (undated), ibid., 456–457; Ward omitted Gilbert's remark that "a great friend" was "moving in that direction," and that Frances was "more likely to be moved . . . by an Anglican or ex-Anglican friend of exactly that type. Fond as we are of each other, I am just a little too Bellocian already . . . to effect the precise thing I mean" (The *Tablet*, December 26, 1953, in I. Ker, *G.K. Chesterton: A Biography*, op. cit., 428).

204. M. Ward, *Gilbert Keith Chesterton*, op. cit., 464.

during his brain illness, and was prepared to act on them should he once again be at risk of death,[205] but when at last he was received into the Church, she wept, and Chesterton believed that taking the step herself would be "much more of a wrench" because she had "been able to practise her religion in complete good faith"—something his "doubts" had prevented him from doing.[206] He feared that Frances was "just at the point where Rome acts both as the positive and the negative magnet; a touch would turn her either way; almost (against her will) to hatred." In due course Frances asked Chesterton to send for Father O'Connor, of whom she was "fond."[207] Despite an apparent preference for Jerusalem over Rome, as Ward notes,[208] eventually she followed in Chesterton's wake, but attributed her conversion to another source, as he much later recalled: "My wife, when asked who converted her to Catholicism, always answers, 'the Devil.'"[209]

Ward says that Frances "thought politics and nothing but politics was 'dull work'"; that "'an intriguer's life must be a pretty poor affair'";[210] she saw Chesterton's political journal as "too great a drain on his time and energy," and although she would not have tried to stop it, knowing how much it meant to him "she would have rejoiced" if he had "let it go."[211] While Frances was a loyal support to her husband during the Marconi court case, a friend said she "worried *dreadfully* over Cecil's libel action while G.K. would only joke over it."[212] Both detested intrusions into their privacy, with good cause,[213] and as Ward

205. Ibid., 385–387; Frances told Maisie Ward's mother Mrs. Wilfrid Ward: "I don't want the world at large to be able to say that he came to this decision when he was weak and unlike himself. He will ratify it no doubt when his complete manhood is restored." (F. A. Chesterton, Letter to Josephine Ward, March 21, 1915, I. Ker, *G. K. Chesterton: A Biography*, op. cit., 359); Gilbert first broached the matter to Father O'Connor in 1912, but O'Connor preferred "to strengthen what faith a man had rather than weaken it" (J. Smith, *The Elusive Father Brown: The Life of Mgr. John O'Connor*, op. cit., 114); alerted to Gilbert's serious situation by Mrs. Wilfrid Ward on December 30, 1914 he went to Beaconsfield to administer the Last Rites; Frances replied: "So that is what Gilbert meant by all the dark hints about being buried in Kensal Green [St. Mary's Catholic Cemetery] . . . I suppose he wanted to put it to me straightforwardly, but couldn't bring himself to the crisis" (J. O'Connor, *Father Brown on Chesterton* (London, 1937), 94–95 [ibid., 115–116]).

206. G. K. Chesterton, Letter to Fr Ronald Knox, (undated), M. Ward, *Gilbert Keith Chesterton*, op. cit., 462.

207. G. K. Chesterton, Letter to Fr Ronald Knox, (undated), ibid., 463–464.

208. On meeting the Chestertons in Rome after their Palestine visit Mrs. Wilfrid Ward remarked: "Frances did rather play off Jerusalem against Rome, didn't she?" (ibid., 444).

209. G. K. Chesterton, *Autobiography*, op. cit., 101.

210. F. Chesterton, Diary of Frances Chesterton, 287–288, I. Ker, *G. K. Chesterton: A Biography*, op. cit., 142.

211. M. Ward, *Gilbert Keith Chesterton*, op. cit., 448.

212. M. Ward, *Return to Chesterton*, op. cit., 135.

213. During one of Gilbert's illnesses Frances begged Father O'Connor: "Please keep this private or all the newspapers in both hemispheres will be ringing up" (ibid., 47).

reveals, she asked Chesterton "to keep her out of" his autobiography, and their taste for "keeping private life private made him call it 'this very Victorian narrative.'"[214] Frances suffered ill health, and her sister Gertrude (Rudyard Kipling's secretary) was killed in an accident in 1899. Their brother George Knollys committed suicide in 1906, having never recovered from the shock. Pearce remarks that this affected Frances so badly that despite Chesterton's disapproval she "sought solace in the cult of spiritualism";[215] but her family history may have concealed a deeper mystery that even she did not suspect, and her husband certainly did not: although he insisted that people recognized Jews as different because they were "foreigners"[216] he did not recognize the possibility of his own wife's Jewish descent.

Born Frances Alice Blogg, according to Ward she was the "daughter of a diamond merchant some time dead. The family was of French descent, the name de Blogue having been somewhat unfortunately anglicised into Blogg. They had fallen from considerable wealth into a degree of poverty that made it necessary for the three daughters to earn a living."[217] For centuries the English diamond trade has been exclusively associated with Jews, thus it is probable that Frances Chesterton, through her father, was ethnically Jewish; the secrecy, name-changing, migrations and endemic insecurity that Chesterton saw as characteristic of Jews, applied to his wife's family history.[218] It is likely that Frances herself knew no more of her background than the "official" family history: her grandfather had married in the Church of England; Frances was brought up an Anglo Catholic and went to an Anglo Catholic convent school;[219] as a sincere Christian she wrote religious poetry and also the words to the well-known Christmas carol *How Far is it to Bethlehem?*[220] What survives from Frances's youthful correspondence with her father George Blogg consists

---

214. M. Ward, *Gilbert Keith Chesterton*, op. cit., 85.

215. J. Pearce, *Wisdom and Innocence: A Life of GKC*, op. cit., 40; 103.

216. See Chapter Seven.

217. M. Ward, *Gilbert Keith Chesterton*, op. cit., 85.

218. The jeweller's shop "Blogg, Geo. & Co." was at 4 Albemarle Street, London W1 (D. Conlon, personal communication; Census and other records). Eighteenth century Dutch circumcision records show Jewish names "Blag," "Bloch," "Blok," and "Blokh" rendered in Dutch as "Blog" or "Blogg," accessed May 23, 2011, http//:www.dutchjewry.org.

219. She was "brought up" in an Anglo Catholic convent school "by accident" (G.K. Chesterton, *Autobiography*, op. cit., 153).

220. Music by Richard Donovan (Chesterton Collection, British Library, Add. 73461 ff. 3–6v); also known as *Children's Song of the Nativity*, it appeared in *The Oxford Book of Carols* (Oxford: Oxford University Press, 1928).

mostly of humorous and affectionate letters from "Puppy" to Frances.[221] George implied that he was well-connected in the City of London and at some point entered the Army; in 1878 he told her that his Regiment had been placed on active service "so I shall have to be quite a real soldier on duty," and that he had been to see Queen Victoria who seemed to him "just like any other lady. But I was very careful not to turn my back upon her but to walk out backwards and to be respectful and polite." At Windsor Castle, he said, he had met a friend, "one of the Governors of the Bank of England; I rather think that the Queen wanted to borrow a little ready money to send . . . to the fleet to pay her sailors and soldiers." There is no corroborative evidence for the Windsor Castle visit[222] but it seems that George Blogg joined the military, leaving his wife to look after the business, perhaps explaining its decline.[223]

As well as the likelihood of Jewish antecedents, Frances was descended from Prussians on her grandmother's side, thus her heritage might have been composed of the two groups of which her husband was most suspicious.[224] Both

---

221. "Poor Puppy can't come . . . he is so sorry as he should very much like to kiss his little girl and tell her how much he loves her. . . . Kiss your brother and sister for Papa. . . . Answer when spoken to, laugh when you're chid, slam the door after you, good little child. Paternal advice from your Aged Parent" (G. Blogg, Letter to Frances Blogg, August 24, 1876 [Chesterton Collection, British Library, 73454]); much later Frances wrote: "Darling father, I think it is very wicked of me not to have written to you before, but we have been having such times here" (F. Blogg, Letter to G. Blogg, August 16, 1887 [Chesterton Collection, British Library, Add. 73454]).

222. G. W. Blogg, Letter to Frances Blogg, April 29, 1878 (Chesterton Collection, British Library, Add. 73454). Queen Victoria's journal for 1878 makes no mention of a visit by Blogg or Lord Aldenham (Henry Hucks Gibbs, Bank of England Governor 1875–77; director 1853–1901), whom he mentions; according to the Court Circular the Queen spent most of April at Osborne House (D. Sulley, Archives Assistant, August 10, 2010, via email).

223. In one letter, written in French, he says Frances's mother Blanche is visiting him in Paris. Baptized at St Stephen Walbrook in the City of London on March 16, 1842, his father George Frederick is recorded as a diamond merchant of 28 Bucklersbury EC4; George W. is listed in the 1861 Census as a diamond merchant, head of household at 33 Peterborough Villas, SW6, with sister Julia, three boarders and servants; he married Blanche Keymer in August 1868, and in 1871 they lived at 20 Baker Street, Marylebone; on May 19, 1879 the Foreign Office issued George W. with a passport; in 1881 Blanche is listed as head of household (not widowed) at Oxford Villas, Kingston upon Thames, Surrey, and as "Jeweller," "Blogg, George & Co." at 4 Albemarle Street in the 1884 and 1886 telephone directories; George W. is listed in telephone directories until 1888, although he died on July 23, 1883 of a "sudden syncope, internal haemorrhage following rupture of an aneurysm. Natural," on "public footway opposite 72 Harley Street," a street noted for fashionable physicians (Census and other records).

224. George W. Blogg's father, George Frederic (later Frederick) Blogg, of uncertain origins, is listed as a diamond merchant at his business address in the City of London, an area noted for its Jewish community; he married Frances Catharine (later Catherine) Ebhart in 1839 at St Luke's church in fashionable Chelsea; as well as George W. they had three daughters, but in 1881 Catherine Blogg was living in Ramsgate, Kent, listed as head of household although not widowed. The Ebhart family was of Prussian military background (Census and other records).

father and daughter were fluent French speakers and in 1878 he wrote from Paris: "Je mis encore dans la plus belle ville de l'Europe."[225] Frances had other family connections that might have made her sensitive to anti-Semitism, for as Ward relates: "After Gilbert's death Frances . . . visited her cousins in Germany, a university professor and his English wife, who were undergoing the persecution of the Swastika. She was deeply moved by their suffering and the peril they stood in."[226] The English wife was Margaret Heaton, Frances's cousin on her mother's side; in 1896, Margaret was staying at the Blogg home, and (a further irony, considering another of Chesterton's aversions) became engaged to a German university professor, Fredrick Ferdinand Paul Arndt.[227] The couple married in London in 1899; he taught for a number of years at Frankfurt am Main University, specializing in economics and trade, and some of his scholarly publications reflected Chesterton's interests.[228] Chesterton wrote an introduction for one of Frau Arndt's many books on German fairy tales, and was godfather to one of their children.[229] One possible reason for the couple "undergoing the persecution of the Swastika" was Professor Arndt being one of the "hundreds and thousands of harmless little fiddlers and schoolmasters and actors and poor students" whom, Chesterton had protested, the Nazis aimed to "hound out" or "exterminate." Having even one Jewish grandparent would mean the loss of a university post, even for baptized Christians, but Professor Arndt, who

225. G. W. Blogg, (Hotel du Helder), Letter to Frances Blogg, June 7, 1878 (Chesterton Collection [British Library, Add. 73454]).

226. M. Ward, *Gilbert Keith Chesterton*, op. cit., 652–653; Gilbert's cousin Alice Chesterton, daughter of his Uncle Arthur, in 1895 was a governess in Berlin (G. K. Chesterton, Letter to E. C. Bentley [ibid., 56–57]).

227. G. K. Chesterton, *Autobiography*, op. cit., 152; Margaret Agnes Mary Heaton's grandmother was Margaret Keymer, Frances's maternal grandmother (Census and other records). Chesterton refers to "Margaret Agnes Mary Arndt who was/ Heaton, a cousin of my blood" (G. K. Chesterton, [*The wedding*], G. K. Chesterton, *G. K. Chesterton Collected Works Vol. X: Collected Poetry Part II*, op. cit., 259); however, on hearing of Frances's engagement, Margaret Heaton, "the cousin living with the Bloggses, begged to be allowed to call [Gilbert] brother-in-law, for Frances was almost a sister to her; and warned him in rather Bedford Park manner that 'Francesca needs a great deal of looking after. She is often very foolish and unkind—to herself! and overworks shockingly (and underfeeds)'" (D. Barker, *G. K. Chesterton: A Biography*, op. cit., 86).

228. Born in Luckenwalde (Brandenburg), September 25, 1870, Arndt obtained his doctorate in Bonn in 1897 and until 1900 was scientific assistant at Cologne's Chamber of Commerce; he specialized in trade and economics, notably the textile industry, home-working and workers' insurance (*Neue Deutsche Biographie* [Archivist, Johann Wolfgang Goethe University, Frankfurt am Main, personal communication]).

229. Dedicated to her daughters Margaret and Barbara and nephews Charles and Stephen Johnson (Frau M. Arndt, *Fairy Tales from the German Forests* [London: Everett's Library, 1913]); Chesterton dedicated his Introduction to Margaret Arndt's *Meadows of Play* to his God-daughter Barbara ("A Letter to a Child" [London, 1909], reproduced in G. K. Chesterton, *G.K.C. as M.C.*, J. P. de Fonseka, ed. [London: Methuen & Co. Ltd., 1929], 59–62).

retired from teaching at that point,[230] may have been one of Bentley's "professors who mysteriously disappeared . . . or went mad, or committed suicide," because they felt unable to comply with Nazism, to be replaced by "unknown men" who taught "frenzied hatred of Jews." Ward later records: "After a visit to Germany which was still further shadowed by the tragic sudden death of her cousin Frau Arndt," Frances wrote once more to Father O'Connor, telling him that "[t]he 'in memoriam' aspect of everything has me beat. I can't think of things like that. I dread going back more than words can say—but I'm pretty much of a coward though I hope a deceptive one."[231] Professor Arndt retired in 1935; Frau Arndt died in Frankfurt in 1937, and after her death Ada Chesterton said that Professor Arndt stayed with Frances "with his young daughter," recalling him as "a kindly, scholarly old gentleman, and a repository of what used to be called German culture, with its fairy lore and understanding of young people."[232] He returned to Germany and died of heart failure in Bad Homburg in 1942.[233] Frances's diary of their Palestine trip reflected her openness to everyone they met—Christian, Jewish, and Muslim—but records her suspicions of Germans.[234] Chesterton's very early condemnations of Nazi anti-Semitism were likely influenced by their German connections.

No correspondence in the Chesterton collection throws any further light on the tantalizing scraps provided by Ward and Ada Chesterton. The Chestertons visited Frances's German cousins but after Gilbert's death she probably destroyed their correspondence.[235] After Frances's death in 1938, Chesterton's secretary and legatee Dorothy Collins, with Ward's help, destroyed correspon-

---

230. *Neue Deutsche Biographie* (Archivist, Johann Wolfgang Goethe University, Frankfurt am Main, personal communication); see: M. H. Kater, "Refugee Historians in America," in Hartmut Lehmann, James J. Sheehan, eds., *An Interrupted Past: German-Speaking Refugee Historians in the United States After* 1933 (Cambridge: German Historical Institute/Cambridge University Press, 1991). The Nuremberg laws (1933) deemed as Jewish persons with three or four Jewish grandparents, and as *Mischling* ("crossbreed") those with one or two Jewish grandparents; all were deprived of citizenship. Some German Jews have borne the name Arndt.

231. M. Ward, *Return to Chesterton*, op. cit., 270.

232. Mrs. C. Chesterton, *The Chestertons* (London: Chapman & Hall Ltd., 1941), 307.

233. "Herzmuskelschwäche" (Fredrick Ferdinand Paul Arndt, death certificate; registered May 26, 1942 [State Archivist, Bad Homburg, personal communication]).

234. An orphanage, established by a "decent" German man, like many such facilities was nonetheless suspected of being set up by "the Germans" for ulterior motives (Frances Chesterton, Diary, British Library [D. Conlon, personal communication]); her enthusiasm for people of all races and religions was expressed in terms now regarded as racist, for example, at Alexandria's Grand Hotel it was "quite wonderful—Arabs—Egyptians, Jordanese, black niggers, all sorts of Europeans passing every morning" (Frances Chesterton, March 5th 1920, Diary of a Visit to Jerusalem 1920, BL Add. MS 73468, fos. 6–9, I. Ker, *G. K. Chesterton: A Biography*, op. cit., 407–408).

235. D. Conlon (personal communication). Quoting part of an early letter from Gilbert to Frances, Ward comments that it was "tragic indeed that the whole of this correspondence was not spared. Dorothy Collins begged Frances to let me at least read it, but she could not prevail"; it was

dence used in her Chesterton biography. Much earlier, Gilbert destroyed his brother's juvenilia, along with all his deceased father's family records.[236]

The family's love of privacy meant that Frances and Ward unwittingly contributed to Chesterton's anti-Semitic reputation, shrouding the target of one satirical rhyme in mystery:

> I am fond of Jews
> Jews are fond of money
> Never mind of whose
> I am fond of Jews
> Oh, but when they lose
> Damn it all, it's funny.

Ward adds: "The name at the head (which wild horses would not drag from me) is the key to this impromptu";[237] it continues to be the subject of speculation, with Godfrey Isaacs a likely candidate.[238] Chesterton's poetry followed a trajectory similar to that of his fiction and non-fiction on the "Jewish question" but, like Belloc, his reputation has led to anti-Semitic interpretations being placed on more innocent meanings, as with his *Song of Quoodle*:

> They haven't got no noses,
> They cannot even tell
> When door and darkness closes
> The park a Jew encloses,
> Where even the law of Moses
> Will let you steal a smell.

The poem appeared in *The Flying Inn* (1914) and during Chesterton's brain illness of 1914–15 Frances sent it to the publisher for inclusion in *Poems* (1915)

Gilbert's "very definite theory" about authors, expressed in *Robert Browning* (1903): "Our wisdom, whether expressed in public or in private, belongs to the world, but our folly belongs to those we love" (M. Ward, *Return to Chesterton*, op. cit., 46–47).

236. The Barker, Ffinch and Coren biographies "reveal the existence of letters and papers . . . no longer" in the British Library Chesterton collection (I. Ker, *G. K. Chesterton: A Biography*, op. cit., ix).

237. Gilbert's doctor asked him to write something to see if he could use a pen after breaking his arm: "After an instant's thought, Gilbert headed his paper with the name of a prominent Jew" (M. Ward, *Gilbert Keith Chesterton*, op. cit., 263–264); D. Conlon (personal communication).

238. "It is not difficult to deduce the name because Chesterton in his open letter to Rufus Isaacs . . . refers to the fact that Godfrey Isaacs had recently *lost* a law suit. Is it so very wicked of Chesterton to find that 'funny'?" (Anthony Cooney, *One Sword at Least: G. K. Chesterton 1874–1936* [London: Third Way Publications, 1998], 28–29); however, the Open Letter was written in 1918; Dr. and Mrs. Pocock became close friends with the Chestertons at Beaconsfield where they moved in 1909 (M. Ward, *Gilbert Keith Chesterton*, op. cit., 262–263); Ada Chesterton recalls Gilbert breaking his forearm "[a]fter they moved to Beaconsfield . . . and as the bones never re-knit properly he could not easily bend the joint" (Mrs. C. Chesterton, *The Chestertons*, op. cit., 256); Dennis Conlon suggests this happened early in 1912 (personal communication); see Chapter Six.

and *Wine, Water and Song*; Denis Conlon notes: "Either she or the publisher, influenced by the libel case against his brother resulting from the Marconi affair, changed lines to avoid any further prosecutions. In *The Song of Quoodle* 'Old Gluck' (Sir Isadore Gluckstein) was censored and replaced by 'The Jew,' thus making a valid comment on the exclusion of the public from parkland seem like an anti-semitic diatribe."[239] Anthony Cooney remarks: "The new meaning implies that Jews smell and a dog can smell them even when they are *enclosed* in a mansion, surrounded by a park. In the original version it is not the landlord who is 'enclosed,' it is he who *encloses*."[240] Quoodle was Chesterton's pet dog, and his love of dogs and fascination with their more acute sensory perception is expressed in the next verse:

> The brilliant smell of water,
> The brave smell of a stone,
> The smell of dew and thunder,
> The old bones buried under,
> Are things in which they blunder
> And err, if left alone. . . .

The poem's opening line, "They haven't got no noses, the fallen sons of Eve" is the key to the interpretation: Chesterton meant that dogs, not sharing Man's fallen state, can smell things that men cannot, including "old bones" in a piece of open countryside enclosed to make a private "park." It also suggests that while secular Jewish "plutocrats" could legally steal a piece of common land from the commoners—an old injustice "buried" in histories that emphasized how the Reformation brought "enlightenment" to England—the Jewish religion ("the law of Moses"), did not criminalize dogs that "steal a smell."[241]

The Religious Puzzle of Chesterton

Like many Jews, Humbert Wolfe found it difficult to comprehend how anyone who claimed to follow the Jewish Jesus could harbor anti-Semitism. Chesterton was raised in a Unitarian family, and argued that the Victorian home, rather than being "stiff with orthodox religion," was "almost the first irreligious home in all human history. Theirs was the first generation that ever asked its children

---

239. Denis J. Conlon, introduction to G.K. Chesterton, *G.K. Chesterton Collected Works Vol. X: Collected Poetry Part II*, op. cit., x.

240. Chesterton "wrote the name of a man who . . . *enclosed* the common land or 'Park' as it is called by country folk. An editor, fearful of libel suits, substituted . . . 'The Jew'" (A. Cooney, *One Sword at Least: G.K. Chesterton 1874–1936*, op. cit., 28–29).

241. G.K. Chesterton, *The Song of Quoodle*, G.K. Chesterton, *The Works of G.K. Chesterton*, op. cit., 150–151; included in *The Flying Inn* (1914) it was published in *Wine, Water and Song* (1915).

to worship the hearth without the altar."[242] The Unitarians also rejected the sacraments and Trinitarian doctrine, and at school he absorbed the English Protestant's identification with—almost appropriation of—the Old Testament. It was only later that he seemed to discover the Old Testament prophets berating the Jewish people for apostasy and "assimilating" with neighboring peoples; that Divine retribution encompassed the innocent as well as the guilty. Some Jewish critics accused the *Chesterbelloc* of planning a resurgent Catholic Church that would relegate Jews to Medieval status, and Adam Gopnik argues that his attraction to the Catholic Church influenced his approach to the "Jewish question."[243] Chesterton had many clerical friends who, it might be supposed, could have influenced his views on the "Jewish question."

Father, later Monsignor, John O'Connor was a close friend of the Chestertons; the prototype "Father Brown,"[244] he assisted in the entry of both into the Church, providing spiritual help to the end.[245] O'Connor reveals Belloc's ambivalence about Chesterton's conversion,[246] relating that just as O'Connor was due to attend Chesterton's reception into the Church, Belloc lured the priest up to London, later admitting that he wanted to keep O'Connor from Chesterton.[247] Some *Father Brown* stories have been criticized regarding anti-Semitism, but unlike the cynical Horne Fisher in *The Man Who Knew Too Much*, Father Brown, while articulating his creator's theories about Jews in Medieval times, is mild, peaceable, and "non-political." There are no references to Jewish issues in O'Connor's memoir, only praise for the Steinthals, with whom he was staying when Gilbert "conceived" Father Brown.[248] He also sums up Chesterton's "whole career" as fighting social workers and "pharisaic atheists" citing *A Ballade of Ephemeral Controversy*.[249]

Consonant with Braybrooke's recollection that Chesterton only expressed anger on issues like divorce, O'Connor maintained that what drew Chesterton

242. G. K. Chesterton, *Autobiography*, op. cit., 23.

243. Adam Gopnik argued that Chesterton "was attracted by the Church's 'authoritarian and poetic solutions' and therefore went for its allegedly endemic anti-Semitism too," but it was "a deeply racial, not merely religious, bigotry; it's not the Jews' cupidity or their class role—it's them" (A. Gopnik, *The New Yorker*, July 2008, quoted in W. Oddie, "The Philosemitism of G. K. Chesterton," in W. Oddie, ed., *The Holiness of G. K. Chesterton*, op. cit., 124); see Chapters Two and Five.

244. M. Ward, *Gilbert Keith Chesterton*, op. cit., 251–256.

245. Ibid., 455. A bundle of Frances's letters showed "how close Father O'Connor was," providing previously unknown details of Gilbert's "last days" (M. Ward, *Return to Chesterton*, op. cit., 269–270).

246. "It is very great news indeed!—and you were the Agent therein" (H. Belloc, Letter to J. O'Connor, August 12, 1922, quoted in J. O'Connor, *Father Brown on Chesterton*, op. cit., 141).

247. I. Ker, *G. K. Chesterton: A Biography*, op. cit., 472–473.

248. J. O'Connor, *Father Brown on Chesterton*, op. cit., 32–33; O'Connor first wrote to Gilbert on February 11, 1903 (J. Smith, *The Elusive Father Brown: The Life of Mgr. John O'Connor*, op. cit., 34); their first meeting was in December 1903 (ibid., 38).

249. J. O'Connor, *Father Brown on Chesterton*, op. cit., 157–158.

to the Catholic Church was its firm stance on moral issues like birth control, divorce and spiritualism, on which Protestant churches were in "utter bewilderment." Chesterton sought moral authority, asking: "Can I go in for cannibalism, or murder babies to reduce the population, or any similar scientific and progressive reform?" He believed that while there were men outside the Catholic Church who would also "denounce these heathen vices," there was no unity and no strong voice.[250] The Church, Chesterton insisted, was the only credible opponent of modern fads like eugenics, birth control, and divorce: "You might unite all High Churchmen on the High Church quarrel, but what authority is to unite them when the devil declares his next war on the world?" Since joining the Church, he had become "conscious of being in a much vaster arsenal, full of arms against countless other potential enemies."[251] The supposition that the "potential enemies" might include Jews was not confirmed by his friendship with Father Ronald Knox.

Monsignor Ronald Knox (1888–1957), who impressed Chesterton with his quiet voice,[252] delivered Chesterton's panegyric at Westminster Cathedral.[253] It was to Knox that Chesterton revealed anxieties regarding the effect of his conversion on Frances, and his inner battle with temptation, religious scruples, and depression: "I am concerned about what has become of a little boy whose father showed him a toy theatre, and a schoolboy whom nobody ever heard of, with his brooding on doubts and dirt and day-dreams of crude conscientiousness so inconsistent as to [be] near to hypocrisy; and all the morbid life of the lonely mind of a living person with whom I have lived"; it was "that story," which "so often came near to ending badly" that Chesterton wanted to "end well."[254] An Anglo-Catholic who converted in 1917, Knox was a brilliant classicist who also wrote detective fiction, drawing up the Detection Club "commandments" warning against Chinamen.[255]

Knox's fiction did, however, include the occasional fleeting stereotype: in *The Footsteps at the Lock* (1928) "Derek Burtell" applies for "financial help to strangers, less Gentile than genteel";[256] the debt-burdened Burtell's inheritance

---

250. Ibid., 140–141.

251. G.K. Chesterton, Letter to Maurice Baring, February 14, 1923, M. Ward, *Gilbert Keith Chesterton*, op. cit., 458–459.

252. Ibid., 269.

253. On June 27, 1936 (ibid., 193).

254. G.K. Chesterton, Letter, (undated), to R. Knox, E. Waugh, *The Life of the Right Reverend Ronald Knox* (London: Chapman & Hall, 1959), 207–208.

255. R.A. Knox, "A Detective Story Decalogue," introduction to *The Best Detective Stories of 1928* (London, 1929), in R.W. Winks, ed., *Detective Fiction: A Collection of Critical Essays* (Englewood Cliffs, NJ: Prentice-Hall, Inc., 1980), 200–202; see Chapter Three.

256. R. Knox, *The Footsteps at the Lock* (Bath: Lythway Press, 1928/1978), 11–12.

Chesterton's Best Friends 447

"all goes to the Jews";[257] but there is also a stereotypical American, Mr. Erasmus Quirk.[258] Knox knew Baring and Belloc, who "had no warmer admirer" than Knox;[259] they met at Oxford, and Baring's friendship "made a new strong bond between them" as it did between Knox and Chesterton.[260] The bond was not political, however: in later years Knox "became an unenthusiastic Conservative."[261] There is no sign of a "Jewish preoccupation" in Knox's non-fiction. In *Difficulties: Being a Correspondence about the Catholic Religion* (1932) Arnold Lunn raises the Dreyfus case as an obstacle to faith in the Church, although he too was received into the Church—by Knox—in 1933;[262] the Jewish Scriptures are discussed but without negative comment, and in Knox's challenge to opponents of religion, *Broadcast Minds* (1932), he pays tribute to "the Jews, a people, as their literature shows, penetrated with the idea of God's government in the national order."[263] His *Nazi and Nazarene* (1940) was written as a Macmillan War pamphlet.[264]

Father (Joseph) Vincent McNabb (1868–1943) was a much more "political" priest, seen by Ward as "the leading Distributist among the clergy ... I have heard him called a Socialist a hundred times." Born in Ireland, his interests were "back to the land," the family and the poor; in the *Witness* papers he denounced eugenics, supported the striking coalminers and campaigned for the "family wage." Like Chesterton he was influenced by St. Thomas Aquinas's philosophy and, like Belloc, *Rerum Novarum*. Firmly against industrialism and the use of machinery, he was popular with parishioners; to Belloc he was saintly, to others eccentric.[265] Ward thought McNabb ranked alongside Chesterton and Belloc "as a really great Distributist writer,"[266] possibly even "the

257. Ibid., 73.

258. Ibid., 122.

259. R. Speaight, *The Property Basket: Recollections of a Divided Life*, op. cit., 374.

260. E. Waugh, *The Life of the Right Reverend Ronald Knox*, op. cit., 197.

261. Ibid., 93.

262. A. Lunn, Letter to R. Knox, September 18, 1931, R. Knox, A. Lunn, *Difficulties: Being a Correspondence about the Catholic Religion* (London: Eyre & Spottiswoode, 1932/19520, 190; after the War Lunn said it was "the fashion among politicians to attribute all our modern evils to political causes," but "Jews were gassed by the hundred thousand" not because Hitler "repudiated democracy" but because he "substituted the worship of race for the worship of Christ"; Dachau was "the by-product not so much of dictatorship as of apostasy" (A. Lunn, Letter to R. Knox, December 22, 1949 [ibid., 252–255]).

263. R. A. Knox, *Broadcast Minds* (London: Sheed & Ward, 1932), 51.

264. R. A. Knox, *Nazi and Nazarene* (London: Macmillan, 1940).

265. M. Ward, *Gilbert Keith Chesterton*, op. cit., 514; M. Ward, *Return to Chesterton*, op. cit., 85; McNabb "maintained that he was not a Distributist—perhaps he meant simply that he was not formally a member of the League" (B. Sewell, *My Dear Time's Waste* [Whitefriars, Kent: St. Albert's Press, 1966], 47).

266. M. Ward, *Gilbert Keith Chesterton*, op. cit., 520.

Father of Distributism." McNabb lived out his commitment to the poor in personal poverty, and his unique contribution was in basing his articles and his social philosophy "closely on the gospels." Despite its subject matter "The Sins of Avarice" in *Nazareth or Social Chaos* (1933) makes no mention of "Jewish finance"; in "Are we living on Capital?" he writes: "The moral standards bequeathed to us by Jewry and Christendom were a precious form of moral Capital."[267] After Chesterton's death, Ward says he provided a much-needed peaceful influence on Distributist meetings.[268]

Father Ignatius Rice (1883–1955), a Benedictine monk at Douai Abbey, was a cricketer and a renowned headmaster of the Abbey School from 1915 to 1952, his influence on education compared to that of Thomas Arnold of Rugby. Rice, a military chaplain on the Western Front, was "another old and dear friend" of Chesterton's who attended his reception into the Church. Their friendship dated back to the beginning of the century, and Ward says that the "Benedictine, as well as the Dominican, outlook and history especially appealed to Gilbert."[269] As seen, Chesterton saw a successful Jewish homeland as economically unsuccessful, and Rice speculated that his "philosophy of failure" was actually a "perverse psychology of sanctity"; he was "never the least interested in the success of his own books," since "his whole being was concentrated on spiritual and supernatural things."[270]

Like Rice the Jesuit Father Cyril Martindale (1879–1963) was not a "political" priest; a convert to the Catholic Church, he was an influential and prolific writer and broadcaster, committed to presenting Christianity to the modern age.[271] Martindale, as seen, was involved in a war-time appeal for Polish Jews suffering under Nazism; according to his biographer Philip Caraman, in the 1930s, on his way to a Eucharistic congress in Manila, he travelled on a German ship; the "maniac Hitlerite captain . . . provoked only a grudging response from his crew when he shot out his arm in the Nazi salute."[272] A delegate to the General Congregation of Jesuits, he was in Rome during Hitler's 1938 visit when, as Caraman describes: "Pius XI left the city for Castelgandolfo, the Vatican museums closed, none of the fathers was permitted to go out, and the public

---

267. The book displayed the *Nihil Obstat* meaning that the Church had no objection (Vincent McNabb, *Nazareth or Social Chaos* [London: Burns, Oates & Washbourne Ltd., 1933], 31). The Chestertons "loved him dearly and their rare meetings were red letter days for both"; besides Distributism, "the two men were united in caring deeply" about St. Thomas Aquinas and his philosophy (M. Ward, *Gilbert Keith Chesterton*, op. cit., 545).

268. M. Ward, *Return to Chesterton*, op. cit., 232.

269. M. Ward, *Gilbert Keith Chesterton*, op. cit., 465; 545.

270. M. Ward, *Return to Chesterton*, op. cit., 232.

271. More than 80 books included *Does God Matter for Me?* (London: Rich & Cowan Ltd., 1937).

272. Philip Caraman, *C.C. Martindale: A Biography* (London: Longmans Green & Co. Ltd., 1967), 192; see Chapter Six.

applause was faked."[273] Visiting Denmark in 1940 he was trapped by the advancing Germans and for the duration of the War shared the Danish people's privations, the perils of civilian resistance and of treachery.[274] Martindale, Caraman says, made friends among both rich and poor; he particularly loved his time in South Africa, which, he told a friend, "would often disgust you"—its "subject and helpless race . . . treated alternately with revolting cruelty and with academic uplift."[275] In Denmark he made a will, requesting that Masses be said for his soul in all the places he had visited or served in, including a hospital, a prison, a ship, a barracks, and a mining village: "Also one in our most purely native mission in Southern Rhodesia, to which I attach special value—I mean to Mass there; I wish thus to identify myself with the whole of the Black race."[276]

Chesterton, Conversion, and the Jews

In *The New Jerusalem* Chesterton quotes an unnamed English priest "more Anti-Semitic" than he, saying that "The people that remembers has a right," but cites this "fine phrase" as his ultimate defense of Zionism.[277] The book was published before Chesterton's conversion and he never exploited the rise of Nazism to expand on the religious significance of his canton idea. If Chesterton's clergy friends influenced him on the "Jewish question," overall the influence was probably not a negative one.

In retrospect Chesterton saw his conversion influenced by deeply personal considerations, beginning in his period of youthful depression— his "period of madness"[278]—not, he added, that he was "mad, in any medical or physical sense," but "simply carrying the scepticism" of the age "as far as it would go."[279] He began to question reality itself, but out of "the darkest depths of the contemporary pessimism" he emerged into what people called his optimism—a "strong impulse to revolt; to dislodge this incubus or throw off this nightmare";[280] he even called himself an optimist, because he was "so horribly near

273. Pius XI "could still have his blue rages, as he did when Cardinal Innitzer welcomed the Anschluss with Germany in March 1938. The Austrian Jesuits immediately left Rome, and the Congregation was quickly wound up" (ibid., 193).

274. Ibid., 216; toward the end of the War "he had to be more careful in his conversation with friends who might repeat his remarks and get themselves, if not him also, into trouble"; spies were everywhere; the Nazis opened the prisons, there was looting and assassination, and constant shooting on the streets (ibid., 218).

275. Ibid., 185.

276. Ibid., 237.

277. See Chapter Seven.

278. G. K. Chesterton, *Autobiography*, op. cit., 79.

279. Ibid., 89.

280. Ibid., 91–92.

to being a pessimist." From this revolt came *The Man Who Was Thursday*[281] and *Manalive*; Chesterton was constructing a version of Thomism, a "rudimentary and makeshift mystical theory" that "mere existence, reduced to its most primary limits, was extraordinary enough to be exciting. Anything was magnificent as compared with nothing." To this he linked his "theory of thanks," for which he thanked his Puritan grandfather who said "he would thank God for his creation if he were a lost soul." Thus Chesterton "hung on to the remains of religion by one thin thread of thanks."[282] As Chapter five found, this theory influenced Chesterton's revision of the "Jewish question," for "the world owe[d] God to the Jews," who "carr[ied] the fate of the world in that wooden tabernacle."[283] This was the debt of gratitude the world owed the Jews.

Nonetheless, Jewish commentators feared that the *Chesterbelloc* approach betokened a resurgence of Christian anti-Semitism,[284] for which sin there had been no "adequate recognition ... by any corporate act of amendment or repentance."[285] Even while persecuting German Christians[286] the Nazis revived the medieval yellow star for Jews, and displayed Martin Luther's savage treatise *On the Jews and Their Lies* (1543) at their Nuremberg rallies.[287] Chesterton and Belloc received the title of Knight Commander of St Gregory with Star for "services ... rendered to the Church" by their writings.[288] On Chesterton's death a telegram from Pope Pius XI praised him as a "gifted defender of the Catholic Faith."[289] But in reiterating his view of the Jews as the Chosen People Chesterton avoided Christian "supercessionism," the belief that Christians were God's new "chosen people."[290] Unlike those who accepted the Old Testament as

---

281. Ibid., 99.

282. Ibid., 91–92.

283. G. K. Chesterton, *The Everlasting Man* (San Francisco: Ignatius Press, 1925/1993), 95.

284. See: A. Roy Eckhardt, *Elder and Younger Brothers: The Encounter of Jews and Christians* (New York: Schocken Books, 1967); R. Wistrich, *Anti-Semitism: the Longest Hatred* (London: Thames Methuen, 1991).a

285. J. Parkes, *Antisemitism* (London: Vallentine, Mitchell, 1963), 60.

286. See: J. S. Conway, *The Nazi Persecution of the Churches* 1933–1945 (Vancouver: Regent College Publishing, 1968/2001).

287. R. L. Rubenstein, J. K. Roth, *Approaches to Auschwitz: The Holocaust and its Legacy* (Atlanta: John Knox Press, 1987), 49; initially sympathetic to the Jewish people, Luther called for the burning of synagogues and the expulsion of Jews (ibid., p. 53).

288. M. Ward, *Gilbert Keith Chesterton*, op. cit., 633; copies of letters, G. K. Chesterton Library, in I. Ker, *G. K. Chesterton: A Biography*, op. cit., 691.

289. W. Oddie, ed., introduction to *The Holiness of G. K. Chesterton*, op. cit., 18.

290. For committing the ultimate sin of Deicide—killing the Messiah—"all Jewish favour with God was lost"; no longer chosen by God, the Jewish people's place would be taken by the Christians (R. L. Rubenstein, J. K. Roth, *Approaches to Auschwitz: The Holocaust and its Legacy*, op. cit., 48); J. Parkes, *Antisemitism*, op. cit., 57–73; however: "I say then, Hath God cast away his people? God forbid" (St Paul's Letter to the Romans 11:1, *The Holy Bible* [King James Version] [London: Collins,

the foundation of Christianity, minus the "bad" Jews,[291] Chesterton saw the origins of morality in the "history of the Jews,"[292] a "mysterious and mystical" people[293] who "would not degrade [the divine] by images."[294] Furthermore, his Zionism was based on the Biblical view of Palestine as the "Promised Land,"[295] reserved by God for the Jews when they were a wandering tribe. The enclave idea might recall St. Augustine's teaching that Jews should live unmolested, but "in a state of condemnation and misery," so as "to be powerless and a living witness to the wrath of God,"[296] but the power of self-defence and a Palestinian homeland went against this teaching, and that of the contemporary Church, which did not favor Palestinian Zionism for practical and theological reasons.[297]

As Parkes notes, Jews had been viewed as "children and emissaries of the devil, vowed to the destruction of Christendom";[298] but Chesterton never quite succumbed to Jewish conspiracy fears. Regarding the belief that "[t]he Jews were a deicide people wholly and eternally under a curse,"[299] he was careful to avoid blaming the Jewish people for the Crucifixion. In his religious opus *The Everlasting Man* (1925) he insisted that in the story of Good Friday "it is the best

1953]); the *Catechism of the Council of Trent* stated: "This guilt [regarding the death of Christ] seems more enormous in us than in the Jews, since according to the testimony of St. Paul: If they had known it, they would never have crucified the Lord of glory; (1 Corinthians 2:8) while we, on the contrary, professing to know Him, yet denying Him by our actions, seem in some sort to lay violent hands on Him" (1545).

291. J. Parkes, *Antisemitism*, op. cit., 63.

292. G.K. Chesterton, *Orthodoxy* (1908) *G.K. Chesterton Collected Works, Vol. I* (San Francisco: Ignatius Press, 1986), 271.

293. G.K. Chesterton, *The Everlasting Man*, op. cit., 86.

294. Ibid., 93.

295. G.K. Chesterton, *Autobiography*, op. cit., 318.

296. R.A. Everett, "The Land: Israel and the Middle East in Jewish-Christian Dialogue," in Michael Shermis, Arthur E. Zannoni, eds., *Introduction to Jewish-Christian Relations* (New York/Mahwah, NJ: Paulist Press, 1991), 96.

297. Sergio I. Minerbi, *The Vatican and Zionism: Conflict in the Holy Land 1895–1925* (New York/Oxford: Oxford University Press, 1990), 179; in 1917 Pope Benedict XV cordially welcomed the idea, a "friendship . . . as tactical as it was atypical: a British-sponsored Jewish enclave in Palestine at least would forestall a Russian Orthodox presence" (H.M. Sachar, *A History of Israel: From the Rise of Zionism to Our Time* [New York: Alfred A. Knopf, 2007], 101); in the 1990s the Vatican recognized the state of Israel: "Jews long suspected" that its long-standing "refusal" stemmed "at least in part" from Church teaching that the Jews had been exiled "as a punishment for not recognizing Jesus and would not return until they had done so"; however, in 1987 the Vatican stated that "the obstacles were purely political. Fear of reprisals by Arab countries," in which there were many Catholic interests, "played a major role" (G. Wigoder, "The Vatican recognizes the State of Israel; Israel-Vatican Agreement Signals an End to 'theological distortion' by Catholic Church," *Jewish Chronicle*, December 31, 1993), in H.P. Fry, ed., *Christian-Jewish Dialogue: A Reader* (Exeter: University of Exeter Press, 1996), 127.

298. J. Parkes, *Antisemitism*, op. cit., 67.

299. Ibid., 65.

things in the world that are at their worst. That is what really shows us the world at its worst. It was, for instance, the priests of a true monotheism and the soldiers of an international civilization."[300]

But Chesterton's other "bible" was the common sense of common people, based on an even deeper truth—*vox populi vox Dei*. The Bible showed that there were bad as well as good Jews: responding to accusations that he portrayed tyrants and traitors, he maintained: "Rehoboam was a tyrant; Jehosaphat was not. In what is perhaps the most celebrated collection of Jews in human history, the proportion of traitors was one in twelve." In the wake of the South Wales riots, his emphasis on "Rehoboams" and "Judas" looks very like anti-Semitism, although he describes the "violent Anti-Semite riots" as "[t]hings fierce and unfamiliar." His defense of the reviled Welsh strikers suggests another clash of underdogs. Furthermore, he did not address the "anti-Irish" viewpoint by discussing Irish "traitors,"[301] but defended the Irish independence campaign even though it cost English lives, viewing the Easter Rising of 1916 not as treachery but evidence of the Irish desire to be "martyrs."[302] Nonetheless, he praised the "Judas Maccabeus" tendencies of Jewish Zionists.

Christian anti-Semitism reached its nadir in the Middle Ages,[303] but Chesterton defended the Medieval Church; he saw popular legend as based in truth,[304] and believed that contemporary anti-Semitism was rooted in Medieval folk memories. Jews had been blamed for disasters like the Black Death, poisoning wells and kidnapping and murdering Christian children for their blood to make Matzos,[305] and Chesterton pointed out that the "Hebrew prophets were perpetually protesting against the Hebrew race relapsing into an idolatry that involved such a war upon children." Black magic, with its "mystical hatred of the idea of childhood," was an "abominable apostasy from the God of Israel," but since Biblical times, it was "probable" that it had "occasionally appeared in Israel" in "the form of what is called ritual murder." Such crimes were not, "of course," committed by the representatives of Jewish religion, "but by individual and irresponsible diabolists who did happen to be Jews." Chesterton also saw birth control and sterilization, as advocated by the modern eugenics campaign, as

300. G.K. Chesterton, *The Everlasting Man*, op. cit., 210.

301. G.K. Chesterton, "Taffy," *Illustrated London News*, September 16, 1911, in *The Uses of Diversity* (London: Methuen & Co. Ltd., 1920/1927), 156–158; see Chapter One.

302. G.K. Chesterton, *Irish Impressions* (1919), *G.K. Chesterton Collected Works, Vol. XX* (San Francisco: Ignatius Press 2001), 114.

303. J. Parkes, *Judaism and Christianity* (London: Victor Gollancz Ltd., 1948), 125; R.L. Rubenstein, J.K. Roth, *Approaches to Auschwitz: The Holocaust and its Legacy*, op. cit., 46–65.

304. See Chapter Two.

305. J. Parkes, *Antisemitism*, op. cit., 68.

"human sacrifice" and, as seen, the New Witness League saw eugenics as a Jewish plot. While defending the Jewish religion from the charge of child killing, he believed that "This sense that the forces of evil especially threaten childhood is found again in the enormous popularity of the Child Martyr of the Middle Ages." Chaucer merely gave "another version of a very national English legend, when he conceived the wickedest of all possible witches as the dark alien woman watching behind her high lattice and hearing, like the babble of a brook down the stony street, the singing of little St. Hugh."[306]

The murder of St. Hugh led to terrible anti-Jewish violence,[307] and as Frances Chesterton describes, when they visited Poland in 1927, in the Wilno Jewish ghetto they heard "the legend that the Jews killed a Christian child 'once a year to get to get the blood for mixing their cake'"; but they also visited a 2000-years-old Jewish sect, and the Wilno synagogue, "where a rabbi dressed in a yellow cloak or cope and a black and white velvet hat was taking the service, and where a blessing was asked for the visitors, who were mentioned by name."[308] Frances had endured an unsuccessful operation to remedy the "abiding tragedy" of childlessness,[309] but as Ker notes, "instead of becoming bitter and jealous of other more fortunate couples" they "lavished the affection they could not lavish on their own children on those of others."[310] This love fuelled Chesterton's defense of children and the family, but ultimately his belief in popular legend did not prevail against his admiration for Jewish family life, an admiration revived by Nazi anti-Semitism. Unlike Shaw and Wells, whose "positive Jew" faded under this challenge, Chesterton was challenged by the totality of biblical truth, and once again saw more clearly the virtues of "Jehosaphat."

Chesterton respected legends because they were "generally made" by the majority of villagers, who were "sane"; tradition meant "giving votes to the most obscure of all classes, our ancestors"—"the democracy of the dead."[311] Fairy tales, he believed, contained a deeper truth: "Jack the Giant Killer" held

---

306. G.K. Chesterton, *The Everlasting Man*, op. cit., 122–123.

307. Little St. Hugh of Lincoln's murder in 1255 was blamed on the Jews after a local Jew, under torture, admitted to ritual murder; a number of Jews were imprisoned in the Tower of London; 18 were hanged for refusing to beg mercy of a Christian jury, and King Henry III acquired their wealth; the rest were pardoned.

308. Based on Frances Chesterton's letters (BL Add. MS 73456, fos. 29–35), Dorothy Collins's Diary (BL Add. MS 43780) and letters to her mother Edith Collins (photocopies, G.K. Chesterton Library), in I. Ker, *G.K. Chesterton: A Biography*, op. cit., 574; M. Ward, *Gilbert Keith Chesterton*, op. cit., 575–576.

309. Ibid., 664; I. Ker, *G.K. Chesterton: A Biography*, op. cit., 286.

310. Ibid., 163.

311. G.K. Chesterton, "The Ethics of Elfland," *Orthodoxy* (1908), *G.K. Chesterton Collected Works, Vol. I*, op. cit., 251.

the "chivalrous lesson" that "giants should be killed because they are gigan-tic"—a "manly mutiny against pride." This "first and last lesson" in philosophy he learned from his nurse—"the solemn and star-appointed priestess . . . of democracy and tradition."[312] He was "impresse[d]" by the Catholic Church's "power of being decisive first and being proved right afterwards," for it was "exactly the quality a supernatural power would have."[313] But much earlier, Chesterton saw the Church's authority foreshadowed in his mother when her warnings were proved right: "[T]he whole world was to me a fairyland of won-derful fulfilments . . . like living in some Hebraic age, when prophecy after prophecy came true."[314]

Unlike "enemies of the Bible" who, he said, described it "as Jewish folk-lore; of course, in a bad sense,"[315] the Hebrew Bible reinforced Chesterton's "popular wisdom" worldview: "Morality did not begin by one man saying to another, 'I will not hit you if you do not hit me'; there is no trace of such a transaction. There *is* a trace of both men having said, 'We must not hit each other in the holy place.' They gained their morality by guarding their religion." Men did not "cultivate courage," but "fought for the shrine, and found they had become courageous"; they did not "cultivate cleanliness" but "purified themselves for the altar, and found that they were clean"; it was only after making "a holy day for God" that they found "they had made a holiday for men." The "history of the Jews" was "the only early document known to most Englishmen"; the facts could be "judged sufficiently from that."[316] In contrast, the Nazis attempted to remove all Hebraic and Old Testament associations from Christianity, leading him to comment: "I cannot . . . understand why the Nazi should particularly dislike the Old Testament, unless it is because it is full of Jews. So, for that mat-ter, is the New Testament."[317]

Chesterton was attracted to the Catholic Church by the need to reconcile faith and reason, a motive deeply personal as well as philosophical. Religion must be reasonable, he said, but reason was "itself a matter of faith";[318] as he

---

312. Ibid., 252–253.

313. G. K. Chesterton, Letter to Maurice Baring, February 14, 1923, M. Ward, *Gilbert Keith Ches-terton*, op. cit., 457–459.

314. G. K. Chesterton, "Authority and the Adventurer," *Orthodoxy* (1908), *G. K. Chesterton Col-lected Works, Vol. I*, op. cit., 360–361.

315. G. K. Chesterton, "The Great Translation," *Daily News*, March 25, 1911, G. K. Chesterton, *The Apostle and the Wild Ducks and other essays*, D. Collins, ed. (London: Paul Elek, 1975), 141.

316. G. K. Chesterton, "The Flag of the World," *Orthodoxy* (1908), *G. K. Chesterton Collected Works, Vol. I*, op. cit., 271.

317. G. K. Chesterton, "Race Religion of the Germans," *The Well and the Shallows* (London: Sheed & Ward, 1935), 27.

318. G. K. Chesterton, "The Suicide of Thought," *Orthodoxy* (1908) *G. K. Chesterton Collected Works, Vol. I*, op. cit., 236.

had found in countless internal arguments, reason alone could lead to madness. In his view, the "madman" was relentlessly logical and would "read a conspiratorial significance" in aimless activity because he saw "too much cause in everything," adding that anyone who had had "the misfortune to talk with people in the heart or on the edge of mental disorder" knew that "their most sinister quality" was a "horrible clarity of detail; a connecting of one thing with another in a map more elaborate than a maze."[319] His brother-in-law Knollys's committal to a lunatic asylum and subsequent suicide[320] provided first-hand knowledge of such problems, and may have influenced his reluctance to embrace conspiracy theories. He insisted: "Morbid and hysterical people . . . imagine all sorts of crimes and conspiracies that do not exist."[321]

For Chesterton, there was no need to reconcile politics and religion, because the "how" of social action sprang naturally from the "why" of the moral imperative. Initially attracted to socialism as a way of putting his Christian beliefs into practice, Chesterton's liberal instinct prevailed. Fearing that socialism would undermine free will, and deploring the absence of joy and humility, the negativity, hopelessness, and yet Utopianism of socialists,[322] by 1896, Ker says, Chesterton "rejected the idea that a Christian must be a Socialist."[323] Like Belloc, he was influenced by the Church's social and economic teaching, embodied in the Papal Encyclical *Rerum Novarum* (1891) which made no mention of Jews and offered a "third way" alternative to socialism and capitalism; initially, however, he took little notice of it,[324] as his politics came under the influence of Belloc's and Cecil's "politicized" Catholicism.

This was long before his conversion, something Chesterton attributed to his spiritual condition and the example of friends like Baring and Belloc—but, long before, Ireland was "dragging" him "in that divine direction." He recalled: "There mingled from the first with all the feelings of a normal patriotic Englishman a sort of supernatural fear of the sorrows of Ireland," and the "suspicion of what they might mean," producing at length the certainty "that the policy of Castlereagh and Carson was at bottom that of Nero and Diocletian." The Irish "were not faultless," but neither were the early Christians,

319. G.K. Chesterton, "The Maniac" (ibid., 221); G.K. Chesterton, "The Suicide of Thought" (ibid., 233–248).

320. I. Ker, *G.K. Chesterton: A Biography*, op. cit., 203–204.

321. G.K. Chesterton, "The Spirits," *The Uses of Diversity* (London: Methuen & Co. Ltd, 1920/1927), 14.

322. M. Ward, *Gilbert Keith Chesterton*, op. cit., 76–82.

323. I. Ker, *G.K. Chesterton: A Biography*, op. cit., 42.

324. G.K. Chesterton, *The Catholic Church and Conversion* (San Francisco: Ignatius Press, 1926/2006), 121–123; see Chapter Six.

and he "knew that we had buffeted Christ." His "political sympathy" with Ireland began long before he had "consciously and theoretically any religious sympathy," but the fact that he could "hold to this political idea while the other Liberals seemed to be abandoning all their Liberal ideas" prompted him to think "it was more than political"; for that reason, it "never changed."[325]

Via the "Irish question," his conversion was linked to England, and also, implicitly, the "Jewish question": England had "got into so wrong a state, with its plutocracy and neglected populace and materialistic and servile morality" that it had to "take a sharp turn," even "a sensational turn." And Christianity was "the religion of repentance," standing "against modern fatalism and pessimistic futurism mainly in saying that a man can go back."[326] But his *Autobiography* maintained: "Whenever people ask me, or indeed anybody else, 'Why did you join the church of Rome?' the first essential answer, if it is partly an elliptical answer, is, 'To get rid of my sins.' For there is no other religious system that does *really* profess to get rid of people's sins."[327]

Jewish commentators would say that one of these "sins" was anti-Semitism, but while criticizing the "Jewish plutocracy" Chesterton defended and even praised the Jewish religion, describing the Jews as "a little and lonely people," in which "paradox" lay their "mission and . . . meaning." It was "true in this sense, humanly speaking, that the world owes God to the Jews." Nonetheless, by strictly demarcating the secular and the religious he could avoid attacking Christianity at its roots, and he adds that the world owed this "truth to much that is blamed on the Jews, possibly to much that is blameable in the Jews."[328] This was because he believed that without limiting counter-pressures, virtues could become vices: loyalty to family—unless one was also loyal to that collection of families, the nation—could lead to nepotism.[329] In 1919 Chesterton told the Irish that nationalism was "nobler" than patriotism, which could be perilous because it was lawless: nationalism appealed to "a law of nations," implying that "a nation is a normal thing, and therefore one of a number of normal things"; he warned against sidelining Christianity and the dangerous patriotism of "race": "Celtism, by itself, might lead to all the racial extravagances

325. G. K. Chesterton, Letter to Maurice Healy, undated, M. Ward, *Return to Chesterton*, op. cit., 239.

326. G. K. Chesterton, Letter to Maurice Baring, February 14, 1923, M. Ward, *Gilbert Keith Chesterton*, op. cit., 458–459.

327. G. K. Chesterton, *Autobiography*, op. cit., 340; Ker infers that Chesterton had been to Anglo-Catholic confession (I. Ker, *G. K. Chesterton: A Biography*, op. cit., 546–548).

328. G. K. Chesterton, *The Everlasting Man*, op. cit., 95.

329. J. Stapleton, *Christianity, Patriotism, and Nationhood: The England of G. K. Chesterton*, op. cit., 215.

which have lately led more barbaric races a dance. . . . In that sense I confess I do not care about Celts; they are too like Teutons."[330] There was a danger even for the Jews as the Chosen People for if they did not submit to being chosen by God they would fall victim to pride, becoming "the thing to be worshipped."

But while arguing that Jews could not be truly English, he dismissed this idea as applied to Catholics.[331] The English saw Catholics as foreign and untrustworthy, like Jews, and the "dual allegiance" of Catholics to England and Rome could have provided a model for his idea of Zionism "absorbing" the loyalties of Diaspora Jewry. His family may not have harbored anti-Catholicism of the "Maria Monk" variety,[332] but his early poems reflect commonly held anti-Catholic hostility and an anti-Catholic view of history. This changed under Belloc's highly colored outsider's view of English history; for many years Chesterton defended the Church, but from the outside—Belloc was the only cradle Catholic in a group of converts that included the Chestertons, Maurice Baring, and E. C. Bentley[333]—and while Chesterton's defenses were welcome to Catholics, few wished to jettison good relations with the Jewish community. His post-conversion religious work *The Thing* (1929) mocked fears of secret Catholic conspiracies while making no mention of Jewish conspiracy and naming the Ku Klux Klan and Freemasons as open conspirators.[334] His conversion, described by Braybrooke as "both an intellectual surrender and a movement towards 'universalism,'"[335] coincided with a milder approach to the "Jewish question." Later, Chesterton would explicitly acknowledge the Jews as the Chosen People, and his ridicule of the Nazi "de-Judaizing" of Christianity echoes Cardinal Faulhaber's famous sermons of Advent 1933 condemning "an anti-Semitic demonstration at Hamburg" and the racial theory of Chamberlain's *The Foundations of the Nineteenth Century;*[336] his anti-Nazi attacks reflect Pope

---

330. G. K. Chesterton, *Irish Impressions* (1919), *G. K. Chesterton Collected Works, Vol. XX*, op. cit., 146.

331. G. K. Chesterton, *The Catholic Church and Conversion*, op. cit., 29.

332. Ibid., 16.

333. D. Barr, introduction to G. K. Chesterton, *G. K. Chesterton Collected Works Vol. VIII*, op. cit., 41.

334. G. K. Chesterton, "Who are the conspirators?" *The Thing* (London: Sheed & Ward, 1929), 140–141; see Chapter Three.

335. P. Braybrooke, *I Remember G. K. Chesterton* (Epsom, Surrey: Dorling & Co., 1938), 66.

336. "When racial research, in itself not a religious matter, makes war upon religion and attacks the foundations of Christianity; when antagonism to the Jews of the present day is extended to the sacred books of the Old Testament and Christianity is condemned because it has relations of origin with pre-Christian Judaism; when stones are cast at the Person of our Lord and Saviour . . . then the bishop cannot remain silent" (M. von Faulhaber, "Judaism, Christianity and Germany," December 3, 1933, in *Judaism, Christianity and Germany* [London: Burns Oates & Washbourne Ltd., 1934], 2–4).

Pius XI's remarks in December 1934 on "the folly of recent attempts to make Law and Justice depend on particular types of national or racial law."[337]

Chesterton agreed with Belloc that England "went wrong" at the Reformation, when the "rebellion of the rich" let loose "a new and wide philosophy" that still ruled society; most of the monks' "mystical virtues" had been "turned into great sins," and the "greatest of these" was charity.[338] Characteristically, loyalty was intrinsic to his decision to convert: one of his "strongest motives was mixed up with the idea of honour"; there was, he said, "something mean about not making complete confession and restitution after a historic error and slander."[339] Jews feared—unsurprisingly, after *The Jews* and *The New Jerusalem*—that the *Chesterbelloc* wished to return them to a Medieval status. Lauer argues that Chesterton wished to awaken the English to the "virtues of medieval culture" without seriously advocating a return to Medievalism.[340] Chesterton insisted in *The New Jerusalem* that "[m]en with medieval sympathies" were "sometimes accused, absurdly enough, of trying to prove that the medieval period was perfect," while "the whole case for it" was that it was "imperfect as an unripe fruit or a growing child is imperfect"; it was, however, "perhaps the one real age of progress in all history": men had "seldom moved with such rapidity and such unity from barbarism to civilisation as they did from the end of the Dark Ages to the times of the universities and the parliaments."[341]

What attracted Chesterton to the Catholic Church was not Christian "supercessionism"—the Church as the new "chosen people"—rather, for his own spiritual security, he needed both Christianity and Judaism to be right. The Church was founded on the Jewish religion—was founded by Jews—but Chesterton believed that its Medieval approach to the Jews had been proved right because Emancipation had highlighted the dangers of a secular "Jewishness,"

337. Philip Hughes, *Pope Pius the Eleventh* (London: Sheed & Ward, 1937), 299; on March 14, 1937 Pius XI wrote *Mit Brennender Sorge* warning against racial ideas; written in German, it was smuggled into Nazi Germany to be read in all Catholic Churches: "Whoever exalts race, or the people, or the State, or a particular form of State, or the depositories of power, or any other fundamental value of the human community . . . above their standard value and divinizes them to an idolatrous level, distorts and perverts an order of the world planned and created by God"; it was drafted by the future Pope Pius XII, whose choice of name indicated his desire to follow in his predecessor's footsteps (David G. Dalin, *The Myth of Hitler's Pope: How Pope Pius XII Rescued Jews from the Nazis* (Washington, DC: Regnery Publishing, 2005), 67; see Chapter Six.

338. G. K. Chesterton, *A Short History of England* (London: Chatto & Windus, 1917), 145.

339. G. K. Chesterton, Letter to Maurice Baring, February 14, 1923, M. Ward, *Gilbert Keith Chesterton*, op. cit., 458–459.

340. Q. Lauer, *G. K. Chesterton: Philosopher without Portfolio* (New York: Fordham University Press, 1988/1991), 139.

341. G. K. Chesterton, *The New Jerusalem* in *G. K. Chesterton Collected Works, Vol. XX* (San Francisco: Ignatius Press), 377–378.

therefore his conversion satisfied his conflicting loyalties to Christianity and Judaism—to Bellocian Catholicism on the one hand and to his Jewish friends and the Jewish religion on the other. In fact, Pope Leo XIII intervened in Captain Dreyfus's support before Chesterton met Belloc,[342] although neither Belloc nor the Church shared Chesterton's Zionism. But Cecil had been a Zionist and also a Catholic convert, thus Gilbert's conversion not only brought him closer to his beloved brother, but also to the Jews. As he himself remarked, the "universal Catholic Church" could "reconcile anybody"—the English and the Irish, and even Cecil and Godfrey Isaacs. And as he told Maurice Baring on his return from Palestine, regarding "certain things" that had been "touched on" between them, he had experienced a momentous spiritual "explosion" in Jerusalem, in the Church of the Ecce Homo.[343]

Chesterton's Religion: The Solution to the Puzzle?

Chesterton's "anti-Semitism" did not originate in his family, his early friendships, or his school. His mature non-Jewish friends, while paying fulsome tributes to Jewish friends, continued to share schoolboy humor about Jews, but none was driven by anti-Semitism. Chesterton's Jewish friendships were undoubtedly sincere, and Humbert Wolfe demonstrates that the admiration could be mutual. Such friendships undoubtedly influenced his approach; his wife Frances restrained him from repeating "Marconi"-type adventures, but also inadvertently contributed to his reputation for anti-Semitism. The perilous position of her German cousins likely influenced his prompt and earnest protests against the Nazis.

Chesterton's clergyman friends did not, apparently, influence him toward anti-Semitism, and his conversion to the Catholic Church coincided with a gentler approach to the "Jewish question" after an atypically bitter "middle period"; for a time the personal became political as Chesterton's defining characteristic, loyalty, came under pressure from two different "old sets": his Jewish friends, his wife, and his "non-political" friends, against his "political" friends and family, notably Belloc and Cecil's "ghost." For a time, too, his Zionism wavered as his "Protestant" soul warred with his need to believe that the Medieval Church was right. Thus religion did play a role in Chesterton's relationship with "the Jews" but, as could be expected from such a complex character, the connection was not a straightforward one. There is no sign that Chesterton was

---

342. "An unseasonably early Pesach? Here's what we were debating back in 1899," *Jewish Chronicle*, March 22, 2013, 4.

343. G. K. Chesterton, Letter to Maurice Baring (undated), M. Ward, *Gilbert Keith Chesterton*, op. cit., 446–447.

a "private" anti-Semite—in fact Humbert Wolfe found him quite the reverse. Personal encounters always had a marked influence on Chesterton, and more contact with Beaconsfield and less with Belloc, as both travelled more extensively, coincided with a mellower, more religiously influenced outlook on the "Jewish question."

9

Conclusion
Chesterton: Prophet or Anti-Semite?

*C*hesterton and the Jews has emphasized the influence of the Holocaust on views of G. K. Chesterton's relationship with the Jewish people not in order to excuse anti-Semitism, but to determine whether views of him as an anti-Semite are justified; and if not, whether at least some aspects of his philosophy deserve to be seen as of lasting value to mankind. The third and final aim of this study is to learn how to recognize and avoid anti-Semitism.

Chesterton's humorous approach meant that his views on the "Jewish question" were treated less seriously than Belloc's severity. But, as might be expected, even Chesterton's humor, which continues to attract, was more complex than would appear at first sight. In 1933 André Maurois commented: "Without his paradoxes, without his jokes . . . Chesterton might perhaps be a cleverer philosopher. But he would not be Chesterton. It has often been supposed that he is not serious, because he is funny; actually he is funny because he is serious. Confident in his truth, he can afford to joke."[1] William Oddie links Chesterton's humor to his humility, and thus to his "holiness," arguing that "[s]o seriously did Chesterton take comedy that he saw it in quasi-religious terms."[2] Chesterton used humor to defuse difficult situations, but after *The New Jerusalem*, his humor began to pall among Jews. As Johnson held, "Of all the griefs that harass the distressed, sure the most bitter is a scornful jest." Since the Holocaust Chesterton's "jests" have appeared scornful of Jewish suffering.

Chesterton's approach to the "Jewish question" was influenced by his reli-

---

1. A. Maurois, *Poet and Prophet* (London: Cassell, 1933), 141–174, quoted in G. K. Chesterton, *G. K. Chesterton Collected Works Vol. X: Collected Poetry Part II*, D. J. Conlon, ed. (San Francisco: Ignatius Press, 2008), xi–xii. Born Émile Salomon Wilhelm Herzog, André Maurois (1885–1967) was a French Jewish author and anti-Nazi.

2. "There is nothing to which a man must give himself with more faith and self-abandonment than to genuine laughter" (G. K. Chesterton, quoted in I. Ker, "Humour and Holiness in Chesterton," in W. Oddie, ed., introduction to *The Holiness of G. K. Chesterton* [Leominster, Herefordshire: Gracewing, 2010], 36).

gious belief, and the Nazis gleefully exploited historical Christian anti-Semit-ism to provide "religious" underpinning for the anti-Semitism leading to Hitler's "final solution"; as will be seen, it was not until much later that the Church formally repudiated such attitudes,[3] making it all the more urgent to explore Chesterton's true attitudes to the "Jewish question." As Michael B. McGarry notes, Christians and Jews especially need "a thoroughgoing under-standing" of the Holocaust,[4] and although Chesterton died before the War, it might be argued that his discourse on the "Jewish question" helped to feed the tributaries that led to that great roaring cataract of evil.

Chesterton drew strict lines of demarcation on the "Jewish question," explic-itly rejecting racism and insisting that he only criticized wealthy Jews and "Jew-ish finance." But while appealing to the commonsense view that some Jews do engage in finance, this approach can easily become tainted by prejudice: as Marconi showed, its proponents tend to look for evidence to support pre-exist-ing opinions rather than basing their opinions on the evidence. In this respect Chesterton's approach fell short of the rationality on which he prided himself, influenced by personal relationships that were themselves highly influenced by prejudice, although his personal relationships with Jews and the Bible itself challenged such prejudices. *Chesterton and the Jews* has scrutinized this approach on its own terms to avoid the danger of its being taken seriously in our own times, even on the plea of averting anti-Semitism.

This was the *Chesterbelloc*'s plea, and it was sincerely made; but it was proved wrong by the very "unthinking" anti-Semitism they condemned, which demanded a scapegoat in troubled times. A better way to avoid the dangers of anti-Semitism, as this work demonstrates, is to study it in historical context, and to deconstruct it in historical context—although not in the sense of "explaining" anti-Semitism as partly caused by the Jewish people, even while striving not to blame the victims. That the *Chesterbelloc* rejected "irrational" anti-Semitism acts as a further warning against the insidious nature of a preju-dice that demands perfection of Jews, alone among the peoples.

Despite such caveats, studying Chesterton in the context of his times shows that anti-Semitism was ubiquitous as well as insidious; that those who accused him of prejudice were not themselves free of it. Such comparisons also show that the "Jewish question" was not the driving force of Chesterton's life. His criticism of the "financial Jew" was the corollary of his defense of the poor, for

---

3. "The decisive Jewish sin . . . was the willful murder of the Messiah. For this deicide no retribu-tion could be too great" (R.L. Rubenstein, J.K. Roth, *Approaches to Auschwitz: The Holocaust and its Legacy* [Atlanta: John Knox Press, 1987], 48); see Chapter Eight.

4. Michael B. McGarry, "The Holocaust: Tragedy of Christian History," in M. Shermis, A.E. Zan-noni, eds., *Introduction to Jewish-Christian Relations* (New York/Mahwah, NJ, Paulist Press, 1991), 82.

whom he felt a genuine sympathy. Unlike Shaw and Wells he did not see the poor as a problem that needed to be diagnosed, solved or in the final analysis eradicated, but as citizens deprived of property and autonomy, who deserved justice. *Chesterton and the Jews* has greatly magnified a small fraction of his total literary output—staggering in its size and scope—the better to examine its significance for his beliefs on the "Jewish question." With characteristic nuance he avoided sweeping anti-Semitic references that he equated with "racism," and throughout his journey from "pro-Semitic" to "anti-Semitic" and back again, he peopled his fiction with diverse Jewish characters, countered common prejudices, and exploded "Jewish conspiracy" theories.

Nonetheless, among Jews, Chesterton never recovered from his reputation as an anti-Semite who wished to return them to a Medieval position of inferiority, and although the vast majority of anti-Semites rejected Zionism, so did many Jews, for vastly different reasons. Despite appearances, his Zionism was heavily influenced by his Jewish Zionist friends—even its negative aspects, including the idea of Jewish enclaves—but it also represented an intellectual compromise between his own fears for Jewish security and Belloc's fears about Jewish influence. As proposals they were as vague as Chesterton's language was precise, simply because he believed that any such decisions were not for him to make. Despite his reputation he had many Jewish friends, some life-long—as did Belloc—but in private, in contrast to Belloc, Chesterton appeared not to indulge in anti-Semitism, and it is highly likely that his best friend, his wife, was of Jewish descent.

Chesterton's patriotism, crucial to his philosophy of the "Jewish question," is the clue to the puzzle of his relationship with "the Jews," for it sprang from his defining characteristic: loyalty. If some of Chesterton's best friends were Jews, some of his other best friends held anti-Semitic views; these included Belloc, but also the poor, for whom he felt deep sympathy. This led to the agony of divided loyalties, and yet Chesterton's fundamental positivity, seen in his theory of thanks—itself closely linked to loyalty—was stronger than any acquired negativity: gratitude to his parents, his brother, his country, his culture and his religion—but also to the Jewish people, who gave God to the world and without whom Christianity would not have existed. In the battle for Chesterton's soul the positive prevailed, in particular the deep longing for reconciliation that motivated his attempts to "explain" the Jews to the poor, and the poor to the Jews, and later prompted his conversion.

A youthful pro-Semite, in his *Autobiography* Chesterton admitted the paradox that Cecil brought him closest to anti-Semitism in the Marconi affair, which also led him to recognize the loyalty of the Isaacs brothers to each other. Cecil's death was a terrific blow; grief transmuted into anger, leading him to assume Cecil's aggressive approach almost as a mark of respect. But Gilbert's conversion helped repair his broken relationship with the Jewish people as well as bridging the chasm of death, for Cecil had converted in the middle of the Marconi trial. After Gilbert's conversion his uncharacteristic abrasiveness on Jewish issues softened; like a piece of grit in an oyster it was gradually covered in layers of qualifications, explanations, excuses, until (in Gilbert's eyes at least) it resembled a pearl.

Although not an anti-Semite he did express beliefs influenced by anti-Semitism—a fine but important distinction; but his private relations with Jews, in contrast to his dealings with his fascist relative A.K. Chesterton, suggest that hatred did not constitute his driving force. Belloc also enjoyed Jewish company and restrained his public discourse on the "Jewish question" but was less restrained in private, revealing at the very least a marked preoccupation with "the Jews." Chesterton tried to be anti-Semitic; Belloc tried not to be anti-Semitic; both failed.

Once the too-flattering gloss and anachronistic graffiti is removed from the portrait of Chesterton and the Jews we see the full depth of the relationship as well as the complexity of its light and shade. We also see through layers of repainting how that relationship changed under the influence of people and events, with first one loyalty and then another coloring the picture and distorting the perspective; but underneath all these layers is the solid unchanging virtue of love. If "love" seems a paradoxical explanation of anti-Semitic expressions, the personally affable and conciliatory Chesterton's attacks were really defenses—according to Stratford Caldecott, his "spirituality of chivalry"; this "warfare" was conducted both in the "heart which is the centre of our soul" and in public in the sphere of politics and economics.[5] Chesterton's populism meant defending the poor, and his liberal love of the underdog meant defending the Jews from the poor; his Zionism especially was the result of trying to reconcile these conflicting sympathies. As he himself argued of the Jews, Chesterton's "vices" sprang from his "virtues."

Chesterton: Failed Prophet?

The fact that Chesterton did not exploit fascist anti-Semitism, or even Distributism, to further his "Medieval" approach to Jews; his swift and unequivocal response to Nazi anti-Semitism; most importantly, his insistence on reserving a place for Jews in his worldview, all militate against the suggestion that anti-Semitism was his primary influence. Just as the tide of English anti-Semitism seemed to be flowing with him, he began to swim against it. Anti-capitalists like Chesterton were accused of anti-Semitism for criticizing "Jewish finance," but

---

5. Stratford Caldecott, "Chesterton's spirituality of gratitude and praise," *The Chesterton Review*, XXXVIII (1 & 2) (Spring/Summer 2012), 90.

by the 1930s the Right was blaming Jews for Bolshevism, while fascists accused them of plotting world domination. No wonder he felt that he and Belloc were the only pro-Semites left. No one needed prophetic powers to predict a recurrence of anti-Semitism; in fact, Chesterton, like Wells warned of a recurrence if his advice was not heeded; but when it did recur, unlike Wells, Chesterton did not blame the Jews; unlike Shaw and Wells, he did not urge their disappearance as a people. While reiterating his theory of Jewish finance, he believed its power had declined. Even during his lifetime Chesterton's patriotism and religion were seen as behind the times, but the more modern Shaw and Wells failed to evolve in response to the times. Chesterton's belief in democracy and revealed religion over fashionable evolutionary theories, Utopias and the "superman," challenged him on the ever-present yet ever-changing "Jewish question"; that he met this challenge in the age of dictators makes him the best prophet of the three.

It could be argued, therefore, that Chesterton should be given credit for his "virtues" even though his "vices" appear to consign him to the past. His view on the evils of rampant capitalism, especially for the poor, might prompt renewed interest in his financial theory, but one of its pitfalls was emphasizing negative examples of Jews and Jewish activity, and following the 2008 "credit crunch," new Jewish conspiracy theorists blamed Jews and Israel for the economic turmoil.[6] It is possible that Chesterton's sincere and self-consciously rational approach might prompt some to regard him as prescient on "Jewish finance," and although the concept has been studied in the context of his time, and rejected in the same context, if any possibility remains that Chesterton's influence may yet lead to negative consequences, albeit unforeseen and unintended by him, his approach should, after all, be examined in the context of the post-Holocaust age.

At first sight, it would appear that thanks to multiculturalism, the overarching idea of twenty-first century Western society, anti-Semitism would not be allowed a recrudescence; that there would be no "repeat" of the Holocaust. Despite this, however, anti-Semitism flourishes anew, and while there is nothing new about the "oldest hatred," and many have no difficulty in diagnosing—or misdiagnosing—it in the past, it is more difficult to recognize in the present age since like a virus it is constantly changing, adapting itself to current concerns;[7] for if multicultural diversity appears to rule out Chesterton, it can also rule out Israel. Chesterton's Zionism placed him in a tiny minority, but after

6. For example, it was alleged that Lehman Brothers bank sent $400 billion to Israel before the bank crashed (*Jewish Chronicle*, October 10, 2008).

7. See: R. S. Wistrich, *Anti-Semitism: The Longest Hatred* (London: Thames Methuen, 1991).

the Holocaust many assumed he was at least right about that; now, some might argue that even if he was prescient regarding the "financial Jew," in his Zionism Chesterton was a failed prophet because the creation of the state of Israel has led to the "friction" he warned about. The *Chesterbelloc* argued that their criticism of "Jewish finance" did not make them anti-Semitic, and now critics of Israel argue the same. The *Chesterbelloc* rejected racism and attacked Nazism, but now, some claim that Israel is a racist, fascist state, heir to the mantle of Nazism.[8] But if Israel's critics argue that Chesterton should be seen as a failed prophet regarding Zionism, it could be argued with equal force that, despite the lessons of the Holocaust, present-day critics of Israel are succumbing to the age-old hatred that they too would reject.

Progressive Postmodernism and the "Israel Question"

Academics Stephen Walt and John Mearsheimer have claimed that an American "Israel lobby" wields disproportionate influence, to the detriment of US interests; that although not composed entirely of Jews—Jewish voters being less attached to Israel than Christian Zionists—this lobby has "inflamed Arab and Islamic opinion and jeopardised not only US security but that of much of the rest of the world." They accused the "Lobby" of intimidating the opposition and manipulating US Middle-Eastern policy to Israel's advantage, including the Iraq war, for which 9/11 served as a pretext; of pushing for action against Iran and Syria. They further alleged that the "Lobby" silenced critics with accusations of anti-Semitism, insisting that anti-Semitism was declining apart from among European Muslims, although it was provoked partly by Israel's treatment of the Palestinians; Israel was even the cause of terrorism, although the "Lobby" also injured Israel. Criticism of Israel, they insisted, was not "new anti-Semitism": Israel was not singled out, or held to higher standards; its right to exist was seldom challenged, merely its treatment of Palestinians on human rights grounds, on which issue, moreover, Israelis themselves agreed.[9] Rebutting their claims, Melanie Phillips[10] noted that terms such as "neo-conservatives" or "neo-cons," accused of directing foreign policy in Israel's favor and

8. "Certain quarters of the left" (J. Goldberg, *Liberal Fascism: The Secret History of the Left from Mussolini to the Politics of Meaning* [London: Penguin Books, 2009], 6); also Professor As'ad Abdul Rahman (Opinion page, *Gulf News*, accessed March 18, 2011, http://www.gulfnews.com/opinions/col umnists/israel-plunging-deeper-into-fascism-1.779065).

9. J. Mearsheimer, S. Walt, "The Israel Lobby," *London Review of Books*, 28 (6), (March 23, 2006), 3–12, accessed March 26, 2011, http://www.lrb.co.uk/v28/n06/john-mearsheimer/the-israel-lobby; they reiterated these views in *The Israel Lobby and U.S. Foreign Policy* (New York: Farrar, Straus & Giroux, 2007).

10. M. Phillips, "The graves of academe," accessed March 26, 2011, http://www.melaniephillips.com/diary/archives/001643.html.

substituting the threat of Islam for the defunct threat of communism, have "become code in Britain for Jews who have corrupted America."[11]

Simplistic media accounts of the Israel/Palestine situation, but also institutional media bias on Middle East issues,[12] have encouraged stereotypical views of Israel as "top-dog" and its supporters as powerful but secretive "wire pullers," but in fact, Jewish organizations openly lobby for Israel, while other Jewish organizations openly lobby for Palestinian rights.[13] Some Jews openly question the legitimacy of the State of Israel,[14] while Israeli academics criticize the Jewish roots of modern Israel;[15] one prominent Jewish commentator has even blamed a "Holocaust industry" for "the falsification and exploitation of the Nazi genocide" partly in order to "justify criminal policies of the Israeli state and US support for these policies."[16] Jewish critics maintain that they are motivated by their greater sensitivity to the problems of Israel,[17] and such criti-

11. M. Phillips, *Londonistan: How Britain is Creating a Terror State Within* (London: Gibson Square, 2006), 200. In addition "neo-con" has been applied to those supporting the Iraq war out of concerns about Saddam Hussein's oppression (Nick Cohen, *What's Left? How Liberals lost their Way* [London: Fourth Estate, 2007], 333–334).

12. The head of BBC TV news admitted: "There are problems with reporting what are considered to be aberrant views. Consensus can work to exclude certain ideas. It is not about being restricted by external forces, but I think that perhaps people can exclude certain ideas from debate because they do not feel comfortable including them and that they do sometimes limit themselves" (P. Horrocks, *Independent on Sunday*, January 8, 2006, in Anthony Browne, *The Retreat of Reason: Political correctness and the corruption of public debate in modern Britain* [London: Civitas, 2006], 96). Commissioned by the BBC into the fairness of its Israeli-Palestinian coverage, the Balen Report's release was barred by the House of Lords after a legal battle costing £227,300 of public money ("We are impartial on Israel, says BBC," *Jewish Chronicle*, May 27, 2011, 6).

13. For example, the American Israel Public Affairs Committee, established in 1951, and the UK-based Jews for Justice for Palestinians, founded in 2002, "a network of Jews who are . . . practising and secular, Zionist and not. We oppose Israeli policies that undermine the livelihoods, human, civil and political rights of the Palestinian people. We support the right of Israelis to live in freedom and security within Israel's 1967 borders. As well as organising to ensure that Jewish opinions critical of Israeli policy are heard in Britain, we extend support to Palestinians trapped in the spiral of violence and repression. We believe that such actions are important in countering antisemitism and the claim that opposition to Israel's destructive policies is itself antisemitic" (accessed October 14, 2014, http://jfjfp. com/?page_id=2).

14. A. Dershowitz, *The Case for Israel* (Hoboken, NJ: John Wiley & Sons, Inc., 2003), 217–221.

15. "Professor [Schlomo] Sand announces that the Jews who now live in Israel are in no sense the descendants of the Jews who dwelt in the kingdom of Judea 2,000 and more years ago" (G. Alderman, "We're not a 'people'? Outrageous: A new Israeli book arguing that there is no 'nation-race' of Jews will be pounced upon by anti-Zionists," review, S. Sand, *When and How Was the Jewish People Invented? Jewish Chronicle*, April 4, 2008, 33).

16. Norman G. Finkelstein, *The Holocaust Industry: Reflections on the Exploitation of Jewish Suffering* (London: Verso, 2001), 7–8.

17. Citing Rabbi Hillel on the Torah: "It is crucial that Jews speak out for Palestinians' human rights. The humanitarian values of Judaism have been corrupted by the Israeli state's human-right's abuses" (Jews for Justice for Palestinians, accessed March 27, 2011, http://www.jfjfp.com/?page_id=2).

cism indicates a commitment to freedom of speech that is lacking in other Middle East countries, whose human rights records attract far less sustained interest in the democratic West.[18] When leaked official communications from Middle-Eastern countries revealed their greatest fear as Iran's nuclear ambitions, the revelation failed to dent the stereotype of Israel as "the problem."[19] According to the director of a progressive human rights organization, British Jews are automatically linked to Zionism, and are increasingly subjected to casual anti-Semitism,[20] while in Europe kosher slaughter is now coming under pressure from animal welfare campaigns.[21] Despite being singled out for physical attack throughout the world,[22] suspicions remain that Jews are secretly influencing world events and plotting world domination, as demonstrated by the enduring nature of "Jewish conspiracy" theories claiming that "the Jews" are "behind everything."[23] Old libels such as *The Protocols of the Elders of Zion*

---

18. A. Dershowitz, *The Case for Israel*, op. cit., 181–184. Despite its human rights record, in May 2010 Libya was elected to the UN General Assembly's Human Rights Council; membership was suspended in March 2011 when Colonel Gadaffi pledged to kill all Syrian rebels.

19. 250,000 classified diplomatic cables on the Wikileaks website showed Arab nations united in fear of Iran, and Saudi Prince Abdullah's repeated requests for the US to destroy the Iranian nuclear program (accessed March 27, 2011, http://www.af.reuters.com/article/energyOilNews/idAFLDE6A50 3L20101129).

20. "[T]he word Zionist" was sometimes used in political discussion "euphemistically and pejoratively" to "mean someone who believes in the State of Israel"; or "assumptions" were made about people's politics "because they are Jewish," or about how people would feel about things "like anti-terror policy, because of their race. I have seen it, I have heard it, I have watched it" ("Casual anti-Semitism is now so prevalent it turns my stomach," Shami Chakrabarti (Director of Liberty), Interview, *Jewish Chronicle*, March 18, 2011, 8).

21. "The beginning of the end for kosher meat?" *Jewish Chronicle*, June 25, 2010, 1; Scottish European Parliament member Struan Stevenson "drafted an amendment to the food information bill which calls for kosher meat to be labelled 'this product comes from an animal slaughtered by the shechitah [ritual slaughter] method" ("New threat to shechitah is '21st century yellow star'" [*Jewish Chronicle*, April 1, 2011, 6]).

22. In Mumbai, India, over 150 died in Islamist attacks, including a Rabbi and his wife, held hostage at a Jewish center (*Guardian*, November 28, 2008, accessed at March 27, 2011, http://www.guardian.co.uk/world/2008/nov/28/mumbai-terror-attacks-india2). Some news outlets, including the BBC, minimized the fact that the attackers spared Muslims but singled out British, American, and Indian citizens, and the Jewish center (T. Gross, "If This Isn't Terrorism, What Is?" *Wall Street Journal Europe*, December 2, 2008, accessed March 27, 2011, http://www.online.wsj.com/article/SB1228168 92289570229.html); M. Phillips, "The Mumbai atrocity is a wake-up call for a frighteningly unprepared Britain," *Daily Mail*, December 1, 2008, accessed March 27, 2011, http://www.dailymail.co.uk/news/article-1090762/MELANIE PHILLIPS-The-Mumbai-atrocity-wake-frighteningly-unprepared-Britain.html). In Toulouse, France, three children at a Jewish school were murdered by a gunman (BBC News, March 19, 2012).

23. M. Phillips, *Londonistan: How Britain is Creating a Terror State Within*, op. cit., 201; for a satirical perspective, see: David Deutsch and Joshua Neuman, *The Big Book of Jewish Conspiracies* (New York: St. Martin's Griffin, 2005).

still resonate,[24] but, just as A.K. Chesterton adjusted his conspiracy theories to take account of Hitler and the War, Jews have been seen as being behind the 9/11 attacks.[25]

The *Chesterbelloc* was fiercely anti-capitalist, and Israel's most vigorous critics come from the anti-capitalist, liberal Left of politics.[26] But, since this worldview favors multiculturalism, which emphasizes the unacceptability of discrimination against minorities and imposes its priorities through the policing of language, anti-Semitism would appear to be excluded. Despite this, as seen, the priorities of those who sympathize with the underdog can change when the interests of underdogs clash, particularly in the case of pro-Israel Jews and pro-Palestinian Muslims.[27] With the Palestinians seen as weaker than the Israelis, as Phillips argues, Jews might be denied "minority status," since under "the prevalent Marxist analysis that racism necessarily involved power," Jews "were seen to be powerful," thus were "part of the majority and so could never be victims."[28] Israel has been accused of being a South African-style "apartheid state,"[29]

24. A 30-part drama series based on the *Protocols, Horseman Without a Horse,* was screened by a number of Middle East television stations ("Ramadan TV Special: The Protocols of the Elders of Zion," December 6, 2001, accessed December 11, 2007, http://www.memri.org/bin/articles.cgi?Area=sd&ID=sp30901).

25. E. Husain, *The Islamist: Why I joined radical Islam in Britain, what I saw inside and why I left,* op. cit., 257.

26. In the West, "sophisticated Marxism became cultural criticism," a cultural trend so influential it was internalized; however, "Weber's prophet" was "replaced by the socialist, egalitarian individual" without containing "a single element of Marx" (Allan Bloom, *The Closing of the American Mind: How Higher Education Has Failed Democracy and Impoverished the Souls of Today's Students* [New York: Touchstone, 1987], 225).

27. Bury Council in Lancashire refused to fly the Israeli flag from the town hall to mark Israel's independence day, although it had for several years flown a Pakistani flag to mark Pakistan's independence day; the Council leader said: "We have had so many requests, from the Polish, Irish, Italian and Indian communities. . . . This is getting a little bit beyond sense" (*Jewish Chronicle,* April 1, 2011, 4). A Scottish male heterosexual Palestinian supporter, fearing his campaign would be "ignored," blogged on the Internet as a young Syrian lesbian: "I wondered if the same ideas presented by someone with a distinctly Arab and female identity would have the same reaction. So I invented her" (*Jewish Chronicle,* June 17, 2011, 6). Homosexual human rights campaigner Peter Tatchell, "founding member of the Palestine Solidarity Campaign," had "a long record opposing anti-Semitism" but claimed that holding the International Lesbian, Gay, Bisexual, Transgender and Queer Youth and Student Organisation's general assembly in Tel Aviv could "'inflame homophobia' in the Arab world by giving the impression that gay and lesbian groups endorsed Israel" (*Jewish Chronicle,* June 24, 2011, 6).

28. M. Phillips, *Londonistan: How Britain is Creating a Terror State Within,* op. cit., 110–111.

29. The "infamous 1975 UN resolution equating Zionism with racism" was "increasingly . . . applied by the student left towards 'Zionist' speakers and against Jewish Student Unions on various campuses," leading to "anti-Zionist resolutions calling for the destruction of the State of Israel, labelling Zionism as racism, and calling for complete support" for the Palestine Liberation Organization (W.D. Rubinstein, *Israel, the Jews, and the West: The Fall and Rise of Antisemitism,* op. cit., 50). In 2010 President Ahmadinejad of Iran, who has expressed doubts about the Holocaust, addressed the UN Conference on Racism (D. Conway, "Expose this ignorant bigotry," *Jewish Chronicle,* January 7, 2011).

despite the fact that all religions are tolerated and its Arab citizens are not excluded from public life,[30] and, as Paul C. Merkley comments: "[O]urs is a secular age, and there are crimes much worse than heresy. The worst crime of all is 'racism.'"[31] Although Western, especially British and American foreign policy is supportive of Israel,[32] in 2012 the UK's Ambassador to Israel warned that "a rising number of Britons saw Israel as 'Goliath' to the Palestinians' 'David.'"[33]

But if modern multiculturalism emerged from concerns about racism, inextricably linked to the Holocaust, Postmodernism was embraced in reaction to the perceived totalitarian connotations of "imposing truths," leading to growing antagonism to the idea of objective truth and those who believe in objective truth: as former Chief Rabbi Jonathan Sacks has noted: "The new dogma of relativism . . . was due less to logical positivism or the breakdown of moral language than to the sincere determination of a post-war, post-Holocaust generation to avoid the possibility of any future 'final solution.'"[34]

In the light of historical Christian anti-Semitism, the decline of Christian influence on society[35] may be seen as a positive augury for the death of anti-

30. Alan Dershowitz, *The Case for Israel* (Hoboken, NJ: John Wiley & Sons, Inc., 2003), 154–157.

31. Paul C. Merkley, *Christian Attitudes towards the State of Israel* (Montreal & Kingston: McGill-Queen's University Press, 2001), 192–193.

32. The relationship was tested when Israel used stolen British identities to assassinate terrorist suspects ("The use of six fake UK passports by the alleged killers of a Hamas commander is an outrage, [Foreign Secretary] David Milliband has said") (BBC news online, February 18, 2010, accessed March 30, 2011, http://www.news.bbc.uk/1/hi/8521246.stm), and when private arrest warrants were taken out in the UK against Israeli government officials on human rights' grounds ("Israel fury at UK attempt to arrest [former Israeli foreign minister] Tzipi Livni," BBC news online, December 15, 2009, accessed March 30, 2011, http://www.news.bbc.co.uk/1/hi/world/middle_east/8413234.stm). Despite little progress over the issue of Israeli construction in the West Bank, seen as an obstacle to the "Peace Process" and prioritized by President Obama, the US/Israel relationship has remained close. Israelis have complained of the European Union's reluctance to confront the problem of terrorism (Raphael Ahren, "Why won't Europe state the obvious about Hezbollah? Everyone knows the Lebanese Shiite group is a terrorist organization, especially the French. But even Bulgaria's indictment may not change what one US legislator calls an 'indefensible' EU policy," *The Times of Israel*, February 6, 2013, accessed February 15, 2013, http://www.timesofisrael.com/why-wont-europe-state-the-obvious-abou t-hezbollah/).

33. "Support for 'Goliath' Israel waning, warns envoy," *Daily Telegraph*, August 4, 2012, 18.

34. J. Sacks, *The Politics of Hope* (London: Vintage, 2000), 34. Dr. Sacks was Chief Rabbi of the United Hebrew Congregations of the Commonwealth from 1991 to 2013.

35. J.G. Davies, *A New Inquisition: religious persecution in Britain today* (London: Civitas, 2010), ix; under new equality laws, two High Court judges agreed that an Evangelical Christian couple who refused to tell foster children that homosexuality was acceptable should not be allowed to continue fostering; the "right of homosexuals to equality" had to "'take precedence' over the right of Christians to manifest their beliefs and moral values"; Britain was a "largely secular" multicultural country whose laws did "not include Christianity"; it was "not yet 'well understood' that British society was largely secular" and that the law had "no place for Christianity" (*Daily Telegraph*, March 1, 2011, 1).

Semitism—but if Christian influence disappears and anti-Semitism does not, even "relativists" may, like Wells, blame anti-Semitism on the continued existence of the Jewish people. Relativism has been enormously influential in the marginalization of religion in post-Holocaust Western society, playing "havoc with our ability to discriminate between good and evil, to justify our beliefs," and this has even affected views on the objective evil of the Holocaust.[36] Consequently, a worldview based on the need to avoid a repeat of the Holocaust, but which denies objective truth, is incapable of condemning the evil of the Holocaust. Dr. Sacks has seen multiculturalism as disastrous because of its unintended consequences;[37] intended to protect the weak from oppression, "political correctness, created to avoid stigmatising speech has done just the opposite," leading Zionists to be "labelled as racists."[38]

Although Jews throughout the world have been subjected to attacks linked to the "Israel problem," the growing belief that the injustice inseparable from its creation "causes" such attacks has encouraged the feeling that Israel is really to blame. But there is no guarantee that if Israel disappeared the world would be free of anti-Semitism. Historically, anti-Semitism gave rise to Israel, rather than the other way round. In 1939, supported by Josiah Wedgwood, Churchill protested against British plans to severely restrict Jewish immigration into Palestine: "This pledge of a home of refugees, of an asylum, was not made to the Jews of Palestine . . . but to the Jews outside Palestine, to that vast, unhappy mass of scattered, persecuted, wandering Jews whose intense, unchanging, unconquerable desire has been for a National Home."[39] As the Rev. James Parkes noted:

> The tree of Israel springs from five roots deeply embedded in the experience of Jewish people. The first and deepest is Judaism as a religion of a community. The second is the messianic hope, intimately connected ever since the destruction of the Jewish state with the expectations of a return to the Promised Land. The third is Jewish history, and the long experience of dispersion and insecurity. The fourth is the continuity of Jewish life in Palestine. The fifth is the unique relationship between the Jewry of Palestine and the whole Jewish people.[40]

It could be argued, however, that since modern Israel has caused "friction" it

---

36. J. Sacks, *The Politics of Hope*, op. cit., 35.

37. See: J. Sacks, *The Home We Build Together: Recreating Society* (London: Continuum, 2007).

38. C. Wolf, "Hail to the Chief for his wise indictment of multiculturalism," *The Jewish News*, October 25, 17.

39. Speech, House of Commons, May 22, 1939, in H. M. Sachar, *A History of Israel: From the Rise of Zionism to Our Time* (New York: Alfred A. Knopf, 2007), 224.

40. J. Parkes, *Israel and the Diaspora* (London, 1952), 3, quoted in R. A. Everett, "The Land: Israel and the Middle East in Jewish-Christian Dialogue," in M. Shermis, A. E. Zannoni, eds., *Introduction to Jewish-Christian Relations*, op. cit., 103.

cannot be the right answer to anti-Semitism. Chesterton noted the antagonism of Arabs to Jewish settlers in Palestine, but his belief, and that of Churchill, Wedgwood, and Jewish Zionists, was that a Jewish homeland was needed to lessen friction in the Diaspora because anti-Semitism was not caused solely by anti-Semites, but by the peculiar position of Jews, a community without a territorial base or recognized center. The creation of the State of Israel was seen as a refuge for Jews when—not if—anti-Semitism reemerged, and the Holocaust reinforced this lesson. Since history has disproved the theory that assimilation is the only way to eradicate anti-Semitism, even if Israel were to disappear peacefully, it would simply mean a return to pre-Israel days: anti-Semitism in the Diaspora but with no Jewish homeland—even an embattled one—to offer sanctuary in the last resort. As in the 1930s, other countries might prove reluctant to shelter displaced Jews,[41] especially if threatened by Islamist terrorism.

"Rational" anti-Israelism or Irrational anti-Semitism?

This does not mean that Palestinian claims to justice should be disregarded, and neither should criticism of Israel be automatically equated with anti-Semitism—often it represents a rational response to perceived human rights issues, but any solution that involves the end of the state of Israel would involve injustice for Jews. Nick Cohen argues that some of the Left/liberal focus on human rights in Israel rather than in totalitarian states is shaped by a desire to appease the greater force, warning that if the experiment of Israel surrendering land failed, history would "judge" such critics "harshly."[42] Critics of Israel believe that Palestinian claims could be accommodated were it not for Israeli intransigence, but Israel's surrender of territory to Palestinian authority in Gaza led not to increased cooperation but to an increase in terrorist attacks.[43]

41. International sympathy for German Jews soon turned to fears of a refugee problem (M. Gilbert, *The Holocaust: The Jewish Tragedy* [London: Fontana Press, 1987], 78–82); an international conference at Evian, France in July 1938 produced a dangerously inadequate response (ibid., 64).

42. N. Cohen, *What's Left? How Liberals lost their Way*, op. cit., 354.

43. After Israel's unilateral withdrawal from Gaza in August 2005 Palestinians set light to an abandoned synagogue amid joyful celebrations; after ejecting rivals Fatah in a bloody battle, Hamas won elections in 2006 and fired rockets at Israel; Israel responded with artillery shells and a military incursion, Operation Cast Lead, from December 2008-January 2009 (BBC news online, September 12, 2005, accessed March 27, 2011, http://www.news.bbc.co.uk/1/hi/4235768.stm). More recent offers of land have been rejected: the "Egyptian government later denied the reports," but "talk persists that Egyptian President Abdel Fattah el-Sisi did in fact offer the Palestinians sovereignty over a large swathe of the Egyptian Sinai adjacent to Gaza as a means of establishing a viable Palestinian state without sovereignty over Judea, Samaria and Jerusalem," an offer that, reportedly, Hamas refused (Caroline B. Glick, "O-BAM-a: American prez does it yet again," *Jewish World Review*, October 3, 2014, accessed October 15, 2014, http://www.jewishworldreview.com/1014/glick100314.php3).

Privately, Palestinian leaders have insisted on a "Jew-free" Palestine,[44] but even open declarations of hostility have received little attention.[45]

Many sincerely see Israel as a powerful irritant, a threat to world peace, but *Chesterton and the Jews* has shown how easy it can be to perceive certain "underdogs" as powerful, thus making it permissible to criticize them. In fighting off seemingly overwhelming military attacks since its inception, Israel may have added to the impression of unassailable power. Perhaps, too, Israel's survival, like the survival of the Jewish people, is baffling to those who see religion as an outdated human construct;[46] in the absence of belief in supernatural power, the only explanation is unnatural, possibly secret power.[47]

44. "You understand that we plan to eliminate the State of Israel and establish a purely Palestinian state . . . I have no use for Jews; they are, and remain Jews" (Yasser Arafat, speaking at the Grand Hotel, Stockholm, January 1, 1996, accessed at http//:www.accessmiddleeast.org, quoted in N. Comay, *Arabs Speak Frankly on the Arab-Israeli Conflict*, op. cit., 79).

45. "We will continue to aspire to the strategic goal, namely, a Palestine from the river to the sea" (Faisal al-Husseini, Palestinian Authority Minister of Jerusalem Affairs, addressing an Arab lawyers' forum, Beirut, March 21, 2001 (Middle East Media Research Institute, http://www.memri.org, quoted in N. Comay, *Arabs Speak Frankly on the Arab-Israeli Conflict*, op. cit., 46); "Stop murdering Israelis until we have an independent Palestinian state" (Abu Mazen, Prime Minister, Palestinian Authority, February 2003, Middle East Media Research Institute, http://www.memri.org, quoted in ibid., 47); "I swear by almighty God, we will not leave a single Jew in Palestine" (Abdel Aziz Rantizi, Hamas leader, June 2003, http://www.seacoastonline.org, quoted in ibid.); see also: Aaron Klein, *Schmoozing with Terrorists: from Hollywood to the Holy Land, Jihadists Reveal their Global Plans—to a Jew* (Los Angeles: WND Books, 2007). "The Islamic Resistance Movement believes that the land of Palestine has been an Islamic Waqf throughout the generations and until the Day of Resurrection, no one can renounce it or part of it, or abandon it or part of it" (Article 11, Hamas Charter); "(Peace) initiatives, and so-called peaceful solutions and international conferences are in contradiction to the principles of the Islamic Resistance Movement. . . . Those conferences are no more than a means to appoint the infidels as arbitrators in the lands of Islam. . . . There is no solution for the Palestinian problem except by Jihad. The initiatives, proposals and international conferences are but a waste of time, an exercise in futility" (Article 13, Hamas Charter) (Cal Thomas, 'Rebuilding Gaza for the next attack,' *Jewish World Review*, October 14, 2014, accessed October 14, 2014, http://jewishworldreview.com/cols/thomas101414.php3).

46. Historian Arnold J. Toynbee (1889–1975) called the Jewish People "the fossils of history," opening a disquisition on Jewish culture by maintaining: "There remains the case where victims of religious discrimination represent an extinct society which only survives as a fossil . . . by far the most notable is one of the fossil remnants of the Syriac Society, the Jews" (Arnold J. Toynbee, introduction to "The Geneses of Civilizations," *A Study of History*, Vol. 1, Section VII [London: Oxford University Press, 1934], 135–139.)

47. "The Lord our God be with us, as he was with our fathers; may he not leave us or forsake us; that he may incline our hearts to him, to walk in all his ways, and to keep his commandments, his statutes, and his ordinances, which he commanded our fathers. Let these words of mine . . . be near to the Lord our God day and night, and may he maintain the cause of his servant [Solomon], and the cause of his people Israel, as each day requires; that all the peoples of the earth may know that the Lord is God; there is no other" (1 Kings: 57–60).

This raises the possibility that disproportionate interest in the injustices inflicted by Israel is also influenced by the recurring problem of prejudice. It is possible that critics, even those motivated by human rights concerns, are in danger of constructing an "all-powerful Israel" just as the *Chesterbelloc* view suggested an "all-powerful financial Jew," while others constructed the even more powerful "elders of Zion." When criticism of the "Israel question" is subjected to the same scrutiny as the *Chesterbelloc* on the "Jewish question" it becomes clear that just as the *Chesterbelloc* held Jewish capitalists to a higher standard than other capitalists, critics tend to hold Israel to a higher standard than other nations.[48]

Critics insist that they criticize Israel, not Jews; the *Chesterbelloc* insisted that they only criticized "financial" Jews, and simply wished to discuss Jewish "faults"; despite this, Chesterton and Belloc were among the earliest critics of Nazi anti-Semitism, and even before that they praised Jewish "virtues" while criticizing Jewish "vices." Israel's critics ignore its "virtues" and concentrate on its "vices," and resent accusations of anti-Semitism, arguing that they simply wish to discuss Israel's faults. As to attacks on Israel, its perceived illegitimacy trumps any attack, no matter how barbaric, for if Israel had not been established the attacks would not have been happened. A false equivalence can be constructed between perpetrator and victim reminiscent of the 1930s, with Jewish settlements in disputed territories, though possibly an obstacle to a peace agreement, viewed more seriously than brutal murders against the "settlers."[49]

The *Chesterbelloc* saw the "Jewish problem" as the result of wealthy Jews causing resentment, although Chesterton was careful to "rationally" "explain" the origin of this "fault" and deplored repercussions on poor Jews. More recently, Israel's security measures have been seen not as a response to terrorism but as causing it, an intrinsic part of the "Israel problem."[50] American support for Israel has also been seen as "causing" terrorist attacks, and some in the West have rationalized the behavior of suicide bombers and even identified

---

48. N. Cohen, *What's Left? How Liberals lost their Way*, op. cit., 353.

49. Following the brutal murder of five members of the Fogel family, Conservative Member of Parliament Louise Bagshawe said the BBC had marginalized the news item, omitting gruesome details of the "barbaric attack" and Hamas's celebrations ("A family slaughtered—doesn't the BBC care?" *Daily Telegraph*, March 24, 2011, 24); the BBC later "admitted that the horrific murders . . . should have been covered on their 24 hours news channel" ("BBC backs down on its Fogel coverage," *Jewish Chronicle*, April 1, 2011, 11).

50. "The most morally depraved response was that the murder [of the Fogel family] was caused by Israel's provocation—the settlements. Blaming the victims for their own suffering is the kind of moral inversion that runs through centuries of Western excuses for the murder of Jews" (*Jewish Chronicle*, March 18, 2011, 3).

with their presumed motivations.[51] In contrast, when the Nazis attacked German Jews, Chesterton and Belloc attacked the Nazis, not the Jews. Chesterton's solution to "Jewish vices" was a Jewish homeland, and his vague idea of Jewish "separation," mooted in 1920, was not resurrected when the Nazis appeared to be putting it into practice. Israel's critics blame Israel for intransigence in the peace process, while overlooking the Palestinian leaders' own rejection of a peaceful solution. They believe that they are defying a powerful Jewish state, and the *Chesterbelloc* believed they were defying the "Jewish money power," but with the advent of Nazi anti-Semitism they defied the Nazis. In contrast, modern critics show signs of rationalizing terrorism, recalling Chesterton's humorous depiction of the progressive Lord Ivywood rationalizing militant Islam in *The Flying Inn*.[52]

Like the *Chesterbelloc*, Western critics of Israel have the luxury of speaking out on issues of injustice, untroubled by totalitarian-style oppression. They have failed to recognize terrorism as a form of totalitarianism, while Chesterton recognized "Prussian" totalitarianism in Nazism, specifically with regard to Jews. Israel's critics would no doubt see his Zionism as proof that he was no prophet, but, unlike them, Chesterton did not blame Jewish settlers for Arab violence—even his controversial enclave idea was partly based on anxieties about Jewish security. Despite this, like many other post-Holocaust commentators, critics of Israel would likely criticize historical figures like Chesterton for their "anti-Semitism."

This need not mean that Israel's critics are anti-Semites, for like Chesterton and Belloc they are not driven by anti-Semitism, but chiefly by a concern for justice; nor should it be supposed (to go to the other extreme of paranoia) that there is a Left/liberal cabal plotting the destruction of Israel, any more than Jews

---

51. The British Prime Minister's wife Cherie Blair apologized after commenting hours after 20 Israelis died in a Jerusalem suicide bombing that young Palestinians "feel they have got no hope but to blow themselves up" (*Independent*, June 21, 2002, in M. Phillips, *Londonistan: How Britain is Creating a Terror State Within*, op. cit., 206–207); former Liberal Democrat Member of Parliament Jenny Tonge was sacked by her party after saying that as a mother and grandmother, if she had to live under Israeli rule: "[A]nd I say this advisedly, I might just consider becoming [a suicide bomber] myself"; she was later elevated to the peerage (*Financial Times*, January 24, 2004, in ibid., 206).

52. Israel is regarded by Islamists as a colonialist project—"little Satan" to America's "big Satan," and far from recognizing a resurgence of totalitarianism the "political left . . . in its anti-imperialist fervours, has lost the ability to stand up to fascism" (Paul Berman, *Terror and Liberalism* [New York/London: W.W. Norton & Company, 2004], 207). In fact, Left/liberal views of Israel now resemble the Islamist sympathies of the 1960s far-Left, when "Arab armies and Palestine guerrillas" were seen as "anti-imperialist and hence 'progressive'"; Israel was a "colonial fact, a 'spearhead' created in the back of the Arab peoples to prevent their emancipation from imperialism"; "expansionist by nature," her Zionist ideology was "racist and her politics fascist"; Hitler "expelled the Jews," but Moshe Dayan was "driving out the Arabs" (R. Wistrich, ed., *The Left Against Zion: Communism, Israel and the Middle East*, op. cit., 260).

defending Israel are proof of a Jewish cabal plotting world domination. None-theless, as with the *Chesterbelloc* the Left/liberal's "rational" approach can provide intellectual respectability for real anti-Semites—although, unlike the *Chesterbelloc*, Israel's critics show little sign of changing direction. While criticism of Israel does not automatically equate with anti-Semitism, to demand unfeasibly high standards of Israel verges on discrimination against Jews, since Israel is a Jewish state. With critics inadvertently conferring intellectual respectability on violent opposition to Israel and Jews worldwide, Western democracies, no doubt fearful of becoming terrorist targets, have become less ready to support Israel.[53] Just as the nations were reluctant to take in Jewish refugees from Nazism, the Jewish homeland may yet become the scapegoat of the nations.

The Holocaust Again?

Despite the fact that concerns about avoiding a "repeat" of the Holocaust have shaped multiculturalism, Chesterton's solution to anti-Semitism is now seen as the cause of anti-Semitism, and the Jewish homeland is under threat from neighbors that include Hamas-controlled Gaza, and Hizbollah in Lebanon, both sponsored by Iran.[54] Holocaust denial is a growing feature of Middle Eastern countries, including Iran, a country on the brink of acquiring a nuclear weapon, whose president has hinted that Israel should be wiped out.[55] With

---

53. "Israel condemns British MPs' vote to recognise Palestinian state: Non-binding vote, supported by 274 MPs with 12 voting against, said to reflect changing public opinion," *The Guardian*, October 14, 2014, accessed October 14, 2014, http://www.theguardian.com/world/2014/oct/14/israel-condemns-british-mps-vote-palestinian-state. "MPs Palestine vote shows Israel had 'lost UK public,'" *Jewish Chronicle*, October 17, 2014, 1.

54. W.D. Rubinstein, *Israel, the Jews, and the West: The Fall and Rise of Antisemitism*, op. cit., 63. Israel intercepted an arms shipment from Syria that included advanced missiles designed in China and made in Iran (*Jewish Chronicle*, March 18, 2011, 15).

55. "Iran's leader's comments attacked: The European Union and Russia have joined condemnation of the Iranian president's public call for Israel to be 'wiped off the map'" (BBC News Online, October 27, 2005, accessed March 28, 2011, http://www.news.bbc.ukh/hi/4378948.stm). President Ahmadinejad wrote to Germany's Chancellor Angela Merkel suggesting that Israel be accommodated within Germany ("Ahmadinejad: Holocaust was made up," *Daily Mail*, MailandGuardianonline, March 28, 2006, accessed March 28, 2011, http://www.mg.co.za/article/2006-08-28-ahmadinejad-holocaust was-made-up); "On December 14, 2005, Mahmoud Ahmadinejad became the first senior Iranian politician to deny the Holocaust" ("Anti-Israel paranoia reaches new heights in Iran," *Jewish Chronicle*, December 31, 2010, 1). Clarifying his remarks, the Iranian President said he favored the "return" of Palestinian refugees and their descendants and a democratic vote on the matter, thus accomplishing Israel's abolition (Ethan Bronner, "Just How Far Did They Go, Those Words Against Israel?" *New York Times*, June 11, 2006, accessed March 28, 2011, http://www.nytimes.com/2006/06/11/weekinreview/11bronner.html).

historical roots going back to Nazism, Holocaust denial[56] now influences Islamist views, which range from denial that it ever happened to approval.[57] "Holocaust revision" has affected prominent individuals of both Right[58] and Left.[59] While religion might act as a prod to the public conscience regarding Holocaust remembrance, "Holocaust revisionism" has received support from a Catholic Bishop.[60] Such views are not widely shared among Christians, but, whereas in the light of the Holocaust many saw Israel's emergence as "a divine

56. A "number of prominent Nazis" spread their propaganda across the Middle East after the War (J. Parkes, *Antisemitism* [London: Vallentine Mitchell & Co. Ltd., 1963], 132).

57. "[D]eep down, we never really objected to the Holocaust. Indeed, in the prayer room we were convinced that the college principal . . . as well as several other members of the management, were Zionist agents. Without question we despised Jews and perceived a Jewish conspiracy against our nascent Islamic Society" (E. Husain, *The Islamist: Why I joined radical Islam in Britain, what I saw inside and why I left*, op. cit., 54); in Syria "Hitler was considered to be a hero and the Holocaust was denied" (ibid., 228).

58. In 2000 right-wing British historian David Irving lost a libel suit against Professor Deborah Lipstadt who had claimed he was "one of the most dangerous spokespersons for Holocaust denial"; the judge described Irving as "anti-Semitic, racist and a Holocaust denier who had 'deliberately misrepresented and manipulated historical evidence.'" Later, Irving served a prison sentence in Austria for claiming that there were no gas chambers at Auschwitz (BBC news online, January 4, 2006, accessed April 1, 2011, http://www.newsbbc.co.uk/1/hi/uk/4578534.stm); see: D. Lipstadt, *Denying the Holocaust: The Growing Assault on Truth and Memory* (New York: Free Press, 1993); *History on Trial: My Day in Court with David Irving* (New York: Ecco Press, 2005). Irving has hosted tours of Nazi death camps in Poland ("'My death camp tours aren't sick': Holocaust denier David Irving defends plans for 'Nazi travel' tourist trail," MailOnline, September 23, 2010, accessed April 1, 2011, http://www.dailymail.co.uk/travel/article-1310819/My-death-camp-tours-arent-sick-Holocaust-denier-David-Irving-defends-plans-Nazi-Travel-tourist-trail.html).

59. Irving has linked hands in friendship with left-wing playwright Rolf Hochhuth who tarnished the War-time reputation of Pope Pius XII with *The Deputy* (1963) and attempted the same with Sir Winston Churchill. See: P. Lapide, *The Last three Popes and the Jews* (London: Souvenir Press, 1967); John Cornwell, *Hitler's Pope: The Secret History of Pius XII* (London: Viking, 1999); D. G. Dalin, *The Myth of Hitler's Pope* (Washington DC: Regnery Publishing, 2005); the Pave the Way Foundation, founded by Jewish couple Gary and Meredith Krupp has worked to restore Pius's reputation ("War-time pope's secret heroism," *Jewish Chronicle*, February 27, 2009, 1). Irving and Hochhuth met in January 1965 and remained friends (D. Irving, *Banged Up*, published online, 2008); Irving's website shows a photograph of the two outside Irving's London home in July 1966 (accessed March 28, 2011, http://www.fpp.co.uk/Irving/photos/index.html). Hochhuth, who drew partly on Irving's work, in his play *Soldiers, Necrology on Geneva* (1967) alleged that Churchill was responsible for the death of Polish Prime Minister Wladyslaw Sikorski in 1943 in a plane crash; the plane's pilot won a libel case against Hochhuth.

60. Bishop Richard Williamson said there were "no lethal gas chambers and that, at most, 300,000 Jews died in the Nazi camps"; he also claimed that *The Protocols of the Elders of Zion* were "authentic." Disgraced historian David Irving, who had met and corresponded with Williamson, said he was no Holocaust-denier: "Like me, he does not buy the whole package" ("Holocaust-denying bishop barred from preaching in UK," *Jewish Chronicle*, February 27, 2009, 2). The English-born Williamson was suspended from ministry until he showed genuine repentance, but "having distanced himself from the management and the government of the SSPX for several years, and refusing to show due respect and obedience to his lawful superiors," he was formally excluded on October 4, 2012

action,"[61] comparable to the Israelites reaching the Promised Land, more recently, the perception of Arabs as victims (and Jews as victimizers) has led to a decline in Christian sympathy for Israel.[62] Christian voices have joined secular calls for boycotts of the Jewish state.[63] Chapter One noted fears about Holocaust remembrance becoming a thing of the past, and well-publicized doubts

_____

("Bishop Williamson is expelled from SSPX," *Catholic Herald*, October 26, 2012, 1). Williamson was ordained in the Society of St Pius X, and Holocaust revisionism featured prominently in the Society's break with Rome. Archbishop Marcel Lefebvre, who founded the SSPX in 1970, incurred excommu-. nication in 1988 when he ordained four bishops, including Williamson. The SSPX never "accepted the liturgical reforms of the Second Vatican Council and its concepts of religious freedom and ecumenism" ("Pressure mounting on bishop to recant views," *Catholic Times*, February 15, 2009, 1); having expelled Williamson, who has since been excommunicated for a second time after consecrating one of his followers as a bishop, SSPX head Bishop Bernard Fellay declared that Jews, with Freemasons, and Modernists, were "the enemies of the Church"; that "Jews opposed the salvific mission of Christ and that he aimed the comments at the heads of 'Jewish organisations'" (*Catholic Herald*, January 11, 2013, 13). Vicomte Leon de Poncins criticized Vatican II's formal overturning of the Church's "Teaching of Contempt," alleging Jewish influence and noting the opposition of Lefebvre, French. Superior General of the Holy Ghost Fathers (Leon de Poncins, *Judaism and the Vatican: An Attempt at Spiritual Subversion* [Sudbury, Suffolk: Bloomfield Books, 1967], 133); Poncin concludes: "The question of six million Jewish victims who died in Hitler's camps can no longer be considered an article of faith" (ibid., 190); the book's publisher was described by an anti-fascist magazine as "one of Britain's leading distributors of anti-Semitic material" (N. Lowles, S. Silver, *Searchlight Magazine*, November 2000, accessed April 1, 2011, http://www.searchlightmagazine.com/index.php?link=template&story=86). The Catholic Church's Second Vatican Council formally repudiated anti-Semitism. "[A]ccording to [St. Paul], the Jews still remain most dear to God because of their fathers, for He does not repent of the gifts he makes nor of the calls He issues (cf. Romans 11:28–29)" ("Declaration on the Relationship of the Church to Non-Christian Religions" [*Nostra Aetate*], October 28, 1965, *The Documents of Vatican II*, Walter M. Abbott, ed. [London: Geoffrey Chapman, 1967], 664); "The Church repudiates all persecutions against any man. Moreover, mindful of her common patrimony with the Jews, and motivated by the gospel's spiritual love and by no political considerations, she deplores the hatred, persecutions, and displays of anti-Semitism directed against the Jews at any time. and from any source"; "if there was anti-Semitism" in earlier Church laws "it is here repudiated" (ibid., 666–667). Pope Benedict XVI emphasized that Matthew's Gospel reference to "the whole" Jewish people ("His blood be on us and on our children" [27:25]) "does not cry out for vengeance and punishment; it brings reconciliation. It is not poured out *against* anyone; it is poured out *for* many, for all" (Joseph Ratzinger, *Jesus of Nazareth Part II: Holy Week From the Entrance into Jerusalem to the Resurrection* [London: Catholic Truth Society/San Francisco: Ignatius Press, 2011], 187); the Pope acknowledged the "grave consequences" of the passage, which had been "used down the centuries to justify Christian antisemitism" (E. Kessler, Director, Woolf Institute of Abrahamic Faiths, Cambridge, "Benedict's benediction," *Jewish Chronicle*, March 25, 2011, 40).

61. I. Markham, "Theological Problems and Israel," in H.P. Fry, ed. *Christian-Jewish Dialogue: A Reader* (Exeter: University of Exeter Press, 1996), 125.

62. Marcus Braybrooke, *Children of One God: A History of the Council of Christians and Jews* (London: Vallentine Mitchell & Co. Ltd., 1991), 55–56.

63. "Uproar over Methodist Israel report," *Jewish Chronicle*, June 18, 2010, 10; "Now Quakers consider a boycott," *Jewish Chronicle*, February 18, 2011, 9. The Palestine Solidarity Campaign has claimed that "blood diamonds"—rough diamonds polished in Israel—are "funding war crimes and crimes against humanity" (*Jewish Chronicle*, March 25, 2011, 16).

about its historical foundations may function as permission for those experiencing "Holocaust fatigue" to shrug off the moral imperative to avoid anti-Semitism,[64] as well as discouraging Jews and Gentiles from citing the Holocaust as a reason for supporting Israel.

Chesterton's support for a Jewish homeland was rooted in his Christian faith, and his visit to the Holy Land was crucial to his conversion; now, Israel's biblical foundations are being physically undermined as archaeological artifacts in Jerusalem and elsewhere are being destroyed.[65] The Jewish homeland, although never a religious project, was to Chesterton the religious answer to the problem of secular Jewry. The only solution to a landless people was to provide them with the Biblical "Promised Land." But what finally delivered the land "promised" by the Balfour Declaration was the Holocaust. Holocaust remembrance is, therefore, inextricably linked to the Jewish homeland; to forget why that homeland was needed is to forget the Holocaust. Chesterton did acknowledge the problems caused by his "solution," but trusted God with the outcomes. As he insisted, the need for a homeland was not simply material, but spiritual, and, regarding the Holocaust, Michael Goldberg maintains that in taking up "a Holocaust master story" Jews should not exclude God from the picture, because to do so would mean being left only with "a litany of inhuman violence, cruelty, and death." He states that if the Jewish people "would continue to be the bearer of a master story about redemption—not only theirs, but the world's, not only humanity's, but God's," they should "recite *Kaddish* once more not as a doleful lament, but as a joyous affirmation, proclaiming the hope of its closing line, 'He who makes peace in his heavens, he *will* make peace for us and for all Israel.'"[66]

As Chesterton, Belloc, Kolnai and others warned during the 1930s, Nazi anti-Semitism was a new manifestation of age-old barbarism; it was not solely an attack on the Jewish people but on Western civilization. Left/liberal responses to terrorist attacks—attacking Western governments rather than the perpetrators[67] and even avoiding the word terrorist altogether—recall Shaw's and Wells' dismissive approach to fascism in the 1930s. Shaw and Wells favored the strong over the weak, the able-bodied over the disabled, the pro-active fascists over the Jewish victims, and it is an uncomfortable reminder that their solution to these lesser mortals, in the interest of breeding a better human race, was for the weaker parties to disappear.

---

64. Anti-Defamation League, *Attitudes Toward Jews in Ten European Countries*, op. cit.

65. Y. Alt Miller, "Airbrushing Jewish History," *Israel and Christians Today*, March 2011, 5.

66. Michael Goldberg, *Why Should Jews Survive? Looking Past the Holocaust Toward a Jewish Future* (New York/Oxford: Oxford Union Press, 1995), 175; *Kaddish* is the Jewish prayer for the departed.

67. N. Cohen, *What's Left? How Liberals lost their Way*, op. cit., 320.

Shaw and Wells, however, constructed their philosophies before the Holocaust, unlike critics of Israel. And although Chesterton cited Jewish Zionist friends, just as critics of Israel can cite Jewish anti-Zionists, Chesterton did at least have a positive answer to anti-Semitism, supporting the idea of a Jewish homeland in the same spirit in which he saved a small Jewish boy from school bullies. To Chesterton, the disappearance of the Jewish people did not represent a Utopian dream but a dystopian nightmare.

A Prophet in His Own Country?

The problem of Holocaust influence is the problem of history; "prevision" makes us see things not as they were but as we think they were.[68] In attempting to avoid the mistakes of the past there is a tendency to see an ever-growing number of people and phenomena "leading to" the Holocaust, and, thanks to Postmodernist relativism, even objective truth is no longer seen as a reliable guide, since it is perceived as underpinning the authoritarian attitudes that "led to" fascism. Worse, relativism has left the world vulnerable to Holocaust denial, but—notwithstanding the rejection of "judgmentalism"—it has not precluded the tendency to judge historical figures rather than learn from them how to recognize and avoid anti-Semitism. And individuals like Chesterton have been judged not against their past, but in the light of current preoccupations, consequently we gain no meaningful insights into how to avoid the repetition of past horrors—not even, as Hegel remarked, learning from history the fact that people never seem to learn from history.

By focusing exclusively on historical anti-Semitism we can fail to recognize similar attitudes in our own times; but by dismissing historical anti-Semitism as "of its times" we risk falling into the same trap. Far from defending the indefensible *Chesterton and the Jews* has explored at length its subject's imperfections on the "Jewish question." But more important than perfection in historical figures is the capacity for humility—the readiness to reassess theories in response to the practical challenges of the day. It is also vitally important, however to realize, as did Chesterton, that "[e]xtreme pragmatism is just as inhuman as the determinism it so powerfully attacks."[69] On its own, common sense can too easily become the utilitarian rationale for the most convenient course of action—or non-action—in the face of evil. Chesterton needed to feel secure in his "rightness" but ultimately the authority he relied on was not his. It was "God-sense" that made him constantly alert to the perils of choosing any

---

68. See: Marc Bloch, *The Historian's Craft*, trans. P. Putnam (Manchester: Manchester University Press, 1992).

69. G.K. Chesterton, "The Suicide of Thought," *Orthodoxy* (1908), *G.K. Chesterton Collected Works, Vol. I* (San Francisco: Ignatius Press, 1986), 239–240.

course of action, but neither was non-action an option, for there were sins of omission as well as commission. His loyalty to orthodox religion helped him recognize counterfeit religions so that long before most others he saw determinism in the Nazis' "wild worship of race." Self-worship was the most dangerous religion of all, and if, beguiled by the modern evolutionary quest, people regarded the "Missing Link" as the "father of mankind," they might see him as "an excuse for being half-human."[70]

Chesterton's chief weakness stemmed from allowing some loyalties to subordinate other loyalties, but ultimately his strength lay in understanding what constitutes true strength in all ages. This understanding, which sprang from humility, was displayed not solely in his serious works but in a myriad of observations scattered carelessly in popular journals. In 1901, in an article about novelettes, he remarked that one of humanity's most ancient "weaknesses" was "the hunger for the strong man";[71] he insisted that "the great man is a man; it is always the tenth-rate man who is the Superman."[72] Later he recognized and responded to this recurring weakness, emerging afresh in the hunger for a dictator. Nazi anti-Semitism was a new and terrible manifestation of the recurring problem of anti-Semitism, and his response was that Nazism must be destroyed and the Jewish people preserved. For this reason, Chesterton can be seen as a man for all seasons.

He also predicted the rise of Postmodernism, which now threatens Holocaust remembrance. His contemporaries did not view totalitarianism—or Jews—in the same light as Chesterton because they were influenced by the heretical philosophies or fashions that he explicitly condemned in 1908. *Orthodoxy* regarded the unalloyed pursuit of Enlightenment Modernism, in the sense of God-less materialist rationalism, as leading to madness.[73] Despite its belief in its own "rightness," rationalism's failure to explain the non-material world and to cure every problem, including anti-Semitism—and also the desire of Jews to remain Jews—had given birth to Postmodernism, the "new humility" that refused to have an opinion on anything.[74] Worse, Postmodernism's relent-

---

70. G. K. Chesterton, "On Monsters," *The Uses of Diversity* (London: Methuen & Co. Ltd, 1920/1927), 188–191.

71. "If any of Nietzsche's followers wish to find the fullest and heartiest acceptance of their master's doctrines, the most unrestrained prostration before masculine pride and violence, they will always find it in the novelettes"; it was "one of the oldest" but "most generous, and most excusable of the weaknesses of humanity"—at least in "the tired sempstress or the overworked shopgirl" (G. K. Chesterton, "Sentimental Literature," *The Spice of Life*, D. Collins, ed. [Beaconsfield, Bucks.: Darwen Finlayson Ltd., 1964], 12–14).

72. G. K. Chesterton, "Questions of Divorce," *The Uses of Diversity*, op. cit., 116.

73. G. K. Chesterton, "The Maniac," *Orthodoxy* (1908), *G. K. Chesterton Collected Works, Vol. I*, op. cit., 221; 225.

74. G. K. Chesterton, "The Suicide of Thought," *Orthodoxy* (1908), ibid., 235.

less process of deconstruction, skeptical "free thought," inevitably ended in the "suicide of thought,"[75] where it did not end in mere superstition: the age of Voltaire, Chesterton said, was "rather beautiful and touching"—a "brief interlude of contented Paganism, during which men thought for a very short time indeed that they could be wholly satisfied with this earth and this life"; that "by being ordinarily humane and reasonably logical and practical, all problems would solve themselves."[76] This "interlude" gave way to superstition, or instinct, as people still held "noble and honourable prejudices" against doing certain things, but could not say why.[77] Wells, the enthusiastic Postmodernist, claimed that morality was constantly changing—that his "new" morality would "happen anyway."[78] But, along with political inevitability, pessimism, and decadence, Postmodernism allowed laissez-faire economics and the evolutionary determinism that destroyed rationalism.[79] Determinism did provoke Nietzsche's "will to power," but as Chesterton noted, the boundless self-belief of Shaw's "supermen," enabling them to determine their own fate, was shared by lunatics,[80] while the "new Pagan" anti-rationalist or emotional approach that privileged "choice" over thinking allowed the unthinking choice of evil.[81] Those who, in spite of Postmodernism, still felt the existence of evil, could adopt the moral response of pacifist Tolstoyean non-resistance,[82] but in this way, the Superman gave birth to dictator and slave, totalitarianism's sadomasochistic twins.

Postmodernists dismissed Chesterton's warnings as influenced by a Christianity obsessed with dogma and encouraging bigotry, although to Chesterton, bigotry was not the holding of dogmas but the "incapacity to conceive seriously the alternative to a proposition." The man who rejected dogmas out of hand, he said, believed in dogmas without realizing it, and in that "strange epoch" there were "no great fighting philosophers . . . because we care only about tastes; and there is no disputing about tastes."[83] The Postmodernist toleration of Chesterton's day has become increasingly intolerant of dissent and is beginning to resemble the totalitarianism it aimed to combat. Perhaps for this reason the

---

75. Ibid., 240–241.

76. G. K. Chesterton, *The Superstitions of the Sceptic* (Cambridge: W. Heffer & Sons Ltd., 1925), 10.

77. Ibid., 16–18.

78. G. K. Chesterton, "The Suicide of Thought," *Orthodoxy* (1908), *G. K. Chesterton Collected Works, Vol. I*, op. cit., 236.

79. Ibid., 237.

80. G. K. Chesterton, "The Maniac," ibid., 216.

81. G. K. Chesterton, "The Suicide of Thought," ibid., 241.

82. G. K. Chesterton, "The Paradoxes of Christianity," ibid., 302–303.

83. G. K. Chesterton, "The Bigot," *Lunacy and Letters* (1958), in *Gilbert Magazine*, 12 (2 & 3), (November/December 2008): 58, accessed May 19, 2011, http://www.209.236.72.127/wordpress/wp-content/uploads/2010/12/gilbert_12.2_5.pdf.

Postmodernist mindset is unable to recognize the reemergence of totalitarianism in terrorism. And if Chesterton is regarded by progressives as a failed prophet on the "Israel problem," Hitler's avowedly sincere opposition to Israel could yet be seen as prophetic.

Against all modern and Postmodern heresies—fragments of the truth, but not the whole truth—Chesterton continued to believe that despite everything, each man, though unique, was essentially the same: created good, the recurring danger of pride in his own goodness led to repeated falls into evil. Chesterton continued to assert that there was such a thing as objective truth; that good and evil did exist—sin was "a fact as practical as potatoes"[84]—and could not, as Nietzsche urged, be transposed. Good did not come disguised as evil, and evil as good. Evil could not be planned away, or left to pass by itself, or safely wielded in the strongest hands; it must not be welcomed as the precursor of the Utopia, or utilized for the greater good, or not resisted for the greater good. Men must fight evil as though the future of Man depended on it; but first it must be recognized, and it must be recognized that it matters.

Life itself was a gift of inestimable value; it mattered that it was prevented from coming into existence, or ceased to exist. It mattered that the Jews existed, and would continue to exist. Unlike some other philosophers, Chesterton never lost touch with reality. Acutely sensitive to the existence of good and evil, as an artist he was acutely aware of the thing that philosophers frequently forgot. Unlike the "philosophic evolutionist" who said: "I am not; therefore I cannot think," he knew that things, as well as thoughts, exist;[85] unlike Shaw and Wells he never thought it sufficient to think away evil. As an artist too he was sensitive to beauty and ugliness, and to his own power to create both; to the importance of seeing things in the right perspective; to the fear of getting things out of proportion.

As in the toy theater that his father created, in Chesterton's universe issues were clear cut; there was a villain as well as a hero; a fair maiden in the castle waiting to be rescued; a skeleton in every cupboard. The meta-narrative was simple and always the same, but each character was individually colored, with its own story-line. The villain was not always "the Jew," and when every evil plot was uncovered not one was strong enough to destabilize his universe because love, not hate, was his "life force." The need to save the things he loved—England, the poor, Christianity, the family, the Jews—to see all men as redeemable—was stronger than the desire simply to do battle. When the curtain came down, everyone was reconciled; as in *The Man Who Was Thursday*

---

84. G. K. Chesterton, "The Maniac," *Orthodoxy* (1908), *G. K. Chesterton Collected Works, Vol. I*, op. cit., 217.

85. G. K. Chesterton, "The Suicide of Thought," ibid., 238.

every fiend shed his mask and became a friend.[86] The recurring sin of pride, the root of racism and eugenics, was still waiting in the wings, lurking deep in the shadowed soul of Everyman—but every man was a child of God, with free will, the bedrock of democracy, enabling him to choose salvation. Every man would live happily ever after because Chesterton was not the Author of the story; the universe he had been arranging was not his after all.

86. "I was not then considering whether anything is really evil, but whether everything is really evil" (G. K. Chesterton, "The Man Who Was Thursday," *G. K. C. as M. C.*, J. P. de Fonseka, ed. [London: Methuen & Co. Ltd., 1929], 205).

Bibliography

Works Consulted

Abbott, Walter M., ed. *The Documents of Vatican II*. London: Geoffrey Chapman, 1967.

Ackerman, Nathan W., and Marie Jahoda. *Anti-Semitism and Emotional Disorder: A Psychoanalytic Interpretation*. New York: Harper and Bros, 1950.

Addison, Paul. *The Road to 1945: British Politics and the Second World War*. London: Jonathan Cape, 1975.

———. *Churchill on the Home Front 1900–1955*. London: Jonathan Cape, 1992.

Adelman, Paul. *The Decline of the Liberal Party 1910–1931*. London: Longman, 1995.

Ahamed, Liaquat. *Lords of Finance: the Bankers who broke the World*. London: Wm. Heinemann, 2009.

Aitken, Robin. *Can We Trust the BBC?* London: Continuum, 2007.

Allen, Charlotte. *The Human Christ: The Search for the Historical Jesus*. Oxford: Lion Publishing, 1998.

Allingham, Margery. *Mystery Mile*. Suffolk: St. Edmundsbury Press Ltd., 1989.

Almog, Shmuel. *Zionism and History: The Rise of a New Jewish Consciousness*. New York: St. Martin's Press, 1987.

Alter, Peter. *Nationalism*. London: Edward Arnold, 1994.

Arendt, Hannah. *Eichmann in Jerusalem: A Report on the banality of evil*. London: Faber and Faber, 1963.

———. *The Origins of Totalitarianism*. San Diego: Harcourt Inc., 1994.

Arndt, Frau. *Fairy Tales from the German Forests*. London: Everett's Library, 1913.

Arkell, Reginald. *Meet these People*. London: Herbert Jenkins Ltd., 1928.

Arnold, Matthew. *Culture and Anarchy: An Essay in Political and Social Criticism*. McLean, Virginia: IndyPublish.com, 1869/n.d.

Arns, Carl. *Gilbert Keith Chesterton: Umniss seiner KünsHerpersön lichkeit und Proben-seiner schaffens*. Dortmund: Würzburg, 1925.

Aronson, Theo. *The King in Love: Edward VII's Mistresses*. London: John Murray, 1988.

Aschheim, Steven E. *Culture and Catastrophe: German and Jewish Confrontations with National Socialism and Other Crises*. London: Macmillan, 1996.

Bagguley, Philip. *Harlequin in Whitehall: A Life of Humbert Wolfe*. London: Nyala Publishing, 1997.

Baker, David. *Ideology of Obsession: A.K. Chesterton and British Fascism*. London: Tauris Academic Studies, 1996.

Ball, Stuart and Ian Holliday. *Mass Conservatism: The Conservatives and the Public since the 1880s*. London: Frank Cass, 2002.

Baring, Maurice. *The Puppet Show of Memory*. London: William Heinemann, 1922.

_____. *Maurice Baring: a postscript (with some letters and verse)*. Edited by L. Lovat. London: Hollis & Carter, 1947.

_____. *Maurice Baring Restored: Selections from his Work*. Edited by P. Horgan. London: William Heinemann Ltd., 1970.

Barkan, Elazar. *The Retreat of Scientific Racism: Changing Concepts of race in Britain and the United States between the World Wars*. Cambridge: Cambridge University Press, 1992.

Barker, D. *G.K. Chesterton: A Biography*. London: Constable, 1973.

Barnett, Henrietta. O. W. *Canon Barnett. His Life, Work and Friends Vol. 2*. London: John Murray, 1921.

Bartov, Omer. *Murder in Our Midst: the Industrial Killing and Representation*. New York: Oxford University Press, 1996.

Bauer, Yehuda. *Jews for Sale: Nazi-Jewish Negotiations 1933–45*. New Haven: Yale University Press, 1994.

Bauman, Zygmunt. *Modernity and the Holocaust*. Cambridge: Polity Press, 1991.

Belloc, Hilaire. *The Path to Rome*. London: Geo. Allen & Unwin Ltd., 1902/1936.

_____. *Emmanuel Burden: Merchant of Thames Street, In the City of London, Exporter of Hardware: A Record of his Lineage, Speculations, Last Days and Death*. London: Methuen & Co., 1904.

_____. *Mr. Clutterbuck's Election*. www.forgottenbooks.org: Forgotten Books, 1908/n.d.

_____. *A Change in the Cabinet*. London: Methuen & Co. Ltd., 1909.

_____. *Pongo and the Bull*. London: Constable & Company Ltd., 1910.

_____. *The Servile State*. London: Constable & Co Ltd., 1912/1950.

_____. *The Jews*. England: Bloomfield Books, 1922/1983.

_____. *The Mercy of Allah*. London: Chatto & Windus, 1922/1973.

_____. *Europe and the Faith*. London: Constable & Company Ltd., 1924.

_____. *Mr. Petre: A Novel*. London: Arrowsmith, 1925.

_____. *The Cruise of the Nona*. Harmondsworth, Middx.: Penguin Books Ltd., 1925/1958.

_____. *A Companion to Wells' 'Outline of History'*. London: Sheed & Ward, 1926.

_____. *A History of England: Vol. II Catholic England: The Early Middle Ages AD 1066–1348*. London: Methuen & Co. Ltd., 1927.

_____. *A History of England: Vol. III Catholic England: The Later Middle Ages AD 1348–1525*. London: Methuen & Co. Ltd., 1928.

_____. *But Soft – we are observed*. London: Arrowsmith, 1928/1930.

_____. *The Missing Masterpiece*. London: Arrowsmith, 1929.

_____. *The Man Who Made Gold*. London: Arrowsmith, 1930.

_____. *The Postmaster-General*. London: Arrowsmith, 1932.

_____. *The Battle Ground*. London: Cassell & Company Ltd., 1936.

_____. *The Crusades: The World's Debates*. Rockford, IL: Tan Books & Publishers, Inc., 1937/1992.

_____. *The Catholic and the War*. London: Burns Oates, 1940.

_____. *On the Place of Gilbert Chesterton in English Letters*. London: Kegan, Paul, Trench, Trubner & Co. Ltd., 1940.

_____. *Letters from Hilaire Belloc*. Edited by R. Speaight. London: Hollis & Carter, 1958.

_____. *Belloc: A Biographical Anthology*. Edited by H. Van Thal and J. Soames Nickerson. London: George Allen & Unwin Ltd., 1970.

_____. And C. Chesterton, *The Party System*. London: Stephen Swift, 1911.

Bentley, E.C. *Trent's Last Case*. New York: Harper & Row, Publishers, 1913/1978.

_____. *Those Days*. London: Constable & Co. Ltd., 1940.

Berenbaum, Michael, ed. *A Mosaic of Victims: Non-Jews Persecuted and Murdered by the Nazis*. London: I.B. Tauris & Co. Ltd., 1990.

Berman, Paul. *Terror and Liberalism*. New York/London: W.W. Norton & Company, 2004.

Billington, James H. *Fire in the Minds of Men: Origins of the Revolutionary Faith*. London: Temple Smith Ltd., 1980.

Black Book (*Sonderfahndungsliste* GB) (facsimile Reprint Series No.2). London: Imperial War Museum, 1989.

Blackbourn, David. *The Fontana History of Germany* 1780–1918. London: Fontana, 1997.

Bland, Lucy and Laura Doan, eds., *Sexology Uncensored: The Documents of Sexual Science*. Cambridge: Polity Press, 1998.

Blinkhorn, Martin. *Fascism and the Right in Europe* 1919–1945. Harlow, England: Pearson Education Ltd., 2000.

Bloch, Marc. *The Historian's Craft*. Trans. P. Putnam. Manchester: Manchester University Press, 1992.

Block, Brian P., and John Hostettler, *Hanging in the Balance: A History of the Abolition of Capital Punishment in Britain*. Winchester, Hants.: Waterside Press, 1997.

Blom, Philipp. *The Vertigo Years: Change and Culture in the West, 1900–1914*. London: Weidenfeld & Nicolson, 2008.

Blond, Phillip. *Red Tory: How the Left and Right Have Broken Britain and How We Can Fix It*. London: Faber & Faber Ltd., 2010.

Bloom, Allan. *The Closing of the American Mind: How Higher Education Has Failed Democracy and Impoverished the Souls of Today's Students* (New York: Touchstone, 1987.

Bloom, Harold. *et al., Deconstruction and Criticism*. New York: Seabury, 1979.

Bloomsbury Guide to English Literature. London: Bloomsbury, 1989.

Bogaerts, Anthony M. *Chesterton and the Victorian Age.* Hilversum: Rosenbeek EnVenemans Uitgeverbsbedr. N.V., 1940.

Booker, Christopher and Richard North. *The Great Deception: Can the European Union Survive?* London: Continuum, 2005.

Bower, Tom. *Blind Eye to Murder: Britain, America and the Purging of Nazi Germany—A Pledge Betrayed.* London: Andre Deutsch, 1981.

Boyd, Ian. *The Novels of G.K. Chesterton: A Study in Art and Propaganda.* London: Paul Elek, 1975.

Braun, Thom. *Disraeli the Novelist.* London: Geo. Allen & Unwin, 1981.

Braybrooke, Marcus. *Children of One God: A History of the Council of Christians and Jews.* London: Vallentine Mitchell & Co. Ltd., 1991.

Braybrooke, Patrick. *Gilbert Keith Chesterton.* London: Chelsea Publishing Company, 1922.

_____. *Some Thoughts on Hilaire Belloc: Ten Studies.* London: Drane's, 1923 (California Digital Library, accessed February 7, 2013, http://www.archive.org/details/somethoughtsonhioobrayrich).

_____. *I Remember G.K. Chesterton.* Epsom, Surrey: Dorling & Co. Ltd., 1938.

Brendon, Piers. *The Dark Valley: a panorama of the 1930s.* New York: Alfred A. Knopf, 2000.

Brodhead, Jane N. *The Religious Persecution in France 1900–1906,* London: Kegan Paul, Trench, Trüber & Co. Ltd., 1907.

Browne, Anthony. *The Retreat of Reason: Political Correctness and the Corruption of Public Debate in Modern Britain.* London: Civitas, 2006.

Buber, Martin. *On Zionism: The History of an Idea.* Edinburgh: T & T Clark Ltd., 1985.

Buchan, John. *The Thirty-Nine Steps.* London: Penguin Books, 1915/1994.

Burleigh, Michael. *Death and Deliverance: 'Euthanasia' in Germany 1900–1945.* Cambridge: Cambridge University Press, 1994.

_____. *The Third Reich: A New History.* London: Macmillan, 2000.

Burleigh, Martin and Wolfgang Wipperman. *The Racial State: Germany 1933–1945.* Cambridge: Cambridge University Press, 2003.

Cammaerts, Emile. *The Laughing Prophet: The Seven Virtues and G.K. Chesterton.* London: Methuen & Co. Ltd., 1937.

Canovan, Margaret. *G.K. Chesterton: Radical Populist.* New York: Harcourt Brace, 1977.

Caraman, Philip. *C.C. Martindale: A Biography.* London: Longmans Green & Co. Ltd., 1967.

Cargas, Harry J., ed. *Problems Unique to the Holocaust.* Lexington, Kentucky: University of Kentucky, 1999.

Casillo, Robert. *Genealogy of Demons: Anti-Semitism, Fascism, and the Myths of Ezra Pound.* Evanston, Illinois: Northwestern University Press, 1988.

Cesarani, David., ed. *The Making of Modern Anglo-Jewry.* Oxford: Basil Blackwell Ltd., 1990.

_____. ed. *The Final Solution: Origins and Implementation*. London: Routledge, 1996.

_____. *The Jews and the Left: The Left and the Jews*. London: Labour Friends of Israel, 2004.

Chesterton, A. K. *The Apotheosis of the Jew: from Ghetto to Park Lane*. Canterbury, England: Steven Books, 1936/1998.

_____. *Oswald Mosley: Portrait of a Leader*. London: Action Press, 1937.

_____. *The New Unhappy Lords: An Exposure of Power Politics*. Hampshire: Candour Publishing Co., 1972.

Chesterton, Cecil. *Gladstonian Ghosts*. London: S. C. Brown Langham & Co. Ltd., 1905.

_____. *G. K. Chesterton. A Criticism*. London: Alston Rivers Ltd., 1908.

_____. *The Prussian Hath Said in his Heart*. London: Chapman & Hall Ltd., 1914.

_____. *A History of the United States*. London: Chatto & Windus, 1919.

Chesterton, Mrs. C. *Sickle or Swastika?* London: Stanley Paul & Co. Ltd., 1935.

_____. *The Chestertons*. London: Chapman & Hall, 1941.

Chesterton, G. K. *Basil Howe: A Story of Young Love*. London: New City, 1893–94/ 2001.

_____. *Twelve Types*. Norfolk VA: IHS Press, 1902/2003.

_____. *Robert Browning*. London: Macmillan & Co. Ltd., 1903.

_____. *G. F. Watts*. USA: Kessinger Publishing, 1904/n.d.

_____. *The Napoleon of Notting Hill*. Ware, Herts.: Wordsworth Classics, 1904/ 1996.

_____. *The Club of Queer Trades*. New York: Dover Pubs. Inc., 1905/1987.

_____. *Charles Dickens*. London: Methuen & Co. Ltd, 1906/1913.

_____. *All Things Considered*. USA: Feather Tail Press, 1908/2009.

_____. *The Man Who Was Thursday*. Harmondsworth, Middx.: Penguin, 1908/ 1967.

_____. *George Bernard Shaw*. London: The Bodley Head, 1909/1961.

_____. *The Ball and the Cross*. London: House of Stratus, 1909/2001.

_____. *Alarms and Discursions*. London: Methuen & Co. Ltd., 1910/1939.

_____. *What's Wrong With the World*. London: Cassell & Company Ltd., 1910.

_____. *Appreciations and Criticisms of the Works of Charles Dickens*. London: J. M. Dent & Sons Ltd., 1911.

_____. *A Miscellany of Men*. Norfolk VA, USA: IHS Press, 1912/2004.

_____. *Manalive*. London: House of Stratus, 1912/2001.

_____. *The Victorian Age in Literature*. London: Williams & Norgate, 1913/1919.

_____. *The Barbarism of Berlin*. London: Cassell & Company Ltd., 1914.

_____. *The Flying Inn*. Harmondsworth, Middx.: Penguin, 1914/1958.

_____. *A Short History of England*. London: Chatto & Windus, 1917.

_____. *Utopia of Usurers*. Norfolk VA: IHS Press, 1917/2002.

_____. *The New Jerusalem*. London: Hodder & Stoughton, 1920.

————. *The Uses of Diversity*. London: Methuen & Co. Ltd., 1920/1927.

————. *Eugenics and Other Evils*. London: Cassell & Company Ltd., 1922.

————. *The Man Who Knew Too Much*. Thirsk, Yorks.: House of Stratus, 1922/2001.

————. *What I Saw in America*. London: Hodder & Stoughton Ltd., 1922.

————. *Fancies Versus Fads*. London: Methuen & Co. Ltd., 1923.

————. *St Francis of Assisi* London: Hodder & Stoughton, 1923.

————. *Tales of the Long Bow*. London: House of Stratus, 1925/2001.

————. *The Everlasting Man*. San Francisco: Ignatius Press, 1925/1993.

————. *The Superstitions of the Sceptic*. Cambridge: W. Heffer & Sons Ltd., 1925.

————. *William Cobbett*. London, Hodder and Stoughton Ltd., 1925.

————. *A Gleaming Cohort*. London: Methuen & Co. Ltd., 1926.

————. *The Catholic Church and Conversion*. San Francisco: Ignatius Press, 1926/2006.

————. *The Outline of Sanity*. London: Methuen & Co. Ltd., 1926.

————. *The Return of Don Quixote*. London: Chatto & Windus, 1927.

————. *Generally Speaking*. London: Methuen & Co. Ltd., 1928/1937.

————. *G.K.C. as M.C.* Edited by J. P. de Fonseka. London: Methuen & Co. Ltd., 1929.

————. *The Poet and the Lunatics: Episodes in the Life of Gabriel Gale*. London: Cassell & Company Ltd., 1929.

————. *The Thing: why I am a Catholic*. London: Sheed & Ward, 1929.

————. *Four Faultless Felons*. Beaconsfield, England: Darwen Finlayson, 1930/1964.

————. *The Resurrection of Rome*. London: Hodder & Stoughton Ltd., 1930/1934.

————. *All is Grist*. London: Methuen & Co. Ltd., 1931.

————. *Sidelights on New London and Newer York & Other Essays*. London: Sheed & Ward, 1932.

————. *Avowals and Denials*. London: Methuen & Co. Ltd., 1934.

————. *The Well and the Shallows*. London: Sheed & Ward, 1935.

————. *As I Was Saying*. London: Methuen & Co. Ltd., 1936.

————. *Autobiography*. Sevenoaks, England: Fisher Press, 1936/1992.

————. *The Paradoxes of Mr. Pond*. New York: Dover Publications Inc., 1937/1990.

————. *The Coloured Lands*. London: Sheed & Ward, 1938.

————. *The End of the Armistice*. London: Sheed & Ward, 1940.

————. *The Common Man*. London: Sheed & Ward, 1950.

————. *A Handful of Authors*. Edited by D. Collins. London: Sheed & Ward, 1953.

————. *Lunacy and Letters*. Edited by D. Collins. London: Sheed & Ward, 1958.

————. *The Spice of Life*. Edited by D. Collins. Beaconsfield, Bucks.: Darwen Finlayson Ltd., 1964.

————. *Chesterton on Shakespeare*. Edited by D. Collins. Henley-on-Thames,

Oxon.: Darwen Finlayson Ltd., 1971.

———. *The Apostle and the Wild Ducks and other essays.* Edited by D. Collins. London: Paul Elek, 1975.

———. *The Complete Father Brown.* London: Penguin, 1981.

———. *G.K. Chesterton Collected Works, Vol. I (The Blatchford Controversies; Heretics; Orthodoxy).* San Francisco: Ignatius Press, 1986.

———. *Thirteen Detectives.* New York: Dodd, Mead & Company, 1987.

———. *Brave New Family.* Edited by A. da Silva. San Francisco: Ignatius Press, 1990.

———. *G.K. Chesterton Collected Works Vol. XVIII (Robert Louis Stevenson, Chaucer, Leo Tolstoy, Thomas Carlyle).* San Francisco: Ignatius Press, 1991.

———. *Father Brown.* Ware, England: Wordsworth Classics, 1994.

———. *Collected Works: Vol. X Collected Poetry Part I.* Edited by A. Mackey. San Francisco: Ignatius Press, 1994.

———. *The Works of G.K. Chesterton.* Ware, England: Wordsworth Library, 1995.

———. *G.K. Chesterton Collected Works Vol. VIII (The Man Who Knew Too Much; Tales of the Long Bow; The Return of Don Quixote)* San Francisco: Ignatius Press, 1999.

———. *G.K. Chesterton Collected Works, Vol. XX (England: A Nation; Explaining the English; Irish Impressions; The New Jerusalem; The Patriotic Idea).* San Francisco, USA: Ignatius Press, 2001.

———. *St Thomas Aquinas; St Francis of Assisi.* San Francisco: Ignatius Press, 2002.

———. *Father Brown.* Edited by I. Ker. London: Penguin, 2003.

———. *G.K. Chesterton Collected Works Vol. X: Collected Poetry Part II.* Edited by D.J. Conlon. San Francisco: Ignatius Press, 2008.

———. *Chesterton on War and Peace: Battling the Ideas and Movements that Led to Nazism and World War II.* Edited by M.W. Perry. Seattle: Inkling Books, 2008.

———. *Collected Works: Vol. X Collected Poetry Part II.* Edited by D.J. Conlon. San Francisco: Ignatius Press, 2008.

———. *The Bodley Head G.K. Chesterton.* Edited by P.J. Kavanagh. London: Bodley Head Ltd., 1985.

Cheyette, Bryan. *Constructions of the Jew in English Literature and Society: Racial Representations 1875–1945.* Cambridge: Cambridge University Press, 1995.

Christie, Agatha. *The Secret of Chimneys.* London: Pan Books Ltd., 1925/1961.

———. *The Body in the Library.* London: HarperCollins, 1942/2000.

———. *An Autobiography.* London: HarperCollins, 1977/1993.

———. *Agatha Christie: the collected short stories.* London: HarperCollins, 2002.

Christie et al, *The Floating Admiral.* New York: Charter Books, 1931/1984.

Churchill, Randolph S. *Winston S. Churchill Vol. II: Young Statesman 1901–1914.* London: Wm. Heinemann Ltd., 1967.

———. *Winston S. Churchill Vol. II Part 2 1907–1911.* London: Heinemann, 1969.

———. *Winston S. Churchill, Companion Vol. II Part 3, 1911–1914*. London: Heinemann Ltd, 1969.

Churchill, Winston. S. *The Second World War: The Gathering Storm*. London: Cassell & Co. Ltd., 1948.

———. *A History of the English-Speaking Peoples* (abridged version). London: Cassell, 2003.

———. *Churchill Speaks: Winston S. Churchill in Peace and War: Collected Speeches, 1897–1963*. Edited by R. R. James. Leics.: Windward, 1981.

Churchill, W. and C. Churchill, *Speaking for Themselves: The Personal Letters of Winston and Clementine Churchill*. Edited by M. Soames. London: Doubleday, 1998.

Clemens, Cyril. *Chesterton as Seen by His Contemporaries*. Webster Grove, Missouri: International Mark Twain Society, 1939.

Clipper, Lawrence. *G.K. Chesterton*. New York: Indiana University, South Bend, Twayne Publishers Inc., 1974.

Coates, John. *Chesterton and the Edwardian Cultural Crisis*. Hull: Hull University Press, 1984.

Cobbett, William. *Rural Rides*. London: Penguin Books, 1830/2001.

Cohen, Michael J. *Churchill and the Jews*. London: Frank Cass, 1985.

Cohen, Nick. *What's Left? How liberals lost their way*. London: Fourth Estate, 2007.

Cohn, Norman. *Warrant for Genocide: The myth of the Jewish world-conspiracy and the Protocols of the Elders of Zionism*. London: Eyre & Spottiswoode, 1967.

Cohn-Sherbok, Dan, ed. *The Future of Jewish-Christian Dialogue*. Lampeter, Wales: Edwin Mellen Press, 1999.

———. ed. *Holocaust Theology: A Reader*. Exeter: University of Exeter Press, 2002.

Collis, Maurice. *Nancy Astor*. London: Futura, 1982.

Comay, Joan, ed. *Who's Who in Jewish History after the period of the Old Testament*. London: Routledge, 1995.

Comay, Naomi. *Arabs Speak Frankly on the Arab-Israeli Conflict*. Great Britain: Printing Miracles Ltd., 2005.

Conlon, D. J., ed. *G.K. Chesterton: The Critical Judgments Part I: 1900–1937*. Antwerp: Antwerp Studies in English Literature, 1976.

———. ed. *G.K. Chesterton: A Half Century of Views*. Oxford: Oxford University Press, 1987.

Connerton, Paul. *How Societies Remember*. Cambridge: Cambridge University Press, 2004.

Conrad, Joseph. *Heart of Darkness*. London: Penguin Books, 1902/1973.

Conway, J. S. *The Nazi Persecution of the Churches 1933–1945*. Vancouver: Regent College Publishing, 2001.

Cook, Chris, and John Stevenson. *Modern European History 1763–1997*. London: Longman, 1998.

Cooney, Anthony. *Hilaire Belloc 1870–1953*. London: Third Way Publications, 1997.

_____. *G.K. Chesterton: One Sword At Least*. London: Third Way, 1998.

Coren, Michael. *Gilbert: The Man Who Was G.K. Chesterton*. Vancouver, British Colombia: Regent College Publishing, 1990.

Cornwell, John. *Hitler's Pope: The Secret History of Pius XII*. London: Viking, 1999.

Corrin, Jay. *G.K. Chesterton and Hilaire Belloc: The Battle against Modernity*. Athens: Ohio University Press, 1981.

_____. *Catholic Intellectuals and the Challenge of Democracy*. Notre Dame, Indiana: University of Notre Dame, 2002.

Croner, Helga, ed. *More Stepping Stones to Jewish-Christian Relations: An Unabridged Collection of Christian Documents 1975–83*. New York: Stimulus/Paulist Press, 1985.

Cross, Colin. *The Fascists in Britain*. London: Barrie and Rockliff, 1961.

Crowther, Ian. *Thinkers of Our Time: G.K. Chesterton*. London: The Claridge Press, 1991.

Cumberland, Gerald. *Written in Friendship: A Book of Reminiscences*. London: Grant Richards, 1923.

Dale, A. Stone. *The Outline of Sanity: A Life of G.K. Chesterton*. Grand Rapids, Michigan: Wm. B. Eerdmans Publishing Company, 1982.

Dalin, David G. *The Myth of Hitler's Pope: How Pope Pius XII Rescued Jews from the Nazis*. Washington, DC: Regnery Publishing, 2005.

Dalin, D., and John F. Rothman. *Icon of Evil: Hitler's Mufti and the Rise of Radical Islam*. New York: Random House, 2008.

Darwin, Charles. *On the Origin of Species*. London: Murray, 1859.

_____. *The Descent of Man*. London: Murray, 1871.

Davies, John Gower. *A New Inquisition: religious persecution in Britain today*. London: Civitas, 2010.

Dawidowicz, Lucy S. *The Holocaust and the Historians*, Camb., Mass./London: Harvard University Press, 1981.

Defries, Harry. *Conservative Party Attitudes to Jews 1900–1950*. London: Frank Cass, 2001.

Dershowitz, Alan. *The Case for Israel*. Hoboken, New Jersey: John Wiley & Sons, Inc., 2003.

Deutsch, David and Joshua Neuman, *The Big Book of Jewish Conspiracies*. New York: St Martin's Griffin, 2005.

Dickens, A. G. *The Age of Humanism and Reformation*. Milton Keynes, Bucks.: Open University Press, 1977.

Dickens, Charles. *Oliver Twist*. Ware, Herts.: Wordsworth Classics, 1837–38/1996.

_____. *Our Mutual Friend*. Ware, Herts.: Wordsworth Classics, 1864–65/2002.

_____. *David Copperfield*, Ware, Herts.: Wordsworth Editions Ltd., 1849–50/2000.

Disraeli, Benjamin. *Alroy. Ixion in Heaven. The Infernal Marriage. Popanilla*, London: Longmans, Green & Co., 1833/1881.

———. *Coningsby: or the New Generation*. London: John Lehmann Ltd., 1844/1948.

———. *Tancred or The New Crusade*. London: Longmans, Green & Co., 1847/1881.

———. *Lothair*. London: John Lane, The Bodley Head Ltd., 1870/1927.

———. *Endymion*. Montreal: Dawson Bros, 1880.

Donaldson, Frances. *The Marconi Scandal*. London: Rupert Hart-Davis, 1962.

Dorril, Stephen. *Black Shirt: Sir Oswald Mosley and British Fascism*. London: Viking, 2006.

Draper, Michael. *H. G. Wells*. London: Macmillan Publishers Ltd., 1987.

Drummond, Andrew L. *The Churches in English Fiction: A literary and historical study, from the Regency to the present time, of British and American fiction*. Leics.: Edgard Backus, 1950.

Dworkin, Dennis. *Cultural Marxism in Postwar Britain: History, the New Left, and the Origins of Cultural Studies*. Durham/London: Duke University Press, 1997.

Eckhardt, Alice L., and A. Roy Eckhardt. *Long Night's Journey into Day: A Revised Retrospective on the Holocaust*. Detroit, Michigan: Wayne State University Press, 1988.

Eckhardt, A. Roy. *Elder and Younger Brothers: The Encounter of Jews and Christians*. New York: Schocken Books, 1967.

———. *Your People, My People: The Meeting of Jews and Christians*, New York: Quadrangle, 1974.

Eder, David. *Memoirs of a Modern Pioneer*. Edited by J. B. Hobman. London: Victor Gollancz Ltd., 1945.

Eldridge, C. C. *Disraeli and the Rise of a New Imperialism*. Cardiff: University of Wales Press, 1996.

Ellis, Marc H. *Beyond Innocence and Redemption: Confronting the Holocaust and Israeli Power: Creating a Moral Future for the Jewish People*. San Francisco: Harper & Row, 1990.

Erikson, Robert P. *Theologians Under Hitler: Gerhard Kittel, Paul Althaus, Emanuel Hirsch*. New Haven/London: Yale University Press, 1985.

Evans, Maurice. *G. K. Chesterton*. London: Cambridge University Press, 1939.

Fackenheim, Emil L. *God's Presence in History: Jewish Affirmations and Philosophical Reflections*. New York/London: New York University Press/University of London Press, 1970.

———. *The Jewish Return into History: Reflections in the Age of Auschwitz and a New Jerusalem*. New York: Schocken Books, 1978.

———. *To Mend the World: Foundations of Post-Holocaust Jewish Thought*. Bloomington, Indiana: Indiana University Press, 1994.

Fagerberg, David W. *The Size of Chesterton's Catholicism*. Notre Dame, Ind.: University of Notre Dame Press, 1998.

Fairfield, Laetitia. *Catholics and the German Law of Sterilisation*. No publisher, 1938.

Fanfani, Amintore. *Catholicism, Protestantism and Capitalism*. Norfolk, VA: IHS Press, 1934/2003.

Farmer, Ann. *By Their Fruits: Eugenics, Population Control and the Abortion Campaign*. Washington, DC: Catholic University of America Press, 2008.

_____. *Prophets & Priests*. London: St Austin Press, 2002.

Faulhaber, M. Von. *Judaism, Christianity and Germany*. London: Burns Oates & Washbourne Ltd., 1934.

Feldman, David. *Englishmen and Jews: Social Relations and Political Culture, 1840–1914*. London: Yale University Press, 1994.

Ferrara, Christopher. *The Church and the Libertarian: A Defense of Catholic Teaching on Man, Authority and the State*. Forest Lake, Minnesota: Remnant Press, 2010.

Ffinch, Michael. *G. K. Chesterton*. London: Weidenfeld & Nicolson, 1986.

Finkelstein, Norman G. *The Holocaust Industry: Reflections on the Exploitation of Jewish Suffering*. London: Verso, 2001.

Fisch, Harold. *The Dual Image: A Study of the figure of the Jew in English Literature*. London: Lincolns-Prager Ltd, 1959.

Fishman, William J., *The Streets of East London*. London: Duckworth, 1992.

Fletcher-Jones, Pamela. *The Jews of Britain: A Thousand Years of History*. Gloucestershire: The Windrush Press, 1990.

Foster, R. F. *Lord Randolph Churchill: A Political Life*. Oxford: Clarendon Press, 1981.

Foxman, Abraham H. *Jews and Money: The Story of a Stereotype*. New York: Palgrave Macmillan, 2010.

Frankel, Jonathan, ed. *Dark Times, Dire Decisions: Jews and Communism*. Oxford: Oxford University Press, 2005.

Friedlander, Henry. *The Origins of Nazi Genocide: from Euthanasia to the Final Solution*. Chapel Hill/London: University of North Carolina Press, 1995.

Friends of Europe. *Germany's National Religion*. London, n.d.

Fry, Helen P. ed., *Christian-Jewish Dialogue: A Reader*. Exeter: University of Exeter Press, 1996.

Furlong, William. *Shaw and Chesterton: The Metaphysical Jesters*. London: Pennsylvania State University Press, 1970.

Gasman, Daniel. *The Scientific Origins of National Socialism: Social Darwinism in Ernst Haeckel and the German Monist League*. London: Macdonald, 1971.

Gellner, Ernest. *Nations and Nationalism*. Oxford: Blackwell, 1992.

Gilbert, M. *Winston S. Churchill Vol. V 1922–1939*. London: Heinemann, 1976.

_____. *The Holocaust: The Jewish Tragedy*. London: Fontana Press, 1986.

_____. *The Righteous: the unsung heroes of the Holocaust*. London: Black Swan, 2003.

_____. *Churchill and the Jews*. London: Simon & Schuster Ltd, 2007.

Goldberg, Bernard. *Bias: A CBS Insider Exposes How the Media Distort the News.* Washington, D.C.: Regnery Publishing, Inc., 2002.

Goldberg, David J. *To the Promised Land: A History of Zionist Thought.* London: Penguin, 1996.

Goldberg, David J., and John D. Rayner. *The Jewish People: Their History and Their Religion.* London: Penguin, 1987.

Goldberg, Jonah. *Liberal Fascism: The Secret History of the Left from Mussolini to the Politics of Meaning.* London: Penguin Books, 2009.

Goldberg, Michael. *Why Should Jews Survive? Looking Past the Holocaust Toward a Jewish Future.* New York/Oxford: Oxford Union Press, 1995.

Goldhagen, Daniel J. *Hitler's Willing Executioners: Ordinary Germans and the Holocaust.* Abacus, 1996.

Goodrick-Clarke, Nicholas. *The Occult Roots of Nazism: Secret Aryan Cults and their Influence on Nazi Ideology.* London: I. B. Tauris & Co. Ltd, 1992.

Gould, Stephen J. *Dinosaur in a Haystack: Reflections in Natural History.* London: Jonathan Cape, 1996.

Grainger, J. H. *Patriotisms: Britain* 1900–1939. London: Routledge and Kegan Paul, 1986.

Grant, George. *Grand Illusions: The Legacy of Planned Parenthood.* Nashville, Tenn.: Cumberland House, 2000.

Greene, Graham. *Brighton Rock: An Entertainment.* Harmondsworth, Middx.: Penguin Books Ltd., 1938/1968.

Griffin, Susan. *Anti-Catholicism in Nineteenth Century Fiction.* Cambridge: Cambridge University Press, 2004.

Griffiths, Richard. *Fellow Travellers of the Right: British Enthusiasts for Nazi Germany* 1933–9. London: Constable, 1980.

Guedalla, Philip. *A Gallery.* London: Constable & Company Ltd., 1924.

Halbwachs, Maurice. *On Collective Memory.* Chicago: The University of Chicago Press, 1992.

Hales, E. E. Y. *The Catholic Church in the Modern World.* London: Eyre & Spottiswoode, 1958.

Hannaford, Ivan. *Race: The History of an Idea in the West.* Baltimore/London: Johns Hopkins University Press, 1996.

Hayek, Friedrich A. *The Road to Serfdom.* London: The Institute of Economic Affairs, 1945/2001.

Hayes, Paul, ed. *Themes in Modern European History* 1890–1945. London: Routledge, 1992.

Hayman, Ronald. *Nietzsche: A Critical Life.* London: Weidenfeld & Nicolson, 1980.

Hertzberg, Arthur. *Jewish Polemics.* New York: Columbia University Press, 1992.

———. *The French Enlightenment and the Jews: The Origins of Modern Anti-Semitism.* New York: Columbia University Press, 1990.

Hilberg, Raul. *The Destruction of the European Jews.* New York: Holmes & Meier, 1985.

Hill, Roland. *Lord Acton*. New Haven/London: Yale University Press, 2000.

Hitler, Adolf. *Mein Kampf*. London: Pimlico, 1925–26/2001.

Hollis, Christopher. *The Mind of Chesterton*. London: Hollis & Carter, 1970.

Holmes, Colin. *Anti-Semitism in British Society 1876–1939*. London: Edward Arnold, 1979.

Holmes, Richard. *In the Footsteps of Churchill*. London: BBC Books, 2005.

Holroyd, Michael. *Bernard Shaw: Vol. I 1856–1898: The Search for Love*. London: Chatto & Windus, 1988.

_____. *Bernard Shaw: Vol. II 1898–1918: The Pursuit of Power*. London: Chatto & Windus, 1989.

_____. *Bernard Shaw: Vol. III 1918–1950: The Lure of Fantasy*. London: Penguin, 1993.

Hughes, Philip. *Pope Pius the Eleventh*. London: Sheed & Ward, 1937.

Hunter, Lynette. *G.K. Chesterton: Explorations in Allegory*. London: The Macmillan Press Ltd., 1979.

Husain, Ed. *The Islamist: Why I joined radical Islam in Britain, what I saw inside and why I left*. London: Penguin Books, 2007.

Huxley, Aldous. *Brave New World Revisited*. New York: Harper Perennial, 1932/2005.

Jacobs, Joseph. *Jewish Contributions to Civilization: An Estimate*. Philadelphia: The Jewish Publication Society of America, 1919.

Jacobs, Louis. *A Tree of Life: Diversity, Flexibility, and Creativity in Jewish Law*, Oxford: Oxford University Press, 1984.

_____. *The Jewish Religion: A Companion*. Oxford: Oxford University Press, 1995.

Jaki, Stanley L. *Chesterton, a Seer of Science*. Urbana & Chicago: University of Illinois Press, 1986.

Jay, Martin. *The Dialectical Imagination: A History of the Frankfurt School and the Institute of Social Research 1923–1950*. London: Heinemann, 1973.

Johnson, Paul. *A History of the Jews*. London: Weidenfeld & Nicolson, 1987.

_____. *Churchill*. New York/London: Viking, 2009.

Jones, G. Stedman. *Outcast London: A Study in the Relationship between Classes in Victorian Society*. Harmondsworth, Middx.: Penguin Books Ltd, 1976.

Judd, Denis. *Lord Reading: Rufus Isaacs, 1st Marquess of Reading, Lord Chief Justice and Viceroy of India 1860–1935*. London: Weidenfeld & Nicolson, 1982.

Julius, Anthony. *Trials of the Diaspora: A History of Anti-Semitism in England*. Oxford: Oxford University Press, 2010.

Kaplan, Marion A. *The Jewish Feminist Movement in Germany 1904–1938*. Westport, CT/London: Greenwood Press, 1979.

Kasun, Jacqueline. *The War against Population: The Economics and Ideology of World Population Control*. San Francisco: Ignatius Press, 1988.

Katz, Jacob. *From Prejudice to Destruction: Anti-Semitism, 1700–1933*. Harvard University Press, 1980.

Katz, Stephen. T. *The Holocaust in Historical Context, Vol. I: The Holocaust and Mass Destruction before the Modern Age.* Oxford: Oxford University Press, 1994.

Kenner, Hugh. *Paradox in Chesterton.* London: Sheed & Ward, 1948.

Ker, Ian. *The Catholic Revival in English Literature, 1845-1961.* Leominster, Herefordshire: Gracewing, 2003.

Ker, Ian. *G. K. Chesterton: A Biography.* Oxford: Oxford University Press, 2011.

Kershaw, Ian. *Hitler: Hubris 1889–1936.* London: Penguin Books, 1998.

Kertzer, Morris. N. *What is a Jew?* New York: Touchstone, 1996.

Kevles, Daniel. J. *In the Name of Eugenics: Genetics and the Uses of Human Heredity.* Harvard University Press, 1985.

Klein, Aaron. *Schmoozing with Terrorists: from Hollywood to the Holy Land, Jihadists Reveal their Global Plans—to a Jew.* Los Angeles: WND Books, 2007.

Knight, Mark. *Chesterton and Evil.* New York: Fordham University Press, 2004.

Knox, Ronald. *The Footsteps at the Lock.* Bath: Lythway Press, 1928/1978.

_____. *Caliban in Grub Street.* London: Sheed & Ward, 1930.

_____. *Broadcast Minds.* London: Sheed & Ward, 1932.

_____. *Nazi and Nazarene* (Macmillan War Pamphlets No. 5). London: Macmillan & Co. Ltd., 1940.

Knox, Ronald and Arnold Lunn. *Difficulties: Being a correspondence about the Catholic Religion.* London: Eyre & Spottiswoode, 1952.

Koch, H. W., ed. *The Origins of the First World War.* London: Macmillan Publishers Ltd., 1984.

Kogel, Renee and Zev Katz. *Judaism in a Secular Age: An Anthology of Secular Humanistic Jewish Thought.* Farmington Hills, MI: KTAV Publishing House Inc., 1995.

Kolnai, Aural. *The War Against the West.* London: Victor Gollancz Ltd., 1938.

Koss, Stephen E. *Fleet Street Radical: A. G. Gardiner and the Daily News.* London: Allen Lane, 1973.

Kuper, Leo. *Genocide: Its Political Uses in the Twentieth Century.* New Haven/London: Yale University Press, 1981.

Kushner, Tony. *The persistence of prejudice: Antisemitism in British Society during the Second World War.* Manchester: Manchester University Press, 1989.

_____. *The Holocaust and the Liberal Imagination: A Social and Cultural History.* Oxford: Blackwell, 1994.

Kushner, T., and Kenneth Lunn, eds. *The Politics of Marginality: Race, the Radical Right and Minorities in Twentieth Century Britain.* London: Frank Cass & Co. Ltd., 1990.

Landau, Ronnie. *Studying the Holocaust: Issues, Readings and Documents.* London: Routledge, 1998.

Lange, Nicholas De. *Judaism.* Oxford: Oxford University Press, 1986.

Langer, Lawrence L., ed. *Admitting the Holocaust: Collected Essays.* New York/Oxford: Oxford University Press, 1995.

Lapide, Pinchas. *The Last Three Popes and the Jews*. London: Souvenir Press, 1967.

Lauer, Quentin. *G.K. Chesterton: Philosopher without Portfolio*. New York: Fordham University Press, 1991.

Lebzelter, Gisela C. *Political Anti-Semitism in England 1918–1939*. London: Macmillan Press Ltd., 1978.

Leftwich, Joseph. *Israel Zangwill*. London: James Clarke & Co. Ltd, 1957.

Lehmann, Hartmut and James J. Sheehan, eds. *An Interrupted Past: German-Speaking Refugee Historians in the United States After 1933*. Washington DC/Cambridge: German Historical Institute/Cambridge University Press, 1991.

Levi, Primo. *The Drowned and the Saved*. London: Michael Joseph, 1988.

Levy, Richard S. *Antisemitism: A Historical Encyclopedia of Prejudice and Persecution*. Santa Barbara, CA: ABC–Clio, 2005.

Lewy, Guenter. *The Catholic Church and Nazi Germany*. London: Weidenfeld & Nicolson, 1964.

Lindemann, Albert S. *Esau's Tears: Modern Anti–Semitism and the Rise of the Jews*. Cambridge: Cambridge University Press, 1997.

Lindqvist, Sven. *Exterminate all the Brutes*. London: Granta Books, 1997.

Linehan, Thomas. *British Fascism 1918-39: Parties, ideology and culture*. Manchester: Manchester University Press, 2000.

Lion, Aline. *The Pedigree of Fascism*. London: Sheed & Ward, 1927.

Lipman, Vivian. D. *A History of the Jews in Britain since 1858*. Leicester: Leicester University Press, 1990.

Lipstadt, Deborah. *Denying the Holocaust: The Growing Assault on Truth and Memory*. New York: Free Press, 1993.

_____. *History on Trial: My Day in Court with David Irving*. New York: Ecco Press, 2005.

Littell, Franklin. H. *The Crucifixion of the Jews: The Failure of Christians to Understand the Jewish Experience*. Macon, Georgia: Mercer University Press, 1986.

Lively, Scott. *The Poisoned Stream: "Gay" Influence in Human History Vol. I, Germany 1890–1945*. Keizer, Oregon: Founders Publishing Corp., 1997.

Lively, Scott and Kevin Abrams. *The Pink Swastika: Homosexuality in the Nazi Party*. Sacramento, Calif.: Veritas Aeterna Press, 2002.

Lodge, David. *The Novelist at the Crossroads and other essays on Fiction and Criticism*. London: Ark Paperbacks, 1986.

Lowndes, Marie Belloc. *The Young Hilaire Belloc*. New York: P.J. Kenedy & Sons, 1956.

_____. *Diaries and Letters of Marie Belloc Lowndes 1911–1947*. Edited by S. Lowndes. London: Chatto & Windus, 1971.

MacDonald, Kevin. *The Culture of Critique: An Evolutionary Analysis of Jewish Involvement in Twentieth-Century Intellectual and Political Movements*. 1st Books Library, 2002.

Mackey, Aidan. *G.K. Chesterton: A Prophet for the 21st Century*. Kempston, Bedford: A. Mackey, 2008.

MacKenzie, Norman and Jeanne MacKenzie. *The Time Traveller: The Life of H. G. Wells.* London: Weidenfeld & Nicolson, 1973.

Malino, Frances and Bernard Wasserstein. *The Jews in Modern France.* Hanover & London: Brandeis University Press/University Press of New England, 1985.

Manchester, William. *The Caged Lion: Winston Spencer Churchill* 1932–1940. London: Cardinal, 1989.

Maritain, Jacques. *Antisemitism.* London: Geoffrey Bles: The Centenary Press, 1939.

Marrus, Michael R. *The Holocaust in History.* Harmondsworth, Middx.: Penguin, 1989.

Marsh, E. *A Number of People: A Book of Reminiscences.* London: William Heinemann Ltd./Hamish Hamilton Ltd, 1939.

Maurois, André. *Prophets and Poets.* Trans. H. Miles. Milton Keynes, Bucks.: Lightning Source UK Ltd., 1935/n.d.

Matheson, Peter, ed. *The Third Reich and the Christian Churches: A Documentary Account of Christian Resistance and Complicity during the Nazi Era.* Edinburgh: T & T Clark Ltd, 1981.

Matthews, Andrew. *Nationalism* 1789–1945. London: Hodder & Stoughton, 2000.

Maybaum, Ignaz. *The Face of God after Auschwitz.* Amsterdam: Polak & Van Gennep Ltd., 1965.

Mayer, Arno J. *Why Did the Heavens not Darken?* London: Verso, 1990.

Mayers, Simon. *Chesterton's Jews: Stereotypes and Caricatures in the Literature and Journalism of G. K. Chesterton.* CreateSpace Independent Publishing Platform, 2013.

McCarthy, John P. *Hilaire Belloc: Edwardian Radical.* Indianapolis: LibertyPress, 1978.

McGrath, Alister E. *Christian Theology.* Oxford: Blackwell Publications Ltd., 1999.

McNabb, Vincent. *Nazareth or Social Chaos.* London: Burns Oates & Washbourne Ltd., 1933.

Merkley, Paul C. *Christian Attitudes towards the State of Israel.* Montreal & Kingston: McGill-Queen's University Press, 2001.

Micklem, Nathaniel. *National Socialism and the Roman Catholic Church: Being an Account of the Conflict between the National Socialist Government of Germany and the Roman Catholic Church* 1933–8. London: Oxford University Press, 1939.

Minerbi, Sergio. I. *The Vatican and Zionism: Conflict in the Holy Land* 1895–1925. New York/Oxford: Oxford University Press, 1990.

Modras, Ronald. *The Catholic Church and Antisemitism: Poland,* 1933–39. Reading, Berks.: Harwood academic publications for the Vidal Sassoon International Center for the Study of Antisemitism, 1994.

Moloney, Thomas. *Westminster, Whitehall and the Vatican: The Role of Cardinal Hinsley* 1935–43. Tunbridge Wells, Kent: Burns & Oates, 1985.

Morris, Kevin L. *Hilaire Belloc: A Catholic Prophet*. London: CTS publications, 1995.

Morse, Arthur D. *While Six Million Died*. London: Secker & Warburg, 1968.

Morton, J. B. *Hilaire Belloc: A Memoir*. London: Hollis & Carter, 1955.

Neuhaus, Richard J. *The Naked Public Square: Religion and Democracy in America*. Grand Rapids, Mich.: Eerdmans/Exeter: Paternoster, 1984.

Nichols, Aidan. *G. K. Chesterton, Theologian*. London: Darton, Longman & Todd Ltd, 2009.

Nicolson, Harold. *Diaries and Letters 1930–39*. Edited by Nicolson. London: Collins, 1967.

Nietzsche, Friedrich. *The Birth of Tragedy*. Oxford: Oxford University Press, 1886/2000.

Niewyk, Donald L. *The Jews in Weimar Germany*. Manchester: Manchester University Press, 1980.

Nordau, Max. *Degeneration*. Lincoln, NE/London: University of Nebraska Press, 1892/1993.

Norman, E. R. *Anti-Catholicism in Victorian England*. London: Geo Allen & Unwin Ltd., 1968.

Norman, Edward. *Secularisation: New Century Theology*. London: Continuum, 2002.

Novick, Peter. *The Holocaust and Collective Memory*. London: Bloomsbury, 2001.

O'Connor, John. *Father Brown on Chesterton*. London: Frederick Muller Ltd., 1937.

Oddie, William. *Chesterton and the Romance of Orthodoxy: The Making of GKC, 1874–1908*. Oxford: Oxford University Press, 2008.

_____. ed. *The Holiness of G. K. Chesterton*. Leominster, Herefordshire: Gracewing, 2010.

Okey, Robin. *Eastern Europe 1740–1985: Feudalism to Communism*. London: Hutchinson, 1982.

Olusoga, David and Casper W. Erichsen. *The Kaiser's Holocaust: Germany's Forgotten Genocide*. London: Faber & Faber Ltd., 2010.

Orwell, George. *As I Please: The Collected Essays, Journal and Letters of George Orwell, Vol. III, 1943–5*. London: Secker & Warburg, 1968.

Parkes, James. *Judaism and Christianity*. London: Victor Gollancz Ltd., 1948.

_____. *Antisemitism*. London: Vallentine, Mitchell, 1963.

Pawlikowski, John T. *Christ in the Light of Christian-Jewish Dialogue*. New York: Paulist Press, 1982.

Pearce, Joseph. *Wisdom and Innocence: A Life of G. K. Chesterton*. London: Hodder & Stoughton, 1997.

_____. *Old Thunder: A Life of Hilaire Belloc*. London: HarperCollins, 2002.

The Persecution of the Catholic Church in the Third Reich: Facts and Documents. London: Burns Oates, 1940.

Peters, Sally. *Bernard Shaw: The Ascent of the Superman*. New Haven/London: Yale University Press, 1996.

Phillips, Melanie. *The Ascent of Woman: A History of the Suffragette Movement and the Ideas Behind It.* London: Abacus, 2003.

_____. *Londonistan: How Britain is Creating a Terror State Within.* London: Gibson Square, 2006.

Poliakov, Leon. *Harvest of Hate: The Nazi Program for the Destruction of the Jews of Europe.* New York: Holocaust Library, 1979.

_____. *The History of Anti-Semitism: From the Time of Christianity to the Court Jews, Vol. I.* Trans. by R. Howard. Philadelphia, PA: University of Pennsylvania Press, 2003.

Poncins, Leon De. *Judaism and the Vatican: An Attempt at Spiritual Subversion.* Sudbury, Suffolk: Bloomfield Books, 1967.

Pontifex, John and John Newton, eds. *Persecuted and Forgotten?* Sutton, Surrey: Aid to the Church in Need (UK), 2011.

Popper, Karl R. *The Open Society and its Enemies: Vol. I: The Spell of Plato.* London: Routledge & Kegan Paul, 1945/1977.

Pound, Ezra. *I cease not to Yowl: Ezra Pound's Letters to Olivia Rossetti Agresti.* Edited by D.P. Tryphonopoulos and L. Surette. Urbana: University of Illinois Press, 1998.

Pugh, Martin. *Hurrah for the Blackshirts! Fascists and Fascism in Britain Between the Wars.* London: Jonathan Cape, 2005.

Pulzer, Peter. *The Rise of Political Anti-Semitism in Germany and Austria.* London: Peter Halban, 1988.

_____. *Jews and the German State: The Political History of a Minority* 1848–1933. Oxford: Blackwell, 1992.

Pundt, Alfred. G. *Arndt and the Nationalist Awakening in Germany.* New York: Columbia University Press, 1935.

Ratzinger, Joseph. *Jesus of Nazareth Part II: Holy Week From the Entrance into Jerusalem to the Resurrection.* London: Catholic Truth Society/San Francisco: Ignatius Press, 2011.

Rauch, Rufus W., ed. *A Chesterton Celebration.* Indiana: University of Notre Dame Press, 1983.

Read, Anthony and David Fisher. *Kristallnacht: Unleashing the Holocaust.* London: Papermac, 1991.

Reckitt, Maurice. *As It Happened: An Autobiography.* London: J. M. Dent & Sons Ltd., 1941.

Rée, Jonathan and J.O. Urmson, eds., *The Concise Encylopaedia of Western Philosophy,* 3rd Edition. London: Routledge, 2005.

Reinharz, Jehuda. *Chaim Weizmann: The Making of a Zionist Leader.* Oxford: Oxford University Press, 1985.

Reuther, Rosemary. Radford. *The Theological Roots of Anti-Semitism.* London: Search Press/New York: Seabury Press, 1975.

Reynolds, Ernest E. *The Roman Catholic Church in England and Wales: A Short History.* Wheathampstead, Herts.: Anthony Clarke Books, 1973.

Robertson, E. *Bonhoeffer's Heritage: the Christian way in a world without religion.* London: Hodder & Stoughton, 1989.

Rogger, Hans. *Jewish Policies and Right-Wing Politics in Imperial Russia.* London: Macmillan/St Anthony's College, Oxford, 1986.

Rose, Norman. *The Cliveden Set: Portrait of an Exclusive Fraternity.* London: Jonathan Cape, 2000.

Rosenberg, Alfred. *The Myth of the Twentieth Century 1925–1930*, accessed March 28, 2004, http://www.ety.com/HRP/booksonline/mythos/mythostoc.htm.

Rosenberg, Edgar. *From Shylock to Svengali: Jewish Stereotypes in English Fiction.* London: Peter Owen, 1961.

Roth, John K., Berenbaum, Michael, eds. *Holocaust: Religious and Philosophical Implications.* St Paul, Minnesota: Paragon House, 1989.

Rothfels, Hans. *The German Opposition to Hitler.* Trans. by L. Wilson. London: Oswald Wolff (Publishers) Ltd., 1978.

Rubenstein, R. L. *The Age of Triage: Fear and Hope in an Overcrowded World.* Boston: Beacon Press, 1983.

_____. *After Auschwitz: History, Theology and Contemporary Judaism.* Baltimore/London: The Johns Hopkins University Press, 1992.

Rubenstein, R. L., and J. K. Roth. *Approaches to Auschwitz: The Holocaust and its Legacy.* Atlanta, Georgia: John Knox Press, 1987.

Rubinstein, W. D. *The Left, the Right and the Jews.* London: Croom Helm, 1982.

_____. *A History of the Jews in the English-Speaking World: Great Britain.* London: Macmillan Press Ltd., 1996.

_____. *The Myth of Rescue: Why the democracies could not have saved more Jews from the Nazis.* London: Routledge, 1997.

_____. *Genocide: A History.* Harlow, Essex: Pearson Longman, 2004.

_____. *Israel, the Jews, and the West: The Fall and Rise of Antisemitism.* London: Social Affairs Unit, 2008.

_____. *The End of Ideology and the Rise of Religion: How Marxism and Other Secular Universalistic Ideologies Have Given Way to Religious Fundamentalism.* London: Social Affairs Unit, 2009.

Rubinstein, W. D., and H. L. Rubinstein. *Philosemitism.* London: Macmillan Press, 1999.

Ryan, Michael., ed. *Human Responses to the Holocaust: Perpetrators and Victims, Bystanders and Resisters.* New York/Toronto: Edwin Mellen Press, 1981.

Sachar, Howard M. *A History of Israel from the Rise of Zionism to our Time.* New York: Alfred A. Knopf, 2007.

Sacks, Jonathan. *One People? Tradition, Modernity, and Jewish Unity.* London: The Littman Library of Jewish Civilization, 1993.

_____. *Faith in the Future.* London: Darton, Longman & Todd, 1995.

_____. *The Politics of Hope.* London: Vintage, 2000.

_____. *The Home We Build Together: Recreating Society.* London: Continuum, 2007.

Salomon, Sidney. *The Jews of Britain*. London: Jarrolds Publishers, 1938.

Salter, F. R. *St Paul's School* 1909–1959. London: Arthur Barker Ltd., 1959.

Sams, Hurbert. A. *Pauline and Old Pauline* 1884–1931. Cambridge: privately printed, Cambridge University Press, 1933.

Samuel, Maurice. *Blood Accusation: The Strange History of the Beiliss Case*. London: Weidenfeld & Nicolson, 1967.

Sayers, Dorothy L. *Three Complete Lord Peter Wimsey Novels*. New York: Wings Books, 1992.

_____. *The Complete Stories*. New York: Perennial, 2002.

Schall, James V. *Schall on Chesterton: Timely Essays on Timeless Paradoxes*. Washington DC: Catholic University of America Press, 2000.

Schmude, Karl. *G. K. Chesterton*. London: Catholic Truth Society, 2008.

Scholder, Klaus. *The Churches and the Third Reich: Vol. I: 1918–1934*. London: SCM Press Ltd., 1987.

_____. *"A Requiem for Hitler" and Other New Perspectives on the German Church Struggle*. London: SCM Press Ltd., 1989.

Scholem, Gershom. *The Messianic Idea in Judaism and Other Essays on Spirituality*. New York: Schocken Books, 1971.

Searle, G. R. *The Quest for National Efficiency: A study in British politics and political thought* 1899–1914. Oxford: Blackwell, 1971.

_____. *Eugenics and Politics in Britain* 1900–1914. Leyden: Noordhoff International Publishing, 1976.

Seton-Watson, Hugh. *The Russian Empire* 1801–1917. Oxford: Clarendon Press, 1988.

Sewell, Brocard. *My dear time's waste*. Aylesford, Kent: St Albert's Press, 1966.

_____. *Cecil Chesterton*. Whitefriars, Faversham, Kent: Saint Albert's Press, 1975.

_____. *"G.K.'s Weekly": An Appraisal*. Maidstone, Kent: The Aylesford Press, 1990.

_____. *The Habit of a Lifetime: An Autobiography*. Padstow, Cornwall: Tabb House, 1992.

Sewell, Dennis. *The Political Gene: How Darwin's Ideas Changed Politics*. London: Picador, 2010.

Sharf, Andrew. *The British Press and Jews under Nazi Rule*. London: Oxford University Press, 1964.

Shatzkes, Pamela. *Holocaust and Rescue: Impotent or Indifferent? Anglo-Jewry* 1938–1945. London: Vallentine Mitchell, 2004.

Shaw, George B. *The Complete Plays of George Bernard Shaw*. London: Odhams Press Ltd., 1937.

_____. *The Bodley Head Bernard Shaw Collected Plays with Prefaces Vol. II*. London: The Bodley Head, 1971.

_____. *The Bodley Head Bernard Shaw Collected Plays with Prefaces Vol. III*. London: The Bodley Head, 1971.

_____. *Plays Extravagant: Too True to be Good; The Simpleton of the Unexpected*

Isles; The Millionairess. Harmondsworth, Middx.: Penguin Books Ltd., 1981.

_____. *Plays Political: The Apple Cart; On the Rocks; Geneva*. Harmondsworth, Middx.: Penguin Books Ltd., 1986.

_____. *Bernard Shaw: Collected Letters 1926–1950 Vol. 4*. Edited by D.H. Laurence. London: Max Reinhardt, 1988.

Shaw, Stanford J. *The Jews of the Ottoman Empire and the Turkish Republic*. London: Macmillan, 1991.

Shermis, Michael and Arthur E. Zannoni, eds. *Introduction to Jewish-Christian Relations*. New York/Mahwah, NJ: Paulist Press, 1991.

Shirer, William. L. *Berlin Diary: The Journal of a Foreign Correspondent, 1934–1941*. Baltimore, Maryland: Johns Hopkins University Press, 1941/2002.

Singer, Peter. *Practical Ethics*. Cambridge: Cambridge University Press, 1993.

_____. *Writings on an Ethical Life*. London: Fourth Estate, 2001.

Skidelsky, Robert. *Oswald Mosley*. London: Macmillan, 1990.

Slezkine, Yuri. *The Jewish Century*. Princeton, US: Princeton University Press, 2004.

Smiles, S. *Self-Help with illustrations of Conduct and Perseverance*. London: IEA Health and Welfare Unit, 1859/1997.

Smith, David. C. *H.G. Wells Desperately Mortal: A Biography*. New Haven/London: Yale University Press, 1986.

Smith, Julia. *The Elusive Father Brown: The Life of Mgr John O'Connor*. Leominster, Herefordshire: Gracewing, 2010.

Smith, Paul. *Disraelian Conservatism and Social Reform*. London: Routledge & Kegan Paul, 1967.

Speaight, Robert. *The Life of Hilaire Belloc*. London: Hollis & Carter, 1957.

_____. *The Property Basket: Recollections of a Divided Life*. London: Collins & Harvill Press, 1970.

Sprug, Joseph W. *An Index to G.K. Chesterton*. Washington DC: Catholic University of America Press, 1966.

Stanislawski, Michael. *Zionism and the Fin de Siècle: Cosmopolitanism and Nationalism from Nordau to Jabotinsky*. California and London: University of California Press, 2001.

Stapleton, Julia. *Christianity, Patriotism, and Nationhood: The England of G.K. Chesterton*. Lanham, MD/Plymouth, Devon: Lexington Books, 2009.

Stone, Dan. *Breeding Superman: Nietzsche, Race and Eugenics in Edwardian and Interwar Britain*. Liverpool: Liverpool University Press, 2002.

_____. *Constructing the Holocaust: A Study in Historiography*. London: Vallentine Mitchell, 2003.

_____. *Responses to Nazism in Britain, 1933–1939: Before the War and the Holocaust*. Basingstoke, Hants.: Palgrave Macmillan, 2003.

_____. *History, Memory and Mass Atrocity: Essays on the Holocaust and Genocide*. London: Vallentine Mitchell, 2006.

Sullivan, John, ed. *G.K. Chesterton: A Centenary Appraisal*. London: Paul Elek, 1974.

Sutherland, Halliday. *The Arches of the Years.* London: Geoffrey Bles, 1933.

Swartz, Helen M., and Marvin Swartz. M. *Disraeli's Reminiscences.* London: Hamish Hamilton Ltd., 1975.

Sykes, Christopher. *Nancy: The Life of Lady Astor.* London: Collins, 1972.

Sykes, Stephen. *The Identity of Christianity: Theologians and the Essence of Christianity from Schleiermacher to Barth.* London: SPCK, 1984.

Symons, Julian. *Bloody Murder: From the Detective Story to the Novel: a History.* London: Pan Books Ltd., 1972/1994.

Taylor, Alan J. P. *English History 1914–1945.* Oxford: Clarendon Press, 1965.

_____. *The Course of German History: A Survey of the Development of German History Since 1815.* London: Methuen & Co. Ltd., 1985.

Taylor, Stan. *The National Front in English Politics.* London: The Macmillan Press Ltd., 1982.

Taylor, Telford. *The Anatomy of the Nuremberg Trials: a personal memoir.* London: Bloomsbury, 1993.

Thomson, Matthew. *Psychological Subjects: Identity, Culture, and Health in Twentieth-Century Britain.* Oxford: Oxford University Press, 2006.

Thompson, E. P. *The Making of the English Working Class.* London: Penguin Books, 1984.

Thurlow, Richard C. *Fascism in Britain: A History 1918–1985.* Oxford: Basil Blackwell, 1987.

Titterton, William. R. *G. K. Chesterton: A Portrait.* London: Douglas Organ, 1936/1947.

Toynbee, Arnold J. *A Study of History,* Vol. 1. London: Oxford University Press, 1934.

Trevor-Roper, H. *Hitler's Table Talk 1941–1944.* London: Phoenix Press, 1953/2000.

Trollope, Anthony. *The Way we live Now.* Oxford: Oxford University Press, 1991.

Trombley, Stephen. *The Right to Reproduce: A History of Coercive Sterilization.* London: Weidenfeld and Nicolson, 1988.

Tuchman, Barbara. *The Proud Tower: A Portrait of the World before the War 1890–1914.* London: Hamish Hamilton, 1966.

Turnbull, Malcolm J. *Victims or Villains: Jewish Images in Classic English Detective Fiction.* Bowling Green Ohio: Bowling Green State University, 1998.

Unterman, Alan, ed. *Dictionary of Jewish Lore and Legend.* London: Thames & Hudson, 1997.

Vergnas, Raymond Las. *Chesterton, Belloc, Baring.* London: Sheed & Ward, 1938.

Vital, David. *Zionism: the Formative Years.* Oxford: Clarendon Press, 1982.

Walker, Martin. *The National Front.* Glasgow: Fontana/Collins, 1977.

Wall, Derek. *Green History: A reader in environmental literature, philosophy and politics.* London: Routledge, 1994.

Wansborough, Henry, ed. *The New Jerusalem Bible.* London: Darton, Longman & Todd Ltd, 1994.

Ward, Maisie. *Gilbert Keith Chesterton.* New York: Sheed & Ward, 1943.

_____. *Return to Chesterton*. London: Sheed & Ward, 1952.

Watson, Colin. *Snobbery with Violence: English Crime Stories and their Audience*. London: Methuen, 1987.

Watson, George. *Politics and Literature in Modern Britain*. London: The Macmillan Press Ltd., 1977.

Watson, Winifred. *Miss Pettigrew Lives for a Day*. London: Persephone Books, 1938/2004.

Waugh, Evelyn. *The Life of Ronald Knox*. London: Chapman & Hall, 1959.

Webster, Nesta. *World Revolution: The Plot Against Civilization*. London: Constable & Co. Ltd., 1921.

Weikart, Richard. *From Darwin to Hitler: Evolutionary Ethics, Eugenics, and Racism in Germany*. Houndmills, Hants.: Palgrave Macmillan, 2006.

Weindling, Paul. *Health, race and German politics between national unification and Nazism, 1870–1945*. Cambridge: Cambridge University Press, 1989.

Weinreich, Max. *Hitler's Professors: The Part of Scholarship in Germany's Crimes against the Jewish People*. New Haven/London: Yale University Press, 1946/1999.

Weintraub, Stanley. *Disraeli: A Biography*. London: Hamish Hamilton Ltd., 1993.

Weizmann, Chaim. *Trial and Error: The Autobiography of Chaim Weizmann*. London: Hamish Hamilton, 1949.

Wells, H. G. *When the Sleeper Wakes*. London: Everyman, 1899/1999.

_____. *Anticipations of the Reaction of Mechanical and Scientific Progress Upon Human Life and Thought*. London: Chapman & Hall Ltd., 1901/1902.

_____. *Mankind in the Making*. London: Chapman & Hall Ltd., 1903.

_____. *A Modern Utopia*. London: Thomas Nelson & Sons Ltd., 1905/1911.

_____. *Tono-Bungay*. London: Penguin, 1909/2005.

_____. *The New Machiavelli*. London: Penguin, 1911/2005.

_____. *Marriage*. London: no publisher, 1912/1933.

_____. *The Wife of Sir Isaac Harman*. London: Odhams Press Ltd., 1914/1986.

_____. *God the Invisible King*. 1917. Accessed April 21, 2011, http://www.on line-literature.com/wellshg/invisibleking/.

_____. *Russia in the Shadows*. London: Hodder & Stoughton Ltd., 1920.

_____. *The Outline of History: Being a Plain History of Life and Mankind from Primordial Life to Nineteen-sixty*. London: Cassell, 1920/1961.

_____. *The Autocracy of Mr. Parham: His Remarkable Adventures in This Changing World*. London: William Heinemann Ltd., 1930.

_____. *The Open Conspiracy and Other Writings*. London: no publisher, 1933.

_____. *The Shape of Things to Come; The Ultimate Revolution*. London: J. M. Dent, 1933/1999.

_____. *Experiment in Autobiography: Discourse and Conclusions of a very ordinary brain (since 1866)*. Vol. I. London: Faber & Faber, 1934/1984.

_____. *Experiment in Autobiography: Discourse and Conclusions of a very ordinary brain (since 1866)*. Vol. II. London: Victor Gollancz Ltd., 1934.

_____. *The Anatomy of Frustration: a modern synthesis.* London: The Cresset Press, 1936.

_____. *The Holy Terror.* London: Michael Joseph Ltd., 1939.

_____. *Travels of a Republican Radical in Search of Hot Water.* Harmondsworth, Middx.: Penguin, 1939/1947.

_____. *The Common Sense of War and Peace: World Revolution or War Unending.* Harmondsworth, Middx.: Penguin Books, 1940.

_____. *You Can't Be Too Careful: A Sample of Life* 1901–1951. London: Secker & Warburg, 1941/1947.

_____. *The Outlook for Homo Sapiens: An unemotional Statement of the Things that are happening to him now, and of the immediate Possibilities Confronting him.* London: Secker & Warburg, 1942.

_____. *Crux Ansata: An Indictment of the Roman Catholic Church.* Harmondsworth, Middx.: Penguin Books, 1943.

_____. *The Last Books of H. G. Wells: The Happy Turning and Mind at the End of its Tether.* Edited by G. P. Wells. London: H. G. Wells Society, 1945/1968.

_____. *The Complete Science Fiction Treasury of H. G. Wells.* New York: Avenel Books, 1978.

_____. *H. G. Wells in Love: Postscript to an Experiment in Autobiography.* G. P. Wells, ed. London: Faber & Faber, 1984.

Wells, H. G., J. Huxley and G. P. Wells, *Science of Life.* London: Cassell, 1931.

Wensley, F. Porter. *Forty Years of Scotland Yard: A Record of a Lifetime's Service in the Criminal Investigation Department* (USA: Kessinger Publishing, 2005) (published as *Forty Years of Scotland Yard: A Record of a Lifetime's Service in the Criminal Investigation Department* [New York, 1968]); originally published as *Detective Days* (London, 1931).

West, Anthony. *H. G. Wells: Aspects of a Life.* London: Hutchinson & Co. (Publishers) Ltd., 1984.

West, Julius. *G. K. Chesterton: A Critical Study.* London: Martin Secker, 1915.

Wheatcroft, Geoffrey. *The Controversy of Zion: or How Zionism tried to resolve the Jewish Question.* London: Sinclair-Stevenson, 1996.

Wheatland, Thomas. *The Frankfurt School in Exile.* Minneapolis, Minnesota: University of Minnesota Press, 2009.

Willebrands, Cardinal J. *The Church and Jewish People: New Considerations.* New York: Paulist Press, 1992.

Wills, Garry. *Chesterton.* New York: Image Books, 1961/2001.

_____. *Papal Sin: Structures of Deceit.* London: Darton, Longman & Todd, 2000.

Wilson, A. N. *Hilaire Belloc.* London: Hamish Hamilton, 1984.

Winks, Robin W., ed. *Detective Fiction: A Collection of Critical Essays.* Englewood Cliffs, NJ: Prentice-Hall, Inc., 1980.

Winn, Dilys. *Murder Ink.* New York: Workman Publishing, 1984.

Wise, Stephen. *Challenging Years: The Autobiography of Stephen Wise.* London: East and West Library, 1951.

Wistrich, Robert S., ed., *The Left Against Zion: Communism, Israel and the Middle East.* London: Vallentine, Mitchell, 1979.

_____. *Anti-Semitism: The Longest Hatred.* London: Thames Methuen, 1991.

Wolfe, Humbert. *Lampoons.* London: Ernest Benn Ltd., 1925.

_____. *Notes on English Verse Satire.* London: The Hogarth Press, 1929.

_____. *Now a Stranger.* London: Cassell & Company Ltd., 1933.

_____. *The Upward Anguish.* London: Cassell & Company Ltd., 1938.

_____. *Out of Great Tribulation—New Poems.* London: Victor Gollancz Ltd., 1939.

Wollaston, Isabel. *A War Against Memory? The Future of Holocaust Remembrance.* London: SPCK, 1996.

Woolf, Leonard. *Sowing: An Autobiography of the Years 1880 to 1904.* London: The Hogarth Press, 1967.

Zahn, Gordon. C. *German Catholics and Hitler's Wars: A Study in Social Control.* London/New York: Sheed & Ward, 1964.

Zangwill, Israel. *The King of Schnorrers.* New York: Dover Publications Inc., 1894/1965.

_____. *The Voice of Jerusalem.* London: Wm Heinemann, 1920.

Archives

Chesterton Collection, British Library.

Eugenics Society Archive, Wellcome Institute, London.

Articles

Guedalla, Philip. "Childe Chesterton," *The Zionist Review*, March 1921, 1990, 199–200.

Kaufman, Gerald. "Chesterton's final solution," *Times Educational Supplement*, January 2, 1998.

Mearsheimer, John, and Stephen Walt "The Israel Lobby," *London Review of Books*, 28 (6), (March 23, 2006): 3–12, accessed March 26, 2011, http://www.lrb.co.uk/v28/n06/john-mearsheimer/the-israel-lobby.

Sheed, Wilfrid. "ChesterBelloc and the Jews," *The New York Review of Books*, 17 (3), September 2, 1971.

Official Publications

Mental Deficiency Act 1913. London: His Majesty's Stationery Office.

Mental Deficiency Act 1927. London: His Majesty's Stationery Office.

Periodicals

The Chesterton Review.

Common Ground.

G.K.'s Weekly.
Gilbert Magazine.
Holocaust and genocide studies.
Jewish Chronicle.
Jewish Historical Studies.
Jewish Social Studies.
The Journal of Holocaust Education.
The New Witness.
Patterns of Prejudice.

Unpublished Papers

Conlon, Denis Joseph. "New and Original Views," 2012.
Farmer, Ann. "Has the Holocaust Influenced Views of G.K. Chesterton's 'Anti-Semitism?'" Anglia Polytechnic University, 2005.
Farmer, Ann. "Churchill and Eugenics," 2009.
Mathews, Race. "Prejudice: Anti-Semitism in the Distributist Weeklies," 2001.
Mathews, Race. "The Beiliss Affair and The New Witness," 2001.

Websites Consulted

The American Chesterton Society, accessed at http://www.Chesterton.org.
David Irving, accessed at http://www.fpp.co.uk.
The Pave the Way Foundation, accessed at http://www.ptwf.org.

Index

CPSIA information can be obtained
at www.ICGtesting.com
Printed in the USA
BVHW032350150319
542849BV00002B/30/P

9 781621 381303